"For over thirty years, Bruce Evans has worked in close consultation with the author of *Buddhadhamma* to refine his English translation, cut out any conceivable excess, and give us *The Essential Buddhadhamma*. A Thai masterpiece of Theravada Buddhism, the scope and meaning of the Buddha's teachings are explained here in a wholly satisfying way. Scriptural knowledge and authentic understanding rarely come together like this, showing us a coherent vision of life, truth, and purpose. Recommend 1000%."

AJAHN HĀSAPAÑÑO, abbot of Vimokkharam Forest Hermitage

"This impressive survey gives us an 'inquire within about everything' for Theravada Buddhism. Practicing Buddhists, students, and scholars will welcome the chance to encounter Ven. Payutto's authoritative discussions on almost any topic you could think of: dependent arising, the five aggregates, theories of not-self, rebirth, and many others that can be so difficult to grasp. Payutto walks us carefully through some of the thorniest areas of debate around these themes—and in a readable style that makes his compendious volume ideal both as a work of reference and as something to read and consider for interest. Chapters on key topics of doctrine and practice are accessible and suitable for beginners as well as those with greater knowledge. *The Essential Buddhadhamma* promises to be a classic manual for many years to come."

SARAH SHAW, author of *The Art of Listening*

"This deep dive into the underpinnings of the Theravada Buddhist path—with its clear, detailed explications—provides trustworthy guidelines for gauging one's development of right view and meditation, and should become a resource that will stand the test of time."

PAUL BREITER, translator of Ajahn Chah's *Being Dharma*

"In *The Essential Buddhadhamma*, Ven. P. A. Payutto offers fundamental Buddhist teachings in practical, lucid, and descriptive prose. Payutto, through the editing and translation of Bruce Evans, reveals the Dhamma's value for our lives, grounded in the authoritative texts of the Pali canon."

BROOKE SCHEDNECK, author of *Living Theravada*

"*The Essential Buddhadhamma* is the book for everyone seeking a comprehensive, practical, and insightful overview of early Buddhist and Theravada teachings. As the early corpus is huge, a comprehensive survey requires length, even in abridged form. Ven. Payutto is judiciously loyal to the texts and wise tradition, beautifully incorporating the Buddha's original teachings throughout. He guides practitioners in thinking through and digesting these profound teachings so that we may put them into practice intelligently. Bruce Evans has managed the abridgment nicely. Appropriately, the emotions it fosters are equanimity, confidence, and contentment.

"Venerable Bhikkhu P. A. Payutto has long been a jewel of the Thai Saṅgha: kind, humble, gracious, and generous. I know of no better overview of early Buddhist and Theravada teachings than his masterpiece."

SANTIKARO UPASAKA, cotranslator of Ajahn Buddhadasa's *Seeing with the Eye of Dhamma*

The Essential Buddhadhamma

The Teachings and Practice of Theravada Buddhism

BHIKKHU P. A. PAYUTTO

Translated and edited by Bruce Evans

SHAMBHALA

Shambhala Publications, Inc.
2129 13th Street
Boulder, Colorado 80302
www.shambhala.com

Cover art: kasamarat / Adobe Stock
Cover design: Claudine Mansour

9 8 7 6 5 4 3 2 1

First Edition
Printed in the United States of America

Shambhala Publications makes every effort to print on acid-free, recycled paper.

Shambhala Publications is distributed worldwide by Penguin Random House, Inc., and its subsidiaries.

LIBRARY OF CONGRESS CATALOGING-IN-PUBLICATION DATA
Names: Phra Thēpwēthī (Prayut), author. | Evans, Bruce, 1952- translator.
Title: The essential Buddhadhamma: the teachings and practice of Theravada Buddhism / Bhikkhu P. A. Payutto; translated and edited by Bruce Evans.
Other titles: Phutthatham. English
Description: First edition. | Boulder: Shambhala Publications, 2024. | Includes bibliographical references and index.
Identifiers: LCCN 2023023339 | ISBN 9781645472353 (hardcover; acid-free recycled paper)
Subjects: LCSH: Buddhism—Doctrines. | Theravāda Buddhism—Essence, genius, nature.
Classification: LCC BQ4132 .P4613 2024 | DDC 294.3/4201—dc23/eng/20231025
LCrecord available at https://lccn.loc.gov/2023023339

Contents

Author's Preface vii

Translator's Preface ix

Introduction 1

BOOK ONE · THE MIDDLE TEACHING

PART ONE · What Is Life?

1. The Five *Khandha*s and the Six Sense Bases 19

PART TWO · What Is Life Like?

2. The Three Characteristics: The Natural Characteristics of All Things 61

PART THREE · How Does Life Work?

3. *Paṭiccasamuppāda*: The Principle of Dependent Arising 127

4. *Kamma* as a Principle Contingent on the *Paṭiccasamuppāda* 203

PART FOUR · How Should Life Be?

5. *Nibbāna* 281

BOOK TWO · THE MIDDLE WAY

PART FIVE · How Should Life Be Lived?

6. Introduction to the Middle Way 359

7. The Precursors of Learning 399

8. The Wisdom Factors of the Middle Way:
Right View and Right Thought 473

9. The Morality Factors of the Middle Way:
Right Speech, Right Action, and Right Livelihood 503

10. The Concentration Factors of the Middle Way: Right Effort,
Right Mindfulness, and Right Concentration 565

Conclusion: The Four Noble Truths
as a Summary of the Buddhadhamma 691

Glossary 737

Abbreviations of Sources 741

Notes 745

Selected Bibliography 813

Index 817

About the Author and Translator 835

Author's Preface

It is highly meritorious that Mr. Bruce Evans has successfully completed this English translation of an abridged version of *Buddhadhamma*, titled *The Essential Buddhadhamma: The Teachings and Practice of Theravada Buddhism*, with a great deal of mental effort and sacrifice.

Mr. Evans has a long and extensive experience in the field of Dhamma, both in his life and in publishing, since before 1992, and his understanding of the Thai language is likewise long and extensive. Importantly, he has made the sacrifice to do the task of summarizing the essentials of Buddhadhamma on his own initiative, for the benefit of students and those interested in learning about Buddhism, with no thought of personal gain. It is a task completed by zeal (*chanda*) for the work and out of goodwill, for the benefit of the people. This is practicing for benefit (*atthacariya*) and a great act of merit done out of true love for the work.

I would like to express my great appreciation to Mr. Evans for completing this skillful action on this occasion, which has led to this new English translation of *Buddhadhamma*. May it be of benefit to a greater audience and lead to the advancement of knowledge and virtue in the world.

Somdet Phra Buddhaghosacariya (P. A. Payutto)
December 17, 2021

Translator's Preface

A translator's job is to become, ideally, an invisible conduit between the source language and the target language. As such, there would seem to be no need to write anything by way of a translator's introduction. But ideals are just that, and there is usually a gap between the ideal and the reality. It would be impossible, after having spent many decades working on this project, to have not inserted myself into the final product through my editorial decisions. Therefore some brief background is called for.

Venerable Prayudh Payutto—also known as P. A. Payutto and by various ecclesiastical titles, currently Somdet Phra Buddhaghosacariya—is widely acknowledged as one of Thailand's foremost Buddhist scholars. His written works in Thai span the gamut of social issues such as Buddhist approaches to economics, administration, education, and science, as well as more traditional Buddhist works, including Buddhist dictionaries and commentaries. He has been a voice of authority when dealing with crises of thought within Thai Buddhist circles. The foundation of his authority is twofold: on one hand there is a thorough knowledge of the core Buddhist teachings based on years of study and research; on the other is a profound understanding of those teachings, and a keen awareness of how to apply them to modern situations, all of which are brilliantly expounded in his most important work, *Buddhadhamma*.

The first Thai edition of *Buddhadhamma* (*Phutthatham: kot thammachat laa khun kha kap cheewit*) was published in 1971. It was a relatively short text, numbering 206 pages, written in response to a request for a contribution of a chapter on Buddhist philosophy to a collection of writings on social sciences and humanities. An English translation of this text by Dr. Grant Olson was published by State University of New York Press in 1995 as *Buddhadhamma: Natural Laws and Values for Life*.

The Thai version was then revised and greatly expanded in a 1982 edition numbering 1,145 pages. This was reprinted a number of times, with additional pages inserted into the original plates, which had remained unchanged from the first printing.

In 2012 the whole manuscript was entered into computer and a further revised edition was made, numbering 1,360 pages. This revised edition has been translated by Robin Moore as *Buddhadhamma: The Laws of Nature and Their Benefits to Life* (Buddhadhamma Foundation, 2021).

The bulk of the translation in this book is based on the first expanded edition of *Buddhadhamma* published in 1982, and follows the structure and format of that edition. The later 2012 edition was revised by the author and contained some structural changes and additional text. While conforming to the structure of the 1982 edition, I have occasionally updated the text of this translation with some material from the 2012 edition (notably the chapter on *sīla*, some additional text in the section on *anattā* in chapter 2, and additional text in the chapter on *nibbāna*, all of which were revised or added at the venerable author's specific request), but some changes in the 2012 edition have not made it into this translation, as the intent is, after all, a condensed version of the original

Editorial cuts have been made on a number of levels, resulting in a word-count reduction of roughly two-thirds. Some chapters have been omitted—specifically, the chapters "Calm and Insight: Liberation by Mind and Liberation through Wisdom"; "Lifestyle and Fundamental Virtues of the Noble Ones"; "Morality and Social Objectives"; "The Paranormal: Psychic Powers and Devas"; "The Problem of Motivation"; and "Happiness." In addition, some chapters have been conflated into single chapters. The first two chapters of the expanded *Buddhadhamma* ("The Five *Khandhas*" and "The Six Sense Bases") have been merged into one; the four chapters on *nibbāna* ("Knowledge, Liberation, Purity, Peace, *Nibbāna*"; "Kinds and Levels of *Nibbāna* and Those Who Attain It"; "Major Features of *Nibbāna*"; and "*Nibbāna*: Summary") have been merged into one chapter; and the two chapters on the precursors of learning ("The Sounds from Outside: The Good Friend," and "*Yoniso-Manasikāra*: Wise Attention") have also been merged into one.

Cuts were also made within each of the chapters. In some sections, discussions of incidental points were reduced, including but not limited to some sections that applied more specifically to the Thai cultural context. In sections where the author provides many excerpts of Buddhavacana (literally, "Buddha's words") from the Pali Tipiṭaka to support his discussion, I have chosen for space reasons to delete some of the excerpts and retain the ones I have deemed most essential for the reader's understanding. Some footnotes were reduced in length, and in the body text I have deleted some sentences and words to make the text more concise.

As the reader may imagine, there is a good deal of subjective decision-making involved in these cuts, and for any shortcomings I ask the reader's patience and forgiveness.

I do not have a particularly academic background; I gained my knowledge of Thai almost entirely by living with Thai bhikkhus (monks) as a bhikkhu disciple of the revered forest meditation teacher Ajahn Chah. Venerable Ajahn Chah famously said, "Put the books away and just read your own mind," and that is a principle I followed faithfully for seventeen years, concentrating on meditation practice in the forests of northeast Thailand. However, it can't be denied that books are indeed a valuable, if not indispensable, stepping stone on the road to understanding, especially for Western practitioners who lack the broad spiritual support enjoyed by people living in traditional Buddhist cultures. When some of Venerable Ajahn Chah's disciples began translating his teachings into English, I quickly joined in and developed both my translation skills and also my love of the Buddhist teachings with a number of books printed for free distribution. Many of those translations have been reproduced in *Food for the Heart: The Collected Teachings of Ajahn Chah*, published by Wisdom Publications.

I began work on translating *Buddhadhamma* while I was still a bhikkhu in 1991. The first results of that work were published by the Buddhadhamma Foundation as *Good, Evil and Beyond: Kamma in the Buddha's Teachings*. I was inspired by the work partly by its elegant structure and also by the venerable author's distinct combination of traditional Buddhist learning tethered with a keen understanding of modern ways of thinking. *Buddhadhamma* struck me as the one volume that could take an earnest student from beginner level in terms of knowledge of the Buddha's teachings up to the level of adept, if not expert.

In 1992 I left the monkhood and took up household life in Bangkok, where I worked full time with the Buddhadhamma Foundation to translate the rest of *Buddhadhamma*, among other things.

Coming from a forest-tradition background, I have always been fond of the "less is more" approach, and while translating the full version of *Buddhadhamma*, it occurred to me that an abridged version, in which the main points were highlighted, would be a useful addition to Buddhist literature. It is especially apt during this day and age in which we are accustomed to ready access to information of all kinds.

It is with a great feeling of pride and accomplishment that I am finally able to offer this project in honor of the venerable author, to at last complete a project that has been thirty years in the making. As it is said in Buddhism, *anākulā ca kammantā ettaṁ maṅgala-muttamaṁ*: "Having no unfinished business is a supreme blessing." I cannot say that I have no unfinished business, but to complete something that has been a presence in my life for three decades is indeed a fine feeling. It is my hope that this volume will be an invaluable aid to students of Buddhism and lead to increased understanding and peace in a world that seems intent on ever-increasing confusion and conflict.

I am indebted to the venerable author for his patience and encouragement throughout, and for giving me the opportunity to complete my project of the condensed version of *Buddhadhamma*. The venerable author availed himself for questions and discussions during the six years I worked with the Buddhadhamma Foundation on the translation of the expanded version, and also continued to encourage me and make himself available for queries in more recent years while revising the text and pulling together *The Essential Buddhadhamma.*

The project would not have been possible without the generous and passionate support of Khun Yongyut Thanapura, president of the Buddhadhamma Foundation, who offered me the opportunity to translate the original text of *Buddhadhamma*. Khun Yongyut also strongly encouraged me during the preparation of *The Essential Buddhadhamma.*

Professor Somsin Chanawangsa of Chulalongkorn University spent a brief but highly influential period advising me on the revision of my translations of the original *Buddhadhamma*, and guided me toward a more disciplined approach to translation, which hopefully enabled me to unload some of the bad habits gained through my self-taught translation practice.

I am indebted to Venerable Hāsapañño of Vimokkharam Forest Hermitage in Melbourne for taking the time to read through the entire manuscript and offering valuable suggestions, even though he was throughout that time also overseeing the construction of a new temple hall, a stressful undertaking under any circumstances.

Venerable Khemānando, formerly of Vimokkharam Forest Hermitage, also did some read-through for me, as did Professor Peter Skilling in Bangkok some decades ago.

For conversion of footnote references from the Thai recension of the Pali Tipiṭaka and commentaries in the source text to the roman-script versions, I have referred to the translation of the full version of *Buddhadhamma* by Robin Moore.

The Essential Buddhadhamma

Introduction

When thinking of Buddhism, many modern readers tend to question whether it is a religion, a philosophy, or merely a way of life. Faced with this problem, arguments or explanations have to be made, drawing out the matter and leading to different conclusions and endless complications.

Here, while I will be expounding on Buddhadhamma in the context of philosophy, I will not deal with this question, but concentrate on explaining only what Buddhism does teach.[1] As for whether Buddhism is a philosophy, I leave this to philosophy itself to sort out whether its scope or meaning can be interpreted as including Buddhism. Buddhism is Buddhism, and will always be Buddhism. The point is that any principle or teaching that merely aims to search for truth for intellectual reasons, without any objective or teaching for practice in real life, cannot be taken as being Buddhism, in particular the original teachings of the Buddha, which I am here referring to as "Buddhadhamma."

It is difficult to compile the teachings of Buddhism as definitively representing the Buddhadhamma taught and intended by the Buddha, even quoting passages from the texts that are accepted as the words of the Buddha (Buddhavacana), because the teachings in the texts are copious, with varying levels and degrees of profundity, and are dependent on the interpretation of each individual's intelligence and sincerity. In some cases, it may be possible to quote sections from the texts to support opposite views. Gleaning the truth is dependent on the accuracy of one's comprehension and the compatibility and conformity with the principles and overall evidence. Even so, that which is given as evidence tends to be insufficiently broad and therefore does not escape the influence of the individual's underlying views and understandings.

In this regard, there is one other factor that needs to be incorporated into the analysis, and that is the life events and conduct of the Lord Buddha himself, the original source of the teaching.

The Buddha's conduct and his actions—that is to say, what the Teacher actually did—in some cases more clearly illustrate the Buddha's real intention than the words in the texts, or at least can be incorporated to obtain a clearer understanding, even though there may be those who counter that these factors are obtained from the texts just the same as the teachings, and are just as subject to interpretation. Even so, it must be accepted that they are a valuable source for consideration.

From the various sources, both textual and historical, we can draw a picture of the social conditions in the Buddha's time as follows.

The Buddha was born in Jambudvīpa (the "Roseapple Land"—that is, modern-day India and Nepal) about twenty-six hundred years ago. He was born into a royal clan (*kṣatriya*) with the name Prince Siddhattha, the son of King Suddhodana, who was the ruler of the Sākya country located in the northeast of Jambudvīpa at the foot of the Himalayas. As a royal prince and the hope for continuing the family line, he was afforded worldly pleasures in full, and he lived in pleasure like this for twenty-nine years. He was married and the couple had one child.

Politically, at that time some of the kingdom states were on the rise and were making wars in attempts to spread their power and dominion. Many other states, in particular those ruled by consensus (republics), felt their power waning. Some had already been absorbed by other states. States that were still strong were under duress, with wars likely to begin at any time. Even large and powerful states were often at war.

Economically, trade was thriving, and one class of people, the merchants, was growing more influential in society, gaining in rights, status and royal influence.

Socially, people were divided into four castes in accordance with the principles of Brahmanism. Their rights, social standing, and livelihoods varied according to their caste. While some Hindu historians have stated that the castes at that time were not very strict, members of the *śūdra* caste, the manual workers, at least, had no right to listen to or recite passages from the Vedas, which were the sacred scriptures of the Brahmanist religion, and those prohibitions became stricter in later times, with extremely violent punishments, such as being sawn in two, prescribed for any *śūdra* who studied the Vedas. The "untouchables," those who were outside the castes, had no right to any education at all. The designation of the castes was defined by birth, and the brahmins held themselves to be the highest caste.

Religiously, the brahmins, traditionally the protectors of Brahmanism, had gradually developed the teaching to comprise increasingly lavish and esoteric, even irrational, ceremonies. They did this not just for religious objectives but also with the aim of responding to the desire of the elites to display their rank and power, in addition to the rewards they themselves would receive from those elites.

These ceremonies mostly encouraged people to look to increase their own personal benefits, with the hope of rewards of wealth and sensual happiness. At the same time, they created suffering for the lower castes, the slaves who had to do the heavy labor, and for the animals involved in cruel sacrificial ceremonies.[2]

During this time, some of the brahmins began to give serious thought to the problem of eternal life and the way to achieve it, and realized that these ceremonies were not capable of giving them the answers they sought. They went so far as to leave mainstream society in their search, seeking solitude in the forests.

The teachings of Brahmanism at this time, which is known as the Upanishads era, contained many contradictions. Some parts gave further explanation of the many ceremonies, while some parts decried those very ceremonies, and there were different views on the matter of eternal life. There were varied and conflicting teachings on Ātman (the higher self). Ultimately the Ātman was Brahma, the source and essence of all things, with a characteristic of being inexplicable, known as "*neti, neti*" ("not that, not that"). This was the ultimate goal of religious practice, and there were attempts to explain and resolve questions about this state and also to retain that knowledge exclusively within their own group.

Meanwhile, another group of renunciants, who were disenchanted with the meaninglessness of life in this world, took to different practices of their own devising, hoping to discover the deathless or to achieve various attainments. Some of them resorted to ascetic practices of various forms, from fasting to torturous and bizarre observances that people today might think were impossible. Some of them developed concentration (*samādhi*) and attained the form and formless absorptions (*jhāna*), and some developed the absorptions to such high levels of skill that it is said that they could perform miracles.

On another level, many groups of the renunciants, known as *samaṇa*, who had renounced the home life and gone to homelessness in their quest for the deathless, wandered throughout the region debating with each other and establishing themselves as cult leaders with their own doctrines.

The efforts to search for the goal and spread the various competing doctrines proceeded with much vigor, until a great number of doctrines had arisen.[3] Of these, six main doctrines are spoken of frequently in the Buddhist texts.[4]

The situation can be briefly summarized as a time in which one group of people was growing in wealth and power, indulging in and enjoying the search for wealth and material pleasures, while many other groups were seeing their status and livelihoods constantly deteriorating and themselves being neglected. Another group had renounced society, striving to search for the truth through philosophy, but also paying no attention to the state of society.

Prince Siddhattha was pampered with all kinds of worldly happiness for a period of twenty-nine years. He was not only pampered but also shielded from the truths of the suffering experienced by ordinary people. But the reality could not be hidden from him forever, and, confronted by the sufferings of humanity, which are most clearly seen in old age, sickness and death, the prince looked for a solution.

Looking at this problem outwardly on a broader scale, we see a society in which one group of people had the advantage and sought opportunities to increase their own pleasure, contending with and fighting each other and fully immersed in those pleasures, with no thought for the suffering of others. They spent their lives as slaves to material things. When times were good, they immersed themselves in their own selfish pleasures, and when times were hard they fell into mindless suffering. Finally, they grew old, got sick, and died meaninglessly. As for the disadvantaged, those with no opportunities, they were oppressed pitilessly until finally growing old, getting sick, and dying meaninglessly.

Prince Siddhattha, seeing this state of affairs, became disenchanted with his own lifestyle. He looked on such pleasures as void of essence, and searched for a solution that would lead to lasting happiness, a happiness that was real. He could think of no solution, and his situation, surrounded as he was by so many temptations and distractions, was not conducive to clear thinking. Eventually he saw some recluses (*samaṇa*) who had removed themselves from society to search for truth, leading simple lifestyles free of worldly concerns, lifestyles that were conducive to the search for knowledge and clear thinking. Such a lifestyle, he thought, could help him in his quest, and some of those recluses who had searched for truth might have something they could teach him.

At this point, Prince Siddhattha left the home life and became one of those recluses. He traveled around, studying all the knowledge and practices that were known to them. He studied the methods of yoga and practiced meditation until he had developed the *jhāna* attainments up until the highest level of formless attainment, and attained expertise in psychic powers, as well as practicing self-torment.

Eventually he decided that none of the methods of these recluses was capable of giving him the answer he desired. Looking back at the life he had lived, it seemed like two extremes. He then turned within and conducted his own search, until he became enlightened.[5] Later, when teaching the truth that he had discovered to others, he called it the "Middle Teaching" (*majjhena dhamma*; or in full, *majjhena dhammadesanā*) and called the practice that he had formulated the "Middle Way" (*majjhimā paṭipadā*).

At this point we can see that Buddhism sees both living in society with delusion, immersed in and abandoned to enslavement by the stream of defilements on one hand, and total escape, living with no connection or social responsibility, and indulging in self-mortification, on the other, as mistaken extremes that are incapable of leading humanity to a truly meaningful life.

Having been enlightened in this way, the Buddha set out to begin the work of earnestly spreading the Buddhadhamma for the benefit of society and worldly beings, and continued this work for the remaining forty-five years of his life.

Putting aside other factors and considering only social aspects, it can be seen that the work of the Buddha for the benefit of society at that time could best be served by working in the status of a homeless one. The Buddha therefore encouraged and invited many members of the higher classes to give up their wealth and comfort and leave the home life in order to realize the truths he had discovered, and then to work together, sacrificing themselves for the benefit of the people by traveling and meeting people of all classes and in all regions to create benefit on a broad scale.

Moreover, the Saṅgha (order of bhikkhus and bhikkhunīs) is an important resource for solving social problems, in the sense that all people, regardless of their caste, including those who were outcasts, could apply for ordination, and all had equal rights to study for the highest goal.

As for the merchants and householders who were not yet ready to give up everything, they could live as male and female lay supporters, helping support the Saṅgha to carry out their duties and using some of their wealth for creating welfare for the people.

The objectives and scope of the work of both the Buddha and his disciples (*sāvaka*) can be gleaned from the Buddha's words spoken at the very first time he sent his disciples forth to spread the teaching:

> "Bhikkhus, go forth and wander for the benefit and happiness of the many folk, for the welfare of the world, for the benefit, welfare and happiness of gods and humans."[6]

The extent that the Buddhadhamma can be used in a social context, and types of people it can benefit, can be seen in the Buddhavacana of the *Pāsādika Sutta*, which can be summarized as follows:

The holy life (i.e., the teaching) can be said to have been successfully spread far and wide, to have benefited the multitude and be solidly established, to the extent that it is well declared among gods and humans, when the following factors are fulfilled:

- The founder (*sāsadā*) is an elder, of long standing, over a long period of time.
- There are bhikkhu followers who are elders, who are knowledgeable and skilled, who have been well trained, who are bold and have realized the secure release from bondage, who are able to teach the Dhamma with real effect and denounce correctly in accordance with the Dhamma any contentious doctrines (*parapavāda*) that have arisen, and they in turn have bhikkhu followers who are of middle and newly ordained status who have the same abilities.
- There are bhikkhuni (female monk) followers who are elders and of middle and newly ordained status who have the same abilities.
- There are male lay followers, both those who live the holy life and those who live the household life and partake of sense pleasures, who have the same abilities.
- There are female lay followers, both those who live the holy life and those who live the household life and partake of sense pleasures, who have the same abilities. Without so much as the female lay followers, the holy life cannot be said to be fully established.[7]

This passage shows that the Buddhadhamma is aimed at all kinds of people, both renunciants and householders; that is, it encompasses all of society.

General Characteristics of Buddhadhamma

The general characteristics of Buddhadhamma can be summarized in two ways:

First, it gives a Middle Teaching, known as the *majjhena dhamma* or *majjhena dhammadesanā*, dealing with the truth based on pure rationality in accordance with the natural processes. It is taught specifically for practical objectives in real life. Attempts to realize the truth through arguments, philosophical debate, and creation of various theories to be attached to and fought over is not encouraged.

Second, it teaches a "Middle Way" of practice known as the *majjhimā paṭipadā*, which constitutes the principles of living for one who is training to know the truth of life. It aims for the objective of happiness, purity, light, peace and freedom, to be seen in this very life. In practice, this Middle Way proceeds in conjunction with other factors, such as the status of being a renunciant or a householder.

Buddhism is a religion of action (*kammavāda* or *kiriyavāda*) and a religion of effort (*viriyavāda*),[8] not a religion of prayer and supplication, or a religion of hope and worry. The Buddha's teaching was aimed at practical results, for all people to deal with their actual lives in this world and in this very moment. The knowledge of the principles known as the Middle Teaching and the practice of the path known as the Middle Way are things that all people, regardless of their situation and station in life, can understand and implement as appropriate to that situation and station. If they are concerned about a life after this world, they should actualize the good life they aspire to by practicing in the present moment, until they are confident that they will definitely fare well without having to worry about or be concerned over that next life.[9]

Everyone has an equal, natural right to reach these attainments, even though their abilities may differ. Everyone should therefore have an equal opportunity to find success in accordance with their ability. That ability is something that can be modified and increased. So it is fitting that all people have an equal chance to develop their abilities as best they can. While ultimately all people must achieve this attainment for themselves, as their own personal responsibility, they can be helped by others. Therefore, the principle of heedfulness (*appamāda dhamma*) and the principle of the good friend (*kalyāṇamitta*) are prominent teachings, and both are given much emphasis in terms of accepting personal responsibility on one hand, and the importance of supportive external factors.

Considering the accomplishments and conduct of the Buddha, we can see many important principles at work, such as acting to dismantle gullible beliefs in regard to meaningless rituals, in particular the sacrificial ceremonies, by pointing out the harm and fruitlessness of those rituals. That the Buddha gave great emphasis to giving up sacrificial ceremonies is because those ceremonies caused people to blindly put their hope in external forces, to crave and concern themselves even more with material benefits, selfish interests and harming other lives with no consideration of the suffering and trouble caused, and to put their hopes in the future to the neglect of the present moment. He taught instead the principle of giving (*dāna*), sharing, and helping each other in society.

The next concept that the Buddha's teaching sought to dismantle was the belief in castes, which divided people on the basis of their birth and restricted their social and intellectual rights and opportunities. He established the Saṅgha, which accepted people from all castes into an egalitarian community, like the great ocean that receives water from all the rivers and brings them together as one,[10] leading to the institution of the Buddhist monastery, which later became an important center for cultural and educational propagation, a model that was adopted by Hinduism around fourteen hundred to seventeen hundred years after the Buddha's time.[11]

According to the Buddhadhamma, both women and men are equally capable of attaining the highest goal of Buddhism. Having established the bhikkhu Saṅgha the Buddha later established the

Saṅgha of bhikkhunis, in spite of a social milieu that was not supportive. He did this with consideration of the difficulties involved and with great care, in order to ensure that the vocation of female renunciants would be able to survive in society at a time when opportunities for study of the mind for females had been severely limited, and almost extinguished, by the Vedic religions.

The next item is that the Buddha taught in the common vernacular, so that people of all levels of education could benefit from it equally. This is in contrast to the Brahmanist religion, which held to the holiness of the Vedas and restricted higher knowledge to their own group in various ways, in particular by using the original Sanskrit language, knowledge of which was limited to their own group, for the purposes of preserving and passing down their religious texts. On being asked to put his teachings into the language of the Vedas, the Buddha refused, and maintained that the teachings should be preserved in the common language.[12]

The next item is that the Buddha absolutely refused to waste time arguing in philosophical debates over truths that could not be verified by logic. When people asked him such questions, he would shut down the question and immediately bring the questioner back to a problem that he or she would have to relate to and deal with in their real lives.[13] That which can be known through speech, he taught through speech; that which can be known through seeing, he pointed out. He did not try to teach through speech that which must be seen directly.

As to this, he taught the Buddhadhamma in multiple ways and on many levels, both for householders, people who were conducting their lives in society, and also those who had renounced the household life, with teachings aimed at both material benefit and more profound mental benefits, so that all people could benefit from it.

That he had to teach the Buddhadhamma surrounded by a Brahmanist culture and the multifarious beliefs and doctrines of the recluses at the time meant that the Buddha had to involve himself with the terminology of the prevailing religions, doctrines, and beliefs, both in the sense that he had to have listened to them and had to refer to them, and also in that he wanted the teaching to quickly spread and to benefit the population on a broad scale. Thus it was that the Buddha developed methods in response to the terminology of these religions. It is noteworthy that he did not tend to tear down the words of previously held beliefs, but only to tear down the beliefs that were behind those words. That is to say, he did not use aggressive methods, but brought about change that arose naturally as a result of understanding and wise reflection, through study and personal development.

In this sense, the Buddha made use of some of the teachings contained in the existing religions, but imbued them with different meanings in accordance with the Buddhadhamma, adding new values to those terms. Examples are using "Brahma" to mean a mortal being in the world, or as a term for one's parents; changing the meaning of the homage to the six natural directions to obligations for preservation of social relationships; changing the meaning of the threefold fire worship in Brahmanist ceremonies to a social responsibility to three kinds of persons; and changing the deciding factor for determining a person as a brahmin, or an *āryan*, from birth status to a way of conduct.

The Buddha occasionally used parts of existing religions in his own teachings, but in a new and beneficial way. He accepted those teachings that were correct and beneficial, deeming such correctness and benefit to be natural universal qualities. In cases where a teaching or practice of the prevailing religions had a number of different meanings, he pointed out which perspective was right and which was wrong, and accepted and taught that perspective that was good and correct.

He also taught that the mistaken and harmful practices of those religions were a deterioration of originally correct teachings, and explained what the original teachings were. Examples of this are ascetic practices (*tapa*), sacrificial ceremonies, the principles of governance, and the duties of the brahmins.[14]

The above shows not only the breadth of the Buddhadhamma and the Buddha's intention to teach only what was true, good, and correct in a neutral way, but it also acts as a caution to be aware of the distinction between the meaning of the teachings used in the Buddhadhamma and those used in other religions.

After the Buddha's passing away, as time went on and the teachings spread to different areas, the understanding of the Buddhadhamma began to stray from the original and take on many variations, due to the differences in the basic knowledge, training, and wisdom of those who were spreading it, contamination of beliefs from other doctrines and religions, influence of local religions and cultures, and increased emphasis on certain aspects of the teaching due to the biases and abilities of the protectors of the teaching. This led to splitting up into different sects, the best-known being the Mahayana and Theravada.

As for Theravada, even though it is known as the sect that has most accurately preserved the original model and teaching, it does not escape aberration. Some parts of the teachings, even those in the texts, still cause problems that people in the present time must debate and research for evidence of affirmation or rejection as being true original teachings. The more the beliefs and practice of people strays into error, the more clearly does the understanding of Buddhism stray. In some cases, it is almost the opposite to the original teaching, or has become another of the doctrines that the original teaching sought to challenge.

To take an example from Thailand, when we say the word *kamma*, the understanding of most people will focus on the past, on actions in past lives, or on phenomena that are results, seeing events that occur in the present as results of past actions, or on the power of past bad actions to produce bad results. Mostly the understanding is according to a mixture of these perspectives, which when considered in accordance with the teaching of *kamma* in the Buddhadhamma can be clearly seen to have strayed far from the real meaning.

In the exposition of Buddhadhamma to follow, the writer has tried to explain the true meaning as taught and intended by the Buddha. To this end, I have completely dispensed with the meaning of terms as understood by the general population [in Thailand] because I believe that this meaning is not required for an understanding of the Buddhadhamma.

The main source for the content and meaning of the Buddhadhamma explained here are the Buddhist texts, which unless otherwise required, consists solely of the Pali Tipiṭaka, because these are the texts that are generally accepted as the most complete and accurate repository of the compiled Buddha's teachings. Even so, I have chosen only those parts that I believe to be the original teachings and the real meaning, adhering to the principle of consistency and compliance with the overall meaning. For additional confidence, I have included the Buddha's conduct and duties in consideration of the correct approach and scope of the Buddhadhamma.

Governed by these principles, I am confident that it is possible to give an explanation of the essence of Buddhadhamma that is extremely close to the real meaning.

Even so, fundamentally, the explanation is still dependent on the wisdom of the writer and any biases I may unknowingly have. Therefore, let it be taken as one attempt to explain the Buddhadhamma as accurately as possible in accordance with the Buddha's own teaching and objectives, relying on a method and principles, as well as evidence, upon which I believe I can have the most confidence.

If we divide Buddhadhamma into two parts, being truth (*saccadhamma*) and conduct (*cariyadhamma*), and define those parts for our purposes here as truth being the reality or features of truth, and conduct being the entirety of the practice, we can see that truth in Buddhism refers to the teachings dealing with the reality of things, or nature and the natural order of things, or natural laws. Conduct refers to making use of the knowledge and understanding of that reality and natural order, or knowing the laws of nature, and putting that knowledge to use in a way that is beneficial. In another sense, truth is nature and the natural laws, while conduct is knowing how to practically apply that truth. These principles are entirely unrelated to any supernatural agent such as a creator.

For that reason, the chapters in this book dealing with natural realities also contain sections dealing with ethical value. For example, having dealt with the knowledge and understanding of life and the world, there is a discussion of the meaning and practical value of such an understanding. Looking on a broader scale, at this book as a whole, the same approach is followed. That is, the first section (book one) deals with the realities and laws of nature, known as the *majjhena dhammadesanā*. The second part (book two) deals with taking the knowledge of reality and natural laws and putting it into practice in actual life, which is called the *majjhimā paṭipadā*.

Even so, if looked at from the perspective of the main principles of Dhamma, the structure of this book conforms with the teaching method of the four noble truths. This teaching emphasizes practical application. It therefore begins with the problem that has arisen, and from there searching for the cause, ascertaining the objective and establishing a solution. In this book, we begin with the nature of life that is a problem and search back to find the factors that cause the problem. There is a discussion of the goal and the methods for solving the problem and attaining that goal, in order. In this sense, even though at first glance it may seem to be a new way of presenting the Dhamma, in essence my approach follows the structure of the original teaching.[15]

BOOK ONE

THE MIDDLE TEACHING

Ete te brāhmaṇa ubho ante anupagamma majjhena tathāgato dhammaṁ deseti: avijjāpaccayā saṅkhārā, sāṅkhārapaccayā viññāṇaṁ...

Here, Brahmin, the Tathāgata, not inclining to those two extremes, teaches the Dhamma in a Middle Way, thus: with ignorance as condition are volitional formations; with volitional formations, consciousness...

PART ONE

What Is Life?

CHAPTER 1

The Five *Khandhas* and the Six Sense Bases

The Five *Khandhas*

Buddhism looks on things as aggregates of component parts. They have no abiding essence. When the components are taken away, no self or entity remains. A simple example that is often cited is the cart: when the various components are put together in compliance with the design, the result is designated a "cart," but when all of those components are separated, no entity "cart" can be found.[1] There is no entity of a cart apart from the components, only the designation "cart" given to the state that results when they are put together.

The components themselves manifest as the result of the compounding of even lesser components, and likewise no real essence can be found within them. When we say that things exist, it must be understood in the sense that they exist as aggregates of components.

Since it sees things as aggregates of components in this way, Buddhism must proceed to show what these components are and what they are like, at least in illustration, and since the teaching has a special concern with life, especially its mental aspect, its explication must encompass both matter and mind, the physical (*rūpadhamma*) and the mental (*nāmadhamma*), and it gives special emphasis to the mind.

There are many ways to present the components of life, depending on the purpose intended,[2] but here we will be explaining the five *khandhas* (groups), which is the model preferred in the sutta discourses.

Analyzing according to the five *khandhas*, Buddhism dissects life, including all of its component parts—which we designate as a "being," an "individual," and so on—into five types or groups of components, referred to in Buddhist terminology as the five *khandhas*.

1. *Rūpa* (physicality).[3] The entire gamut of physical components; the body and all its manifestations, or matter and physical energy, together with their properties and activities.
2. *Vedanā* (feeling or sensation).[4] The feelings of pleasure, suffering, and indifference that arise from contact through the five physical senses and the mind.
3. *Saññā* (perception).[5] Determining or perceiving—that is, apprehending or recognizing modality, signs, and features that enable the remembrance of cognitive objects (*ārammaṇa*).
4. *Saṅkhārā* (mental formations or volitional activities).[6] The factors and qualities of the mind, led by intention, that condition the mind to be good, evil, or neutral. In simple terms, it is the various good and bad thoughts, such as faith (*saddhā*), recollection or mindfulness (*sati*), goodwill (*mettā*), compassion (*karuṇā*), equanimity (*upekkhā*[7]), wisdom (*paññā*), delusion (*moha*), greed (*lobha*), and hatred (*dosa*).
5. *Viññāṇa* (consciousness).[8] Awareness of objects through the five physical senses and the mind: seeing, hearing, smelling, tasting, experiencing sensations through the body, and awareness of mental objects.

The last four *khandhas*, which are all mental conditions, require further explanation:[9]

Saññā is a form of knowledge.[10] It refers to "perception," the "apprehension" of the attributes of an object of awareness, such as its features, figure, color, and shape, and also names, conventions, and concepts such as "green," "red," "loud," or "soft." This registering of sense objects is done by juxtaposition or comparison of old experiences and new ones. If the new experience corresponds with an old one, for example in seeing or hearing a familiar person or object, this is called "recognition" (note here that "recognizing" is not "remembering"; see page 26, "*Saññā*, *Sati,* and Memory"). If the new experience does not correspond with an old one, old experiences are used as a frame of reference to see in what ways they are similar and dissimilar. That object is then registered according to what has been found out or noted. This is the action of "noting" or "perceiving as."

There are many different levels of this noting: noting in accordance with conventions based on ordinary knowledge, such as "green," "white," "yellow," "red"; noting in accordance with worldly, social, cultural or traditional values, such as "polite" or "impolite"; noting in accordance with personal preferences and ideas, as in "this doesn't look good" or "that is beautiful"; noting on two levels—for example, "two strikes of the bell signals meal time"; and even noting on the basis of one's study and practice of Dhamma, as when noting impermanence or selflessness. There are simple levels of noting and complex levels of noting (in that they are more involved with other *khandhas*); there are noting of material objects and noting of mental objects.

The words that are commonly used to translate *saññā*—"recognizing, marking, noting, regarding, registering, perceiving as"—all show different shades of meaning for the *saññā* group. In simple terms, *saññā* is the process that collects, collates, and stores the data of experience as raw materials for the thinking process. *Saññā* is useful in the conduct of human life, but it is also not without its dangers, because people tend to cling to things according to their perceptions. Then *saññā* becomes an obstruction to seeing the true nature of things.

For convenience of study, *saññā* can be divided into two broad levels: basic or simple *saññā*, which notes the features of objects of awareness as they generally arise, and derived or complex *saññā*, which is sometimes referred to by other names, especially *papañca-saññā* , which is *saññā* derived from objects of awareness fabricated and complicated by desire, conceit, and views, which are the leading kinds of malignant *saṅkhāra*. Analyzing *saññā* in this way helps to show more clearly the meaning of *saññā* in operation and its relationship to the other *khandhas* within the natural processes.

In the monastic tradition, *viññāṇa* is glossed as "knowing clearly." It is the consciousness of sense objects, the fundamental kind of knowledge, the "standing awareness," as it were. It is both the base from which, and the medium through which, the other mental *khandhas* function and are interconnected with one another. It is both preliminary awareness and subsequent awareness. By "preliminary awareness" is meant the initial awareness of seeing, hearing, and so on (the arising of consciousness), depending on which there are the feelings (*vedanā*) of pleasure or stress, recognition as "this" or "that" (*saññā*), and volitional response and fabrication (*saṅkhāra*).

By "subsequent awareness" is meant awareness in conjunction with the activities of other *khandhas*. For example, when one feels happy and contented (which is *vedanā*) there is also an awareness (*viññāṇa*) of that happy feeling (note that feeling happy and awareness of the feeling of happiness are not the same); when one feels depressed (*vedanā*), there is an awareness (*viññāṇa*) of this unpleasant feeling. In perception of happiness and suffering (*saññā*), there is awareness (*viññāṇa*) involved; whenever there is thinking or intention (*saṅkhāra*), there is also an awareness of that. The fundamental stream of awareness, which is constantly and continuously arising and ceasing in conjunction with the other mental *khandhas* or activities of the mind, is called *viññāṇa*.

Another distinctive feature of *viññāṇa* is that it is a distinguishing awareness, or an awareness in the light of specific meaning. This may be illustrated through some examples: when one sees a striped piece of cloth, the actual seeing, even without any noting of what the object is, also entails an awareness of some of its existing characteristics, such as some specific and distinctive colors. This is awareness on the level of *viññāṇa*. Because *viññāṇa* sees that distinction, *saññā* can perform the function of recognizing those distinctive features, as in identifying the striped object as a hand towel. When one is eating a piece of fruit, even if one does not recognize a specific sweet or sour taste, there is an awareness of that distinctive taste itself, whether sweet or sour. Moreover, even in a sweet or sour taste, there is an awareness of the distinctive taste even if there is no recognition of the taste as the sourness of a mango, a plum, a tamarind, a lemon, or a pineapple, or the sweetness of a particular kind of banana or an apple.

This kind of awareness is *viññāṇa*. It is the fundamental awareness that acts as the base on which function the other mental *khandhas*, as in experiencing a taste as pleasant or unpleasant (*vedanā*), or recognizing it as a particular kind of sweetness or sourness (*saññā*).

Viññāṇa as awareness in the light of a specific meaning can be briefly explained thus: when *viññāṇa* arises, such as in seeing or hearing, it is actually only seeing or hearing some specific aspects or meanings of what is seen or heard. In other words, it is seeing or hearing in the light of the specific aspects or meanings we assign to it, depending on the mental activities (*saṅkhārā*) that condition it.[11]

For example, in the middle of a large, open field stands a solitary mango tree. It is a large tree, but it has only a few mangoes, sparse leaves, and hardly any shade. Five people approach that tree in different circumstances: one is fleeing a dangerous animal, one is starving, one is seeking shelter from the hot sun, one is looking for fruits to sell, and one is looking for a place to tether her cow while she goes off to tend to some business nearby. All five of those people see the big mango tree, but each will be conscious of the sight from a different perspective and within the context of different meanings. *Viññāṇa* arises for them all, but it is different for each of them, according to the intention each has in relation to the tree. At the same time, the perceptions (*saññā*) of each of those people will differ according to the context of meaning in which he or she sees the tree, as too will the feelings (*vedanā*) that arise.

For instance, the person who is fleeing a dangerous animal might be pleased at the sight of such a big tree, because he sees in it an escape from danger. The starving person might also be pleased, because only three or four mangoes will be sufficient to save her life. The person suffering from the hot sun might be disappointed on finding that the tree has less shade than could be expected for one of its size. The person looking for fruits to sell will be unhappy on finding the number of fruits so small. The person looking for a place to tie up her cow may feel pleased, but only mildly so, simply relieved that she doesn't have to lead the cow any further or find somewhere else to tether it.

Vedanā is commonly translated as "having a sensation" or "experiencing the *flavor* of a sense object." It is a feeling toward an object of awareness, and it arises every time an awareness occurs. The feeling may be one of pleasure (such as comfort, happiness, or delight), pain (oppression, suffering, and so on), or indifference.

To prevent confusion with *saṅkhārā*, it should be understood that *vedanā* is a passive function of the mind. It involves the effects that experiences have on the mind.[12] *Vedanā* is not included within the mind's intentions toward or responses to objects of awareness, as that is the domain of the *saṅkhārakhandha*. Thus, such words as *like* and *dislike* are usually used to describe activities of the *saṅkhārakhandha*, as movements contingent on, but distinct from, *vedanā*, because *like* and *dislike* have elements of intention. They are active responses to objects of awareness.

Vedanā is important in that when it is pleasant it is aspired to and sought after, and when it is unpleasant it is abhorred and shunned. Each time awareness arises, *vedanā* is the pivotal link that influences the direction in which other factors will proceed. If one becomes aware of a sense object and pleasant feeling arises, one will note that object intensely and in such a way that the feeling is prolonged, and will create ways of repeating or extending the experience.

Saṅkhārā includes both the conditions, led by intention (*cetanā*), that fashion the mind's qualities or states, and the process of volition that directs, selects, and organizes those qualities in conditioning actions, speech, and thoughts, resulting in bodily, verbal, and mental *kamma*. However, in explaining *saṅkhārā* as one of the five *khandhas*, the objective is to show the state of nature—that is, what life is made up of—rather than the process of nature—that is, how life functions. Thus, the explanation of *saṅkhārā* in the five *khandhas* is usually limited to a description of the mind's conditioners—for example, what they are and what they are like. The explanation of *saṅkhārā* as a process of conditioning, which deals with the functional level, is given in the teaching on the principle of dependent arising (*paṭiccasamuppāda*), which shows how life functions. Thus, in the teaching of dependent arising, *saṅkhāra* is described as an operation, divided into *kāyasaṅkhāra* (the conditioning through which intention expresses itself in bodily actions, or the intention that conditions bodily actions), *vacīsaṅkhāra* (the conditioning through which intention expresses itself in speech, or the intention that conditions speech), and *cittasaṅkhāra* (the conditioning through which intention expresses itself in thinking, or the intention that conditions thought). By contrast, the explanation of *saṅkhārā* in terms of the five *khandhas* describes the various factors that do the conditioning, such as faith (*saddhā*), mindfulness (*sati*), goodwill (*mettā*), greed (*lobha*), anger (*dosa*), intention (*cetanā*), and concentration (*samādhi*). The explanation of *saṅkhārā* in terms of the five *khandhas* is like a car on display showing its various components, while the explanation in terms of the principle of dependent arising (which will be dealt with later) is like a description of a car in operation.

Of all the factors that condition the mind, intention is foremost. No matter how many conditioning factors arise at any one time, intention will always be at the core. Sometimes the word *cetanā* is even used to represent *saṅkhāra* as a whole, thus giving us another definition of *saṅkhāra*: "*Saṅkhāra* is intention (*cetanā*) and its associated qualities (*sampayutta dhamma*), which condition the mind into good, evil, or neutral states; mold thinking, speech, and actions; and cause *kamma* through body, speech, and mind." The word *cetanā* alone is sometimes used as a synonym for *saṅkhāra* or is used in defining *saṅkhāra*. *Cetanā* is also used to define *kamma*.

Thus, in this sense, the words *saṅkhāra*, *cetanā*, and *kamma* have roughly the same meaning.

Apart from the importance already described, the factor of intention is also what distinguishes *saṅkhārā* from the other *khandhas*. *Vedanā*, *saññā*, and *viññāṇa* work on cognitive objects already arisen; they are contingent on cognitive objects, dependent on them in order to function, and passive, whereas *saṅkhāra* can be self-initiating: it exerts will on cognitive objects and acts upon them.[13]

In this light, it is easier to see why it is that pleasure and pain are classified as *vedanā*, while like and dislike, which arise subsequent to pleasure and pain, are classified as *saṅkhārā*; why *saññā* and *sati*, which are both connected to memory, are nevertheless classified into different *khandhas* (*sati* is classed as *saṅkhāra*), and why *paññā*, which, like *saññā* and *viññāṇa*, is a kind of knowledge, is put into the *saṅkhārakhandha*.

Saññā, *Sati*, and Memory

Confusion often arises as to which *khandha* the functioning of memory is classified into. The word *saññā* is often translated as "memory," while the word *sati* is generally translated as "recollection" and is sometimes translated as "memory." A notable example of this is the case of Venerable Ānanda, who was declared the foremost among those who could remember the Buddha's words (Buddhavacana). The Pali word used in this case was *sati*: "Ānanda is the foremost of my disciples in regard to being endowed with *sati*."[14] No confusion exists here: memory is not a function of one specific factor but is the result of a whole process, and within this process, *sati* and *saññā* are the main factors; both have meanings that overlap with memory. That is, one function of *saññā* is also an aspect of memory; another function of *saññā* lies beyond the scope of memory. The same with *sati*: one function of *sati* corresponds with one aspect of the meaning of memory, while another function of *sati* lies beyond the bounds of the process of remembering. Importantly: *saññā* and *sati* perform different functions within the memory process.

Saññā notes or marks an object of awareness. When another object arises, it compares it with the data already observed. If the two are marked as the same, there is "recognizing." If there are discrepancies, they are further noted. Both the act of noting, marking, or recognizing an object as this or that (in comparing and collecting data) and the object that is noted (the data so formed and collected) are called *saññā*. This corresponds to memory insofar as it provides the conditions for remembering to take place. The important feature of *saññā* is that it operates on objects that have already arisen: only when an object appears before one can there be noting, marking, or recognition of it.

The function of *sati* is to bring an object of awareness to mind, or hold it to the mind, holding the mind to its object and not allowing the object to slip by. It may be the bringing to awareness of an object that has already passed by, or it may be the retaining of an object that is just about to pass. The meaning of *sati* thus encompasses recollecting, bringing to mind, bearing in mind, being able to recall, being able to remember, being without lapses of concentration. It corresponds to memory specifically in recollecting and its capacity to recollect. For this reason, *sati* is said to find its opposite in *sammosa*, "to forget" (*saññā* is not the opposite of *sammosa*). *Sati* is an initiative from within, driven by intention, even when no object of awareness appears. *Sati* involves an intention on objects of awareness and as such is classified as *saṅkhāra*.

Saññā records and stores data, while *sati* brings it forward for use. Both good *saññā*, the clear and systematic noting and collation of data into a meaningful and coherent form (which in turn depends, for example, on attention and understanding), and good *sati*, which is the ability to recollect, are factors contributing to good memory.

Imagine two people who are old acquaintances but have not met for many years. After ten years, Ms. Black meets Mr. Green and recognizes him. Later she recalls that she and Mr. Green visited certain places together. Ms. Black's recognizing Mr. Green when they meet is *saññā*, while her subsequent recollections of their past experiences are *sati*.

A telephone is situated in one corner of a room; a telephone book is in another corner. A woman opens the telephone book, searches for a number, and makes a mental note of the number she wants. She then walks to the other side of the room to make her call, keeping the telephone number in mind. Her reading and noting the number are functions of *saññā*, whereas her bearing the number in mind while walking across the room is a function of *sati*.

When an object of awareness is present, it can be immediately noted, but when an object is not present, and if it is a mental object (stored as a memory), *sati* is used to retrieve it for noting. Moreover, *sati* may recollect old *saññā*; that is, it can retrieve old impressions or memories and make them objects of the mind. *Saññā* will note those impressions again to make them clearer and firmer, or make further notes about them in light of a different objective.

The Interaction between the *Khandhas*

The five *khandhas* are interdependent. The *rūpakhandha* is corporeal and the four *nāmakhandhas* are mental. There must be both body and mind for there to be life. When body and mind are functioning normally and harmoniously, life proceeds smoothly. For example, the activities of the mind require knowledge of the world, which arises on the basis of the sense objects of sight, sound, taste, smell, and touch through eye, ear, nose, tongue, and body. The five kinds of sense objects, as well as their respective sense organs, are all physical, belonging to the *rūpakhandha*.

Here the focus will be on the mental *khandhas*. The mind is the center of the activities of life—vast, complex, and profound. It is the quality that imbues values and meaning into life and directly concerns the Buddhadhamma that will be dealt with in the following pages.

The four *nāmakhandhas* are closely related and exert an influence on each other. Their arising normally follows this sequence:

> "With sense contact (*phassa*; eye, ear, etc. + form, sound, etc. + consciousness) as condition there is feeling (*vedanā*); what

> one feels, that one perceives (*saññā*); what one perceives, that one thinks about (*saṅkhāra*)."[15]

For example, a man hears the sound of a bell (ear + sound + aural consciousness), feels the sound to be pleasing (*vedanā*), and perceives that it is a melodic sound, that the sound is of a bell and that it is a melodic sound (*saññā*). He likes the sound and wants to hear it again; he may think of striking the bell himself, think of going to buy a similar bell, or of stealing that bell (*saṅkhāra*).

Note that *vedanā* plays an important role within this process. *Saññā* will tend to note any object that produces pleasant feeling. The stronger the pleasant feeling produced by the object, the stronger the noting. That feeling is also the impetus for mental fabrications and actions directed at experiencing more of it. The ongoing phenomenon is a simple, basic process of nature. Within this process, *vedanā* is the bait that seduces the mind, suggesting, in a sense, whether the object is worth obtaining or avoiding. *Saññā* is like a collector of data, the raw material. *Saṅkhāra* is like a person who works on the data and raw material, or processes it for use. *Viññāṇa* is like the owner of the work, the person who is aware of everyone else's work: it is both the provider of the opportunity to work and the recipient of the work's results.[16]

The process is complex. It is not only that *vedanā* influences other *khandhas*; other *khandhas* also condition *vedanā*. For example, the sound of the same piece of music or song might be pleasing to one person but distressing to another. Even the same person might feel pleased on hearing the sound at one time, but at another time find it unpleasant. As a rule, experiencing things that are to our liking, which conform with our desires, produces pleasant feelings, while experiencing things that are not to our liking, which conflict with our desires, produces unpleasant feelings. In this instance, *saṅkhārā*, as liking and disliking, wanting and loathing, conditions *vedanā*.

But *saññā* is also involved in this process. *Saṅkhāras* condition *saññā*, and thereby condition *vedanā*. For example, we see certain mannerisms in people we like or admire and perceive that those mannerisms are graceful or endearing; we see some mannerisms in other people that we don't like and perceive those mannerisms as repugnant (*saññā*). Later when we again see the mannerisms that we have taken a liking to and perceived to be graceful or endearing, or that we have perceived to be repugnant as the case may be, we feel pleased or distressed (*vedanā*) and then we like them or hate them accordingly (*saṅkhāra*).

More complicated would be the case of some kinds of work or study that are inherently difficult. On their own, such tasks would cause suffering, which would discourage people from doing them. However, people's interest can be awakened by an incentive. Such incentives may be in the form of pleasant feeling during the actual work, such as some way of making the task more pleasant, or they may be something more complicated, involving the expectation of future happiness, such as a perceived reward, future success, or benefit to oneself, to others or to the community at large, depending on what kind of *saṅkhāra*—desire, pride, or wisdom, for example—is doing the conditioning. Incentive imbues the work being done with meaning, value, or importance, and also enables us to enjoy the work. Even though there may be some physical discomfort, the mind is suffused with gladness, and the worker or student can continue the tasks with energy.

When the school bell rings in the afternoon, the students all hear it (*viññāṇa*). Many of them may feel indifferent (*vedanā*) to the sound because they have heard it often enough before. They all realize that it is the signal to go home (*saññā*). One student may feel pleased at the sound (pleasant feeling + *saṅkhāra*) because he can go and play and does not have to sit uncomfortably in his seat any longer (complex *saññā*), while another might feel upset (unpleasant feeling + *saṅkhāra*) at stopping a valuable lesson, missing out on potential benefit, or because he has to go home and face a fearsome parent or guardian (complex *saññā*).

In this sense, the whole sequence that begins with *viññāṇa* is a process of entirely interrelated, intricate causal factors that together build up each individual's personality and determine his or her destiny and the directions their lives take. Within this process, it is *saṅkhāra* that is the conditioning factor, and *saṅkhāra*, represented by intention, is the "personal name," as it were, of the term *kamma*. It is for this reason that *kamma*, the official or working title of *saṅkhāra*, is referred to as having such a prominent role in such statements as "*Kamma* is that which divides beings, making them coarse and refined"[17] and "All beings fare according to *kamma*."[18]

The Five *Khandhas* and the Five *Khandhas* of Clinging: Life and Life That Is a Problem

In the Buddhavacana defining the four noble truths, which encompass all of the Buddha's teachings, there is an especially noteworthy passage dealing with the five *khandhas*. It occurs in the section on the first noble truth, the truth of suffering.

In that first noble truth, the Buddha explains or defines suffering with events that are readily seen and commonly occur in everyday life, each of which is shown to be suffering. At the end of this list, the Buddha summarizes them all into one: the five *khandhas* of clinging (*upādāna*) are suffering.

> "Bhikkhus, this is the truth of suffering: birth is suffering, aging is suffering, death is suffering, association with the unloved is suffering, separation from the loved is suffering, not getting what one wants is suffering; in short, the five *khandhas* of clinging (*upādānakkhandhā*) are suffering."[19]

Not only does this passage show the place of the five *khandhas* in the Buddhadhamma, but it also contains the noteworthy statement that the meaning of suffering can be easily remembered with this briefest of summaries, "the five *khandhas* of clinging."

What needs to be noted here are the words *khandha* and *upādānakkhandha*, in regard to which the following lines of Buddhavacana should be considered:

> "Bhikkhus, I will expound the five *khandhas* and the five *khandhas* of clinging (*upādānakkhandhā*). Listen well.

> "What are the five *khandhas*? Any form...feeling...perception...mental formation...consciousness, whether past, future, or present; internal or external; gross or subtle; coarse or refined; far or near...these are called the five *khandhas*...
>
> "What are the five *khandhas* of clinging? Any form...feeling...perception...mental formation...consciousness, whether past, future, or present; internal or external; gross or subtle; coarse or refined; far or near, that contain the outflows (*āsava*), that are objects of clinging (*upādāna*)...these are called the five *khandhas* of clinging."[20]
>
> ---
>
> "*Rūpa*...*vedanā*...*saññā*...*saṅkhārā*...*viññāṇa* are the bases of clinging. *Chandarāga* (affection to the degree of attachment) in that *rūpa*...*vedanā*...*saññā*...*saṅkhāra*...*viññāṇa* is the clinging (*upādāna*) to that."[21]

This principle is an important foundation for our understanding of the Buddhadhamma to come.

Practical Value

People have a tendency to believe that their real self exists in one form or another. Some believe it is the mind;[22] others believe that there is a separate self concealed within the mind, an owner or agent that controls and directs body and mind from another level.

The teaching of the five *khandhas* aims to show that what we call a being, an individual, a self, and so on, when taken apart, is merely these five component parts. Nothing is left that could be a separate self. And each of those five *khandhas* exists only in an interdependent relationship. They are not independent and do not exist by themselves. Thus, none of the five *khandhas* is the self either.

Essentially, the teaching of the five *khandhas* illustrates the truth of not-self (*anattā*), showing that life is the coming together of various components. The combination of these components is not a self, each of the components is not a self, and there is no self apart from them.[23] Seeing in this way, attachment to the issue of self can be uprooted. Not-self can be seen more clearly when one understands the process of the five *khandhas* in the cycle of dependent arising (*paṭiccasamuppāda*), which will be explained later.

When the five *khandhas* are seen as existing in interrelationship and interdependence, the wrong views of annihilationism, known as *ucchedadiṭṭhi*, and eternalism, known as *sassatadiṭṭhi*, will not arise. Moreover, understanding all things in this way also enables a proper understanding of how the law of *kamma* operates. This process of interrelationship and interdependence is explained, once again, in the teaching on dependent arising.

Furthermore, seeing things by dissecting their components as described by the five *khandhas* is a way of training the thought processes, developing the habit of analytical thinking. When we experience or associate with things, our thought responses are not limited or fixed on only their external appearance. Instead, we develop the habit of inquiring into and examining things and searching for truth, and, most importantly, seeing things objectively, as they are, not holding on to them with desire and clinging, which cause us to see things subjectively, as we would want them to be or not be.

This last value is the attainment of the objective of the Buddhadhamma and the teaching of the five *khandhas*: non-attachment, relating to things not through desire and attachment but through wisdom.

However, in the Buddha's teaching the five *khandhas* are usually not presented on their own, as they are simply posited as bases for observation, and that observation must accord with other teachings that are types of natural laws, through which to discern and examine how the five *khandhas* exist and function. The five *khandhas* should therefore be taught in relation to these other teachings, such as the principle of not-self, before their value in practical terms is fully realized. For that reason, we will here finish our discussion of the five *khandhas*, having established them as the bases for further examination in the light of the principles that follow.

The Six Sense Bases: The Spheres of Awareness

Although life is composed of the five *khandhas*, which can be dissected into a large number of subsidiary components, in practical terms human beings are not directly concerned with all of those components in their everyday lives. Many of these components exist and function without our knowledge, and even those we do know we rarely think about. On the physical side, for example, the internal organs of the body carry out their functions almost entirely without the awareness or interest of their owners. Sometimes they malfunction or some irregularity arises, and then we take some interest in them. The same applies to the components of the mental processes.

The study and analysis of the parts of the body and the physical processes are usually left to students of medicine and biology, while the study and analysis of the component factors within the mental processes are usually left to Abhidhamma experts and psychologists.

But for the average person the meaning of life lies in the practical concerns of everyday life, which is contact and interaction with the world. This is what gives life its meaning. In other words, life as understood by human beings is life as it relates to the world.

This life in relation to the world can be divided into two sectors. In each sector there is a system of operation that depends on channels through which life can have contact and involvement with the world, known as *dvāra* (doors, channels), as follows:

1. The sector of awareness and experience of the world makes use of the six channels (*dvāra*) of eye, ear, nose, tongue, body, and mind to cognize and experience the world, which appears to us as the attributes and features known as the six cognitive objects (*ārammaṇa*)—forms, sounds, smells, tastes, tangibles, and mental objects.
2. The sector of expression or action upon the world makes use of the three channels (*dvāra*) of body, speech, and mind (*kāyadvāra, vacīdvāra, manodvāra*) to make responses to the world,

expressed in bodily actions, speech, and thoughts (*kāyakamma*, *vacīkamma*, *manokamma*).

With the first sector, the word *dvāra* is usually dropped in favor of the term *āyatana*, which means "sphere of connection that gives rise to knowledge," or "path of awareness." For the purposes of this discussion, we will use the word *āyatana* rather than *dvāra*.

Regarding the second sector, the process is included in the fourth *khandha*, *saṅkhāra*, described in the previous section. The volitional activities (*saṅkhāra*) of the *saṅkhārakhandha*, of which there are many—divided into good, evil, and neutral—will emerge and operate via intention, as their leader or representative, choosing or assigning the factors to condition expression or activities through the three *dvāra*—body, speech, and mind—constituting the *kamma* of deeds, speech, and thoughts. In this case, *saṅkhāra* are reclassified, in conformity with the role they play, according to the paths through which they function, as follows:

kāyasaṅkhāra (volitional activities through body)
vacīsaṅkhāra (volitional activities through speech)
manosaṅkhāra (volitional activities through mind)

They are also called *kāyasañcetanā*, *vacīsañcetanā*, and *manosañcetanā* (meaning "intention through body, speech, and mind") after their leading or representative factor, or *kāyakamma*, *vacīkamma*, and *manokamma,* after the work they do (see diagram 1.1).

Saṅkhāras as factors for conditioning the quality or features of the mind have already been covered in the discussion of the five *khandhas*. *Saṅkhāras* as the process of conditioning, expressing, and acting upon the world constitute the activities of life to be separately covered in the section "How Does Life Work?"

Here the intention is simply to show the constituents of life together with their functions, so our discussion will be confined to the first sector of interaction with the world—that is, the six sense bases (*āyatana*).

What Are the Sense Bases?

The word *āyatana* means "connector" or "sphere." It refers to the connection where consciousness arises, the source of knowledge. Simply put, they are the six paths of cognition, known simply as eye, ear, nose, tongue, body, and mind.

When we say "connectors" or "connections to knowledge," what is it that they connect to? They connect to the world, the external environment. However, the world appears to us only in parts or aspects, only as much as our human tools of cognition, the six sense bases, will allow. The six senses thus have their respective counterparts in the outside world as the objects that are cognized. These external cognitive objects or features of the world are also called *āyatana*, because they, too, are connectors to knowledge or sources of knowledge, but they are external.

In order to clearly distinguish between the two, the scriptures call the former group the "internal *āyatana*" and the latter group the "external *āyatana*."

The six external *āyatana* are forms, sounds, smells, tastes, tangible objects, and mental objects. They are usually called "cognitive objects" (*ārammaṇa*), meaning objects that the mind holds onto. *Ārammaṇa* can be simply translated as objects of awareness or "things known."

When (internal) *āyatana*, which are the spheres of cognition, contact (external) *āyatana*, which are the cognitive objects, or the things known, the awareness specific to the respective *āyatana* will arise. For instance, eye contacts a visual form, and the awareness known as "sight" results; when ear contacts sounds, the resulting awareness is known as "hearing." The awareness in these specific spheres is called *viññāṇa*, consciousness.

Thus, just as there are six sense bases and six objects, there are six consciousnesses—visual consciousness (seeing), aural consciousness (hearing), olfactory consciousness (smelling), gustatory consciousness (tasting), tactile consciousness (touching), and mental consciousness (cognizing a mental object).

kāyasaṅkhārā	= *kāyasañcentanā* ———	*kāyadvāra* →	*kāyakamma*
(that which conditions bodily actions)	(volition expressed through body)	the body door	bodily kamma
vacīsaṅkhārā	= *vacīsañcentanā* ———	*vacīdvāra* →	*vacīkamma*
(that which conditions verbal actions)	(volition expressed through speech)	the speech door	verbal kamma
manosaṅkhārā	= *manosañcentanā* ———	*manodvāra* →	*manokamma*
(that which conditions mental actions)	(volition expressed through mind)	the mind door	mental kamma

Fig. 1.1. Process of kamma creation.

All in all, the six sense bases, six objects, and six consciousnesses are referred to and related to each other as follows:[24]

eye (*cakkhu*)	is the sphere that cognizes	forms (*rūpa*)	the awareness that arises is seeing (*cakkhuviññāṇa*)
ear (*sota*)	is the sphere that cognizes	sounds (*sadda*)	the awareness that arises is hearing (*sotaviññāṇa*)
nose (*ghāna*)	is the sphere that cognizes	odors (*gandha*)	the awareness that arises is smelling (*ghānaviññāṇa*)
tongue (*jivhā*)	is the sphere that cognizes	flavors (*rasa*)	the awareness that arises is tasting (*jivhāviññāṇa*)
body (*kāya*)	is the sphere that cognizes	tangibles (*phoṭṭhabba*)	the awareness that arises is touching (*kāyaviññāṇa*)
mind (*mano*)	is the sphere that cognizes	mind objects (*dhamma*)[25]	the awareness that arises is cognizing mental objects (*manoviññāṇa*)

Although consciousness must depend for its arising on contact between the *āyatana* and its object,[26] the appearance of an object to a sense base does not always lead to consciousness. There must be the factor of attention, intention, or interest for consciousness to arise.[27] For example, at certain times, as when one is deeply asleep, distracted, absent-minded, immersed in some task or other, or even in states of deep concentration (*samādhi*), many sights and sounds that arise within range of sight or hearing are not seen or heard. When concentrating on writing, one may not be aware of the parts of the body contacting the chair or desk, the hand touching the paper, or a finger on pen or pencil.

When a sense base and its object come within range of each other but no consciousness arises, cognition is not yet said to have arisen.

Cognition arises only with the arising of all three factors: sense base (*āyatana*), object (*ārammaṇa*), and consciousness (*viññāṇa*). This condition is technically called *phassa*. Literally, *phassa* means "contact," but in Buddhism it specifically refers to the meeting or convergence of sense base, cognitive object, and consciousness. Simply speaking, *phassa* is awareness.

This *phassa*, or cognition, is named according to the organ through which it functions, giving six kinds of contact: eye contact, ear contact, nose contact, tongue contact, body contact, and mind contact.

Phassa is an important stage in the cognitive process: when contact has been made, a process is set in motion, beginning with a feeling in response to the object, and then to other mental reactions: noting, fabrication around the object, and all the ensuing outward expressions.

Within this process, the factor of particular interest is the feeling that arises immediately following contact. This feeling is called *vedanā*, which means the "experiencing" or "tasting" of an object. It is an impression of that sense object, either as pleasant, unpleasant, or indifferent.

Divided according to the channels of cognition, *vedanā* is of six kinds: the feelings that arise from visual contact, the feelings that arise from auditory contact, and so on.[28] However, if classified according to quality, there are three kinds of feeling: *sukha* (comfortable, happy, pleasant); *dukkha* (uncomfortable, painful); *adukkhamasukha* (neither pleasant nor unpleasant, indifferent; also called neutral feeling, *upekkhā*).[29] Another classification is into five kinds: *sukha* (pleasant bodily feeling); *dukkha* (unpleasant bodily feeling, pain); *somanassa* (pleasant mental feeling, happiness); *domanassa* (unpleasant mental feeling, sorrow); and *upekkhā* (indifference, neither pleasant nor unpleasant feeling).

The cognitive process so far described can be illustrated thus:

> *āyatana* + *ārammaṇa* + *viññāṇa* = *phassa* → *vedanā*
> sense door + object + consciousness = contact → feeling

So cognitive objects are the world as it appears to humans through the sense bases. The cognition of these objects enables us to interact with the world, to function and survive. Feeling is an important factor in this cognitive process, serving as the mechanism that informs us what is harmful to life and to be avoided and what is supportive to life and to be benefited from. Thus, feeling enables the subsequent cognitive process to acquire more comprehensive and profitable knowledge and understanding.

For the ordinary, unenlightened person (*puthujjana*), however, that is not all that feeling is. It is not just an additional factor in the cognitive process to complement knowledge and thereby increase our ability to lead a good life. It also represents something the world has to offer as a reward or prize. This reward is the delicious taste, the pleasure that arises from cognitive objects known as *sukhavedanā*.

Once the cognitive process has advanced to feeling, if we become attached to feeling in this sense, we will deviate from the cognitive process, allowing another process to take over, in which *vedanā* becomes the prime factor for producing further consequences. At the same time, the cognitive process, which has assumed a secondary role, is corrupted by the force of this new process and veers away from the truth.

The process that has taken over usually operates according to a simple and basic model: when an object is cognized and a pleasant feeling arises, it is followed by desire (*taṇhā*). When there is desire the mind becomes involved and attached to the extent that clinging (*upādāna*) arises—the mind becomes obsessed and cannot let go, even though the object cannot really be held onto since it has already passed away.

From there, the mind begins to imagine itself to be in possession of that cognitive object and to devise ways and means of acquiring it, prompting actions through body and speech to obtain the desired results so as to experience more of the pleasant feeling. Within this process there arises complex and intense pleasure and pain, which are products of human creation, which spin off new cycles starting with *vedanā*. It becomes the spinning of the wheel of birth in pleasure and pain (*saṁsāravaṭṭa*), and it cannot advance to realizing the higher benefits that can be attained in this life.

In this light, the continuation of the process from contact is clearly a crucial moment, the turning point in which feeling plays the key role. The direction the process will take (for ordinary people) depends on the nature of the feeling. In this respect, the following observations can be made:

First, the process that continues on from contact is the turning point between a pure cognitive process and the *saṁsāric* process (*saṁsāravaṭṭa*). In the pure cognitive process, feeling is a minor factor contributing to accurate and thorough knowledge. In the *saṁsāric* process, feeling is the main factor, with the power to dominate the outcome of the entire process. It could be said that whichever way human beings think and act, or however life proceeds, is because of, and for the sake of, feeling. Moreover, in the *saṁsāric* process, human beings do not stop at simply cognizing objects, learning about the world in order to relate to and deal with their environment in the most effective way, but proceed to become "tasters" of the world.

As for the pure cognitive process, to be technically precise, it must also be taken to branch off at the point immediately after contact, given that cognition has completely arisen at contact. The process continuing on from here can therefore be distinguished as a separate part of the process altogether, and I would like to call it a process of direct knowledge and vision (*ñāṇadassana*), or a process of "unwinding" (*vivaṭṭa*), as opposed to the process of "winding" (*saṁsāravaṭṭa*). This process of unwinding is concerned with solving life's problems, so it will be dealt with later in this book, in part four, "How Should Life Be?" and part five, "How Should Life Be Lived?"

Second, the process that follows on from contact is the ethical turning point between good and evil, between the skillful (*kusala*) and the unskillful (*akusala*), and between liberation and enslavement to the winding of *saṁsāra*.

Having discussed other parts of the cognitive process, we must now come back to the six sense bases, because all the processes discussed here depend on and start at the sense bases. When other factors are said to be important, we must accept that the six sense bases are also important. For example, when we say that feeling is a crucial factor in the process of tasting the world, it follows that the six sense bases are also crucial, because they are the sources or pathways of feeling.

Feeling is something that human beings aspire to, and the sense bases are the channels that provide the objects of these aspirations.

Summarizing, the six sense bases serve human beings in two ways.

First, they are the pathways to cognition of the world, or the medium through which the world is presented to human beings. They are the tools of communication through which human beings receive the information necessary to their proper dealing with the world in order to survive and lead a good life.

Second, they are the channels for "tasting" the world, or the doors that human beings open out to receive and experience those cognitive objects that are the delicious taste of the world, by looking, listening, smelling, tasting, and touching pleasure and entertainment, and also imagining pleasurable things.

The two functions are connected. The former is the primary or fundamental function, and is indispensable. The latter is secondary. It could be said to be complementary or even superfluous. The functioning of the six senses is identical in either case. The only difference lies in the volition, whether it is directed to cognition or to feeling. For the ordinary person, the importance of the senses tends to jump over to the second kind of function, the tasting of the world, to such an extent that the first function is simply a support for the second. In other words, the cognitive process is only a factor for supporting the process of tasting the world, or for serving the *saṁsāric* process.

Moreover, people's relationship with the world in active expression through deeds, speech, and thoughts will also become actions for serving the *saṁsāric* process: doing, speaking, and thinking to seek and procure cognitive objects for enjoyment. The thicker the delusion that enshrouds them, the more their sensory activity will be bogged down in the secondary functions of the senses, such that life and the world for them revolve entirely around the six sense bases.

It can be seen that even though the six senses are merely one portion of the five *khandhas* and do not encompass all there is to life, as do the five *khandhas*, they play a vital role in the process of our lives. They also have a lot of power over the directions of our lives, such that it may be said that life, as far as we know it and live it, is the contact and relationship with the world through these sense bases, and that life has meaning through them. Once these sense bases no longer function, the world "goes out," and life no longer has any meaning.

The following passage in the Pali Tipiṭaka succinctly shows the process described here and also helps connect the explanation given here with our discussion of the five *khandhas* to show the process more comprehensively:

> "Dependent on eye and visual form, eye consciousness arises. The convergence of these three is contact. With contact as condition there is feeling. What a person feels, that one perceives (*saññā*); what one perceives, that one thinks about (*vitakka*); what one thinks about, that one imagines about (*papañca*). When one imagines about an object, on account of that imagination, the manifold kinds of complex perception (*papañcasaññā*)[30] in regard to forms cognizable by the eye, past, future, and present, spring up and beset one."[31]

The text then proceeds to cover other sense bases and objects to the same effect until all six pairs are covered.

Once *papañcasaññā* arises, there is even greater and more elaborate thinking (*vitakka*), which leads to the arising of defilements such as like, dislike, possessiveness, and jealousy, which permeate the thought processes.[32]

Correct and Incorrect Knowledge

In discussing the spheres of cognition, we should know something about correct and incorrect knowledge.

The Two Levels of Truth

Students are sometimes confused by some of the Buddha's teachings. For example, in some texts we are told not to associate with fools, to associate with the wise; that a fool has these attributes and a wise person has those attributes; that we should be contented with what we have and not go coveting the belongings of others; that the self is the refuge of the self; or that people should help each other. But then elsewhere we are told to examine and see as it is that the body is simply a body, not a being, an individual, a self, not ours or ourselves, to know as it is that it is not ours and not our self and that all things are not-self (*anattā*).

We may conclude from this that there are contradictions in the Buddha's teachings, and become confused: when it is time to speak or act in accordance with the everyday knowledge of the average person, we speak or act out of attachment to our knowledge of how things really are, leading to confusion and problems for ourselves and for others.

The Abhidhamma texts, hoping to prevent this kind of confusion, teach us to distinguish truth into two levels:[33]

1. *Sammatisacca*: conventional truth (otherwise called *vohārasacca*: truth in a manner of speaking, the spoken word). It is truth according to the common consensus, as agreed upon or collectively perceived. It is a tool of communication for use in everyday life. An example is the use of the words *water* and *salt* in everyday speech.
2. *Paramatthasacca*: ultimate truth, truth in its highest sense, according to the ultimate level of truth that can be expressed in words. It is the knowledge of reality (*saccadhamma*) that

causes all attachments and delusions to dissolve and enables one to establish a correct attitude toward the world, transcending defilements and suffering and having a mind that is free, unhindered, clear, buoyant, and truly happy.

Some of the things that are ultimately true are, for example, mentality (*nāmadhamma*), physicality (*rūpadhamma*), *vedanā*, *saññā*, *saṅkhāra*, *viññāṇa*; or mind (*citta*), mental concomitants (*cetasika*), form (*rūpa*), *nibbāna*, contact (*phassa*), volition (*cetanā*), one-pointedness (*ekaggatā*), and the life principle (*jīvitindriya*). An example that conveys the general idea is how in science the words *water* and *salt* are more specifically referred to as hydrogen oxide (H_2O) and sodium chloride (NaCl) respectively.

In any case, the ideas of conventional truth and ultimate truth coined in the Abhidhamma cite passages from the suttas, indicating that these ideas were in existence from the earliest times. However, in early times the concepts were probably readily understood, so there was no necessity to specify the two terms. The passage of the sutta cited in the Abhidhamma is a statement by the Bhikkhuni Vajirā, as follows:

> "So, Māra, how can you conceive of a being? This is nothing but a pile of formations; no being can be found here. Just as when there is an assemblage of components there is the word *cart*, so, when there are the aggregates, there is the convention of a 'being.'"[34]

Similar words can be found in many of the Buddhavacana in the Pali canon. For example:

> "A bhikkhu who is an arahant, a vanquisher of the outflows (*khīnāsava*)... might say, 'I said,' or 'he said to me,' [but] he is clever, he knows the language of the world, and merely speaks in accordance thereof."[35]

> "These are worldly perceptions, worldly language, worldly speech, worldly concepts, which the Tathāgata uses in speech but does not attach to."[36]

The writers of the commentaries describe the nature of the suttas as *vohāradesanā*, since they are largely given in terms of the spoken word, or in conventional terms, while the Abhidhamma is *paramattha desanā*, because its content is mostly given in ultimate terms, in terms of reality.[37]

*The Three Distortions (*Vipallāsa*)*

Vipallāsa is distorted knowledge, knowledge that deviates or errs from the truth. It refers to knowledge distorted on the fundamental level, which leads to misunderstandings, delusions, self-deception, and incorrect mental attitude and conduct in regard to life and the world. There are three kinds of *vipallāsa*:

1. *Saññāvipallāsa*: distorted perception; perceiving in error of the truth
2. *Citta vipallāsa*: distorted mind; thinking in error of the truth
3. *Diṭṭhi vipallāsa*: distorted view; views in error of the truth

Examples of *saññāvipallāsa*: a frightened person seeing a rope as a snake; crows and deer perceiving a scarecrow guarding a field as a person; a lost person mistaking north for south, south for north; someone seeing a row of stationary, blinking lights on a neon sign as if they were moving.

Examples of *citta vipallāsa*: a person suffering from psychosis thinking that grass is food; a person suffering from paranoia thinking that whoever approaches is intent on harming him; someone seeing a shadow moving in a dark place and imagining it to be a ghost.

Normally *diṭṭhi vipallāsa*, distorted view, follows on from distorted perceptions and distorted thinking. However wrongly we perceive things, so we believe; however wrongly we think and conceive, so we believe. For example, misperceiving a rope to be a snake, we may come to the conclusion and firm belief that there are many snakes in that area; perceiving the land around us to be flat, extending outward in a straight line, we come to the conclusion that the earth is flat; thinking that for all things to arise, fare, and move around, there must be a controller and mover behind them, we may develop the firm belief that thunder, lightning, earthquakes, rain, and floods are watched over and controlled by gods.

These examples are on a coarse level that is easily seen. They may be called "distortion to the point of eccentricity." In the Buddha's teaching, the meaning of *vipallāsa* is examined in its most subtle sense, penetrating to the fundamental level, referring to the distorted knowledge that is not only within certain individuals or groups of people, but also within almost all people without their knowing it. People fall under its power, and the three kinds of distortion become one homogeneous group. The subtle or fundamental levels of distortion are explained in the texts as follows:

> "Bhikkhus, distortion of perception, distortion of thinking, and distortion of view are of four kinds. What are the four? [They are as follows:]
>
> 1. "Distortion of perception, distortion of thinking, and distortion of view that what is impermanent is permanent.
> 2. "Distortion of perception, distortion of thinking, and distortion of view that what is stressful (*dukkha*) is happy.
> 3. "Distortion of perception, distortion of thinking, and distortion of view that what is not-self is self.
> 4. "Distortion of perception, distortion of thinking, and distortion of view that what is not beautiful is beautiful."[38]

These distortions are obstacles to the cultivation and development of wisdom, and destroying them is the target of wisdom cultivation. The methods for cultivation of wisdom and knowledge discussed in the Buddha's teachings are all useful for the correction and removal of these distortions, especially the use of wise attention (*yoniso-manasikāra*) of the kind that delves into causes and conditions, and analyzes component factors as they are with mindfulness (*sati*).[39]

The Buddha's Words Concerning the Sense Bases

All Things, the World and Names

"Bhikkhus, I will teach you 'the all.' Please take heed. What is the all? Eye and form, ear and sound, nose and smell, tongue and taste, body and tangible, mind and mental object—these I call 'the all.'"[40]

"Revered Sir, they say 'world, world.' On what condition is there the world; what is said to be conception as the world?"

"Herein, Samiddhi, wherever there is eye, form, eye consciousness, and things to be known through eye consciousness, there is the world or what is said to be the world. Wherever there is ear... nose...tongue...body...mind, mental object, mind consciousness and a condition to be known through mind consciousness, there is the world or what is said to be the world."[41]

"Bhikkhus, I do not say that the end of the world is something that can be known, seen, or attained through traveling, but I also do not say that the person who has not reached the end of the world can make an end of suffering."

[Ānanda replied:] "This teaching that has been given in brief by the Blessed One, not yet explained in detail, I understand to mean in full this: 'By whatever the worldling conceives the world to be the world, and holds the world to be the world, that is called 'world' in the discipline of the Noble Ones [*ariyavinaya*]."

"And by what do people conceive the world to be the world, and hold the world to be the world? By eye...by ear...by nose... by tongue...by body...by mind do people conceive the world to be the world, and hold the world to be the world."[42]

"Bhikkhus, I will expound the arising and the setting of the world, please take heed. What is the arising of the world? Dependent on eye and form, visual consciousness arises. The convergence of those three is contact. With contact as condition is feeling; with feeling as condition, desire; with desire as condition, clinging; with clinging as condition, becoming; with becoming as condition, birth; with birth as condition are aging and death, sorrow, lamentation, pain, grief, and despair: this is the arising of the world.

"Dependent on ear...dependent on nose...dependent on tongue...dependent on body...dependent on mind and mental object, mind consciousness arises...this is the arising of the world.

"And what is the setting of the world? Dependent on eye and form, eye consciousness arises. The convergence of these three is contact. With contact as condition is feeling; with feeling as condition, desire. With the total abandoning of that desire without remainder, there is the cessation of clinging; with the cessation of clinging, there is the cessation of becoming; with the cessation of becoming, there is the cessation of birth; with the cessation of birth, there is the cessation of aging and death, sorrow, lamentation, pain, grief and despair. Thus is the cessation of the whole mass of suffering. This is the setting of the world.

"Dependent on ear...dependent on nose...dependent on tongue...dependent on body...dependent on mind and mental objects, mind consciousness arises...This is the setting of the world."[43]

"Revered Sir, they say 'Māra, Māra,'...they say 'being, being'... they say 'suffering, suffering'...What is the condition for this 'Māra,' or the concept 'Māra'...for this being, or the concept 'being'...for this suffering, or the concept 'suffering'?"

"Herein, Samiddhi, wherever there is eye, form, visual consciousness, and a condition to be known through visual consciousness...there is mind, mental object, mind consciousness, and a condition to be known through mind consciousness, there is to be found Māra or the concept *Māra*...a being or the concept 'being'...suffering or the concept 'suffering.'"[44]

"When there is eye, the enlightened ones [arahants] say there are happiness and suffering. When eye is not, the enlightened ones do not say there are happiness and suffering. When there is ear...nose...tongue...body...mind, the enlightened ones say there are happiness and suffering. When ear...mind are not, the enlightened ones do not say there are happiness and suffering."[45]

The One Truth for the Deluded and Those Who Know

"Bhikkhus, just as when the rice plants are ripe and full and the farmer guarding the rice is heedless, the cattle eat the rice plants, go down into the rice and recklessly indulge to their hearts' content, so when the unlearned, unenlightened being fails to guard contact through the six sense bases, he recklessly indulges to his heart's content in the five kinds of sense pleasures."[46]

"Bhikkhus, these six bases of contact (*phassāyatana*), when untrained, untended, uncared for, and unrestrained, are instruments for the arising of suffering...These six bases of contact, when well trained, well tended, well cared for, and well restrained, are instruments for the arising of happiness..."[47]

"Is eye a bind on forms, and forms a bind on the eye; ear... sounds; nose...smells; tongue...tastes; body...tangibles; is mind a bind on mental objects, and mental objects a bind on the mind?

"[No.] Eye is not a bind on forms, forms are not a bind on the eye; it is rather *chandarāga* (affection to the degree of attachment) contingent on both eye and forms that is a bind on both eye and forms...the mind is not a bind on mental objects and mental objects are not a bind on the mind; it is rather *chan-*

darāga arising contingent on mind and mental objects that is a bind on both mind and mental objects.

"If the eye were a bind on forms, or forms were a bind on the eye, the living of the holy life for the complete destruction of suffering would not be possible. But because the eye is not a bind on forms, and forms are not a bind on the eye, but rather it is *chandarāga* arising contingent on eye and forms that is a bind on eye and form, the living of the holy life for the proper cessation of suffering is possible.

"The Blessed One has eyes, the Blessed One sees forms with his eyes, [but] *chandarāga* does not arise for the Blessed One. The Blessed One has a heart that is well released. The Blessed One has ears...nose...tongue...body...mind..."[48]

The Expansive Mind Led by Wisdom Living with Mindfulness

"On what account can a person be said to be one who does not guard the sense doors? Some people, seeing forms with the eye, incline and surrender the mind to forms that are attractive and are angered and offended by forms that are unattractive. They do not guard the mind with mindfulness, and abide with minds that are of small measure. They do not understand as it is the release and liberation of the mind and the release and liberation through wisdom that would make evil, unwholesome conditions arisen within them cease without remainder. Hearing sounds with the ear...smelling odors with the nose...tasting flavors with the tongue...experiencing tangibles in the body... cognizing mental objects in the mind, they incline and surrender the mind to mental objects that are attractive and are angered and offended by mental objects that are unattractive...

"On what account can a person be said to be one who guards the sense doors? A bhikkhu, seeing forms with the eye, does not incline and surrender the mind to forms that are attractive and is not angered or offended by forms that are unattractive. He guards his mind with mindfulness and abides with a mind that is broad and boundless. He understands as it is the release and liberation of the mind and the release and liberation through wisdom that make evil, unwholesome states already arisen within him cease without remainder. Hearing sounds with the ear... cognizing mental objects in the mind, he does not incline the mind to surrender to attractive mental objects, and is not angered or offended by unattractive mental objects..."[49]

Advancing on the Path of Freedom and Happiness

"Bhikkhus, before the enlightenment, when I was still an unenlightened *bodhisatta*, I reflected to myself thus: 'What is the attraction [the sweetness, the pleasant taste] of eye? What is the danger [the flaw, the fault] of the eye? What is the escape [freedom, independence] of the eye? What is the attraction... the danger... the release of ear... nose... tongue... body... mind?'

"I thought to myself: 'Happiness (*sukha*) and gladness (*somanassa*) arisen on account of the eye is the attraction of the eye. The fact that the eye is impermanent, suffering, naturally subject to change: this is the danger of eye. The destruction of affection, the abandoning of affection contingent on the eye, is the escape from eye.' [The same said for ear, nose, tongue, body, and mind.]

"As long as I had not realized truly as it is the attraction of the six internal sense bases as the attraction, the danger as the danger, and the escape as the escape, I did not declare that I had realized the complete and unexcelled enlightenment (*anuttara sammā sambodhiñāṇa*)..."[50]

[The attraction, the danger, and the escape of the six external sense bases are then explained in the same manner.]

"Bhikkhus, one who sees eye as it is, who sees forms as they are, who sees eye consciousness as it is, who sees visual contact as it is, who sees feeling, be it pleasant, painful, or neither pleasant nor painful, arisen contingent on condition of eye contact as it is, does not attach to eye, does not attach to forms, does not attach to eye consciousness, does not attach to visual contact, does not attach to feeling, be it pleasant, painful, or neither pleasant nor painful, that arises contingent on condition of eye contact.

"Since he is not attached to, not immersed in, and not deluded, is wise to their fault, the five *khandhas* of clinging do not form or grow.

"Moreover, desire—which brings renewal of being, is accompanied by delight and lust (*nandirāga*), and delights in this and that—is abandoned.

"Restlessness of the body and restlessness of the mind, distress of the body and distress of the mind, rankling of the body and rankling of the mind, are all abandoned by him. That person experiences well-being both in body and in mind.

"The view of such a one is right view; the thinking of such a one is right thought; the effort of such a one is right effort; the recollection of such a one is right recollection; the concentration of such a one is right concentration. As for that person's bodily deeds, verbal deeds, and livelihood, they are already purified. On this account, that person is said to have developed the noble eightfold path to the full." [The same said for ear, nose, tongue, body and mind.][51]

Practical Value

In terms of *kusala* and *akusala*, good and evil, the sense bases are the beginning, and the crucial point of divergence between them. One path leads to heedlessness, intoxication, bad deeds, and infatuation in the world; the other to understanding, good deeds, and liberation.

The important point here is that without any training to develop an understanding of the sense bases and deal with them correctly, most people will usually be seduced into leading lives aimed at consuming the world, going around doing things purely for the sake of seeking pleasant forms, sounds, smells, tastes, and tangibles, and various kinds of pleasures and entertainment to feed their eyes, ears, nose, tongue, body, and mental desires, accumulating greed, hatred, and delusion and creating confusion and trouble for themselves and others.

It is not difficult to see that the ever-increasing exploitation, conflict, oppression, and social problems in the world are mostly a result of people allowing themselves to be seduced into the path of habitual, ever-more sensual gratification. Many people have never stopped to reflect on the meaning of their actions and the nature of the senses they are so busily feeding, and have never taken on any practices for training or restraining their sense bases or sense faculties, so they are left with ever-increasing delusion and indulgence.

The practical solution lies partly in creating an understanding of the meaning of the sense bases and the things contingent on them to appreciate their true role and importance in our lives. Another part of the solution lies in training according to a method for controlling, restraining, using, and serving the senses in a way that is of real benefit to one's own life and to society.

The sense bases are the source of both happiness and suffering, which in turn become the rationale for the way life is generally conducted, and almost all striving in the tasks of the ordinary person: in the case of happiness, there is seeking; in the case of suffering, there is avoidance.

Apart from their connection in regard to the problem of good and evil conduct, happiness and suffering are also problematic in themselves, in terms of their value, their substantiality, and their capacity to be real refuges in life.

Many people, having thrown the time and energy of their lives into running after happiness through worldly pleasures, meet with disappointment—from not getting what they want, from finding that the sweet taste is mixed with bitterness (sometimes the more the happiness attained, the more intense the sorrow and pain that follow), from finding that the price they have paid to attain their happiness is greater than what they have received, from attaining what they want but finding it does not give them the joy they expected, or, having attained their goal, finding that happiness runs further off away from them and they never seem to catch up with it. Some finish their lives still running, never having found real or sufficient happiness.

Studying the sense bases is for the objective of knowing the truth of things and practicing with a proper attitude that does not lead to excessive harm for ourselves or for others. In addition to being careful in the methods we use to seek happiness, we also understand the limitations and different levels of happiness, and then know how to attain happiness on the subtler levels. When we practice correctly in relation to happiness and suffering and progress to subtler levels of happiness, this is progress in morality.

In terms of cultivating wisdom, the sense bases involve ethics from the outset, because if we practice wrongly at the first arising of awareness our cognition will be impure. It will instead become a cognitive process in service of enjoying the world, or a component in the process of "winding" (*saṁsāravaṭṭa*, the wheel of rebirth). It leads to knowledge that is distorted, partial, or prejudiced, not in accordance with the truth or with the real state of things.

A practice that is of help in this regard is the technique of maintaining the mind in equanimity (*upekkhā*), keeping the mind even, so that it is not overpowered by defilements such as like and dislike.

In terms of general practice, there are many methods that either directly or indirectly concern the six sense bases. Some are specifically for particular stages, depending on where the problem tends to arise, or the point at which suffering or evil tend to find their ways through. However, emphasis is usually placed on the method of guarding against or preventing defilements right from the very first, which is when contact is made through the sense bases. This will mean that problems do not arise at all, making it the safest of all methods. If problems have arisen and evil, unwholesome states have already found their way in, they are often difficult to correct. For example, if we allow cognitive objects to stir up and fashion the mind so that lust (*rāga*), or greed, hatred, and delusion arise, even though we know what is right and what is wrong, and we have a sense of conscience, we cannot resist the allurement, and give in to the force of defilements and create bad *kamma*.

For this reason, the emphasis is on the method of guarding and securing the senses from the outset. An important tool for guarding at the earliest point of awareness is mindfulness (*sati*), which is what holds the mind to its base of normalcy, like a rope for holding the mind down. The use of *sati* for guarding the sense bases occurs in the teaching known as restraint of the sense faculties (*indriya-saṁvara*). It is also called control of the sense doors. It means being armed with mindfulness when becoming aware of an object through a sense faculty—such as seeing a form with the eye—and not allowing the mind to apprehend that object by means of such features that would be the cause for the arising of attachment or aversion, like or dislike, so that the mind gets overwhelmed by unwholesome states. This practice helps in preventing the arising of unskillful, harmful thoughts, preventing suffering, and preventing the creation of distorted and prejudiced knowledge and ideas.

However, it is not possible to utilize this teaching at will, because in order for *sati* to be firm and constantly ready for action, training is essential. Thus, restraint of the faculties needs constant application. The training of the faculties is called *indriyabhāvanā* (usually translated as "cultivation of the faculties"). One who has trained or developed the faculties is safe from evil, unwholesome conditions, suffering, and prejudiced and distorted knowledge, because one has set up a protection before they can arise.[52] Even if like and dislike do manage to slip through, one is able to speedily subdue or abandon them. Restraint of the sense faculties is a factor of morality (*sīla*), but its main component factor, *sati*, is classified as part of the concentration (*samādhi*) group, because it leads to use of mental effort and constant control of the mind. Thus it is also a training in *samādhi*.

Wise attention (*yoniso-manasikāra*), which is a wisdom method, is another principle recommended for practice in this regard, seeing or examining in such a way as to derive knowledge from cognitive objects, seeing the truth or seeing in a way the leads to benefit, such as reflecting on the benefits and drawbacks, merits and defects, together with the state of freedom and security, in which there is happiness without any need to rely on cognitive objects.

Some of these practices have been touched on in the Buddhavacana above, and some will be dealt with later, so I have here treated them only in brief.

PART TWO

What Is Life Like?

CHAPTER 2

The Three Characteristics

The Natural Characteristics of All Things

In saying that all things exist only as combinations of component parts, this doesn't mean that those components are in any way substantial, nor that their amalgamation results in real objects as their appearance suggests. In fact, they exist as a stream. The so-called component parts are themselves composed of lesser components, none of which has any independent existence. They are all constantly arising and ceasing, unstable and changing.

This process is dependent only on natural causal relationships. There is no external agent in the form of a creator or controller, so the process is simply called "laws of nature."

There are two groups of Buddhist teachings presented as natural laws: the three characteristics (*tilakkhaṇa*) and the law of dependent arising (*paṭiccasamuppāda*). In fact, the two teachings show two different perspectives of the one law: the teaching of the three characteristics describes the properties things display as they fare according to the process of interdependent relationships known as dependent arising; the principle of dependent arising shows how all things are related and interdependent in a stream-like process that reveals them to be subject to the three characteristics.

The natural laws are described as *dhammadhātu*—maintained in the natural course of things; *dhammaṭṭhiti*—naturally fixed and certain; and *dhammaniyāma*—laws of nature, directed by nature, involving neither a creator nor the arising of religions or prophets.

That the laws of nature are this way indicates that the role of a religious founder, in Buddhism, is the discoverer and proclaimer of those truths to the world.

> "Whether or not the Tathāgata arises in this world, these principles are the norm (*dhammadhātu*); they are fixed and certain truths (*dhammaṭṭhiti*), natural laws (*dhammaniyāma*), as follows:
>
> 1. All formations (*saṅkhārā*) are impermanent...
> 2. All formations are stressful (*dukkha*)...
> 3. All things (*dhammas*) are not-self...
>
> "The Tathāgata is enlightened to and penetrates these principles, then states them, shows them, formulates them, reveals them and clarifies them, saying, 'All formations are impermanent...all formations are *dukkha*...all things are not-self...'"[1]

The three characteristics are also known as *sāmaññalakkhaṇa*, meaning "common characteristics," or characteristics that apply equally to all things.

The Three Characteristics in Brief

1. *Aniccatā* (impermanence): instability; the characteristic of being born, changing, and inevitably proceeding to dissolution
2. *Dukkhatā* (stress and conflict): the state of being oppressed by birth and dissolution; the state of stress and conflict within things because of changes to the determinants that cause them to be the way they are, so that they are unable to maintain their condition; the state of imperfection and being flawed, providing no real fulfillment or satisfaction to those who have desires for them, and creating suffering to those who cling to them with desire and attachment (*upādāna*)
3. *Anattatā* (soullessness): not-self, voidness of an intrinsic self

Things exist only in the form of a stream of interrelated determinants that are constantly arising and ceasing. For that reason, they have the characteristic of impermanence (*anicca*). Since they are unstable, always arising and passing away according to causes and determinants, there must be friction, stress, conflict, and the manifestation of imperfection and deficiency (*dukkha*) within this process. Since all conditions exist as interrelated components, they are not-self (*anattā*), and it is impossible for them to have any fixed identity.

In the case of individual beings, they can be seen to be made up entirely and exclusively of the five *khandha*s, and apart from them there is nothing. So we can dispense with the question of a free and independent self existing outside of the *khandha*s. Now, when we analyze each of these five *khandha*s, we find them all to be impermanent (*anicca*). Being impermanent they are *dukkha*, subject to affliction and stress for whoever clings to them. Being *dukkha*, they are not-self and do not belong to self because (1) they are entirely arisen from determinants, void of intrinsic entity; and (2) they do not come under anybody's absolute control, they are ownerless:

> "Bhikkhus, form...feeling...perception...volitional formations...consciousness are not-self. If form...feeling...perception...volitional formations...consciousness were the self, they would not be subject to affliction, they would conform to desires thus: 'May my form...feeling...perception...volitional formations...consciousness be this way, may they not change from this.' But because form...feeling...perception...volitional formations...consciousness are not-self, they are subject to affliction and it is not within the power of anybody to control them thus: 'May my form...feeling...perception...volitional formations...consciousness be this way, may they not become otherwise.'
>
> "Bhikkhus, how do you conceive this? Is form permanent or impermanent?"
>
> "It is impermanent, Lord."

> "Is what is impermanent stressful or pleasant?"
> "It is stressful, Lord."
> "And of that which is impermanent and stressful, is it proper to conceive of it 'that is mine,' 'I am that,' 'that is my self'?'"
> "No, it is not proper, Lord."
> "Therefore, bhikkhus, for that reason, form...feeling...perception...volitional formations...consciousness, in any condition, be they of the past, the future, or the present, internal or external, coarse or fine, inferior or superior, far or near, should all be seen with right wisdom as they are thus, 'That is not me, I am not that, that is not my self.'"[2]

Many Western and Hindu scholars have sought to demonstrate that the Buddha did not deny the existence of a self, or *ātman*, on the highest level, only within manifestations. In this sutta, for example, the Buddha rejects the five *khandhas* as being the self. Perhaps, they say, this simply means that the real self lies outside of the *khandhas*. Supporters of this view explain that *nibbāna* has the same state as *ātman*. In other words, *nibbāna* is the real self.

It is natural for worldlings, especially those educated within a belief system that holds to the concept of self, to cling to or search for a self in some form or other. It is a way of satisfying a deep-seated need that people unknowingly hold. No sooner do they give up one notion of self (one or more of the five *khandhas*) than they proceed to fill the vacuum with another. However, the Buddha did not teach letting go of one attachment in order to become enslaved by another. Something that contains a self cannot possibly exist, while whatever exists must have no self.

Scriptural Explanations of the Three Characteristics

Let us look at the definitions of the three characteristics, or common characteristics, again in more detail, as explained in the scriptural sources.

All formations (*saṅkhārā*) are impermanent.

All formations are *dukkha.*

All things (*dhammā*) are not-self.

All formations are impermanent, or, in the Pali, *anicca.* Impermanence, temporality, or the state of impermanence in Pali is called *aniccatā.* The characteristic describing things as impermanent is called *aniccalakkhaṇa.*

All formations are *dukkha*, unsustainable. The state of being subject to stress or unsustainability in Pali is called *dukkhatā.* The characteristic describing things as *dukkha* is called *dukkhalakkhaṇa.*

All things are not-self. The state of being not-self, of being *anattā*, in Pali is called *anattatā.* The characteristic describing things as not-self is called *anattalakkhaṇa.*

Within the three characteristics there are some points that warrant further examination, as follows.

The Terminology

Regarding "all formations" and "all things," notice that in the first and second characteristics, all "formations" (*saṅkhārā*) are said to be impermanent and *dukkha*, while in the third characteristic, all "things"(*dhammā*) are said to be not-self. The difference in terminology here indicates a discrepancy in meaning between the first and second characteristics and the third. This discrepancy becomes clearer once the meanings of the words *saṅkhārā* and *dhammā* are understood.

The word *dhammā* (or *dhammas*) has the broader meaning, incorporating within its scope all things there may be, that can be and have been, as well as nonexistence, the opposite of existence. All things that can be spoken of, conceptualized or known, both physical and mental, good and evil, mundane and supramundane, are *dhammas*. To make a more specific meaning, explanatory words can be added to the word *dhamma* to give the required shade of meaning or specify the type of *dhamma.* Or the single word *dhamma* is used, but in a sense accepted or acknowledged within a specific context. When it is paired with *adhamma*, for example, or used in connection with moral behavior, *dhamma* means "goodness" (*puñña*) or "virtue"; when paired with the word *attha*, it means "principle" or "cause"; when used in relation to learning, *dhamma* (Dhamma) means the written or spoken teachings, the Buddha's words.

In the three characteristics, the word *dhamma* is used in its fullest and broadest sense, which includes all states and conditions without limitation. It may be more easily understood when it is analyzed into different categories, such as *rūpadhamma* (material or physical properties) and *nāmadhamma* (abstract or mental properties); *lokiya* (mundane) *dhammas* and *lokuttara* (supramundane) *dhammas*; *saṅkhata* (conditioned) *dhammas* and *asaṅkhata* (unconditioned) *dhammas*; *kusala* (skillful) *dhammas*, *akusala* (unskillful) *dhammas*, and *abyākata* (indeterminate) *dhammas*. Each of these groups includes all things, but the analysis that is of particular interest here is the conditioned (*saṅkhata*) *dhammas* and unconditioned (*asaṅkhata*) *dhammas*.[3]

Saṅkhatadhamma (conditioned things) are objects or states that arise from, and are conditioned by, determinants. They are also known as *saṅkhāras*, which has the same etymological root and meaning as *saṅkhata*. This category includes all things, both physical and mental, material and immaterial, mundane and transcendent, good, evil, and neutral, with the single exception of *nibbāna*.

Asaṅkhata-dhamma (the unconditioned) is that which has no determinants, is not arisen from determinants and is not subject to determinants. This is also known as *visaṅkhāra* (meaning that which is void of *saṅkhāras*), the unconditioned, or *nibbāna*.

It can be seen that *saṅkhāras* (formations), which are *saṅkhata-dhamma*, are only one portion of that which is *dhamma*. The word *dhamma* includes both the conditioned and the unconditioned, formations and that which is beyond formations. Bearing this in mind, we can more easily see the difference in extent of the first two characteristics, impermanence and *dukkha*, as compared to the third, as follows:

All formations, all *saṅkhatadhamma*, are impermanent and

dukkha according to the first two of the three characteristics (and are not-self according to the third), whereas the unconditioned, *asaṅkhata-dhamma*, or *nibbāna*, is not subject to these two characteristics.

All things—that is, both the conditioned and the unconditioned, both formations and that which is beyond formations, including *nibbāna*—are not-self.

Anattatā, not-self, is the only characteristic that is common to both the conditioned and the unconditioned. As for *aniccatā* and *dukkhatā*, these characteristics are found only in conditioned things, and this differentiates them from the unconditioned.

In the Pali canon the Buddha described the characteristics of conditioned things and the unconditioned in the *saṅkhatalakkhaṇa* (characteristics of the conditioned) and the *asaṅkhatalakkhaṇa* (characteristics of the unconditioned), thus:[4]

Saṅkhatalakkhaṇa are the signs or indications that tell us something is conditioned. There are three of these:

Arising is manifest.

Dissolution is manifest.

While existing, change is manifest.

The characteristics of the unconditioned (*asaṅkhatalakkhaṇa*) are the signs that indicate something is unconditioned. As above, there are three of these also:

Arising is not manifest.

Dissolution is not manifest.

While existing, change is not manifest.

It must be emphasized that the unconditioned, *visaṅkhāra* or *nibbāna*, transcends the qualities of impermanence and suffering but is still not-self. All conditions apart from that are entirely impermanent, *dukkha*, and not-self, as is supported by this verse from the Vinaya Piṭaka:

> All formations (*saṅkhāra*) are impermanent, all conditioned things (*saṅkhatadhamma*) are *dukkha* and not-self. *Nibbāna* and concepts (*paññatti*) are not-self. This is the teaching.[5]

Saṅkhāras *in the Five* Khandhas *and* Saṅkhāras *in the Three Characteristics*

The word *saṅkhāras* is used in no less than four different senses in Buddhadhamma, but here I would like to acquaint the reader with two in particular: *saṅkhāras* as one of the *khandhas*, and *saṅkhāras* in the three characteristics. These two senses of the word occur in important teachings and are similar, with overlapping meanings.

1. *Saṅkhāras* in the five *khandhas*: form (*rūpa*), feeling (*vedanā*), perception (*saññā*), volitional formations (*saṅkhārā*), and consciousness (*viññāṇa*).
2. *Saṅkhāras* in the three characteristics: All formations (*saṅkhārā*) are impermanent, all formations are *dukkha*, all *dhammas* are not-self.

Comparing these two meanings, note first that *saṅkhāras* as the fourth *khandha* refers to the qualities that condition the mind into good, evil, and neutral states. They are mental qualities that, led by intention, shape the thinking process and expression through body and speech as the agents of *kamma*. In short, *saṅkhāras* in the five *khandhas* refers to the conditioners of the mind, such as faith, mindfulness, shame (*hiri*), fear of wrongdoing (*ottappa*), goodwill, compassion, wisdom, delusion, greed, and aversion (the Abhidhamma gives fifty of these among a total of fifty-two mental concomitants, or *cetasika*), which are all the mental qualities apart from feeling (*vedanā*), perception (*saññā*) and consciousness (*viññāṇa*).

Saṅkhāras in the three characteristics refers to all conditioned things—that is, all things that arise from determinants, be they physical or mental, animate or inanimate, within the mind or in external objects. *Saṅkhāras* in this sense is also called *saṅkhata-dhamma* (conditioned things). It includes everything with the single exception of *nibbāna*.

That Which Conceals the Three Characteristics

Although the characteristics of impermanence, *dukkha,* and not-self are the common characteristics of all compounded things, and are truths that are plainly evident at all times, we don't usually see them. There is something that conceals them. Without a conscious effort to reflect on conditions as they really are, the truths of the three characteristics remain hidden, concealed by the following:[6]

santati: continuity, which conceals the characteristic of impermanence
iriyāpatha: (the changing of) positions, which conceals *dukkha*
ghana: perception of mass, which conceals not-self

It is said that because we do not attend to birth and death, or arising and ceasing, *santati*, continuity, hides the characteristic of impermanence. All things that we see are constantly arising and ceasing, but this process takes place continuously, which causes us to perceive what we are looking at as stable and unchanging. This is evident in our perception of ourselves, or of people that we see often, such as members of our family: because we see them every day, they seem to remain the same, but when we see them after a long absence it is easy to see a change. Actually, that change is occurring continuously, little by little. Another example is a propeller. When it is spinning rapidly it appears as a stationary, flat disk. The slower it spins, the more easily the movement of the individual blades can be distinguished. In the stationary propeller, the individual blades are obvious. When looked at with the right tools or keen discernment, things can be seen to comprise a process of constant arising and ceasing, and thus point to impermanence, instability, and constant change—they are *anicca.*

It is also said that because we do not attend to the stress and pressure that are always present, *iriyāpatha*, the shifting of position, hides the characteristic of *dukkha*. It usually requires a passage of time before the quality of stress—the inability to preserve any one state for any length of time due to the pressure and conflict within component factors—becomes obvious to our awareness. If there is movement or a change of circumstances, or the object of observation is removed from our field of awareness, the state of stress, pressure, and conflict remains unnoticed. Most events in nature tend to be like this, so the characteristic of *dukkha* is hidden.

A simple example is our own body: you don't have to wait for it to get sick or die before suffering becomes apparent—even within our own everyday lives, stress and conflict are constantly affecting every part of the body, making it impossible for us to endure any one position for any length of time. If for some reason we are forced to stay in one position for a long time—to stand unmoving, to sit unmoving, or to lie down unmoving—the stress within the body will gradually increase to the point where we experience the feeling of stress and conflict commonly known as pain, and we are forced to move.

When that stress and conflict, which is the ordinary stress of nature, subsides, the feeling of pain also subsides. (When this feeling of suffering subsides, a comfortable feeling, known as pleasure, usually arises in its place, but this is simply an impression. In fact, the suffering has merely abated, giving way to a state of absence of suffering.)

In our everyday lives, as soon as a sensation of pain arises we change positions; we constantly change positions so that we avoid many feelings of suffering, in the absence of which we tend to overlook the truth of the inherent stress in things. For this reason, it is said that [the changing of] positions conceals the characteristic of *dukkha*.

Finally, it is said that because we do not attend to the compounded nature of things, *ghana*, the appearance of mass or solidity, conceals their true nature, and the characteristic of not-self is not seen. All things without exception arise from the compounding of components. When these components are separated and broken down, the object that resulted from their collection is found to be nonexistent. Human beings in general do not see this truth because of the effect of *ghanasaññā*, the perception of mass, which hides the true nature of things.

When a little girl looks at a doll, she sees only a doll, she doesn't see the plastic that is its real substance. There is no "doll," only plastic, and the plastic, once again, is compounded of components. In this way *ghanasaññā* hides the truth of not-self. Careful consideration and analysis of things into their constituent parts results in a realization of not-self, and *anattā* is understood.

Analyzing the Three Characteristics

Notice that the teachings about the five *khandhas* and the six sense bases stress the study of life from the perspective of the personal life experience—the internal *khandhas* and the internal sense bases. In the teaching of the three characteristics, the scope is expanded outward to include everything, both the internal and external *khandhas* and the internal and external sense bases. Thus, it includes both personal life and all the things related to it, or the world in general.

Now that each of the three characteristics has been explained in brief, let us analyze them more closely according to the references available in the texts.

Aniccatā *and the Characteristic of Impermanence (*Aniccalakkhaṇa*)*

In the Paṭisambhidāmagga, the meaning of *aniccatā* is given simply as "It is *anicca* because of its ceasing (*khayaṭṭhena*)."[7] That is, wherever and whenever a condition arises, it ceases then and there. Physical properties (*rūpadhamma*) in the past cease in the past, they do not continue on into the present. Physical properties in the present cease in the present, they do not continue on into the future. Physical properties in the immediate future will cease there, not continuing onward.

The commentaries, to clarify this point, have expanded on this basic definition to cover many different perspectives and levels, from the coarse to the refined, on a moment-to-moment basis.

Initially they point out the change over a whole cycle of human life, beginning with birth and ending in death. On progressively subtler levels, this quality of arising and ceasing is analyzed more closely in the arising and ceasing of ages [infancy, childhood, youth, adulthood, middle age, and old age], of decades, of years, of seasons, of months, and of cycles of the day, and finally to every instance of movement—a level difficult to perceive for most people.

Nowadays, with the advances of modern science, impermanence, particularly on the physical plane, is much easier to understand, and in fact has become a readily accepted concept: all modern scientific theories—from that of stellar evolution to atomic physics—can be used to illustrate the law of impermanence.

The commentaries have expanded on the definitions of *anicca* in many ways. It is written, for example: "It is *anicca* because it is not stable or permanent (*aniccantikatāya*), because it has a beginning and an ending (*ādi antavantatāya*)."[8] One commonly used and simple definition: "It is *anicca* in that it is gained and then lost (it appears and disappears—*hutvā abhāvaṭṭhena*)."[9] Sometimes a number of meanings are incorporated, such as in "It is *anicca* because it arises, decays and becomes otherwise, or because having been gained, it is lost (*uppādavayaññathattabhāvā hutvā abhāvato vā*)."[10] The most comprehensive definition, however, is found in the four meanings of *anicca*, meaning the four reasons that something is said to be *anicca*:[11]

1. *Uppādavayappavattito*: it is *anicca* because it fares subject to birth and dissolution, arising, and ceasing.
2. *Vipariṇāmato*: it is *anicca* because it changes and becomes otherwise.
3. *Tāvakālikato*: it is *anicca* because it is temporary.
4. *Niccapaṭikkhepato*: it is *anicca* because it denies permanence; that is, its impermanence in itself refutes permanence. When we look at something as it really is, we can find no permanence. No matter how we may try to see it as permanent, it cannot become so. Thus, it is said to deny permanence.

Dukkhatā *and the Characteristic of Stress (*Dukkhalakkhaṇa*)*

The Paṭisambhidāmagga defines the characteristic of *dukkhatā* simply as "It is *dukkha* because it is fearsome (*bhayaṭṭhena*)."[12] All formations are of the nature to disintegrate. They provide no security or peace of mind; in themselves they contain the threat of disintegration and decay, and therefore they bring danger—that is, fear and insecurity—to all who come into contact with them.

The commentaries expand on the definition in numerous ways. Two definitions frequently encountered are as follows: "It is *dukkha* because it is continually oppressed by birth and disintegration (*uppādavayapaṭipīḷanaṭṭhena*[13] or *uppādavayapaṭipīḷanatāya*[14])." There is stress and conflict within the things that comprise it, and it also is stressed and conflicted by the things that comprise it.[15] "[It is called *dukkha*] in that it is the base for suffering to arise (*dukkhavatthutāya*[16] or *dukkhavatthuto*[17])." Conditioned things are receptacles for suffering; it is through them that the feeling of suffering arises. In other words, "they are suffering (*dukkha*) because they cause the feeling of suffering"; or "they are said to be *dukkha* because they cause the feeling of stress to arise." The most comprehensive definition is found in the four reasons a thing is said to be *dukkha*:[18]

1. *Abhiṇhasampatipīḷanato*: because it is constantly stressed; that is, it is continually stressed by the arising, decay, and disintegration of the things within and around it.
2. *Dukkhamato*: because it cannot endure. Things cannot maintain any one state; they inevitably change because of the arising and disintegration of determinants.
3. *Dukkhavatthuto*: because it is a base for suffering; it is something that creates suffering. (The commentaries say that it is a receptacle for the three *dukkhatā*[19] and the suffering of *saṁsāra*.)[20]
4. *Sukhapaṭikkhepato*: because it denies happiness. In reality, so-called happiness is simply a temporary impression. The intrinsic

> state is one of suffering, stress and conflict. These external characteristics of stress produce the feeling of stress known as suffering (*dukkhavedanā*). When the stress eases, suffering is relieved, and the result is a feeling of happiness. The greater the stress and the feeling of lack or want, the greater is the resulting feeling of happiness when that stress is relieved, just as a person who has been walking in the hot sun for some time might feel when entering into a cool room. Conversely, if there has been an intense feeling of happiness, when suffering arises it is felt that much more acutely. Even a minor amount of discomfort, which would normally not be noticed, can be felt as extreme discomfort, just as people who work in air-conditioned rooms feel the outside heat more intensely than those who don't.

The feeling known as happiness is not really an escape from suffering, but simply another level of it. When the relief of stress reaches a certain level, we call it "happiness," because that is the feeling it creates, but if the state is increased beyond that level it becomes intolerable, and another feeling of suffering arises. In fact, there is only suffering, the increasing and decreasing of stress and conflict. It is like heat and cold. In reality there is no such thing as coolness. The basic condition is a presence of more or less heat. No heat at all is intolerable. If the amount of heat is increased to a certain level, it becomes tolerable, even comfortable, but if the heat is increased beyond that, the result is not more happiness, but suffering. Thus, the feeling of happiness (*sukhavedanā*) is said to be a form of suffering, both in the sense that it is one level of suffering, merely a feeling, and in the sense that it is bound to the characteristic of stress, change, and disintegration. It is as if *dukkha* as a natural condition prevents happiness from lasting.

The Paṭisambhidāmagga, which defines *dukkha* in the three characteristics simply as "something that harbors danger (fear; *bhayaṭṭhena*)," explains *dukkha*, in the first of the four noble truths, as "It has the meaning of 'stressed' (*pīḷanaṭṭha*), it has the meaning of 'conditioned' (*saṅkhataṭṭha*), it has the meaning of 'burning' (*santāpaṭṭha*), it has the meaning of 'changing' (*vipariṇāmaṭṭha*)."[21] These four meanings can also be used with *dukkha* in the three characteristics, so I will include them here. After omitting the redundant definitions, we are left with an extra two:

1. *Saṅkhataṭṭha*: because it is compounded, a result of the combination of numerous constituent factors, dependent on determinants, and is not stable.
2. *Santāpaṭṭha*: because it burns; within themselves conditions contain the state of burning, they burn themselves to disintegration. Moreover, they burn deluded beings who grasp onto them.[22]

Dukkha in the Three Characteristics and *Dukkha* in the Four Noble Truths

The word *dukkha* appears in three important Buddhist teachings: in the types of feeling (which can be either three—unpleasant, pleasant, and neutral—or five—physical pain, physical pleasure, mental suffering, mental happiness, and equanimity), where it is called *dukkhavedanā* (painful feeling); in the three characteristics where it is called *dukkhalakkhaṇa* (the characteristic of *dukkha*); and in the four noble truths (*ariyasacca*), where it is called *dukkha ariyasacca* (the noble truth of *dukkha*).

While the meaning of *dukkha* in these three teachings overlaps, there are differences in scope. The broadest sense of the word, which encompasses all senses of the term, is *dukkha* in the three characteristics, *dukkhalakkhaṇa*: the state of instability, the inability of things to maintain any single state because of the stress and conflict resulting from the arising and ceasing of things. This applies to all formations. In this sense, its scope is equal to that of *anicca*: whatever is impermanent is also *dukkha*.

In its narrowest sense, as one aspect of a conditioned state, *dukkha* is the painful feeling known as *dukkhavedanā*; it is the *dukkha* that arises as a result of the *dukkha* in the three characteristics, the feeling of pain that arises on a personal basis as a result of the stress (*dukkha*) of the three characteristics. It is conditioned by the state of each person's physical and mental makeup. The feeling of suffering, just like other kinds of feeling, is included in the *dukkha* of the three characteristics. That is, all kinds of feeling, be they pleasant, unpleasant or neutral, are without exception *dukkha* according to the common characteristics of existence.

Dukkha in the noble truths is specifically that aspect of *dukkha* in the three characteristics that causes problems on the personal level. That is, all formations are in a state of stress according to the three characteristics, and those formations (not all of them, and not equally) cause stress for human beings, which is *dukkha* in the four noble truths. They cause stress on an experiential level because they are stressful according to the three characteristics.

Simply speaking, the *dukkha* of the four noble truths refers specifically to the five *khandhas*, or the five clung-to *khandhas*. It is that part of *dukkha* that is contingent on the faculties (*indriyabaddha*), and excludes any suffering that is not contingent on the faculties (*anindriyabaddha*). (Note that *dukkha* in the four noble truths is also *dukkha* in the three characteristics, while the second noble truth (*samudaya,* the cause of suffering) and the fourth noble truth (*magga,* the way leading to the end of suffering) are *dukkha* in the three characteristics but not *dukkha* in the four noble truths.)

The following observations may help to clarify the extent of *dukkha* in the four noble truths:

It is contingent on the sense faculties, related to life and the human problem. It does not include inanimate things and therefore is not the same as *dukkha* in the phrases "all formations are *dukkha*," or "whatever is impermanent is *dukkha*," both of which refer to *dukkha* in the three characteristics.

It arises from deeds (*kamma*) and defilements (*kilesa*). (In the texts it is said that it arises from the cause of *dukkha*, which is desire.)

It is contingent on the *pariññā* duty, the task to be done in relation to the first noble truth. *Pariññā* is comprehension or understanding. Thus, *dukkha* in the four noble truths is specifically that which must be known and understood.

In reference to the definitions of *dukkha* given above, the *dukkha* of the noble truths is that which is a receptacle or base for suffering (*dukkhavatthutāya*), not the stress and conflict within all conditions as a result of constant arising and ceasing (*udayabbaya-paṭipīḷanaṭṭhena*), which is *dukkha* in the three characteristics.[23]

Kinds of *Dukkha*

The greatest number of definitions of *dukkha* occur in the teachings on the four noble truths, because this is the subject that relates directly to human experience. *Dukkha* is (in this sense) a problem that must be corrected, something to be examined and transcended through appropriate practice. Teachings on the three characteristics cover *dukkha* only briefly to convey a general idea. Here I will present only the most important or commonly mentioned groupings.

First Group: The Three Dukkhatā.[24] This important grouping is based on the Buddha's own words, and it covers the entire range of meanings of *dukkha* in the three characteristics:

1. *Dukkhadukkhatā*: *dukkha* that is a feeling; that is, stress in both body and mind, as is normally understood by the word *suffering*. Examples: pain, discomfort, tiredness. This is *dukkhavedanā*.

2. *Vipariṇāma-dukkhatā*: the *dukkha* contingent on, or inherent in, change. This is the feeling of happiness (*sukhavedanā*), which in fact is merely another level of suffering. The feeling of pleasure is tainted with suffering, and the feeling will manifest fully as *dukkhavedanā* as soon as that pleasure changes. It could be said that happiness causes the arising of suffering because of its own instability and transience. (It could also be said that *sukhavedanā* is a modified form of suffering.)

3. *Saṅkhāra-dukkhatā*: the stress that is the natural state of all things that arise from causes and determinants. That is, the whole of the five *khandhas* (internal and external) are stressful, in that the arising and dissolution of conflicting conditions makes it impossible for them to maintain any one state for any length of time. This third kind of suffering incorporates the entire range of meaning of the *dukkha* of the three characteristics.

Second Group: The Twelve Kinds of Dukkha.[25] This group is an expansion of the definition of *dukkha* in the four noble truths:

1. *Jāti*: birth is *dukkha* because it is the condition for many kinds of suffering—for example:

- *Gabbhokkantimūlaka dukkha*: the stress of taking birth in a womb, being in a place that is incredibly cramped, dark and full of repulsive substances; the fetus is compared to a worm in slime.
- *Gabbhapariharaṇamūlaka dukkha*: the stress arising from the treatment of the womb. Whichever way the mother moves about, and whatever she eats or drinks, be it hot, cold, sour, or spicy, has an effect on the fetus.
- *Gabbhavipattimūlaka dukkha*: the suffering that arises from accidents within the womb, such as miscarriages and stillbirths, and operations to procure the child.
- *Vijāyanamūlaka dukkha*: the suffering of delivery. Before the baby can pass through the tiny channel available, it must endure intense pain.
- *Bahinikkhamamūlaka dukkha*: the stress of emerging into the outside world. A newborn baby has such a sensitive body and soft skin, it is like a fresh wound, every touch exceedingly painful.
- *Attupakkamamūlaka dukkha*: suffering at one's own hand, such as suicide, observing ascetic practices, becoming angry and refusing to eat, or injuring oneself.
- *Parupakkamamūlaka dukkha*: suffering at the hands of others, such as being murdered, imprisoned, or beaten.

2. *Jarā*: aging—organs of the body become frail and weak, the faculties of eye, ear, nose, and so on are impaired, strength fails, agility disappears, the skin wrinkles, the memory fades, and self-sufficiency deteriorates, all of which support the arising of suffering.

3. *Maraṇa*: death. At the time of approaching death, an image of one's evil actions appears; loved ones and possessions must all be abandoned; the organs of the body cease to function; bodily suffering is often intense and without remedy.

4. *Soka*: sorrow, grief, such as when bereaving a lost loved one.

5. *Parideva*: lamentation, such as when losing loved ones.

6. *Dukkha*: suffering in the body, pain, illness, and so on.[26]

7. *Domanassa*: pain in the mind, the kind that leads to tears, beating of the chest and head, falling in a heap, slashing the wrists, or suicide.

8. *Upāyāsa*: despair, hopelessness, the feeling of anguish when grief becomes unbearable.

9. *Appiyasampayoga*: association with things or people not liked.

10. *Piyavippayoga*: separation from things or people that are dear.

11. *Icchitālābha*: not attaining things hoped for.

12. *Upādānakkhandhā*: the five *khandhas* that are a base of clinging; all the kinds of suffering so far mentioned are suffering of the five clung-to *khandhas*. In summary, then, the five clung-to khandhas are suffering.

Third Group: Two Kinds of Dukkha.[27]

1. *Paṭicchannadukkha*: concealed or hidden suffering, the suffering that does not appear outwardly, such as toothache, earache, and the agitation of the mind when it is beset with lust or anger.

2. *Appaṭicchannadukkha*: unconcealed or overt suffering, such as being pricked by a thorn, whipped, or stabbed.

Fourth Group: Two Kinds of *Dukkha.*[28]

1. *Pariyāyadukkha*: suffering by extension, or indirect suffering, which is all of the suffering mentioned above, apart from *dukkhavedanā*.

2. *Nippariyāyadukkha*: direct suffering, the feeling of suffering, or *dukkhavedanā*.

In the *Mahādukkhakkhandha Sutta* and the *Cūḷadukkhakkhandha Sutta*,[29] the Buddha mentions many groups of suffering resulting from sensual desire. In essence, these are as follows:

1. The suffering and torment, exhaustion and even loss of life resulting from trying to make a living.

2. The disappointment and sadness that arise when the rewards of one's efforts are not forthcoming.
3. The suffering of having to protect possessions.
4. The sadness and woe when possessions cannot be successfully protected and are lost, such as when they are stolen by bandits or destroyed by fire.
5. The arguments and contention, struggle and even death, between king and king, householder and householder, parent and child, sibling and sibling, and friend and friend.
6. War and battle between two sides, resulting in death and injury.
7. War resulting from invasions of one country by another and the resulting death and injury.
8. The suffering of punishment, sometimes resulting in death, for dishonest activities, such as robbery and adultery.
9. The suffering in the hell realms that results from dishonest behavior through body, speech, and mind.

More varieties of suffering are scattered throughout the Tipiṭaka and commentaries. There are suttas that expound on the characteristics of suffering (such as in the *Mahādukkhakkhandha* and *Cūḷadukkhakkhandha Suttas* mentioned above) without actually referring to the word *dukkha*. In some places it is given specific names, such as *samsāra-dukkha*,[30] *abāyadukkha*, *vaṭṭamūlaka-dukkha*, *āhārapariyeṭṭhidukkha*,[31] and so on.

The subject of *dukkha* can be expanded on in many more ways than those mentioned here, because the problems of human existence are countless. There are common kinds of *dukkha* that apply everywhere and there are those that are specific to particular times, locations, and situations. It is not necessary to mention them all but rather to understand the objective of listing all these forms of *dukkha*, which is to recognize the existence of *dukkha* as it is in reality and to relate to it in a proper way. The proper way to relate to *dukkha* is to acknowledge its reality, not to ignore it or try to convince ourselves that it does not exist, or try to comfort ourselves with the thought that it will not come to us. This only creates more *dukkha*. We are rather encouraged to face up to the truth of *dukkha*, to acknowledge it and study it, until we are able to transcend it or prevent it from arising, at first temporarily and then permanently, ultimately attaining liberation.

Anattatā *and the Characteristic of Not-Self* (Anattalakkhaṇa)

The Paṭisambhidāmagga defines *anattā* with these simple words: "It is *anattā* in that it has no essence (*asārakaṭṭhena*)."[32] Having no essence means void of pith or substantiality: there is nothing that is a permanent entity. The definition states: "'Having no essence' means there is no intrinsic being or pith (*attasāra*) that could be thought to be a self (*attā*), an occupant (*nivāsī*), an agent or doer (*kāraka*), one who feels or experiences (*vedaka*), or a controller (*sayaṁvasī*), because whatever is impermanent is *dukkha* (stressful). It is not possible to forbid impermanence or stress, conflict, dissolution and disintegration from happening. Since this is so, how can there be a creator? For that reason, the Blessed One said, 'Bhikkhus, if this form were the self, it would not be subject to affliction...'"[33]

Note that the definition of not-self as having no essence is linked to the definition "cannot be created" or "having no power." If there were a permanent entity, then it could oppose change and not be subject to those changes. If there were an owner, that owner would have the power to force the things within its control as it wished, but in reality this is not the case.

Voidness of self or owner, then, specifically means having no power to control. Things are beyond control, they deny desires, as the commentaries state: "It is *anattā* because it is not controllable (*avasavattanaṭṭhena* or *avasavattanato*)."[34] This is further explained as meaning that nobody has the power to force (that is, to constrain according to one's desires rather than determinants) formations (*saṅkhārā*) that have arisen not to exist, those that exist not to age, and those that have aged not to disintegrate, or to prevent them from being battered by arising and cessation.[35] The Buddha's words are cited: "A person cannot have (as desired) of form (and the other *khandhas*), thus, 'May my form be like this, may it not be like that.'"[36]

After careful analysis, on an absolute level, no real and permanent entity can be found within phenomena. There are merely processes (*dhammapavatti*), the process of formations or a process of physical and mental properties (*khandhapavatti*) that arise from components brought together, and each of those components is subject to arising, decay, and cessation, faring according to a relationship of interrelated determinants, both within what can be identified as discrete processes, and between other processes. About this state, four observations can be made:

1. There is no real or essential self within this process.
2. It is a result of the collection and compounding of components.
3. Those components are constantly arising and ceasing and are threaded into a process.
4. If this is analyzed into lesser streams of processes, the lesser streams are also interdependent.

The definition of *anattā* as the characteristic of all things arising from components coming together, interrelated and interdependent, void of substantial entity or creating or controlling force, is a fundamental one that can be supported by many passages in the texts:

> "Dependent on the timber, lashings, mortar, and thatch, and a surrounding space, there is what is called a house; in the same way, dependent on bones, tendons, flesh, skin, and enclosure of space, is the condition known as body (*rūpa*)."[37]
>
> ---
>
> [Māra asks Bhikkhunī Vajirā]
>
> "Who created this being, where is its creator, where is it born, where does it cease?"
>
> [The bhikkhuni answers:]

> "So, Māra, you call this 'a being'? This is [simply] a pile of conditions; no being can be found within it. Just as when certain conditions are brought together the result is called 'a cart,' so too, when the five *khandhas* arise, the result is called 'a being.' In fact, only *dukkha* (the condition of instability) arises, continues, and ceases. Apart from *dukkha*, nothing arises, nothing continues, and nothing ceases."[38]
>
> ---
>
> "When elephants, horses, soldiers, and chariots are brought together they are called 'an army;' when buildings, houses, people, and numerous activities are brought together, it is called 'a town'; when the fingers and the hand are brought together in a certain form, the result is called a 'fist.' In reality there is no 'fist,' only the fingers and the hand. Even the fingers and the hand, when analyzed and dissected, do not really exist; they are made up of smaller constituents. This dissection can go on indefinitely and no solid entity can be found. The suttas teach only of mind and form (*nāma* and *rūpa*), they do not speak of a being or a person."[39]

In summary, the commentators have grouped the various meanings of the word *anattā* into four perspectives:[40]

1. *Suññato*: because it is empty, void of self or essence (*attasāra*), or empty of individuality. There is no occupier, creator, or consumer, other than the stream of interrelated factors proceeding according to cause and effect, except by conventional terms. Simply speaking, *suññato* means empty of a being, person, and all other conventional appendages.
2. *Assāmikato*: because it is ownerless; it is not anyone's self and does not belong to a self, and there is no self manipulating formations from outside. There is only a stream of interrelated factors, proceeding according to determinants (it has no owner, belongs to no one, and is no one's self).
3. *Avasavattanato*: because things do not lie within anyone's

(absolute) power, they are not obligated to anybody, there is no one with the power to force them to be any way other than according to causes and determinants. Other words that are used are *anissarato*—because they are not their own master, they cannot manipulate or direct themselves, they can only follow causes and determinants—and *akāmakāriyato*—because they cannot be bent to the will or intimidated by desires, but must conform to causes and determinants. For desires to be satisfied, the causes and determinants must be arranged accordingly.

4. *Attapaṭikkhepato*: because it denies *attā*. Things in themselves refute the existence of a self. The fact that they are a process, a stream of factors, with all the factors causally related, in itself denies the possibility of the existence of a self hidden anywhere within or outside of the process that could interfere with, control, or oppose it. If there were such a self, there could be no faring according to determinants, because things would follow its orders. Moreover, the causal process is perfect in itself. There is no need for, and cannot be, a self giving any orders.

There are two further definitions of *anattā* which, although covered within the definitions already given, do have some special connotations, and are therefore worthy of separate mention:

5. *Suddhasaṅkhārapuñjato* or *suddhadhammapuñjato*: because they are a heap of mere formations, or a heap of mere *dhammas* (*rūpadhamma*, *nāmadhamma*, or both); or *aṅgasambhārato*: because they are a compounding of lesser parts, they are not specific, perfect, unique entities, and there is no real being or person apart from those components (this interpretation is already covered in the first point above).
6. *Yathāpaccayapavattito*: because they proceed according to causes and determinants; the components are interrelated. In short, the process fares according to causes and determinants, not to desires. It cannot contain a self, either internally or exter-

nally, that could oppose or direct it. (This context is included in all four points mentioned above, particularly the third and the fourth.)

In summary, then, things proceed according to causes and determinants. When there are determinants (for things to be a certain way), they arise (in that way). When those determinants (for being that way) are no more, then there is cessation (from that state). Things do not listen to people's desires, they are not the entities (they appear to be) and do not belong to anyone.

One common misunderstanding is the perception of a thinker as separate from the thought, an intender as distinct from the intention, an experiencer of feeling as distinct from the feeling, or a committer of deeds (*kamma*) as distinct from the deed. Even famous philosophers have fallen into this trap, and failed to arrive at the pure truth that transcends habitual self-oriented thinking. The fifteenth-century French philosopher René Descartes, for example, deliberated long and hard about this question and concluded: "I think, therefore I am."[41] The feeling of self is a normal perception for all unenlightened beings, and it seems reasonable in accordance with normal thinking, but careful consideration reveals some contradictions.

Questions such as "Who is it who makes contact (*phassa*)?" "Who experiences feeling?" "Who desires?" "Who clings?" were put to the Buddha thousands of years ago. He said that such questions are useless because they are wrongly phrased. They are founded on a feeling or an impression, not on reality. To phrase it correctly, the questions must be put this way: "What is the determinant for the arising of contact?" "What is the determinant for the arising of feeling?" "What is the determinant for the arising of desire?" "What is the determinant for the arising of clinging?"[42] The answer is, the Buddha said, that thinking, intention, desire, and the experience of feeling are all factors in a process of mental and physical properties. In the same way, the feeling (of being a thinker, one who intends) is also a factor within that process, and all of those factors are related through cause and effect. There is merely the thought and the feeling of one who thinks (that is, it is the mistaken perception of a thinker, not an actual thinker), which arises naturally within the whole cause-and-effect process. The feeling of one who thinks is simply another instance of thinking as part of the thought process.

The reason for this false perception of self is the inability to analyze the interdependent cause-and-effect stream, and to perceive the functioning of that stream on a momentary basis. At the moment of thinking (about any given subject) there is no feeling of "one who thinks," and while there is the feeling of "one who thinks," there is no thinking about other subjects. The thought and the concept of a thinker are separate instances of thought within one overall process. The "one who thinks" is simply a feeling or impression that arises momentarily within the process.

This misunderstanding arises from unwise attention (*ayoniso-manasikāra*) and falls within one of six schools of thought mentioned in the following passage from the Buddha:

> "When an unenlightened being attends unwisely (*ayoniso-manasikāra*) in this way, one of these six views will arise: either the fixed view that 'I have a self'...'I do not have a self'...'Through self I am aware of self'...'Through the self I am aware of that which is not-self'...'With not-self I am aware of that which is self,' or, if not one of these, then the view will arise that 'This self of mine is the director, the experiencer, the receiver of good and evil *kamma*.'"[43]

It has been stated that the names added conventionally to the collective image have no bearing on or relation to the process, other than through clinging. Although there is no real self, the clinging to the concept of self can cause problems. Such clinging becomes a factor within the process, and as such is a determinant in how it fares. This effect is unhelpful (*akusala*), because it is born of ignorance (*avijjā*) of the true nature of things, and arises as an obstruction to the stream, in that while it does not, and cannot, ultimately alter causes and determinants, at the same time it does not conform to them, with deleterious results.

On one level, this clinging causes conflict within the process, which results in the feeling of stress known as *dukkhavedanā*. One who does not know things as they are clings to conventions (*sammati*), clings fast to concepts of self, and is battered about by that clinging, leading to much suffering. One who understands conventions does not cling blindly to the self, but sees merely a stream of conditions flowing according to cause and effect. The wise person uses names according to the convention, but when it is time to act, that person does so according to the relevant causes and determinants. He or she does not let desire and clinging create problems and suffering, and therefore is not harmed by clinging (this is to know how to use conventions effectively), and also is freed of having to receive the *kamma* resulting from clinging to conventions.

Clinging to self encourages the arising of unskillful mental qualities known as *kilesa* (defilements), especially desire for objects to gratify the senses (*taṇhā*), pride and conceit (*māna*), and clinging to personal views (*diṭṭhi*). They are factors for the arising and spread of stress and conflict, both internally and externally.

Those who do not know the truth of conventions and cling fast to the concept of self will allow these defilements to control their behavior and their lives, and suffering grows and spreads both internally and outward to others. Those who know the truth of conventions do not deludedly cling to self, and therefore they are freed of the power of these defilements and do not cling to concepts of owning or being anything. They live wisely, with awareness of conventional truth, and act in harmony with causes and determinants. This is the basis for a safe and trouble-free life for both oneself and others.

Another kind of delusion that leads people to cling to things is swinging to either one of the two extreme views. One view is that there is a permanent and immutable soul, being, or self. Even when the life span comes to an end, this soul continues on unchanged. Some say that this self wanders from birth to birth, some say it is waiting to go to eternal heaven or hell, depending on God's will. This view in Pali is called *sassatadiṭṭhi*, or *sassatavāda*—the eternalist view, the belief that the self is permanent and unchanging.

Another group believes that there is a self but that it is not permanent, it is destroyed at death. When a person dies, the being is annihilated. This view in Pali is called *ucchedadiṭṭhi*, or *ucchedavāda*, the annihilationist view.

Even students of Buddhism, if they do not truly understand the teaching, can fall into one of these two views. Specifically, those who study the law of *kamma* as it applies to the round of rebirth (*saṁsāravaṭṭa*) can easily fall into the eternalist view; those who study the teaching of *anattā*, not-self, can easily fall into the annihilationist view. The mistake common to both of these extreme views is the belief in or attachment to a self of some form. One side believes the self to be permanent and unchanging, while the other believes that it is annihilated at death.

In addition to these two views is another extreme view: that there is no self—that is, nothing. No being or person means no one who receives the fruits of actions. When there is no one to receive the fruits of actions, then all actions are void of consequence, and there is no karmic responsibility. In short, there is no *kamma*. This view can be analyzed into three main kinds. One is the belief that actions are void, as if not done, known as *akiriyadiṭṭhi* or *akiriyavāda*. The second is the belief that all things are random, entirely accidental and void of causal relationship. In short, there are no causes. It is called *ahetukadiṭṭhi* or *ahetukavāda*. The third is that there is nothing at all, nothing exists. This view is called *natthikadiṭṭhi* or *natthikavāda*.

Since things are a process arising from the compounding of components, functioning according to the effects of causes and determinants, there can be neither a permanent self nor a self that is annihilated. Right now, there is no being or self, so where is the self that can be eternal or the self that can be destroyed? This reflection refutes both *sassatadiṭṭhi* and *ucchedadiṭṭhi*.

Since the process is functioning with its related and interdependent components, how can it be said that there is nothing or that things are random, void of cause and determinants? This refutes the views of *natthikadiṭṭhi* and *ahetukadiṭṭhi*.

Since the process fares according to causes and determinants and changes according to events within it, there must be results, and deeds are not void. The fruition of actions occurs without the need for a "self" to be the receiver of results. That is, results, such as pleasant and unpleasant feeling and the changes within mind and personality, arise naturally within the process itself. In semi-conventional terms, we might say that the process is what receives the fruit of actions. This is a fruition of results that is much more certain than if a self were involved. If there were a real and permanent self, it might choose not to receive the fruits of certain actions. Since things fare according to causes and determinants, since results arise naturally within that process, and since the stream of events changes accordingly, how can it be said that actions are as if not done, or that actions are void of fruit? This refutes *akiriyadiṭṭhi* or *akiriyavāda*.

The following excerpts from the Visuddhimagga may serve to clarify the foregoing points:

> In reality there are only mental properties (*nāma*) and physical properties (*rūpa*) in this world. Within these physical and mental properties no being or self can be found. *Nāma* and *rūpa* are empty, concocted by determinants, like a machine. They are a mass of suffering [unstable], like grass and kindling.[44]
>
> ---
>
> There is suffering, but no one who suffers. There is deed, but no one who does it. There is *nibbāna*, but no one who attains it. There is a path, but no one who walks it.[45]
>
> ---
>
> There is no one who makes *kamma*; there is no one who receives the result. There are only conditions faring on their way. This is right view. Since *kamma* and result, as well as their causes, are like this, it is impossible to know the beginning and ending, as

in before the seed and after the tree. Even in the future, as long as there is *saṁsāra*, no ending [to *kamma* and *kamma* result] can be seen.

Followers of other sects, not knowing this truth, are not free (*asayaṁvasī*) [meaning they are powerless, or they are not independent; they must rely on others because of their wrongly held views]. Holding to the views based on the perception of a being (*sattasaññā*), of permanence, of annihilation, or the sixty-two kinds of view, they dispute. They are tied up in the net of views and are swept along by the current of desire, and therefore they cannot transcend suffering. A bhikkhu who is a follower (*sāvaka*) of the Buddha, knowing this clearly, understands fully and attains to the profound void.

There is no *kamma* in result (*vipāka*), there is no result in *kamma*. Each of them is entirely void of the other. But without *kamma* there is no result. Just as fire is not in sunlight, in a magnifying glass, or in dried cow dung—but is also not outside of those three objects, and arises from the combination of the three—in the same way, *vipāka* cannot be found within *kamma*, but it also cannot be found outside *kamma*. *Kamma* is not found within result; it is void of result. Result is not within *kamma*, but it depends on *kamma* and arises from *kamma*. For that reason, in truth, in the process of *saṁsāra*, among the *devas* and *brahmas*, no creator of the world can be found. There are only things (*dhammas*) proceeding in conformity to the relevant causes and conditions.[46]

Nature arises entirely due to causes. It is *dukkha*, impermanent, wavering, temporary, not lasting. All things are causally arisen from determinants (*dhamma*). Neither self nor other can be found within this process of events.

Things lead to the arising of things through the interaction of causes and determinants. The Buddha gave the teaching for the cessation of all causes. When causes are subdued, the circuit (*vaṭṭa*) is broken and no longer spins. The higher life (*brahma-*

> *cariya*) is lived for this cessation of suffering. When no being can be found, there is no annihilation and no eternity.[47]

Anattā means all things are not-self and have no self. They are all rather natural conditions, which is to say they each have their own particular nature. They are, and fare according to, natural conditions, such as arising, ceasing, and changing in accordance with determinants. Therefore they do not belong to anyone and are not subject to anyone. They are not a self and they do not contain a self anywhere that could own them or control them to be any particular way in accordance with the desires of anyone or anything. Some examples may help to clarify this.

An example from among conditioned things (*saṅkhatadhamma*): We may say "my arm" or "their arm," because we can control our arm to pick up, lift, and do other things in accordance with our wishes. But in reality, that the arm can move in those various ways is in accordance with the related determinants. If the determinants are missing or proceed differently, for instance if the nerves, muscles, or tendons are damaged, even though we may say "my arm, my arm," we can't control that arm. It is our own only by convention or attachment; it doesn't really belong to us.

None of us can have as we wish of the things that we hold to be ourselves or belonging to us to be this or that, because those things are only "us" or "ours" according to our attachments or accepted views.

When we know that they are not-self, that things are only conditions in and of themselves, we won't suffer when those things do not follow desires, but we know in accordance with determinants whether they can be corrected or not, and we can fix them according to those determinants.

As for not-self in relation to the reality that is the unconditioned (*asaṅkhata*), the cessation of determinants (*paccakkhaya*), or the non-formed (*visaṅkhāra*), it is clearly a state in and of itself that does not fare according to determinants; there is no self inside, outside, or anywhere else to own or control it. It is a thing of itself in the natural order.

In summary, the teaching of *anattā* helps to clarify and substantiate the following principles:

It refutes the eternalist (*sassatadiṭṭhi*) and annihilationist (*ucchedadiṭṭhi*) views.

It refutes the belief that a higher being created the world and controls the destinies of beings (*issaraniramitavāda*).

It supports the teaching of *kamma* in the Buddhist sense, while refuting the schools of thought that believe actions to be without consequence (*akiriyavāda*), the "old *kamma*" school (*pubbekatavāda*, as in the Jains), the view of *kamma* as created by a self (*ātman*) or tied to social class (as in the Hindu teaching), the accidentalists who believe that all things are random (*ahetukavāda*) and the nihilists (*natthikavāda*).

It distinguishes Buddhism's highest teaching or objective from those of the religions that adhere to self (*ātmavāda*).

The three characteristics are interrelated and causally connected. This is borne out in the oft-quoted words: "Whatever is impermanent, that is *dukkha*; whatever is *dukkha*, that is not-self (*yad'aniccaṁ taṁ dukkhaṁ, yaṁ dukkhaṁ tad'anattā*)." The Buddha often followed this statement with "Whatever is not-self should be seen with right understanding as it is thus: 'That is not mine, I am not that, that is not my self.'"[48]

The connection and relationship of these three characteristics can perhaps be most briefly conveyed like this: All things arise from the compounding of interrelated components. All of those components are related in the sense that they all arise and cease, are constantly changing, and are all affecting one another. They are a process faring according to causes and determinants.

Within this state: The fact that component factors are constantly arising and ceasing is *aniccatā*. The fact that the components or process are oppressed by this constant arising and ceasing and cannot maintain any state for long is *dukkhatā*. The fact that none of the components within the process contains any abiding essence or self, and that the components are subject only to causes and determinants, is *anattatā*.

If we look at these three characteristics together, we see the things conventionally known as discrete entities as collections of innumerable components crowded together, invariably arising and ceasing, being separated and scattered about. The process is full of stress and conflict, which causes it to change and to be unstable; it is dependent on causal relationships that control it and keep it within the form of a single stream or process. There is no self within it, and it all fares according to causes and determinants, not according to anyone's desires.

Attā—Anattā and *Attā—Nirattā*

In the Suttanipāta there are frequent references to the arahant, one who has attained to the goal of the holy life, as one who "has neither *attā* nor *nirattā*."[49] In simple terms it means having neither self nor negation of self. The Mahāniddesa explains this to mean that *attā* refers to the belief in a permanent self (*sassatadiṭṭhi*), while *nirattā* refers to the belief that the self is annihilated (*ucchedadiṭṭhi*). Another interpretation states that *attā* means that which is held onto, while *nirattā* means that which must be let go of. This means that the arahant is free of both attachment to a self and the belief that there is no self, having neither something held onto nor something to give up. The Mahāniddesa goes on to explain that whoever is holding on to something still has something to let go of; whoever has something to let go of is holding on to something. An arahant has transcended holding on and letting go.[50]

The ordinary person usually clings firmly to the belief in self. On the coarsest level, this belief centers on the body. However, when the body is closely examined, its change is undeniable, so it is obviously not the self. Clinging then transfers to the mind, or some of its qualities, such as feeling, memory, wisdom, or awareness. In Buddhist terminology we would say that there is clinging to one or another of the five *khandhas* as a self. Sometimes the clinging is to the overall image given by all of them. Some, looking a little deeper, reason that the five *khandhas* cannot be the self, so the real self must be separate from the five *khandhas*, either subliminally inherent within them or controlling them from a superior position.

Philosophers and religious leaders have pondered the question of self over the ages, and there are seers who have claimed to have attained states of ultimate truth, which they called the True Self, the highest Ātman, Paramātman, Brahma, or God. These are profound schools of thought, and the states they speak of are indeed sublime, but no state that is tainted with or connected to the feeling of self can be ultimate, because it still contains clinging.

Reality does exist, and it is not a state of total negation, but it also cannot be attained or realized with knowledge that is distorted by mistaken conceptions. The reason so many religious seekers have not been able to attain the highest reality is that, while they know clearly that the body, and even the five *khandhas*, cannot be the self, they are still blinded by the following two distortions that are inherent in the unenlightened makeup and influence their search for ultimate reality:

- Concept (*paññatti*) of self, the image of self rooted in attachment to the body, which is a smear that stains them right from the coarsest attachment to self as the body. No matter how refined the mental image may become, it is still an image just the same, and a mistaken image. It attaches itself to all states experienced, thus creating a distortion on all objects of awareness.
- Clinging and attachment (*upādāna*) to self. This attachment is brought to their relationship with ultimate reality and keeps them from attaining that ultimate reality.

In short, these religious seekers have not been liberated because they have not transcended concepts and attachment. Both of these conditions are related and are in fact two aspects of the same condition. Bringing them together, we have a picture of deludedly clinging to conditioned images of self that have resulted from attachment, and pasting them onto the reality of natural processes.

Liberation is an important prerequisite for attaining ultimate reality, because the ultimate reality, or unconditioned, is diametrically opposed to the conditioned, and can only be seen when conditioned things have ceased and attachment to self has been given up. The self is a concept, while ultimate reality is beyond concepts. They are opposites. The self is conceived for use in the conventional world. Only when the conventional is transcended can reality be realized. Simply speaking, reality cannot be self, and self cannot be reality.

The important factors in this delusion are the concept or image of self, and attachment to it. The self only exists on a conventional level; it is simply an attachment. Therefore, in the passage quoted from the Suttanipāta above, *attā* can be translated in two ways: first, as "self," or "attachment to self," and second, as "that which is attached to." The self is merely an attachment; it is not reality. Moreover, in that passage, *attā* is used in conjunction with *nirattā*, in the statement that "the arahant has neither *attā* (self) nor *nirattā*." *Nirattā*, like *attā*, can be translated in two ways: as "the attachment (to the view) that there is no self, or that the self ceases," or as "that which must be let go of."

This means that once the attachment to self and all misconceptions in regard to the conventional world are given up, that is the finish. There is nothing else to do. It isn't necessary to proceed to attach to the idea that there is no self. You are free and untroubled; you do not attach to anything else that would be a cause for more delusion. Having given up attachment, that is the end of the matter. In the Buddha's words: "When nothing is attached to, what is there to let go of [*natthi attā kuto nirattaṁ vā*]?"[51]

Note that the phrase "attachment to self" is not strictly correct. It should rather be "attachment to the concept of self," because that is all the self is—a concept or convention. It doesn't really exist. Since it is nonexistent, not-self is realized simply by not attaching to the concept of self; there is no need to give up or let go of self. If there is no self to hold on to, what is there to let go of? To attach to self is to create an image and paste it over the actuality of the present moment. Even if one kind of concept is given up, the image of self will be pasted over whatever remains, and reality will be blocked from view. Thus, by giving up old images of self, not attaching to anything new as self, and avoiding the trap of *nirattā*, all that remains is the reality, which is not related to, controlled by, or dependent on attachment to self.

The Buddha's responsibility in teaching the Dhamma is simply to show the way to give up the concepts of self that we attach to; that is, to give up attachment to the five *khandhas* as self. When the self is no longer clung to, that is the end of the matter as far as self goes. Then it is simply a matter of looking at what does exist, or reality—the unconditioned (*asaṅkhata*), which is no longer affiliated with self.

A harmful result of attachment to the concept of self is linking self to the concept of an all-powerful essence. When the concept of self becomes so subtle that it reaches its highest level, the self is made to be a great or universal self that creates and controls everything, and there is imagined a creator god, unnecessarily imposed onto the process of causes and determinants. It is unnecessary because reality is self-sustaining, the process faring according to causes and determinants, without the need for a creator or director of events. If it were to be said that there must be a creator god, then let the realities themselves be that which exists beforehand, instead of God (because the reality changes according to causes and determinants; simply put, it is self-creating), and then we are relieved of such obvious (and difficult) questions as "What existed before God?" or "Where did God come from?"

It is natural for people to see things in terms of self and a creator god, a director of life's events. It is a deduction that arises naturally because we usually see things arising from a creator. To see the causes and determinants that lie behind the image of a creator is a profound level of insight, and this explains why in ancient times natural phenomena such as thunder, lightning, floods, and earthquakes were attributed to the work of divine beings.

Little wonder, then, that so many religious seekers have become stuck on the concepts of self and God. Those who were exceptionally wise were able to formulate extremely subtle and profound teachings, but in essence they were still running along the same old concepts.

That the Buddha, who one might expect to have adhered to the old way of thinking, perhaps transforming the self to new and subtler heights, declared instead the truth of *anattā*, transcended attachment to self, and showed how processes fare according to causes and determinants with no need for a creator, and how the unconditioned, the highest truth, can exist without the need for a self or a creator, was a momentous step forward in the history of human intellectual development, removing the concept of liberation from the great trap into which people had fallen until that time. Many truth seekers before the Buddha had realized the truths of impermanence and suffering, but they had invariably become stuck on the idea of self.

Not-self is a truth that is extremely hard to see. Before giving a teaching on it, the Buddha often resorted to teachings on impermanence and *dukkha.* That not-self is such a difficult teaching to see, and the fact that not-self was such a momentous development not to be found before or outside of the Buddha's teaching, were truths that the writers of the commentaries were well aware of, as can be seen in the following passages:[52]

> Truly, when the Fully Enlightened Buddha taught the principle of not-self, he did so through the teaching of impermanence, the teaching of *dukkha*, and the teachings of both *dukkha* and impermanence.
>
> The Fully Enlightened Buddha taught the principle of not-self through the teaching of impermanence in this passage: "Bhikkhus, whoever should say, 'Eye...[ear...nose...tongue...body] is the self,'" is speaking incorrectly, because eye...displays arising and decay. [In that case], that person, possessed of such arising and decay, would have to conclude that "my self has arisen and it decays." For that reason, the statement that eye... is the self is not correct. Eye...is not-self.[53]

The Fully Enlightened Buddha taught the principle of not-self through the teaching of *dukkha* in this passage: "Bhikkhus, form is not-self. If form were self, it would not be subject to affliction [that is, stress and conflict], and we would be able to control it as we wished thus, 'May my form be like this, may it not be like this,' but because form is not-self, it is subject to affliction and cannot be controlled as we desire…"[54]

The Fully Enlightened Buddha taught the principle of not-self through the teachings of both impermanence and *dukkha* in this passage: "Bhikkhus, form is impermanent. Whatever is impermanent is suffering (*dukkha*). Whatever is suffering, that is not-self. Whatever is not-self should be seen with right understanding as it is, thus: 'That is not mine, that I am not, that is not my self.'"[55]

Why did the Buddha teach in this way? Because impermanence and *dukkha* are observable conditions. Observe how, when cups, plates, dishes or other objects fall from the hand and break, people tend to cry out, "Oh, *anicca*!" In this way, impermanence is manifest. When boils and sores break out on the body, or when people are pricked by thorns or stub their toes, they cry out, "Oh, how painful!" *Dukkha* is thus apparent. As for the characteristic of not-self, this is not apparent, it is not easily seen. It is not clear, it is difficult to comprehend, difficult to explain, difficult to proclaim.

Whether the Tathāgata appears in the world or not, the characteristic of impermanence and the characteristic of *dukkha* are apparent, but the characteristic of not-self is not apparent unless a Buddha appears in the world. The truth of not-self only becomes revealed in a Buddha Age. Truly, those religious seekers and wanderers with great power, such as (the prophet) Sarabhaṅga, are capable of teaching the characteristics of impermanence and *dukkha*, but they cannot teach the characteristic of not-self. If teachers from other sects, such as Sarabhaṅga, could teach the characteristic of not-self, it is possible that some of their listeners would become enlightened. Truly, the articulation of the characteristic of not-self is beyond the capabilities of all except a fully enlightened Buddha. This is how the characteristic of not-self is not apparent.

Practical Value

In terms of practical value, Buddhism's teachings stress the concept of impermanence more than the other two characteristics, because it is clearly manifest, easily seen. *Dukkha* is of medium visibility, and therefore is second-most common in the teachings. Not-self is subtle, hardest to see, and is the final level. The concept of impermanence is used as a base from which to explain the other two characteristics.

There are two Buddhavacana that serve as good examples of the ethical perspective of the three characteristics:

1. "All formations are impermanent, of the nature to arise, decay, and cease. Having arisen they pass away. The calming and abandoning of those formations is happiness."[56]
2. "All formations have decay and cessation as a natural condition. Strive to do what must be done with heedfulness."[57]

The first passage illustrates the value in terms of having an attitude toward life and the world based on knowing their true nature. It is impossible to hold formations indefinitely in any one state. They cannot be controlled by desires, but fare according to causes and determinants, and that is their natural way. Knowing this, the mind develops a proper attitude toward things that is free of clinging. Even though the things encountered may change and disappear, the mind is not overwhelmed by events, but maintains its openness, buoyancy, and clarity through knowledge of the way things are. This value emphasizes the liberation of the mind. It is the transcendent (*lokuttara*) level. In short, we could call this the "value in relation to mind development."

The second passage indicates the value in terms of practice, having a life that can be said to be for the benefit and happiness of both oneself and others, and also aimed at attaining the ultimate goal of life, by knowing the truth that every single thing in life and the world arises from component factors, exists only temporarily with stress and conflict, and inevitably decays and ceases. When all things are seen to be subject to causes and determinants rather than whims and desires, and inevitably destined for decay and dissolution, there is an appreciation of the fleetingness of existence. When this is known, there arises a sense of urgency that inspires one to quickly strive to do what must be done, to abandon what must be abandoned, and not to allow one's time to pass in vain. One corrects any mistakes that have been made, taking care to prevent them occurring again, and creates that which is fine and good, reflecting and acting with wise understanding of the causes and determinants, leading to good results both in terms of one's actions and in one's mind. This value emphasizes heedfulness, which is a mundane quality. In brief we could call it "the value in relation to performing tasks."

This second value must be used in relation to all levels of life and conduct in the world, from minor personal concerns to beneficial actions on the social level, from the immediate benefits to the highest, from the economic concerns of the householder's life to the practice and striving for full enlightenment of the Buddha, as is brought out by the following Buddhavacana:

> "Bhikkhus, seeing the benefit to yourselves, it is fitting that you bring about that benefit with heedfulness; seeing the benefit to others, it is fitting that you bring about that benefit with heedfulness; seeing the benefit to both sides, it is fitting that you bring about that benefit with heedfulness."[58]
>
> ---
>
> "Your Majesty, there is a thing (*dhamma*), the attainment of which creates the two kinds of benefit—namely, the immediate benefit (or mundane benefit; *diṭṭhadhammikattha*) and the fur-

> ther benefit (or profound benefit; *samparāyikattha*). That thing is heedfulness (*appamāda*). The heedful person is wise, creating both kinds of benefit, the immediate one and the further one. By realizing them, that person is a victor and a sage."[59]
>
> ---
>
> "Bhikkhus, as to this, one who has morality (*sīla*), who is endowed with morality, relying on heedfulness, procures a great treasure."[60]
>
> ---
>
> "Bhikkhus, that enlightenment which I have attained through heedfulness, if you strive toward it without retreating, in no long time you too will realize that goal of the holy life and enter therein with your own wisdom in this very life."[61]

The two values of mental development and heedfulness are mutually supportive, and when both are fully developed there can be full attainment of benefit. Now let us look into them in more detail, as follows.

The Value of the Teaching in Terms of Mental Development or Liberation

The value in terms of mental development or liberation and the practices for attaining it are related to the highest goal of Buddhism. Not only is this value broad in scope, but the details of its practice need special understanding, and the texts deal with it in depth. Some texts, such as the Visuddhimagga, organize the practice of mental development into an ordered system. In this book, too, the subject is dealt with in many chapters, for which reason I will not go into it in detail here, but give instead a general overview.

Usually, a practitioner who is developing wisdom through contemplation of the three characteristics will clarify understanding of life and the world, and experience changes in mental state in two distinct stages of development:

With the development of a medium level of understanding of the nature of formations as impermanent, stressful, and not-self, the response is a reaction against what has previously been felt toward the world. Whereas previously the tendency was attachment and delight in sights, sounds, smells, and so on, after the three characteristics are seen, this feeling changes to one of disenchantment, disgust, and a desire to escape these things. The feeling may even manifest as fear or loathing. At this stage feelings are stronger than knowledge; it is a case of "heart over mind." Even though at this stage wisdom is still not fully developed and feelings are biased, it is an important, even necessary, stage to be passed through in order to free the mind from the powerful effect of clinging, and therefore be able to progress to the perfect state of the second level. Stopping at this stage, in fact, can lead to deleterious results.

When understanding develops into a clear perception of the truth, wisdom is fully developed. The feelings of disenchantment, loathing, and wanting to escape disappear, and the heart settles into an impartial awareness, neither delighted nor disgusted, neither attracted nor averse, neither involved nor repulsed. There is simply knowing things clearly as they are, a feeling of clarity and freedom, and an attitude of responding to things in accordance with causes and effect, according to determinants. In the stages of insight, this level is called *saṅkhārupekkhāñāṇa* (direct knowledge accompanied by impartiality toward all formations). It is an important and essential stage in reaching the truth and perfect liberation of mind.

The value in terms of mental liberation, especially at the level of full development, has two features and effects. The first is absence of suffering: the mind is free of all feelings of stress and conflict that result from clinging. It is imbued with a happiness that is not dependent on objects or inducements; there is openness, clarity, joy, buoyancy, and freedom from worry. The mind does not waver or experience feelings of sorrow and depression over the ups and downs known as the worldly conditions (*lokadhamma*). It is not affected by loss and deprivation. This feature has an effect on moral conduct also, in that there is no compulsion to relieve personal suffering outwardly on other people, which is one of the main causes of behavioral problems. Moreover, the enlightened mind is a fertile field for the arising of virtues, especially goodwill and compassion, which are of immense benefit to moral conduct.

The second is absence of defilements: the mind is free from the influence, stress, and domination of defilements such as greed, anger, jealousy, and ambitious desire. It is clear, calm, and pure. This feature has a direct result on moral conduct, internally in the thinking and use of pure, detached wisdom that is not biased by like, dislike, and selfish desires, and externally in not acting wrongfully or badly under the dictates of defilements, and ultimately being able to fully and truly do things that are good and in accordance with causes and results.

However, as long as it is still in the developing stages, this first ethical value is not totally comprehensive. In itself it can still go bad—that is, have a harmful effect—in accordance with the principle of the skillful (*kusala*) being a determinant for the unskillful (*akusala*).[62] When the mind has been developed to a certain degree and experiences calm and happiness, one may indulge in that happiness or become content with merely that attainment, and give up striving to do what needs to be done and neglect to attend to external problems. This is called living with heedlessness, as described by the Buddha:

> "Nandiya, how is it that a noble disciple lives with heedlessness? Herein, a noble disciple in this teaching and discipline is possessed of unshakable faith in the Buddha, the Dhamma, and the Saṅgha, he is possessed of morality that is praised by the enlightened ones...and that noble disciple is satisfied with that unshakable faith...and the morality praised by the enlightened ones, and makes no effort to exceed that attainment. This, Nandiya, is a noble disciple who lives with heedlessness."[63]

The way to avoid this is to practice in such a way that also develops the second value.

The Value in Terms of Heedfulness

The second value, the value in terms of heedfulness, is associated with two tendencies that unenlightened beings are prone to. One is that only when faced with stress, danger, or necessity are they motivated to attend to the problem or task that needs doing. Then they struggle frantically to deal with the situation. Sometimes they are successful, sometimes not, and they suffer loss or even calamity. If they are able to solve the problem or avert a danger, it is only at the expense of much confusion, and it is difficult to solve the problem completely. It may even take the form of a "crushing success."

The other is that when things are normal and going well, or a problem has been averted, they drop their guard and spend their time either looking for pleasure or simply fall into complacency. They do not think of preparing for decline or dangers that may arise in the future. Anything that does not demand urgent attention tends to be put off until a future time. When danger threatens again, they are forced once more to do something; then, when the threat has passed, they lie down and take it easy again.

This is the cycle of behavior for the ordinary, unenlightened being, and it continues on in this way until such time as an event occurs that cannot be rectified, or it takes the form of a "crushing success," at which point the matter comes to a close.

This kind of life is called *pamāda*: heedlessness, negligence, carelessness, disinterest, apathy. *Pamāda* is linked with laziness and lack of effort.

The opposite quality to this is called *appamāda* (heedfulness). To live heedfully is to live with effort, alerted by mindfulness, continuously heedful of what must be avoided and what must be done, and applying oneself to them. There is an appreciation of the importance of time, and there is care with all matters and tasks, even minor ones. The heedful person doesn't allow himself or herself to slide into decline, nor does that person allow an opportunity for goodness or progress to pass by in vain. The heedful person does not procrastinate and plans actions thoroughly. Heedfulness has three important characteristics:

1. Seeing the value and importance of time, which is relentlessly moving by, and not allowing time and opportunities to pass by; utilizing time as thoroughly and skillfully as possible.
2. Non-intoxication (in sensual pleasures), care and watchfulness against error; not allowing a fall into decline or bad actions.
3. Quickly creating goodness and well-being, application to tasks; not being careless but striving to develop the mind and acting with thoroughness (this is called "heedfulness in regard to wholesome things").

Knowledge of the three characteristics is a direct aid to heedfulness, because when we know that all things are unstable, constantly changing, and subject to determinants, it naturally follows that the only correct action is to speedily act in accordance with determinants. This means urgently guarding against decline that has not yet set in, rectifying problems or decline that have arisen, generating benefit and preserving the benefit that has been generated. It is achieved by studying causes and determinants and acting accordingly.

With the understanding that all things are impermanent and subject to causes and determinants, if we want welfare and benefit we must make a concerted effort to create the causes for maximum goodness and bring about as much benefit as possible. This is the value of the three characteristics in regard to heedfulness.

The Value Contingent on Liberation, or in Terms of Purity and Virtue

A third value, the value contingent on liberation, or in terms of purity and virtue, is included in the first value, the value in terms of mental development, in the sense of the mind being free of defilements, but as it has its own unique importance, we will examine it separately.

The first two values are usually mentioned in relation to the characteristic of impermanence, because that characteristic is easily seen. Even beginners in Buddhist practice can derive some benefit from reflecting on the three characteristics in terms of the first two values. The third value, however, tends to come with attention on not-self.[64] See, for example:

> "A bhikkhu sees as it is with right wisdom that all form... feeling... perception... volitional formations... consciousness, whether of the past, the present or the future,... are entirely ownerless, seeing 'I am not that, that is not my self.' Knowing and seeing in this way, he is free of [thoughts of] me (*ahaṁkāra*) and mine (*mamaṁkāra*) and the tendency to conceit (*mānānusaya*), both in regard to the body and consciousness, and in regard to all external images."[65]

Ahaṁkāra is the defilement known as views (*diṭṭhi*); *mamaṁkāra* is the defilement known as desire (*taṇhā*); *mānānusaya* is the defilement known as conceit (*māna*).

The Buddhavacana quoted above in essence says that one who clearly sees *anattā* is freed of the defilements that are bound to or centered on the self—that is to say, desire, conceit, and views. These three kinds of defilements are also referred to as *papañca*, or *papañcadhamma*. *Papañca* means "that which slows down." It can be simply translated as "churning": churning the mind into suffering, churning the head into lots of problems, entanglements, confusion, and complexity, causing it to stray from the simple and obvious truth. Where there was no problem, these defilements cause one to arise; where there is already a problem, they prevent any simple and straightforward correction and instead make the problem more complicated. They are the factors that cause people to run around in conflict, contention, and even war. Not only are these defilements the causes of all kinds of evil actions, but they are behind good actions too, imbuing those actions with an ulterior motive. Those actions become impure and cannot be fully carried out, since these defilements slow them down or put them off course.

By understanding the three characteristics, and in particular the characteristic of not-self, the influence of these self-based tendencies is weakened, and, depending on the level of wisdom and liberation, ultimately completely destroyed. Without the interference of these defilements the path to goodness is clear, wide, and open. Virtues such as goodwill, compassion, generosity, moral rectitude, and service (*atthacariya*) can be developed unhindered.

Seeing the three characteristics through clear and proper attention leads to the arising of the moral values of virtue and personal growth as corollaries of happiness; that is, virtue as a result of wholesome conditions functioning smoothly and unhindered by unwholesome conditions; growth as a result of wisdom that perceives the world and life as they are, such perception making the mind clear, radiant, joyful, and free. Although happiness is not in itself morality, it can be a strong supporting factor for moral conduct. The happiness that supports moral conduct is exclusively that known as *nirāmisasukha*—the happiness independent of externals. This kind of happiness does not depend on personal profit of any kind, unlike materialistic kinds of happiness, which tend to lead to decadence and selfishness and eventually bring more harm than good.

To see the three characteristics is to know the way things really are and to achieve the independent kind of happiness, which guarantees virtuous conduct. Even though those who have this insight may still experience sensual happiness, they are not so attached to it that it will cause serious problems. Their indulgence in sensual pleasure does not exceed the limits of moderation or lead to exploitation, and when happiness disappears they maintain their mental equilibrium and are not overwhelmed by suffering. They can experience happiness on every level in the most thorough and fluent way, because there is no anxiety or confusion resulting from the interference of the defilements. There is no attachment to happiness, no matter how refined or exceptional it is.

With this understanding of the practical value of the three characteristics as a group, we will now examine their value individually.

Aniccatā: *The Characteristic of Impermanence*

The principle of *aniccatā* describes impermanence—the arising, establishment, and ceasing of things—up until the most refined level, both in the physical and mental spheres. The impermanence of components, as it appears to us, is known as "change." The common perception is that things have an essential being, which was originally one way and then becomes another. This perception is an illusion, and a cause for clinging and attachment, leading us to bind ourselves to an image we have created that is not in accordance with reality. When we live in ignorance of the way things are, we are dragged into struggling after the images of our own creation. This is living as a slave. Those who know reality live freely and are able to derive benefit from the natural laws. In terms of ethics, the principle of impermanence can be used in many ways, as follows.

Although impermanence is intrinsically neutral, neither good nor evil, in terms of human life one kind of change is called "prosperity," and another is called "decline." All changes must proceed at the direction of determinants. In terms of ethics, the principle of impermanence can be used to teach, in accordance with the understanding of prosperity and decline, that whatever prospers can also decline, whatever declines can also prosper, and whatever prospers can prosper even further, depending on causes and determinants. And among these causes and determinants, humankind is one. In this context, prosperity and decline are not random but are things that human beings can interact with and create, as causes and determinants allow. There is no question of external interference above and beyond the ordinary natural processes, because there is no such supernatural agent. Thus, the natural law of impermanence or change, being impartial, gives hope, because it is neutral: whichever way we want things to be, it is up to our ability to create the causes and determinants. Change for the better, whether it be in terms of material progress or mental development (from the level of making a dull person clever to that of changing an unenlightened being into an enlightened one), is a possibility, subject to the understanding of causes and determinants and appropriate action within them.

Summarizing, impermanence as "change" warns us that prosperity can degenerate into decline. Anyone who does not want decline must heedfully avoid or remove those determinants that cause decline and create and facilitate those determinants that cause and foster prosperity. Those changes that are conducive to prosperity can be developed and enhanced by increasing the determinants that cause prosperity and guarding against the causes and determinants that cause decline, such as heedlessness, and at the same time not heedlessly indulging in that prosperity to the point of being completely blind to the possibility of decline.

It is at this point that we find that most important of teachings, the link between reality and ethics, and that is the necessity of wisdom, which is required for the recognition of the nature of decline and prosperity and the causes and determinants that bring about the desired changes, and also required in developing our ability to interact with and manipulate those determinants. The quality of impermanence is thus extremely meaningful for ethics. It provides hope for prosperity and endorsement for the law of *kamma*, and it necessitates the use of wisdom in order to interact with change in the most effective way.

In terms of internal life, or the value in terms of mentality, the principle of impermanence helps us to live our lives in full knowledge of reality, while in terms of the external life we are able to use wisdom to avoid decline and create prosperity. Within the mind we abide with detachment, enslaved by neither decline nor prosperity, knowing how to make use of the laws of nature and how to interact with them without being thrown around aimlessly through attachment and clinging to particular parts of the process so much that we can hardly help ourselves, let alone others.

One who has a free mind understands things as they really are. Only through not clinging to things with desire and attachment can one clearly see real prosperity and decline, not just the kind of prosperity that is used as an excuse to bind oneself and others even more. Only then can one really reap benefit from the prosperity one has created and, in so doing, become a mainstay for others.

In the initial stages of practice, the principle of impermanence teaches us to know the norm of things, and therefore prevents us from falling into extreme forms of suffering when confronted with decline or loss, and from heedlessness and delusion in times of prosperity. In the more advanced levels, it leads to progressively higher levels of awareness of the truth, culminating in insight into the principle of *anattā*, enabling us to live with a free mind, with no attachment or suffering, and perfect mental health.

In brief, ethical utilization of the teaching of impermanence has two stages: in the first stage, when confronted with undesirable changes, suffering can be mitigated by reflecting on the truth of impermanence; when confronted with changes that are agreeable, one is not deluded by them because one knows the truth. The second stage is the urgent effort to do what needs to be done to the best of one's abilities, and with a mind that is free, knowing that change fares according to causes and determinants. Those who, seeing that all things are ephemeral and subject to change, let their lives flow at random, leaving things go as they will, have wrong understanding and wrong application of the principle of impermanence, and neglect the Buddha's final instruction, which states, "All formations are of the nature to decay and dissolve; strive on with heedfulness."[66]

Dukkhatā: *The Characteristic of Suffering*

There are two measures for gauging the ethical value of *dukkhatā*, the characteristic of suffering.

Since all things arise from the accumulation of components, and each of those components is impermanent, constantly arising, changing and ceasing according to the law of impermanence, each group of these determinants is simply a mass of change and conflict, ready to fall into decay and dissolution at any time. Subsequently, the containment of those changing and decaying components into a collective image, either according to one's desires or in any desired form, requires energy and some organization of those components as further determinants. The more numerous and complicated those components are, the more energy and organization required. Efforts to influence things must be made in accordance with causes and determinants, with a clear awareness of the factors involved in success, failure, and management of those determinants. This is the way to practice in relation to things without being caught up in them. Such practice does not lead to suffering. The opposite way of practice is to act out of attachment and desires, tying oneself to conditions and being oppressed by them. Not only does this cause suffering for oneself, it leads to no fruitful result.

In the four noble truths, the only task in relation to *dukkha* is to observe or understand it (*pariññā*). This important teaching is often overlooked. Buddhism teaches that we must relate to *dukkha* as an object of study: we "know suffering" in order to know the problems with which we have to deal, not in order to have suffering, but in order to practice correctly in relation to it and therefore not have suffering. To put it simply, the teaching on the four noble truths tells us that whatever is a problem must be studied and clearly understood before any effective corrective action can be taken. Studying problems does not mean creating or looking for them, but finding a way to resolve them. Those who do not know the task in relation to the noble truths may practice mistakenly in relation to *dukkha*, veering from the path and increasing their suffering by looking at the world in a negative way.

Anattatā: *The Characteristic of Not-Self*

Understanding *anattatā*, the characteristic of not-self, has the following ethical values.

On the most basic level, in relation to desire, the teaching of not-self helps to decrease the influence of selfishness by encouraging a perception of that which is useful on a broader level, not just to oneself. The nature of all things having no intrinsic self, arising from components and faring according to determinants, teaches us that whatever form things may take depends on conditioning, the creation of determinants, and the guiding of their relationship so that it fares according to objectives and efficacy. For this reason, the teaching reiterates the necessity to relate to things according to causes and determinants, with an independent attitude, which is the best way to ensure attainment of the goal without the problems created by desire and clinging.

On the middle level, in relation to view, an understanding of not-self broadens our outlook, enabling us to understand and act on all concerns without the interference of selfish desires, personal opinions, and beliefs. Instead, we are able to reflect on things as they are, in accordance with causes and results. We can maintain equanimity and impartiality, see things as they really are, stop the rule of the self (*attādhipatteya*) and practice according to the rule by Dhamma (*dhammādhipatteya*).

On the highest level, to know the teaching of *anattā* is to know things as they really are, to know the principles of nature comprehensively. Such a comprehensive knowledge enables one to completely relinquish clinging and attain complete liberation, the goal of Buddhist practice.

In general, the principle of not-self, as with the principles of impermanence and *dukkha*, is a guarantee of any true practical teachings, such as the law of *kamma* and the practice for liberation. For example, it is because all things have no self that they proceed in the form of a stream of interrelated causes and determinants and *kamma* can operate, and because all things have no intrinsic self, liberation is possible. However, our consideration of these points must be left until the section on dependent arising in the next chapter.

Textual References

Knowing the Truth of the Three Characteristics

> "Bhikkhus, form...feeling...perception...volitional formations...consciousness are impermanent. Whatever is impermanent is stressful (*dukkha*). Whatever is stressful is not-self. Whatever is not-self should be seen with right wisdom thus: 'That is not mine; I am not that; that is not my self.'"[67]
>
> ---
>
> "Bhikkhus, form...feeling...perception...volitional formations

...consciousness are impermanent...stressful...not-self. Those determinants that enable the arising of form...feeling...perception...volitional formations...consciousness are also impermanent...stressful...not-self. How can form...feeling...perception...volitional formations...consciousness that are arisen from factors that are impermanent...stressful...not-self be conceived of as permanent...happiness...self?"[68]

"Friend, a learned, noble disciple, conversant with the noble ones, well versed in the noble teaching, well trained in the noble teaching (*ariyadhamma*), conversant with the true persons, well versed in the true teaching (*sappurisadhamma*), well trained in the true teaching, does not see form, feeling, perception, volitional formations, and consciousness as the self; does not see self as having form, feeling, perception, volitional formations, and consciousness; he does not see form, feeling, perception, volitional formations, and consciousness in the self, and does not see the self in form, feeling, perception, volitional formations, or consciousness. That noble disciple clearly knows form, feeling, perception, volitional formations, and consciousness, which are impermanent, stressful, not-self, concocted, and true murderers, as they really are, as impermanent, stressful, not-self, concocted, and true murderers. That noble disciple does not attach to, does not adhere to, does not aspire to, form, feeling, perception, volitional formations, and consciousness as self. Those five *khandhas*, to which that noble disciple does not cling or attach, are of much benefit and happiness for a long time to come."[69]

"And what, householder, is it to be sick in the body and sick in the mind? Herein, the unenlightened being, not conversant with the noble ones, not well versed in the noble teaching, not trained in the noble teaching...sees form, feeling, perception, volitional formations, and consciousness as the self and sees the self as having form, feeling, perception, volitional formations, and consciousness; he sees form, feeling, perception, volitional formations, and consciousness in the self and sees self in form, feeling, perception, volitional formations, and consciousness. He lives beset by the notion that 'form is me, form is mine; feeling is me, feeling is mine; perception is me, perception is mine; volitional formations are me, volitional formations are mine; consciousness is me, consciousness is mine.' Since he is beset by this notion that 'form is me, form is mine...consciousness is me, consciousness is mine,' when form, feeling, perception, volitional formations, and consciousness change and become otherwise, that person experiences sorrow, distress, suffering, grief, and despair on account of that changing and becoming otherwise of form...consciousness.

"And what, householder, is it to be sick in the body but not in the mind? Herein, a noble disciple...does not see form, feeling, perception, volitional formations, and consciousness as the self, and does not see self as having form, feeling, perception, volitional formations, and consciousness; he does not see form, feeling, perception, volitional formations, and consciousness in the self, and does not see the self in form, feeling, perception, volitional formations, or consciousness. He does not live beset with the notion that 'form is me, form is mine; feeling is me, feeling is mine; perception is me, perception is mine; volitional formations are me, volitional formations are mine; consciousness is me, consciousness is mine.' Since that noble disciple does not live beset with the notion that 'form is me, form is mine; feeling is me, feeling is mine; perception is me, perception is mine; volitional formations are me, volitional formations are mine; consciousness is me, consciousness is mine,' when form, feeling, perception, volitional formations, and consciousness change and become otherwise, he is not sorrowful, he does not experience distress, suffering, grief, or despair on that account."[70]

"Bhikkhus, how is one to attain the non-confusion that arises from non-clinging? Herein, a learned, noble disciple...does not see form as the self, does not see the self as having form; does not see a self in form and does not see a form in self. No matter how that disciple's form may change and become otherwise, his consciousness does not follow after the changes of that form on account of its becoming otherwise. Confusion and the mass of thinking that arises from consciousness's following of the vicissitudes of form cannot overwhelm his mind. Because his mind is not overwhelmed, he has no fear or trepidation, no agitation or regret. Because he does not cling, he is not confused."[71] [The same passage is repeated for feeling, perception, volitional formations, and consciousness.]

"Bhikkhus, knowing *anicca*, the change, decay, and cessation of form, seeing as it is with right wisdom that form from previous times and form in the present are entirely impermanent, stressful, of the nature to change, one throws off sorrow, lamentation, pain, grief, and despair. Through discarding sorrow...there is no confusion. When there is no confusion, one dwells at ease. A bhikkhu who dwells at ease, I say, is one who experiences *nibbāna* in that moment (*tadaṅganibbuta*)."[72] [Same words for feeling, perception, volitional formations, and consciousness.]

"An unenlightened, unlearned being, attends unwisely (*ayoniso-manasikāra*) in this way: 'In the distant past, did I exist?...Or did I not exist?...What was I?...How was I?...Having been what did I become what? In the distant future, will I exist?... Or will I not exist?...What will I be?...How will I be?...Having been what will I become what?' Or, considering the present, he doubts, thinking, 'Do I exist?...Or do I not exist?...What am I?...How am I?...Where does this being come from?...Where will this being go to?'

"When that unenlightened being attends unwisely in this way, one of the six kinds of view will arise for him. He will conceive the certain belief that 'I have a self'...'I do not have a self'...'I observe the self with the self'...'I observe that which is not-self with the self'...'I observe the self with that which is not-self,' or if not, then the view that 'This self is the one who controls, the one who experiences, the one who receives the fruits of good and evil actions. It is a condition that is permanent, everlasting, unchanging and eternal.' Bhikkhus, this is called view, the tangle of views, the desert of views, the thicket of views, the squirming of views, the binding of views. The unlearned, unenlightened being, tied and bound by such views, does not transcend birth, aging, death, sorrow, lamentation, pain, grief, and despair. I say he does not escape suffering.

"Bhikkhus, as for the learned noble disciple...he knows clearly what things should be attended to, and he knows clearly what things should not be attended to. He does not attend to what should not be attended to, and he attends to what should be attended to.

"And what are those things that should not be attended to that are not attended to by the noble disciple? Whatever thing, being attended to by that noble disciple, causes the arising of the outflows (*āsava*) of sensual desire, becoming and ignorance not yet arisen, or those outflows already arisen to increase, these are the things that should not be attended to, that are not attended to by that noble disciple.

"And what are those things that should be attended to, that are attended to by that noble disciple? Whatever things, having been attended to by that noble disciple, cause the non-arising of as yet unarisen outflows of sensual desire, becoming and ignorance, and the relinquishment of those already arisen, these are the things that should be attended to, that are attended to by the noble disciple. Since that noble disciple does not attend to those things that should not be attended to, and attends to those things that should be attended to, any outflows that have not yet arisen do not arise, and those that have arisen are relinquished.

"That noble disciple attends wisely that 'this is suffering (*dukkha*)...this is the cause of suffering...this is the cessation of suffering...this is the practice leading to the cessation of suffering.' When that noble disciple attends wisely in this way, three of the fetters can be given up. They are self view (*sakkāyadiṭṭhi*), doubt (*vicikicchā*), and grasping at rites and rituals (*sīlabbataparāmāsa*)."[73]

The Impermanence of Life and the Preciousness of Time

The Kinsman of the Sun [the Buddha] has said that form is like bubbles in a river, feeling is like froth in rain, perception is like a mirage, volitional formations are like a banana tree, and consciousness is like a conjurer's trick. A bhikkhu, considering this, attending wisely to the five *khandhas*, finds only a state of emptiness. He with wisdom as mighty as the earth, using the body as a base, taught the relinquishment of three conditions (greed, hatred and delusion; or desire, conceit, and views) thus: "Venerables, see how this body is thrown off. When life, warmth, and consciousness leave the body it is discarded, void of consciousness, to become food for other creatures. Life is like this: it is a trick to deceive fools. It has been said that the five *khandhas* are like a band of vicious murderers. No essence can be found within them. A bhikkhu, arousing effort, should consider the *khandhas* in this way, with self-awareness and firm recollection, both day and night. He should throw off the fetters and build himself a mainstay. With *nibbāna* as his goal, he should strive toward it as if his hair were on fire."[74]

"Bhikkhus, the human life span is short; all must go to the next world. Consider this situation with heedfulness, develop goodness, live the holy life. There is no one born who does not die. Even the most long-lived people only make it to one hundred years; if they exceed that it is only by a little.

"The human life span is short. The wise should scorn such a short span of years, practicing as if their heads were on fire. There is no escaping the King of Death. The days and nights are passing; life is getting shorter all the time. The lives of beings are constantly ebbing away, like water in a drying stream."[75]

"Like four mighty mountains of rock as tall as the sky, rolling inward from the four directions and crushing all in their path, aging and death overwhelm all living beings. Kings, brahmins, merchants and artisans, outcasts, and garbage rakers too are all crushed by aging and death—no one is exempt. At the time of death, there is no battleground for battalions of elephants, chariots, or infantry; magical charms and bribery are of no avail. That is why the wise, seeing that which is (truly) useful, awaken faith in the Buddha, the Dhamma, and the Saṅgha. Those who practice the Dhamma with body, speech, and mind are praised by the world. Passing from this world, they delight in heaven."[76]

"Worldlings, slaughtered by the Lord of Death, captured by aging, and stabbed by the dart of desire, run around chasing their desires. Worldlings, constantly smashed by the Lord of Death, trapped by aging, have nothing with which to protect themselves and suffer interminably, as if they were criminals being punished. Death, sickness, and aging are like three balls of fire following on their heels, and they have neither the strength to oppose them nor the speed to escape them. [For that reason], do not let the days pass by in vain. Whether much or a little, at least derive some benefit from your time, because the days and nights are relentlessly passing, and people's lives are getting further from benefit, becoming shorter and shorter. While walking, standing, or sitting, the final moment is advancing closer and closer, do not waste your time."[77]

"I see your sons, crying 'Mummy,' 'Daddy,' lovely children, hard begotten, dying even before they get old. I see your daughters, pretty young maidens, lovely to behold, dying like young bamboo shoots torn from the clump. Verily, male and female can die even in their youth: who can rest assured that they are still young? The days and nights are passing, our lives are getting shorter all the time, like the lives of fish in a drying pond. Where is the guarantee in youth?...Worldlings are slaughtered by death, trapped by aging. The days and nights pass by in vain...

The more cloth the weaver has spun, the less thread remains to be woven: such are the lives of worldlings. Just as a mighty river, full to the brim, never flows upward, so do the lives of human beings never flow back to childhood. As a mighty river, full to the brim, sweeps the trees along its bank to destruction, so do aging and death sweep all before them... As a ripe fruit is in constant danger of falling to the ground, so all beings, born into this world, are in constant danger of death. We see many people in the morning, but come evening some are gone. We see many people in the evening, but come morning some are gone. Quickly practice, begin today! Who knows if we will not die tomorrow? There is no bargaining with the Lord of Death."[78]

"It would be better for you to lament for yourselves, still in the clutches of the Lord of Death, than to lament for the deceased. Time is not heedless, like living beings who are standing, sitting, reclining, or walking; the ages pass with every blink of the eye. Since the ages are passing in this way, there is no need to doubt that separation is in store. It is better to look on those beings who still remain with kindness than to grieve over those who have passed on."[79]

"Bhikkhus, these five eventualities (*ṭhāna*) are things that cannot come to be for a recluse (*samaṇa*), brahmin, angel (*devatā*), demon (*māra*), deity (*brahma*), or anyone in this world. What are the five? They are that 'may the things that are of the nature to age not age; may the things that are of the nature to sicken not sicken; may the things that are of the nature to die not die; may the things that are of the nature to cease not cease; may the things that are of the nature to go to destruction not go to destruction.'

"For the unlearned, unenlightened being, that which is subject to aging ages, that which is subject to sickness becomes sick, that which is subject to death dies, that which is subject to cessation ceases, and that which is subject to destruction is destroyed. That unenlightened being...[confronted with this situation] does not consider 'It is not only I [who must suffer this], but truly, as long as there are beings coming and going, being born and dying, it will always be, for all creatures, without exception, that that which is subject to aging ages...and that which is subject to destruction is destroyed. Since that which is subject to aging ages...and that which is subject to destruction is destroyed, if I were to sorrow, grieve, lament, become distressed and beat my breast, I would not be able to eat, my body would become haggard, my work would suffer, my enemies would be gladdened and my friends saddened.' [Not reflecting in this way, when this situation arises], they sorrow, grieve, and lament, crying and beating their breasts. Thus is the unlearned, unenlightened being pierced with the poisoned dart of sorrow, gone to grief.

"But for the learned, noble disciple, that which is subject to aging ages...that which is subject to destruction goes to destruction. That noble disciple reflects in this way: 'It is not only I (who must suffer this), but truly, as long as there are beings coming and going, being born and dying, it will always be, for all creatures, without exception, that that which is subject to aging ages...that which is subject to destruction is destroyed. Since that which is subject to aging ages...and that which is subject to destruction is destroyed, if I were to sorrow, grieve, lament, become distressed and beat my breast, I would not be able to eat, my body would become haggard, my work would suffer, my enemies would be gladdened and my friends saddened.' [When such situations do indeed arise,] that noble disciple does not sorrow, grieve, lament, cry, or beat his breast. The learned noble disciple has removed the poisoned dart of sorrow, which pierces all unenlightened beings. Being free of this piercing, poisonous dart, he does away with distress and agitation, and remains cool and calm."[80]

"When you die, you go alone; when you are born, you come

alone. Relationships are mere momentary meetings. For that reason, for those who have learned much, who are learned, who see this world and the next, who understand the Dhamma, loss and sorrow, no matter how great, do not agitate them. 'I will manage my status and wealth, support my wife and family, my relatives, and all beings'... this is the duty of a wise person."[81]

"Fools think only, 'In the rainy season I will live here, in the winter and the summer I will live there.' They do not consider the danger. Delighting in their children, nephews, and nieces, with minds preoccupied with livestock, wealth, and possessions, they are taken away by the Lord of Death, just as sleeping villagers are swept away by a mighty flood. When you are trapped by the Lord of Death, neither sons, fathers, relatives, nor friends can help; there is no refuge in a circle of relatives. The wise man, restrained in moral conduct, knowing this truth, quickly prepares himself for the way to *nibbāna*."[82]

"My city is Kapilavatthu. The king, my father, was named Suddhodana; my mother, the queen, was Māyādevī. I lived the home life for twenty-nine years. I had three palaces, named Sucanda, Kokanuda, and Koñca. I had eighty-four thousand dancing girls, beautifully dressed. My queen was Yasodharā; my son was Rāhula. Seeing four visions, I left the home life to become a mendicant on the Royal Steed, and practiced austerities for six years. I set rolling the wheel of truth in the Isipatana Deer Park near the town of Bārāṇasī. I am the perfectly enlightened Buddha, Gotama, the refuge of all living beings... My age in this period of time is not so great, at most only one hundred years. Even though I have lived for so brief a time, I have helped a great number of people to overcome suffering, lighting the torch of truth so that later generations can come to realization. In no long time, I and the order of disciples will go to final *nibbāna*, like a fire that goes out when all the fuel is spent. This body with all its special qualities, endowed with the thirty-two characteristics, with its incomparable power, with the ten powers and the six radiant rays lighting in all directions like a sun, will be completely destroyed. All formations are truly void of essence and empty."[83]

"Bhikkhus, seeing your own benefit, it is fitting that you procure that benefit with heedfulness. Seeing the benefit to others it is fitting that you procure that benefit with heedfulness. Seeing the benefit to both sides, it is fitting that you procure that benefit with heedfulness."[84]

Exhortations to Diligence and Preparing for the Future

"Heedfulness is the path to the deathless; heedlessness is the way to death. One who is heedful does not die; one who is heedless is as if already dead... the heedful one, ardently reflecting, experiences perfect happiness."[85]

"One gone to the homeless life should constantly reflect, 'The days and nights are passing—how am I spending my time?'"[86]

"Do not waste your chance—remove the dart that pierces your heart with heedfulness and knowledge (*vijjā*)."[87]

"When he should be rising to work, he does not rise. Even though he is young and strong, he is listless and lets his thinking sink into laziness and torpor. He does not encounter the path of wisdom."[88]

"One who learns little ages like an old bull: his meat increases, but his wisdom does not."[89]

"While still young they do not practice the holy life, they do not amass treasure. [When they get old], they sit forlorn, like old herons with their beaks stuck in mud that has no fish.

"While still young they do not practice the holy life, they do not amass treasure. [When they get old], all they can do is sleep and think of the past, like poisoned darts that have already been fired [their poison is spent]."[90]

"All benefit is based on two principles: obtaining that not yet obtained, and looking after that which is."[91]

"Bhikkhus, a family that has become materially prosperous can maintain itself for long through one or more of these four principles: knowing how to replace what is destroyed; repairing what is broken; knowing moderation in use of things; and appointing a man or woman who has morality as their leader."[92]

"Bhikkhus, it is through knowing clearly the (value of) two things—insatiability in respect to the skillful (*kusala*) and unrelenting practice—that I obtained enlightenment through heedfulness, and unexcelled clarity and deliverance."[93]

"A bhikkhu who has not yet attained the cessation of the outflows should not be satisfied with mere morality and practices, an abundance of learning, the attainment of *samādhi*, the enjoyment of solitude, or (even) the realization that he has experienced the pleasure of renunciation that is not known to normal persons."[94]

"Herein, Sāriputta, the blessed ones Kakusandha, Konāgamana, and Kassapa were not idle in regard to teaching the Dhamma in detail to their disciples, and the teachings (sutta, *geyya*, *vedalla*) of those blessed ones were numerous; the training rules were laid down by them for their disciples, and the Pāṭimokkha[95] was recited. When those blessed ones and their enlightened disciples passed away, the later generations of disciples, which were of many different names, families, and professions, were able to maintain the teaching for a long time. It is like many different kinds of flowers, well garlanded and laid on a floor. The wind cannot scatter them because they have been well garlanded... This is the reason why the teachings of the blessed ones Kakusandha, Konāgamana, and Kassapa were long-lived."[96]

"At that time the Venerable Mahā Kassapa said to the bhikkhus, 'Friends, let us all rehearse (*saṅgāyanā*) the teaching (*dhamma*) and the discipline (*vinaya*), before what is not the teaching thrives and the teaching is obstructed; before what is not the discipline thrives and what is the discipline is obstructed; before the speakers of what is not the teaching thrive and the speakers of the teaching become weak; before the speakers of what is not the discipline thrive and the speakers of the discipline become weak.'"[97]

"Ānanda, as long as the Vajjians meet together regularly...as long as the Vajjians convene and adjourn in harmony, and perform their duties in harmony, (then) the Vajjians can be expected to have only prosperity, not decline...

"Bhikkhus, as long as the bhikkhus meet regularly...as long as the bhikkhus convene and adjourn in harmony and harmoniously perform the duties of the Saṅgha, then the Saṅgha can be expected to have only prosperity and no decline...

"Bhikkhus, as long as the bhikkhus are possessed of faith... shame...fear of wrongdoing...learning...ardent practice... mindful restraint...wisdom, then the bhikkhus can be expected to experience only prosperity, and no decline."[98]

PART THREE

How Does Life Work?

CHAPTER 3

Paṭiccasamuppāda

The Principle of Dependent Arising

The *paṭiccasamuppāda* (principle of dependent arising) is a teaching that was given by the Buddha in the form of a natural law, a truth that exists as the norm, independent of the arising of teachers.

The Buddhavacana dealing with the *paṭiccasamuppāda* as a natural law are as follows:

> "Whether the Tathāgata arises or not, this law (principle) exists and is a certainty (*dhammaṭṭhiti*), a law of nature (*dhamma-niyāma*); that is, the law of conditionality (*idappaccayatā*).[1]
>
> "The Tathāgata, having been enlightened to this principle, tells it, teaches it, formulates it, establishes it, reveals it, makes it known, clarifies it, and points it out, saying, 'See here,
>
> "'With ignorance as condition are volitional formations…'
>
> "This actuality (*tathatā*), bhikkhus, this invariability (*avi-tathatā*), this immutability (*anaññathatā*)—that is to say, this law of conditionality—is called the *paṭiccasamuppāda* (principle of dependent arising)."[2]

The importance of the *paṭiccasamuppāda* can be gleaned from the following Buddhavacana:

> "Whoever sees the *paṭiccasamuppāda* sees the Dhamma; who-ever sees the Dhamma sees the *paṭiccasamuppāda*."[3]

> "Truly, bhikkhus, a learned noble disciple has direct knowledge for himself, without having to believe others, that 'when there is this, then there is that; with the arising of this, that arises...'
>
> "When a noble disciple thus fully sees the arising and cessation of the world as it is, this noble disciple can be said to be endowed with perfect view and perfect vision, to have attained to the true Dhamma, to possess the initiate's (*sekha*) direct knowledge (*ñāṇa*), to possess the initiate's knowledge, to have entered the stream of Dhamma, to be a noble one endowed with the knowledge that penetrates defilements, to be one who is at the very door of the deathless."[4]
>
> ---
>
> "Whatever recluses or holy ones know these things, know the originating cause of these things, know the cessation of these things, and know the way leading to the cessation of these things... those recluses or holy ones are worthy of recognition as 'recluses among recluses' and recognition as 'holy ones among holy ones,' and of them it can be said, 'They have realized the benefit of the recluse's life and the benefit of the holy one's life due to their own higher wisdom, and abide therein.'"[5]

Be that as it may, there are Buddhavacana warning us not to underestimate the profundity of the *paṭiccasamuppāda*, as can be seen in the following exchange with Venerable Ānanda:

> "How amazing, how unheard of, Lord! This *paṭiccasamuppāda* principle, although such a profound teaching and appearing to be so profound, yet seems to me to be so simple!"
>
> "Say not so, Ānanda, say not so. This *paṭiccasamuppāda* is a profound teaching and appears to be profound. It is through not knowing, not understanding, and not fully penetrating this truth that beings are confused like a tangle of threads, thrown together like a bundle of threads, like a mass of knotted thread, and do not rise above the netherworlds, the woeful bourns, hell, and the round of birth and death (*saṁsāra*)."[6]

Those who have studied the life of the Buddha may recall his reflections shortly after the enlightenment, before going out to spread the teaching. As related in the Pali canon, the Buddha was at that time inclined not to teach:

> "Bhikkhus, the thought arose in me thus: 'This truth that I have realized is profound, difficult to see, difficult to know, calming, subtle, not attainable through logic, refined, accessible only to the wise.
>
> "'But people revel in attachment, take pleasure in attachment and abandon themselves to attachment. For people who (thus) revel in and abandon themselves to attachment, this eventuality (*ṭhāna*) is an extremely difficult thing to see: that is, the law of conditionality (*idappaccayatā*), the principle of *paṭiccasamuppāda*. Moreover, this eventuality is also an extremely difficult thing to see: the calming of all formations (*saṅkhārā*), the casting off of all clinging (*upadhi*), the end of desire, dispassion, cessation, *nibbāna*. If I were to give this teaching and people did not thoroughly understand me, that would only cause me weariness, and only cause me trouble.'"[7]

This passage mentions two teachings, the *paṭiccasamuppāda* and *nibbāna*, stressing both their difficulty and also their importance as things the Buddha became enlightened to and taught to the world.

The Format and the Relationships within the *Paṭiccasamuppāda*

The Buddhavacana forming the textual descriptions of the *paṭiccasamuppāda* can be divided into two categories: the general description, in which no factors are specified, and the detailed description, in which the specific conditions are shown linked together in an ordered process. The former format is often used to precede the latter as a central or general principle. The latter is frequently encountered and mostly expressed on its own, without the former preceding it. It may be regarded as the formal elaboration, since it shows the details, or as the practical description, since it shows how the natural process conforms to the general principle.

Each of these two main categories can further be divided into two sections, the first showing the process of origination, the second, the process of cessation. The first section, showing the process of origination, is called origination mode (*samudayavāra*) and is considered to be the sequence in forward order. It corresponds to the second of the four noble truths, the cause of suffering (*dukkhasamudaya*). The second section, showing the process of cessation, is called the cessation mode (*nirodhavāra*) and is considered to represent the sequence in reverse order. It corresponds to the third noble truth, the cessation of suffering (*dukkhanirodha*).

The two descriptions are as follows:

The General Principle

Origination:

Imasmiṁ sati idaṁ hoti	When there is this, that is.
Imassuppādā idaṁ uppajjati	With the arising of this, that arises.

Cessation:

Imasmiṁ asati idaṁ na hoti	When this is not, neither is that.
Imassa nirodhā idaṁ nirujjhati	With the cessation of this, that (also) ceases.[8]

This general principle conforms with the Pali term *idappaccayatā*.

The Specialized Principle, or Principle in Operation

Origination:

Avijjāpaccayā saṅkhārā
With ignorance as condition, there are volitional formations.[9]
Sāṅkhārapaccayā viññāṇaṁ
With volitional formations as condition, consciousness.

Viññāṇa-paccayā nāmarūpaṁ
With consciousness as condition, mind-body (*nāmarūpa*).
Nāmarūpapaccayā saḷāyatanaṁ
With mind-body as condition, the six sense bases.
Saḷāyatana-paccayā phasso
With the six sense bases as condition, sense contact.
Phassa-paccayā vedanā
With contact as condition, feeling.
Vedanā-paccayā taṇhā
With feeling as condition, desire.
Taṇhāpaccayā upādānaṁ
With desire as condition, clinging.
Upādāna-paccayā bhavo
With clinging as condition, becoming.
Bhava-paccayā jāti
With becoming as condition, birth.
Jāti-paccayā jarāmaraṇaṁ
With birth as condition, aging and death,
Soka-parideva-dukkha-domanassupāyāsā sambhavan'ti
sorrow, lamentation, pain, grief, and despair.
Evametassa kevalassa dukkhakkhandhassa samudayo hoti
Thus is the arising of this whole mass of dukkha.

Cessation:

Avijjāya tveva asesa virāga nirodhā saṅkhārā nirodho
With the complete fading away and cessation of ignorance, volitional formations cease.
Saṅkhārā nirodhā viññāṇa nirodho
With the cessation of volitional formations, consciousness ceases.
Viññāṇa nirodhā nāmarūpa nirodho
With the cessation of consciousness, mind-body ceases.
Nāmarūpa nirodhā saḷāyatana nirodho
With the cessation of mind-body, the six sense bases cease.
Saḷāyatana nirodhā phassa nirodho
With the cessation of the six sense bases, contact ceases.

> *Phassa nirodhā vedanā nirodho*
> With the cessation of contact, feeling ceases.
> *Vedanā nirodhā taṇhā nirodho*
> With the cessation of feeling, desire ceases.
> *Taṇhā nirodhā upādāna nirodho*
> With the cessation of desire, clinging ceases.
> *Upādāna nirodhā bhava nirodho*
> With the cessation of clinging, becoming ceases.
> *Bhava nirodhā jāti nirodho*
> With the cessation of becoming, birth ceases.
> *Jāti nirodhā jarāmaraṇaṁ*
> With the cessation of birth, aging, and death,
> *Soka-parideva-dukkha-domanassupāyāsā nirujjhan'ti*
> sorrow, lamentation, pain, grief, and despair cease.
> *Evametassa kevalassa dukkhakkhandhassa nirodho hoti*
> Thus is there a cessation to this whole mass of *dukkha*.[10]

Note that the summarizing words of this *paṭiccasamuppāda* show it as a process of the arising and cessation of suffering (*dukkha*). Such summaries are the ones most commonly found in the texts, but in some places the summary describes it as the arising and cessation of the world, using the Pali words *ayaṁ kho bhikkhave lokassa samudayo*—"Thus, bhikkhus, is the arising of the world"—and *ayaṁ kho bhikkhave lokassa aṭṭhaṅgamo*—"Thus, bhikkhus, is the dissolution of the world";[11] or *evamayaṁ loko samudayati*—"Thus does this world arise"—and *evamayaṁ loko nirujjhati*—"Thus does this world cease."[12] However, essentially both of these summaries state the same thing and are of the same scope. The problem lies with how the terms are defined, and this remains to be explained.

In the Abhidhamma and commentaries, the *paṭiccasamuppāda* principle is also known by the term *paccayākāra*, meaning "mode of conditionality."

In the full description of the principle there are altogether twelve factors. These factors are interdependently linked in the form of a beginningless and endless cycle. That is, there is no first cause (*mūlakāraṇa*). Putting *avijjā*, ignorance, at the beginning does not imply that it is the first cause, or genesis, of all things; it is put there simply for ease of understanding, by intercepting the cycle at a factor considered to be most appropriate, counting that as the first, and then counting the other factors from there. In fact, we are cautioned not to take ignorance as a first cause with the following description of the arising of ignorance: *āsava samudayā avijjā samudayo, āsava nirodhā avijjā nirodho* (ignorance arises with the arising of the outflows [*āsava*], and ceases with their cessation).[13]

The twelve factors of the *paṭiccasamuppāda* format are counted from ignorance through to aging and death only: that is, *avijjā* → *saṅkhārā* → *viññāṇa* → *nāmarūpa* → *saḷāyatana* → *phassa* → *vedanā* → *taṇhā* → *upādāna* → *bhava* → *jāti* → *jarāmaraṇa*. As for sorrow, lamentation, pain, grief, and despair, these are simply byproducts that arise in a person with outflows and defilements (*kilesa*) when aging and death occur, becoming "fertilizer" for the outflows, which in turn are factors for ignorance and the further turning of the cycle.

In describing the *paṭiccasamuppāda* in application, the Buddha did not always describe the cycle in sequence or in full (from beginning to end). The complete, ordered sequence tended to be used when he was explaining the principle, but in terms of practice, where it started from a particular problem, he usually applied it in reverse order, thus: *jarāmaraṇa* ← *jāti* ← *bhava* ← *upādāna* ← *taṇhā* ← *vedanā* ← *phassa* ← *saḷāyatana* ← *nāmarūpa* ← *viññāṇa* ← *saṅkhārā* ← *avijjā*.[14]

In such practical applications, a description might have begun at any one of the intermediate factors, depending on which of them was the problem in question. For example, the Buddha would start at birth (*jāti*),[15] feeling (*vedanā*),[16] or consciousness (*viññāṇa*),[17] following the steps forward up to aging and death (from middle to end), or tracing backward to arrive at ignorance (from middle to beginning). Or he might have begun with some other factor altogether than the twelve, which was then worked into the *paṭiccasamuppāda* cycle.[18] Thus, a description of the *paṭiccasamuppāda* need not necessarily contain all of the above twelve factors or come in the one fixed form.

Note that the conditioning of these factors does not mean "causing" as such. The factors that make a tree grow, for instance, are not only the seed, but also include the soil, moisture, fertilizer, air, temperature, and so on. These are all factors. Furthermore, being factors does not mean that they necessarily follow any chronological or circumstantial sequence.[19]

Interpreting the *Paṭiccasamuppāda*

The principle of *paṭiccasamuppāda* has been interpreted in a number of ways, which can be summarized into the following two broad categories: first, as an explanation of life- and world-evolution, based on a literal interpretation of Buddhavacana such as *lokasamudaya*[20] (arising of the world); and second, as a demonstration of the arising and cessation of individual life and suffering. This second category can further be divided into two interpretations:

- Demonstrating a long-term process from lifetime to lifetime—that is, a trans-lifetime model. This is another literal interpretation and is the explanation found throughout the commentaries, which expand on the subject in minute detail, giving the process a formulaic character, with so many fixed stages and special terms that the new student is likely to become confused.
- Demonstrating a process that is continually turning every moment of our lives. It is an interpretation that is implied within the previous explanation, but stressing a more profound or practical interpretation of the terms, considered to be the Buddha's objective (or real aim of the teaching), with emphasis on the present moment. This kind of interpretation finds support in the Buddhavacana of many suttas, such as the *Cetanā Sutta*,[21] the *Dukkhanirodha Sutta*,[22] and the *Lokanirodha Sutta*.[23] In the Abhidhamma Piṭaka the *paṭiccasamuppāda* process is described as occurring in its entirety in one mind moment, an interpretation that forms the subject of one whole section of that text.[24]

In the first kind of explanation, there are attempts to interpret the *paṭiccasamuppāda* principle as a world-origin theory, taking ignorance (*avijjā*) as the first cause[25] and tracing an evolutionary process through all twelve factors. This kind of interpretation implies that the Buddhist teachings are in part similar to other religious teachings and philosophical systems, which postulate an origination principle, such as a creator god, as a supernatural originator of the world. According to this interpretation, the teachings of Buddhism describe the faring of things as simply a form of evolution proceeding according to the natural processes of causes and conditions. However, this interpretation can certainly be ruled out as being against the Buddha's teaching, since any teaching or doctrine that shows a world originating from a first cause (*mūlakāraṇa*) is contrary to the principle of conditionality (*idappaccayatā*), or *paṭiccasamuppāda*. The *paṭiccasamuppāda* gives the impartial explanation that all things are interdependent factors for each other, arising continually through the ceaseless process of causes and effects. Any first cause, be it a creator god or anything else, is impossible. An interpretation of the *paṭiccasamuppāda* principle as a description of life- and world-evolution can only be conceded when it shows the unfolding of the natural processes of growth and decline according to causes and conditions, with no beginning and no end.

An important rationale to be considered in assessing the plausibility of these interpretations is the Buddha's objective in teaching the Buddhadhamma, which is therefore also his objective in teaching the principle of *paṭiccasamuppāda*. In teaching the Buddhadhamma, the Buddha aimed for and taught only that which could be usefully put into practice in real life, which is related to life, to addressing life's problems, and to practical application. He did not encourage trying to realize truth through cogitation on or debate over metaphysical problems. For this reason, assessing a teaching as authentically Buddhist necessarily involves an assessment of its ethical or practical value. Interpreting the *paṭiccasamuppāda* principle as a beginningless and endless wheel of evolution, although seemingly acceptable, can still be seen to have little ethical value (i.e., value in terms of practical application for real benefit in life), providing merely a general view of life or the world as faring according to causes and effects and bound to the conditions found in the natural process itself. Thus, it can be said that:

1. There is no creator or "appointer," nor is the world a series of aimless accidents. Goals cannot be realized through mere wishing, supplication to gods or supernatural forces, or through waiting for luck, but must be effectuated through action; that is, people must rely on themselves by creating the causes and conditions that will bring about the desired result.
2. It is only possible to create the right causes and conditions for effectuating desired results when there is proper knowledge and understanding of those causes and conditions and their relationship within the natural processes. Thus, wisdom (*paññā*) is an important factor: that is, we must relate to and deal with things with wisdom.
3. An understanding of the natural processes as subject to the flow of causes and conditions can be effective in reducing or destroying the delusions that are responsible for clinging to things as self, enabling us to relate more correctly and beneficially with things in accordance with their purpose, not becoming enslaved to the things we deal with, and thereby maintaining our independence.

These world- and life-evolution views, while entirely correct and of value in accordance with Buddhism's objectives, are nevertheless fairly superficial; they are not firm or convincing enough to guarantee the arising of the three values (especially the third) in their entirety.

To make this interpretation more valuable, it is necessary to examine nature's cyclic processes in more detail—that is, to understand the nature of this process at all stages as it actually occurs before us, and to see the flow of continuous and interdependent causes and conditions even in brief instances, at all times. When the state of things as they arise at every instant is clearly seen in this way, the full arising of those three benefits will be assured. Such a perspective also encompasses the long-term model of evolution.

In interpreting the life-and-world-evolution model of *paṭicca-samuppāda* discussed above, regardless of whether it be in the coarse or more subtle senses, the attention is directed outward; it is an outward consideration. The origination-and-cessation-of-suffering interpretation of *paṭiccasamuppāda* places emphasis on the inner life. What is under consideration is the process of continuation of life and the suffering of the individual; it is an inner consideration.

The interpretation described in the trans-lifetime model dealing with the origination and cessation of suffering is the one most accepted and expanded on in the commentarial texts.[26] There it is treated in minute detail and given added technical terms in order to more clearly show the process as a formalized, sequential system. At the same time, however, this trans-lifetime model may be so fixed that we end up attaching to it or getting stuck on the system. It also becomes a matter of mystery and complexity for the newcomer. Here it will be given its own section, followed by the interpretation with emphasis on the present moment.

Preparatory Explanation

In order to gain a simple and general overview, a brief summary of the meaning of the *paṭiccasamuppāda* is in order.

The concluding lines of the *paṭiccasamuppāda* formula on page 132 show that the entire process is of the arising and cessation of *dukkha*. *Dukkha* figures prominently in several other key teachings, such as the three characteristics (*tilakkhaṇa*) and the four noble truths (*ariyasacca*). The word *dukkha* has already been defined in the chapter on the three characteristics. It now requires further explanation.

In order to understand the meaning of *dukkha* as it is used in Buddhist teachings, it is necessary to consider it in the light of the broad meaning of the Buddhavacana, in which *dukkha* is divided into three kinds,[27] which, together with the commentarial explanations,[28] are as follows:

1. *Dukkha-dukkhatā*: the *dukkha* that is a feeling of suffering—that is, physical and mental suffering—aches, pains, sadness, and so on—as is usually understood by the word *suffering*. It is the suffering both in name and in quality known specifically as *dukkhavedanā* (the feeling of suffering that ordinarily arises whenever a disagreeable sensation is experienced).
2. *Vipariṇāma-dukkhatā*: the *dukkha* inherent in change, or the *dukkha* concealed within the inconstancy of happiness—that is, the happiness that changes into suffering, or leads to suffering, because of its own changeability. This is the situation in which when things are normal, one feels fine, not suffering at all, but once one has experienced some pleasure, and that pleasure is taken away or disappears, the original state of comfort and normality changes into suffering. It is like a covert form of suffering, revealing itself as soon as the happiness fades away or diminishes. The more happiness there is, the more extreme the suffering that results, as if the "covert suffering" increases in proportion to the happiness. If the pleasant feeling had not arisen, the suffering on account of it would likewise not have arisen. Even while experiencing pleasant feeling, as soon as one reflects that it may vanish, one suffers from fear and anxiety. Once the pleasant feeling passes away, one yearns for it with the longing, "I used to have such happiness; now it is gone."
3. *Saṅkhārā-dukkhatā*: the *dukkha* inherent within formations—that is, the nature of formations themselves, or all things that arise from conditions, specifically the five *khandhas* (including *magga* and *phala*, which are *lokuttara*)—are suffering. In other words, they are subject to stress from conflicting conditions, to arising and cessation. They are not perfect within themselves but exist only as part of the continuum of causes and conditions. As such, they are likely to cause suffering (that is, the feeling of suffering, *dukkhavedanā*) to whomever is ignorant of their

> nature and their workings and, rather than relating to and dealing with them with wisdom, stubbornly and ignorantly opposes the flow because of desire and clinging (*taṇhā upādāna*).

The important kind of suffering is the third kind, which describes the nature of formations. This state assumes a psychological significance in the sense that formations are incapable of providing any perfect contentment, and can lead to suffering at any time for anybody who relates to them through ignorance, desire, and clinging (*avijjā-taṇhā-upādāna*).[29]

The *paṭiccasamuppāda* principle shows how the natural processes become human problems through ignorance, desire, and clinging. At the same time, the natural processes show how all things are interrelated and interdependent in the form of a stream. As a stream, the meaning can be expanded on to show a number of different perspectives: all things are interrelated and interdependent; all things exist in relationship; all things exist dependent on conditions; all things have no constancy, even for a moment; all things do not exist in themselves—that is, they have no real intrinsic being; all things are without first cause, or genesis. To put it another way, the fact that all things appear in their diverse forms with their different kinds of growth and decline shows their true nature as being a stream or process; their being a stream indicates their nature of being compounded from numerous components; the stream arises because the various component factors are interrelated and interdependent; the flow can proceed and change form because its component factors have no constancy, even for a moment; the component factors have no constancy, even for a moment, because they have no intrinsic being; since they have no intrinsic being, they are entirely dependent on conditions; because the conditions are interrelated and interdependent, they maintain the form of a stream, and being interrelated and interdependent indicates that they have no first cause. To render it in reverse form: if things had any intrinsic being they would have some constancy; if things were constant, even for a moment, they could not be conditions for each other; if they could not be conditions for each other they could not form a stream; if there were no stream of causes and conditions, the workings of nature would be impossible; and if there were some real intrinsic self within that stream there could be no true interdependent faring according to conditions. The stream of causes and conditions, which enables all things to exist and fare as they do, can only operate because things are impermanent, unstable, arising, and ceasing, without intrinsic being of their own and interdependently related.

The characteristic of impermanence, instability, arising, and dissolving, is called *aniccatā*. The characteristic of being oppressed by arising and dissolution, of being imbued with stress and conflict and intrinsically imperfect, is called *dukkhatā*. The characteristic of being void of any real intrinsic self is called *anattatā*. The *paṭiccasamuppāda* reveals these three characteristics in all things and shows their interrelatedness and interdependence to produce the diverse events in nature. The state and faring of the *paṭiccasamuppāda* principle applies to all things, both in the material world and in life, complete with its physical and mental properties, expressing itself through a number of natural laws, which are the laws of the relationship between cause and effect (*dhammaniyāma*), the natural laws pertaining to inanimate things (*utuniyāma*), the natural laws pertaining to living things and heredity (*bījaniyāma*), the laws of the workings of the mind (*cittaniyāma*), and the law of *kamma* (*kammaniyāma*), which is particularly relevant to the subject of happiness and suffering and directly involves the subject of ethics.

What needs to be particularly stressed, since it tends to conflict with the common human perception, is that *kamma*—and indeed all other natural cause-and-effect relationships—can only function because all things are impermanent (*anicca*) and have no intrinsic being (*anattā*). If things were permanent and had intrinsic being, none of the natural laws, including the law of *kamma*, could operate. Moreover, these laws affirm that there is no first cause, or genesis, such as a creator god.

Things have no real being because they arise dependent on conditions and exist in relationship to each other. A simple, concrete illustration: a bed arises from compounding various components into a designated form. An entity of "bed" separate from these components does not exist. When all the components are dismantled, there is no longer any "bed." All that is left is the mental concept of bed. Even that concept does not exist in and of itself, but must relate to other concepts. For example, the concept "bed" has no meaning of itself if divorced from its relationship to sleeping, a flat surface, a base, empty space, and so on. In common human perception, the knowledge of concepts arises in conjunction with understanding of the conditions and association of relationships involved. But once there is the formulation of a concept, the habits of desire (*taṇhā*) and clinging (*upādāna*) fix onto that concept and create the sense of a fixed entity, blocking off true recognition and isolating that object from its relationship with other things. It leads to a failure to see things as they are, and notions of "me" and "mine" (*ahaṁkāra*, *mamaṁkāra*) proliferate.

It is an actuality that things have no first cause, root cause, or first arising. Whatever we propose for investigation, if we trace back along the stream of causes ad infinitum, we will find no root cause. Yet common human perception tends to try to find some kind of original cause, which is a perception that conflicts with the natural actuality, and so we do not perceive things truly. It may be called a form of distorted perception (*saññāvipallāsa*), a result of the human habit of trying to ascertain the causes of any given thing by stopping their search at its immediate apparent causes and searching no further. This habit causes the common understanding of cause and effect to be impeded, and to lead to thinking that is contrary to the laws of nature, with the idea that there must be an original cause for things. Common sense leads us to further ask, "What is the cause of that so-called first cause?" and so on. Since all things exist in interrelationship and interdependence, there is naturally no first cause or root cause. The question should rather be asked, "Why should things have a root cause anyway?"

Another kind of thinking that contradicts nature and arises from human habits, and is related to the idea of a root cause, is the idea that in the beginning there was nothing. This kind of thinking arises from the habitual self-clinging, noting the appearance of something and attaching to the concept, which leads to the feeling that it is an entity that previously did not exist.

This kind of thinking that fixes on one thing, one aspect, or one perspective and does not flow is the habitual thought known as "attachment to conventions" or "not knowing the truth of conventions," which becomes not knowing things as they are. This leads to the search for something permanent to serve as a root cause, as a source or creator of all manifestations. This produces such contradictions as "How can that which is permanent be the source or creator of impermanent things?" and "If that which is permanent is the source of impermanent things, why is it that those impermanent things are not permanent?"

In fact, within the process of the stream of interrelated causes and conditions there is no problem of whether there is or is not an entity, be it in the beginning or now, except as a manner of conventional speech. We should rather encourage fresh consideration with the question "Why does there have to be a beginning anyway?"

The commonly accepted belief that all things have a creator is another idea that contradicts the actuality. The belief is based on the observation of the human creation of tools, goods, utensils, arts, and so on. These things are products of human creation. The conclusion follows that therefore all things in the world must have a creator. In this case, people deceive themselves by isolating the concept of "creating" from the normal causal process, thus taking a falsehood as their basic premise. In fact, "creating" is only one sense of the expression "being conditioned." Human beings can only create anything at all by becoming one of the conditions in the process of causal relationships that produces the desired result. Human beings differ from the purely physical conditions of the process only in that there are added mental factors, involving intention. Even so, those factors retain their status as conditions working together with other conditions, and must also proceed according to the process of causes and conditions in order to produce a desired result. For instance, when we wish to build a skyscraper, we must deal with conditions and manipulate them along the process to completion. If human creation meant bringing things into existence independent of the cause-and-effect process, we could create a house or skyscraper anywhere simply by thinking it into existence. Thus, "creating" has no meaning beyond being a description of one kind of causal process. And since things proceed smoothly along the natural process of conditions, the problem of a creator is no longer relevant at any point along the process.

In any case, examining the arguments regarding the question of a root cause or a creator god has little value in the Buddhadhamma, because it is not essential to a beneficial course of conduct in life. Even though it may help to provide a wider world- or life-view, it can still be passed over, as examining the ethical value of the *paṭiccasamuppāda* is sufficient benefit in itself. We should therefore direct our attention more toward the aspect of its practical application in real life.

As mentioned in chapter 1, life is made up only of the five *khandhas*. There is nothing apart from the five *khandhas*, either hidden within them or outside of them, which could serve as the owner or controller of the five *khandhas*. In examining life, the five *khandhas* are a comprehensive enough base from which to work.

The five *khandhas* are a process that functions in conformity with the law of *paṭiccasamuppāda*; that is, they exist in the form of a flow of interrelated and interdependent conditions. No part of that flow can remain fixed; there is only arising and dissolution and the determination of further arising and dissolution. The various parts are related, interdependent and act as conditions for each other, thus causing the flow or process to fare rationally and maintain some continuous form.

In this state, the five *khandhas*, or life, are subject to the three characteristics: they are in a condition of *aniccatā*—impermanent and unstable; *anattatā*—containing no intrinsic self and not tenable as a self; and *dukkhatā*—oppressed by constant arising and dissolution, and always ready to cause suffering whenever there is association through ignorance.

The process of the five *khandhas* faring thus with constant change and without abiding entity proceeds entirely according to the flow of interrelated conditions in accordance with the natural way. But for the unenlightened person, resistance occurs when the appearance of the flow, or one or another of its parts, is mistakenly clung to as being the self, and there is the desire for this "self" to be or proceed a certain way. At the same time, the twists and changes that arise within the flow conflict with desires, creating stress and stimulating the arising of even more intense desire and clinging. The struggle and desire intensifies to have a self in some form or other, and to have that self exist in some form or other, or to have it constantly and eternally in the desired state. When things do not proceed as one wished, stress manifests as disappointment, suffering, and despair. In addition, the dim awareness of the truth that change will inevitably occur in some form or other, and that the self that one clings to may not exist, or will dissolve, intensifies one's attachment and desire, along with fear and anxiety.

These states of mind are *avijjā* (ignorance of the truth, mistakenly believing in a self), *taṇhā* (wanting this imagined self to attain, be or not be something or other), and *upādāna* (attaching that imagined self to various objects). These defilements are deeply hidden within the mind, and they are the agents that direct and control all personal behavior, consciously and subconsciously, and also shape personality and have a significant impact on the fortunes of our individual lives. In general, they are the cause of suffering for all unenlightened beings.

Summarizing, we are here describing the discord or friction between two processes:

1. The process of life, proceeding subject to the fixed law of the three characteristics—that is, *aniccatā*, *dukkhatā*, and *anattatā* which are expressed as birth, aging, and death, both in their superficial and more profound senses.
2. Ignorance of the process of life as it really is, mistakenly conceiving it to be a self and clinging to it, together with the concomitant fear and restlessness.

In short, it is a conflict between the laws of nature and deluded clinging to self—or more bluntly, "creating a self with which to obstruct the flow of the natural laws."

This is a life lived with ignorance, lived with clinging, lived in bondage, lived in conflict and opposition to the law of nature, or lived with suffering.

The way of life described above, apart from instilling fear and anxiety deep into the mind, there to control one's behavior and depriving the life process of its independence, also has numerous harmful repercussions:

- It causes desire and selfishness, the endless search for objects to gratify one's wants and the avaricious grasping of them with no concern for the interests of others.[30]
- It causes adherence to views, theories, or attitudes, evaluating them as self or belonging to self, and tightly clasping and cherishing them as if one were protecting one's very self. It is like building a wall to block oneself away from the truth, or even hiding from truth altogether.[31]
- It produces credulous and irrational beliefs and practices, clinging blindly to them through a vague perception of their interrelationship. Lacking inner certainty and concerned for the false self that one has created and now attaches to, one desperately tries to grasp at something as a source of security, no matter how vague and obscure it may be.[32]
- It produces [the notion of] an independent self, which must be held onto, carried around, cherished and protected from conflict or disappearance.[33]

Thus, conflict, stress, and suffering not only arise within one individual but also radiate outward to become conflict, stress, and suffering in and between other people in society. It may be said that clinging is the source of all the human-made suffering, troubles, and problems in society.

The *paṭiccasamuppāda* principle in its practical mode shows the origin of the stressful life, or the arising of life with a self, which inevitably results in suffering. Breaking the *paṭiccasamuppāda* cycle is tantamount to destroying the life of suffering, or destroying all the suffering that arises from life with a self. It is the opposite state: a life lived with wisdom, lived without clinging to a self, lived with freedom, lived in harmony and integration with nature, or lived without suffering.

To live with wisdom means to live in full awareness of the way things are and to know how to derive benefit from nature; to derive benefit from nature is the same as living in harmony and integration with nature; to live in harmony and integration with nature is to live freely; to live freely is not to fall into the power of desire and clinging, or to live without clinging; to live without clinging means to live with wisdom, or to know, relate to, and manage things through the way of causes and conditions.

A life of wisdom can be looked at from two perspectives: inwardly, it is characterized by serenity, openness, clarity through wisdom, and freedom. When experiencing pleasure, the mind does not sink into or abandon itself to it; when separated, denied, or deprived of pleasurable conditions, it is firm, secure, unshaken, not depressed, saddened, forlorn, or thrown into despair. One does not invest one's happiness and suffering into the hands of external objects to direct one's fortunes. Outwardly, there is fluency, efficiency, readiness to relate to and manage things appropriately, with pure rationale, free of complexes or internal attachments.

There are a number of Buddhavacana illustrating some of the differences between the life lived with clinging and the life of wisdom, such as the following:

> "The unlearned, unenlightened being (*puthujjana*), bhikkhus, experiences pleasant feelings, unpleasant feelings and neither pleasant nor unpleasant (neutral) feelings. The learned, noble disciple also experiences pleasant feelings, unpleasant feelings and neither pleasant nor unpleasant feelings. In this case, bhikkhus, what is the distinction, the difference, the contrast between the learned, noble disciple and the unlearned, unenlightened being?

"When an unlearned, unenlightened being encounters unpleasant feeling, he grieves, laments, wails, moans, beats his chest, and is distraught and distracted therein: he experiences both kinds of feeling—namely, bodily and mental.

"It is as if an archer, having fired one arrow into a certain man, were then to fire a second arrow. In that case, that man would experience pain on account of both arrows—that is, both in the body and in the mind. Such is the unlearned, unenlightened being...He experiences both kinds of pain, bodily and mental.

"Moreover, experiencing that unpleasant feeling he feels displeasure. Displeased over that unpleasant feeling, tendencies to aversion (*paṭighānusaya*) contingent on that unpleasant feeling are accumulated. Confronted with unpleasant feeling he turns to delight in sense pleasures.[34] Why so? Because the unlearned, unenlightened being knows of no other way out of unpleasant feeling than sense pleasures. Delighting thus in sense pleasures, tendencies to greed (*rāgānusaya*) contingent on those pleasant feelings are accumulated. He does not know as they are the arising, the dissolution, the attraction, the liability, and the release from those feelings. Not knowing...[these things] as they really are, tendencies to delusion (*avijjānusaya*) contingent on neither pleasant nor unpleasant feelings (*upekkhāvedanā*) are accumulated. Experiencing pleasant feeling he does so with bondage; experiencing unpleasant feeling he does so with bondage; experiencing neutral feeling he does so with bondage. Thus, bhikkhus, is the unlearned, unenlightened being entangled in birth, aging, death, sorrow, lamentation, pain, grief, and despair. He is, I say, entangled in suffering.

"As for the learned, noble disciple, bhikkhus, experiencing unpleasant feeling he neither grieves, laments, wails, moans, beats his chest nor feels distraught and distracted on that account. He experiences pain only in the body, not in the mind.

"Just as if an archer, having shot one arrow into a certain man, were then to shoot a second arrow but miss the mark: in this case that man would experience pain only on account of the first arrow. Such is the learned, noble disciple... he experiences pain in the body, but not in the mind.

"Moreover, he experiences no displeasure on account of that unpleasant feeling. Not being displeased over that unpleasant feeling, tendencies to aversion contingent on that unpleasant feeling are not accumulated. Experiencing that unpleasant feeling he does not turn to distraction in sense pleasures. Why not? Because the learned, noble disciple knows of a way out of unpleasant feelings other than sense pleasures. Not distracting himself with sense pleasures, tendencies to greed contingent on pleasant feelings are not accumulated. He knows as they are the arising, the dissolution, the attraction, the liability and the release from feelings. Knowing [these things] as they really are, latent tendencies to delusion contingent on neither pleasant nor unpleasant feelings are not accumulated. Experiencing pleasant feeling he does so without bondage; experiencing unpleasant feeling he does so without bondage; experiencing neutral feeling he does so without bondage. Bhikkhus, thus is the learned, noble disciple liberated from birth, aging, death, sorrow, lamentation, pain, grief, and despair. He is, I say, without suffering.

"This, bhikkhus, is the distinction, the difference, the contrast between the learned, noble disciple and the unlearned, unenlightened being."[35]

The Scriptural Explanation

The scriptural explanation is subtle, profound, complex, and extensive. It is an academic concern, for which the student requires a fundamental knowledge of Buddhism and many Pali terms. There are also entire texts devoted exclusively to the subject.[36] Here I will only briefly summarize the basic factors.

Factors and Structure

All the factors have already been covered in the beginning of the chapter; the following diagram reiterates them in brief:

1	*2*	*3*	*4*	*5*	*6*
avijjā	*saṅkhārā*	*viññāṇa*	*nāmarūpa*	*saḷāyatana*	*phassa*

7	*8*	*9*	*10*	*11*	*12*
vedanā	*taṇhā*	*upādāna*	*bhava*	*jāti*	*jarāmaraṇa*

soka parideva dukkha domanassa upāyāsa
the cause of suffering (dukkha samudaya)

Fig. 3.1. Links of the *paṭiccasamuppāda* cycle.

The cessational mode, *dukkhanirodha*, proceeds according to the same factors.

Since the *paṭiccasamuppāda* process works as a cycle, with no starting or ending point, it should rather be represented as follows:

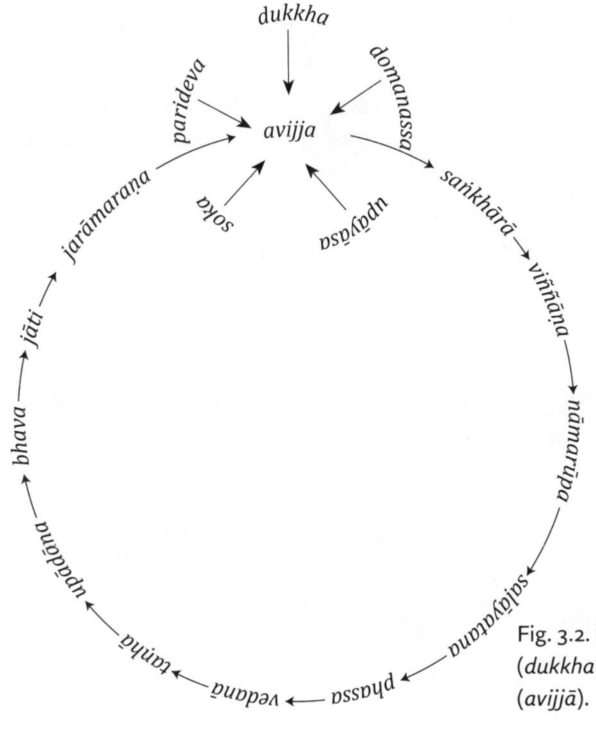

Fig. 3.2. Creation of suffering (*dukkha*) from ignorance (*avijjā*).

DEFINITION OF THE FACTORS[37]

1. *Avijjā* = not knowing suffering (*dukkha*), its cause (*samudaya*), its cessation (*nirodha*), and the way leading to its cessation (*magga*)—that is, not knowing the four noble truths—and (according to the Abhidhamma) not knowing what comes before, what goes after, what comes both before and after,[38] and the principle of *paṭiccasamuppāda*.
2. *Saṅkhārā* = bodily formations (*kāyasaṅkhārā*); verbal formations (*vacīsaṅkhāra*); mental formations (*cittasaṅkhārā*); and (according to the Abhidhamma) meritorious formations (*puññābhisaṅkhārā*), non-meritorious formations (*apuññābhisaṅkhārā*), and imperturbable formations (*āneñjābhisaṅkhārā*).
3. *Viññāṇa* = consciousness through eye, ear, nose, tongue, body, and mind (the six consciousnesses).
4. *Nāmarūpa* = *nāma* (feeling [*vedanā*], perception [*saññā*], intention [*cetanā*], contact [*phassa*], attention [*manasikāra*]) or, according to the Abhidhamma, *vedanā-khandha*, *saññā-khandha,* and *saṅkhārā-khandha*; + *rūpa* (the four great elements or material properties [*mahābhūtarūpa*] of earth, water, wind, and fire and all forms dependent on the great elements [*upadāyarūpa*]).
5. *Saḷāyatana* = the six sense bases: eye (*cakkhu*), ear (*sota*), nose (*ghāna*), tongue (*jivhā*), body (*kāya*), and mind (*mano*).
6. *Phassa* = visual contact, auditory contact, olfactory contact, gustatory contact, tactile contact, and mental contact (the six contacts).
7. *Vedanā* = feelings (of pleasure, pain, and indifference) arising from contact on eye, ear, nose, tongue, body, and mind (the six feelings).
8. *Taṇhā* = desire for sights (*rūpataṇhā*), desire for sounds (*saddataṇhā*), desire for odors (*gandhataṇhā*), desire for tastes (*rasataṇhā*), desire for bodily sensations (*poṭṭhabbataṇhā*), and desire for mind objects (dhammataṇhā)—the six desires.
9. *Upādāna* = clinging to sense objects—that is, sights, sounds, odors, tastes, and bodily sensations (*kāmupādāna*); clinging to views, doctrines, theories, and so on (*diṭṭhupādāna*); clinging

to rules and practices, believing they make one pure (*sīlabbatupādāna*); clinging to self; creating a self and clinging to it with delusion (*attavādupādāna*).

10. *Bhava* = *kāmabhava* (the sense/sensual realm); *rūpabhava* (the realm of form); *arūpabhava* (the realm of formlessness). An alternative definition: *kammabhava* (the realm of action, or actions that condition birth), which comprises meritorious actions (*puññābhisaṅkhārā*); demeritorious actions (*apuññābhisaṅkhārā*); and imperturbable actions (*āneñjābhisaṅkhārā*); and *upapattibhava* (realms of existence), which comprises the sense realm; the realm of form; the formless realm; the realm of perception; the realm of non-perception; the realm of neither perception nor non-perception; the realm of single-faculty beings (i.e., beings with only one *khandha*: *ekavokārabhava*); the realm of beings with four *khandhas* (*catuvokārabhava*); the realm of beings with five *khandhas* (*pañcavokārabhava*).
11. *Jāti* = the appearance of the *khandhas*; the obtaining of the sense bases, or birth; the manifestation of things.
12. *Jarāmaraṇa* = *jarā* (decline of life, the fading of the faculties) and *maraṇa* (breaking up the *khandhas*, cutting off the life principle); or the dissipation and dissolution of things.[39]

Examples of the Model on the Long Term

Āsava → *Avijjā*: Believing that birth in heaven is the highest happiness; believing that to kill someone will bring happiness; believing that to kill oneself will bring happiness; believing one can attain *nibbāna* by practicing austerities; believing that this very self will be reborn in various states due to certain actions; believing that after death there is nothing. From there…

→*Saṅkhārā*: Thinking and formulating intentions in accordance or conformity with those beliefs; formulating methods and acting on those intentions, producing good *kamma* (*puñña*), bad *kamma* (*apuñña* or *pāpa*), and imperturbable (*āneñjā*) *kamma*. From there…

→*Viññāṇa*: The arising of the realization and awareness of the specific cognitive objects that accord with or conform to those intentions. To put it simply, mind or consciousness is shaped into having a particular quality or form. At death, the momentum of *saṅkhārā*—that is, the *kamma* that has been created—causes an appropriate relinking consciousness (*paṭisandhi viññāṇa*) to take birth in an appropriate sphere and level of existence. That is, birth takes place. From there…

→ *Nāmarūpa*: The process of birth moves on and formulates a life-form primed to generate more *kamma*. As a result, there are the *rūpa*, *vedanā*, *saññā*, and *saṅkhārā khandhas* in their entirety, containing the distinct virtues and failings endowed on them by the fashioning influence of *saṅkhārā*—that is, the *kamma* that has been made, and within the limitations of the particular sphere of existence (*bhava*), be it human, animal, divine, and so on…

→ *Saḷāyatana*: But a life that is to respond to its wants and be ready to act in response to the external world must have a channel of communication with that world, through which the cognitive process can function. Thus, supported by mind and body (*nāmarūpa*), the process of life proceeds, in conformity with karmic momentum, to the arising of the six sense bases, the organs of eye, ear, nose, tongue, body, and mind. From there…

→ *Phassa*: The cognitive process can now operate, through the contact or convergence of three factors: the internal sense bases (eye, ear, nose, tongue, body, and mind), cognitive objects (*ārammaṇa*) or external sense bases (sights, sounds, odors, tastes, bodily sensations, and mind objects), and consciousness (eye consciousness, ear consciousness, nose consciousness, tongue consciousness, tactile consciousness, and mind consciousness). Whenever cognition arises,…

→ *Vedanā*: Feeling, the "tasting" of sense objects, must arise in some form or other—that is, comfortable and pleasant (*sukhavedanā*); uncomfortable, painful, and stressful (*dukkhavedanā*); or indifferent (*adukkhamasukhavedanā* or *upekkhāvedanā*)—and in keeping with the nature of unenlightened beings, the process does not stop there, but goes on to…

→ *Taṇhā*: If feeling is comfortable and pleasant, one takes a liking to it and wants to have it or have more of it, and so desire and seeking arise. If the feeling is unpleasant one is aggravated, annoyed, and wants to be rid of it by destroying or escaping from it, and so there arise restlessness and struggle to be rid of the cognitive object that causes suffering or conflict, and to turn to other cognitive objects that will produce pleasant feeling. If there is neutral feeling, equanimity, which is a subtle kind of feeling, this is classed as being on the pleasant side because it does not disturb the mind; it is a diluted form of happiness, a kind of complacency. From there...

→ *Upādāna*: As desire intensifies, it becomes clinging, attachment, and giving in to its object. As long as an object is unattained it is desired through *taṇhā*; once attained it is clung to through *upādāna*. This clinging involves not only desirable objects (*kāmupādāna*) but also clinging to views, theories, and opinions (*diṭṭhupādāna*), clinging to modes of behavior and practices for achieving desired goals (*sīlabbatupādāna*), and clinging to self (*attavādupādāna*). On account of this clinging there follows...

→ *Bhava*: Intention and deliberate action to obtain and control things in accordance with that clinging, and leading to the whole process of behavior (*kammabhava*) once more, being good *kamma*, bad *kamma*, or imperturbable (*āneñjā*) *kamma*, in conformity with that desire and clinging. For example, wanting to go to heaven, and firmly believing that to go to heaven one must perform certain actions, one carries out those actions as one wishes, thus preparing the basic states of life, the five *khandhas*, to appear in the state (*bhava*) appropriate to those actions (*upapattibhava*). With the process of creating *kamma* thus in motion, when one life span ends, the momentum of accumulated *kamma* (*kammabhava*) induces the continuation of the next stage of the cycle, which is...

→ *Jāti*: Beginning with the relinking consciousness (*paṭisandhi viññāṇa*), with features conforming to that karmic momentum, there is birth (*paṭisandhi*) into a sphere of existence (*bhava*) appropriate to that *kamma*, and the arising of the five *khandhas*. A new life continuum begins—that is, there arises another cycle of body and mind, the six sense bases, contact, and feeling. And when there is birth, what inevitably follows is...

→ *Jarāmaraṇa*: the decline and disintegration of that life process. For the unenlightened being, aging and death are constantly threatening life, both overtly and covertly (subconsciously). Therefore, in the life cycle of the unenlightened being, old age and death inevitably bring with them...

→ *Soka* (sorrow), *parideva* (lamentation), *dukkha* (stress), *domanassa* (grief), and *upāyāsa* (despair), which can all be summed up in the one word: *suffering*. Thus the summarizing words of the *paṭiccasamuppāda* formula: "Thus is the arising of this whole mass of suffering."

However, as the process is a cycle (*vaṭṭa*), it does not stop here. In fact, the factors of this last stage become a crucial link in the further turning of the cycle. Specifically, sorrow, lamentation, pain, grief, and despair are all manifestations of defilements that fester in the subconscious, known as the outflows (*āsava*), as follows: the concern with gratifying desires of the five senses and the mind (*kāmāsava*); views and opinions, for example that the body is the self or belongs to self (*diṭṭhāsava*); esteem for certain states as being excellent and happy, and the hope and aspiration to obtain and maintain those states and experience happiness for as long as possible (*bhavāsava*); and ignorance of things as they are (*avijjāsava*).

Aging and death aggravate these outflows. For example, in relation to *kāmāsava*, aging and death cause unenlightened beings to feel they are being separated from, or deprived of, that which they love and cherish; in relation to *diṭṭhāsava*, when there is attachment to the idea that the body is ours or belongs to us, and that body changes, they experience disappointment and despair; in relation to *bhavāsava*, aging and death remind them that they must be deprived of, disappointed by, or lose the opportunity to preserve the life that they esteem; in relation to *avijjāsava*—that is, lacking understanding on the primary level, beginning with what life is, what aging is, and how they should be related to, as soon as they think of or associate with aging and death, they feel and respond with delusion and fear, and experience melancholy and depression. Thus, these outflows are the "fuel" for sorrow, lamentation, pain, grief, and despair to arise as soon as aging and death become involved.

Sorrow, lamentation, and so on are also indications of the dullness of the mind: whenever these forms of suffering arise, the mind becomes confused, agitated, and muddled. Thus, when they arise, it is tantamount to the arising of ignorance, as written in the Visuddhimagga: "Sorrow, pain, grief, and despair are not separate from ignorance, and lamentation is normal for the deluded being. For that reason, when sorrow, and so on come to a head, so also does ignorance come to a head."[40] "Regarding ignorance, know that it comes to a head with the arising of conditions such as sorrow..."[41] "Ignorance is present as long as sorrow and so on are present."[42] Thus, it is said, "With the arising of the outflows, ignorance is arisen,"[43] and it can be concluded that the aging and death of the unenlightened being—which bring with them sorrow, lamentation, pain, grief, and despair—are conditions for the arising of ignorance, thus turning the cycle once more.

From these explanations, there are a number of observations and points to be especially understood, as follows:

1. This explanation of the *paṭiccasamuppāda* is often called the wheel of existence (*bhavacakka*) or wheel of rebirth (*saṁsāracakka*). Note that the explanation spans three lifetimes—ignorance and volitional formations in one lifetime, consciousness to becoming in a second, while birth and aging and death (including sorrow, lamentation, and so on) are in a third. If the middle life span—that is, from consciousness to becoming—is taken as the present life, the three life spans, containing the entire twelve factors (headings), can be divided into three time periods, thus:

   Past (= ignorance, volitional formations)
   Present (= consciousness, mentality and physicality, sense bases, contact, feeling, desire, clinging, becoming)
   Future (= birth, aging, and death, along with sorrow, lamentation, etc.)

2. Dividing the process into these three periods, the middle period, the present life, is taken as the base. When the middle section is taken as the base, it shows the relationship of the past section as purely causal—that is, tracing back from results that appear in the present to see the causes in the past that led to their arising (= past cause → present result)—and at the same time the future section specifically shows resultant factors—that is, extending from causes in the present to see the results that will arise in the future (= present cause → future result). In this light, the middle section, the present, contains both causal and resultant factors. Thus, it can be represented in four sections (known as the four *saṅgaha*, or synopses):
   Past cause= ignorance, volitional formations
   Present result = consciousness, mentality and physicality, sense bases, contact, feeling
   Present cause = desire, clinging, becoming
   Future result = birth, aging, and death (+ sorrow, lamentation, etc.)

From the descriptions of each of the factors, we can see a connection of meaning in some of the factors, which can be grouped as follows:

Avijjā and *Taṇhā-Upādāna*

From the description of ignorance (*avijjā*), it is obvious that desire (*taṇhā*) and clinging (*upādāna*), especially clinging in relation to self, are involved in all examples: not knowing life as it truly is, and mistakenly believing that there is a self, there is desire and the various forms of clinging on behalf of that self; and in the words "with the arising of the outflows (*āsava*), there is the arising of ignorance," the outflows of sensual desire (*kāmāsava*), desire for being (*bhavāsava*) and attachment to views (*diṭṭhāsava*) are all matters of desire and clinging. Thus, when speaking of ignorance, the meaning invariably includes or involves desire and clinging.

The same applies to the explanations of desire and clinging—it can be seen that ignorance is always involved with or connected to them, in the sense that because of the deluded assumption of self, one wants and clings on account of that self; because one does not know things as they are, one desires them and clings to them as being the self or belonging to self, or wants to obtain them for oneself; and while one is desiring and clinging in this way, the more intense the desire and clinging, the more are reason overlooked, things not seen as they are, and mindful and rational conduct toward them neglected. Thus, when speaking of desire and clinging, ignorance is automatically implied.

In this light, ignorance within past causes, and desire and clinging within present causes, can be interpreted as being the same in those senses, but ignorance is classed as a past factor, while desire and clinging are classed as present factors, in order to indicate the prominent or leading factor in relationship with other factors in the wheel of becoming (*bhavacakka*).

Saṅkhāras and *Bhava*

Saṅkhārā and *bhava* have similar explanations within the cycle. Volitional formations (*saṅkhārā*) occur in the past-life section, while becoming (*bhava*) occurs in the present-life section. Each is an important agent for shaping life to arise in different states, and therefore they have similar meanings. In fact, they are almost the same, differing only in the scope of their emphasis. *Saṅkhārā* focuses on the factor of intention (*cetanā*), or volition, the shaper of actions, as the leading factor in the creation of *kamma*. *Bhava* has a broader meaning, incorporating both *kammabhava* and *upapattibhava*. While *kammabhava*, like *saṅkhārā*, has intention as its main agent, it carries a more comprehensive meaning than *saṅkhārā* by focusing on the entire behavioral process. As for *upapattibhava*, it refers to the five *khandhas* arising as a result of *kammabhava*. In this respect, when either *saṅkhārā* or *kammabhava* is spoken of, the other can be included.

Viññāṇa to *Vedanā*, and *Jāti Jarāmaraṇa*

The section of the cycle from *viññāṇa* to *vedanā* is the present life, which is the result of causes in the past. It is described in sequence, point by point, because the aim is to break up the process to reveal how the components of life, which are present resultant conditions, interact with each other to produce other factors that are present causal conditions and that will lead to resultant conditions in the future.

Jāti jarāmaraṇa are shown as future results, the aim being to show simply that as long as there are causes in the present, there will have to be results in the future. Thus, it is briefly stated as "birth" and "aging and death," which in effect refers to the arising and cessation of consciousness up to feeling, but in condensed form. The objective here is to emphasize the perspective of the arising of suffering, showing the point that will lead to the turning of the cycle once again. Thus, it is said that the sections from consciousness to feeling, and from birth to aging and death, are virtually the same and synonymous.

Bearing this in mind, each of the four stages of cause and effect in the middle section of the process, the present, can be divided into five factors, thus:

1. Five past causes: ignorance, volitional formations, desire, clinging, becoming.
2. Five present results: consciousness, mind-body, sense bases, contact, feeling (= birth, aging and death).
3. Five present causes: ignorance, volitional formations, desire, clinging, becoming.
4. Five future results: consciousness, mind-body, sense bases, contact, feeling (= birth, aging and death).

Counting the factors thus gives us twenty in all, and these are together called the twenty "attributes" (*ākāra*). The twelve factors of the *paṭiccasamuppāda* can be divided, according to their functions within the cycle, into three groups, called the threefold *vaṭṭa*, or cycle, as follows:

1. *Avijjā-taṇhā* and *upādāna* are defilements (*kilesa*), the causes that motivate thoughts and actions. They are called the cycle of defilements (*kilesavaṭṭa*).

2. *Saṅkhārā* and (*kamma-*) *bhava* (birth-conditioning actions) are *kamma*, the deed-committing process, or the deeds that shape life into its various forms. They are called the cycle of *kamma* (*kammavaṭṭa*).
3. *Viññāṇa*, *nāmarūpa*, *saḷāyatana*, *phassa*, and *vedanā* are *kamma* result (*vipāka*), the states of life resulting from the fashioning of *kamma,* which in turn become conditions for *kilesa.* They are called the cycle of *kamma* results (*vipākavaṭṭa*).

These three *vaṭṭa* are continuously spinning around as conditions for each other, so that the cycle of life proceeds unbroken.[44] It may be depicted like this:

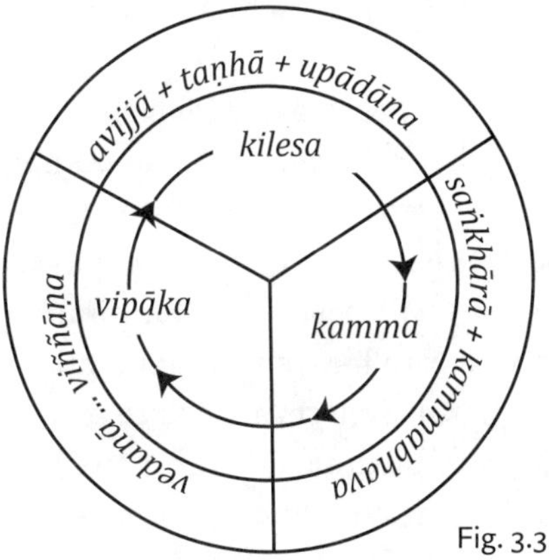

Fig. 3.3. Threefold cycle of kamma creation.

Since they are the originating factors of the deeds that shape how life proceeds, defilements are positioned at the starting point of the cycle. Thus, we have two starting points, known as the two roots (*mūla*) of the wheel of becoming (*bhavacakka*):

1. *Avijjā* is the past initiating factor, sending results to the present, up to *vedanā.*
2. *Taṇhā* is the present initiating factor, extending from *vedanā* and sending results to the future, up to aging and death.

The rationale behind presenting ignorance in the former section and desire in the latter is as follows: *avijjā* follows on from sorrow, lamentation, and so on, while *taṇhā* follows on from *vedanā*. Thus, *avijjā* and *taṇhā* are the predominant defilements for each case.[45]

In terms of birth into new states of existence, the explanation according to this model distinguishes between cases where ignorance is the predominant defilement and those where desire is the predominant defilement, as follows:

- Ignorance is the specific agent for beings taking birth into woeful states, because those who are enveloped in ignorance do not know what is good or evil, what is right or wrong, what is useful or harmful, or what are the causes for ruin and downfall. As a result, they commit actions on the basis of delusion and unknowing. Having no standards, the chances for erroneous deeds are great.
- Desire for being (*bhavataṇhā*) is the specific agent for beings taking birth into pleasant states. When *bhavataṇhā* is the leading factor, a person thinks of and aspires to fortuitous life situations. If it is a future existence, the desire is for birth in a heavenly or divine state, for example. If it is present existence, the aspiration is to become rich, to be famous, or to have a good reputation. With such aspirations, one plans and effects actions to realize those objectives: if one aspires to birth in a divine state, one develops *jhāna*;[46] if one aspires to heaven, one practices generosity and maintains moral precepts; if one wants to be rich, one diligently seeks wealth; if one aspires to a good reputation, one performs good works, and so on. Such aspirations encourage one to control one's mind and be heedful, to diligently apply oneself to doing what is good. As a result, the chances of doing good actions are greater than for one who lives under ignorance.

That ignorance and desire for being are placed at the beginnings of the cycle but are not the first cause is borne out by this Buddhavacana:

> "No ultimate beginning can be found, bhikkhus, to ignorance, thus: 'Before this there was no ignorance, but then it arose.'

> In this case, it can only be said, 'Dependent on this, ignorance manifests.'"[47]

There is also a Buddhavacana with the same meaning for *bhavataṇhā.*[48]

That ignorance and desire are originating factors and arise together is borne out by this Buddhavacana:

> "Bhikkhus, this body arises in its entirety to a fool...a sage, oppressed by ignorance and bound by desire. This body, together with external mental and physical properties (*nāmarūpa*), makes two things. Dependent on these two things there is contact within the range of the six sense bases. The fool...sage, receiving impingement through one or another of those sense bases, experiences pleasure or pain."[49]

The way the factors of the *paṭiccasamuppāda* relate to and condition each other accords with one or more of the twenty-four modes of relationship given in the explanation known as the *paṭṭhānanaya.*[50]

Again, each of the factors has its own extensive details and scope of meaning. For example, *viññāṇa*, or mind (*citta*), can be further analyzed into those that are good, evil, or endowed with various qualities, on various different levels, or leading to birth in various states. In regard to physicality (*rūpa*), there are many details: for example, the number of kinds of physicality, what qualities each of those kinds has, and in what states particular kinds will arise.

However, it is not necessary to go into the twenty-four kinds of relationship or the intricacies of the various factors here in full. Those who are interested may refer to the texts of the Abhidhamma.

From the above explanations, we may schematize the process as shown in figures 3.4 and 3.5 (pages 162 and 163).

Note that in terms of the four noble truths, the causal section is called *samudaya*, because it is the agency that causes suffering, while the resultant section is called *dukkha*. Alternatively, the causal section is referred to as *kammabhava*, because that is the part of the process that creates causes, and the resultant section is called

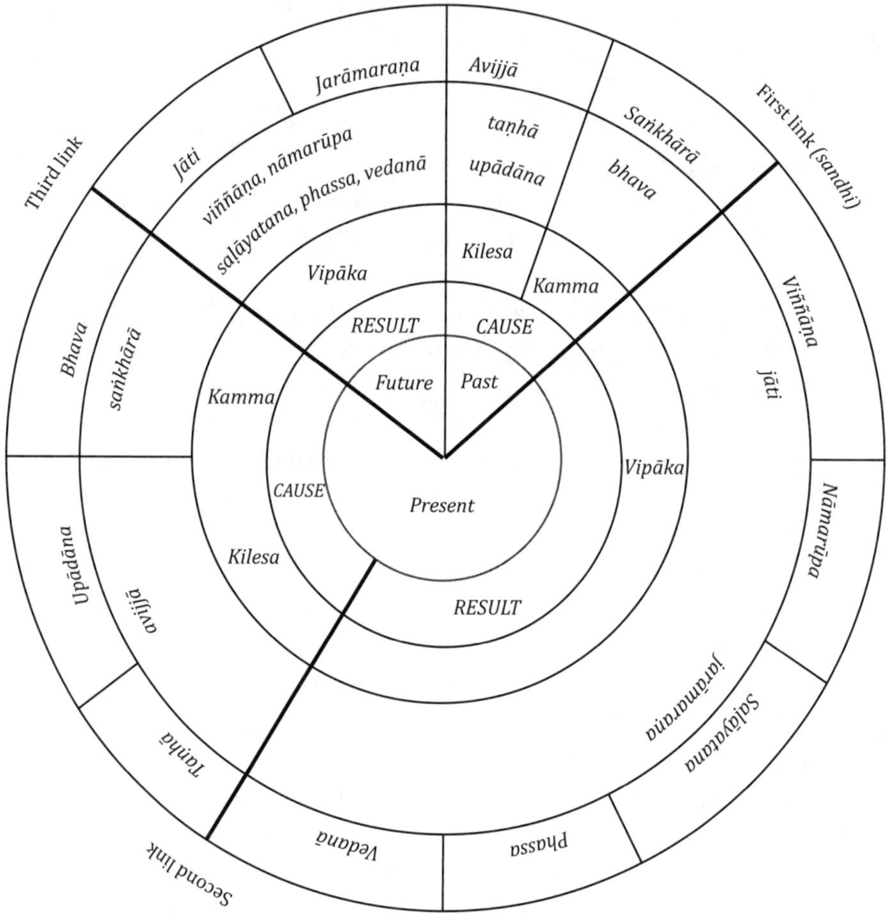

Fig. 3.4. Process of rebirth, circular.

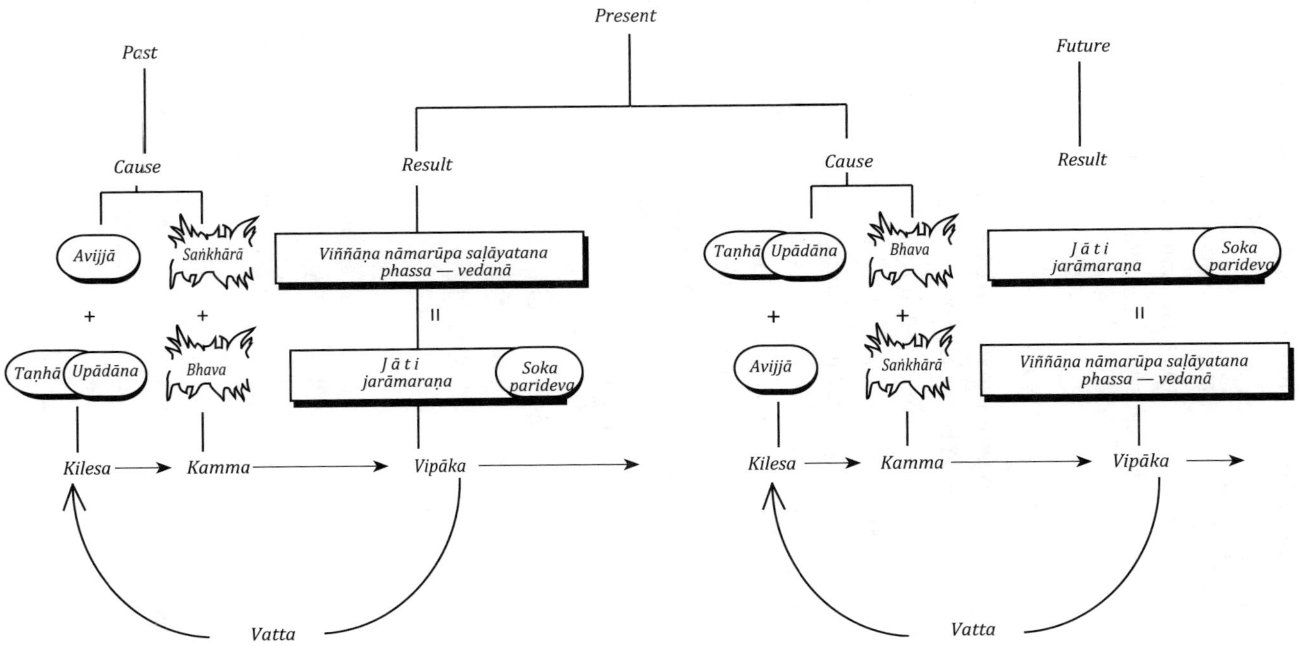

Fig. 3.5. Process of rebirth, linear.

upapattibhava, as that is that part of the process in which results arise.

The links between cause and result and result and cause are called *sandhi*. There are three of these: first *sandhi* = cause to effect; second *sandhi* = effect to cause; third *sandhi* = cause to effect.

The Meaning in Everyday Life

The explanation so far given is called the explanation according to the model, that given in the commentaries and adhered to as the standard ever since. It can be seen that this kind of explanation has been systematized into a fixed form that seeks to explain the *paṭiccasamuppāda* in terms of the *saṁsāravaṭṭa*, the round of birth and death, from lifetime to lifetime, showing the continuity over three lifetimes—past, present, and future.

Those who are not content with this interpretation, and want an explanation that is meaningful in every moment of everyday life, can not only refer to the teachings in the Abhidhamma Piṭaka, which describes the entire principle of *paṭiccasamuppāda* occurring in one mind moment, but can also interpret the very same Buddhavacana used to support the formal explanation to support their own view. In addition, it is also possible to cite other arguments and sources in the texts to support and give weight to these views. Since this explanation has its own special interest, it is here discussed separately.

The arguments that can be used to support this interpretation are many. For instance, the cessation of suffering and the sorrowless life of the arahant are states that occur in this very life: we do not have to die first before we can transcend renewed birth, aging, and death, and thus sorrow, lamentation, pain, grief, and despair in a future life. Those things are gone in this very life. The whole of the *paṭiccasamuppāda* cycle in the arising or cessation of suffering is a concern of this very life. It is not necessary to delve into past lives or wait for a future life. Moreover, once the cycle as it operates in the present is clearly understood, it follows that the cycle in the past and the cycle in the future are also clearly understood, because they are all of the same nature.

For scriptural reference, the following Buddhavacana can be cited:

"Listen, Udāyī, whosoever can recall the various *khandhas* that previously existed in great number... such a person would be fitted to question me about the past (past lives),[51] or I could question that person about the past; that person could satisfy me with an answer about the past, or I could satisfy that person with an answer about the past. Whosoever sees beings, both those passing away and those taking birth, with the Divine Eye... such a person would be fitted to question me about the future (future lives),[52] or I could question that person about the future; that person could satisfy me with an answer about the future, or I could satisfy that person with an answer about the future.

"But, Udāyī, enough of former times, and enough of future times. I will teach you the essence of Dhamma: When there is this, there is that; with the arising of this, that arises. When there is not this, that is not; when this ceases, so does that."[53]

The householder known as Gandhabhaka, having sat down at a respectful distance, addressed the Blessed One thus: "Revered Sir, may the Blessed One explain to me the arising and ceasing of suffering."

The Blessed One replied, "Householder, if I were to teach the arising and the cessation of suffering to you by referring to the past thus, 'In the past there was this,' doubt and perplexity as to that might arise in you. If I were to teach you the arising and the cessation of suffering by referring to the future thus, 'In the future there will be this,' doubt and perplexity as to that might also arise in you. So, householder, I, sitting right here, shall teach the arising and the cessation of suffering to you, as you sit right here."[54]

"Sīvaka, some feelings arise with bile as cause... some with phlegm as cause... some with wind as cause... some with a confluence of factors as cause... some with changes in the weather

> (*utu*) as cause…some with irregular exercise as cause…some with external dangers as cause…some with *kamma* results as cause. That feelings…arise with these different factors as origin is something you can know for yourself, and that people everywhere acknowledge as fact. On this account, whatever recluse or brahmin possesses the teaching or view that 'Any feeling experienced by a person, be it pleasant or unpleasant, all of that feeling is entirely on account of previous *kamma*,'[55] can be said to have exceeded what he himself can know and to have exceeded what people everywhere acknowledge as fact. Thus, I say that this is a wrong view on behalf of those recluses and brahmins."[56]
>
> ———
>
> "Bhikkhus, whatever one intends, fixes one's mind on and ponders, that becomes the base upon which consciousness is maintained. With a cognitive object, consciousness has an abiding. When consciousness is firmly established, when consciousness is developed, birth in a new state (*bhava*) ensues. When there is arising into a new state of existence, birth, aging and death, sorrow, lamentation, pain, grief and despair follow. Thus is there the arising of this whole mass of suffering."[57]

While the meaning of this interpretation of *paṭiccasamuppāda* must be understood in its own right, we nevertheless do not discard the pattern established by the basic model. Therefore, before going into its meaning, we should first come to an understanding of the meaning according to the model already described, in order to establish a basis of understanding and to aid in the comparisons to be made later.

Definition of Factors[58]

1. *Avijjā* (ignorance, lack of knowledge) = unknowing, not seeing things as they are, not being wise to the actuality (*sabhāva*); being deluded by nominal realities; the ignorance connected with beliefs; the state of lack of wisdom; failure to think ratio-

nally; not using wisdom, or wisdom not functioning at a given time.

2. *Saṅkhārā* (volitional formations) = mental fabrication, intention, will, decision-making, and the manifestation of intentions through actions; the organization of the thinking process, the search for cognitive objects to serve thoughts in accordance with one's accumulated habits, abilities, preferences, beliefs, and attitudes; the shaping of the mind, shaping of the thinking process, or the shaping of *kamma* by the "conditioners"—habituated or accumulated qualities.
3. *Viññāṇa* (consciousness) = sense consciousness—namely, seeing, hearing, smelling, tasting, touching, and cognizing objects in the mind; also includes the fundamental state of the mind in any given moment.
4. *Nāmarūpa* (animated organism) = the presence of physical and mental properties within a person's awareness; the state of coordination and functioning of all parts of body and mind to respond and function in conformity with the consciousness that arises; the components of body and mind that develop or change as a result of mental states.
5. *Saḷāyatana* (the six sense bases) = the state in which the relevant sense bases function in conformity with a given situation.
6. *Phassa* (contact) = connection between awareness and the outside world; cognition of sense objects.
7. *Vedanā* (feeling) = feelings of comfort or pleasure; suffering or discomfort; or indifference, neither comfort nor discomfort.
8. *Taṇhā* (desire) = wanting, ambition, desire for pleasurable objects and avoidance of what causes unpleasant feeling, expressed as wanting to have, wanting to be (wanting for something to always be in a certain condition), or wanting things to cease or be destroyed.
9. *Upādāna* (attachment, clinging) = clinging to the feelings that one likes or dislikes; gathering to oneself the life states that precipitate such feelings; affixing to things that produce pleasant or unpleasant feelings to such an extent that one adopts an

attitude toward or evaluates them in terms of their potential to satisfy desires.

10. *Bhava* (process of becoming) = the entire behavioral process generated to serve that desire and clinging (*kammabhava*: the active/dynamic process); also the life states that manifest (*upapattibhava*: the passive/static process) in conformity with clinging and its behavioral process.[59]
11. *Jāti* (birth) = the arising of the clear recognition of a self that has or has not emerged in a particular state of existence; adopting that life state or identifying with that behavioral process, consciously recognizing them as one's own.
12. *Jarāmaraṇa* (decay and death) = recognition of lack, or of deprivation or separation of the self from a life state; the feeling that the self is threatened with annihilation or separation from certain life states or from having or being something, resulting in sorrow, lamentation, pain, grief, and despair—for example, feelings of oppression, frustration, despair, depression, despondency, disappointment, agitation, and various forms of suffering.

The Relationships between Factors

1–2. *Ignorance as a condition for volitional formations*: Not knowing in accordance with the truth, not seeing the truth, not knowing the facts, not clearly understanding or using wisdom to investigate when experiencing a situation, we go into various kinds of thinking and build expectations in accordance with our beliefs, fears, or accumulated tendencies, eventually intending and planning on actions to be done and words to be said in relation to that situation. It is like a person in a dark place seeing the light reflected from the eyes of an animal. Believing in ghosts (ignorance), that person sees it as a face or the form of a ghost, is frightened by it (volitional formations) and thinks of various responses, such as running away. Someone who does not know the true nature of formations as impermanent, not lasting, arisen from the shaping of components, and inevitably subject to causes and conditions, and therefore sees them as fine, attractive, and desirable, imagines about them, makes plans about them, and devises ways to obtain them.

2–3. *Volitional formations as conditions for consciousness*: When there is the intention, aim, or choice to relate to or become aware of something, consciousness arises—that is, seeing, hearing, smelling, tasting, touching, or thinking about that matter or object. Intention, in particular, will guide consciousness to think repeatedly about the object of focus. At the same time, it conditions the basic state of mind (consciousness) into being good or bad, virtuous or immoral, or other qualities in accordance with the intention, be it good or bad. Without intention, or the turning of the mind toward an object, even when one is in a position to be aware, consciousness will not arise. For example, when we are absorbed in a book, our consciousness receives only the subject matter of the book; nearby sounds that are audible go unheard, and mosquito bites may go unnoticed. Looking at one and the same object in different circumstances, with different intentions, we see it differently, depending on the context of the intention. For example, a vacant plot of land seen with the thinking of a child wanting to play will carry certain perceptions and implications. Seen again with the intentions of a property developer, a farmer, or an industrialist, it will carry yet different features and implications.

3–4. *Consciousness as a condition for mentality and physicality*: Consciousness and body and mind are interdependent, as Venerable Sāriputta said: "Like two sheaves of reeds standing, leaning on each other, with mind and body as condition there is consciousness; with consciousness as condition, mind and body... Of those two sheaves of reeds, if we remove the first, the other falls down; if we remove the other sheaf, the first will tumble. In the same way, with the cessation of mind and body, consciousness ceases; with the cessation of consciousness, mind and body cease."[60] Since there is a consciousness that cognizes, sees, and hears, for example, there must also be corporeal properties (*rūpadhamma*) and mental properties (*nāmadhamma*) to be known and seen. When consciousness operates, the corporeal and mental properties that function with, and exist dependent on, consciousness, such as the relevant physical organs, as well as *vedanā*, *saññā*, and *saṅkhāras*, must also operate in conformity with their functions. Moreover, however consciousness is conditioned at that time, with whatever qualities, only those mental and corporeal properties that are of similar nature or have similar qualities to that consciousness will manifest in conjunction with it. For instance, when consciousness is conditioned by formations of the angry type, the perceptions that come into play as a result will be those dealing with violent words, abuse or even weapons. Corporeal properties, such as the facial expressions, will be fierce and severe, the muscles tense, the blood racing. Feelings will be oppressive and unpleasant. When consciousness takes on any particular state repeatedly, the subsequent mental and corporeal properties that arise and cease will create the corresponding traits of body and mind known as character.

4-5. *Mentality and physicality as conditions for sense bases*: When corporeal and mental properties spring into action in any particular mode, form, or direction, they must be served by the relevant sense bases, which are the media through which knowledge is fed, or the channels by which human beings conduct their behavior; the sense doors are roused into readiness for action. For instance, in the case of a football player on the field, the sense organs responsible for attending to objects directly concerned with the game being played, such as eye and ear, will be in a state of alertness, while those senses not directly concerned will not.

5-6. *Sense bases as conditions for contact*: When the sense bases perform their function, awareness arises, comprising the convergence of three factors: internal sense bases (eye, ear, nose, tongue, body, mind), external cognitive objects (sights, sounds, smells, tastes, bodily feelings, and mental impressions), and consciousness (through eye, ear, nose, tongue, body, and mind). Awareness arises in conformity with each particular sense base.

6-7. *Contact as a condition for feeling*: When there is cognition of a sense object, there must also be feelings, *vedanā*, of one kind or another: if not pleasant or unpleasant, then neutral.

The *paṭiccasamuppāda* from the third link to the seventh—that is, from consciousness to feeling—is the *vipāka*, or *kamma* result, section of the process. Factors 5, 6, and 7 (sense base, contact, feeling), in particular, are neither wholesome nor unwholesome, good nor bad, in themselves, but can be causes for the arising of subsequent good and bad states.

7–8. *Feeling as a condition for desire*: When the cognition of any sense object leads to a pleasant and comfortable sensation, we enjoy it, become attached to it, and want to have it, so sensual desire (*kāmataṇhā*) arises. We want to keep it, to be in a position to control and indulge in pleasant feelings from that cognitive object, and therefore desire for being (*bhavataṇhā*) arises. When the experience of any object produces feelings of suffering, stress, or discomfort, we hate it, are offended by it, and want to be rid of it; we want to destroy it or make it go away, and therefore desire for non-being (*vibhavataṇhā*) arises. If the feeling is neutral, we react with indifference or dullness; it is a state of delusion (*moha*) and it can be attached to as a subtle form of pleasant feeling, liable to evolve into desire for pleasurable feeling.

8–9. *Desire as a condition for clinging*: As desire becomes stronger it becomes clinging, holding onto objects in the mind and not being able to let go. We adopt attitudes to objects: if we like something, we tie ourselves to it as if it were our self; our mind falls for it, and whatever is connected with that object is seen to be fine and good, while whatever clashes with it also clashes with us. If we dislike something, it seems to clash with us as if it were an enemy. Whatever is related to that object produces feelings of friction and rejection. Nothing connected with it seems to be good, and any movement it makes seems to be a direct affront to us. Simultaneously, any attitude we adopt, be it in the direction of approval or disapproval, tends to become a reinforcement and an adjunct to clinging, exalting the value and importance of the following things: objects that nurture the happiness to be obtained or taken away (*kāma*); views and understandings about things related to us and with life and the world (*diṭṭhi*); systems, methodologies, practices, ceremonies, and techniques for realizing success, both in terms of obtaining and in terms of escaping (*sīlavatta*); and the belief in a self (*attavāda*) to either attain or be thwarted.[61]

9–10. *Clinging as a condition for becoming*: When there is clinging, a position toward a particular thing, person, or state, we create life situations accordingly, both in terms of the entire behavioral process (*kammabhava*), from systems or habits of thought outward, and also in terms of character, both the corporeal and mental properties that are the features or status of our lives at that time (*upapattibhava*)—the behavioral process (*kammabhava*) and character traits (*upapattibhava*), for example, of one who aspires to be rich, or who desires power, fame, or beauty, who wants to be fashionable, or who hates society. For example, if one wants to acquire a valuable object belonging to someone else, one clings to the state of being the owner of that object. Clinging to the activities or methods that will enable one to obtain it, not reflecting on the danger or fault of wrong methods, one thinks, intends, and acts accordingly, leading to theft or crime. The original aim of becoming an owner becomes the actuality of being a thief. In this way, in pursuit of what they want, people will make bad *kamma* or good *kamma*, in accordance with the force of their beliefs and understanding, right or wrong as the case may be.

This stage of the *paṭiccasamuppāda* is pivotal in the creation of *kamma* and receiving its results, and in the development of habit and character traits.

10–11. *Becoming as a condition for birth*: Given a particular life state to be occupied and possessed, a self arises as the clear recognition of living in, occupying, or assuming that life state, expressed as holding or adopting ownership of it, being the receiver of results, the doer of the deed, the victim of adversities, the victor, the defeated, the gainer or the loser within that state. We might say that a "self" has arisen within that state of existence, resulting in "I who am the owner," "I who am a thief," "I who have no honor," "I who am a failure." In daily life, birth, or the arising of the self, can be most easily observed in times of conflict, which tend to exacerbate clinging. For example, in arguments or discussions, if defilements are used instead of wisdom, a distinct sense of self will arise in the form of such thoughts as "I am the boss," "I am the honored person" (together with the corresponding concepts "they are my subordinates," "they are of lower status"), "this is my view," "I am being challenged," thus discrediting, threatening, or destroying the identity. Birth is therefore most obvious at times of decay and death, but it is only on condition of birth that decay and death can arise.

11–12. *Birth as a condition for aging and death*: When a self arises to occupy a particular life state, there will naturally be the experiences, both of decline and of prosperity, within that state. This will include decline within that state, experiences of adversity, and the fall from that state, especially the constant threat from and worry about the possibility of loss of that life state and the necessity of having to constantly see to its preservation. Decline, loss, and the constant threat of danger inevitably bring sorrow, lamentation, pain, grief, and despair—that is, suffering can arise at any moment.

In this sense, when the self arises in a life state or situation that is not desired, or when it arises in a desired life state but is deprived of it, or when it is threatened with loss, failure, and separation from a desired life state, suffering arises in its various forms—for example, sorrow, lamentation, pain, grief, and despair. In this state of suffering there are only unknowing and non-understanding of things as they are, which are features of ignorance. Thus, there follows the struggle to escape based on the methods of ignorance within the *paṭiccasamuppāda* cycle.

A simple example in everyday life: When victory occurs in a competition, for the unenlightened person it is not simply victory as a social phenomenon with its attendant social implications, but also the identity of being a victor, which is attached to in conjunction with the implications afforded it by clinging (*bhava*). Sometimes the feeling of self springs up— "I am the victor" = "I have been born as a victor (*jāti*)." However, our identity as victor in its full sense must entail honor and praise, receiving recognition from others. The minute the successful being is born, together with its attendant concepts and implications, there are fulfillment and disappointment. When there is success it is followed by the compulsion to tie oneself tightly to the identity of victor because of the fear that one's victory will be taken away, and that all the adulation and recognition one once received as a victor will not last, or will diminish or disappear. Whenever one does not receive the expected signs of honor and recognition, or less than expected, or when the adulation one once had begins to diminish, one becomes despondent. That is, the self is being threatened with decline (*jarā*) and separation (*maraṇa*) from the identity of being a victor, and all the related values (*bhava*) it has attached to. When the situation reaches this point, all the feelings of depression, worry, and disappointment that have arisen and not been removed by mindfulness and clear comprehension (*sati sampajañña*) will amass in the subconscious (*santāna*), influencing character and behavior in accordance with the *paṭiccasamuppāda* cycle.

An Example in Everyday Life

Rosa and Celeste are close school friends. Every day when they meet at school they smile and greet each other. One day Rosa sees Celeste, and approaches her with a friendly greeting as usual, but Celeste is sullen and does not smile or respond in any way. Rosa is slighted by this and stops talking to Celeste. In this case, the process of events might unfold in the following way:

1. *Avijjā*: Seeing Celeste's grim face, surliness, and silence, and not knowing the true reason for it, Rosa fails to examine the matter wisely to find out the facts behind Celeste's behavior—that Celeste may have some problem on her mind or is experiencing a mood carried over from somewhere else.

2. *Saṅkhārā*: As a result, Rosa proceeds to fashion and formulate images in her mind, conditioned by her temperament, attitudes, or habitual thinking, that Celeste must be feeling this or that way about her, and therefore confusion, anger, and pride, dependent on her particular defilements, arise.

3. *Viññāṇa*: Rosa's mind is clouded by the defilements that have

arisen within it and fashion it, and she notes and interprets Celeste's actions and gestures in such a way as to feed the feelings she is then experiencing—as they say, "The more I think about it, the plainer it gets." Celeste's every action and gesture seems to affront Rosa.

4. *Nāmarūpa*: Rosa's feelings, thoughts, moods, facial expressions, and gestures—that is, the mind and body together—begin to form together the overall features of an angry, piqued, or hurt person (depending on the *saṅkhāras* doing the conditioning), primed to function in accordance with that consciousness.

5. *Saḷāyatana*: Rosa's sense organs, such as the eyes and ears, especially those connected to receiving data related to the situation, are in a state of alertness, primed to perform their functions in receiving information.

6. *Phassa*: There is sense contact with Celeste's behavior that is particularly noteworthy in relation to the case, such as the frowning, the surliness, the disdainful, disrespectful, or insulting attitude.

7. *Vedanā*: There are unpleasant feelings, stress, hurt, or despair.

8. *Taṇhā*: Desire for non-being (*vibhavataṇhā*) arises—the desire for the offensive images that cause pain to go away or to disappear, to be repressed, expunged, or destroyed.

9. *Upādāna*: There is clinging and obsession in relation to Celeste's behavior, that it applies especially to herself (Rosa), as a personal affront, and Celeste is seen as an adversary who must be dealt with one way or another.

10. *Bhava*: Rosa's subsequent behavior falls under the influence of clinging and becomes a behavioral process specifically for serving that clinging, the behavior of an enemy to Celeste (*kammabhava*). The life states, both physical and mental, that support that process of behavior are also in conformity with that—in other words, it is the state of being Celeste's enemy (*upapattibhava*).

11. *Jāti*: Rosa takes on the identity of being an enemy as she becomes clearly aware of the hostility between herself and Celeste and the distinction between "me" and "her"; there is a self that will confront and clash with Celeste.

12. *Jarāmaraṇa*: For this "self" of enmity to continue and grow

there must be certain related concepts, such as ability, honor, power, and victory, all of which have their opposing states, such as inferiority, inadequacy, dishonor, and defeat. As soon as that self arises, it is threatened with the absence of any guarantee of attaining what it wants and, if the desired state is attained, of maintaining it for any definite length of time. That is, it may not be Rosa the able, powerful, and victorious adversary she wants to be but rather the adversary who loses, who is weak and unable to preserve her honor, power, and victory. Various forms of suffering are always interfering, beginning with the suffering resulting from fear of failure, the stress and agitation of struggling to attain the desired state, and the disappointment at failure. These various forms of suffering influence subsequent behavior and the entire conduct of life. In Rosa's case, for example, she may feel unhappy for the whole day, finding her ability to study impaired, and exhibiting unpleasant mannerisms and speaking impolitely to other people she meets, leading to more unpleasant incidents with other people.

If Rosa were to practice correctly from the start, the problematic cycle would not arise. Seeing her friend's surliness and lack of greeting, she could wisely reflect that Celeste may have some problem on her mind—she may have been scolded by a parent, she may be in need of money, or she may be depressed about something. Thinking in this way, Rosa would not see Celeste's actions as a personal affront; her mind would remain expansive and untroubled, and she would instead feel compassion and try to help Celeste. She might go to ask her what the trouble is and comfort her, or help her look for a solution, or just give her the space to be by herself for a while.

Even if the negative cycle had been set in motion, it could still be corrected. For instance, if the cycle had continued on up to sense contact, where Celeste's unpleasant actions were perceived and Rosa had experienced an unpleasant reaction as a result, Rosa could set up mindfulness right there: instead of falling under the power of the subsequent desire for non-being or annihilation (*vibhavataṇhā*), she could cut the cycle by instead wisely considering the facts of the situation and thereby gaining a fresh awareness of Celeste's behavior, reflecting on both her friend's actions and her own appropriate responses. Her mind would be relieved of its stress and confusion and instead be clear, and directed to helping alleviate Celeste's problems.

Thus, when wisdom or *vijjā* arises, it frees the mind, and a self to be battered about does not arise. In addition to causing no problems or suffering for oneself, this also serves to encourage the compassion to help relieve other people's suffering. This is the opposite to *avijjā*, which is what leads us into the cycle of birth and death (*saṁsāravaṭṭa*), causes desire and clinging, creates a self within which to confine us and subject us to the tribulations of the world, and causes suffering as a problem for oneself and for others on a wider scale.

Before leaving this example, it might be useful to reiterate some salient points in order to provide a broader view of the *paṭiccasamuppāda*:

- In real-life situations, the complete cycle or process mentioned in the above examples occurs rapidly, the whole sequence taking only an instant. For example, a student finding out that she had failed an exam, a man hearing of the death of a loved one, or a woman discovering her husband with another woman may feel such intense sorrow or shock as to go weak at the knees, scream, or faint on the spot. The more intense the attachment and clinging, the more intense the reaction will be.
- It should be stressed once again that the interdetermination within this process does not necessarily have to be in sequential order: for example, chalk, a blackboard, and writing are all conditions for the white letters on a blackboard's surface.
- The explanation of the *paṭiccasamuppāda* is meant to clarify the laws of the norm, or the natural processes, in order to identify the causes and points to be corrected. As for the details of how that correction is actuated, or the method of practice, they are not a direct concern of the *paṭiccasamuppāda*, but rather of *magga* (the path), or the Middle Way, which will be discussed later.

In any case, the examples given here are only for clarification, and do not convey the meaning deeply or clearly enough. Some sections of it only scratch the surface, especially those more subtle points, such as ignorance as a condition for volitional formations, and sorrow, lamentation, and despair conditioning the further turning of the cycle. The example given for *avijjā* is not something that commonly arises every day, and this can induce us to think that for the common unenlightened being it is possible to live one's everyday life without *avijjā* arising, or that the *paṭiccasamuppāda* is not a teaching describing the truth of actual life. It is therefore necessary to explain the profound meaning of some of the factors in more detail and more clearly.

The More Profound Meaning of Some of the Factors

In general, all unenlightened beings, finding themselves confronted with a particular experience or situation, will interpret and act on that experience or situation through the following biases or influences:

1. The concern with satisfying desires for the five kinds of sense objects (*kāma*).
2. The concerns or hopes around the existence and preservation of the self, its identities and the preservation of desired states (*bhava*).
3. Acquired, accumulated, and grasped-at views, beliefs, understandings, theories, and ways of thinking (*diṭṭhi*).
4. Delusion, non-understanding—that is, not recognizing or observing the causes, results, implications, values, objectives of, and relationships between things or events as they really are in nature; the deluded idea that there is a self that acts and is acted upon by things; not seeing the relationships of things as a process of causes and conditions; in short, not seeing things as they are, and instead seeing them as one thinks they are or wants them to be (*avijjā*).

The third and fourth of these, in particular, are obviously related: not observing, not understanding, or being deluded, one's actions are guided by acquired and accumulated views and beliefs, or by habitual thought and behavior patterns.

Ignorance and views are concealed deeply within people and are continually and subconsciously exerting an influence over their behavior. We think that we ourselves are performing all our actions, fully in accordance with our own desires, but this is in fact an illusion. If we drill down and ask ourselves, "What is it that we really want, why do we want such things, and why do we do the things we do?" we would find nothing that is really our own. We would find instead behavior patterns inherited from education, training, culture, religious beliefs, and social values. We simply choose and act within the parameters of these criteria, or make variations on them by using them as a point of reference for comparative purposes. What people feel to be their self is none other than the sum total of these four influences or biases, which, apart from having no intrinsic identity, are powerful forces over which most people have no control, and so they have no way of being independent.

In Buddhism the four qualities mentioned above are called *āsava*. Literally, *āsava* means "floods" or "outflows"; another interpretation is "that which ferments," meaning these things "curdle" or muddy the subconscious. They foul the mind and are what floods and colors it whenever it experiences a cognitive object. No matter what may be experienced through any of the sense doors or thought in the mind, these outflows spread their influence over it, discoloring and staining it accordingly. Those sensations and thoughts, instead of being pure objects of mind and intelligence, become instead objects of the *āsava*, blocking off any pure awareness or thinking, and becoming the causes for subsequent suffering and problems. The first *āsava* is called *kāmāsava*, the second *bhavāsava*, the third *diṭṭhāsava*, and the fourth *avijjāsava*.[62]

These outflows are the sources of behavior of all unenlightened human beings. They are the agents that cause people to deludedly identify something or other as their self, which is the most fundamental level of ignorance, and then force them to unknowingly think, behave, and act under its power. This is the very beginning of the *paṭiccasamuppāda* cycle: with the arising of *āsava* ignorance arises, and ignorance is a condition for the arising of volitional formations (and so on). While human beings live under the delusion that they are their own masters, we may in fact retort that they are not their own masters because their behavior is controlled by subconscious volitional formations.

Briefly summarizing at this point, the state of ignorance is not seeing the three characteristics, especially not-self (*anattā*), according to the *paṭiccasamuppāda*—that is, not realizing that the states taken to be a being—a person, a self, an "us" or a "them"—are simply a flow of innumerable lesser physical and mental properties, which are related and interdetermined, constantly arising and ceasing, causing the flow to be in a state of constant flux. To put it more simply, we could say that a "person" is simply the sum of feelings, thoughts, desires, habits, tendencies, attitudes, knowledge, understanding, beliefs (from the coarse level, such that are wrong or irrational, to the subtle level, such that are right and rational), opinions, values, and so on at any given time, which are products of cultural transmission, education and training, and reactions, both internally and in relation to the environment, which are all constantly in operation. Not clearly realizing this, there is clinging to one or another of these things at any given time as one's self. Clinging to these things as self is in effect being deceived by them, which is tantamount to falling under their control, being led and forced by them to see the self going through various changes, all the time understanding that the self is acting according to its wishes.

This is an explanation of "ignorance as a condition for volitional formations" on a more detailed and profound level than previously explained. As for the remaining headings from here up until *vedanā* (feeling), there should be no difficulty understanding them from the explanations already given. Therefore, we will pass over them to another important section: "desire as a condition for clinging," which is another of the phases of defilement (*kilesa*).

The three kinds of desire already mentioned are all expressions of the one desire, and all are commonly experienced in everyday life by all unenlightened beings, but they can only be seen when the workings of the mind are subjected to deep analysis, beginning with ignorance of the process of relationships between conditions in nature. This leads to the fuzzy notion of having a self in some form or other. Thus, human beings have an important fundamental level of desire, and that is the desire to have or be, the desire to live, which in effect means wanting the self of one's fuzzy notions to be ever constant. This wanting to be is related to wanting to have—it is not simply wanting to be, but wanting to be in order to consume objects of desire, in order to experience those objects that will produce pleasant feelings and feed one's desires. So it can be said that one desires existence because one wants to have, and with desire to have the desire to exist is intensified.

When desire to be is intense, it may produce a number of situations: for one, if the desired object is not obtained at the desired time, the reaction is that the *bhava*, or life state at that time, is no longer delightful. It seems adverse, intolerable, and one wants it to end. The desire for annihilation follows. But then desire to have manifests itself again, and one fears that if one ceases to exist one will no longer be able to experience the pleasant feelings one desires. And the desire to be arises again. A second possibility is not obtaining the desired object at all; a third, obtaining it but not as much as one wants; while a fourth is obtaining it but then desiring something else. In all cases the process follows the same pattern, but the situation that is fundamental and includes all the others is one of ever-growing desire.

At any given moment, human beings can be seen to be constantly seeking a state happier than that moment. As a result, they are constantly brushing off, or pushing themselves away from, each present moment. Each moment of present time is an intolerable life state. We want it to cease, want to escape it and find another state that will answer our desires. Wanting to have, wanting to be, and wanting to not be are constantly spinning around in the daily life of unenlightened beings. But the cycle is so subtle, on the level of moments of consciousness, that people are unaware that every moment of their personal lives is a constant struggle to escape a life state in the preceding moment and seek out objects of fulfillment in new life states.

Tracing back along the process, we can see that these forms of desire originate from ignorance—not knowing things as they really are, not seeing them as processes of interdependent and interrelated conditions, leading to the fundamental misconception of self in one form or another: either seeing things as separate entities, fixed and enduring,[63] or, if not, seeing things as becoming completely and utterly annihilated.[64] All unenlightened beings have these two subtle forms of wrong view within them, and therefore they have the three kinds of desire. That is, having the distorted understanding deep down in their minds that things have fixed and enduring being, that they are individual entities, they conceive desire for existence (*bhavataṇhā*). On the other hand, with unknowing and uncertainty, the other misconception arises that all things are actual, individual entities that can come to an end or disappear. Thus, the desire for nonexistence (*vibhavataṇhā*).

These two wrong views are related to desire insofar as they pave the way for it. If there is understanding and perception of things as a process of interrelated causes and conditions, there can be no permanent self as an actual entity, and nor can there be an actual entity that disappears. Thus, desire has no ground on which to stand. As for sensual desire (*kāmataṇhā*), it is also a result of those two wrong views: because of fear that one's self or pleasant feeling will disappear and come to an end, one frantically struggles to find more pleasant feeling, and because of the perception that all things are actual, separate entities there is the struggle to procure for and preserve those entities.

In the event of having studied, trained, and received a religious teaching, of possessing right views and adhering to worthy principles (within the scope of *avijjā*), desire can be guided toward a good direction, and as a result people do good actions in order to be good people, and make efforts to attain long-term goals, performing good works for enhancing their reputation or for birth in heaven, using their spare time constructively, and, ultimately, using desire to abandon desire.

The defilement that follows on from desire is called *upādāna*, of which there are four kinds:

1. *Kāmupādāna*, clinging to sensuality:[65] When there is desire and effort to seek, there are clinging and attachment to the objects desired. Once an object is attained, there is clinging to it again, with the fear that it will disappear or be taken away from one. When one suffers disappointment or separation, attachment increases through longing. Clinging is strengthened by the fact that objects of desire never really give full satisfaction, so one strives to attain a state of fulfillment through further efforts, and since those objects are not really one's own, one has to hold on to them with the heartening notion that they really are one's own in one sense or another.

2. *Diṭṭhupādāna*, clinging to views: Wanting to be or not be some way according to one's desires leads to bias and attachment to views, theories or philosophical principles that are compatible with those desires. Wanting objects of desire causes one to adhere firmly to principles, ways of thinking, views, doctrines or teachings that provide or facilitate the provision of those objects. Once an idea or principle has been attached to as a personal possession, it becomes assimilated into one's "self," with the result that not only does one think and act in conformity with those views, but when another theory or view conflicts with one's own, it is seen as a threat to the self, and therefore one has to fight to preserve one's views for the sake of one's dignity, and so on.[66]

3. *Sīlabbatupādāna*, clinging to mere rule and ritual: Wanting to have, wanting to be and fear of the annihilation of self through not understanding the process of causes and conditions in nature, coupled with attachment to some view or other, leads to gullible behavior in relation to things thought to be capable of satisfying one's desires, even though no rational connection can be seen. Wanting the self to exist and continue, and attachment to the self, express themselves outwardly or socially in the form of fixed attachment to modes of conduct, customs, disciplines and methods, traditions, doctrines, ceremonies, and even institutions, believing that they must be that way, not realizing their meaning, value, objectives, or rational connection. As a result, human beings create these things

to obstruct, confine, and calcify themselves. It is difficult for them to make any improvement or to derive any benefit from the things they deal with.

On the subject of *sīlabbatupādāna*, the late Venerable Buddhadāsa has given an explanation that may help clarify the matter:

> When coming to the practice of morality or any other form of Dhamma practice, not knowing its objective or reflecting on its rationale, people simply decide that the practice is sacred, and that sacred practices will automatically produce good results. Thus, they take on moral observances or Dhamma practice merely according to the texts, according to the letter, according to tradition, according to examples maintained by tradition. They do not penetrate to the real reasons for these practices, but because they have followed them until they are habituated, their attachment to them is firm. This is a kind of clinging (*upādāna*) that is difficult to redress...unlike the second kind of clinging, which is the attachment to views, or wrong thoughts. This kind of clinging is attachment to the actual forms of practice, or external modes of behavior.[67]

4. *Attavādupādāna*, clinging to the ego-belief: The feeling of a true self is a fundamental delusion, and this feeling is enhanced by other factors, such as language, which induces people to see things as separate and fixed entities. This feeling becomes clinging because of the factor of desire—that is, wanting something, one clings to the idea of a self who will be the recipient and experiencer of the desired object, a self to be the owner of the thing obtained. Importantly, that wanting is related to the feeling of an owner who controls, a self that is the master, manipulating things to accord with desires. Sometimes this manipulation is indeed successful, so one mistakenly thinks that there is an "I" or "myself" who owns and can actually control those things. In fact, such control is only partial and temporary. What is adhered to as self is one condition within a process of causes and conditions. It cannot direct or force things to fully and lastingly conform to desires. The feeling that one

is an owner with some, but not complete, control in fact strengthens attachment and the struggle to reinforce the feeling of self. Clinging to the self, one does not know how to organize things in conformity with causes and conditions, and instead misconceives the relationship, putting the self up on a pedestal as the owner of things, to manipulate them as it wishes. Not acting in accordance with the cause-and-effect process, and conditions not behaving in accordance with desires, the self is oppressed with lack, decline, inferiority, and loss. This clinging to self is an important kind of clinging, the foundation for all other kinds.

One simple perspective indicating the relationships involved within this section of the *paṭiccasamuppāda* cycle is that, when the experience of something leads to reception of an appealing feeling, desire—liking and wanting that object—arises followed by *kāmupādāna*, clinging to the desired object, thinking that one must consume it, must possess it. *Diṭṭhupādāna* follows, clinging to the idea that only this object is good, that only by obtaining it will there be happiness, that one must consume or possess this object or kind of object for life to have any meaning, and that only the principles and teachings that encourage the search for and procurement of this object are correct. *Sīlabbatupādāna* arises when, observing any particular discipline (*sīla*), religious observance, custom, or method, one looks on it as a means for obtaining the object of one's desires, or feels that one will only practice it if it can be a means for obtaining what one wants. And there arises *attavādupādāna*, clinging to the self that will consume or possess that desired object.[68]

From clinging the process continues up to becoming (*bhava*), birth (*jāti*), and aging and death (*jarāmaraṇa*), resulting in sorrow, lamentation, and so on, as already explained. With the arising of sorrow, lamentation, and so on, people try to find a way out by thinking, deciding, and acting on habits, biases, beliefs, and accumulated opinions, and the cycle begins once again at ignorance.

Although ignorance is the fundamental defilement, the foundation upon which all other defilements are built, in terms of expression through actual behavior, desire is the instigator; it is the director and plays a more intimate and obvious role. Therefore in practical teachings, such as the four noble truths, desire is singled out as the cause of suffering.

When ignorance proceeds blindly and randomly and desire goes unguided and uncontrolled, one lives in order to realize desires, and therefore bad *kamma* is more likely to exceed good *kamma*. But when ignorance is tempered by good beliefs, right thinking and rational understanding, desire is redirected to good goals; it is controlled, processed, and impelled toward those goals, and therefore good and useful *kamma* can easily arise. Moreover, if desire is correctly directed it becomes a support for the eventual destruction of ignorance and desire. The former way is that of bad *kamma* and unwholesomeness, while the latter is the way to goodness and wholesomeness. Both good and bad people have their own kinds of suffering, but only the good way is capable of leading to the cessation of suffering, to liberation and freedom.

There is an example of desire used in a beneficial way, for ultimate benefit, in the following passage:

> "Sister, a bhikkhu in this teaching and discipline hears that such and such a bhikkhu has realized the deliverance of mind (*cetovimutti*) and deliverance by wisdom (*paññāvimutti*) that is void of outflows...He then considers to himself, 'When will I also be able to realize that deliverance of mind and deliverance by wisdom...?' Later, that bhikkhu, relying on desire, abandons desire. It was on account of this that I said, 'This body is born of desire. Relying on desire, one should abandon this desire.'"[69]

If one has no alternative than to choose between different kinds of desire, the good kind is the preferable incentive for action. But, if possible, one should avoid both good and bad desires and choose the path of wisdom, which is the ideal path that is pure, free, and without suffering.

Paṭiccasamuppāda *as a Middle Teaching*

Understanding the *paṭiccasamuppāda* is said to be right view (*sammādiṭṭhi*), and this right view is an impartial kind of view, one that does not tend to extremes. The *paṭiccasamuppāda* is a principle or law that shows the truth in an impartial and unbiased way, which is known as the "Middle Teaching" (*majjhena dhammadesanā*).[70] The impartiality of this truth stands in reference to various extreme doctrines, and for a correct understanding of the *paṭiccasamuppāda* it must be differentiated from these extreme theories. I will now present some of these theories for comparison, arranged in pairs, accompanied by extracts from the Buddhavacana as explanation and keeping further commentary to a minimum.[71]

First Pair

Atthikavāda: The doctrine that all things really exist (extreme realism).

Natthikavāda: The doctrine that all things do not exist (nihilism).

"Revered Sir, it is said ' right view, right view.' To what extent is view said to be right?"

"Herein, Venerable Kaccāna, this world mostly tends (its views) toward two states—*atthitā* (existence) and *natthitā* (nonexistence). When the cause of the world is seen as it is with right understanding, there is no 'nonexistence' in the world. When the cessation of this world is seen as it is with right understanding, there is no 'existence' in the world. The world mostly clings fast to expedience and is bound by dogmas. As for the noble disciple, he does not go to, fix onto, or attach to expedience, fixations, dogmas, or the conceit 'my self.' He doubts not that 'suffering arises' when it arises, and 'suffering ceases' when it ceases. That noble disciple has direct knowledge in regard to this, independently of others. Just this is having 'right view.'

"Kaccāna! To say 'all things do exist' is one extreme. To say 'all things do not exist' is another. The Tathāgata proclaims a teaching that is balanced, not attaching to these two extremes, thus, 'With ignorance as condition there are volitional formations; with volitional formations as condition, consciousness...with the complete abandoning of ignorance, volitional formations cease; with the cessation of volitional formations, consciousness ceases...'"[72]

A brahmin who was a materialist approached the Buddha and asked, "Revered Gotama, do all things exist?"

The Buddha replied, "The view that all things exist is the first materialistic view."

Question: "Then all things do not exist?"

Answer: "The view that all things do not exist is the second materialistic view.

Question: "Are all things, then, a unity (*ekatta*)?"

Answer: "The view that all things are a unity is the third materialistic view."

Question: "Are all things, then, a plurality (*puthutta*)?"

Answer: "The view that all things are a plurality is the fourth materialistic view.

"Brahmin, the Tathāgata, not attaching to these two extremes, proclaims a teaching that is balanced, thus, 'With ignorance as condition there are volitional formations; with volitional formations as condition, consciousness...with the complete abandoning of ignorance, volitional formations cease; with the cessation of volitional formations, consciousness ceases...'"[73]

Second Pair

Sassatavāda: The doctrine of eternalism.
Ucchedavāda: The doctrine of annihilationism.

Third Pair

Attakāravāda or *sayaṅkāravāda*: The doctrine that happiness and suffering are entirely self-determined (self-generationism or karmic autogenesism).

Parakāravāda: The doctrine that happiness and suffering are entirely caused by external agents (other-generationism or karmic heterogenisism).

These second and third pairs are important in terms of the teaching of *kamma*. If studied and clearly understood, they help prevent a lot of misunderstandings about *kamma* and therefore should be considered in light of the following Buddhavacana:

> Question: "Is suffering (*dukkha*) self-caused?"
>
> Answer: "Do not put it that way."
>
> Question: "Is suffering then caused by other agents?"
>
> Answer: "Do not put it that way."
>
> Question: "Is suffering then caused both by oneself and other agents?"
>
> Answer: "Do not put it that way."
>
> Question: "Is suffering then caused neither by oneself nor other agents, but randomly arisen (*adhiccasamuppanna*)?"
>
> Answer: "Do not put it that way."
>
> Question: "In that case, is there no suffering?"
>
> Answer: "It is not that there is no suffering; suffering does exist."
>
> Question: "In that case, does Venerable Gotama neither know nor see suffering?"
>
> Answer: "It is not that I neither know nor see suffering. I do indeed know and see suffering."
>
> Question: "...May the Blessed One please tell me then, please instruct me, about suffering."
>
> Answer: "To say 'suffering is caused by the self,' as you first stated, is the same as saying 'He who acts experiences [the results] (suffering).' It is the eternalist view (*sassatadiṭṭhi*). To say 'suffering is caused by other agents,' as a person who experiences sharp and painful feelings would feel, is just like saying, 'One person acts, another experiences (suffering).' This is the annihilationist view (*ucchedadiṭṭhi*). The Tathāgata, not attaching to those two extremes, proclaims a teaching that is balanced, thus, 'With ignorance as condition there are volitional formations; with volitional

formations as condition, consciousness...with the complete abandoning of ignorance, volitional formations cease; with the cessation of volitional formations, consciousness ceases...'"[74]

"Ānanda, I say that happiness and suffering are dependently arisen (*paṭiccasamuppanna dhamma*). Dependent on what? Dependent on contact (*phassa*).

"When there is a body, on account of volition in relation to the body, internal happiness and suffering can arise. When there is speech, on account of volition in relation to speech, internal happiness and suffering can arise. When there is a mind, on account of volition in relation to mind, internal happiness and suffering can arise.

"With this very ignorance as condition, a person forms volitional bodily actions that are conditions for internal happiness and suffering; on account of other people [at the instigation or suggestion of other people or agents], one forms volitional bodily actions, a cause for internal happiness and suffering; knowingly, one forms volitional bodily activities, the cause of internal happiness and suffering; unknowingly, one forms volitional bodily activities, the cause of internal happiness and suffering...volitional speech...volitional thoughts...on account of other people...knowingly...unknowingly: in [all] these cases, ignorance is involved."[75]

Fourth Pair

Kārakavedakādi-ekattavāda:[76] The belief that the doer of the deed and the experiencer of the result are one and the same (the extreme view of a self-identical soul or the monistic view of subject-object unity).

Kārakavedakādi-nānattavāda: The belief that the doer of the deed and the experiencer of the result are separate (the extremist view of individual discontinuity or the dualistic view of subject-object distinction).

Question: "Are the doer and the receiver [of the result] one and the same thing?"

Answer: "Saying that the doer and receiver [of the result] are one and the same thing is one extreme."

Question: "Are, then, the doer one thing, the receiver [of the result] another?"

Answer: "To say the doer is one thing, the receiver (of the result) another, is another extreme. The Tathāgata, avoiding these two extremes, proclaims a teaching that is balanced, thus, 'With ignorance as condition there are volitional formations; with volitional formations as condition, consciousness...with the complete abandoning of ignorance, volitional formations cease; with the cessation of volitional formations, consciousness ceases...'"[77]

Question: "Revered Sir, what are aging and death? To whom do aging and death belong?"

Answer: "You have put the question wrongly. To say either, 'What are aging and death, to whom do they belong,' or 'Aging and death are one thing, the owner of aging and death another,' is to say the same thing; the statements differ only in the letter. When there is the view, 'Life and the body are one and the same thing,' the living of the holy life (*brahmacariya*) cannot be. When there is the view, 'Life is one thing, the body another' the living of the holy life cannot be. The Tathāgata, not attaching to these two extremes, proclaims a teaching that is balanced, thus, 'With birth as condition are aging and death.'"

Question: "Revered Sir, birth...becoming...clinging...desire ...feeling...contact...the sense bases...mind and body...consciousness...volitional formations...What are they? To whom do they belong?"

Answer: "You have put the question wrongly....[same as for aging and death]...With the complete abandoning of ignorance, whatsoever views there be that are distorted, vague, and contradictory—such as 'What are aging and death, to whom do they belong?' 'Aging and death are one thing, the experiencer another,' 'The life principle and the body are one thing' 'The life principle is one thing and the body another'—all of those views are destroyed, uprooted, obliterated, made to not be and unable to arise again.[78]

"Bhikkhus, this body does not belong to you, nor does it belong to another. You should understand it as old *kamma*, formed by conditions, willed into being [arisen from or based on volition], a base for feeling.

"In regard to that, bhikkhus, the learned, noble disciple wisely considers and traces (*yoniso-manasikāra*) thoroughly the dependent arising (*paṭiccasamuppāda*) of things, thus: 'When there is this, there is that. With the cessation of this, that ceases.' That is, with ignorance as condition are volitional formations; with volitional formations as condition, consciousness... With the complete abandoning and cessation of ignorance, volitional formations cease; with the cessation of volitional formations, consciousness ceases."[79]

The *paṭiccasamuppāda* demonstrates the truth of nature, that all things have the characteristics of impermanence, stressfulness, and not-self, known as the three characteristics, and fare according to the process of causes and conditions. There is no need for questions about the existence or nonexistence of things, whether they are eternal or whether they are annihilated and so on. Those who do not clearly understand the *paṭiccasamuppāda* tend to misunderstand the three characteristics, especially the characteristic of not-self. Quite often they listen to the teaching superficially and proceed to interpret not-self as nothingness, which is the nihilist (*natthika*) view, a pernicious form of wrong view.

One who understands the *paṭiccasamuppāda* is free of the various kinds of wrong views that branch out from the theories described above, such as the view that all things have a genesis or first cause, and belief in the supernatural. This is illustrated in the following Buddhavacana:

> "Bhikkhus, when a noble disciple sees clearly as they are, with right wisdom, the *paṭiccasamuppāda* and the dependent arising of things (*paṭiccasamuppanna dhamma*), it is impossible for that noble disciple to fall into such extreme views in relation to the beginning as, 'Did I exist in the past? What was I in the past? How was I in the past? Having been what in the past did I become what?'; or such views in relation to the end as, 'In the future, will I be? In the future what will I be? In the future how will I be? In the future what will I proceed to become?'; or even to entertain such doubts in relation to the present as, 'Do I exist? What am I? How am I? Where did this being arise from, and to where will it go?'—none of these can arise for him. Why? Because that noble disciple has seen this *paṭiccasamuppāda* and the dependent arising of things clearly, as they are, with perfect wisdom."[80]

In this respect, one who sees the *paṭiccasamuppāda* will have no doubts about the various metaphysical questions known as *antagāhikadiṭṭhi*, and this is why the Buddha remained silent when asked about such issues. He called them *abyākatapañhā*—questions better left unanswered. Once the *paṭiccasamuppāda* is seen, and one understands how all things fare according to the process of causes and conditions, such questions become meaningless. Here we may consider an example of the Buddhavacana explaining why the Buddha would not answer such questions:

> "Revered Gotama, what is the cause or condition that recluses of other sects, when questioned thus—
>
> 1. Is the world permanent (eternal)?
> 2. Is the world impermanent?
> 3. Is the world finite?
> 4. Is the world infinite?
> 5. Are the life principle and the body one thing?
> 6. Are the life principle one thing and the body another?

7. Does a being[81] exist after death?
8. Does a being not exist after death?
9. Does a being both exist and not exist after death?
10. Does a being neither exist nor not exist after death?

—give such answers as 'The world is eternal,' or 'The world is not eternal,'...'A being neither exists nor does not exist after death.'? [But] what is the cause and the reason that the Revered Gotama, being so questioned, does not answer that 'The world is eternal,' 'The world is not eternal,'...?"

"Herein, Vaccha, these recluses of other sects believe that form is the self, or that the self has form, or that form lies in the self, or that the self lies in form; or they believe that feeling...perception...volitional formations...consciousness is the self, or that the self has consciousness, that consciousness lies in the self or that the self lies within consciousness. It is for this reason that those recluses of other sects, being so questioned, answer that 'The world is eternal,'...

"But the Tathāgata, Arahant, Perfectly Self-Enlightened Buddha, does not apprehend form to be the self or self as having form, or that form lies in the self, or that the self lies within form...that consciousness is the self, or that the self has consciousness, or that consciousness lies within the self, or that the self lies within consciousness. For this reason, the Tathāgata, Arahant, Perfectly Self-Enlightened Buddha, being so questioned, does not answer that 'The world is eternal' or 'The world is not eternal'..."[82]

Of the wrong theories or doctrines that clash with the *paṭiccasamuppāda* principle, there are others that have a special connection with *kamma*. They are not covered here since that subject is explained in its own separate chapter, and it is there that those theories or doctrines will be discussed.

OPPOSITE: Fig. 3.6. Divergence of dependent-arising process into the social level.

Paṭiccasamuppāda *as Conditionality on the Social Scale*

In the *Mahānidāna Sutta*,[83] an important, indeed the longest, sutta dealing with *paṭiccasamuppāda*, the Buddha explains the principle of conditionality functioning both in the individual mind and also in human relations or in the social context. So far we have dealt exclusively with conditionality as it occurs in individual human consciousness, or the conditionality of life. Before passing on from this subject it would therefore be appropriate to mention, at least briefly, the *paṭiccasamuppāda* as conditionality on the social scale.

The *paṭiccasamuppāda* of social suffering proceeds in the same way as that for the arising of personal suffering, but from desire onward it diverges into a description of external events. Here is the relevant Buddhavacana:

> "In this way, Ānanda, on condition of feeling there is desire; on condition of desire there is seeking (*pariyesanā*); on condition of seeking there is gain (*lābha*); on condition of gain there is evaluation (*vinicchaya*); on condition of evaluation there is fondness (*chandarāga*); on condition of fondness there is possessiveness (*ajjhosāna*); on condition of possessiveness there is ownership (*pariggaha*); on condition of ownership there is covetousness (*macchariya*); on condition of covetousness there is guarding (*ārakkha*); on condition of guarding, and resulting from guarding, there are the taking up of the stick, the taking up of the knife, arguments, contention, dispute, abuse, slander, and lying. Evils of many a kind thus appear in profusion."[84]

How the process diverges into two directions is simply rendered as follows:

ignorance → volitional formations → consciousness → mind & body → sense bases → contact

↗ clinging → becoming → birth → aging & death → sorrow, lamentation, pain, grief and despair = personal suffering

feeling → desire

↘ seeking → gain → evaluation → fondness → possessiveness → ownership → covetousness → guarding → dispute, contention, abuse, slander, lying = suffering in society

In studying the above process, we may incorporate an investigation into some of the minor processes described by the Buddha in other places for clarification. For example, there is the process of variation or profusion (*nānatta*), which can be briefly summarized thus:

Variations within the elements (*dhātunānatta*) → variations within contact (*phassanānatta*) → variations within feeling (*vedanānānatta*) → variations within perception (*saññānānatta*) → variations within thought (*saṅkappanānatta*) → variations within desire (*chandanānatta*) → variations within agitation (*pariḷāhanānatta*) → variations within seeking (*pariyesanānatta*) → variations within gain (*lābhanānatta*).[85]

The first section, from *dhātu* to *saññā*, can be simply rephrased thus: because of the manifold variation of elements, there arises the manifold variation of perceptions. Elsewhere in the canon the following sequence of events is described:

Variations of the elements (*dhātunānatta*) → variations of perception (*saññānānatta*) → variations of thought (*saṅkappanānatta*) → variations of impingement (*phassanānatta*) → variations of feeling (*vedanānānatta*) → variations of desire (*chandanānatta*) → variations of agitation (*pariḷāhanānatta*) → variations of seeking (*pariyesanānatta*) → variations of gain (*lābhanānatta*).[86]

This kind of *paṭiccasamuppāda* illustrates a process connecting events in the individual mind with external events in terms of human interaction. It shows the source of social problems or evils arising from human defilements. It is a basic process, showing a broad unfolding of events. The explanations that more specifically emphasize external happenings on a social level appear in other suttas, such as the *Aggañña*,[87] *Cakkavatti*,[88] and *Vāseṭṭha Suttas*.[89] Those suttas may be said to be the definitive examples of descriptions of the *paṭiccasamuppāda* process on the social scale. Here, however, it is not my intention to go onto social conditionality in depth, so I will not expand on the subject here. Instead I would like to make two observations.

· Let us emphasize once more the meaning of conditionality: with feeling as condition, for example, there is desire. This means that for desire to exist there must be feeling, or there must be feeling before desire can be. However, the presence of feeling does not always necessitate the presence of desire. It is important to understand this, and this point is a crucial one in the cessation of the *paṭiccasamuppāda* cycle, or *vaṭṭa*, as demonstrated in the various suttas quoted above, where the experience of feeling is described without the arising of desire, in which case there must be mindfulness and clear comprehension (*sati sampajañña*) or mindfulness and wisdom (*satipaññā*). That is, when an experience of feeling is accompanied by mindfulness and clear comprehension, the process is cut off, and desire does not arise. The stage "feeling as a condition for the arising of desire" is a critical internal factor in determining human social behavior, and, by extension, the evolution of society as a whole.

· The suttas named above describe events in human society, such as the formulation of the caste system and the variations within human lives, as results of the mutual interaction between human beings and their respective natural environments. In other words, they are a result of the evolutionary process arising from interdependent conditionality between human beings (from internal mental factors outward), society, and the whole natural environment. For example, the feelings people experience are dependent on sense contact (*phassa*), which comprises social or environmental factors in conjunction with preexisting internal factors such as *saññā* (perception or memory). Once feeling is experienced and desire arises, there is behavior. This may be expressed in actions toward other people or the natural environment, within the limitations of social status and the situation. Results arise and in turn have an effect on all other factors involved. Human beings are not the only determining factors on society or the natural environment, society is not the only determining factor on human beings, and the natural environment is not the only determining factor on human beings and society. It is a process of interdependence.

Some sections of the *Aggañña Sutta* illustrate the sequence of social evolution according to the principle of conditionality:

People become lazy and begin to hoard rice (previously rice was plentiful and there was no need to hoard it) and this becomes the preferred practice → people begin to apportion off and protect private stores of rice → greedy people steal other people's shares to enlarge their own (stealing arises) → censure, lying, punishment, and fighting ensue → the wise see the need for authority; there is an election and the word *king* comes into being → some of the people, being disillusioned with the evils of society, decide to do away with evil and go off into the forests to cultivate meditation practice. Some of these live close to the city and study and write scriptures. They become the brahmins. Those who have families and earn their living by various occupations become the artisans. The remaining people, being coarse and inept, are called *śūdra*, the plebeians. → From among these four groups, a smaller group breaks off, renouncing tradition and household life and taking to the homeless life. These become the *samaṇa*, the religious mendicants.

The aim of this sutta is to show that the arising of the various social classes is a matter of events in accordance with causes and conditions and the law of relationship, not commandments from an almighty god. All people are equally capable of good and evil behavior, and all receive results equally according to the natural law. And they are all equally capable of attaining enlightenment when they practice the Dhamma correctly.

The *Cakkavatti Sutta* shows the arising of crime, social evils, and troubles according to the following sequence of conditionality:

[The king] does not apportion some of his wealth to the poor → poverty spreads → theft spreads → the use of weapons spreads → killing and maiming among people [*pāṇātipāta*] spreads → lying spreads → slander...sexual infidelity...abusive and frivolous speech...covetousness and hatred...wrong view → greed for what is wrong (*adhammarāga*), avarice, wrong teachings, disrespect for parents, elders, and religious persons spreads, disrespect for position spreads → longevity and appearance degenerate.

A Note on Interpreting the Paṭiccasamuppāda

As referred to in endnote 26 of this chapter, in the commentary to the Abhidhamma Piṭaka (Sammohavinodanī) the *paṭiccasamuppāda* process is shown occurring entirely within the space of one mind moment. This point needs to be repeated because established study of the *paṭiccasamuppāda* always interprets it on a lifetime-to-lifetime basis. Accordingly, when people interpret and explain the *paṭiccasamuppāda* as a process occurring in everyday life, those who adhere to the scriptural basis may have misgivings about these interpretations. For mutual ease of mind, therefore, I have included this reference to show that the everyday-life interpretation of the *paṭiccasamuppāda* has a scriptural basis. However, it is worth noting that the basis that does exist may be merely a trace from the past that is slowly fading away or being forgotten, and what does remain only does so because it is demanded by the scriptural basis in the Tipiṭaka.

In explanation, the description of the *paṭiccasamuppāda* as a lifetime-to-lifetime process that has been adhered to in Buddhist academic circles comes from the Visuddhimagga, written by Ācariya Buddhaghosa around B.E. 900 (roughly C.E. 460). But there is another text that deals with the *paṭiccasamuppāda*: the Sammohavinodanī mentioned above. The explanation of *paṭiccasamuppāda* given in the Sammohavinodanī is divided into two sections. The first explains it on a lifetime-to-lifetime basis, as in the Visuddhimagga, but the second explains it as occurring in one mind moment. The Sammohavinodanī is also the work of Ācariya Buddhaghosa and is believed to have been written after the Visuddhimagga. It differs from the Visuddhimagga only in that whereas the latter is Buddhaghosa's own work, the Sammohavinodanī is a commentary on the Abhidhamma Piṭaka. In his introduction to the Sammohavinodanī, Buddhaghosa writes: "I have sifted the essence of the ancient commentaries to compile this work."[90] Even in the Visuddhimagga, which was his own work, when it comes to the section dealing with the *paṭiccasamuppāda*, he excuses himself by saying: "It is extremely difficult to explain the *paṭiccasamuppāda*" and "Today I would like to expound on the *paccayākāra* (principle of conditionality), even though I have no foundation, like stepping into a flowing river with no stepping stone. However, the *paṭiccasamuppāda* is rich with interpretations, not to mention the explanations handed down from the ancient teachers in an unbroken line. Thus, relying on these two sources, I will now proceed to expound on the meaning of *paṭiccasamuppāda*."[91]

The explanation of the *paṭiccasamuppāda* given in the Visuddhimagga, unlike the Sammohavinodanī, contains only one section—that is, the first section explaining the principle on a lifetime-to-lifetime basis. There is no section explaining the principle on a one-mind-moment basis. The explanation of the lifetime-to-lifetime version is almost identical to that given in the Sammohavinodanī, differing only in that it expands a little on some points.[92] This being the case, it may be asked why in the Visuddhimagga is there no section explaining the *paṭiccasamuppāda* in one mind moment, as there is in the Sammohavinodanī? It may be that even in the time of Buddhaghosa, study and teaching of the *paṭiccasamuppāda* subscribed only to the lifetime-to-lifetime interpretation, thus the Visuddhimagga stuck to that perspective. It may also be that the author felt more comfortable with the lifetime-to-lifetime explanation because, difficult as it was, as he noted in his introduction, there were the teachings handed down from former times to rely on. The one-mind-moment interpretation, on the other hand, was not only difficult but had also disappeared from scholastic circles. This can be surmised from the Sammohavinodanī itself, where the description of this interpretation is extremely brief. Perhaps any explanation of it that does occur is simply because the Tipiṭaka mentions it and as such it demanded at least some explanation. Since there were traces of it in ancient commentaries, Buddhaghosa treated the subject only as far as given in those sources.

Now let us consider the explanation given in the Sammohavinodanī. The Sammohavinodanī is a commentary on the Vibhaṅga, the second volume of the Abhidhamma Piṭaka. The section of the

Vibhaṅga that describes the principle of *paṭiccasamuppāda* is called the Paccayākāra Vibhaṅga. It is divided into two sections: the first called Suttantabhājanīya (sutta-like explanation), the second, Abhidhammabhājanīya (Abhidhamma-like explanation). The Sammohavinodanī, the commentary to this book, is likewise divided into two sections. It describes the difference between the two explanations thus:

> Since the *paccayākāra* is not limited to numerous minds but can occur even in one mind moment, the Teacher, having expounded the *paccayākāra*...in terms of various moments of consciousness in the Suttantabhājanīya, then seeks to explain in various ways how the *paccayākāra* occurs in one mind moment in the Abhidhammabhājanīya.[93]

And elsewhere he states:

> In the Suttantabhājanīya the *paccayākāra* is divided into different mind moments. In the Abhidhammabhājanīya it is described as occurring in one mind moment."[94]

An example of an explanation in the form of one mind moment in everyday life is:

> With birth and so on [birth, aging, and death] here refers to birth [aging and death] of immaterial (*arūpa*) things. Thus [the Buddha] was not referring to the decaying of the teeth, the graying of the hair, the wrinkling of the skin, dying, the action of leaving (existence)."[95]

It is noteworthy that in the Vibhaṅga—that is, in the Tipiṭaka—the Suttantabhājanīya, which describes the principle of conditionality in terms of different mind moments (lifetime-to-lifetime interpretation), covers only five pages. The Abhidhammabhājanīya, which describes the principle of conditionality in one mind moment, covers seventy-two pages.[96] In the Sammohavinodanī, however, it is the reverse: the section explaining the Suttantabhājanīya interpretation is long, covering ninety-two pages, while the section explaining the Abhidhammabhājanīya interpretation covers only nineteen pages.[97] That the commentary on the Abhidhammabhājanīya is so short may be because the commentator, Ācariya Buddhaghosa, did not have much to say about it. Perhaps he thought it had already been explained comprehensively and in sufficient detail in the Tipiṭaka and there was no need for much further commentary. Whatever the case, it is apparent that the interpretation of *paṭiccasamuppāda* in everyday life is one that existed from the very beginning, in the Tipiṭaka, and there are traces of it remaining in the commentaries, but in later times those traces have gradually faded and been all but forgotten.

CHAPTER 4

Kamma as a Principle Contingent on the *Paṭiccasamuppāda*

Buddhism teaches the truth that all things, be they people, animals or objects, corporeal or mental, physical objects or mental events, be it life or the things around it,[1] are entirely subject to the direction of causes and conditions, and are interdependent. This natural course of things is looked on by human beings as "the law of nature." In Pali it is called *niyāma*, literally meaning "certainty," "fixed way," or "ordered process," because it appears that specific determinants inevitably lead to corresponding results.

Those laws of nature, or *niyāma*, while sharing the one general characteristic of faring according to causes and conditions, can be classified according to the specific features of their modes of relationship. This classification helps to make their study easier. In terms of the Buddhist perspective, the commentaries give five kinds of *niyāma*, as follows:[2]

1. *Utuniyāma*:[3] the natural law pertaining to physical events, especially events and changes in the natural environment, such as the weather, the seasons, rain and thunder, the blooming of the lotus in the day and its folding up at night, the way soil, water and nutrients help a tree to grow, and how things disintegrate and decompose. The commentators' perspective emphasizes the changes brought about by heat or temperature.
2. *Bījaniyāma*:[4] the natural law pertaining to reproduction, or

what is known as heredity, best described by the adage, "as the seed, so the fruit": a mango seed, for example, leads to a mango fruit.

3. *Cittaniyāma:*[5] the natural law pertaining to the workings of the mind; for example, how the mind works when an object (stimulant) impresses on a sense base and cognition arises.
4. *Kammaniyāma:*[6] the natural law pertaining to human behavior—that is, the process of the generation of deeds and their results, as in the adage "good deeds bring good results, bad deeds bring bad results."
5. *Dhammaniyāma:*[7] the natural law governing the relationship and interdependence of all things, especially that which is referred to as "the norm." For example, all things have arising, continuation, and ceasing as a norm. Regardless of whether a Buddha arises in the world or not, it is the norm for things to be impermanent, oppressed by determinants, and not-self.

The first four *niyāma* are contained within or derived from the fifth one, *dhammaniyāma*. It may be questioned why it is that when *dhammaniyāma* is divided into minor laws there is still *dhammaniyāma* within the subdivisions? The answer to this question can be conveyed with an analogy. It is like all the people in this country of Thailand: they can be divided into different categories, such as the king, the government, public servants, merchants, and the people; or into police, military, public servants, students, and the people; or in other ways. In fact, the words "the people" include all the other groups of people in the country: civil servants, police, the military, merchants, and students are all equally "people," but they are separated into categories because the people in each of those groups have their own characteristics and duties peculiar to themselves. Those without any particular feature or duty relevant to the analysis are grouped under the general heading "the people." Moreover, although those groupings may change according to the particular design of the analysis, they will always include the words "the people," or "the citizens," or a similar generic term for the people who do not need to be given any separate category. The five *niyāma* should be understood in the same way.

Whether or not the analysis of the natural laws into five sublaws is a complete analysis, or should contain other categories, is not a problem here because the commentators have detailed the most outstanding groupings relevant to their needs, and any other groupings can be included under the fifth one, *dhammaniyāma*, in the same way as in the example above. The important point to understand is the commentators' design or objective in pointing out these five *niyāma*. I would like to emphasize a number of these points, as follows:

First, it highlights the Buddhist perspective, which sees the course of things, or of life and the world, according to causes and conditions. No matter how minutely this law is analyzed, we see only the workings of the norm, the state of causal interdependence. This means that we learn, live, and practice with a clear and firm understanding of the way things are, without having to worry about a creator god coming to divert the flow of the norm (unless by becoming one of the determining factors within it). We need not bother trying to answer such questions as "Without a being to create them, how can the natural laws come to be?" but need only reflect that if left to themselves all things must fare in some way, and this is the way they fare, because there is no other way for them to go than according to causes and conditions. We humans, observing and studying this state of things and incorporating it into our thinking, proceed to call them "laws." But whether they are called laws or not does not change their actual operation. If we were to insist on positing a creator or arbiter of the natural laws we would have even more difficulty, having to ask ourselves under what laws does the maker of the laws live, and who created them, or who controls the creator. If we were to say that no one controls the creator, and that creator is free to act as it pleases, then it could choose to change the laws at any time. (In fact, if there were a creator of the laws, and it was compassionate, it would probably help change many of the minor laws so that, for example, people were not born with physical or mental deficiencies.)

Second, in analyzing the law into many minor laws, we must by no means make the mistake of separating events off as solely results of single laws. In fact, any given event may arise from a combination of these laws. For example, the blooming of the lotus in the day and its folding up at night are not the effects of *utuniyāma* (physical laws) alone, but are also subject to *bījaniyāma* (heredity). When a person sheds tears, it may be mainly because of *cittaniyāma*, such as feelings of gladness or sadness, but it may also be the workings of *utuniyāma*, such as smoke in the eyes. A person may sweat as a result of *utuniyāma*, such as in hot weather, or it may be a result of *cittaniyāma* and *kammaniyāma*, such as in feeling fear or anxiety over some wrong doing. A headache may be a result of *utuniyāma*, such as in hot or muggy weather or being in a stuffy place, or it may be a result of *bījaniyāma*, such as some congenital physical trait, or of *kammaniyāma* in conjunction with *cittaniyāma*, such as feeling depressed or worrying over something.

Third, and most important, here the commentators are showing us that within those natural laws, there is also the law of *kamma*. From the human perspective, *kammaniyāma* is the most important of the natural laws because it directly concerns human beings. Human beings are the creators of *kamma*, and *kamma* in turn shapes the lives and fortunes of human beings. If we divide the spheres of influence in the world into the natural sphere and the human sphere, we find that *kammaniyāma* falls within the human sphere. The other *niyāma* are entirely nature's domain. Human beings are born from nature and are part of nature, but they have a special capacity that is purely their own, and that is this *kammaniyāma*, through which they have created a society and human inventions constituting a world, so to speak, separate from the natural one.

Within the domain of *kammaniyāma*, the essence, the actual entity of *kamma*, is *cetanā* (intention) or volition. Thus, the law of *kamma* is the law that covers the workings of volition, or the world of all thought, fabrication, creation (and destruction) arising from the human hand. Whether or not we deal with other *niyāma*, we stand on *kammaniyāma*, to the extent that however we deal with and use other *niyāma* is dependent on *kammaniyāma*. *Kammaniyāma* is a human capacity, the domain within which human beings have the power to shape, control, and create.

To put it more correctly, we could say that the human capacity to enter into and join other causal factors within the natural processes, leading to the expression that human beings are able to control nature or have conquered it, is all due to this *kammaniyāma*. That is, human beings interact with other *niyāma* by examining their truths and acting on or using them in accordance with their own volition. In addition to that, human beings use volition to define their personal interactions in the way they relate to other people. And while they are interacting with each other, with other things, and with the natural environment, and fashioning the natural world, human beings, or more specifically, their volitions, are also shaping themselves, shaping their own characters, their ways of life and their fortunes.

Because *kammaniyāma* is the leading factor in the shaping of each person's life, directing human society and the outcome of human creation and destruction, as explained above, Buddhism gives great emphasis to its importance, as shown in the Buddhavacana, stating *Kammunā vattatī loko*: "The world fares according to *kamma*," or "The world is moved by *kamma*."[8] *Kamma* is thus one of the most important teachings in Buddhism.

Be that as it may, the inclusion of *kammaniyāma* as one of the five *niyāma* reminds us that *kammaniyāma* is merely one among many natural laws. Thus, when any event arises, we should not just put it all down to *kamma*,[9] as shown above. Even in the Buddha's statement that the world fares according to *kamma*, the reference is to the world of beings—that is, worldly beings. To use modern terminology, it is like saying *kamma* directs society, or *kamma* defines the ways of life in society. It may be said that *kammaniyāma* is only one of the laws in nature, but it is the most important one for human beings.

Apart from the five kinds of natural law mentioned above, there is another kind of law that is specifically a human concern. It is not found in nature, and is not directly concerned with nature. It is the law that human beings establish and fix in the form of social agreements for controlling human behavior, so that we can live together in peace. They are social conventions, comprising standards, decrees, regulations, laws, customs, and rules. This kind of law could be placed at the end of the above list as a sixth kind of law. We could call it social determination,[10] or conventional laws (*samattiniyāma*).[11]

These social regulations are products of human invention, and as such are products of *kamma* and subject to the *kammaniyāma*, but they are simply additions to *kammaniyāma*, not *kammaniyāma* as such. Thus, they do not have the characteristics in terms of causality and natural truth as does *kammaniyāma*. However, because social determination is interconnected with the law of *kamma*, it tends to become confused with it, and misunderstandings frequently arise as a result. Because both kinds of law—*kammaniyāma* and conventional laws—are concerns of human beings and are intimately related with human beings, the subject is an important one deserving discussion in its own right.

To begin with, we might say that in general *kammaniyāma* is the natural law that deals with human deeds, whereas conventional or social laws are created by human beings themselves. They are related to nature only insofar as they are a product of human action or invention. In another sense, through the law of *kamma*, human beings receive the fruits of their actions via the natural processes, whereas in conventional laws human beings take responsibility for their actions via a process established by themselves. Points for consideration other than this will be dealt with in the sections on the problem of good and evil and the problem of the fruition of *kamma* to follow.

Definition of *Kamma*

Etymologically, *kamma* means "work" or "deed," but technically speaking we must define it more specifically as "deeds done with intention" or "deeds willfully done." Deeds that are without intention are not considered to be *kamma* in the technical sense.

This definition is, however, a general one, covering a broad area. If we wish to clarify the content and extent of *kamma*, we must consider an analysis of it into different perspectives, or levels, as follows.

Kamma *as Intention*

Looking at the true essence of *kamma*, or its source, *kamma* is *cetanā*, meaning intention, volition, will, choice, decision, the will to act. Intention or volition is that which instigates, defines, and directs human actions. It is the agent or leader in all kinds of initiation, creation, and invention. Thus, it is the essence of *kamma*, as expressed in the Buddhavacana, *Cetanāham bhikkhave kammaṁ vadāmi*: "Bhikkhus, intention, I say, is *kamma*. Having willed, a person creates *kamma*, through body, speech, and mind."[12]

Kamma *as Conditioning Factor*

Looking outward to other factors—that is, looking into the life process of each individual—we find *kamma* as a factor playing a role in the whole life process, being the agent responsible for conditioning the shape of life and the direction it takes. *Kamma* in this sense corresponds with the word *saṅkhārā*, as it appears in the *paṭiccasamuppāda*, where it is described as "mental conditioners," meaning the factors or qualities of the mind, with intention at the lead, that make the mind good, evil, or neutral, and that fashion thinking and outward expressions through body and speech as *kamma*. Simply translated, this is "thinking" and "mental fabrication." Even in this definition we still take intention as the essential factor, and sometimes we see the word *saṅkhārā* translated simply as "intention."[13]

Kamma *as Personal Responsibility*

Looking further outward, in the sense of life as the collective unit conventionally referred to as a person living in the world, *kamma* refers to the deeds, speech, and thoughts for which each individual must accept responsibility and personally reap the results, be it in the immediate present or from the broader perspective of the past and the future. *Kamma* in this sense conforms to the broad, general definition given above, and it is the sense that is most often referred to, appearing in injunctions encouraging people to accept responsibility for their actions and try to do only good deeds, such as the Buddhavacana:

> "Bhikkhus, these two things are a cause of remorse. What are the two? Some people in this world have not done good, have not done the skillful, have not made merit as a safeguard against fear. They have done only bad, made only foul *kamma*, only harmful *kamma*. They experience remorse as a result, thinking, 'I have not made good *kamma*' or 'I have made only bad kamma'..."[14]

It is worth noting that these days not only is *kamma* almost exclusively taught from this perspective, but it is also treated largely from the perspective of past lives.

Kamma *as Social Activity or Career*

Looking even further outward—that is, from the perspective of activities of the human community—we see *kamma* in its sense of livelihood, work, making a living, and the various human undertakings that are results of volition and creative thought and that lead to the events in society we see around us, as stated in the Buddhavacana of the *Vāseṭṭha Sutta*:

> "Listen, Vāseṭṭha, you should understand it thus: Among people, one who depends on farming for a livelihood is a farmer, not a brahmin...one who makes a living with the arts is an artist...one who makes a living by selling is a merchant...one who makes a living serving others is a servant...one who makes a living through stealing is a thief...one who makes a living by

> the arrow and the sword is a soldier...one who makes a living through the duties of ministering ceremonies is a minister of ceremonies, not a brahmin...one who rules the land is a king, not a brahmin...I call one who has no defilements lingering in the mind, who is free of clinging, a brahmin...One is not a brahmin on account birth, but by *kamma* is one a brahmin, by *kamma* is one not a brahmin. One is a farmer because of *kamma* (work, livelihood, conduct, lifestyle). Whether one is an artist, a merchant, a servant, a thief, a soldier, an officiator of ceremonies, or even a king, it is all because of *kamma*. The wise, seeing *paṭiccasamuppāda*, skilled in *kamma* and its results, see *kamma* as it is in this way. The world fares according to *kamma*. Human beings fare according to *kamma*..."[15]

Be that as it may, even though we have looked at these four different meanings of the word *kamma*, it must be stressed that the meaning always has intention at its core, because intention is what guides our relationships with other things and defines the way we deal with them; whether we make ourselves a channel for the expression of unskillful qualities via desire (*taṇhā*), or greed, hatred, and delusion, or whether we will bring skillful qualities to the fore in creating happiness and benefit, are all at the free discretion of intention. Any act that is without intention has no result in terms of the *kammaniyāma*: that is, it is not subject to the law of *kamma*, but becomes the domain of one of the other *niyāma*, especially *utuniyāma* (physical laws). Such actions have as much ethical significance as earth caving in, a rock falling from a mountain, or a dead branch falling from a tree.

Kinds of *Kamma*

Analyzed in terms of its qualities, *kamma* can be divided into the following two main kinds:[16]

1. *Akusala kamma*: *kamma* that is unskillful, deeds that are not good, bad *kamma*; it refers to actions born from the roots of

unskillfulness (*akusalamūla*), which are greed, hatred, and delusion.

2. *Kusalakamma*: *kamma* that is skillful, good deeds, or good *kamma*; it refers to actions that are born from the roots of skill (*kusalamūla*), which are non-greed, non-hatred, and non-delusion.[17]

If we classify *kamma* according to the paths or channels through which it occurs, there are three:[18]

1. *Kāyakamma*: deeds done with the body, or bodily actions.
2. *Vacīkamma*: deeds done with speech, or verbal actions.
3. *Manokamma*: deeds done with the mind, or mental actions.

When distributed according to both of these principles, there are altogether six kinds of *kamma*: bodily, verbal, and mental *kamma* that is unskillful; and bodily, verbal, and mental *kamma* that is skillful.[19]

Again, *kamma* is classified according to its relation with *vipāka*, or its fruition, into four categories:[20]

1. Black *kamma* with black result: bodily formations (*kāyasaṅkhāra*), verbal formations, and mental formations that are harmful. Examples: killing, stealing, sexual infidelity, lying, and drinking intoxicants.
2. White *kamma* with white result: bodily formations, verbal formations, and mental formations that are not harmful. Examples: practicing in accordance with the ten courses of skillful action (the *kusalakammapatha*).[21]
3. *Kamma* both black and white, with results both black and white: bodily formations, verbal formations, and mental formations that are partly harmful, partly not, such as the actions of people in general.
4. *Kamma* neither black nor white, with results neither black nor white, which leads to the cessation of *kamma*: the intention

to abandon the three kinds of *kamma* mentioned above; in terms of factors, it is developing the seven enlightenment factors (*bojjhaṅga*) or the noble eightfold path (*ariyaṭṭhaṅgikamagga*).

In commentarial literature there is another kind of division of *kamma* that has been adhered to over the ages and in later times has become well known, and that is the twelvefold classification of *kamma*, or four groups of three, described in the Visuddhimagga, but that level of detail will not be included here.

Of the three channels of *kamma*—bodily, verbal, and mental—described above, mental *kamma* is the most important and has the strongest and most far-reaching consequences, as given in the Pali:

> "Listen, Tapassi. Of these three types of *kamma* so analyzed and differentiated by me, I say that mental *kamma* has the heaviest consequences for the committing of evil deeds and the existence of evil deeds, not bodily or verbal *kamma*."[22]

The reason mental *kamma* is considered to be the most significant is that it is the starting point. A person thinks before speaking or acting. Thus, bodily and verbal deeds are derived from mental *kamma*. Mental *kamma* is said to have the most far-reaching and intense consequences because mental *kamma* includes the beliefs, views, theories, attitudes, and values known as *diṭṭhi*. *Diṭṭhi* is what determines people's general behavior, the events of their lives and the direction of society as a whole. Whatever one believes, sees, or prefers, one plans, speaks, instructs, encourages, and acts accordingly. If the view is wrong (*micchādiṭṭhi*), thinking, speech, and actions proceed in a wrong direction; they are also wrong (*micchā*). If the view is right, thinking, speech, and actions proceed in a right direction; they are *sammā*.[23]

For example, a people and society that hold material wealth to be the most valuable thing, the worthiest goal, would strive to seek abundance of material possessions, and hold such abundance to be the gauge for measuring progress, prestige, and honor. Their way of life and the development of their society would assume one form. In contrast, a people and society that valued peace of mind and contentment as its goal would have a different way of life and development.

There are many Buddhavacana describing the importance of right view and wrong view, including the following:

> "Bhikkhus, I see no other condition that is so much a cause for the arising of as yet unarisen unskillful qualities, and for the development and growth of unskillful qualities already arisen, as wrong view...
>
> "Bhikkhus, I see no other condition that is so much a cause for the arising of as yet unarisen skillful qualities, and for the development and growth of skillful qualities already arisen, as right view..."[24]
>
> ---
>
> "Bhikkhus, when a person has wrong view, bodily *kamma* adhered to and put into practice in accordance with that view, verbal *kamma* adhered to and put into practice in accordance with that view, mental *kamma* adhered to and put into practice in accordance with that view, intentions, aspirations, wishes and volitional impulses—all are productive of results that are undesirable, unpleasant, disagreeable, of that which is not beneficial, of suffering. Why is that? Because of that pernicious view. It is like a margosa seed, a seed of the luffa, or a seed of the bitter gourd, planted in moist earth: all the nutriment taken in through the soil and water are wholly converted into a bitter taste, an acrid taste, a foul taste. Why is that? Because the seed is not good...
>
> "Bhikkhus, when a person has right view, bodily *kamma* adhered to and put into practice in accordance with that view, verbal *kamma* adhered to and put into practice in accordance with that view, and mental *kamma* adhered to and put into practice in accordance with that view, intentions, aspirations, wishes, volitional impulses—all are productive of results that are

desirable, pleasant, agreeable, producing benefit, conducive to happiness. Why is that? It is because of those good views. It is like a seed of the sugar cane, a seed of wheat, or a nutmeg seed planted in moist earth: the water and soil taken in as nutriment are wholly converted into sweetness, into refreshment, into a delicious taste. Why is that? Because of the good seed..."[25]

"Bhikkhus, there is one whose birth into this world is for the non-benefit of the many, for the non-happiness of the many, for the decline from benefit and the non-benefit of the many, for the suffering of both devas and men. Who is that person? It is the person with wrong view, with distorted views. One with wrong view leads the many away from truth (*saddhamma*) and into falsehood...

"Bhikkhus, there is one whose birth into this world is for the benefit of the many, for the happiness of the many, for growth and benefit of the many, for the happiness of devas and men. Who is that person? It is the person with right view, who has undistorted views. One with right view leads the many out of falsehood and establishes them in truth...

"Bhikkhus, I see no other condition that is so harmful as wrong view. Of harmful things, bhikkhus, wrong view is the greatest."[26]

"Bhikkhus, what is right view? I say that there are two kinds of right view: the right view (of one) with outflows (*āsava*), which is good *kamma* and of beneficial result to body and mind; and the right view (of one) without outflows, which is transcendent, and is a factor of the noble path.

"And what is the right view that contains outflows, which is good and of beneficial result to body and mind? This is the belief that offerings bear fruit, the practice of giving bears fruit, reverence is of fruit, good and evil *kamma* give appropriate results; there is this world, there is an after-world; there is a mother, there is a father; there are spontaneously arisen beings; there are mendicants and religious seekers who practice well and who

> proclaim clearly the truths of this world and the next. This I call the right view that contains the outflows, which is good, and is of beneficial result to body and mind..."[27]
>
> ---
>
> "All conditions have mind as forerunner, mind as master, are accomplished by mind. If one has a defective mind, whatever one says or does brings suffering in its wake, just as the cart wheel follows the ox's hoof...If one has a clear mind, whatever one says or does brings happiness in its wake, just as the shadow follows its owner."[28]

Criteria for Good and Evil

The definitions of the terms *good* and *evil* are fraught with problems. What, for example, is "good," and how is something said to be good? What is it that we call "evil," and how is something said to be evil? These questions are a problem of language, but in the Buddha's teaching, which is based on the Pali language, the meaning and standards are quite clear, as will now be shown.

The English words *good* and *evil* have broad meanings, particularly the word *good*, which has a broader usage than *evil*. A virtuous and moral person is said to be a good person; eating a delicious food, we might say "This is a good meal" or "The food at this restaurant is good." A block of wood that has fulfilled some purpose might be called a "good" block of wood. In the same way, something that is good to one person might not be good to many others. Some things may be good from one perspective, but not from another. Certain kinds of behavior or expression that are considered good in one area or society might be considered bad in another. There seems to be no agreement, or at least little clarity. It might be necessary to divide "good" into "good" in an ethical sense, "good" in an aesthetic sense, "good" in an economic sense, and so on. The reason for this difficulty and confusion is because it is a concern of values, and the words *good* and *not good* in English can be used with all kinds of values. Therefore, we will not use the words *good* and *not good* or *evil*, thus eliminating the necessity of having to deal with all the different value systems talked about above.

In our study of good and evil in relation to *kamma* the following points should be borne in mind:

- Our study of good and evil will be from the perspective of the *kammaniyāma*, and we will use the specialized terms *kusala* (skillful) and *akusala* (unskillful). These terms have precise meanings and standards.
- The study of *kusala* and *akusala*, in terms of Buddhist ethics, is a concern of *kammaniyāma*, thus the study is in terms of realities (*sabhāva*), not in terms of social values as commonly understood.[29] To study in terms of values is to study on the level of conventional laws, which is a distinctly different domain from that of *kammaniyāma*.
- The faring of *kammaniyāma* is related to other *niyāma* and conventions. Especially noteworthy are that, within the individual, *kammaniyāma* is dependent on *cittaniyāma*, while outwardly *kammaniyāma* is related to conventional laws.

The Meanings of Kusala *and* Akusala

Although *kusala* and *akusala* are sometimes translated as "good" and "evil" or "bad," these are not precise translations. Some things are *kusala* but may not be called good in English, while some things are *akusala* and yet not known as evil in English, as will now be shown.

Kusala and *akusala* are conditions that arise in the mind, producing results initially in the mind, and from there to external actions and physical features. The meanings of *kusala* and *akusala* therefore have the state, the contents, and the events of mind as their basis.

Kusala literally translates as "clever, skillful, wholesome, comfortable, beneficial, fitting, meritorious, fluent, removing affliction, or removing that which is evil and despicable." *Akusala* is defined as the opposite to *kusala*, as in "unskillful, unwholesome," and so on.

There are four explanatory meanings of *kusala* in the teachings that can be taken as fundamental:

1. *Ārogya*: free of illness, a mind that is free of illness, as we say, mental health; it refers to states or factors that are beneficial to mental health, that make the mind healthy, not oppressed or restless, that render the mind strong, fluent, comfortable, well fitted for work.
2. *Anavajja*: free of blame, faultless; it indicates a mind that is whole, perfect, undamaged or containing no impurities, unclouded, clean, immaculate, fresh, glowing.
3. *Kosalasambhūta*: born from wisdom or intelligence; it refers to states in which the mind contains wisdom or qualities that are based on knowledge and understanding, illumination, seeing or being wise to the truth. It conforms with the teaching that *kusala* conditions have *yoniso-manasikāra*, wise attention, as proximate cause (*padaṭṭhāna*).
4. *Sukhavipāka*: resulting in well-being. *Kusala* is a condition that produces happiness. When *kusala* conditions arise in the mind, there is immediately a sense of well-being and ease, without any need to wait for any external reward. Just as when the body is strong and untroubled by disease (*ārogya*), unaffected by blemishes, defects, stains, or pollutants (*anavajja*), and one knows that one is in a secure and safe place (*kosalasambhūta*), there is a sense of well-being and contentment, even without experiencing any particular kind of pleasure.

The meaning of *akusala* should be understood in just the opposite way from above: as the mind that is diseased, defective, arisen from ignorance, and resulting in suffering. Briefly, in another sense it is the state that causes the mind to decline both in quality and efficiency, as opposed to *kusala*, which promotes the quality and efficiency of the mind.

In order to further clarify these concepts, let us expand on the attributes of a mind that is good, disease-free and blameless, and then consider how it is that *kusala* conditions give the mind such qualities, or how *kusala* conditions lead to such states of mind, and how it is that *akusala* conditions cause the mind to lose such qualities, or lead to the decline of such states of mind.

The characteristics of a good mind can be summarized into the following groups.

- *Firm*: resolute, stable, constant, unwavering, focused, undeviating.
- *Pure and clear*: free of stains, not cloudy or gloomy, spotless, immaculate, clear, smooth, bright, luminous.
- *Secure and free*: unhindered, not narrow, unrestricted, not oppressed or repressed, not frustrated, expansive, boundless.
- *Fit for work*: pliant, soft, light, not heavy, malleable, resilient, not brittle, not stubborn, straight, undeviating, not bent, not distorted, not straying.
- *Calm and content*: relaxed, serene, not tense, not oppressed, untroubled, not restless or agitated; not lacking, not craving, contented.

Now that we know the qualities of a whole mind, one that is healthy and free of blemishes and fault, we must now look at the qualities known to be *kusala* and *akusala* and see whether and how the qualities that are *kusala* really do foster the quality and efficiency of the mind and whether and how the qualities that are *akusala* cause the mind to decline in quality and efficiency.

Some examples of *kusala* conditions: *sati*, mindfulness or recollection, the ability to keep the mind on what it should attend to or whatever task is to be done; *mettā*, love, goodwill, the desire for others to be happy; *alobha*, non-greed, absence of desire and attachment, including thoughts of sharing with others; *paññā*, clear knowledge, understanding, being wise to the truth; *passaddhi*, relaxation and calm, coolness of body and mind, non-tension, non-agitation; *kusalachanda*, predilection for that which is wholesome, desire to know and put that knowledge into effect, having a mind that thinks according to causes and conditions; *muditā*, gladness at the good fortune and happiness of others.

Examples of *akusala* conditions are *kāmachanda*, desire to have, to obtain;[30] *byāpāda*, ill will, aversion, or enmity; *thīnamiddha*, depression, despair, melancholy, listlessness, sleepiness; *uddhacca-kukkucca*, distraction, irritation, worry, restlessness, annoyance and anxiety; *vicikicchā*, doubt, irresolution; *kodha*, anger; *issā*, jealousy, vexation when seeing others thrive or prosper; *macchariya*, miserliness or possessiveness.

When there is goodwill, the mind is naturally happy, cheerful, clear, and expansive. This is a condition that is beneficial to the psyche, supporting the quality and efficiency of the mind. Goodwill is therefore *kusala*. *Sati* enables the mind to focus on whatever it is involved in or must do, recollecting the proper course of action in that situation, and helping to prevent *akusala* conditions from arising, thus putting the mind in a condition that is well prepared to work. *Sati* is therefore *kusala*.

Jealousy (*issā*) oppresses the mind, making it uncomfortable and unclear, and obviously damages its quality and health. Jealousy is thus *akusala*. Anger (*kodha*) burns the mind and oppresses it so that it cannot be at ease, and it has a rapid resulting effect on the health of the body. It is clearly *akusala*. Sensual desire (*kāmachanda*), or even general kinds of greed (*lobha*), cause the mind to become obsessive, obstructed, worried or devious, cloudy and unclear. This is also *akusala*.

Once we understand the words *kusala* and *akusala*, we can now understand good *kamma* and bad *kamma*—that is, *kusala kamma* and *akusala kamma*. As already stated, intention is the essence of *kamma*. Thus, an intention that contains *kusala* is a skillful intention and is skillful *kamma*, and an intention that contains *akusala* is unskillful intention and unskillful *kamma*. When those skillful or unskillful intentions are expressed through the body, speech, or mind, they are known as *kusala* and *akusala kamma* through body, speech, and mind respectively, or, alternatively, bodily *kamma*, verbal *kamma* and mental *kamma* that are *kusala* and *akusala*, as the case may be.

Salient Features of Kusala *and* Akusala

Kusala and *akusala* can be catalysts for each other. In some people, or on some occasions, there is faith, or an act of generosity, moral conduct, or wisdom, which are all *kusala*, but then conceit arises on account of those virtues. They are used as a means by which to exalt oneself and disparage others. Conceit and self-exaltation are *akusala*. This is called "*kusala* as a condition for *akusala*." Some people practice meditation and attain *jhāna* states (*kusala*), but then greed arises and they attach to those states (*akusala*). Some people cultivate thoughts of goodwill (*kusala*), looking at others in a positive way, but then, when encountering a desirable object, their *mettā* becomes a channel through which desire can easily arise (*akusala*), and this may be followed by other kinds of *akusala* conditions, such as preferential bias (*chandāgati*). This is called *kusala* as a condition for *akusala*.

Some people have a desire or greed (*rāga*) to be born in heaven and as a result apply themselves to moral conduct; some people have a desire for peace of mind and tranquility, so they devote themselves to cultivating concentration and attain the *jhāna* states; some children have a desire to earn the admiration and praise of their elders, and so strive to be good; some students have a desire to pass their exams in order to get ahead in the world, and are zealous and diligent in their studies;[31] some people experience such intense anger that it seems to burn them up, and they see clearly its harmful effects; some people, angered at an enemy, will sympathize and help others; some people experience intense fear of death and as a result give up possessiveness and become generous and helpful to others; other people experience strong depression that becomes the cause for faith in the Dhamma. These are all called *akusala* as a condition for *kusala*.

A teenage boy is warned by his parents not to consort heedlessly with others, but he takes no notice and is eventually lured into drug addiction by errant friends. On realizing his situation, he is both angered and grieved; then, remembering his parents' warnings, he is moved by their kindness and good wishes (*akusala* as a condition for *kusala*), but this in turn merely aggravates his own anger and self-hatred (*kusala* as a condition for *akusala*).

In these situations, at the moment *kusala* arises, the mind is in a healthy state, while when *akusala* arises, the mind will be in a damaged and oppressed state. These good and bad states of mind may arise and interchange rapidly, so it is necessary to distinguish them on a moment-by-moment basis.

Standards for Gauging Good and Bad Kamma

It has been mentioned that the *kammaniyāma* has an intimate relationship with both *cittaniyāma* and conventional laws, and this close relationship can easily lead to misunderstandings. Thus, in order to understand the subject of *kamma* and the nature of good and evil more clearly, it is necessary to first distinguish the boundaries of these respective *niyāma* and conventions.

Kammaniyāma depends on *cittaniyāma*, and is superimposed, as it were, upon it, but the point of distinction between *kammaniyāma* and *cittaniyāma* is clear: *cetanā* (intention) is the essence and active principle of *kammaniyāma*. *Cetanā* is what makes *kammaniyāma* a separate *niyāma* in its own right, or what allows human beings to have their own independent role, separate from the other *niyāma*, able to build their own world of volition—to such an extent that they put themselves on the same level as nature, and perceive themselves as having their own world of creation and invention separate from nature. Intention needs the mechanics of *cittaniyāma* in order to function, and whenever *cetanā* creates an act of *kamma*, the process of fruition must also work through *cittaniyāma* in order to proceed.

An analogy can be made of a person driving a motor boat. The "driver" is intention, which is in the domain of *kammaniyāma*; the entire boat engine is comparable to the mechanics and factors of the mind that come within *cittaniyāma*. The driver must depend on the boat engine, but where and how the boat engine will lead the "boat," life and the body, is entirely at the discretion of the "driver" (intention), and it is the driver who takes responsibility. The driver depends on and makes use of the boat, and also takes responsibility for the welfare of the boat, both vessel and engine. In the same way, *kammaniyāma* both depends on and makes use of *cittaniyāma*, and also accepts responsibility for the welfare of life, both body and mind.

As far as the relationship between *kammaniyāma* and *cittaniyāma* goes there is not much problem, because these are not matters in which people take much interest, and regardless of whether or not human beings take any interest or understand it, or even know that it exists, the process invisibly continues on its way.

The issue that is the problem and source of confusion is the relationship between *kammaniyāma* and conventional laws, which tends to cause problems with good and evil: what is good, what is evil? Are there really good and evil actions? What is the standard for measuring good and evil? We often hear it said that good and evil are human or social inventions: one and the same action may be regarded as good in one location or time but bad in another. One and the same action may be one community's recommended behavior but another's prohibition.

For example, some religions teach that to kill animals for food is not bad, while others teach that harming animals in any way is never good. To say that good and evil are matters of human and social convention holds a good degree of truth. Even so, it has no bearing on the *kammaniyāma* in any way, and it should not be a point of confusion with *kammaniyāma*. The "good" and "evil" of social conventions are matters of conventional laws or social determination. The "good" and "evil," or more correctly *kusala* and *akusala*, of *kammaniyāma* are concerns of *kammaniyāma*. Even though the two are related, they are in fact separate, and there is a very clear dividing line between them. The confusion results from mixing the good and evil of conventional laws with the good and evil, or *kusala* and *akusala*, of *kammaniyāma*.

That which is at once the builder of that relationship and the point of distinction between this natural law (*niyāma*) and the convention is the same as that between *cittaniyāma* and *kammaniyāma*—intention, or volition. As to how this is so, let us now consider.

In terms of the law of *kamma*, the conventions made by society may be divided into two types. First are *those conventions that have no direct relationship to* kusala *and* akusala *of the* kammaniyāma but are determined by society for its own specific objectives, such as to enable its people to live together harmoniously and in peace and happiness. Conventions that have no direct relationship to *kusala* and *akusala* come in the form of mutual agreements or contracts. In this respect, the conventions may indeed be instruments for creating social harmony or they may not. They may indeed be beneficial to society or they may be harmful. This depends on whether or not those conventions are established with sufficiently broad knowledge and understanding, or whether or not the authority who established them was honest. These kinds of conventions take various forms: they may be traditions, customs, or laws. "Good" and "evil" in this case are strictly matters of conventional laws. They may change and take different forms, but however they change or vary is not a concern of *kammaniyāma*, and must not be confused with it. And when a person disobeys or violates these conventions, however that person is punished by society is also a matter of conventional laws, not *kammaniyāma*.

With this distinction in mind, we can now consider the area in which these conventional laws may encroach on the domain of *kammaniyāma*. When a member of the society does not conform to a convention, opposes it, or violates it, that person will be acting on some kind of intention.[32] This intention is the first step in *kammaniyāma* and is a concern of *kammaniyāma*. In many societies there may be an attempt to ascertain this intention and incorporate it into the judgment of a case. However, that is a concern of conventional laws, indicating that that particular society is wise and knows how to utilize the *kammaniyāma*. It is not a concern of *kammaniyāma*. As for *kammaniyāma*, regardless of whether society investigates the intention or not, or even whether or not society is aware of the violation, *kammaniyāma* goes into action from the instant the person conceives the intention, and on the basis of that intention commits the violation. That is, the process of fruition has been set in motion, and the person begins to receive results from that moment on.

Simply speaking, the deciding factor in *kammaniyāma* is whether the intention is *kusala* or *akusala*. Generally speaking, or in most cases, not to conform with any social regulation can only be said to constitute no violation, or intention to violate, when that society agrees to abandon or reform that convention. In other words, only then will there be no violation of the public agreement.

This can be illustrated by a simple example. Suppose two people decide to live together. In order to render their living arrangement smooth, convenient, and mutually beneficial, they establish a set of regulations, such as having the evening meal together even though they work in different places and return from work at different times. As it would be impractical to wait for each other indefinitely, they agree that each of them should not eat before 7 p.m. Of those two people, one likes cats and doesn't like dogs, while the other likes dogs and doesn't like cats. For mutual peace of mind, they agree not to bring any kind of pet into the house.

Having agreed on these regulations, if either of those two people acts in contradiction to them, there is the arising of an intention to violate, and *kamma* arises in accordance with the *kammaniyāma*, even though in fact eating food before 7 p.m., or bringing pets into a house, cannot be said to be intrinsically good or evil. Another couple might even establish regulations that are directly opposite to these. And if later one of those people considers their regulations to be not helpful to their living together, that person could raise the matter with the other person and they could together agree to abandon or correct that regulation. Only then would any nonconformity on that person's part be free of the intention to violate or offend. The bhikkhus' discipline (Vinaya) is of this nature. This is how the distinction and the connection between "good," "evil," "right," and "wrong," which are changing and uncertain social conventions, and the faring of *kusala* and *akusala* in the *kammaniyāma*, which is fixed, are to be understood.

The second type of conventions made by society are *those conventions that relate to* kusala *and* akusala *in the* kammaniyāma *process.* In such cases, society may define good and evil with or without a clear understanding of *kusala* and *akusala*—that is, what is of benefit and what is harmful to the human psyche—but regardless of how society does define them, the proceeding of the *kammaniyāma* continues along its normal course regardless. It does not change along with those social conventions. For example, suppose a society considered that taking addictive drugs and intoxicants was a good thing and was to be encouraged, that having extreme emotions was good, that people should be aroused, incited, and triggered with desire and ambition, and therefore get a lot of things done; that killing people of other societies was good, or, on a lesser scale, that to kill animals is not bad. In these examples, the good and evil of conventional laws are at odds with *kusala* and *akusala* in the *kammaniyāma*. Looked at from a social perspective, those conventions or attitudes may cause both positive and negative results. For example, lives filled with stress and constant competition with others may cause a society to leap forward in terms of material development, but also produce much mental illness and heart disease, there may be a high suicide rate and an unusually high number of other kinds of mental and social problems. Many of these kinds of repercussions on the social level may be traced to *kammaniyāma*.

Conventional laws and *kammaniyāma* are separate and distinct. The fruits in *kammaniyāma* proceed according to the law of *kammaniyāma*, independent of any social conventions that are at odds with it, as explained above. However, because there is some relationship between the convention and the law, one who is practicing correctly in terms of the *kammaniyāma*, by acting according to what is *kusala*, might still experience problems from contrary social determinations. For example, one who lives in a society that favors taking intoxicants but who abstains from taking them receives the fruits dictated by the *kammaniyāma*—that person does not experience the loss of mental clarity due to those intoxicants—it is true, but in the social context, as opposed to the *kammaniyāma*, that person may be ridiculed or ostracized, called a weakling, or looked at in some other unfavorable social light. And even within the *kammaniyāma*, that person may experience problems from his or her intentional opposition to this social convention, in the form of mental stress, more or less depending on that person's wisdom and ability to free the mind from its conflict.

Civilized societies with intelligent citizens tend to make use of the experience accumulated from previous generations, who have made a study of what is truly beneficial and what is harmful to the human psyche, to lay down the standards and regulations in relation to the good and evil of conventional laws in conformity with the principle of *kusala* and *akusala* of *kammaniyāma*. The ability to establish social principles in conformity with the principles of *kammaniyāma* would seem to be a sound gauge for true progress in a society.

In this respect, when we need to appraise any convention in terms of good or evil, it would best be considered on two levels: first, in terms of conventional laws, by determining whether or not it has a beneficial result to society, and second, in terms of the *kammaniyāma*, by determining whether or not that convention is *kusala*—that is, beneficial to the psyche.

Some conventions, even though long held by societies, are in fact not at all beneficial to them, even from the perspective of conventional laws, let alone from the perspective of the *kammaniyāma*. Those societies should agree to abandon such conventions, or it may be necessary for a wise being with a pure heart to compassionately lead the people away from them, as did the Buddha in respect to the traditions of sacrifice and the caste system in ancient Indian society.

In a case where consideration reveals a regulation or convention to be helpful from the social perspective, leading to prosperity for the human community but not in conformity with the principle of *kusala* according to the *kammaniyāma*, it might be questioned whether the people of that society have not gone astray and mistaken that which is not truly beneficial to society as being beneficial. They may be delighting in a wrong kind of progress, one that seems favorable in the short term but that will lead to harmful repercussions in the long term. Something that is truly beneficial should be harmonious from both the perspectives of conventional laws and *kammaniyāma*.

There is a general principle that something that is beneficial to the psyche should also be beneficial on a general level: that is, if it is beneficial to one life it should be beneficial to all. In this regard we can take a lesson from the creation of material progress. Human beings have striven for material progress and prosperity, with the understanding that material abundance and convenience will lead them to the highest welfare and happiness. In their striving for material progress, they have destroyed many lives and ecosystems that obstructed their progress. In the end we find that our actions were in large part done with delusion: while society appears to be prosperous, we have created so many physical dangers that if we continue on this path it may spell our destruction.

In assessing what is good and what is evil, on a practical level the Buddha taught to reflect on *kusala* and *akusala* as the basic standard. From there he expanded outward to allow the use of our own appreciation in relation to good and evil, known as conscience (*manodhamma*), and referring to the dicta of the wise as supplementary standards (these two are the basis of shame (*hiri*) and fear of wrongdoing (*ottappa*)). In addition, he recommended pondering the fruits of deeds that will arise for oneself and for others, or for the individual and society. If that is still not clear, one can look simply at the results of actions, even those that arise in accordance with social conventions. For most people investigating according to these three standards represents a multi-faceted method of investigation for gaining the most thorough understanding.

Prior to addressing the question of the fruition of *kamma* in the next section, the following references from the Pali canon are offered in support of the points just dealt with.

> "What are skillful (*kusala*) conditions? They are the three roots of skillfulness—non-greed, non-aversion and non-delusion—

the *khandhas* of feeling, perception, mental formations and consciousness that contain those roots of skillfulness; bodily *kamma*, verbal *kamma*, and mental *kamma* that have those roots as their base: these are skillful conditions.

"What are unskillful (*akusala*) conditions? They are the three roots of unskillfulness—greed, aversion and delusion—and all the defilements that are based in those roots of unskillfulness; the *khandhas* of feeling, perception, mental formations and consciousness that contain those roots of unskillfulness; bodily *kamma*, verbal *kamma*, and mental *kamma* that have those roots of unskillfulness as their base: these are unskillful conditions."[33]

"There are two kinds of danger, the overt danger and the covert danger.

"What are the 'overt dangers'? These are lions, tigers, panthers, bears, leopards, wolves...bandits...eye diseases, ear diseases, nose diseases...cold, heat, hunger, thirst, defecation, urination, contact with gadflies, mosquitoes, wind, sun, and crawling creatures: these are called 'overt dangers.'

"What are the 'covert dangers'? They are bad bodily, verbal, and mental actions (*kāya-vacī-mano ducarita*); the hindrances of sensual desire, ill will, sloth and torpor, restlessness and worry, and doubt; greed (*rāga*), aversion, and delusion; anger, enmity, pettiness (negating or hiding the goodness of others), arrogance, jealousy, meanness, deception, boastfulness, stubbornness, contention, pride, scorn, delusion, heedlessness; the mass of defilements, the mass of bad habits; the mass of confusion; the mass of lust; the mass of trouble; the mass of thoughts that are unskillful: these are the 'covert dangers.'

"They are called 'dangers': for what reason are they called dangers? For the reason that they overwhelm...for the reason that they cause decline...for the reason that they are a shelter.

"Why are they called dangers in that they overwhelm? Because those dangers force down, tyrannize, overwhelm, repress, weaken, and crush a person...

"Why are they called dangers in that they cause decline? Because those dangers bring about the decline of skillful qualities...

"Why are they called dangers in that they are a shelter? Because those evil, unskillful qualities born from within take shelter within one, just as a hole-dwelling animal takes shelter in a hole, a water-dwelling animal takes shelter in water, or a tree-dwelling animal takes shelter in trees..."

"When greed, aversion, and delusion arise within his mind, they destroy the evil-minded one, just as the bamboo flower spells the ruin of the bamboo plant..."[34]

"See here, Your Majesty. These three things arise in the world not for welfare or benefit, but for suffering, for an unpleasant abiding. What are those three? They are greed...aversion... delusion..."[35]

"Bhikkhus, there are these three roots of unskillfulness. What are the three? They are the greed root of unskillfulness, the aversion root of unskillfulness and the delusion root of unskillfulness...

"Greed itself is unskillful. When a person is possessed by greed, the *kamma* created through body, speech, or mind is also unskillful. When a person is possessed by greed, overwhelmed by greed, has a mind infested with greed, that person seeks ways to cause trouble for others by killing them, imprisoning them, dispossessing them, decrying them, and banishing them, thinking, 'I am powerful, I am mighty.' That is also unskillful. These many kinds of evil, unskillful qualities, arising from greed, having greed as their cause, having greed as their source, having greed as condition, arise for that person in this way.

"Aversion itself is unskillful; when a person is possessed by aversion, the *kamma* created through body, speech, or mind is also unskillful. When a person is possessed by aversion... that person seeks ways to cause trouble for others...That is also unskillful. These many kinds of evil, unskillful qualities...arise for that person in this way.

"Delusion itself is unskillful; when a person is possessed by delusion, the *kamma* created through body, speech, or mind is also unskillful. When a person is possessed by delusion... that person seeks ways to cause trouble for others...That is also unskillful. These many kinds of evil, unskillful qualities...arise for that person in this way.

"One who is like this, overwhelmed by the evil, unskillful qualities arisen from greed...aversion...delusion, whose mind is infected, experiences suffering, stress, agitation, and anxiety in the present. At death, at the breaking up of the body, that person can expect a woeful bourn, just as a sal tree, a crepe myrtle tree, or a soapberry tree that is entwined to the top with three creepers comes to non-abundance, to destruction, to decline, to annihilation...

"Bhikkhus, there are these three roots of skillfulness. What are the three? They are the non-greed root of skillfulness, the non-aversion root of skillfulness, and the non-delusion root of skillfulness..."[36]

"Bhikkhus, there are three root causes for the origination of deeds [*kamma*]. What are the three? They are greed...aversion...delusion...

"Whatever *kamma* is performed out of greed...aversion... delusion, is born from greed...aversion...delusion, has greed... aversion...delusion as its root and as its source, that *kamma* is unskillful, that *kamma* is harmful, that *kamma* has suffering as a result, that *kamma* is for the creation of more *kamma* (*kammasamudaya*), not the cessation of *kamma* (*kammanirodha*).

"Bhikkhus, there are these three root causes for the origination of deeds. What are the three? They are non-greed...non-aversion...non-delusion...

"Whatever *kamma* is performed out of non-greed...non-aversion...non-delusion, is born of non-greed...non-aversion... non-delusion, has non-greed...non-aversion...non-delusion as its root and as its source, that *kamma* is skillful, that *kamma* is not harmful, that *kamma* has happiness as a result, that *kamma* is for the cessation of *kamma*, not the creation of more *kamma*..."[37]

"Listen, Kālāmas, when you know for yourselves that these things are unskillful, these things are harmful, these things are censured by the wise, these things, if acted upon, will not be for benefit but for suffering, then you should abandon them.

"Kālāmas, how do you consider this matter? Do greed...aversion...delusion, having arisen in a person, arise for benefit or for non-benefit?"

[Answer: "Non-benefit, Lord."]

"One who is gone to greed...who is angered...deluded, who is overwhelmed by greed...aversion...delusion, whose mind is so infected, deprives of life, takes things not given, commits adultery, utters falsehoods, or encourages others to do so, which is for non-benefit, non-welfare and suffering for a long time to come."

[Answer: "That is true, Lord."]

"Kālāmas, how say you, are those things skillful or unskillful?"

[Answer: "They are unskillful, Lord."]

"Are they harmful or not harmful?"

[Answer: "Harmful, Lord."]

"Praised by the wise, or censured?"

[Answer: "Censured by the wise, Lord."]

"If these things are acted upon, will they be for harm and suffering, or not? What do you think about this?"

[Answer: "When acted upon, these things are for harm and suffering, this is our view on this matter."]

"Thus, Kālāmas, when I said, 'Come, Kālāmas, do not believe simply on the basis of word of mouth...nor simply because this recluse is your teacher, but when you know for yourselves that these things are unskillful...then you should abandon them,' it is on account of this that I thus spoke."[38]

The following passage is an exchange between King Pasenadi Kosala and the Venerable Ānanda, a series of questions and answers relating to the meaning of good and evil, from which it can be seen that Venerable Ānanda incorporates all the standards mentioned above.

> King: Venerable Sir, when people who are foolish, unintelligent, not thinking, not considering, speak in praise or criticism of others, I do not give weight to their praise or criticism. As for those who are learned, clever and astute, wise, who think and consider before praising or criticizing others, I give weight to their praise and criticism.
>
> Venerable Ānanda, what kinds of bodily conduct...verbal conduct...mental conduct would be censured by wise recluses and brahmins?
>
> Ānanda: It is that conduct through body...speech...mind that is unskillful, Your Majesty.
>
> King: What is that conduct of body...speech...mind that is unskillful?
>
> Ānanda: It is that conduct of body...speech...mind that is harmful.
>
> King: What is that conduct of body...speech...mind that is harmful?
>
> Ānanda: It is that conduct of body...speech...mind that is oppressive.[39]
>
> King: What is that conduct of body...speech...mind that is oppressive?
>
> Ānanda: It is that conduct of body...speech...mind that results in suffering.
>
> King: What is that conduct of body...speech...mind that results in suffering?
>
> Ānanda: It is that conduct of body...speech...mind that serves to hurt oneself, to hurt others, or to hurt both oneself and others, [as a result of which] unskillful qualities increase considerably and skillful qualities decrease and wane. Your Majesty, just this kind of conduct of body...speech...mind is censured by wise recluses and brahmins.
>
> Venerable Ānanda then answered the king's questions in relation to skillful qualities in the same way, summarizing with:

"That conduct of body...speech...mind that results in happiness, is the conduct...that does not serve to hurt oneself, to hurt others, or to hurt both sides, [as a result of which] unskillful qualities decrease and wane and skillful qualities increase considerably. Your Majesty, just this conduct of body...speech...mind is not censured by wise recluses and brahmins."[40]

"One wanting and desirous...angered...deluded...overwhelmed by desire...aversion...delusion, with mind so infected, plans for one's own hurt, plans for the hurt of others, plans for the hurt of both sides, and suffers misery in mind. Having given up desire...aversion...delusion, that person does not plan for the hurt of oneself, does not plan for the hurt of others, does not plan for the hurt of both sides, and does not have to suffer misery in mind.

"One wanting and desirous...angered...deluded...acts dishonestly (*ducarita*) through body...speech...mind. Having given up desire...aversion...delusion, that person does not act dishonestly though body...speech...mind.

"One wanting and desirous...angered...deluded...with mind infected, does not know as it is one's own welfare...the welfare of others...the welfare of both sides. Having given up desire... aversion...delusion, that person knows as it is one's own welfare...the welfare of others...the welfare of both sides."[41]

"The *kamma* one makes one sees for oneself."[42]

"Bad *kamma* is like freshly squeezed milk: it does not 'go off' immediately. Bad *kamma* follows and burns the evildoer just like hot coals buried in ash."[43]

"One who previously made bad *kamma*, but who reforms and counters it with good *kamma*, brightens the world like the moon emerging from the clouds."[44]

"The good *kamma* one has made is like a good friend at one's side."[45]

"Ānanda, [in regard to] that bad bodily conduct, bad verbal conduct, and bad mental conduct wholly discouraged by me, whoever commits them can expect the following consequences: one is blameworthy to oneself;[46] the wise, on careful consideration, find one censurable; an evil reputation spreads; one dies confused; and at death, on the breaking up of the body, one goes to the nether realms, the woeful bourns, hell...

"Ānanda, [in regard to] that good bodily conduct, good verbal conduct, and good mental conduct wholly encouraged by me, whoever practices it can expect the following results: one is not blameworthy to oneself; the wise, after careful consideration, find one praiseworthy; a good reputation spreads; one dies unconfused; and at death, on the breaking up of the body, one attains a pleasant bourn, heaven..."[47]

"Bhikkhus, abandon unskillful qualities. Unskillful qualities can be abandoned. If it were impossible to abandon unskillful qualities, I would not tell you to do so...but because unskillful qualities can be abandoned, thus do I tell you...Moreover, if the abandoning of those unskillful qualities was not for benefit but for suffering, I would not say, 'Bhikkhus, abandon unskillful qualities,' but because the abandoning of unskillful qualities is for benefit and happiness, thus do I say, 'Bhikkhus, abandon unskillful qualities.'

"Bhikkhus, cultivate skillful qualities. Skillful qualities can be cultivated. If it were impossible to cultivate skillful qualities, I would not tell you to do so...but because skillful qualities can be cultivated, thus do I tell you...Moreover, if the cultivation of those skillful qualities was not conducive to benefit but to suffering, I would not say to you, 'Cultivate skillful qualities.' But because the cultivation of skillful qualities is conducive to benefit and happiness, thus do I say, 'Bhikkhus, cultivate skillful qualities.'"[48]

"Bhikkhus, there are those things that should be abandoned with the body, not through speech; there are those things that should be abandoned through speech, not with the body; there are those things that should be abandoned not with the body, not through speech, but must be clearly seen with wisdom [in the mind] before they can be abandoned.

"What are those things that should be abandoned with the body, not through speech? Herein, a bhikkhu in this teaching and discipline [Dhamma Vinaya] incurs certain offenses that are unskillful through the body. His wise companions in the holy life, having considered the matter, say to him, 'Venerable friend, you have incurred certain offenses that are unskillful with the body. It would be well if you were to abandon this wrong bodily conduct and cultivate good bodily conduct.' He, being thoughtfully remonstrated with by his wise companions in the holy life, abandons that wrong bodily conduct and cultivates good bodily conduct. This is a condition that should be abandoned by body, not through speech.

"What are the things that should be abandoned through speech, not with the body? Herein, a bhikkhu in this teaching and discipline incurs certain offenses that are unskillful through speech. His wise companions in the holy life, having considered the matter, say to him: 'Venerable friend, you have incurred certain offenses that are unskillful through speech. It would be well if you were to abandon this wrong verbal conduct and cultivate good verbal conduct.' He, being thoughtfully remonstrated with by his wise companions in the holy life, abandons that wrong verbal conduct and cultivates good verbal conduct. This is a condition that should be abandoned through speech, not by body.

"What are the things that should be abandoned not by body and not through speech, but must be clearly seen with wisdom before they can be abandoned? They are greed...aversion... delusion...anger...enmity...disdain...arrogance...meanness. These should be abandoned neither by the body nor through

> speech, but must be clearly understood with wisdom before they can be abandoned…"[49]

Problems Relating to the Fruition of *Kamma*

The point of most contention in relation to *kamma* is its fruition, where doubts exist about the truth of the principle, "Good actions bring good results, bad actions bring bad results." Some people try to produce evidence to show that in the "real world" there are many people who obtain good results from bad actions and bad results from good actions. In fact, this kind of problem arises from confusion between *kammaniyāma* and conventional laws, by confounding the workings of the law (*niyāma*) with the convention, not clearly separating and defining their respective areas. This can be seen from the way people misunderstand even the meaning of the words "Good actions bring good results; bad actions bring bad results." Instead of understanding the meaning of "good actions bring good results" as "doing good, one attains the good," "in doing good there is goodness," "doing good is a cause for the arising of goodness," or "doing good deeds brings about good results in accordance with the *kammaniyāma*," they take the meaning to be "doing good, one gets good things" or "having done good, one attains an advantage or desired material gain." Bearing this in mind, it is necessary to consider the matter in more depth.

The point that causes doubt is confusion about the distinction, and the relationship, between *kammaniyāma* and conventional laws. To clarify this point, let us first consider the fruition of *kamma* on four different levels:

1. The inner, mental level: the results *kamma* has within the mind itself, the accumulation of the qualities of *kusala* and *akusala* and the quality and efficiency of the mind, the influence *kamma* has in shaping thinking, biases, preferences, likes, and experiences of happiness, suffering, and so on.

2. The level of character: the results *kamma* has in terms of building character and affecting mannerisms, bearing, attitudes, responses, relationships with other people, and with situations and surroundings in general. The results on this level are derived from the first level, and their domains overlap, but here we are considering them separately in order to further clarify how they produce results.
3. The level of individual life experiences: how *kamma* sways the events of a person's life, causing one to have both desirable and undesirable experiences and to undergo external consequences, encountering prosperity and decline, failure and success, wealth, status, happiness, praise and the losses that are their opposites, which are together known as the *lokadhamma* (worldly conditions). The results of *kamma* on this level can be seen in two aspects:
   - consequences arising from environmental factors other than people.
   - consequences arising from factors of other people and society.
4. The social level: the results individual and collective *kamma* has on the faring of society, such as the occurrence of decline, prosperity, harmony, difficulty and trouble for human communities, including the results of human actions on the environment that bounce back on humanity.

We can clearly see that levels 1 and 2, the results within the mind and character, are the fields in which *kammaniyāma* is dominant. The third level is where *kammaniyāma* and conventional laws meet, and it is here that confusion arises, creating the problem we will now consider. The fourth level, while important, is beyond the scope of this discussion.

Generally, when people consider the results of their actions, or examine other people to see whether their good actions have led to good results or bad actions to bad results, they tend to take note only of the results on the third level, that part of the events of life that is affected by external consequences. This means they overlook results on levels one and two, even though these first two levels are of great importance. They are important both in themselves, comprising the happiness or suffering of the mind, inner strength or weakness, and the maturity or weakness of the faculties, and also as major sources of results on the third level. That is to say, that portion of results on the third level that comes into the domain of the *kammaniyāma* is derived from the *kamma* results on the first and second levels.

For instance, through results on the first level, the individual's states of mind—interests, preferences, tendencies, the search for happiness or internal handling of suffering—influence one to look at any given object or matter in a certain way, draw one toward certain situations and responses, and lead one to conduct one's life in a certain way, further leading to particular experiences, consequences, and responses. In particular they produce results on the second level (character), which in turn promote results on the first level in producing results on the third level, as already explained. This includes the direction and manner of one's actions, whether one completes an action, one's persistence with it, the particular obstacles in face of which one will yield and in face of which one will persist, whether one succeeds, how coarse or refined the action is, and even how one appears to others, which in turn reflects back on one in the form of the help, cooperation, or opposition they give. This is not to deny other factors, particularly social ones, in influencing one via the *kammaniyāma*, but here we are concerned solely with observing the *kammaniyāma* from the inside outward. Fruits of *kamma* on the third level, in the permutations of life and their consequences, are in fact a concern of *kammaniyāma*, and mostly derived from fruits on the first and second levels.

For example, if a person loves one's job, works honestly and diligently, and manages the work well, we could expect that person to do good work and be well rewarded, at least better than another person who was lazy or dishonest. Honest and capable public servants who applied themselves to their duties and obtained good results would be expected to advance in their careers, at least more so than those who were inept and irresolute in their duties. But that is not always the case. This is because events on the third level do not always arise from *kammaniyāma*. There are factors involved from other *niyāma* and conventional laws, especially social conventions. If we look only at *kammaniyāma*, not considering all the other factors, and fail to distinguish the areas of relationship between the *niyāma* and the conventions, we will become confused, and the idea "Good actions bring bad results, bad actions bring good results" will follow.

If there were only *kammaniyāma* working on its own, there would be no problem, and results would arise directly in consequence of the deed. For example, if you are interested in learning, and pick up a book and read it attentively to the end, you obtain knowledge. But sometimes you may feel tired, have a headache, or the weather is too hot, and you can't finish the book, or you read it but don't take it in. Or an accident may occur while reading so that you can't finish the book.

However, we must realize that, for human beings, *kammaniyāma* is undoubtedly the core determining factor for life's permutations, the leading factor for receiving the good and bad results in life. If you have suffered disappointments, or see other people doing good deeds but not getting good results, even without clearly looking at all the determining factors in other areas, you can still reflect simply: "If I hadn't done that good *kamma* my situation would probably be much worse than this," or "If they hadn't done any good *kamma*, they would probably have fallen even further down." By looking in this way, you may begin to gradually see things more clearly, realizing that, come what may, good deeds are never void of consequence. You can also delve into the results within the mind and on character as explained above.

As to the misunderstandings of the fruition of *kamma*, let us begin by looking at and correcting them with the passage that describes the basic principle itself. The phrase that Thai people like to repeat, "Good actions bring good results, bad actions bring bad results," is based on a Buddhist proverb:[50]

Yādisaṁ vapate bījaṁ *Tādisaṁ labhate phalaṁ*
Kalyāṇakārī kalyāṇaṁ *Pāpakārī ca pāpakaṁ*

Which translates as "As the seed sown, so the fruit: the doer of good receives good; the doer of bad receives bad."

The verse is given in the form of *isibhāsita* (words of a sage) and *bodhisattabhāsita* (words of a *bodhisatta*), recounted by the Buddha in the Tipiṭaka. The statement succinctly and clearly expresses the Buddhist doctrine of *kamma*.

Note that in the first part of the analogy, *bījaniyāma*, the law of heredity, is used. Simply by clearly considering this illustration we can immediately dispel all the confusion between *kammaniyāma* and conventional laws. That is to say, the phrase "As the seed, so the fruit" describes the natural law pertaining to plants: if tamarind is planted, you get tamarind; if grapes are planted, you get grapes; if lettuce is planted, you get lettuce. It does not at all describe results in terms of conventional laws, such as in "If tamarind is planted, you get money" or "Planting lettuce will make you rich," which are stages of different processes. *Bījaniyāma* and conventional laws become related when, for example, you plant grapes, harvest the grapes, the time is one in which grapes are in demand, your grapes fetch a good price, and you get rich that year. At another time you plant watermelons and reap a good harvest, but that year many people plant watermelons, watermelons are in abundance, supply exceeds demand, the price of watermelons goes down, and you make a loss and have to throw away a lot of watermelons. Apart from the factor of market demand, there may also be other factors, such as the middle man and price manipulation, but the essential point is to see the immutability of the *bījaniyāma*, and the domains of *bījaniyāma* and conventional laws—both in their distinction and their relationship.

In the same way, people tend to confuse the *kammaniyāma* and conventional laws, saying, "Good actions bring good results" in the sense that "Good actions will make us rich," or "Good actions will earn a promotion," which seems quite reasonable, but does not always eventuate. It is like saying, "Plant mangoes and you'll get a lot of money," "Planting coconuts will make you rich," or "They planted custard apples, that's why they're poor." Such statements may or may not be true, but the truth is that they jump ahead of the facts and do not describe the entire process. Statements like this may be sufficient to communicate on an everyday level, but if you wanted to speak accurately, you would have to analyze the pertinent factors in more detail.

Factors Affecting the Fruition of Kamma

The way *kammaniyāma* gives results on the level of life events, leading to various events and responses from the outside, sometimes satisfactory, sometimes not, is said in the canon to be subject to four pairs of factors, known as the four advantages (*sampatti*) and the four disadvantages (*vipatti*).[51]

Sampatti translates simply as "asset," and refers to a ripeness and readiness of factors to support and facilitate the ripening of good *kamma* and prevent the ripening of bad *kamma*. In brief, *sampatti* are factors that help to augment good *kamma*. There are four *sampatti*, as follows:

1. *Gatisampatti*: The asset of birthplace, endowment of birthplace, or support of birthplace; to be born into a suitable or favorable existence, realm, locality or country; in the short term, to conduct one's life in, or go to, a favorable place.
2. *Upadhisampatti*: The asset of body, endowment of body, or support of body; for example, to have a beautiful or imposing appearance, an attractive face and bearing that are endearing, likable, or inspiring; a strong and healthy body.
3. *Kālasampatti*: The asset of time or occasion, endowment of time, or support of time; to be born at a time when the country is at peace and harmonious, the government is good, people live virtuously, when good people are praised and bad people not; on a short-term level, it means to do things at the right time, at the right moment.

4. *Payogasampatti*: The asset of enterprise, endowment of enterprise, or support of enterprise; doing what is appropriate to the need; doing what accords with one's skill or capability; doing something that fulfills and accords with the principles or criteria concerned, not half-heartedly, sloppily, or wrongly; knowing how to organize or carry out the task.

Vipatti translates simply as defect or failure, and refers to a fault of factors so that they do not support the ripening of good *kamma* but open the way for the ripening of bad *kamma*. There are four *vipatti*, as follows:

1. *Gativipatti*: Defectiveness of birthplace, or failure of birthplace; to be born into an existence, realm, locality, country, or environment that is unsuitable or unbeneficial; a lifestyle or destination that is unsupportive.
2. *Upadhivipatti*: Defectiveness of the body, or failure of the body; having a body that is disabled, sickly, of unpleasant appearance, having an ugly bearing that does not inspire praise, having bad health, or being subject to illness.
3. *Kālavipatti*: Defectiveness of time, or failure of time; to be born into an age in which the country is in the throes of a crisis, or there is social unrest, bad government, a society fallen from moral ways, which is full of oppression, praises bad people and suppresses the good. This also includes doing things at the wrong time, choosing the wrong moment.
4. *Payogavipatti*: Defectiveness of enterprise, or failure of enterprise; for example, putting effort into a misguided enterprise or concern; doing something for which one is not suited or qualified; or doing something half-heartedly.

The first pair consists of *gatisampatti* and *gativipatti*. *Gatisampatti*: being born into an affluent locality with good educational services, even without being of particularly high intelligence or diligence, one attains a better education and can procure a higher position in society than another person who, although brighter and more diligent, is born into a backwoods community. *Gativipatti*: At a time when a Buddha is born into the world and expounding the Dhamma, if one is born in a primitive jungle, or as a being in hell, one has no chance of hearing the teachings; possessing learning and ability but living in a locality or community where such things are not appreciated, one cannot fit in with others, and one is scorned and lives miserably.[52]

The second pair consists of *upadhisampatti* and *upadhivipatti*. *Upadhisampatti*: Being born with a beautiful and attractive appearance, even in a poor family living in a remote area, one's physical appearance can be a stepping stone to a position in which one attains honor and happiness. *Upadhivipatti*: being born in a locality or family that is rich and well-off, but being born with a major disability, one may not receive the honor and happiness befitting one's position; where two people have otherwise equal attributes, but one is imposing or beautiful while the other is ugly or sickly, in cases where the body is a qualifying condition, the person with the better physical condition may be chosen.

The third pair consists of *kālasampatti* and *kālavipatti*. *Kālasampatti*: Being sincere, honest and upright, and born at a time of good government and good society in which good people are praised and promoted, one is respected and advances in society; at a time when poetry is socially preferred, a skilled poet becomes famous and successful. *Kālavipatti*: At a time when society has fallen from righteousness and the government is corrupt, or during times of political unrest or war, people who do good may not be praised and may even be oppressed and harassed; at a time when society prefers harsh music, a musician skilled at cool and relaxing music receives little attention or respect.

The fourth pair consists of *payogasampatti* and *payogavipatti*. *Payogasampatti*: One may not be a good or talented person, but if one knows how to approach people, how to evade what needs to be evaded, and relinquishes what needs to be relinquished, one can gain advancement, and one's defects will not come to light; one may have an aptitude for forging documents but turn that aptitude to a beneficial use, such as inspecting documentation. *Payogavipatti*: One may have knowledge, abilities, and good qualities in every other area but be addicted to gambling, and therefore not be chosen for a position; one may be a fast runner, capable of becoming a champion athlete, but use that talent for running away with other people's possessions; one may be talented in mechanical things but go to work in a clerical position for which one is unsuited.

The fruits of *kamma* on this third level are mostly concerns of worldly conditions, which are in a state of constant flux. They are superficial, external concerns, not the core of life. How heavily or lightly they affect us depends on the extent of our attachment to them. If we do not attach, we can balance our minds and dwell at ease, or at least not be greatly distressed by them, and be able to weather those changes well. For this reason, Buddhism encourages us to be wise to the norms of this world, to have mindfulness and not be deluded, heedless or reckless: in times of happiness or gain, not to become inflated over them, and in times of suffering or loss not to become downhearted or anxious, or allow ourselves to slide into bad ways, but to carefully rectify problems with wisdom.

If one still aspires to favorable worldly goals and to desirable things, one should take note of one's assets and defects, one's strengths and weaknesses, then choose and organize the factors that are assets and avoid the defects, and try to attain one's goals through skillful actions (*kusala kamma*). Such actions will have a lasting and profound effect on all levels of one's life. One should not create results through unskillful actions, or use occasions when one's assets are favorable for creating unskillful *kamma*, because these four pairs of assets (*sampatti*) and defects (*vipatti*) are constantly changing: when favorable opportunities have passed, bad *kamma* will ripen. One should rather utilize favorable conditions for creating skillful *kamma*, adhering only to those portions of these four principles that are wholesome and blameless.

In this respect, we may conclude that for any given action, when factors from many different *niyāma* are involved, one should at least see to it that the factors of *kammaniyāma* are good. This is what we can firmly and confidently adhere to before anything else. As for the factors from other *niyāma*, we can intelligently study, consider, and make use of them, so long as their use is not harmful from the perspective of the *kammaniyāma*. If we can do this, we can be said to know how to make use of skillful qualities and the four assets (*sampatti*), or to know how to use both the *kammaniyāma* and conventional laws to our benefit.

Even so, when we consider the real teaching of the Buddha, one who is doing good should not stay on the level of merely aspiring for worldly results (wealth, status, happiness, praise) for oneself, because true skillful *kamma* arises from the three roots of skillfulness: non-greed, non-aversion and non-delusion. Thus one acts with sacrifice (*cāga*), relinquishing the unskillful within the mind and sharing with and helping others; one acts with goodwill and compassion, helping others to be free of suffering and encouraging them to live together harmoniously and amicably; and one acts with wisdom, in order to know and understand things as they really are, for enlightenment, and for the spread of the Dhamma and its dominion over people and society, which is regarded as the highest kind of *kamma*—the *kamma* that leads to the cessation of *kamma*, in accordance with the teaching already discussed.[53]

Kamma Fruition on a Long-Term Basis

Whenever an intention containing skillful or unskillful qualities arises in the mind, movement has arisen in the mind. Emulating the terminology of physics, we may call this the arising of "volition energy." How this energy works, what process it works by, and what other determinants affect it, we rarely understand or take much interest in. We tend to devote more interest to the end results that manifest as "finished products," especially that "volition energy" that manifests in the material world and human society, which can be clearly seen. We have a good knowledge of the origins of our inventions, and of the systems and models that the mind has created through volition, from the first inception in thought to their successful implementation, but about the actual nature of the psyche itself, the seat of volition, what happens to the psyche conditioned by volition, and how the process of conditioning works, we have scant knowledge indeed. It would not be wrong to say that for most people the subject is a mystery shrouded in darkness, in spite of the fact that the workings of life are something that concerns them directly, and most deeply affects them.

Because of this obscurity and ignorance, when confronted with conditions or situations that are the end products of conditioning, people tend to be unable to join the scattered threads of cause and effect, and either fail to see the relevant determining factors, or see them incompletely, and then put the blame on other things, rejecting the law of *kamma*. This is tantamount to disbelieving the law of cause and effect, or the natural faring of causes and conditions. And this rejection and blaming other factors are in themselves acts of *kamma*, which bring their own unfavorable results. Specifically, one loses any chance of correcting and improving oneself and manipulating and transforming the process so as to achieve the results one desires. Even worse, one may give vent to extreme forms of anger, leading to more intense forms of *kamma* and their subsequent results.

In any case, it is recognized that the process of *kamma* fruition is complex and intricate, beyond the capacity of mere thought, not readily seen through thought. In the Pali it is said to be one of the "unfathomables" (*acinteyya*), something not to be thought about.[54] It is said that insisting on thinking about such things could drive one crazy. This does not mean to say that the Buddha forbade us from thinking, but it is rather pointing out the plain truth that some things cannot be grasped or successfully understood through rational thought, but can only be understood through direct knowledge. And if by thinking about them a person were to go crazy, that is not a result of the Buddha or anyone else punishing them or driving them crazy, but simply a result of their own actions in insisting on racking their brains over those subjects.

Although it is *acinteyya*, this does not mean that we cannot touch the subject at all. The doorway through which we can access it is that of knowing, and knowing what we can know, and having a firm conviction in accordance with that knowledge, by examining those things that we can know—the things that are actually manifesting in the present moment—from the minor or smallest level outward. This is the process of thought or volition already described, beginning with noticing how good and skillful thoughts benefit the psyche and how bad and unskillful thoughts harm it. From there, seeing how the fruits of these thoughts spread outward to affect other people, society, and the world at large, and how they rebound in good and bad ways, and to see the intricate and complex process of fruition as a result of many factors on many sides, until one begins to see the indications of a complexity that is indeed beyond the ken of ordinary thinking, and to develop a firm conviction in the faring of things according to causes and conditions. Once the process is understood on an immediate short-term basis, one can begin to understand the long-term basis in the same way, because events in the long term are derived from, and extend from, the short term. Without the short term, the long term could not be. This is the arising of understanding in accordance with the Dhamma. Once one is confident of the faring of causes and conditions in terms of *cetanā* or volition, one has conviction in the law of *kamma*, or believes in *kamma*.

Once we have a conviction in the law of *kamma*, and aspire to desired goals through our own actions, then act in conformity with causes and conditions though knowledge of those causes and conditions, the results arise accordingly. To achieve goals, we should study the relevant conditions or factors included in both the *kammaniyāma* and other *niyāma* in full, and carefully bring about the right conditions in full, as explained in the previous section. Even in external matters, a clever inventor or creator does not only consider one's own thoughts and intentions, but also the relevant determinants or factors from other *niyāma* and conventions. For example, an architect, making use of the detail of his own volitions, designs a beautiful timber house: in bringing forth the design in his mind into an actual house, he must consider what kind of timbers he will use for particular areas; whether, for example, he will use hard or soft woods. If he designates a soft wood for use where a hard wood is needed, no matter how beautiful the design may be, the house may collapse without fulfilling the purpose for which it was intended. If the design he has made calls for fine appearance but he uses ugly materials, the beauty of his design is lost.

It should be emphasized that in order to use *kammaniyāma* in a wholesome and stable manner, we must try to bring forth or encourage a predilection for the skillful (*kusalachanda*) or predilection for Dhamma (*dhammachanda*)—wanting one's life, for example, to be pure and wholesome, wanting human society to be a wholesome society, wanting everything that one is connected with or that one does to attain a state of wholesomeness and excellence, to grow to its full potential, or wanting goodness to spread far and wide.[55] If people lack this *kusalachanda* or *dhammachanda*, and are only greedy for the worldly results, they will be forever trying to manipulate *kammaniyāma*, or cheat the laws of nature, and that will lead to ongoing adverse repercussions for their own lives, for society, and for humanity as a whole.

Heaven and Hell

Many teachers feel that in order for people to believe in the law of *kamma* and be established in moral conduct they must first be convinced of the fruition of *kamma* on the most long-term basis, in terms of results from past lives and in future lives. They see a need to investigate the existence of an afterlife, or at least to present some evidence to support it. Partly to this end, and partly in pursuit of knowledge, scholars and interested parties have attempted to explain the principle of *kamma* and the wheel of rebirth by referring to scientific laws, such as the law of the conservation of energy, looking at intention as an activity or a movement of the mind. Or they refer to the theories of modern psychology,[56] or try to delve into data concerning recollection of past lives.[57] Some even go so far as to use mediums and séances to support their claims. These accounts and kinds of explanations will not be cited here, as the aim of this book is to deal only with the Buddha's teaching according to Buddhist thought. Those who are interested in such approaches and explanations can refer to the sources given here. Here, I will give only a few reflections on the matter.

The idea that if it could be convincingly demonstrated to ordinary people that there is life after death and there are future lives, and that *kamma* really does follow one and give fruit, moral teachings would be truly effective, does carry some weight: if people really did believe in those things, the practical outcome would likely be for the most part as they say. Supporters of this view are well-intentioned and they stand on rationality, so there should be nothing against allowing them to continue their study and research, as long as that research lies within the bounds of reason and does not stray onto the paths of credulousness and error, by, for example, rather than bringing things out of the realm of mystery into the realm of verification, putting verifiable truths into the realm of unverifiable mystery, or rather than bringing that which is mysterious and beyond people's control out into a form that people can control, instead rendering people powerless to do anything for themselves and having to resort to the mysterious. If investigation and research is within the bounds of reason, at least we may expect some gain in terms of academic knowledge. Even so, ordinary people do not need to involve themselves in such research, but can simply await any results that may be forthcoming. Moreover, scholars who are delving into the subject should not become so engrossed in their research that they are blinded by it, seeing only the importance of their research into future lives and overlooking the importance of the present moment, which becomes an extreme view. They must also be aware of both the good and bad effects of this kind of focus. Apart from the good result to be expected from their research, they must also realize the bad result: for instance, placing too much emphasis on fear of rebirth into woeful realms and a desire for rebirth into heaven realms encourages people to worry about results in a future life, and give all their attention only to those activities that are concerned with reaping results in a future life, neglecting the benefit and the good that they and the community should aspire to in the present life.

Again, without mindfulness and careful attention, an original intention to encourage people to fear the results of bad deeds, to be confident of receiving the results of good actions in a future life, and to have an unshakable faith in the law of *kamma* will result instead in doing the kind of actions that are aimed specifically at results in future lives, becoming greed for future results. People become "profiteering merit-makers." When this happens, another kind of bad result arises: overemphasizing the importance of good and bad results in future lives is overlooking the principle of cultivating *kusalachanda* or *dhammachanda*, which in turn becomes a denial of, or even an insult to, the human aspiration for righteousness or love of the good. This is like saying that human beings are incapable of giving up evil actions and doing the good out of an aspiration for goodness, that they can only renounce evil and do good out of greed for rewards.

Even though there are some grounds for the idea that if people could be convincingly shown that after death there is another life they would agree to lead more virtuous lives, still there is no reason why they should have to wait for the results of this research before they will lead more moral lives. It is impossible to tell when the big "if" of this scientific research will be verified. We do not know when the research will be completed, and if we consider the matter strictly according to the meaning of the word *verification*, as being a clear demonstration, then the word is invalid in this case: it is impossible for one person to show rebirth to another. Rebirth is something that each person must see for oneself. This "verification" that is spoken of is merely on the level of searching for and analyzing available evidence. The essence of the matter remains *acinteyya*: it cannot be rationally thought out and lies beyond the ken of normal capacity. No matter how much we try to verify it and how many facts are shown to support the issue, for the ordinary person it will remain a matter of faith or belief, any change taking place being only from disbelief to belief or from believing little to believing much. And since it is only a matter of belief, there will always be those who disbelieve, and there will always be the possibility of uncertainty and doubt within those who do believe. The same applies to those who do not believe: they are still on the level of belief, since they do not really know, so there is always room for them to doubt until their doubts are eliminated with the attainment of stream entry (*sotāpanna*).

Attempting to make rational proofs and produce evidence to convince people on the issue of life after death has some benefit, and those who are working in such fields should continue to do so. But to say that moral practice or a life that accords with Buddhist principles must be subject to their verification is neither appropriate nor correct.

Kamma *Fruition in the* Cūḷakammavibhaṅga Sutta

Having established this understanding, let us now look at an important Buddhavacana dealing with the fruition of *kamma* from the present into future lives appearing in the *Cūḷakammavibhaṅga Sutta*:[58]

> "See here, young man. Beings are the owners of their *kamma*, they are heirs to their *kamma*, are born of their *kamma*, have *kamma* as their lineage, have *kamma* as their support. *Kamma* it is that distinguishes beings into the coarse and the refined.
>
> 1.a. "A woman or a man is given to killing living beings (*pāṇātipāta*), is cruel, bent on killing, and lacking in goodwill or compassion. At death, on account of that *kamma*, developed and brought to a head, that person goes to the netherworlds, a woeful bourn, to hell, or, if not reborn in hell but as a human being, wherever reborn, he or she will be short-lived.
>
> b. "A woman or man who shuns killing, is possessed of goodwill and compassion, and tends to help other beings, at death, on account of that *kamma*, developed and brought to a head, goes to a good bourn, to a heaven realm, or, if not reborn in heaven but as a human being, wherever reborn, is long-lived.

2.a. "A woman or man who is given to harming and hurting other beings by the hand and the weapon, at death, on account of that *kamma*, developed and brought to a head, goes to the netherworlds, a woeful bourn, to hell, or, if not reborn in hell but as a human being, wherever reborn, is one with many illnesses [sickly].

b. "A woman or man who is not given to harming and hurting other beings, at death, on account of that *kamma*, developed and brought to a head, goes to a good bourn, to a heaven realm, or, if not reborn in heaven but as a human being, wherever reborn, is one with few illnesses [healthy].

3.a. "A woman or man who is of ill temper, is quick to anger, offended at the slightest criticism, harbors hatred and displays anger, at death, on account of that *kamma*, developed and brought to a head, goes to the netherworlds, a woeful bourn, to hell, or, if not reborn in hell but as a human being, wherever reborn, is one with inferior complexion [unattractive].

b. "A woman or a man who is not easily angered, at death, on account of that *kamma*, developed and brought to a head, goes to a pleasant bourn, a heaven realm, or, if not reborn in heaven but as a human being, wherever reborn, is of pleasant appearance.

4.a. "A woman or man who has a jealous mind—when others receive awards, honor, and respect, he or she is ill at ease and resentful—at death, on account of that *kamma*, developed and brought to a head, goes to the netherworlds, a woeful bourn, to hell, or, if not reborn in hell but as a human being, wherever reborn, is one of little influence [inferior in power].

b. "A woman or a man who harbors no jealousy, at death, on account of that *kamma*, developed and brought to a head, goes to a good bourn, to a heaven realm, or, if not reborn in heaven but as a human being, wherever reborn, is powerful and influential.

5.a. "A woman or man who does not practice giving, does not share out food, water, and clothing, at death, on account of that *kamma*, developed and brought to a head, goes to the netherworlds, a woeful bourn, to hell, or, if not reborn in hell but as a human being, wherever reborn, is one with little wealth.

b. "A woman or a man who practices giving, who shares out food, water, and clothing, at death, on account of that *kamma*, developed and brought to a head, goes to a good bourn, to a heaven realm, or, if not reborn in heaven but as a human being, wherever reborn, is one with much wealth.

6.a. "A woman or man who is stubborn and unyielding, proud, contemptuous, and disrespectful to those who should be respected, at death, on account of that *kamma*, developed and brought to a head, goes to the netherworlds, a woeful bourn, to hell, or, if not reborn in hell but as a human being, wherever reborn, is born into a low family.

b. "A woman or man who is not stubborn or unyielding, not proud, but pays respect and takes an interest in those who should be respected, at death, on account of that *kamma*, developed and brought to a head, goes to a good bourn, to a heaven realm, or, if not reborn in heaven but as a human being, wherever reborn, is born into a high family.

7.a. "A woman or man who neither visits nor questions recluses and brahmins about what is good, what is evil, what is harmful, what is not harmful, what should be done and what should not be done, about which actions lead to suffering, which actions lead to lasting happiness, at death, on account of that *kamma*, developed and brought to a head, goes to the netherworlds, a woeful bourn, to hell, or, if not reborn in hell but as a human being, wherever reborn, is of little intelligence.

b. "A woman or man who seeks out and questions recluses and brahmins about what is good, what is evil, for example, at death, on account of that *kamma*, developed and brought to a head, goes to a good bourn, to a heaven realm, or, if not reborn in heaven but as a human being, wherever reborn, is of much intelligence."

We can see that in this sutta, although the fruits to be experienced in a future life are spoken of, the emphasis is on the actions of the present moment, particularly those actions that have the characteristic of being regular conduct, conduct that builds qualities of mind, conditions the features of personality and character and is a direct factor for the respective results in each case. The rewards are not fantastic, such as in doing one single good deed, an act of giving, for example, one receives some boundless reward fulfilling all wishes and desires. Emphasizing this idea would cause people to put all their efforts into doing good deeds like putting money in a bank, and sitting around waiting for the interest to grow, or like playing the lottery, putting down only a little investment and obtaining tremendous profits, and therefore paying no attention to making good *kamma* in their daily conduct and conducting a wholesome life as explained in this sutta.[59]

In summary, the *Cūḷakammavibhaṅga Sutta* maintains the fundamental principle that any deliberation about *kamma* results to be received in a future life should be in the form of conviction based on the *kamma*—that is, the quality of the mind and the quality of conduct—in the present moment, and its fruition on a long-term basis is such that it plays out in a causal relationship.

One basic principle for considering this matter can be briefly stated as follows: The correct belief in regard to results of *kamma* in future lives must be one that promotes and strengthens *dhammachanda*. Any belief in *kamma* results in a future life that does not strengthen *dhammachanda*, but instead serves to strengthen only greed or desire, should be recognized as a mistaken kind of belief that should be corrected.

The *Kamma* That Ends *Kamma*

When describing the different kinds of *kamma* earlier in this chapter, especially in the last group, *kamma* was divided into four kinds, classified according to their relationships with their respective results:

1. Black *kamma* with black result.
2. White *kamma* with white result.

3. *Kamma* both black and white with result both black and white.
4. *Kamma* neither black nor white with result neither black nor white, being the *kamma* that brings about the cessation of *kamma*.[60]

All of the varieties of *kamma* results so far described are within the confines of the first three categories, called white *kamma*, black *kamma*, and both white and black *kamma*. We may simply refer to them as good *kamma* and bad *kamma*. The fourth kind of *kamma* remains to be explained. This fourth kind of *kamma* gives results in a completely different way from the first three kinds, so it is here discussed separately.

Most people, including Buddhists, tend to take an interest only in the first three kinds of *kamma*, disregarding the fourth kind, even though the fourth kind of *kamma* is an important principle of Buddhism and is the practice leading to its ultimate goal.

Black *kamma* and white *kamma*, or good and bad deeds, are generally described as the numerous kinds of action included within the teaching known as the ten ways of unskillful action (*akusalakammapatha*), such as killing living beings, infringing on the property rights of others, sexual misconduct, and bad or malicious speech, and their respective opposites as skillful actions (*kusalakammapatha*). These kinds of *kamma* are the causes for various kinds of good and bad results as explained above, and they are conditioning factors on life and lifestyle, causing the commitment of further good and bad deeds, and furthering the spinning in *saṁsāra*. The fourth kind of *kamma* is characterized by producing exactly the opposite kind of result: it is a kind of *kamma* that does not lead to further accumulation but that causes there to be no more *kamma*, or brings on the cessation of *kamma*. Simply speaking, it is *kamma* that does not lead to more *kamma*.

This *kamma* that leads to the cessation of *kamma* is in effect the practices that lead to the highest goal of Buddhism. In terms of the four noble truths, it is the fourth truth, the noble eightfold path, which can also be arranged into other practices, such as the seven enlightenment factors (*bojjhaṅga*) or the threefold training (*tisikkhā*: morality, concentration and wisdom). Sometimes it is spoken of as the intention to abandon the other three kinds of *kamma*, which is action based on the volition or mind-set that causes the first three kinds of *kamma* to not arise. In terms of its roots, it is the *kamma* arising from non-greed, non-hatred, and non-delusion.

Any discussion of *kamma* will usually include happiness and suffering, because happiness and suffering are fruits of *kamma*. *Kamma* is the cause, and happiness and suffering the results. As long as there is *kamma* there will be spinning around in the whirlpool of happiness and suffering. If we are aiming for the highest state of wholesomeness, one that is devoid of every flaw, any condition tainted with happiness (pleasant feeling) and suffering (unpleasant feeling) does not transcend *dukkha*. Thus, *kamma* is still involved with *dukkha*, and is still a cause of *dukkha*. However, this applies only to the first three kinds of *kamma*. The fourth kind of *kamma* is an exception, because it leads to the cessation of *kamma*, and thus it is the *kamma* that leads to the complete cessation of *dukkha*, or the complete absence of any remaining *dukkha*.

The cessation of *kamma* was taught in a number of other religions in the Buddha's time, notably the Niganthas (Jains). The Niganthas taught the principles of old *kamma* (*pubbekatavāda*), the cessation of *kamma* (*kammakaṣaya*), and discipline of the self through the practice of austerities for the cessation of *kamma*. If we do not clearly distinguish these three principles from the Buddhist teachings, we can easily confuse them with Buddhist principles. The Niganthas taught:

> "'All happiness, suffering, and neutral feeling experienced by a person are entirely results of *kamma* previously done. Thus, by doing away with old *kamma* through the practice of austerities, and making no new *kamma*, *kamma* will no longer have a controlling influence. *Kamma* no longer having a controlling influence, it is done away with. *Kamma* being done away with, suffering is done away with. With the cessation of suffering,

> feeling ceases. With the cessation of feeling, all suffering is completely quelled.' Bhikkhus, the Niganthas are of this view." [61]

The Niganthas believed that everything is caused by old *kamma*. To be free of suffering it is necessary to destroy old *kamma* by practicing austerities, "burning up" the defilements, drying up old *kamma*, and not accumulating new *kamma*. Buddhism teaches that old *kamma* is merely one part of the causal process, that we must be wise to the way things are in order to conduct ourselves correctly. One can do away with suffering through *kamma*, but it must be the right kind of *kamma*, the kind that prevents the arising of more *kamma* and thus leads to its cessation. Therefore, in order to nullify *kamma*, instead of merely stopping still or doing nothing, one who is practicing according to the Buddhist teaching must strive to act through wisdom, understanding things as they are, which leads to clarity, freedom, and transcendence of actions directed and controlled by desire.

To understand this fourth kind of *kamma* more clearly, its general features may be briefly summarized thus:

1. It is the way to the cessation of *kamma*, or the practice leading to the cessation of *kamma* (*kammanirodhagāminīpaṭipadā*). At the same time, it is in itself a kind of *kamma*.
2. It is known as the *kamma* that is neither black nor white, with results neither black nor white, leading to the cessation of *kamma*.
3. It is *kamma* arisen from non-greed, non-hatred, and non-delusion; thus, it automatically precludes evil actions because they no longer have any determinants.
4. It is action based on wisdom, done through knowledge and understanding, seeing the benefits and the flaws of things as they really are. Thus, it is a wholesome kind of action, encouraging quality of life and leading to benefit appropriate to causes and conditions.
5. It is action of the wholesome and supportive kind that is strong,

ardent, or full because effort, mindfulness, and wisdom arise to support it and can directly guide it; it is not directed by desire, either in the form of exploitative action through selfishness, or holding back from action through attachment to personal happiness.

6. It is *kusalakamma*, skillful action, on the level known as transcendent skillful action (*lokuttara kusala kamma*) or direct knowledge of the path (*maggañāṇa*); thus it is called the *kamma* that ends *kamma*, because it does not lead to the arising of more *kamma*.
7. In terms of the principles of practice, it is the eightfold path to the cessation of suffering (*dukkhanirodhagāminīpaṭipadā*)—that is, the fourth of the four noble truths. It may also be referred to by other names, such as the seven enlightenment factors (*bojjhaṅga*) or the threefold training (*tisikkhā*), depending on the context. It can also be referred to generally as the intention to abandon the first three kinds of *kamma*.

In regard to point 5 above, it is noteworthy that most people mistakenly believe that *taṇhā*, or desire, is the force that motivates their actions—the more desire there is, the more ardent and competitive is the resultant action, and without desire there would be no motivation to act, and people would become lazy.

This kind of understanding is looking at human nature only partially. In fact, desire can be a motivation for action or a motivation for inaction. When one is searching for sense pleasures, desire is a motivation for action. Action in such cases tends to be in the form of exploitation or competition with others, or it entails some personal gain but also some bad result for society or other beings. However, at a time when wholesome actions, actions that are useful to life and society, are called for, which entail no sense pleasure, desire will become a motivation for inaction, because it binds one to concern for the sense pleasures or personal comfort, such as the pleasure of sleeping and doing nothing. In this case, desire will become an encumbrance or hindrance, preventing one from stepping out and doing what should be done. Desire in this case is a cause for laziness. The greater the ignorance and lack of understanding of the value or benefit of those actions, the more desire will cause one to be inactive and listless. For this reason, desire may be a motivation for either an exploitative kind of activity, or a lethargic kind of inactivity, depending on the how sensual pleasure will be better served.

The practice that supports quality of life and true benefit is completely different from this delight in sense pleasures, and in many cases calls for a relinquishment of personal pleasures and comforts. This kind of practice cannot be achieved through desire (except if we first lay down certain conditions), but must arise through an understanding and appreciation of the real value or benefit of such practice. This appreciation, or desire for action, in Pali is called *chanda* (known in full as *kusalachanda* or *dhammachanda*).

Chanda is the real and true motivation for any action that encourages quality of life and true benefit and happiness. However, action through *chanda* may be opposed, impeded, or obstructed by desire (*taṇhā*), the delight in lethargy or sense pleasures. In this case, desire leads to suffering, because the action must be done under stress and compulsion, but if the wisdom that sees the value of those actions is clear, and appreciation (*chanda*) is sufficiently strong so that it transcends the dragging influence of desire, *chanda* becomes, in addition to a motivation for action, a determinant for happiness. It is a new kind of happiness, clear and expansive rather than the murky and constrictive happiness resulting from desire. It allows one to make creative actions with a mind that is happy and free of suffering. In this case, *samādhi* will arise in that action, with effort, mindfulness, and wisdom coming to the fore to fully support and guide those actions. This kind of action is *kamma* of the kind known as "the *kamma* that ends *kamma*."

The essence of the process of *kamma* that ends *kamma* may be simply described thus: When practicing according to the noble eightfold path or the seven enlightenment factors (or any other kind of Dhamma practice), where understanding of the value and the reality of things is the guide, desire is removed, having no channel through which to function. Greed, hatred, and delusion do not arise. When there is no desire, no greed, hatred, or delusion, the *kamma* that could lead to results and take over the mind does not arise. With no *kamma* to bind the mind, there is a state of clarity and freedom from suffering. The life that was once lived like a slave waiting on the orders of desire changes to one that is lived with wisdom, in which one is the free master of one's actions.

Below are some of the Buddhavacana dealing with the *kamma* that ends *kamma*:

> "Bhikkhus, know *kamma*, know the cause of *kamma*, know the variations of *kamma*, know the results of *kamma*, know the cessation of *kamma* and know the practices leading to the cessation of *kamma*...Bhikkhus, intention, I say, is *kamma*. A person wills before making *kamma* through body, speech, or mind. What is the cause of *kamma*? [Sense] contact (*phassa*) is the cause of *kamma*. What are the variations of *kamma*? There are the *kamma* that gives fruit in hell, the *kamma* that gives fruit in the animal realm, the *kamma* that gives fruit in the realm of hungry ghosts, the *kamma* that gives fruit in the human realm, and the *kamma* that gives fruit in the heaven realms. These are known as the variations of *kamma*. What are the results of *kamma*? I teach three kinds of *kamma* result. They are results in the present, results in the next life (*upatti*), or results in a future life. These I call the results of *kamma*. What is the cessation of *kamma*? With the cessation of contact, *kamma* ceases. This very noble eightfold path is the practice leading to the cessation of *kamma*. That is, right view, right thought, right speech, right action, right livelihood, right effort, right mindfulness, and right concentration.
>
> "Bhikkhus, when a noble disciple thus clearly understands *kamma*, the cause of *kamma*, the variations of *kamma*, the results of *kamma*, the cessation of *kamma* and the practice leading to the cessation of *kamma*, he then clearly knows the holy

life (*brahmacariya*), which comprises keen wisdom and is the cessation of this *kamma*."[62]

"Bhikkhus, this body does not belong to you, nor does it belong to another. You should see it as old *kamma*, formed by conditions, born of volition, a base of feeling."[63]

"Bhikkhus, there are these three causes of *kamma*. Greed... hatred...delusion are causes of *kamma*. *Kamma* performed on account of greed, born from greed, with greed as cause, and formed from greed, gives fruit wherever that person is born. Wherever that *kamma* ripens, there the doer must experience the fruits, be it in the present, in the next life, or in a future life... *Kamma* performed on account of hatred...*kamma* performed on account of delusion...[the same as for greed].

"Bhikkhus, there are these three causes of *kamma*. Non-greed...non-hatred...non-delusion are causes of *kamma*. *Kamma* performed on account of non-greed, born from non-greed, with non-greed as cause, formed from non-greed, being devoid of greed, is given up, cut off at the root, made like a palm tree stump, completely gone with no possibility of arising again...*Kamma* performed on account of non-hatred...on account of non-delusion..."[64]

"Bhikkhus, there are these four kinds of *kamma*...What is black *kamma* with black result? Some people in this world are given to killing, given to stealing, given to sexual misconduct, given to lying, given to drinking intoxicants that lead to heedlessness. This is called black *kamma* with black result.

"Bhikkhus, what is white *kamma* with white result? Some people in this world dwell aloof from killing...from stealing... from sexual misconduct...from lying...from the drinking of intoxicants that lead to heedlessness. This is called white *kamma* with white result.

"Bhikkhus, what is *kamma* both black and white with result

both black and white? Some people in this world create bodily formations...verbal formations...mental formations that are both hurtful and not hurtful. This is called *kamma* both black and white with result both black and white.

"Bhikkhus, what is *kamma* neither black nor white, with result neither black nor white, which leads to the cessation of *kamma*? Of those three kinds of *kamma*, the intention to abandon (those kinds of *kamma*), this is called the *kamma* that is neither black nor white, with result neither black nor white, which leads to the ending of *kamma*."[65]

"Herein, Udāyī, a bhikkhu in this teaching and discipline cultivates the mindfulness enlightenment factor...the equanimity enlightenment factor, which inclines to seclusion, inclines to dispassion, inclines to cessation, and is well developed, boundless, free of hurtful intent. Cultivating the mindfulness enlightenment factor...the equanimity enlightenment factor...desire is abandoned. With the abandoning of desire, *kamma* is abandoned. With the abandoning of *kamma*, suffering is abandoned. Thus, with the cessation of desire there is the cessation of *kamma*; with the cessation of *kamma* there is the cessation of suffering."[66]

Some Noteworthy Points for Consideration

Who Causes Happiness and Suffering?

According to the Buddhavacana, "With ignorance as condition, a person creates bodily formations (*kāyasaṅkhāra*)[67]...verbal formations (*vacīsaṅkhāra*)[68]...mental formations (*manosaṅkhāra*)[69] of one's own accord...as a result of external agents...knowingly... unknowingly."[70] There is also the Buddhavacana refuting both the theory of the *attakāravādins* that happiness and suffering are self-caused, and the theory of the *parakāravādins* that happiness and suffering are caused by external agents.[71] This highlights the need to see *kamma* as a process of causes and conditions. The extent of any involvement, either of oneself or of external agents, must be considered properly according to this process, and not adjudged too simplistically. This is said to prevent the extreme misunderstanding that often arises in respect of *kamma* that all events are caused by personal actions, ignoring the other agents and environmental factors involved.

However, on another level we must distinguish between *kamma* as a natural law or reality, and *kamma* in the context of ethics. The previous paragraph is stated in reference to *kamma* as a law, but from the ethical perspective, the individual must accept full responsibility for the actions one intends and acts on, and for which one creates results accordingly, as in the Buddha's words "Oneself is one's own mainstay." Here the emphasis is on the accountability of the individual, looking from the individual outward. In this case, apart from meaning that one must help oneself and do things for oneself, in terms of relationships with other people it also refers more broadly to help arising from others, how it is maintained, and its fruition being dependent on how self-reliant is the individual in soliciting and inspiring actions from others, in ensuring the continuation of those actions and in accepting or responding to them. Thus, the principles of *kamma* as natural law and in terms of ethics do not conflict, but actually support each other; but they must be properly understood.

Beliefs That Are Contrary to the Principle of Kamma

There are three doctrines of wrong view about happiness, suffering, and human life that are contrary to the principle of *kamma* and must be carefully distinguished from its teaching:

1. *Pubbekatahetuvāda*: the belief that all happiness and suffering arise from previous *kamma* (past-action determinism). It is called in short *pubbekatavāda*.
2. *Issaranimmānahetuvāda*: the belief that all happiness and suffering are caused by the directives of a supreme god (theistic determinism). It is referred to as *issarakaraṇavāda* or *issaraniramitavāda*.

3. *Ahetu-apaccayavāda*: the belief that all happiness and suffering are dependent on random luck, having no cause or determinant (indeterminism or accidentalism). It is called in short *ahetukavāda*.

Concerning these three, we have the Buddhavacana:

> "Bhikkhus, these three outsider sects, on being questioned and pressed by the wise, fall back on tradition and stand fast on inaction (*akiriyā*). They are as follows:
>
> 1. "One group of recluses and brahmins teaches and is of the view that all pleasant, unpleasant, and neutral feelings experienced by people are entirely a result of deeds done in a previous time (*pubbekatahetu*).
>
> 2. "One group of recluses and brahmins teaches and is of the view that all pleasant, unpleasant, and neutral feelings experienced by people are entirely the creations of a supreme being (*issaranimmānahetu*).
>
> 3. "One group of recluses and brahmins teaches and is of the view that all pleasant, unpleasant, and neutral feelings experienced by people are entirely without cause or determinant (*ahetu-apaccaya*).
>
> "Bhikkhus, of those three groups of recluses and brahmins, I approach (the first group) and say to them, 'I hear that you uphold this teaching and this view... Is that so?' If those recluses and brahmins, on being thus questioned by me, answer that it is so, then I say to them, 'If that is so, then you must have killed living beings as a result of *kamma* done in a previous time, you must have stolen as a result of *kamma* done at a previous time, you must have engaged in sexual misconduct... have uttered false speech... have held wrong view as a result of *kamma* done in a previous time.'
>
> "Bhikkhus, adhering to previously done *kamma* as the essence, motivation (*chanda*), and effort that 'this should be done, this should not be done' do not arise... Not attending closely to what should be done and what should not be done, those recluses

> and brahmins live as if deluded, lacking a control, and they are incapable of having any true teaching from their own experience. This is our first legitimate refutation of those groups of recluses and brahmins holding these views.
>
> "Bhikkhus, of those three groups of recluses and brahmins, I approach (the second group)...and say to them, 'You must have killed living beings because of the directives of a supreme being...stolen the goods of others...engaged in sexual misconduct...uttered false speech...have held wrong view because of the directives of a supreme being.'
>
> "Bhikkhus, adhering to the will of a supreme being as the essence, motivation, and effort that 'this should be done, this should not be done' do not arise...
>
> "Bhikkhus, of those groups of recluses and brahmins, I approach (the third group)...and say to them, '[Then] you must have killed living beings without cause, without condition, stolen the goods of others...engaged in sexual misconduct...uttered false speech...have held wrong view without cause, without condition.'
>
> "Bhikkhus, adhering to accidentalism as the essence, motivation, and effort that 'this should be done, this should not be done' do not arise..."[72]

In addition, there is the Buddhavacana cited in the chapter on *paṭiccasamuppāda*, which emphasizes the same point:

> "Sīvaka, some feelings arise with bile as cause...some with changes in the temperature as cause...some with irregular exercise as cause...some with external dangers as cause...some with *kamma* results as cause...Whatever recluse or brahmin is of the teaching or view that 'Any feeling a person experiences, be it pleasant or unpleasant, all of that feeling is entirely on account of previous *kamma*,'...I say that this is a wrong view on behalf of that recluse or brahmin."[73]

These Buddhavacana discourage us from going to the extreme of seeing *kamma* entirely in terms of past *kamma*, and therefore passively waiting for the results of old *kamma* to ripen, taking things as they come rather than thinking to correct or improve oneself. This is a harmful form of wrong view. We can clearly see here that the Buddha holds effort to be a crucial factor in deciding the ethical value of the principle of *kamma* and all of these teachings.

These Buddhavacana do not dismiss previous *kamma*, because it does play a part in the process of causes and conditions, and thus has an effect on the present, in keeping with its capacity as one of the determinants. But *kamma* is simply a matter of causes and conditions, not a supernatural force to be clung to and passively submitted to. One who understands the *paṭiccasamuppāda* and knows the causal process will have no problems in understanding this.

It is like a man walking up to the top of a three-story building. It is undeniably true that his arriving is a result of past action—namely, walking. And having arrived there, it is impossible for him to stretch out his hand and touch the ground below, or drive a car around that small building as if it were a road. That is because he has gone up to the third floor. This also cannot be denied. Again, having arrived at the third floor, whether he is too exhausted to go any further is also undeniably related to having walked up the stairs. His arrival there, what he is able to do there and the situations he is likely to encounter on account of having gone up there, are all certainly connected to his having walked up the stairs, but exactly what actions he will perform, how he responds to the things he encounters there, and whether he will take a rest before walking on, or walk straight back down the stairs and out of that building, are all matters that he decides afresh for himself, acts on and reaps the results of. Even though the action of walking up the stairs may still be influencing him—for example, he may be too tired by the climb to effectively do anything further—whether he decides to give in to that tiredness or try to do something about it are all matters of the process of causes and conditions.

Thus, old *kamma* should be understood only as far as it actually goes. In terms of practice, whoever understands the *paṭiccasamuppāda* can learn from old *kamma*, to rationally gain an understanding of oneself and situations, and a knowledge and understanding of one's current foundation, on the basis of which one's actions (*kamma*) in the present can be planned and ways sought to make corrections and improvements for the future.

Can Kamma *Be Erased?*

Regarding whether *kamma* can be erased, on one occasion the Buddha said:

> "Listen, householder, some teachers give the teaching and are of the view that all those who kill living beings must go to the woeful states and fall to hell; that all those who take what is not given must go to the woeful states and fall to hell; that all those who commit sexual misconduct must go to the woeful states and fall to hell; that all those who lie must go to the woeful states and fall to hell. Followers with faith in those teachers, thinking, 'Our teacher gives the teaching and is of the view that all those who kill living beings must go to the woeful states and fall to hell,' conceive the view thus, 'I have already killed living beings. Therefore I, too, must go to the woeful states and fall to hell.' Not relinquishing that speech and that view, they indeed go to hell, just as if pushed there by force...
>
> "As for the Tathāgata, the Fully Enlightened Buddha, he arises in the world... He speaks in many a way in dispraise of killing living beings... taking what is not given... sexual misconduct... and lying, and teaches, 'Killing of living beings... taking what is not given... sexual misconduct... lying should be abandoned.' A follower with faith in the Teacher, reflecting thus, 'The Blessed One speaks in dispraise of killing living beings... in many a way, and says, "Give up the killing of living beings." I have already killed so many beings. That I have already killed so many living beings is not good, not worthy. I will truly suffer on account of those actions, and on their account it will not be possible to say that I have not committed evil *kamma*.' Reflecting in this way,

that follower gives up killing of living beings, and is one who abandons the killing of living beings from that moment on. Thus does [that follower] abandon that bad *kamma*...

"He abandons the killing of living beings and refrains from killing...lying...malicious tale-bearing...coarse speech...frivolous speech...covetousness...enmity...wrong view, and is one with right view. He, the noble disciple, has a mind free of covetousness (*abhijjhā*), free of thoughts of hurtfulness (*byāpāda*), and is not deluded, but possessed of clear comprehension and firm mindfulness. He dwells with a mind spreading goodwill to the first...second...third...the fourth direction, above, below, far and wide to the whole world, to all kinds of beings in all places, with a mind full of goodwill that is expansive, grand, boundless, free of enmity, free of ill will. Having so thoroughly developed the mind deliverance through goodwill (*mettācetovimutti*), any moderate amount of *kamma* previously done will no longer remain, it cannot continue in that mind deliverance through goodwill..."[74]

Do Kamma *and Not-Self Contradict Each Other?*

One question that tends to linger in the minds of many newcomers to the study of Buddhism is whether the principles of *kamma* and not-self contradict each other. If everything, both body and mind, is not-self, then how can there be *kamma*? Who is it who commits *kamma*? Who receives the results? These doubts are not simply phenomena of the present time, but have existed from the time of the Buddha, as can be seen in the following example:

A certain bhikkhu conceived the following doubt:

"We know that form, feeling, perception, volitional impulses and consciousness are not-self. If so, how can the *kamma* made by 'non-self' affect one?"

At that time, the Blessed One, knowing the thoughts of that bhikkhu, addressed the bhikkhus thus:

> "Bhikkhus, it may be that some foolish people in this teaching and discipline, with minds fallen into ignorance and overwhelmed by desire, might conceive the teaching of the master thus: 'We know that form, feeling, perception, volitional impulses, and consciousness are not-self. If that is so, how can the *kamma* made by 'non-self' affect one?' All of you now, having been thoroughly instructed and tested by me on points of Dhamma and on other matters, how do you consider these matters: is form permanent or impermanent?" "Impermanent, Lord." "Are feeling, perception, volitional formations, consciousness permanent or impermanent?" "Impermanent, Lord." "That which is impermanent, is that stressful or happy?" "Stressful, Lord" "Of that which is impermanent, stressful, and normally subject to change, is it proper to see that as 'that is mine, that is me, that is my self'?" "No, it is not proper, Lord." "For that reason, form, feeling, perception, volitional impulses, and consciousness, of whatever description... are merely form, feeling, perception, volitional impulses, and consciousness. They are not 'mine,' not 'me,' not 'my self.' You should see this thus with right wisdom. The learned, noble disciple, seeing in this way, loses attachment to form, feeling, perception, volitional impulses and consciousness... is free... and has no further task to do."[75]

Before analyzing this scriptural citation or going into further explanations, consider the following analogy: Suppose that right now we are standing looking at a river. The water flows in a mostly flat area, therefore it flows slowly. The soil in the areas through which the river flows is mostly red, which gives this body of water a reddish color. In addition to this, the water passes many heavily populated areas, and people have long thrown refuse into the river, making the water dirty. Moreover, in recent times factories have been built and they release daily flows of industrial waste into the water. The water therefore has not much animal life. All in all, the body of water we are looking at is reddish-colored, dirty, highly polluted, sparsely inhabited, and slow-flowing. All of these together are the unique features of this body of water. Some of these characteristics might be similar to other rivers, but the sum total of these characteristics is unlike any other river.

Eventually someone tells us that this body of water is called the Tha Wang River. Different people describe it in different ways. Some say the Tha Wang River is dirty and doesn't have many fish. Some say the Tha Wang River does not flow swiftly. Some say that the Tha Wang River is red-colored. We observe that the body of water we are looking at is actually complete within itself. Its various attributes, such as being slow-flowing, red-colored, dirty, and so on, are all caused by various conditioning factors and events. The events that arise themselves condition their own results. Moreover, as we are standing looking at the river, the water is constantly flowing by. The water that we first saw in front of us and the water we see later are not the same. Even so, the river has its own unique features, which may be said to remain the same because the conditioning factors that affect it have not changed.

But we are told, then, that this is the Tha Wang River. Not only that, they say that the Tha Wang River does not flow swiftly, its water is dirty, and it does not have many fish. We can see no separate "Tha Wang River" apart from this body of water we are looking at. We can see no "Tha Wang River" possessing this body of water. Yet they tell us that the Tha Wang River breaks up the red earth as it flows, which makes the water turn red. It's almost as if this Tha Wang River does something to the red earth, which causes the earth to "punish" it by turning its water red. We can clearly see that the body of water we are looking at fares subject to a process of cause and effect complete within itself. The water that splashes against the red earth and the red earth dissolving into the water are causal conditions, the result of which is that the water turns red. We can find no "body" doing anything or receiving any results.

What is more, we can see no actual Tha Wang River anywhere. If there were an actual and fixed Tha Wang River, the flow of water could not proceed according to its various determining factors. Finally, we see that this name "Tha Wang River" is actually superfluous. We can fully describe the process of that body of water without having to bother with the name "Tha Wang River." In fact, there is no Tha Wang River at all.

As time goes by we travel to another district, where we meet many people. Wanting to describe to them the body of water we once saw, we are stumped. We don't know how to describe it in such a way that they will understand what we are talking about. Then we recall someone telling us that that body of water was known as the Tha Wang River, and so we can relate our experience to those people fluently, and they can listen with understanding and interest. We tell them that the Tha Wang River has dirty water and not many fish, flows slowly, and flows past red earth, making its waters reddish-colored. Then we understand clearly that this "Tha Wang River" is simply a conventional term used for communication in the world. Whether the convention of Tha Wang River exists or not, or whether we use it or not, has no effect on that body of water. That body of water continues to be a stream-like process flowing according to its factors and conditions. We can clearly distinguish between the convention and the actual reality. Now we can both understand and use those conventional terms comfortably.

Both reality and convention are necessary. Reality (often referred to as *paramattha*) is a concern of nature. Convention is a concern of utility in human life. Problems arise when people confuse the reality and the convention, clinging to the reality and trying to make it follow conventions. As can be seen in the passage cited above, the bhikkhu who conceived the doubt was confusing his knowledge of the reality, which he had learned, with the convention, to which he still clung. This was the cause of his bewilderment. Referring to the original wording, his doubt goes something like this: "How can the deeds created by not-self affect the self?" The first part of the sentence is spoken according to his acquired knowledge of the reality, while the second part is spoken according to the convention to which he still attached. Naturally they don't fit.

Practical Value

In conclusion, the desired values in terms of ethics of the teaching of *kamma* are as follows:

- It enables us to stand fast on reason, to know how to look at deeds and their results according to causes and conditions, not credulously believing in things or being gullible over such things as holy rivers.
- It shows us that the success of any aspiration, the aspired objective, will be attained through action: Thus, we must rely on ourselves and make the effort ourselves; we should not wait for luck or expect to obtain results by praying to or supplicating external forces.
- It gives us a sense of responsibility to ourselves in giving up bad actions, and to others in doing good deeds.
- It encourages us to see that all individuals have a natural and equal right to act to improve themselves; all people are capable of making themselves worse or better, and all people can improve themselves to a level of excellence that exceeds the gods (*deva*) or *brahmas*.
- It encourages us to see that mental qualities, abilities, and conduct are the measuring sticks of human baseness or refinement and that we should not discriminate on the basis of caste or race.
- In terms of old *kamma*, we can use it as a lesson and reflect on ourselves according to reason, not simply finding fault with others, ascertaining our present position in order to know how to correct and improve on it, and determine the proper actions for supporting our continued improvement.
- It gives hope for the future for people in general.

These values can be considered in the light of the following Buddhavacana.

The General Meaning

> "Bhikkhus, intention, I say, is *kamma*. Having willed, a person acts through body, speech, and mind."[76]
>
> ---
>
> "Beings have *kamma* as their own, are heirs to their *kamma*, are born of their *kamma*, have *kamma* as their lineage, have *kamma* as their support. *Kamma* it is that distinguishes beings into the coarse and the refined."[77]
>
> ---
>
> "Whatever seed one plants one reaps the fruit thereof. One who does good receives good; one who does evil receives evil."[78]

Rationality over Superstition

> "If it were possible to escape evil *kamma* simply by bathing [to wash away bad deeds], then the frogs, turtles, otters, crocodiles, and other animals that pass through the river would certainly be destined for rebirth in a heaven realm...If these rivers were capable of carrying away the evil deeds you have done in the past, they would also carry away your good *kamma*."[79]
>
> ---
>
> "Whoever holds not to superstition and rumor, who holds not to omens, dreams, and good or bad signs, that person is freed from the fault of holding to superstition and rumor, has overcome the barriers of defilements that bind beings to existence (*bhava*), and is never again reborn."[80]
>
> ---
>
> "Benefit slips by while the fool counts the stars. Benefit is the harbinger of benefit; what can the stars do?"[81]

Putting into Action rather than Waiting for Fulfillment of Prayers

> "Do not pine for that which is done and gone, dream not of what is to be. The past is done and gone; the future has yet to come.

One who sees clearly the present moment, which is certain and unwavering, understanding the matter, should strive to practice in that very moment. Strive to practice today, who knows whether tomorrow will bring death? No one can bargain with the Lord of Death, the great commander. One who lives in such a way, ardent, not lazy, day and night, even for a single day, that one is called excellent by the Peaceful One."[82]

"Listen, householder, these five conditions are desirable, likable, satisfying, and hard to come by in this world. They are longevity...pleasant appearance (*vaṇṇa*)...happiness...status... heaven. These five conditions...I say, are not to be had by mere supplication or aspiration. If the obtaining of these five conditions were possible through mere supplication or aspiration, then who in this world would ever lack for anything? Listen, householder, the noble disciple who desires longevity should not merely supplicate or indulge in the wish for longevity on account of that desire for longevity. The noble disciple desiring longevity should maintain the practices that produce longevity, because only the practices leading to longevity will procure longevity. That noble disciple will thus be one who has longevity, both divine and human...who desires pleasant appearance... happiness...status...heaven, should maintain the practices that produce (pleasant) appearance...happiness...status... heaven..."[83]

"Bhikkhus, even though a bhikkhu were to conceive the wish, 'May my mind be freed from the outflows (*āsava*),' if that bhikkhu does not diligently devote himself to the training of the mind he will be unable to free the mind from the outflows... Just like a clutch of eight eggs, ten eggs, or twelve eggs that the mother hen does not sit on, warm, or hatch: even though that hen might conceive the wish, 'May my chicks, using their feet and beaks, break the shells of their eggs and come out safely,' those chicks would not use their feet or their beaks to break the shells and come out of those eggs."[84]

Upholding Conduct rather than Race or Class

"Listen, Vāseṭṭha, you should understand it thus: Among people, one who depends on farming for a livelihood is a farmer, not a brahmin. One who makes a living with the arts is an artist, not a brahmin. One who makes a living by selling is a merchant, not a brahmin. One who makes a living working for others is a servant, not a brahmin. One who makes a living through stealing is a thief, not a brahmin...One who rules the land is a king, not a brahmin.

"I do not call one a brahmin on the basis of his birth. Such a person still has defilements. That is simply the *bho* formality.[85] I say that it is rather the one who has no defilements and no clinging who is a brahmin.

"Names and clans are only worldly conventions, arisen in accordance with the designations applied to them at a given time following the views long held by ignorant beings. Ignorant beings are always saying that they are brahmins because of their birth, but one does not become a brahmin on account of birth, nor is one not a brahmin through birth. One is a brahmin through action (*kamma*), and is not a brahmin through action. One is a farmer through action (the work one does[86]), an artist through action, a merchant through action, a servant through action, a thief through action...a king through action. The wise, seeing the *paṭiccasamuppāda*, skilled in *kamma* and its results, see *kamma* clearly as it is, that the world fares according to *kamma*, beings fare according to *kamma*...Beings are bound together by *kamma*, just as a running cart is bound by its couplings."[87]

"One is not evil because of birth and is not a brahmin because of birth, but is evil because of *kamma*, and is a brahmin because of *kamma* (deed, conduct)."[88]

"From among these four castes—the nobles, the brahmins, the merchants, and the plebeians—all who have left home and gone forth in the teaching and discipline declared by the Tathāgata dispense with their original name and family, and are all regarded as recluses, Sons of the Sakyans."[89]

"From among these four castes, any who are bhikkhus, freed of defilements and outflows, who have completed the holy life, done what was to be done and laid down the burden, who have attained their own benefit, done with the fetters to existence, and attained liberation through true wisdom, they are more excellent than any of those castes."[90]

"Practice is your own responsibility; the Tathāgata only points the way."[91]

"One self is one's own mainstay; who else could be your mainstay? Being well trained within oneself, one attains a mainstay hard to come by."[92]

"Purity and impurity are personal concerns; no one else can make you pure."[93]

"Bhikkhus, be a refuge unto yourselves, take nothing else as your refuge. Take the Dhamma as your refuge, take nothing else as your refuge."[94]

"Women, men, householders, and those gone to homelessness should regularly reflect that 'We are the owners of our *kamma*, the heirs of our *kamma*, are born of our *kamma*, descended from our *kamma*, supported by our *kamma*. Whatever *kamma* we do, whether good or bad, we will receive the results thereof.'"[95]

"If you fear suffering, do not make bad *kamma*, either in public or in private. If you wish to make bad *kamma*, or have made it, even if you fly into the air you will be unable to escape suffering."[96]

"Grain, wealth, money, and anything else you cherish; servants, employees, associates, and dependents—none of them can you take with you. They must all be cast aside.

"But whatever *kamma* a person makes, whether by body, speech, or mind, that is your real possession, and that is what you take with you. That *kamma* will follow you like a shadow.

"Therefore, one should do good actions, gathering benefit for the future. Goodness is the mainstay of beings in the hereafter."[97]

PART FOUR

How Should Life Be?

CHAPTER 5

Nibbāna

When the cycle of *saṁsāra*[1] (wheel of rebirth) is no more, it automatically becomes *vivaṭṭa* ("unraveling"). There is no leaving *saṁsāra* in one place to arrive at *vivaṭṭa* in another, except as a figure of speech. When ignorance, desire, and clinging cease, *nibbāna* automatically appears in their place. In other words, the cessation of ignorance, desire, and clinging is itself *nibbāna*.

Ignorance, desire, and clinging are constantly controlling and clouding the mind of the unenlightened person. When they cease, wisdom arises, there is the light of knowledge (*vijjā*), and we see all things—that is, life and the world—clearly as they really are. Our views and perceptions of the world change, as do our feelings and attitudes, and thence our character. Phenomena that we have never seen, known, or even imagined, because they were previously covered over or hidden away, or because we were too preoccupied with other concerns, appear to us, and a new kind of knowledge and perception arises. The mind becomes expansive, boundless, spacious and free, in a state that is clear, bright, peaceful, subtle, and profound—states that would be inconceivable for a mind dominated by ignorance, desire, and clinging. When such a state is reached, one clearly knows it for oneself, as described in one of the characteristics of *nibbāna*:

> "*Nibbāna*, which the attainer sees for oneself, timeless, inviting inspection, to be internalized and experienced by the wise, each for oneself."[2]

The reason unenlightened beings are incapable of conceiving the state of *nibbāna* is that people usually try to understand the unknown on the basis of what they do know, using their previous perceptions. Like a woman who has never seen or heard of an elephant: if someone were to describe an elephant to her, she would find it impossible to picture. She may think that the speaker was talking rubbish, or speaking another language, or that he was deranged. If the speaker says, "I saw an elephant," the listener can at least surmise that an elephant is something that can be seen. If the speaker says, "An elephant is a kind of animal," the listener's understanding is increased again. If the speaker states that an elephant is a large animal, the picture is narrowed down even more. From there the speaker may go on to describe the characteristics of the elephant—the big ears, the small eyes, the tusks, the long trunk, and so on, and the listener obtains an even more definite image in her mind. That image may be similar to the real thing, or it may be so far off the track that it is like something out of a fantasy story. The image that the listener does conceive is dependent, on one hand, on the accuracy of the speaker's description and, on the other hand, on the perceptions incorporated by the listener in making the new perception.

Such terms as "seeing," "animal," "land," and "large" are all concepts that the listener already has, but if the object being described is totally different from anything the listener has ever experienced there is nothing to compare it with, and one has no way of conceiving or understanding it. When pressed for an analogy, all the speaker can do is say what it is not like. If the speaker insists on trying to describe the object based on perceptions that the listener can use, there is a great risk of the listener creating misconceptions around it, or even refuting the description altogether and accusing the speaker of trying to deceive her. But it would be wrong for the listener to refute that object simply because she has never seen it or experienced it, or because it does not correspond with her previous perceptions.

Nibbāna is a state that transcends all that an unenlightened being can conceive. It is beyond the ken of a knowledge that is dominated by ignorance, desire, and clinging. When the Buddha was newly enlightened, before he had begun to teach, he reflected to himself, "This Dhamma (truth) that I have realized is profound, difficult to see, abstruse, calming, refined, not attainable through logic, subtle, known only to the wise."[3] There is also the following verse: "This Dhamma that I have attained with great difficulty—now is not the time to teach it. This Dhamma is not something that beings dominated by greed and hatred can easily understand. Beings who are stained by greed and enveloped in the mass of darkness (*avijjā*) cannot see the state that goes against the stream, which is refined, profound, abstruse, and extremely subtle."[4] The word *Dhamma* here refers to the *paṭiccasamuppāda* and *nibbāna.* (It could also be said to refer to the four noble truths, which essentially means the same thing.)

In spite of its being so difficult, the Buddha did make a great deal of effort to teach and explain it. Thus, the statement that *nibbāna* is inconceivable for an unenlightened being should be taken more as a caution, warning us not to simply try to conceptualize or argue about *nibbāna*, which would only lead to wrong perceptions. The right approach is to attain it as a personal realization. Although *nibbāna* is inconceivable and incomprehensible for one who has not yet experienced it, it can be experienced and attained, albeit with difficulty. Having agreed on this, we may change the words often used to describe *nibbāna* as "inconceivable" or "incomprehensible" (or even, as some would say, "impossible to put into words") and use the words of the Buddha himself, who said that it is "difficult to see, hard to know."

Since *nibbāna* is difficult to see and hard to know, it cannot be imagined, and as long as it is not directly realized, it is incomprehensible. There are no words to directly describe it or perceptions with which to determine it. Thus, it is worth finding out just what words are used to describe *nibbāna.* As far as can be gathered, in essence the ways of describing *nibbāna* can be divided into four categories.

1. *By negation.* Defining in terms of relinquishing, destroying, or

removing that which is not wholesome, not beneficial, or not useful, which lies within the bounds of *vaṭṭa*. Examples: "*nibbāna* is the cessation of greed, the cessation of aversion, and the cessation of delusion;[5] "*nibbāna* is the cessation of becoming (*bhava*);[6] "*nibbāna* is the end of desire;[7] or "... the end of the road for suffering."[8] Sometimes a word that describes the exact opposite of a characteristic of *saṁsāra* is used—for instance, as in "it is the unconditioned (*asaṅkhata*)," "the ageless" or "the deathless."

2. *By synonym, or according to its features*. Describing *nibbāna* in words that are already in use and understood, and that are related in meaning to the state of perfection or the highest good, to show some of its characteristics—for example, "peaceful" (*santa*), "subtle" (*paṇīta*), "pure" (*suddha*), and "secure" (*khema*).

3. *By analogy*. Analogies are more commonly used to describe the state and characteristics of one who has attained *nibbāna* rather than the state of *nibbāna* itself. For example, the arahant is compared to a cattle herder who has led the herd across a swiftly flowing river and reached the other shore,[9] and to a person who has crossed the ocean or a vast expanse of water, full of dangers, and safely reached the other side,[10] and it is said that an arahant can neither be said to be reborn or not reborn and so on, like a fire going out when the fuel is spent.[11] There are, however, some direct analogies for *nibbāna*, such as: *nibbāna* is like a placid and joyful land;[12] like a further shore that is free of danger;[13] and like a message that is true.[14] There are many words used as descriptors for *nibbāna*, such as *ārogya* (perfect health), *dīpa* (an island, a refuge), and *leṇa* (a cave, a shelter). In the times of the later commentaries, which are teachings of the disciples (*sāvakabhāsita*), *nibbāna* is even described as a city, such as in the words *uttamapurī* (Perfect Town)[15] and *nibbānanagara* (City of Nibbāna),[16] and such terms have become commonly used in Thai sermons and literature. However, these later terms cannot be regarded as accepted terms for the state of *nibbāna*.

4. *By direct description*. These are rare, but they are of great interest to students and researchers, especially those who study Bud-

dhism as a philosophy, and the terms are variously interpreted, often resulting in disputes. The direct descriptions of *nibbāna* are given here:

> "There is, bhikkhus, that sphere (*āyatana*) in which there is no earth element, no water, no fire, no wind, no sphere of limitless space (*ākāsānañcāyatana*), no sphere of limitless consciousness (*viññāṇañcāyatana*), no sphere of nothingness (*ākiñcaññāyatana*), no sphere of neither perception nor non-perception (*nevasaññānāsaññāyatana*), no this world, no further world (*paraloka*), neither sun nor moon. I do not say of that sphere that there is any coming, any going, any stopping, any cessation, or any arising. That sphere has no standing, (but it) does not proceed, and needs no support. That is the end of suffering."[17]
>
> ---
>
> "There is, bhikkhus, the unborn (*ajāta*), the unexisting (*abhūta*), the uncreated (*akata*), the unconditioned (*asaṅkhata*). If there were no unborn, unexisting, uncreated, and unconditioned, there would be no escape in this world from the state of having been born, existing, having been created and been conditioned. But because there is the unborn, unexisting, uncreated, and unconditioned, there is an escape from having been born, existing, having been created and conditioned."[18]
>
> ---
>
> "As long as there is dependence, there is wavering; with no dependence, there is no wavering; where there is no wavering, there is perfect stillness; where there is perfect stillness, there is no fluctuation; where there is no fluctuation, there is no coming and going; where there is no coming and going there is no ceasing (*cuti*) and arising (*upatti*); where there is no ceasing and arising there is no this world (*bhava*), there is no other world, and there is no in between: that is the end of suffering."[19]
>
> ---
>
> "The state that can be known (*viññāṇa*) but cannot be seen with

> the eye (*anidassana*),[20] which is limitless, all radiant,[21] to which the earth-ness of the earth element cannot affix, the fluidity of the water element... the heat of the fire element... the movement of the wind element cannot affix, the being-ness (*satta*) of beings cannot affix... the heavenliness of the heavenly beings... the lordship of the lord of beings (*pajāpati*)... the Brahma-ness of Brahma... the radiance of the radiant *brahmas*... the refulgent glory (*subhakiṇha*) of the Subhakiṇha *brahmas*... the great fruit (*vehapphala*) of the Vehapphala *brahmas* cannot affix, the omnipotence of gods cannot affix, and to which the all-ness of the all cannot affix.
>
> "The state that can be known (*viññāṇa*) but cannot be seen with the eye (*anidassana*), which is limitless, which can be entered from every angle (*sabbatopabha*)—here it is that earth, water, fire, and wind find no footing; here long and short, large and small, beautiful and ugly find no footing; here mind-body (*nāmarūpa*) cease without remainder. When consciousness ceases, mind-body ceases.'"[22]

These passages dealing with the state of *nibbāna* have spawned different interpretations and been the cause of some discussion and debate. This is partly due to interpreting and conceptualizing things that cannot be conceptualized, but must be realized through practice, as already explained. In addition, the translations of some of the Pali words used in these passages have affected the interpretation of the passages. For example, some scholars, translating the word *āyatana* in the first passage as "sphere," interpret *nibbāna* as being a locality or place, or another dimension. The word *viññāṇa*, in the fourth and fifth passages, has been interpreted by some scholars in the same sense as eye consciousness, ear consciousness, and so on, and therefore *nibbāna* is interpreted as a kind of consciousness, translating the passage as "*nibbāna* is a kind of consciousness (*viññāṇa*) that cannot be seen with the eye." However, in the commentaries[23] it is explained that the word *viññāṇa* is here used in reference to *nibbāna*, meaning "that which can be known," as translated above. In the fifth passage, the word *viññāṇa* occurs twice. The first occurrence refers to *nibbāna* and is here rendered accordingly, while the second occurrence, in the phrase "when *viññāṇa* ceases," refers to the *viññāṇa* that is a determinant for the arising of mind-body in the *paṭiccasamuppāda.*

One of the most important words used to describe the state of *nibbāna* is *asaṅkhata*, meaning unconditioned, that which is not born from the conditioning of determinants. Some thinkers have posited that *nibbāna* must have some cause, since it is a result of the practice of the path. This doubt can be briefly answered with an analogy: if we compare the practice leading to *nibbāna* to traveling to a certain city—let us say Chiang Mai—it can be seen that Chiang Mai, which is the objective of the journey, is not the result of the path or the journey as such. Regardless of whether the road or the journey exist, the city of Chiang Mai still exists. The road and the journey are simply causal conditions for reaching the city of Chiang Mai. It is the same with the path and the practice of the path: they are conditions for the attainment of *nibbāna*, not for *nibbāna* itself.

The following Buddhavacana is the Buddha's guarantee that the attainment of *nibbāna* and other higher levels of Dhamma really do exist and can take place when the "wisdom-eye" is opened. It is said in refutation of a brahmin who held the view that it was impossible for a human being to attain to superhuman knowledge and vision:

> "Listen, young man, it is like a man blind from birth. He sees no black, white, green, yellow, red or pink forms, no smooth and rough forms; he sees not the stars, the moon, or the sun. If he were to say, 'White and black forms do not exist and there are no people who see white and black forms; green forms do not exist and there are none who see green forms;...the moon and sun do not exist and there are none who see the moon and sun. I do not know or see those things; thus they do not exist.' Speaking in this way, could we say he was speaking rightly?" The young man answered, "No, not rightly." The Buddha then continued, "This is the same. The brahmin Pokkharasāti Opamañña, the

> chief of the Subhaga forest, is one blind, without eyes. That he would see or attain that special knowledge and vision attainable only to superhuman abilities is impossible."[24]

As long as we have not practiced, attained, and experienced *nibbāna* for ourselves, we should be aware that all our concepts of it are much the same as the image of the elephant in the story, which goes:

> At one time in Sāvatthī there were many different recluses, brahmins, and wanderers of different doctrines and theories, all holding their own views to be right and all others false. Arguments and contention were rife and they stabbed each other with the spears of their tongues, saying, "The truth (*dhamma*) is like this, not like that. The truth is not like that, it is like this." The bhikkhus brought the matter to the Buddha, and he told them this story:
>
> "Such a situation has already occurred. A king in Sāvatthī ordered his advisers to assemble all the men blind from birth who were at that time living in Sāvatthī. Then he had an elephant brought forward and told the blind men to acquaint themselves with it. The adviser let one group of blind men examine the elephant's head, and told them, 'This is what an elephant is like.' Then he showed another group the elephant's ears, saying, 'This is what an elephant is like.' Other groups he let touch the elephant's tusks, trunk, body, feet, back, tail, and tail-tip, telling each that 'an elephant is like this.' Then the adviser told the king, 'The blind men have all familiarized themselves with the elephant, Sire.' Then the king went to where the blind men were assembled and asked them, 'You have all seen the elephant, is that so?' The blind men answered, 'We have all seen the elephant, Sire.' The king then said to them, 'Then tell me what an elephant is like.'
>
> "Then the blind men who had touched the elephant's head said that an elephant was like a pot; those who had touched the elephant's ears said that an elephant was like a winnowing

basket; those who had touched the elephant's tusks said that an elephant was like a plowshare; those who had touched the elephant's trunk said that an elephant was like a plow handle; those who had touched the elephant's body said that an elephant was like a granary; those who had touched the elephant's feet said that an elephant was like a post; those who had touched the elephant's back said that an elephant was like a mortar; those who had touched the elephant's tail said that an elephant was like a pestle; those who had touched the elephant's tail-tip said that an elephant was like a broom. In the end the blind men got into a heated argument, saying, 'An elephant is like this, not like that,' 'An elephant is not like that, it is like this,' giving the king cause for great merriment."

At the end of the story, the Buddha gave the following utterance in verse:

"Thus do some recluses and brahmins get stuck on these theories and views. Those who see only a part of the truth hold different views and inevitably fall into argument."[25]

The State of One Who Attains *Nibbāna*

Because Buddhism places emphasis on things that can actually be put into practice, practicing for clear knowledge and results in real life,[26] speculation and debate over things that must be known through experience is not encouraged any more than is needed as a foundation of understanding for their attainment. Thus, when it comes to the subject of *nibbāna*, studying the state of one who attains *nibbāna* and the visible benefits of its attainment, which can be seen in life or in the character of the enlightened person, is of more practical value and more in keeping with Buddhist principles than trying to describe the state of *nibbāna* itself.

The state of one who has attained *nibbāna* may be gleaned from the terms used to refer to the characteristics of the enlightened being, which can comprise both positive or negative meanings.

Many of these terms are words of praise and respect for one who has qualities of purity, excellence, or attainment of the highest, such as *arahant* (worthy one, one far from defilements), *khīnāsava* (vanquisher of the outflows), *asekha* (one who has finished learning, or one who possesses the *asekhadhamma*, the qualities of one beyond learning), *parikkhīṇabhavasaṁyojana* (one who is done away with the fetters[27] that bind to existence), *vusitavanta* or *vusitabrahmacariya* (one who has completed the holy life), *katakaraṇīya* (one who has done what was to be done), *ohitabhāra* (one who has laid down the burden), *anuppattasadattha* (one who has realized one's own benefit), *sammadaññāvimutta* (one who is freed through right knowledge), *uttamapurisa* (the highest being, a most excellent person), *mahāpurisa* (one who is great in virtue), *sampannakusala* (one endowed with complete skillfulness), *paramakusala* (one who has the greatest skillfulness).

Not a few of the terms make reference to terms used in previous doctrines and religions, but given a new meaning that accords with the teachings and practice of Buddhism, such as a true "brahmin" (one who has cast off unskillful qualities; originally = the name given to a member of the highest caste in the caste system); *dakkhiṇeyya* (one who is worthy of offerings; originally = name given to the brahmin worthy of payment for performance of sacrifices); *nahātaka* (one bathed in Dhamma, who creates clean *kamma*, and provides security for all beings; originally = a name given to a brahmin who performs a bathing ceremony for anointing a higher-ranked brahmin); *vedagū* (one attained to or completed in learning, who is liberated from attachment to all feelings; originally = a title given to a brahmin who has completed study of the three Vedas); *samaṇa* (a peaceful one, one who has calmed the defilements; originally = a religious wanderer); *kevalī* (a completed one; originally = name given to one who has attained perfection in Jainism); *ariya* (a civilized or noble one, one who practices harmlessness toward all beings; originally = the name given to the top three *vaṇṇa* [castes], or *āryan* by birth).[28]

Among many Buddhists, the preference is to discuss the qualities of an arahant and a noble one in negative terms, defined by the defilements that are given up or abandoned. For instance, a stream enterer (*sotāpanna*) gives up three fetters (*saṁyojana*); a once-returner (*sakadāgāmī*) gives up those three fetters and also reduces the level of greed (*rāga*), anger, and delusion; a non-returner (*anāgāmī*) gives up all five of the lower level of fetters, and an arahant gives up all ten of the fetters. Or the arahant is described in brief as "one who has given up desire, anger, and delusion," or "given up defilements." The advantage of this kind of terminology is that it is clear and easy to measure, but it is a narrow perspective. It doesn't clearly show what special qualities, characteristics, lifestyle, or benefits toward the world are possessed by the arahant and the noble ones.

In fact, there are several words describing the positive attributes of the arahant, but as an explanation or teaching this approach tends to be broad, and it is difficult to narrow it down to define the qualities in order or in levels or specific points.

Here I would like instead to choose a descriptive term that shows the qualities and characteristics of the arahant in a broad and comprehensive manner that is systematic, easily summarized, and clearly expanded on, as an alternative for all the other terms. It is also a word that was used by the Buddha himself.

That word is *bhāvitatta*, which is directly translated as "a person whose self is well trained" or "a developed person." It is a word that was used with all arahants: the Buddha, the "silent buddhas" (*paccekabuddha*), and all the arahant disciples, as for example in the *Mahāparinibbāna Sutta* when describing the Buddha's journey to the place of his decease, where the Buddha is referred to as "the Developed One."

> "The Buddha...journeyed to the Kakudhā River, which had clear water, fresh and clean, and went down to bathe in and drink the water. The Buddha, surrounded by the bhikkhu retinue... journeyed to Ambavana and said to the bhikkhu Cundaka, 'Help fold my outer robe into four layers for me to lie down.' Venerable Cundaka, having been so ordered by the Developed One (Bhāvittata), immediately spread the outer robe in four layers."[29]

The *Loka Sutta* (also called the *Bahujanahita Sutta*) has similar content but with a broader range, and is well worth studying:

> "Bhikkhus, these three kinds of persons, arising in the world, arise for the welfare of many, for the happiness of many, for the support of the world, for the benefit, for welfare, for the happiness, of devas and humans. What are the three?
>
> "Bhikkhus, the Tathāgata arises in this world, an arahant, rightly self-enlightened, endowed with knowledge and conduct, well gone, a knower of the world, an unsurpassed trainer of trainable men, teacher of devas and humans, open-hearted, dispenser of the truth. That Tathāgata teaches the Dhamma that is fine in the beginning, fine in the middle, and fine in the end; he declares the holy life in the letter and meaning, utterly pure and complete.
>
> "Bhikkhus, this first type of person, arising in the world, arises for the welfare of many, for the happiness of many, for the support of the world, for the benefit, for the welfare, for the happiness, of devas and humans.
>
> "Moreover, a disciple of that teacher, an arahant, vanquisher of the outflows (*khīnāsava*)... liberated through full knowledge, teaches the Dhamma, fine in the beginning, fine in the middle, fine in the end; he declares the holy life in the letter and meaning, utterly pure and complete.
>
> "Bhikkhus, this second type of person, arising in the world, arises for the welfare of many, for the happiness of many, for the support of the world, for the benefit, for welfare, for the happiness, of devas and humans.
>
> "Moreover, bhikkhus, a disciple of that disciple of the teacher, who is still a learner, is still practicing, is learned, possessed of morality and discipline, teaches the Dhamma, fine in the beginning, fine in the middle, fine in the end, declares the holy life in the letter and the spirit, utterly pure and complete.
>
> "Bhikkhus, this third type of person, arising in the world, arises for the welfare of many, for the happiness of many, for

> the support of the world, for the benefit, for the welfare, for the happiness, of devas and humans.
>
> "The Teacher, seeker of the highest good, is the first type of person in the world. Following him there are the followers (*sāvaka*), the *bhāvitatta*, and from there are the learning disciples (*sekhasāvaka*), who are still practicing, who are learned and possessed of morality.[30]

The adjective *bhāvitatta* used to describe the Buddha and the arahants, expanded on as *bhāvitakāya*, *bhāvitasīla*, *bhāvitacitta*, and *bhāvitapaññā*, is connected to the teaching known as the four cultivations (*bhāvanā*), which are *kāyabhāvanā*, *sīlabhāvanā*, *cittabhāvanā*, and *paññābhāvanā* (*bhāvita* being the adjectival or adverbial form and *bhāvanā* being the noun).

So, from what has been already discussed, we can say that the arahants have completed the four *bhāvanā*, as follows:

1. *Kāyabhāvanā*: bodily development, which is developing the relationship with the material or physical environment, particularly through the five senses (eye, ear, nose, tongue, and body) by practicing toward it in a way that is beneficial, not leading to harm, that causes the arising of skillful qualities (*kusaladhamma*) and the decline of unskillful qualities (*akusaladhamma*).
2. *Sīlabhāvanā*: moral development, which is development of behavior and social interaction by being established in disciplines, not harming or causing trouble, living harmoniously and supportively with others.
3. *Cittabhāvanā*: mental development, which is training the mind to be strong and stable, growing in good qualities such as kindness and compassion, possessed of predilection for the good (*chanda*), effort, patient endurance, concentration and cheerfulness, buoyancy, happiness, and clarity.
4. *Paññābhāvanā*: wisdom development, which is training wisdom to grow into clear awareness of the truth of things, knowing and understanding things as they are, knowing them in full,

clearly seeing the world and life as they actually are, able to free the mind, to make oneself pure of defilements and be free of suffering, able to solve problems and do things with wisdom of their causes and conditions.

Now that we know the meaning of the word *bhāvanā*, which is a teaching on four kinds of practice, we can better understand the *bhāvita*, which are qualities of those who have completed the practice, as follows.

*Developed in Body (*Bhāvitakāya*)*

As already stated, while the Buddha referred to *bhāvitakāya* on many occasions in the Tipiṭaka, the word is not explained. It is as if taken as understood. However, sometimes there were outsiders, wanderers and members of other sects, who bought up this issue and spoke of it according to their own understanding, which caused the Buddha to give his explanation.

The *Mahācakka Sutta* relates that one morning Saccaka Niganthaputta, who was well known at the time, had a discussion with the Buddha, beginning by bringing up the subject of bodily development (*kāyabhāvanā*) and mental development (*cittabhāvanā*). He said that according to his view, the disciples of the Buddha practiced only mental development, not bodily development.

The commentaries explain that Saccaka had this view because he saw the bhikkhus isolating themselves in peaceful places and not practicing austerities. When he gave this view, the Buddha asked him what, as he understood it, was *kāyabhāvanā*. Saccaka gave the example of practicing austerities, ascetic practices, and self-mortification (*attakilamathānuyoga*).

The Buddha then asked what he had learned about *cittabhāvanā*. At this point Saccaka was unable to answer. The Buddha stated that even the *kāyabhāvanā* that he had described was not the development in body as practiced by the noble ones. Not knowing development in the body, how could he understand development of the mind? From there he explains to Saccaka what is and is not development of the body and development of the mind.

> "Here, Aggivessana, what is *bhāvitakāya* and *bhāvitacitta*? A noble disciple in this teaching and discipline, one who has learned, experiences pleasant feeling. Even though that disciple experiences pleasant feeling, he is not enamored or desirous of that pleasant feeling; he does not become one who is desirous or covetous of pleasant feeling. [When] that pleasant feeling ceases, on account of its cessation, unpleasant feeling (*dukkhavedanā*) arises. Experiencing that unpleasant feeling, he does not sorrow, does not become depressed, does not grieve, does not lament or beat his chest; he is not driven to distraction.
>
> "In this way, Aggivessana, because he is developed in body, that pleasant feeling, even though it arises, does not overcome and take hold in his mind; because he is developed in mind, unpleasant feeling, even though it arises, does not overcome and take hold in his mind.
>
> "Aggivessana, for a noble disciple, even though pleasant feeling arises, it does not overcome or take hold in the mind, because he is developed in body; even though unpleasant feeling arises, it does not overcome or take hold in the mind, because he is developed in mind. Having both, Aggivessana, a person can be said to be one who is developed in body and developed in mind."[31]

Kāyabhāvanā is in essence the development of the five senses, contact through the senses of eye, ear, nose, tongue, and body. In this sense, *kāyabhāvanā* seems to be the same as the development of the faculties (*indriyabhāvanā*). Development of the faculties begins with sense restraint, which the Buddha emphasized in the training of newly ordained bhikkhus. It can be called an initial practice, continuing on from moral training (later commentaries indeed coined the term *indriyasaṁvarasīla*, "the morality of sense restraint"). Let us first look at this initial teaching in the following Buddhavacana:

> "Now, Your Majesty, how is it that a bhikkhu is said to be one who guards the senses? Herein, Your Majesty, a bhikkhu in this teaching and discipline, having seen a form with the eye, does not attach to the overall image, does not attach to the detail. He practices for the restraint of the faculty that is the eye, which, if left unrestrained, would be a cause for coarse, unskillful conditions such as covetousness and dejection (*abhijjhā domanassa*) to overwhelm the mind. He maintains his eye faculty, becoming one who is restrained in the eye faculty. Hearing a sound with the ear... smelling an odor with the nose... tasting a flavor with the tongue... feeling a sensation in the body... knowing a mental state with the mind [as before]. That bhikkhu is possessed of sense restraint that is noble. He experiences unblemished happiness within. Your Majesty, thus is a bhikkhu known as one who is restrained in the faculties."[32]

There is a restraint of the faculties that is more profound, or described in a different way, which I wish to present for comparison. This kind of restraint of the faculties, when well developed, causes the fulfillment of the three *sucarita* (avenues of good conduct); the three *sucarita*, when well developed, cause the fulfillment of four foundations of mindfulness; the four foundations of mindfulness cause the fulfillment of the seven enlightenment factors (*bojjhaṅga*); the seven enlightenment factors, when well developed, cause the fulfillment of knowledge (*vijjā*) and liberation (*vimutti*), the final rewards.

This was spoken to Kuṇḍaḷīya the Wanderer:

> "Kuṇḍaḷīya, and how does a person develop and make much of restraint of the faculties to perfect the three *sucarita*? Herein, Kuṇḍaḷīya, a bhikkhu in this teaching and discipline, on seeing a visual object that is pleasing to the eye, is not enamored, not carried away, does not allow greed (*rāga*) to build, and his body is stable, his mind unwavering and firm within, well freed. Again, seeing a visual object that is not pleasing to the eye, he

> is not cowed, not offended, not oppressed, not angered, and his body is stable, his mind unwavering within, well freed. Again, a bhikkhu hears a sound with the ear... smells an odor with the nose... tastes a flavor with the tongue... feels a sensation with the body... knows a mental state in the mind... [as before]. See here, Kuṇḍalīya, in this way does a person develop and make much of restraint of the faculties to perfect the three *sucarita*."[33]

Now let us look at an even higher level of training, called *indriya-bhāvanā*, the teaching given in the *Indriyabhāvanā Sutta*. In this sutta, after discussing the practice, the Buddha goes on to explain the difference between the training of a noble one who is still practicing (*sekha paṭipadā*) and that of an arahant, one who has finished the training (*bhāvitindriya*).

The story goes that at one time when the Buddha was staying in the forest at Kajaṅgala Nigama, the young man Uttara, a disciple of Pārāsiriya the brahmin, approached the Buddha. The Buddha asked him how Pārāsiriya the brahmin taught development of the faculties to his disciples. The young man answered that Pārāsiriya the brahmin taught development of the faculties by not allowing the eye to see forms, not allowing the ear to hear sounds. The Buddha answered that if the truth was as taught by this brahmin, then blind and deaf people would be developed in the faculties (*bhāvitindriya*). He explained that development of the faculties as taught by Pārāsiriya the brahmin differed from the supreme development of the faculties in the practice of the noble ones. From there, Venerable Ānanda then asked the Buddha to explain the teaching of the supreme development of the faculties in the practice of the noble ones, and here is a summary of the Buddha's reply:

> "Herein, Ānanda, and what is the ultimate development of the faculties in the practice of the noble ones? Ānanda, on seeing a form with the eye, a pleasant state arises, an unpleasant state arises, or a both pleasant and unpleasant state arises in a

bhikkhu in this teaching and discipline. He knows clearly in this way that a pleasant state, an unpleasant state, a both pleasant and unpleasant state has arisen. But that pleasant state, unpleasant state, or both pleasant and unpleasant state is conditioned, it is coarse, arisen dependent on determinants. However, this state is calm, this state is subtle—that is, equanimity (the mind neutral through knowledge and comprehension in balance). The pleasant state, unpleasant state, and both pleasant and unpleasant state that have arisen for him are extinguished, and equanimity is firmly established. Ānanda, any bhikkhu within whom, when a pleasant state, an unpleasant state, or a both pleasant and unpleasant state arises, those states, having arisen, are extinguished and equanimity is firmly and quickly established, instantly, without difficulty, as if a man with good eyes were to open his eyes and close them, or close his eyes and open them, this, Ānanda, is called the supreme development of the faculties in visual forms in the discipline of the noble ones.

"Ānanda, and again, on hearing a sound with the ear... smelling an odor with the nose... tasting a flavor with the tongue... feeling a sensation in the body... knowing a mental state in the mind [as before]. Ānanda, any bhikkhu within whom, when a pleasant state, an unpleasant state, or a both pleasant and unpleasant state arises, those states, having arisen, are extinguished and equanimity is firmly and quickly established, instantly, without difficulty, just as if a strong man were to slowly pour two or three droplets of water into a hot frying pan for an entire day, those droplets of water would doubtless be instantaneously evaporated and disappear, this, Ānanda, is called the supreme development of the faculties in mental states in the discipline of the noble ones.

"This, Ānanda, is the supreme development of the faculties in the discipline of the noble ones."

The Buddha next relates to Venerable Ānanda the practice of the learner (*sekha paṭipadā*):

> "Ānanda, and how is it for the learner (*sekha*) bhikkhu, one who is still practicing? Ānanda, on seeing a form with the eye, a pleasant state arises, an unpleasant state arises, a both pleasant and unpleasant state arises to a bhikkhu in this teaching and discipline. He is oppressed, wearied, disgusted with the pleasant state, the unpleasant state, and the both pleasant and unpleasant states that have arisen. On hearing a sound with the ear... on smelling an odor with the nose...on tasting a flavor with the tongue...on feeling a sensation in the body...on knowing a mental state in the mind...he is oppressed, wearied, disgusted with the pleasant state, the unpleasant state, and the both pleasant and unpleasant states that have arisen. Ānanda, this is the learner bhikkhu, one who is still practicing."

The Buddha finally relates to the practice of one who is fully developed:

> "Ānanda, and how is it for the noble one (*ariya*) who is developed in the faculties? Ānanda, on seeing a form with the eye, a pleasant state arises, an unpleasant state arises, a both pleasant and unpleasant state arises to a bhikkhu in this teaching and discipline. If he reflects thus: 'I will perceive that which is abhorrent (*paṭikūla*) as not abhorrent,' he is able to perceive that thing as not abhorrent. If he reflects thus: 'I will perceive that which is not abhorrent as abhorrent,' he is able to perceive that thing as abhorrent. If he reflects thus: 'I will perceive that which is both abhorrent and not abhorrent as not abhorrent,' he is able to perceive that thing as not abhorrent. If he reflects thus: 'I will perceive that which is neither abhorrent nor not abhorrent as abhorrent,' he is able to perceive that thing as abhorrent. If he reflects 'I will refrain from perceiving as either abhorrent or not abhorrent and dwell in equanimity with mindfulness and self-awareness (*sati sampajañña*),' he is able to dwell with equanimity in that thing with mindfulness and self-awareness.

> "Ānanda, again, on hearing a sound with the ear...on smelling an odor with the nose...on tasting a flavor with the tongue...on feeling a sensation in the body...on knowing a mental state in the mind..., a pleasant state arises, an unpleasant state arises, a both pleasant and unpleasant state arises to a bhikkhu in this teaching and discipline...If he reflects 'I will refrain from perceiving as either abhorrent or not abhorrent and dwell in equanimity with mindfulness and self-awareness,' he is able to dwell with equanimity toward that thing with mindfulness and self-awareness.
>
> "Herein, Ānanda, just this is the noble one, one who has developed the faculties."[34]

*Developed in Morality (*Bhāvitasīla*)*

In terms of general conduct, which we refer to as "morality" (*sīla*), there are not many descriptions of the characteristics of an enlightened being. This may be because, according to the teaching, morality is an elementary level of training (*sikkhā*). The noble ones have all attained perfect morality from the very first level of noble one, the stream enterer (*sotāpanna*),[35] and the liberation in mind (*cetovimutti*) and liberation in wisdom (*paññāvimutti*) attained by an enlightened being are such that any violations (*dussīla*) or immorality no longer remain.[36] All that remains to be considered, then, is to define what kinds of lives the arahants live and what duties or activities they perform, and how.

First, arahants are people who have extinguished[37] or done away with[38] *kamma*. Their actions are no longer referred to as *kamma*. In the Abhidhamma texts their deeds are called *kiriyā* (action).[39] By "extinguishing *kamma*," we mean that deeds are not committed under the influence of ignorance (*avijjā*), desire (*taṇhā*), and clinging (*upādāna*), but with a mind that is free, with wisdom that is totally aware of things in terms of cause and effect, no longer acting as an unenlightened person and acting like a noble one (*ariyajana*). Instead, one does things in accordance solely with that action's direct objective by cause and effect, and therefore it is action that is freed from, and transcends, good *kamma*. As for bad *kamma*, it does not come into the discussion, since any delusion, greed, and aversion that would be the causes for such bad deeds are gone.[40]

Even so, whenever we do something there is usually some motivation for doing it, and the essential core of that motivation is usually aspiration or wanting, which should be included under the term *desire*, or *taṇhā*. Since enlightened beings have given up *taṇhā*, one might think that they would be without motivation, so how could they do anything? They would become inactive. True, they may not do bad actions, but they wouldn't do good actions either, so what use would that be?

To put it simply, we have two kinds of motivation: the motivation of *taṇhā*, which is a motivation that arises from feeling. It is desire and wanting in accordance with likes, such as wanting to taste a delicious flavor. It is a kind of wanting that doesn't require any knowledge of right or wrong, benefit or harm. The second kind of motivation is the motivation arising from wisdom. It is the motivation that arises from knowledge—that is, aspiration or wanting that is in accordance with knowledge and understanding of cause and effect, and in accordance with what is right in actuality—as, for example, seeing a road surface that is damaged, unclean, obstructed, or slippery, understanding that a road as a means of travel should be clean, orderly, and safe, and wanting to clear it and make it unobstructed. This kind of wanting is the second kind of motivation. It has its own special name to distinguish it from the motivation of *taṇhā*, and that is the motivation of *chanda*.

Chanda is wanting or wishing in accordance with the reality—that is, wanting something to be good, perfect, and as it should be—which is not related to like or dislike, or gaining or losing in order to feed one's sense of self. The wanting or aspiration that is the motivation of *chanda* develops in accordance with the development of wisdom.

Chanda when related to people expresses itself in the wish for a person to be good, perfect, strong, happy, and admirable, including wanting that person to live in a state that is correct, appropriate, and without fault or error. In terms of relating to people, *chanda* is split up into different streams, according to the situation: goodwill (*mettā*), wanting people to be happy and well in normal times; compassion (*karuṇā*), wanting people to be free of their suffering in times when they have fallen low or are troubled; sympathetic joy (*muditā*), wanting to support people to further happiness and success in good times; and equanimity (*upekkhā*), wanting people to maintain themselves in what is correct, just, and not harmful.

For the enlightened being, in particular, who is freed of suffering and is fully liberated, having a motivation that arises from wisdom pushes the force of *chanda*, in the form of compassion, to the fore, and therefore the Buddha and the arahants have compassion as one of their main qualities.

The feeling that expands outward to help others, known as compassion, is an important motivating factor in the life of one who has attained *nibbāna*. Compassion is contingent on wisdom and having a free mind. Wisdom in this sense is known by the specialized term *vijjā* (knowledge). The possession of a free mind is called *vimutti* (liberation). As a set, these three qualities are *vijjā* (the wisdom of reality, which gives no footing for self to stand on), *vimutti* (liberation, clarity, and freedom), and *karuṇā* (the outward-going sympathy of the mind as it feels for the suffering of others, and the desire to make them free). They are the opposites to *avijjā* (ignorance of reality, which leads to the feeling of self), *taṇhā* (the desire for the self to relate to some thing or state in a way that caters to the lack or imperfection of the self, or nourishes and expands it) and *upādāna* (clinging fast to things or states that are seen to be important to the service of the self, or to the greatness and stability of the self).

One who attains *nibbāna* gives up ignorance, desire, and clinging, leaving only wisdom and compassion as motivations for action. In this sense, we can see that if desire were the only motivation for action, real altruistic actions would be impossible. Similarly, as long as desire is the motivation for helpful actions, such actions will not be true compassion.

In fact, desire (as also ignorance and clinging) is not only a dangerous motivation, but also one that causes us to be blind to our own benefit and that of others. Even if we do see them, we see them distortedly—what is beneficial we instead see as not beneficial, and what is not beneficial we see as beneficial—manifesting as greed (*rāga*), aversion (*dosa*) and delusion (*moha*), or as the five hindrances,[41] which obstruct the functioning of the mind. When the mind is free of these defilements it is calm and smooth, and sees real benefit.[42]

The final reason that those who attain *nibbāna* have no need to think of their own benefit, or concern themselves with themselves, and can thus fully devote themselves to the benefit of others, is that they have already achieved their own benefit. An arahant is described as one who has realized one's own benefit (*anuppattasadattha*) and one whose task is done (*katakaraṇīya*). The arahants' work is finished. Having fulfilled personal benefit (*attattha*) and being endowed with their own benefit (*attahitasampatti*), they no longer have to bother themselves with their own concerns, and can devote themselves fully to the benefit of others (*parattha*), leading the lives that remain to them for the benefit of others (*parahitapaṭipatti*).[43] Equipped with such preparation, an arahant is capable of truly fulfilling the qualities of being a friend to all (*sabbamitta*, *sabbasakha*) and having concern for all beings (*sabbabhūtānukampaka*).[44]

Now let us consider the life conduct of one who has attained *nibbāna* in two ways: first, in performance of duty, and second, in personal conduct.

In performance of duty, the arahant, as one who has been released from all bondage, is the exemplary member of the Saṅgha, able to perform the duties of a disciple of the Buddha to the utmost.

The work of a Buddhist disciple (*sāvaka*) is clearly indicated in the exhortation often given by the Buddha, beginning with his message to the first group of realized disciples before they were sent out to spread the teaching, in the first year of the Buddha's mission:[45] "for the benefit and happiness of the many, for the welfare of the world, for the benefit, welfare and happiness of gods and humans." This phrase illustrates an important objective of the holy life (*brahmacariya*), or Buddhism,[46] a gauge for measuring the conduct of a bhikkhu,[47] and the benefits to be expected from one who can be said to have attained excellence according to the Buddhist teachings.[48]

The duty or fundamental task of one who has attained *nibbāna* is thus teaching and imparting knowledge, fostering wisdom, mindfulness (*satipaññā*) and virtues, and living and behaving as an example, in a way that embodies happiness and virtue, in a life that is wholesome and can be used as an example by later generations. The duty of teaching and imparting knowledge to others, in particular, may almost be regarded as obligatory for one who has realized *nibbāna*.[49]

In terms of personal conduct, a similar principle applies: the aim is for the benefit of others. Although an arahant is said to have completed one's task, and the various observances one maintained in order to attain *nibbāna* are no longer necessary, it seems that if there were cause for it, the arahants would continue these practices. On a personal level, such practices were their way of maintaining a pleasant abiding (*diṭṭhadhammasukhavihāra*). In relation to others, they were for the benefit of later generations, as good examples to be followed. Examples of this are the Buddha continuing to live in forest areas after his enlightenment[50] and Mahā Kassapa maintaining the allowable ascetic (*dhutaṅga*) practices.[51]

Even for those who are the elders in the community, who may not yet be enlightened, there are injunctions to think of one's conduct as an example for later generations.[52] Thus, for the arahant, who is the highest paradigm, such considerations would have to be especially keen. Note also that some of the training rules in the monastic discipline were laid down not in regard to bad conduct as such, but to behaviors that were simply considered improper from the perspective of later generations.[53]

All in all, the conduct of the arahants, both in their performance of duty and in their personal conduct, was aimed at the benefit of others, with regard to being a good example for later generations: this is the concern of cultivating benefit for others, conforming with the virtue of compassion as a motivating force.

However, if we were to look for examples from the lives of the arahant disciples in the time of the Buddha, it is difficult to find relevant information. It must be gleaned from scattered sources throughout the teachings, in the regulations of the Vinaya, and stories from the later texts. Even then, the records are not complete, because the texts give emphasis to teachings or explanations of the Dhamma and Vinaya.

The stories of the foremost disciples (*etadagga*),[54] which the commentators hold to be appointments of distinction, and where the names of many arahants are compiled, are virtually announcements and celebrations of special qualities possessed by some of the disciples, or unusual features for which some of them were well known. If they do deal with the performance of duty, it is only in those respects where certain of the arahants were unusually gifted. For example, Venerable Dabbamallaputta was the foremost in assignment of dwellings (*senāsanapaññāpaka*); however, no foremost assigner of meal invitations (*bhattudesaka*) or robes (*cīvarabhājaka*) or construction overseer (*navakammika*)—which, like the dwelling assigner, are also positions conferred on individual bhikkhus by the Saṅgha—are mentioned.

An arahant bhikkhu who was mentioned as foremost in a certain area may have had some particular regular activity for which the quality he was extolled was merely a support. Moreover, there are problems with the meaning of some of the titles of *etadagga*, which are not yet clearly understood. Thus, the list of foremost disciples[55] is not sufficiently pertinent to describe the kinds and extent of the duties of the arahants. Even so, among the names of the *etadagga*, we find that many of the qualities for which bhikkhus are extolled were related to teaching. It may be said that the task of teaching, counseling, and training others is one that should be performed by all who have attained *nibbāna*, each according to his or her abilities. Other tasks and duties vary according to the background in training and temperament (*dhātu*) of the individual.

Those who were gifted at teaching and commanded respect accumulated groups of followers and became preceptors (*upajjhāya*) and teachers (*ācariya*) with large followings. In addition to their general teaching duties, they were also required to give training to their followers, as illustrated in many stories of the great disciples traveling around followed by large retinues.[56]

Apart from responsibility to the work of teaching, providing education and administration, the sources and stories appearing in the texts show that the arahants also conducted themselves as examples of conscientiousness, communal responsibility and respect for the Saṅgha. Such thinking is important, since the Buddhist social system holds the Saṅgha, the community, as of major importance, and the Buddha always stressed the harmony of the group in teachings such as the conditions for non-decline (*aparihāniyadhamma*),[57] adherence to the Dhamma,[58] and regulations of the monastic discipline (Vinaya), especially those dealing with duties of the order (*saṅghakamma*).[59]

There are many stories indicating that the arahants took an interest, and were required to take an interest, in communal responsibilities, and that they respected the Saṅgha. For example, when the Buddha allowed the Saṅgha to perform the *uposatha* ceremony, chanting the Pāṭimokkha (the core code of discipline for bhikkhus and bhikkhunis) and proving their purity every half-month, the Venerable Mahā Kappina had a doubt as to whether or not he should attend the ceremony, since he was an arahant and already completely pure. Knowing of his train of thought, the Buddha cautioned him: "If you, who are a brahmin (that is, an arahant), do not respect the *uposatha*, who will respect the *uposatha*? Go to the *uposatha* and *saṅghakamma*."[60]

Venerable Dabbamallaputta had attained arahantship from an early age. He thought to himself, "I attained arahantship from the time I was seven. Whatever there is for a disciple to attain, I have attained already. There is no further task for me to do, and no need to go back and add to what has already been done. In what way can I be of service to the order?" He then thought, "I should help to organize lodgings for the order and distribute the meals." He then went and informed the Buddha of his intention. The Buddha gave his approval, and had the order convened in order to formally appoint him as the *senāsanapaññāpaka* (assigner of dwellings) and the *bhattudesaka* (assigner of meals).[61]

When events arose that may have had an adverse effect on the peace and harmony of the teaching (*sāsanā*), the arahant elders made efforts to resolve the situation, even though they were normally inclined to peace and seclusion. Mahā Kassapa, for example, began the proceedings of the First Great Council,[62] and Venerables Yasakākaṇḍaputta, Sambhūtasāṇavāsī, and Revata instigated the Second Great Council.[63]

At the First Great Council, the meeting passed a motion imposing an offense on the elder Ānanda for a number of failings in his service as the Buddha's attendant. Even though Ānanda could fully explain that he had done his duty flawlessly, he nevertheless obeyed the motion of the order, first clearly giving the reasons for his actions.[64] When the order convened to settle a dispute in the Second Great Council, two of the arahants failed to arrive at the meeting on time. The elders at the meeting imposed a punishment on those two by appointing them to perform certain duties.[65]

When King Milinda, the Greek king who ruled over the northwestern region of India and who was well versed in matters of religion and philosophy, was holding debates with various religions and doctrines, he caused great insecurity for the order. The arahant elders held a meeting to see what could be done to counter the situation. One of the arahants, Rohaṇa, had entered into the meditative state of cessation (*saññāvedayitanirodha samāpatti*) in the Himalaya mountains and did not know of the meeting, so he did not attend. The meeting sent a messenger to invite him, at the same time conferring on him a punishment consisting of taking on the responsibility of ordaining and training the young boy Nāgasena.[66]

Regardless of how true the details of these stories are, especially the latter ones, they are clear indications of the concept that the arahants are the paradigms of conduct in relation to respect for the order and attention to communal activities, and this is a longstanding Buddhist tradition. The rationale (it could be called the motivation) upon which this is based is the same one mentioned above: "to ensure the leading of the holy life (*brahmacariya*) for a long time to come, for the benefit and happiness of gods and humans."[67]

*Developed in Mind (*Bhāvitacitta*)*

The principal mental quality of an enlightened being is that of freedom, or transcendence. This state arises from wisdom: when the mind sees things as they really are, and is wise to conditioned things, it escapes the grip of defilements. The attainment of this state is often described in the scriptures thus: "The mind cultivated by wisdom is freed from the outflows,"[68] or "Knowing this and seeing this, his mind is freed from the outflow of sensual desire (*kāmāsava*), the outflow of becoming (*bhavāsava*) and the outflow of ignorance (*avijjāsava*)."[69]

One aspect of freedom is that the mind is not enslaved by alluring or inciting mental objects that are bases for desire or greed, aversion and delusion.[70] Moreover, a corollary of the absence of desire, aversion, and delusion is absence of fear, fright, shock, or trembling.[71] Not only is there no longer any cause for committing any gross bad actions, there is also a guarantee of honest (*sucarita*) intentions in one's conduct. One is able to be the master of one's moods (*ārammaṇa*), such that one becomes "one whose faculties are trained": when objects such as sights, sounds, smells, or tastes are cognized and the feeling arises that they are either likable, not likable or neutral, one is able to control one's perceptions, to see things that are abhorrent (*paṭikūla*) as not abhorrent and to see things that are not abhorrent as abhorrent, for example, and even to discard perceptions of not abhorrent and abhorrent altogether, and therefore be impartial with mindfulness and clear comprehension, as one wishes,[72] as already explained in relation to development of the faculties in the section "Developed in Body." This is one who is controlled by mindfulness. Someone like this is said to be well trained,[73] to have conquered oneself, which is the greatest victory.[74]

In addition, one has a mind that is solid and unwavering in the face of agreeable and disagreeable sensations, like a rocky mountain that stands steadfast even in the strongest wind,[75] or like the great earth, which supports everything without aversion or resentment regardless of whatever good or bad, clean or filthy things are thrown onto it.[76]

Another facet of liberation is transcendence, not attaching to things. A common analogy is that of a lotus leaf, which is not blemished by water, or a lotus flower, which takes root in mud but is itself clean, beautiful, and pure, untainted by the mud.[77] It begins with non-attachment to sensuality, non-attachment to merit and demerit, and non-attachment to mental objects that would cause hankering for the past and hoping for the future, as is said in the Tipiṭaka: "Those who attain the Dhamma do not pine for what is past and do not hanker for what is yet to come. They abide in the present; that is why their complexion is radiant. As for those who are weak in wisdom, they hanker for things not yet come and pine over that which has passed away, and therefore they are haggard, like reeds uprooted and left in the sun."[78]

What is noteworthy here is that this "not pining for the past" and "not hankering for the future" are given as mental qualities rather than intellectual states. In Western terminology we would call them emotional qualities. Thus, it does not mean that an arahant does not use wisdom to consider tasks to be done in the future, or make use of knowledge of the past. On the contrary, because the state of mind of the arahants is clear of the past and the future, they are fully able to utilize their knowledge of those things rationally. There are words describing the conduct of an arahant in relation to the past and the future, but they are concerned with the wisdom faculty. Examples are *pubbenivāsānussatiñāṇa* (recollection of past lives), *cutūpapātañāṇa* (direct knowledge of the death and rebirth of other beings), *atītaṁsañāṇa* (direct knowledge into the past), and *anāgataṁsañāṇa* (direct knowledge into the future),[79] as well as the tendency of the arahants to do things for the benefit of future generations, as will be described below.

Some of the mental characteristics of an enlightened being may seem negative to an unenlightened being. One of the more conspicuous of these is the quality known in Pali as *nirāsa* or *nirāsā*,[80] which, translated into common speech, means "hopeless" or "without hope." The hopelessness or lack of hope of one who has attained *nibbāna* has a much more profound meaning than what is normally understood by the term. Unenlightened beings usually live on hope, and that hope is founded on wanting: because they want to have and to be certain things, they entertain the hope of achieving and being those things. This hope is one of the driving forces of their lives. People who are disappointed because their hopes have not been fulfilled, or who give up hope because there is no longer any chance of fulfilling it, are considered losers, sufferers. Those who have their hopes fulfilled by getting what they want, or who have hope because they can see that their desire is likely to be fulfilled, are regarded as fortunate and happy.

Enlightened beings are similar to the first kind of person, the one without hope, but their case is different. The hopelessness or lack of hope of enlightened beings results from their no longer having the desires that cause hope. That is, not desiring this or that, not wanting to be this or that, there is nothing to be hoped for. Since there is nothing hoped for, they live without hope, having transcended both fulfillment and hopelessness as normally understood. They are fulfilled and whole in themselves. They transcend hope because they have complete happiness in each and every moment. It is impossible for them to be disappointed or to experience hopelessness or despair (compare this with the quality of "without faith" [*assaddha*], which is a quality of the wisdom type).

There are many other mental qualities that are related to those mentioned, such as "free of worry and concern"; "nothing lingering in the mind" (*akiñcana*); not thinking excitedly, free of agitation, free of fury and irritation, not depressed, not afraid, free of fear, calm (*santa*); happy, free of sorrow (*asoka*); stainless, immaculate (*viraja*); secure (*khema*); clear, cool (*sītibhūta, nibbuta*); contented, satisfied (*santuṭṭha*); satiated (*nicchāta*);[81] light-hearted and at ease whether walking, standing, sitting, or lying down.[82]

One quality that is worthy of special mention, and is often mentioned in the Tipiṭaka, is happiness. For example, "*Nibbāna* is the ultimate (*parama*) happiness,"[83] "those who attain *nibbāna* (*parinibbāna*) always sleep happily,"[84] "I have no worries, therefore I am happy."[85] Practitioners of Dhamma must see *nibbāna* as a kind of happiness in order for their practice to be properly directed, as stated in this Buddhavacana:

> "Bhikkhus, that a bhikkhu who sees *nibbāna* as suffering will be possessed of thoughts conducive to seeing the truth is not possible. That a bhikkhu who does not have reflections that are conducive to seeing the truth will progress to *sammattaniyāma* (certain determination of what is right, or the standard for what is right) is not possible. That a bhikkhu who has not progressed to *sammattaniyāma* will attain the fruit of stream entry, once-returner, non-returner, or arahant is not possible."[86]

Although *nibbāna* is happiness, and one who attains *nibbāna* is happy, those who attain it do not attach to happiness of any kind, including the happiness of *nibbāna*.[87] When cognizing external objects through eye, ear, or nose, for example, the arahants do experience the feeling (*vedanā*) contingent on those sense objects, be it pleasant, unpleasant or neutral, just as ordinary people do, but their experience differs in that it is not bound by defilements. They do not indulge in or attach to those feelings, so those feelings do not lead to desire. It is the experience of feeling on only one level. In short, they experience only bodily suffering, but not mental suffering. Feelings do not lead to agitation in the mind, and are thus said to be cooled.

The experience of feeling by the arahant is of a kind that does not harbor latent tendencies (*anussaya*), unlike the unenlightened being in whom, when experiencing pleasant feeling, the latent tendency of greed (*rāga*) is accumulated; when experiencing unpleasant feeling the latent tendency of aversion (*paṭigha*) is accumulated; and when experiencing neutral feelings the latent tendency to delusion (*avijjā*) is accumulated, increasing the habituation and intensity of those defilements.[88] For the arahant, it is impossible for external happiness and suffering to affect the inner calm, coolness, and happiness of the mind. The arahant's happiness is thus independent of external conditions. It is called "great *nirāmisasukha*," or "exceeding *nirāmisasukha*."[89]

When one's happiness is not dependent on external conditions, the vicissitudes of things according to the natural way of formations do not cause one suffering. No matter how the six kinds of sense objects may change, the arahant lives happily.[90] No matter how the five *khandhas* may change, the arahant is not distressed.[91] Wisdom to the truth of impermanence and change leads to peace and calm, and the mind is free of confusion and agitation. The arahant is always at ease. This state is said to be one meaning of the statement "being a refuge unto oneself" or "having the Dhamma for refuge."[92]

Another important word indicating the state of the enlightened mind, which incorporates many of the characteristics already mentioned, is *ārogya*, meaning "without illness," or "the state of having no illness," which we normally refer to as "health" or "being healthy." *Ārogya* is one of the epithets for *nibbāna*.[93] Absence of illness here refers to absence of mental illness, or mental health: "Reflect to yourself thus: 'Even though my body may be sick and ailing, my mind will not ail along with it.'"[94] The Buddha also spoke of two kinds of illness, illness of the body and illness of the mind: "Beings who can assert that they have lived without mental illness for even an instant are hard to find, except among the vanquishers of the outflows (*khīnāsava*)."[95] This Buddhavacana indicates that the arahant is one with perfect mental health.

Describing the state of one who has attained *nibbāna* as one of perfect mental health is a good way of indicating the value of attaining *nibbāna*. Unenlightened people may wonder how it is that an enlightened being, void of the seeking and indulgence in happiness that most people cherish, can be happy, and what it is that is good about *nibbāna*.

Absence of illness and good health is happiness and perfect within itself. It is far better than being sick or having a chronic illness. Whenever the illness arises, one is agitated, discomforted, and distressed. As soon as one obtains medicine or treatment to suppress the symptoms, one gains some relief. The more severe the symptoms, the more intense is the feeling of happiness when they are relieved. The happiness that is simply the security and inner ease, perfect within itself, of having no illness—which means one does not experience the frequent or temporary happiness when agitation and stress of illnesses are relieved—can be compared to the happiness of *nibbāna*.

The happiness resulting from temporarily suppressing the symptoms of an illness can be compared to the unenlightened being's search for happiness. The analogy is given of a man with eczema, who has broken out in a rash, with sores all over his body. The bacteria are constantly eating at his sores, and he is always scratching them and basking by fire. As he scratches and roasts his sores, the sores become itchier and more infected. The happiness and pleasure he obtains is from having sores to be scratched. He continues on like this until a skilled doctor comes along and prepares some medicine and cures the disease. The man then becomes cured of his eczema and is healthy, happy, free, independent, and at liberty to go anywhere he pleases.

The scratching of those sores and the sitting and roasting at the fireside, which that man once felt to give so much pleasure, no longer seem to be pleasurable at all. In fact, if he were to continue doing those things now that he no longer has the illness, they would be painful and unpleasant. However, this would not have been apparent to him while he still had the eczema.

Unenlightened beings gain pleasure from obtaining objects to feed their desires, but they are then more incited, roused, and agitated by the "spark" of desire. Living in this way, their happiness, pleasure, and delight revolve around titillating, heating up, and intensifying the sparks of desires, and then seeking something to feed them, and so extinguish the resulting agitation and confusion from time to time. When *nibbāna* is attained, the spark of desire that caused the excitement, agitation, and confusion has gone out. The enlightened being is free and independent, and no longer sees any happiness in the various actions aimed at pacifying that excitement and agitation.[96]

The unenlightened being is like someone with an itch that must be scratched, and their happiness lies in scratching it. The itchier it is, the more they scratch; the more they scratch, the itchier it gets. The itchier it is, the more happiness they feel from scratching, and the itchier it is, the more they can scratch. So the unenlightened being likes to raise the level of happiness by searching for ways to increase the agitation of the itch, and thereby experience more happiness in the "scratching." The liberated being is like a person who is cured of the itch, whose body is whole and healthy. Theirs is the happiness of having no itch to scratch. They may, however, be criticized by unenlightened beings for losing the happiness of scratching.

Attainment of arahantship also leads to a change in one's character, and in attitude to life and the world in general. The change that mental development brings about can be readily understood when compared to the growth of a child into an adult: the toys that were once loved and cherished, and once seen to be so real, important, and vital to a child, lose their attraction when the child grows to adulthood. They no longer excite any emotion. To an adult, the sight of children eagerly admiring and competing for such things may seem comical, and the ways children find pleasure seem meaningless. In the same way, those who attain *nibbāna* have reached a higher level of development than the ordinary person. Their attitude to life and the world, to the things that are valued and cherished by unenlightened beings and their ways of life, is changed.[97]

*Developed in Wisdom (*Bhāvitapaññā*)*

The important feature of the intellectual foundation of one who has attained *nibbāna* is the perception of things as they really are, beginning with the cognition of objects via the sense bases with a mind that is impartial and mindful, unmoved by likes and dislikes. The enlightened being is able to look at those objects as they really are, from their arising to their cessation, without attachment, obstruction, confusion, or trauma resulting from being "tripped up" by that object. The unenlightened being gets tripped up by mental objects, and distorted knowledge and understanding arise: things are seen through the conditioning of defilements (*kilesa*) rather than as they really are. For example, one and the same event described by someone who likes it, with words of praise, may seem agreeable and produce a favorable impression in the listener, but when described by another person without the support of that bias, may seem disagreeable. When we hear one and the same piece of information from someone we like, we might say that it is good and proper, but when we hear it from someone we do not like, we may see it as wrong and unacceptable.[98]

On a deeper level, the wisdom of the enlightened being is knowledge of the true nature of conditions in accordance with the universal characteristics, as impermanent, *dukkha* and not-self. The enlightened being is wise to conventions and concepts, not hypnotized by the mere external appearance of things, and accepts all aspects of the truth, rather than sticking to only one.

Knowing things as they are helps to counter the misunderstanding of Buddhism as a pessimistic religion. One who has penetrated the Buddhadhamma knows that the five *khandhas* are neither entirely pleasant nor entirely painful.[99] One knows that "[it is rather] the sensual desire born from people's thinking that is sensually enticing (*kāma*)... the fascinating objects of this world are not in themselves sensually enticing... the fascinating objects of this world are simply established as they are. Thus, the brave ones do away with (only) the liking for those objects."[100]

To be enlightened, one must first understand both the positive or delightful aspect (*assāda*, "the sweet taste"), the bad aspect or fault (*ādīnava*, "the danger"), and the way to escape from (*nissaraṇa*) sensual objects, the world, and the five *khandhas*, seeing the good aspect as the good aspect, the bad aspect as the bad aspect, and the way to transcend them as the way to transcendence. The renunciation of sensual desire, attachment to the world and the five *khandhas* is achieved through seeing the way to transcendence and freedom (*nissaraṇa*), the way that enables one to lead a happy life independent of both those good and bad aspects. It is also a nobler and more refined kind of happiness.[101]

Being wise to conventions and concepts includes understanding the techniques of language known as "worldly speech," knowing how to use language as a vehicle for communication without becoming attached to the conventions of language, as described in the following Buddhavacana.

> "A bhikkhu who is an arahant, a destroyer of the outflows... may say, 'I say this,' 'He said this to me,' [but] he is clever; he knows the words used in the world and only speaks according to the conventions."[102]

When wisdom arises into things as they are, one sees things as coming from interdependent causes and conditions, and understands life and the world as they really are. There is proper worldview and life view; views, metaphysical opinions and theories, and doubts about the unanswerable questions (*abyākatapañhā*), such as whether the world is eternal or temporal, automatically disappear, as described in the following passages:

> "Bhikkhus, with the utter remainderless cessation of ignorance, contention, stubbornness, and confusion over one or another of the following views—What are formations (*saṅkhārā*)? To whom do these formations belong? Formations are one thing, the owner of formations another. The body and the life principle are one and the same thing. The body is one thing, the life principle another—all these views are entirely done away with..."[103]
>
> When a bhikkhu asked, "What is the cause and condition that a learned, noble disciple does not conceive doubts about those questions that the Lord has not answered (*abyākatapañhā*)?" the Buddha answered:

> "Because views have ceased, that learned, noble disciple does not conceive doubts about those questions not answered by me...The unlearned, unenlightened being does not clearly know [the truth of] views, does not clearly know the cause of views, does not clearly know the cessation of views and does not clearly know the practice that leads to the cessation of views, and therefore his views increase. He does not escape birth, aging and death, sorrow, lamentation, pain, grief, and despair."[104]

Another intellectual characteristic of one who has reached truth is that one no longer has to believe anything: one is no longer dependent on faith (*saddhā*). In Pali this quality is called *assaddha.* It is diametrically opposed to "non-belief" or "having no faith" in the normal sense, which refer to not believing out of lack of knowledge, or not being inspired by the speaker, or just plain stubbornness.

In this case, not believing is a result of directly knowing the truth as a personal experience, seeing for oneself and therefore having no need to rely on the knowledge of others. *Saddhā* is a voluntary dependence on the knowledge of another for as long as one has not yet seen it for oneself. When one knows for oneself, what need is there to believe? It is a level that is greater than, or transcends, belief, as expressed in the following passage:

> "In regard to those things that he knows for himself and realizes for himself, (he) does not believe through anybody else, be it recluse or holy man, *deva*, *māra*, or *brahma*. He does not believe through others regarding those things that he knows for himself and realizes, thus: all formations are impermanent; all formations are *dukkha*; all things are not-self; dependent on ignorance are volitional impulses..."[105]

Or as Venerable Sāriputta said to the Buddha:

> "In regard to this, I do not believe simply through faith in the Blessed One...This I know, I see, I clearly know, I realize and

> I have touched with my own wisdom. Thus, I have no doubts, I have no uncertainties."[106]

The qualities of one who attains *nibbāna*, regardless of how they are described, including as described in the four developments (*bhāvita*), are based on three core qualities: wisdom (*vijjā*), freedom (*vimutti*), and compassion (*karuṇā*). If we compare the unenlightened being to a man bound and tied, *vijjā* is like a knife for cutting his bonds, *vimutti* is the freedom he gains when the bonds are cut, and *karuṇā* is the compassion he feels when he sees others still bound once he is freed from the trouble and confusion of his own concerns.

According to the teaching, *vijjā* is regarded as the path (*magga*), while *vimutti* is generally regarded as fruit (*phala*). However, *vimutti* is divided into two stages, being both path and fruit. The action of transcending bondage, the moment of liberation, is said to be path; the state of freedom experienced on having been liberated is called fruit.[107] The attainment of *nibbāna* is completed with just *vijjā* and *vimutti*. As for *karuṇā*, it is a concern of actions done for other people. In other words, personal benefit (*attattha*) is completed through *vijjā* and *vimutti*, while the benefit of others (*parattha*) is realized through *karuṇā*.

Note that among those three qualities, liberation is a resultant condition. That is, it is the state of completion of the task, and it is the state that facilitates further work. It is not in itself work. Wisdom and compassion are factors of work.

Wisdom is the factor that functions in the successful attainment of *nibbāna* for oneself, while compassion is the quality that functions in the successful completion of the concerns of others. It is for this reason that wisdom and compassion are considered to be the Buddha's fundamental qualities: wisdom being the essence of actions for personal benefit, while compassion is the essence of actions for the benefit of others. Thus, the Buddha's qualities can be summarized as two: conduct for personal benefit, which is done through wisdom, and conduct for the benefit of others, which is done through compassion.[108]

However, both personal benefit and benefit for others can only be meaningful and authentic when supported by liberation (*vimutti*). Liberation is the quality that denotes the attainment of *nibbāna*, and is regarded as a synonym for *nibbāna*.

The Kinds of *Nibbāna*

There is only one *nibbāna*, but it is divided into different kinds in order to describe the qualities of people associated with it, or to describe it from different perspectives.[109]

Etymologically, *nibbāna* is derived from *ni*, "opposition" (meaning to be expelled, or expired, to be without or given up) and *vāna* (meaning to sweep, to go, to fare, or a bond). Used in relation to fire, it is "putting out" or "extinguishing heat"; "cooled" (but not "annihilated"). In describing a state of mind, it refers to its cooling, refreshment, extinguishing of mental heat, lack of confusion and agitation.[110] It is also translated as "that which extinguishes defilements," meaning that which removes desire, aversion, and delusion. In the supplementary texts, commentaries, and subcommentaries, it is mostly translated as "without the bondage of desire," or "gone from desire, which is the bondage to existence."[111]

Nibbāna is generally divided into two elements (*nibbānadhātu*), following the Itivuttaka,[112] thus:

1. *Sa-upādisesanibbānadhātu*: the *nibbāna* element with remaining *upādi* (residue).
2. *Anupādisesanibbānadhātu*: the *nibbāna* element with no remaining *upādi*.

The distinguishing criterion for these two kinds of *nibbāna* is *upādi*, which is explained by the commentaries as the state that is occupied by *kamma-kilesa*, or that which is clung to by *upādāna*, meaning the five *khandhas*.[113] According to this definition, the two kinds of *nibbāna* thus mean:

1. *Sa-upādisesanibbānadhātu*: *nibbāna* in which the five *khandhas* are still remaining, or *nibbāna* that is still associated with the five *khandhas*.
2. *Anupādisesanibbānadhātu*: *nibbāna* in which the five *khandhas* are no longer present, or *nibbāna* that is not associated with the five *khandhas*.[114]

The first kind of *nibbāna* is further defined as the extinguishing of defilements, but with the five *khandhas* remaining. It is the *nibbāna* of an arahant who is still alive, and corresponds with the word *kilesaparinibbāna* (the final extinguishing of defilements) coined in the commentaries. The second kind of *nibbāna* is further defined as the cessation of defilements with no *khandhas* remaining. It is the *nibbāna* of an arahant who has passed away. This corresponds with the word *khandhaparinibbāna* (the final cessation of the *khandhas*) coined in the commentaries.[115]

Examining these two *nibbāna* elements, we can see that they describe *nibbāna* in terms of the person who attains it. In other words, the attainer of *nibbāna* is used as a means to understand *nibbāna*. They are not direct descriptions of *nibbāna* itself. This is because the state of *nibbāna* itself is *sandiṭṭhika*—to be seen by each person for oneself—and *paccattaṁ veditabbo viññūhi*—known only to the wise who experience it. In this respect, the division of *nibbāna* into two kinds tells us nothing further or more profound than what has already been explained. However, before going into this matter further, we must emphasize once more the words of the commentary, stating that in the highest sense, or in reality (*paramattha*), *nibbāna* is not divided into different kinds. It is divided into two only in a relative sense.[116]

If we were to make a comparison, we might say that unenlightened people are as if swimming against the current, waves, and wind in a great ocean, while those who have attained *nibbāna* are like those who have reached the shore. The state of having made it to the shore, a state that is one of perfect contentment and wholeness, security, and ease, and that is experienced within and realized by those who reach it, is comparable to *anupādisesanibbāna*. The state of not being oppressed or threatened, not obstructed or confined within the ocean's waves, not being tossed around by them, not being under the power of the waves and wind and able to relate to the things around one freely and effectively, is comparable to *sa-upādisesanibbāna*.

To use an analogy closer to home, unenlightened beings can be compared to sick people, while those who have attained *nibbāna* are like people who are cured of their sickness. Having no illness, or being in good health, are states that are whole within themselves, which that person experiences and realizes for oneself. How whole, refreshing, secure, comfortable, and fluent this state is can only be experienced by those who are healthy. Other people may guess at what it may be like according to its features and make rational conclusions, but they cannot experience it for themselves. This state of health is comparable to *anupādisesanibbāna*. As for the various conditions that are contingent on good health, and which may manifest externally or have an effect on outward expressions in the conduct of life or in contacting and relating to the external environment, such as not being pressured by disease, the non-oppression, non-weakness, non-obstruction, non-impediment, or non-hindrance from pain and weakness, and therefore being able to move freely in the world, can be compared to *sa-upādisesanibbāna*.

The process of cognition through the five senses, contact with and relation to the outside world, and the conduct of everyday life usually cease decisively and clearly when a person dies. Thus, when an arahant dies and cognition through the five senses comes to final cessation, there is only one *nibbāna* element to experience, and that is *anupādisesanibbāna*.

In general speech, *anupādisesanibbāna* has become a specialized term referring to the death of an arahant, changing the emphasis from being a description of a state to a description of an event, and this can be seen from the use of *anupādisesanibbāna* in other texts, where it is exclusively used in reference to the death of the Buddha or an arahant. The word *sa-upādisesanibbāna* cannot be used to describe an event, and it is not really required (as there are already many words available for such specific purposes). Thus, the word does not appear anywhere else in the Tipiṭaka.[117]

Be that as it may, it must be realized that sources in the Pali canon do not indicate that the issue of these two kinds of *nibbāna* was of great interest. The point that was given more attention is that which can be practiced in order to realize *nibbāna* for oneself. Excessive academic explanations of the two *nibbānas* may simply be complicating something that the teachers did not overly concern themselves with, and may cause the student to develop a distorted idea of the actual amount of attention given to this subject in the Tipiṭaka. The explanation given so far should be sufficient to convey the general idea, so I will bring the discussion to a close at this point.

Attributes of the Arahant

To speak entirely in academic terms on the state of *nibbāna* is not only burdensome, but also runs the risk of creating misconceptions, since it is not possible to translate some of the key terms clearly and comprehensively. Moreover, the student may have previous conceptions about these terms or teachings that do not particularly conform with the true meaning. For example, having read the passages describing the qualities of an arahant, one may perceive an arahant as being some lifeless kind of person, cold-hearted, without feeling or interest in the world.

In order to prevent such misunderstandings, having looked at the state of *nibbāna* according to the texts, we should also compare it with the results that appear in actual life in order to see how the academic descriptions and practical results in actual life conform to each other, and how even contradictory parts of the teaching can be reconciled and can mutually support each other. This will be an investigation of the content and meaning of the texts by looking at the actual experience of *nibbāna* itself, which can be gleaned from the following passages.

External Features and Community Life

In the *Dhammacetiya Sutta*, King Pasenadi Kosala declares his reverence to the Buddha, extolling the reasons for his faith in the Triple Gem (the Buddha, the Dhamma, and the Saṅgha). The Buddha acknowledged his words as a Dhammacetiya ("Dhamma monument"), useful as an elementary principle for the holy life, and encouraged the Saṅgha to study and memorize it. Among King Pasenadi's statements, one of them describes the features of the conduct of the bhikkhus in the Buddhist religion as follows:

> "Revered Sir, there is also this point: I often tour around sanctuaries and parks, and at those places I see one group of recluses and brahmins, thin, gloomy, of dull complexion, yellowish, the veins standing out, a sight not inviting to behold.[118] The thought occurs to me that these venerables must certainly be unhappy in leading the holy life, or otherwise they are suffering the fruits of some evil past *kamma* that they have committed and are covering up...But I see the bhikkhus in this teaching and discipline cheerful, with minds buoyant, of pleasing appearance and attitude, with faculties radiant, unconfused, with hairs laid flat [with minds calm and confident, not frightened], supporting themselves on what is offered,[119] with minds like deer [gentle-minded, not given to thoughts of disturbing or taking advantage of others, loving freedom, free to go anywhere]. The thought occurs to me that these venerables must certainly have realized some special, higher quality in the Buddha's teaching (*sāsanā*)...This also (is a cause) for my faithful reverence of the Dhamma of the Blessed One thus: 'The Blessed One is truly the Fully Enlightened Buddha, the Dhamma [is] well expounded by the Blessed One, the order of the Blessed One's disciples are well-practiced.'"[120]

Having Mental Freedom and Happiness

> "Those whose minds are unwavering, who clearly know the truth, have no mental fabrication, they have given up all yearning

and therefore see only clarity in all directions. They do not exalt themselves, be it among equals, inferiors or superiors."[121]

"The noble ones have no agitation and irritation in their minds; they have transcended all concern with becoming or not becoming this or that. They are without fear, and have only happiness, no sorrow. Even the devas cannot see their minds."[122]

Mastery of Mind and Thinking

"When those who are great beings (*mahāpurisa*), who have much wisdom, wish to think any thought, they think that thought; when they wish to not think a thought, they do not think that thought. When they wish to consider any point, they consider that point; when they wish to not consider a point, they do not consider that point. They have attained to a state of mastery over mind (*cetovasī*) and the thought processes."[123]

Being at Ease with Life and Death, and Having Goodwill and Compassion toward All Beings

"Alive, I am not troubled; when I die, I will not be sorrowful. The sage, seeing the goal, lives without sorrow, even amid sorrow."[124]

"Death I do not prize; to life I do not cling. I will cast aside this body with clear comprehension and firm mindfulness. Death I do not prize; to life I do not cling. I bide my time just as a worker, his work done, awaits his wage."[125]

At one time, the Thera Upasena was sitting in a cave in the Sīta forest. Two snakes were chasing each other across the ceiling of the cave when one of them fell down onto the bhikkhu's shoulder and bit him. The poison spread rapidly. The elder knew that he would die, but he gave no expression out of the ordinary. He even told his fellow bhikkhus to lay his body on a bench where he could pass away (*parinibbāna*) outside the cave.[126]

At one time Ānanda asked Venerable Sāriputta, the Buddha's

chief disciple, whether he would feel sorrow if something happened to the Great Teacher—that is, if he died. Sāriputta answered: "Even were something to happen to the Blessed One, sorrow, lamentation, pain, grief, and despair on that account would not arise in me. I would rather reflect: 'The Great Being, who has such mighty power, has passed on. If the Blessed One had lived longer, it would have been for the benefit of the many, for the happiness of the many, for the welfare of all beings.'" [127]

"Bhikkhus, even were a group of vicious bandits to (catch you and) take a two-handed saw and cut off your large and small limbs, if any one of you were to give rise to a thought of anger toward those bandits, he could not be said to be practicing according to my teaching."[128]

"Spread friendship to all beings thus: 'May all beings be happy; may they be secure...Just as a mother protects her only child, even at the cost of her own life, just so should you develop boundless goodwill for all beings."[129]

"Even those people whose hearts are pierced with the dart can sleep—how then could I, who am free of darts, not sleep well? When I journey through areas with dangerous animals, I have no fear, and even when I sleep in such places, I fear no danger. Day or night, there is nothing that troubles me. I see nothing to be lost anywhere in this world; thus, when I sleep, I think only of helping others."[130]

The canonical passages above are given not only with the aim of allowing readers to see the various meanings from their own examination, but also to emphasize two points: first, if the descriptions of the mental state of the arahants are interpreted according to the feelings of unenlightened beings, it may give rise to the deluded conception of an arahant as one who has no interest in others, who allows things to slide along their way as if he had no heart, and as such be a peculiar kind of person. This is why it is necessary to compare the internal characteristics with the external manifestations, to see that the arahants had conduct and ways of life that entailed a sense of responsibility and rationality, and to see what kinds of thoughts, feelings, and ways of conduct will result for a person who has no defilements dominating the heart and whose mind is free.

In fact, the more strange and unusual attributes tend to occur only among those who had attained some levels of "deliverance in mind" (*cetovimutti*). As for those arahants who were "delivered through wisdom" (*paññāvimutta*), there is not even the attachment to the concept that they are not attached. There is no new clinging (such as to some kind of mental attainment) that would cause them to exhibit neglect of, or inattention to, those things they have, with difficulty, already discarded (such as material supports), and there is not even the defilement that would cause them to show aversion or contempt. Thus, they conduct or express themselves rationally, appropriately as their wisdom reveals it, at the very least to support skillful mental states (*kusalacitta*) in others.

The second point is that absence of fear and fright[131] is an important mental attribute of the arahant, since an arahant has done away with the greed, aversion, and delusion that would cause fear and fright. Fear and fright arise from causes, which are the defilements deeply hidden in what is known as the subconscious. They are reactions that arise spontaneously when objects that are causes for fear suddenly and unexpectedly come into awareness. Fright is hard to conceal, because it arises before one has established mindfulness. As such it is an excellent sign of subtle defilements remaining hidden in the mind, about which one can neither fool oneself nor others. In Dhamma practice such fear and fright have been used as proofs of the attainment or non-attainment of arahantship in subtle cases where daily conduct has indicated attainment, and even the bhikkhu in question believed he had attained enlightenment, as in the story of an elder who had attained great proficiency in the meditation attainments (*samāpatti*). His defilements being suppressed by the power of his absorption, he believed himself to be an arahant. He went on believing this for sixty years from his attainment of concentration, until one day he saw in his meditation an image of an enraged rogue elephant trumpeting loudly and was startled. Only then did he realize that he was unenlightened.[132]

I would now like to discuss some other kinds and levels of *nibbāna.*

The Levels of *Nibbāna* Attainment

The absorption meditation states (*jhāna samāpatti*) are not only good foundations for the practice for the attainment of *nibbāna*, but also are sometimes referred to as "*nibbāna* by extension" (*pariyāya*)—that is, indirectly or in certain senses. For example, there are Buddhavacana referring to each of the four *jhānas* of form, the four formless *jhānas* and the state of cessation (*saññāvedayitanirodha*; also known as *nirodhasamāpatti*)[133] as "*nibbāna* on account of (neutralizing defilements through) opposite qualities, or temporary *nibbāna*" (*tadaṅganibbāna*); as "*nibbāna* in the here and now" (*diṭṭhadhammanibbāna*); and as "*nibbāna* realized by personal experience" (*sandiṭṭhikanibbāna*),[134] as in the canonical passage: "A bhikkhu, removed from sensual desire, removed from unskillful qualities... enters into the first *jhāna*. Just this is called by the Blessed One *nibbāna* by extension in the here and now (*diṭṭhadhammanibbāna*);... a bhikkhu utterly transcends the sphere of neither perception nor non-perception and enters into the cessation of perception and feeling (*saññāvedayitanirodha*). By seeing with wisdom, his outflows are entirely destroyed. Just this is called by the Blessed One *nibbāna* in the here and now directly (*nippariyāya*)."[135]

One who sees the five *khandhas* as impermanent, stressful, and not-self is done with all fear and dwells at ease. That person is said to have attained the *tadaṅganibbāna.*[136]

There is one noteworthy Buddhavacana to the effect that one whose mind is dominated by desire, aversion, and delusion thinks in ways that lead to trouble for oneself, to trouble for others, and to trouble for both oneself and others, and experiences mental distress.

When one has given up desire, aversion, and delusion, one does not think in ways that lead to trouble for oneself or for others, or for both oneself and others, nor does one experience mental distress. This is *sandiṭṭhikanibbāna*. Whenever that person experiences the total removal of desire, the total removal of aversion, and the total removal of delusion (*rāgakkhaya*, *dosakkhaya*, *mohakkhaya*), this is the *nibbāna* that is *sandiṭṭhika* (experienced by its attainer for oneself), *akālika* (independent of time), *ehipassika* (inviting verification), *opanayika* (to be brought within), *paccattaṁ veditabbo viññūhi* (known by the wise each for oneself).[137]

In the Paṭisambhidāmagga, *nirodha*, one of the important synonyms for *nibbāna*, is analyzed into five kinds or levels:[138]

1. *Vikkhambhananirodha*: the suppression of the hindrances by one who develops first *jhāna* (the eight attainments—the four *jhānas* of form and the four formless *jhānas*—are all *vikkhambhananirodha*, because from the attainment of first *jhāna* upward all unskillful qualities, such as the hindrances [*nīvaraṇa*], are suppressed and in abeyance, but only so long as the *jhāna* is maintained). Simply speaking, the conditions that are adversaries to skillful qualities, being defilements such as the hindrances, are suppressed by mundane concentration (*lokiya samādhi*), just as a stone suppresses the grass beneath it.

2. *Tadaṅganirodha*: the arrival at the level of the penetration of defilements[139] and cessation of wrong views of one who develops concentration by means of the opposite quality. This refers to the stopping of defilements on the level of insight (*vipassanā*)—that is, the use of wisdom to investigate the true state of things: investigating, for example, impermanence. Whatever perspective is contemplated leads to corresponding direct knowledge (*ñāṇa*), which destroys the opposing view that obstructs that perspective of the truth. For example, contemplating ourselves and others as merely mentality and physicality can lead to the stopping of self view (*sakkāyadiṭṭhi*); contemplation of impermanence can lead to stopping the perception of things as permanent; contemplation of stressfulness (*dukkha*) can lead to stopping the perception of

things as happiness; contemplation of not-self can lead to stopping the perception of self. This cessation of defilements is like lighting a lamp to destroy darkness, but it is still temporary, just as the darkness returns when the lamp goes out.

3. *Samucchedanirodha*: the cessation of defilements by total severance of one who develops the transcendent path that destroys defilements. This refers to the four noble paths: the paths of stream enterer (*sotāpattimagga*), once-returner (*sakadāgāmimagga*), non-returner (*anāgāmimagga*), and arahant (*arahattamagga*), which extinguish defilements such as the fetters absolutely and irreversibly, just like a tree struck by lightning or dug up by the roots.

4. *Paṭipassaddhinirodha*: the cessation of the defilements in the attainment of fruition, a state in which the defilements are already annihilated. This refers to the four noble fruits: the fruits of stream enterer (*sotāpattiphala*), once-returner (*sakadāgāmiphala*), non-returner (*anāgāmiphala*), and arahant (*arahattaphala*), which are profoundly serene, since the defilements have been completely uprooted and brought to cessation by the path.[140]

5. *Nissaraṇanirodha*: the cessation of defilements, which is a state utterly beyond them, which lies separately, is far removed from defilements, and which is totally unconcerned with defilements. This kind of cessation is *nibbāna*, or the deathless element, a state that is clear and free.

Of these five levels of cessation, the first two are mundane, the last three transcendent. The first four are said to be *nibbāna* by extension (*pariyāya*)—that is, indirectly or in part—while the last, *nissaraṇanirodha*, is said to be direct *nibbāna* (*nippariyāya*)—that is, real *nibbāna* in the direct and full sense of the term.

The Paṭisambhidāmagga similarly divides the terms *pahāna* (destruction), *viveka* (seclusion), *virāga* (dispassion), and *vossagga* (relinquishment) into five levels, just as in the five levels of *nirodha*. The kinds and definitions are all the same.[141] The commentarial literature also tends to divide *vimutti* (liberation) into five levels, with the same kinds and definitions as the five kinds of *nirodha*.[142]

The stages or levels of attaining *nibbāna* that are most familiar are the division into paths and fruits, or the four paths and four fruits, which are stream entry path (*sotāpattimagga*), stream entry fruit (*sotāpattiphala*); once-returner path (*sakadāgāmimagga*), once-returner fruit (*sakadāgāmiphala*); non-returner path (*anāgāmimagga*), non-returner fruit (*anāgāmiphala*); arahant path (*arahattamagga*), arahant fruit (*arahattaphala*). This kind of division is usually reserved for those who do the attaining, and as such will be dealt with in the next section dealing with the kinds of levels of those who have attained *nibbāna*. Here I will simply emphasize that the path and fruit are not *nibbāna* but are merely stages or levels of its attainment. It should also be noted that the first level of path attainment, stream entry path, is also called *dassana* (seeing), because it is the first vision of *nibbāna*. The three higher levels of the path—the once-returner path, the non-returner path, and the arahant path—are together also known as *bhāvanā* (cultivation), because they are a cultivation of that which has been seen by the stream enterer.[143]

The Kinds and Levels of Persons Who Attain *Nibbāna*

People who have attained the goal of *nibbāna*, as well as those who have advanced along the right path to a level from which they can see the goal before them and are assured of its attainment, are included in the community of the Buddha's true disciples, known as the *sāvaka saṅgha*, as used in the passage for recollection on the qualities of the Saṅgha: *supaṭipanno bhagavato sāvaka saṅgho* and so on. There are many other words used to describe the particular qualities of these true disciples of the Buddha. The term widely used and best known in Thailand is probably *ariyapuggala*, or simply *ariya*, meaning "noble one," "excellent one," or "one far from the enemy of defilements." *Ariyapuggala* was not the original term used to describe this level of person.[144] The term used in the canon was *dakkhiṇeyya*, or *dakkhiṇeyyapuggala*. These two words are Brahmanical terms, which were adopted by the Buddha, along with many other words.

The word *ariya* corresponds with the Sanskrit *ārya*, the word used to designate a group of people who migrated to the north-west of India many thousands of years ago and drove the original inhabitants to the south and into the mountains and forests. These Aryans considered themselves to be civilized, and looked down on the original inhabitants as *milakkha* or *maleccha*—savages, forest or mountain people. They were used as slaves. Later, as the Aryans gained firm control of the area and organized their community into a fixed caste system, placing the original inhabitants into the *sūdra* caste, the terms *ariya* or *ārya* came to mean the people of the other three castes: the nobles (*kṣatriyas*), the brahmins, and the merchants. The menials and all other people were *anāryan* (not noble, uncivilized).[145] This system was a racial one; it went by birth and left no room for choice or alteration.

When the Buddha began to spread his teaching, he introduced the concept that being *ariya* was not defined by birth but by the qualities practiced and cultivated in a person's mind: regardless of race or caste, if one practiced according to the noble qualities, one could be an *ariya*, and whoever did not so practice was not an *ariya*. Truth was no longer the exclusive prerogative of the brahmins but instead is neutral and is to be found naturally: whoever realizes this natural truth is an *ariyan*, even if that person did not study the Vedas, and it is this realization of the truth that makes people *ariyans*. Thus, the truth was called *ariyasacca* (the noble truths).[146] According to Buddhist principles, one who understands the noble truths is anyone from a stream enterer upward. Thus, *ariya* in the texts has the same meaning as *dakkhiṇeyyapuggala*.

Dakkhiṇeyya translates as "one worthy of offerings" (*dakkhiṇā*, Sanskrit *dakṣiṇā*).[147] According to the original brahmin sense, it meant payment for a ceremony, especially a sacrificial ceremony. These payments were prescribed in the Vedas, consisting of possessions, gold and silver, tools, furniture, vehicles, grains, livestock, beautiful maidens, and land or jurisdiction over certain districts of the kingdom. The bigger the sacrificial ceremony, the more lavish the offering became. For example, in the ceremony of horse sacrifice, a king would prepare offerings consisting of plunder seized from conquered lands, including ladies of the harem, as offerings to those who performed the ceremony. The *dakkhiṇeyya*, those deserving the offerings, in this case were the brahmins, because they were the only ones who were entitled to perform the ceremony.

When the Buddha began his teaching, he instructed that these sacrificial ceremonies should be abandoned. He redefined the terms *yañ* ("sacrifice") and *dakkhiṇā*. *Yañ* became a ceremony of alms giving in which no harm was done to either people or animals, while *dakkhiṇā* became things that should be given or relinquished as *dāna*, things offered out of faith.[148] No longer was it a payment or reward. If it was to be called a payment, it was payment for goodness, although it would be more correct to say "offerings to goodness." The *dakkhiṇā* given in these cases were not lavish or outlandish, but simply the four simple and basic supports of life (food, clothing, shelter, and medicine).

The *dakkhiṇeyya*, the persons deserving of these offerings, in this case were those who were devoting themselves to training in virtuous conduct. They became the exemplars of a wholesome and happy life, the mere presence of whom in the world was in itself a sufficient benefit to humanity. Their value was even greater when they traveled widely and spread the teaching, instructing others how to obtain such a wholesome life for themselves, a benefit far exceeding the value of any material reward. Moreover, these people demanded or expected no reward. They lived on the four basic supports in a quantity sufficient to maintain their lives.

The offerings given to these people for their maintenance are *dakkhiṇā*, and those people rendered such offerings to be fruitful, because they served to help virtue, wholesomeness and living examples of the happy life to manifest in this world and spread far and wide. These are the persons said to be worthy of offerings, because they caused the offerings to bear fruit. They were later called "the most fertile field of merit in the world,"[149] because they are the place from which wholesomeness grows and from where it spreads throughout the world, leading to benefit for the people of the world.[150]

The *dakkhiṇeyyapuggala* must be truly *dakkhiṇeyya*: that is, they must maintain the virtues and wholesomeness that render them "worthy of offerings," as will be discussed below. Those who are not truly *dakkhiṇeyya* are considered not fully entitled to receive and use the offerings given to them. For example, as long as they are *puthujjana* (unenlightened), the receiving and consuming of alms food from the laypeople by bhikkhus and novices, even though they be of good conduct, maintain their morality and devote themselves to practicing the Dhamma, are considered to be "eating as a debtor," being in debt to the people, a debt that they must quickly strive to be free of by applying themselves to the practice for becoming *dakkhiṇeyyapuggala*. Venerable Mahā Kassapa declared that he ate the alms food of the people as a debtor for only seven days before realizing the truth.[151] That is, from the time he took ordination as a bhikkhu and dedicated himself to the practice, he spent only seven days as a *puthujjana* before attaining arahantship, thus becoming a *dakkhiṇeyyapuggala*.

In the commentarial literature, the bhikkhus' and novices' use of offerings of food and material supports given by householders is divided into four groups. In the first group are those who transgress the precepts and are void of any of the virtues befitting their status. They have only the clothing and the outward appearance of their vocation. Such people have no right to the offerings given to them, and their receiving and use of offerings is called "using as a thief" (*theyyaparibhoga*).

The second group consists of those who are possessed of morality, but use the supports without reflecting on them. For instance, when eating food, they do not reflect that such eating is merely to maintain the body, to maintain life, in order to have the strength to practice the Dhamma, not for the purpose of being stylish, or for fun, indulgence, or attachment to flavors. Such consumption is called "consumption as a debtor" (*iṇaparibhoga*). If, however, they use the supports with reflection, they are not said to be debtors. (This is more lenient than the canonical passage, which states that as long as one is unenlightened, one consumes offerings as a debtor.)

The third group are the "learners" (*sekha*), the first seven levels of *dakkhiṇeyyapuggala* (of the eight that will be detailed below). Having received offerings, their use of them is called "using as an heir" or "rightfully" (*dāyajjaparibhoga*), as heirs of the Buddha, who is the ultimate *dakkhiṇeyyapuggala*.

The fourth group consists of the arahants, who are liberated from enslavement to desire, and whose virtue renders them truly deserving of offerings. They have a full right to receive and make use of *dakkhiṇā*. Consumption by the arahants is called "use as an owner" (*sāmiparibhoga*).[152]

The use of the word *dakkhiṇeyya* emphasizes both economic and social factors. The concepts of offerings and those worthy of them (and indeed, some perspectives of the subject of generosity) are included in one of Buddhism's key social principles, and that is the existence of an independent community that is not subject to the systems of mainstream society. This community gains its independence in exchange for not involving itself in the affairs of society and not becoming directly involved in social institutions. This community has its own system of living based upon freedom of mind, and it helps society by preserving and transmitting the Dhamma within it. And through their independent lifestyle, the members of this community forsake any rewards for their work. They live solely on the offerings provided by the members of the larger community in such forms, for example, as the alms round (*piṇḍapāta*), in a way that does not disrupt the daily lives of that larger community. They are compared to bees, who journey far and wide to collect pollen and nectar from the various flowers to make honey and build their hives, but do not damage the flowers, their color, or their fragrance.[153] Indeed, the bees also help the flowers to germinate and multiply far and wide.

The members of the community known as the Saṅgha are dependent on people for their existence, as a result of which they have a moral obligation to them, and by means of which they are freed to practice for the benefit of people everywhere. Their lives are dependent on all people, but are dependent on no one person;

they rely on all people and therefore belong to all, but they belong to no one. In a society that is organized fairly, there should be no poor people, and thus no beggars.[154] In such a society the members of this independent community would be the only group whose livelihood depended on others through offerings, in such forms as the alms round.

The criteria for analyzing the *dakkhiṇeyya* or *ariyapuggala* can be divided into two main models. The first is an eightfold division (classified according to the stages or levels of destruction of defilements; it may be called a "negative classification"), and the second is a sevenfold division (classified according to levels or stages of virtue attained, which can be called a "positive classification").

First Arrangement: The Eight Dakkhiṇeyyapuggala *or* Ariyapuggala

This division is organized according to the defilements or "fetters" (*saṁyojana*) abandoned on each level of advancement in the practice of the threefold training of morality, concentration, and wisdom. *Saṁyojana* literally means "fetter" or "bond." The word refers to the defilements that bind the mind, or the unskillful qualities that bind worldly beings to suffering in the wheel of rebirth, just as oxen are harnessed to a cart. There are ten fetters: five lower (or coarse) fetters and five higher (or subtle) fetters.[155]

The five lower, or coarse, fetters (*orambhāgiyasaṁyojana*) are as follows:

1. *Sakkāyadiṭṭhi*: self view, the view that is firmly attached to the concept of self, to "us" and "them," and to being this or that; failing to see the reality that beings are merely collections of component factors.[156]
2. *Vicikicchā*: hesitation, doubt, and perplexity, such as doubt in the teacher (*sāsadā*), the teaching (Dhamma), or those who practice it (Saṅgha), and doubt in the practice (*sikkhā*), about the origin and destination of life, about the *paṭiccasamuppāda*.

3. *Sīlabbataparāmāsa*: grasping at rites and observances—that is, mistakenly holding that one can become pure and liberated simply through disciplines and observances, undertaking them out of desire and views.
4. *Kāmarāga*: sensual desire; attachment to sense pleasures.
5. *Paṭigha*: resentment, irritation, aversion or agitation.

The five higher, or subtle, fetters (*uddhambhāgiyasaṁyojana*) are as follows:

6. *Rūparāga*: attachment to fine material form, such as attachment to the objects of the absorptions of form (*rūpajhāna*); enjoying the pleasant and peaceful "taste" of concentration on the level of the *jhāna* of form; attachment and desire for the material sphere.
7. *Arūparāga*: attachment to formless things; attachment, for example, to the objects of the four formless absorptions; attachment and desire for the formless spheres.
8. *Māna*: conceit, or the conception of oneself as being a certain way, such as "superior to," "equal to" or "inferior to."
9. *Uddhacca*: restlessness, disquietude, confusion, scattered thinking.
10. *Avijjā*: ignorance of the truth, not understanding the natural laws of cause and effect, or not knowing the noble truths.

The eight kinds of *dakkhiṇeyyapuggala* or *ariyapuggala* are, in terms of their main levels or stages, only four, and they are related to the fetters as follows.[157]

The *sekha* (learners), or *sa-upādisesapuggala* (those with traces of clinging remaining), constitute the first three levels of *dakkhiṇeyyapuggala* or *ariyapuggala*:

1. The stream enterers (*sotāpanna*): they have entered the stream—that is, entered the path. They are truly walking on the right way, or really practicing correctly on the noble path;[158] they have perfected morality (*sīla*), have developed concentra-

tion (*samādhi*) to a moderate degree and developed wisdom (*paññā*) to a moderate degree. They have given up three of the fetters: *sakkāyadiṭṭhi*, *vicikicchā*, and *sīlabbataparāmāsa*.[159]

2. The once-returners (*sakadāgāmī*): after returning to this world only once they will destroy all suffering. They have perfected morality, developed a moderate degree of concentration, and developed a moderate degree of wisdom. In addition to giving up the first three fetters, they have weakened desire, aversion, and delusion.[160]
3. The non-returners (*anāgāmī*): those who will attain *parinibbāna* in the sphere of their next arising, not returning to this world. They have perfected morality and concentration but developed wisdom only to a moderate degree. They have given up two further fetters: sensual desire and aversion (thereby abandoning all five of the lower fetters).

The fourth level of *dakkhiṇeyyapuggala* or *ariyapuggala* consists of *asekha* (those done with learning) or *anupādisesapuggala* (those with no remaining taint of clinging):

4. The arahants, those worthy (of *dakkhiṇā* or special reverence), those who have broken the spokes of the wheel of rebirth. They have destroyed the outflows, perfected all three trainings—morality, concentration, and wisdom—and further given up all five higher fetters (meaning they have given up all ten fetters).

Sekha means one who is still learning; that is, the *sekha* still has a task to do in relation to personal development. Thus, they are the first three levels of *dakkhiṇeyyapuggala*, who must continue practicing in the training in order to give up the fetters and attain realizations on higher levels until they attain arahantship. *Asekha* means those who are no longer learning; they have done their task in terms of personal development and fully realized their own benefit. They have no further training to do, have no further defilements to give up and no higher states to strive for. They are the arahants.

Sa-upādisesapuggala are those who still have clinging (*upādi*) remaining. That means they still have defilements remaining. They are the first three levels of *dakkhiṇeyyapuggala*. The *anupādisesa-puggala* are those who have no remaining clinging, which means they have no remaining defilements. Note that here the word *upādi* is glossed as *upādāna*, which is clinging, defilements,[161] to differentiate it from the *upādi* in *sa-upādisesanibbāna* and *anupādisesanibbāna*, where it means "that which is attached to," referring to the five *khandhas*.

Those suttas dealing with important practices, such as the four foundations of mindfulness (*satipaṭṭhāna*), the four pathways to success (*iddhipāda*), and the five faculties (*indriya*), usually conclude with the Buddha's summary that when that practice is developed, one can expect one of two fruits: "arahantship in the here and now, or, if there is still remaining attachment [*upādi*], the attainment of non-returner."[162] This clearly shows that the word *upādi* in this case refers to *upādāna*, or broadly speaking, defilements.

The eight kinds of *dakkhiṇeyyapuggala* or *ariyapuggala* are those very individuals on the four levels but arranged in pairs, as follows:[163]

1. *Sotāpanna*: one who has realized, or attained, the fruit of stream entry (*sotāpattiphala*).
2. One who is practicing for the realization of the fruit of stream entry.
3. *Sakadāgāmī*: one who has realized the fruit of the once-returner.
4. One who is practicing for the realization of the fruit of the once-returner.
5. *Anāgāmī*: one who has realized the fruit of the non-returner.
6. One who is practicing for the realization of the fruit of the non-returner.
7. Arahant: one who has realized the fruit of arahantship.
8. One who is practicing for the realization of the fruit of arahantship.[164]

These four pairs of *dakkhiṇeyyapuggala* are collectively referred to as the order of the Buddha's disciples (*sāvaka saṅgha*), which is one arm of the Triple Gem—the ideal Buddhist community, as recited in the verses for recollection of the qualities of the Saṅgha: *yadidaṁ cattāri purisayugāni aṭṭha purisapuggalā, esa bhagavato sāvaka saṅgho*[165] ("that is, the four pairs of noble beings, the eight individuals, the order of this Blessed One's disciples..."), and it is this *sāvaka saṅgha* that later became known as the *ariyasaṅgha*, the Noble Saṅgha.

Second Arrangement: The Seven Kinds of Dakkhiṇeyyapuggala *or* Ariyapuggala

The seven kinds of *dakkhiṇeyyapuggala* are arranged according to the faculties (*indriya*) most instrumental in the practice and are related to the escapes (*vimokkha*), so we must first acquaint ourselves with the faculties and the escapes.

Indriya translates literally as "that which is responsible," referring to the qualities that are responsible for controlling or overthrowing the obstacles to Dhamma practice, which are lack of faith, laziness, indifference, confusion or unknowing, and delusion or not using wisdom. The faculties are forces that support the practice of the Dhamma. There are five *indriya*: faith (*saddhā*), effort (*viriya*), recollection or mindfulness (*sati*), firm establishment of mind or concentration (*samādhi*), and wisdom (*paññā*). Each of these faculties will be present to different degrees in different people. Three of the faculties are critical in determining attainment of Dhamma and are thus criteria for distinguishing the different levels of *dakkhiṇeyyapuggala* or *ariyapuggala*. They are faith, concentration, and wisdom.

Vimokkha translates as escape, and refers to the mind's escape from adverse qualities because of its great delight in, and absorption with, the object being attended to. At that time the mind is free of evil, unskillful qualities, and therefore it is said to be an "escape." However, it is an escape achieved through the power of concentration and as such is temporary, lasting only so long as those absorption attainments last.[166] It is not *vimutti*, complete liberation from defilements and suffering, which is a synonym for *nibbāna*.[167] The eight levels of escape are as follows:[168]

1. One with form perceives forms: this refers to the four form absorptions of one who attains *jhāna* via a meditation device (*kasiṇa*) based on something within one's own body, such as the color of the hair.
2. One without internal form perceives external material form: this refers to the four form absorptions in one who attains *jhāna* through a device based on an external object.
3. One absorbs into the idea "beautiful": this refers to absorption attained by one who develops concentration with a colored device (*vaṇṇakasiṇa*), attending to an attractive color as object or, according to the Paṭisambhidāmagga, the absorption of one who develops attention to the limitless abodes, which are the four divine abodes (*brahmavihāra*)—goodwill (*mettā*), compassion (*karuṇā*), sympathetic joy (*muditā*), and equanimity (*upekkhā*)—which cause one to see all people and beings as attractive and pleasant, none of them objectionable.
4. By utterly transcending all perceptions of form, through the cessation of all disagreeable perceptions (*paṭighasaññā*), through not attending to perceptions of variation (*nānattasaññā*), one enters into the sphere of limitless space (*ākāsānañcāyatana*).
5. By utterly transcending the sphere of limitless space, one enters into the sphere of limitless consciousness (*viññāṇañcāyatana*).
6. By utterly transcending the sphere of limitless consciousness, one enters into the sphere of nothingness (*ākiñcaññāyatana*).
7. By utterly transcending the sphere of nothingness, one enters into the sphere of neither perception nor non-perception (*nevasaññānāsaññāyatana*).
8. By utterly transcending the sphere of neither perception nor non-perception, one enters into the state of cessation of perception and feeling (*saññāvedayitanirodha*).

In practice, the faculties are related to the escapes thus: at the beginning stages of practice, the practitioner will be guided primarily by either the faith faculty or the wisdom faculty. If the practitioner develops the *vimokkha*, the leading factor will then become the concentration faculty. The phrase "attaining the *vimokkha*" here refers to the fourth *vimokkha* and higher. Those who are led primarily by the faith or wisdom faculties may attain the fourth form absorption, but cannot attain the formless absorptions. Generally speaking, they do not attain the *vimokkha*. (However, even when concentration is the leading faculty, eventually that concentration faculty must become a base for the wisdom faculty. The only difference is that the concentration faculty helps produce the *vimokkha* in the process.)

The seven *dakkhiṇeyyapuggala* or *ariyapuggala* are related to the faculties and the escapes shown below. Usually the seven *dakkhiṇeyya* are shown in descending order from the highest downward. Here, to keep the presentation in conformity with the first arrangement, it is shown in ascending order:[169]

The *Sekha*, or *Sa-upādisesapuggala*:

1. *Saddhānusārī* (one who uses faith, or one who follows through faith) are those who are practicing for the attainment of stream entry, who have strong faith faculty. They develop the noble path with faith as the leading factor. (If they have attainment, they become known as "liberated through faith," *saddhāvimutta*.)
2. *Dhammānusārī* (one who uses the Dhamma, or one who follows through Dhamma) are those who are practicing for the attainment of stream entry who have a strong wisdom faculty. They develop the noble path with wisdom as the leading factor. (If they have attainment they become "attained to right view," *diṭṭhippatta*.)
3. *Saddhāvimutta* (liberated through faith) are those who rightly understand the noble truths and clearly see the truth (Dhamma) taught by the Tathāgata. They practice well and properly, and some of their outflows have ceased through seeing (the noble

truths) with wisdom, with faith as the dominant faculty. (This refers to those who have attained the fruit of stream entry upward to the level of those who are practicing for the attainment of arahantship, who have strong faith faculty. If they attain arahantship, they become "liberated through wisdom," *paññāvimutta*.)

4. *Diṭṭhippatta* (those who attain right view) are those who rightly understand the noble truths and clearly see the truth taught by the Tathāgata. They practice well and properly, and some of the outflows have ceased through seeing (the noble truths) with wisdom. (This refers to those who have attained stream entry and upward to the level of those who are practicing for arahantship, with wisdom as the dominant faculty. If they attain the fruit of arahantship they become "liberated through wisdom," *paññāvimutta*.)
5. *Kāyasakkhī*[170] (those who are witnesses in body, or who experience for themselves) are those who have experienced the eight *vimokkha* for themselves and some of the outflows have ceased through seeing (the noble truths) with wisdom. (This refers to those who have attained the fruit of stream entry and upward to those who are practicing for the fruit of arahantship, who have strong concentration faculty. If they attain the fruit of arahantship they become "freed in both ways," *ubhatobhāgavimutta*.)

Asekha or *Anupādisesapuggala*

6. *Paññāvimutta* (those liberated through wisdom) are those who have not experienced the eight *vimokkha* for themselves, but all the outflows have ceased through seeing (the noble truths) through wisdom. (This refers to the arahants whose practice has been led by insight until completion of the path.)
7. *Ubhatobhāgavimutta* (those liberated both ways) are those who have attained the eight *vimokkha* for themselves and in whom the outflows have all ceased through seeing (the noble truths) with wisdom. (This refers to the arahants who have first developed concentration (*samatha*) to a high degree as a base

for the further development of insight up to completion of the practice.)

Types of Arahants

Among the *dakkhiṇeyapuggala*, which have been divided into all these many categories, the arahants—as those who have attained the highest level, completed the training, and attained the goal, and have nothing further to do for their personal benefit, but who strive for the benefit of others—are worthy of analysis separately in their own right.

The arahants are of two main types, and those types can be further divided according to the qualities they either have or do not have, as follows:

1. *Paññavimutta*: the arahants liberated by wisdom. These are those who have focused on the development of insight (*vipassanā*), using only sufficient concentration (*samatha*) to serve as a base for insight and the attainment of knowledge of the cessation of the outflows. They attain *samatha* no higher than the four *jhānas* of form and have no special powers. For instance, they can't enter the cessation attainment (*nirodhasamāpatti*) and do not have the mundane superknowledges (*abhiññā*). They can be divided as follows

    - *Sukkhavipassaka*: those who develop insight only. They achieve the *jhāna* level of concentration at the moment of attaining the path.
    - *Paññāvimutta*: They have attained at least one of the levels of four *jhānas* of form before developing insight and attaining the fruit of arahantship.
    - *Paṭisambhidappatta*: those who attain the four specialized knowledges (*paṭisambhidā*):

        Atthapaṭisambhidā: special knowledge of the meaning and implication,

Dhammapaṭisambhidā: special knowledge of the principle.

Niruttipaṭisambhidā: special knowledge of language and expression.

Paṭibhānapaṭisambhidā: special knowledge of ready wit.

2. *Ubhatobhāgavimutta*: this means "those who have been liberated in both ways"—that is, liberated from the physical body by formless *jhānas*, and liberated from the "mental body" via the noble path. It is a liberation in two steps—that is, by *vikkhambhana* (suppressing defilements with the power of *samādhi* or *jhāna*) and by *samuccheda* (uprooting defilements with wisdom). They can be subdivided as follows:
   - *Ubhatobhāgavimutta*: the arahants who have developed *samatha* to at least one of the four formless *jhānas*, but not the mundane knowledges (*vijjā*) or mundane superknowledges *(abhiññā)*
   - *Tevijja*: the *ubhatobhāgavimutta* arahant who has also attained the three *vijjā*:

     Pubbenivāsānussatiñāṇa: direct knowledge that enables the recollection of the *khandhas* occupied in the past; simply speaking, the ability to recollect past lives.

     Cutūpapātañāṇa: direct knowledge revealing the passing away and arising of beings in accordance with their *kamma*. It is said to correspond with clairvoyance (*dibbacakkhu*).

     Āsavakkhayañāṇa: direct knowledge of the cessation of the outflows, or the knowledge that causes the outflows to cease.
   - *Chaḷabhiññā*: the *ubhatobhāgavimutta* arahant who has also attained the following six superknowledges:

     Iddhividhā or *iddhividhi*: the knowledge enabling the demonstration of psychic powers (such as the ability to fly, walk on water, pass through walls).

Dibbasota: direct knowledge enabling the divine ear (clairaudience).
Cetopariyañāṇa: direct knowledge enabling the perception of others' minds; ability to read others' minds.
Pubbenivāsānussati: direct knowledge enabling the recollection of past lives.
Dibbacakkhu: direct knowledge enabling the divine eye (clairvoyance).
Āsavakkhayañāṇa: direct knowledge enabling the cessation of the outflows.

- *Paṭisambhidappatta*: an *ubhatobhāgavimutta* arahant who also attains the four wisdom skills mentioned above.

Bringing them together into one group and in order of the names used to refer to them, there are six kinds of arahants, as follows:

3. *Sukkhavipassaka*: one who develops insight exclusively.
4. *Paññāvimutta*: one who is liberated through wisdom (apart from the *sukkhavipassaka*).
5. *Ubhatobhāgavimutta*: one who is liberated in both ways.
6. *Tevijja*: one who attains the three knowledges.
7. *Chaḷabhiññā*: one who attains the six superknowledges.
8. *Paṭisambhidappatta*: one who attains the four wisdom skills.[171]

An arahant who is both *chaḷabhiññā* and *paṭisambhidappatta* is one who has all the qualities of an arahant in full.

Qualities of a Stream Enterer

Nowadays the general understanding and feeling among Buddhists about *nibbāna* and arahantship have changed a great deal. The perception of *nibbāna* as a jeweled city of eternal perfect happiness of ancient times has become a perception of *nibbāna* as a state of annihilation. The more people have strayed from the Buddhist teachings and are conditioned by the values of materialism, the more negative is their attitude toward *nibbāna*, seeing it as something to be turned away from. At best they see it as something remote, for which there is no reason to get involved.

In this situation, in addition to developing a proper knowledge and understanding of *nibbāna*, there is a state that people should be encouraged to take an interest in, and that is the state of stream entry. This is the first level of noble one, the first group of members of the noble community. In fact, the state of stream entry is not only of interest in terms of its relationship with *nibbāna* and arahantship, but also something that should always be given emphasis in the teaching. However, it is often neglected or overlooked. The Buddha said:

> "Bhikkhus, you should invite and teach all people, both those who should be helped by you and those who are capable of hearing the teaching, be they friends, associates, relatives or kin, to be established in and maintain these four qualities of a stream enterer."[172]

The state and life of a stream enterer are not too remote or forbidding for ordinary people, even in the present time, and are in fact very attractive. Many of the Buddha's stream-enterer disciples were householders. They lived wholesome, moral lives in the midst of worldly society. They had happy family lives and worked for the benefit of the community, the religion and their country. Their life stories are inspiring and exemplary. Even though these people had attained high states, they still had subtle defilements remaining. When confronted with loss, they still experienced sorrow and cried;[173] they still had love and anger like ordinary people, but it was gentler and lighter, and they would not commit wrong doings of the extreme kind. The suffering that remained for them was very little when compared with the greater amount of suffering that they had already given up. They had a firm foundation that would lead their lives along the path of blameless happiness and perfect goodness (*kusaladhamma*).

Some of the Buddha's noteworthy stream enterer disciples are King Bimbisāra, the great king of Magadha who offered the Bamboo Grove as the first Buddhist monastery, and who observed the *uposatha* precepts four times a month;[174] Anāthapiṇḍika the merchant, the famous builder of the Jetavana Monastery, and peerless supporter of bhikkhus and helper of the poor;[175] Lady Visākhā, the foremost female lay supporter who, even though she had twenty children, was still able to do beneficial works for the community, play an important role in the activities of the order (Saṅgha), and live as a prominent personality in Kosalan society;[176] Jīvaka Komārabhaca the doctor, physician to the Magadhan king, to the Buddha and to the order, who has been immortalized in the circles of ancient medicine;[177] and Nakulapitā and Nakulamātā, the husband and wife who maintained their love together faithfully until old age and who aspired to meet each other in every life thereafter.[178]

The quality of a stream enterer that is best known is the abandoning of the first three fetters—self view (*sakkāyadiṭṭhi*), doubt (*vicikicchā*), and grasping at rites and observances (*sīlabbataparāmāsa*)—which is a quality in terms of what is renounced or given up. But there are also qualities in terms of what is acquired, and in the scriptural sources it seems that these acquired qualities were given a great deal of emphasis.

There are many of these acquired qualities, but in brief they are included within five important criteria: faith (*saddhā*), morality (*sīla*), learning (*suta*), relinquishment (*cāga*), and wisdom (*paññā*). Here I will compile the qualities, both those given up and those acquired, describing only their main points.[179]

Qualities Acquired

1. In terms of faith: believing firmly in the truth, in the efficacy of goodness, and in the natural law of cause and effect; confidence in the ability of human wisdom to extinguish suffering or solve problems in accordance with a rational path; and believing in the virtuous community of people developing that path. These kinds of confidence express themselves as faith firmly rooted in wisdom in the Triple Gem.[180] It is a faith that is resolute, firm,

and unalterable because it is founded on direct knowledge and understanding.

2. In terms of morality: having bodily conduct, verbal conduct, and livelihood that are honest, pleasing to the noble ones; having a morality that is free in that it is not enslaved by desire;[181] acting in accordance with the teachings and their true meaning, for that which is good, gracious, impeccable, for reducing defilements, for peace and for concentration. In general, it is correct observance of the five precepts, which is regarded as the level on which morality can be perfectly developed.
3. In terms of learning: being a learned, noble disciple (*sutvā ariyasāvaka*); to have learned the noble qualities is considered to be "learned."
4. In terms of relinquishment (*cāga*): living the household life with a heart void of meanness; being willing to share and give.
5. In terms of wisdom: having the wisdom of a "learner" (*sekha*): knowing clearly the four noble truths, seeing the *paṭiccasamuppāda*, and understanding well the three characteristics of impermanence, *dukkha* and not-self, until one can cast off wrong view in its various forms entirely, having gone beyond doubt in regard to the four noble truths. In the terminology of the Dhamma it is called being "one who really knows the world."
6. In terms of society: a stream enterer is one who can fully practice according to the six principles for creating harmony and unity in the community known as the *sārāṇīyadhamma*, by being able to correctly practice in accordance with the last of them, which is considered to be their culmination and to encompass all the others, which is *diṭṭhisāmaññatā*. The *sārāṇīyadhamma* practices are as follows:
   - *Mettākāyakamma*: friendly bodily expressions, such as helping each other, and exhibiting polite and respectful behavior.
   - *Mettāvacīkamma*: friendly verbal expressions, such as giving well-intentioned advice or admonishment; addressing each other with polite words.
   - *Mettāmanokamma*: friendly thoughts toward each other,

such as looking on each other in a good light; thinking of each other's benefit, being cheerful.

- *Sādhāraṇabhogī*: sharing rightful gains; dividing gains throughout the community.
- *Sīlasāmaññatā*: having moral conduct on a par with one's fellows, not allowing oneself to become an object of censure to the community.
- *Diṭṭhisāmaññatā*: having harmonious view in the noble teaching (*ariyadiṭṭhi*) which leads to the removal of suffering.

7. In terms of happiness: beginning to know transcendent (*lokuttara*) happiness that is subtle and profound, and which is independent of material objects (because one has attained the noble liberation).

Qualities Given Up

1. The stream enterer gives up three of the ten fetters:
   - *Sakkāyadiṭṭhi*: the wrong view of something as one's self
   - *Vicikicchā*: doubts and uncertainties about the Teacher (Buddha), the teaching (Dhamma), the order (Saṅgha), or the practice (*sikkhā*)
   - *Sīlabbataparāmāsa*: blind following of rules, observances, practices, and forms that is not in accordance with their wholesome objective
2. The stream enterer gives up the five kinds of *macchariya* (= meanness, narrow-mindedness, possessiveness, exclusiveness):
   - *Āvāsamacchariya*: meanness in regard to dwelling place, locality
   - *Kulamacchariya*: meanness in regard to family, group, affiliation, tribe
   - *Lābhamacchariya*: meanness in regard to material gain
   - *Vaṇṇamacchariya*: meanness in regard to reputation, meanness in regard to praise
   - *Dhammamacchariya*: meanness in regard to teaching, in regard to learning or knowledge; meanness in regard to special qualities one has attained[182]

3. The stream enterer gives up the four *agati*, the four biases:
   - *Chandāgati*: bias on account of like
   - *Dosāgati*: bias on account of dislike
   - *Mohāgati*: bias on account of delusion or foolishness
   - *Bhayāgati*: bias on account of fear[183]
4. The stream enterer gives up desire, aversion, and delusion, or greed, hatred, and delusion, on the gross or extreme levels that would lead to the netherworlds; one commits no bad *kamma* extreme enough to cause rebirth in the lower realms.[184]
5. The stream enterer overcomes the dangerous consequences, distress, and various forms of mental suffering that would normally arise from not keeping the five precepts. A stream enterer has utterly transcended the nether realms. The greater body of suffering is done away with; the suffering that remains is merely a small fraction that is virtually negligible.[185]

In fact, the qualities given up and those acquired by the stream enterer are essentially the same. That is to say, *sakkāyadiṭṭhi* can only be given up through having sufficient penetrating wisdom of the reality faring according to causes and conditions; when this sort of clear understanding arises, *vicikicchā*—doubt and uncertainty—naturally disappears, and the faith based on that wisdom is made firm. At the same time, one can now observe the precepts properly in accordance with their principles, so it becomes the morality praised by the noble ones (*ariyakantasīla*). Thus, *sīlabbataparāmāsa* comes to an end. As relinquishment (*cāga*) develops, meanness disappears. As desire, aversion, and delusion are reduced, one no longer falls into the power or the biases (*agati*), and the weakening of desire, aversion, and delusion through the wisdom that sees the true nature of life and the world causes attachment to unwind. When clinging is reduced, suffering is relaxed, and one comes to know a subtler kind of happiness.

In short, the state of stream entry is a level of life that can be acknowledged as satisfactory both in terms of virtue and happiness. In terms of virtue, there is sufficient goodness to guarantee that one will not cause danger, trouble, decline, or ruin for society or for others; on the contrary, one will have conduct that is useful and conducive to the maintenance and well-being of one's own life and society. That virtue is stable because it has arisen as the natural result of its own causes and conditions—because it is based on the keen understanding that leads to a new vision of life and the world.

In terms of happiness, the stream enterer encounters a new kind of happiness that is subtle and profound, which is realized to be of inestimable value—as a result of which even though the stream enterer may experience sensual or other kinds of worldly happiness, he or she would never allow such grosser forms of happiness to exceed their bounds and ruin the subtler kind of happiness. That is, the stream enterer would never give up the subtler transcendent happiness in order to increase the bounds of the grosser worldly happiness; the grosser, worldly kinds of happiness are balanced by the subtle, transcendent happiness. This kind of happiness is both a result of, and also a conditioning factor on, the virtues a stream enterer maintains; thus it is a guarantee of not regressing and only advancing further. Since the value of stream entry attainment is pleasing both to the one who attains it and to society, the stream enterers are designated the first group of members of the community of noble ones.

The Buddha gave many teachings stressing the value and importance of stream entry, such as the following:

> "Greater than being a universal emperor with dominion over all the land, greater than birth in heaven, greater than power over all worlds, is the attainment of stream entry."[186]

If *nibbana* feels too unattainable and difficult to understand, if speaking of it leads to feelings of emptiness or despondency, the level of stream entry serves as a bridge toward it, something that doesn't seem too remote and is easier to understand. At the same time, stream entry is connected to *nibbāna*, having entered the stream leading to *nibbāna*, and is referred to in the commentaries as the first glimpse of *nibbāna*.[187]

If a person is still hesitant and doesn't yet dare to really embark on the journey, he or she may still advance to the level of being ready to step onto the path, known as being a *kalyāṇaputhujjana* (a "good *puthujjana*"),[188] or one who has morality and "good qualities" (*kalyāṇadhamma*),[189] and therefore begin to be called a "learned noble disciple" (*sutvā ariyasāvaka*),[190] one who has learned the noble Dhamma, who knows the noble Dhamma, or one who has heard the call. It is the beginning of being learned, the level of being one who knows the beginning of the path, has prepared the equipment needed for the journey and is in the process of walking out of the forest in which one has been lost and stepping onto the path. Even though one may still be hesitant, one is ready for the journey.

For life on this beginning level, the *kalyāṇaputhujjana*, whose faith, morality, relinquishment, and wisdom are not in themselves stable or firm, there is *suta*, learning. Learning is the important requisite for the journey. It shows us where the path begins[191] and is an important factor for the further enhancement of faith, morality, relinquishment, and wisdom, because when there is correct knowledge, faith arises, and with faith comes the energy to begin the development of the other qualities. When learning is incorporated into faith, morality, relinquishment, and wisdom, to whatever extent they are developed at this point, they are known as the five *sampadā* (attainments, attributes, endowments)[192] or five mundane treasures.[193] When a practitioner becomes a stream enterer, these five attainments or treasures automatically become transcendent.

Names, Descriptive Terms, and Synonyms for the Stream Enterer

> The Buddha: "Sāriputta, it is said 'stream, stream' (*sotā*): what is this 'stream'?"
>
> Sāriputta: "Revered Sir, the noble eightfold path is the stream—namely, right view, right thought, right speech, right

action, right livelihood, right effort, right mindfulness, right concentration."

The Buddha: "That is correct, Sāriputta. It is said 'stream enterer, stream enterer.' What is the stream enterer?"

Sāriputta: "Revered Sir, whoever is possessed of the noble eightfold path is called a stream enterer: the stream enterer of this name, of this clan."

The Buddha: "That is correct, Sāriputta, that is correct."[194]

"This noble disciple can be called one endowed with right view (*diṭṭhisampanna*), endowed with right vision (*dassanasampanna*), to have attained to the true Dhamma (*saddhamma*), to have seen the true Dhamma, to be endowed with the direct knowledge of a learner (*sekhañāṇa*), to be endowed with the knowledge of a learner, to have attained the stream of Dhamma (*dhammasota*), to be a noble one with the wisdom to penetrate the truth, and to be one who is at the threshold of the deathless."[195]

"The learned, noble disciple who has seen the noble ones and is skilled in the noble Dhamma, is well trained (*suvinita*) in the noble Dhamma, has seen the true persons (*sappurisa*), is skilled in the Dhamma of the true persons, is well trained in the Dhamma of the true persons."[196]

"He has seen the Dhamma, attained the Dhamma, realized the Dhamma, arrived at the Dhamma, crossed over doubt, has no more questions to ask (or has no points of doubt) and has arrived at courage, with no need to rely on others in the teaching of the Teacher."[197]

"One who follows the teaching (*sāsanakāra*), who practices in accordance with the instruction, who has crossed over doubts... in the teaching of the Teacher..."[198]

"A noble disciple who has obtained the fruit [realized the

Dhamma], who clearly knows the teaching,"[199] "attained to confidence in the Tathāgata, sees the deathless and realizes the deathless Dhamma,"[200] "...is a stream enterer, naturally not falling low (it is impossible for that person to fall low), one assured of advancing to enlightenment."[201]

BOOK TWO

THE MIDDLE WAY

Ete te bhikkhave ubho ante anupagamma majjhimā paṭipadā tathāgatena abhisambuddhā... ayameva ariyo aṭṭhangiko maggo seyyathidaṁ sammādiṭṭhi sammāsaṅkappo sammāvācā sammākammanto sammā-āvjīvo sammāvāyāmo sammāsati sammāsamādhi...

Bhikkhus, the Tathāgata, not inclining to these two extremes, has realized the practice that is the Middle Way...that is, the noble eightfold path: right view, right thought, right speech, right action, right livelihood, right effort, right mindfulness, and right concentration...

PART FIVE

How Should Life Be Lived?

CHAPTER 6

Introduction to the Middle Way

The Middle Teaching (*majjhena dhammadesanā*) is the teaching presented by the Buddha impartially according to nature—that is, according to the reality that all things fare of their own accord following causes and conditions—discarding the extreme views or theories that human beings contrive in accordance with their distorted perceptions, attachments, and desires. The Middle Teaching is the teaching of *paṭiccasamuppāda*, the process of dependent arising. The *paṭiccasamuppāda* process comes in two modes or streams: the first stream describes the arising of suffering. It is called the *samudayavāra* (origination mode), and is considered to be a definition of the second noble truth (*samudaya ariyasacca*). The second stream describes the cessation of suffering. It is called the *nirodhavāra* (cessation mode), and is considered to be a definition of the third noble truth (*nirodha ariyasacca*).[1]

In essence, then, the *majjhena dhammadesanā* describes both routes of the process:[2]

1. *Samudaya* = The origination mode of the *paṭiccasamuppāda*: ignorance → volitional formations → consciousness → mind-body → sense bases → contact → feeling → desire → clinging → becoming → birth → aging and death, sorrow...despair = the arising of suffering
2. *Nirodha* = The cessation mode of the *paṭiccasamuppāda*: cessation of ignorance → cessation of volitional formations → cessation of consciousness →...cessation of aging and death, sorrow...despair = the cessation of suffering

The teaching of *samudaya* (arising or cause) is given because there is the problem of suffering. It is the starting point from which we must trace back to find the original cause. Therefore I have described the realities that are the bases for the problem, suffering, from the outset in the section on *majjhena dhammadesanā*. *Nirodha* (cessation) has a broad meaning: it refers not only to the process that produces the cessation of suffering, which is the *paṭiccasamuppāda* in cessation mode, but also encompasses *nibbāna*, which is the state of suffering's cessation. Thus, in the section on the *majjhena dhammadesanā* I discussed both the process of suffering's cessation and the state of *nibbāna*.

Having described suffering, the cause of suffering, the process of suffering's cessation, and the state without suffering, this would seem to cover the entire process and bring Buddhadhamma to a close, but that is not the case. This is because the *majjhena dhammadesanā* describes only realities as they exist, according to the natural causes and conditions, and does not cover practical application. In learning the *majjhena dhammadesanā* and understanding the process of suffering's cessation, we may come to understand the principles of the cessation of suffering, but we still need practical guidance as to the methods for achieving the objective. This is the connection between the natural processes and human practice.

The point to be emphasized here is that the methods of practice must be in conformity with the processes of nature; the practice must lead to results through the natural process. Only then will the desired objective be realized. The principle here is learning and understanding the natural processes, and then applying a method based on that knowledge. In other words, as far as the natural processes are concerned, our only duty is to know them. As for the practice, we follow the directions that have been formulated according to that knowledge. Having come to this understanding, we can now proceed from the processes of nature to the level of human application.

The practices, methods, or way of life for attaining the cessation of suffering are known by the specialized term *paṭipadā*. The Buddha established such a *paṭipadā* in conformity with the natural process of cessation described in the *majjhena dhammadesanā*, and called that practice *majjhimā paṭipadā*, meaning "the Middle Way of practice," or just "the Middle Way." It refers to the practices, methods or way of life that are centered according to nature, that conform to the laws of nature, and that are just right for bringing about results according to the natural process, not inclining to the two extremes that would cause one to get stuck or stray from the path.

This Middle Way is called simply "the path" (*magga*). The path has eight components and it transforms those who follow it into noble ones (*ariya*). Thus, it is called in full the noble eightfold path (*ariyaṭṭhaṅgikamagga*). The Buddha stated that this path, also known as the Middle Way, is an ancient path along which many had previously traveled and arrived at the goal. The Buddha was merely the discoverer of this ancient path and its proclaimer to humanity. He performed the duty of pointing it out to trainable beings.[3] This path is a humanly devised method of practice for bringing about results according to the natural process of the cessation of suffering: that is, causing the factors and conditions to interact with each other until the result is accomplished according to that process. Having attained this way, we have gone beyond the natural process under the heading of *nirodha* to the humanly devised technique under the heading of *magga*. In other words, we have passed on from the level of knowing the truth of the natural laws to the level of applying that knowledge in a systematic method of practice.

In order to more clearly illustrate this step from a natural process of *nirodha* to the human practice of *magga*, we may use this schematic representation:

> *Nirodha*: ignorance ceases → formations cease → consciousness ceases → mind-body ceases → sense bases cease → contact ceases → feeling ceases → desire ceases → clinging ceases → becoming ceases → birth ceases → aging and death, sorrow, lamentation, pain, grief, and despair cease = the cessation of suffering

> *Magga*: right view + right thought + right speech + right action + right livelihood + right effort + right mindfulness + right concentration[4] = cessation of suffering

Although this *magga* or Middle Way is said to have only eight factors, they are simply the core factors, which can all be further expanded on and reorganized into many forms, levels, and stages in accordance with different objectives, individuals, situations, conditions, and levels of maturity, and therefore it entails studying a great deal of material. The Middle Way is therefore a vast subject and is here given its own separate section.

Before going on to examine the path itself, let us consider some of the other forms in which there is a procession from natural reality to human practice, or from natural process to human methodology.

There are Buddhavacana describing these two ways of practice:

1. Wrong practice (*micchāpaṭipadā*), or the wrong way; the way leading to suffering
2. Right practice (*sammāpaṭipadā*), or the right way; the way leading to the cessation of suffering

In some places the Buddha classed the origination mode of the *paṭiccasamuppāda* as wrong practice, and its cessation mode as right practice. They can be simply represented like this:

> Wrong practice: ignorance → volitional formations → consciousness . . . → birth → aging and death, sorrow, lamentation, pain, grief, and despair = the arising of suffering
>
> Right practice: cessation of ignorance → cessation of volitional formations → cessation of consciousness . . . → cessation of birth → cessation of aging and death, sorrow, lamentation, pain, grief, and despair = the cessation of suffering[5]

Elsewhere, however, the Buddha showed the practices that are directly opposed to the factors of the path as wrong practice, and the eightfold path as right practice, thus:

> Wrong practice: Wrong view + wrong thought + wrong speech + wrong action + wrong livelihood + wrong effort + wrong mindfulness + wrong concentration
>
> Right practice: Right view + right thought + right speech + right action + right livelihood + right effort + right mindfulness + right concentration[6]

The *paṭiccasamuppāda* is a natural process, depicting only realities, not a way of practice. However, the first set of right and wrong practices given above describes them in terms of the *paṭiccasamuppāda*. Is there a contradiction here? The likely answer is that the *paṭiccasamuppāda* illustrated here (and it is only illustrated as a way of practice in this one sutta) seeks to indicate or connect to practical application. The commentary that explains this sutta asks the question: ignorance can be a condition for good or meritorious actions (*puññābhisaṅkhāra*), or it can inspire the mind to a high level of concentration and stability (*āneñjābhisaṅkhāra*): why then is it said to be wrong practice? In answer, the commentary states that when people desire becoming (*bhava*) and are intent on gaining or becoming something, whatever they do, even if they develop the five mundane superknowledges (*abhiññā*) or the eight levels of concentration (*samāpatti*), it is all wrong practice, while those who aspire to *nibbāna*, who are intent on relinquishment (the mind clear and liberated) rather than gaining or being something, will always have right practice, even when making a small offering.[7]

My intention in presenting these two kinds of right and wrong practice is to incorporate them into an examination of the progression from the natural process in *nirodha* to the humanly devised technique of practice known as *magga*. Here there is the added observation that apart from the process and practice on the good side, the Buddha also described the process and the practice on the harmful or wrong side.

There is a Buddhavacana describing the *paṭiccasamuppāda* as a process of the cessation of suffering in yet another form, which differs from those mentioned above. The beginning half describes the process of suffering's arising according to the *paṭiccasamuppāda* in origination mode in full, up to the arising of suffering, but from there, instead of describing the process of suffering's cessation according to the cessation mode of the *paṭiccasamuppāda*, it proceeds to describe a procession of skillful factors that condition each other in a sequence culminating in liberation. This is a wholly new process with no reference to the cessation of the factors of the origination mode. This kind of process may be taken as an important example of using the factors of the path in a practical, real-life situation. In other words, it is a process that may arise for one who successfully practices the path and attains the goal. This process of liberation is given in many places throughout the texts in different variations. I would like to present each of them here:

> Ignorance → volitional formations → consciousness → mind-body → six sense bases → contact → feeling → desire → clinging → becoming → birth → suffering → faith (*saddhā*) → gladness (*pāmojja*) → rapture (*pīti*) → tranquility (*passaddhi*) → happiness (*sukha*) → concentration (*samādhi*) → direct knowledge and vision of the way things are (*yathābhūtañāṇadassana*) → disenchantment (*nibbidā*)→ dispassion (*virāga*) → liberation (*vimutti*) → direct knowledge of destruction [of the outflows] (*khayañāṇa*)[8]

Note that this process begins with ignorance and proceeds up to suffering according to the standard origination mode of the *paṭiccasamuppāda*, but once it reaches suffering, instead of turning around to begin again at ignorance, it instead continues on with faith taking over from ignorance. From there the process proceeds in a good direction, leading ultimately to the objective of direct knowledge of destruction (*khayañāṇa*), no more to return to ignorance.

For those who well understand the nature of ignorance, the progression above will not seem strange. The process can be divided into two stages: (1) from ignorance to suffering and (2) from faith to direct knowledge of destruction. Those who have studied the *paṭiccasamuppāda* in chapter 3 will understand the meaning of faith here, simply speaking, as a suppressed or weakened form of ignorance: at this stage, ignorance is no longer the totally blind kind but is replaced by a grain of understanding, which serves as a medium for encouraging advancement to a good destination, eventually leading to knowledge of reality and liberation.

Simply explained, this means that once the process has gone from ignorance to suffering, we search for a way out. In this case, we hear a true teaching, or intuitively develop an appreciation of it, and therefore we develop a confidence in its good qualities and wholesomeness, and gladness and rapture result. They then encourage us to strive forward in virtue on progressively higher levels up to the highest.

In fact, this latter process corresponds with the format for the cessation mode of the *paṭiccasamuppāda*, which states "cessation of ignorance → cessation of volitional formations → cessation of consciousness," and so on, but here the details of the prominent factors in the process are shown more clearly, and the intention is to show a connection between the process of suffering's arising and the process of its cessation.

The Nettipakaraṇa,[9] citing the following Buddhavacana, states that it is also a *paṭiccasamuppāda* describing cessation:

> "Ānanda, in this way, skillful moral conduct has absence of remorse (*avipaṭisāra*) as objective (*attha*) and reward (*ānisaṁsa*); absence of remorse has gladness as objective and reward; gladness has rapture as objective and reward; rapture has tranquility as objective and reward; tranquility has happiness as objective and reward; happiness has concentration as

> objective and reward; concentration has direct knowledge and vision into the way things are as objective and reward; direct knowledge and vision into the way things are has disenchantment as objective and reward; disenchantment has dispassion as objective and reward; dispassion has direct knowledge and vision of liberation as objective and reward. It is thus that skillful moral conduct gives rise to and brings about the fulfillment of these respective factors for the attainment of arahantship."[10]

The process related in this Buddhavacana can be written like this:

> Skillful moral conduct → absence of remorse → gladness → rapture → tranquility → happiness → concentration → direct knowledge and vision into the way things are → disenchantment → dispassion → direct knowledge and vision of liberation

This sequence is clearly the same as the previous one, except that it describes only the process of suffering's cessation and not its arising. Let us look once more at the previous sequence:

> Ignorance → volitional formations → consciousness . . . → birth → suffering → faith → gladness → rapture → tranquility → happiness → concentration → direct knowledge and vision into the way things are → disenchantment → dispassion → liberation → direct knowledge of destruction

Although both sequences of factors are similar, they are not identical. One begins with faith, the other with skillful moral conduct, followed by absence of remorse. From there they are the same. In fact, the difference is only in wording and in emphasis, but the meanings agree. One sequence is based on the situation in which faith is predominant. But when there is faith—that is, the mind has full confidence in rationality, is inspired in something good, and confident of virtue—that mental state is also connected to behavior at that time. Faith being supported by good conduct leads to gladness (*pāmojja*). The other sequence, which begins with skillful moral conduct and absence of remorse, is based on the situation in which conduct is the predominant factor. In this case, the mind has a foundation of confidence in the rationality of goodness; that is why there is good conduct. With morality and absence of remorse, there is the arising of self-assurance and confidence in the goodness of one's practice, which is a characteristic of the faith that makes the mind confident and clear. From there, faith becomes a condition for the arising of gladness, just as in the previous sequence. In the final part, one of the sequences finishes with "liberation" and "direct knowledge of destruction," while the other finishes with "direct knowledge and vision of liberation." They are the same, except that the latter sequence includes "liberation" and "direct knowledge of destruction" under the one heading.

There is a similar process of liberation, except "faith" is replaced with "wise attention" (*yoniso-manasikāra*):

> Wise attention → gladness → rapture → calmness → happiness → concentration → direct knowledge and vision into reality → disenchantment → dispassion → liberation[11]

This sequence is no different from the previous ones except that it begins with knowing how to think, consider, and use one's own rational wisdom, instead of beginning with faith. When one thinks properly and understands in accordance with reality, seeing the actuality, the mind is gladdened, which is the arising of gladness (*pāmojja*). From there the factors are the same as in the previous sequence.

These sequences of factors clarify the approach to practice and help to understand what needs to be done, but they are not a sufficiently detailed and systematic description of the practice. The question still remains as to what needs to be done to initiate the arising of such a sequence.

Initial Explanation of the Middle Way

The Middle Way, the last of the four noble truths, is a codification of all the practices or ethical systems taught in Buddhism. It is the practical teaching for aiding advancement to the objectives of the process we have studied and understood in the form of tangible results. For an initial understanding of the Middle Way, consider the following Buddhavacana and brief explanations:

The Path as the Middle Way

> "Bhikkhus, these two extremes should not be indulged in by one gone to homelessness. They are immersion in sensual pleasure, which is lowly, vulgar, common, ignoble, and leads to no benefit; and devotion to difficulty and torment, which is suffering, ignoble, and leads to no benefit.
>
> "The Tathāgata has become enlightened to the Middle Way, which does not incline to those two extremes, and is the way leading to direct knowledge and vision, and inclines to peace, to superknowledge, to enlightenment, and to *nibbāna*.
>
> "What is that... Middle Way? It is the noble eightfold path—right view, right thought, right speech, right action, right livelihood, right effort, right mindfulness, and right concentration."[12]

This Buddhavacana from the first discourse (*Dhammacakkappavattana Sutta*) encapsulates the entire meaning, content, and objective of the Middle Way. Note that the Middle Way is called such because it does not deviate to the two extremes of (1) *kāmasukhallikānuyoga*—immersion in sensual pleasures, or the extreme of hedonism—and (2) *attakilamathānuyoga*—devotion to self-mortification, or the extreme of asceticism.

Sometimes the Middle Way is interpreted in a broad sense, referring to any actions or thoughts that lie somewhere in between these two forms of action or thought, or two groups of people—that is, taking the halfway mark between these two sides. But this should be known as a false Middle Way, not the real thing.

The real Middle Way has a fixed principle, and that lies in its clearly defined objective or goal. Once there is a distinct goal or objective, whatever way leads to it, whatever action accords with it, which is just right to produce the results accordingly, is by definition the Middle Way. It can be compared to shooting an arrow at a target. There must be a point to serve as the target. The straight shot is whatever way of shooting that is just right to guide the arrow to its target. The "Middle Way" is determined by the shot that is just right for hitting that target. All shots that miss the target are wrong. As opposed to the many kinds of wrong shots that veer off to the side, there is only one true point of aim, and that is the "middle" one. That is the sure spot. Similarly, the Middle Way has a sure objective—the cessation of suffering, the state of liberation and freedom from problems. The path is the system of thought and action, or the way of life, that is perfectly attuned to achieving the result of that goal, the cessation of suffering; that is why it is called the Middle Way.

Because the Middle Way is determined by its clear and sure objective, it is essential to know what that objective is. When setting out on a path, you must know where you are going. Thus, the Middle Way is a way of wisdom and begins with right view—understanding one's problem and knowing the way out of it. In this respect, the Middle Way is the way of knowledge and reason, the way of understanding, acknowledging and daring to face up to the truth. When people have knowledge and understanding and dare to look at the truth of the world and life, they will be able to organize their lives appropriately for themselves, without the need to look to occult forces or external higher powers. Equipped with the confidence resulting from this knowledge, they no longer have to preoccupy themselves with things they fear may exist beyond human capacities.

This attitude of confidence is one of the characteristics of the Middle Way. One who walks the Middle Way, having understood the problem and determined the direction in which the objective lies, will gain the subsequent understanding that the Middle Way leading to this objective is a way of life in which one does not value oneself so lowly as to sink completely into the flow of the world, allowing one's life to be enslaved by the delights (*āmisa*) of the world to the extent that happiness and suffering, goodness and the value of life are totally dependent on material things and the vicissitudes of external factors.

The Middle Way also does not incline to mental extremes. It does not see everything as dependent on spiritual practices and mental achievements to the extent that material and physical concerns are neglected, leading to self-torment. This Middle Way of life is characterized by not tormenting oneself or others, and comprises knowledge and understanding of actualities as they really are, both material and mental, and practicing wisely, commensurate with causes and conditions and perfectly attuned to attaining the results of the path. It is not merely doing things for the pleasure to be obtained from material objects or in imitation of others, believing blindly that they must be this or that way.[13] The Middle Way has these important features. Whoever speaks of a Middle Way or traveling a Middle Way should be asked whether that person understands the nature of the problem that is there, and the objective of that Middle Way one is walking.

The Path as a Way of Life for Both Renunciants and Householders

> "Bhikkhus, I do not praise wrong practice, be it of a renunciant or a householder. A renunciant or a householder who practices wrongly does not, on account of that wrong practice, achieve the skillful path (*ñāyadhamma*). And what is wrong practice? It is wrong view...wrong concentration.
>
> "I do praise right practice, be it of a renunciant or a householder. A renunciant or a householder who practices rightly may, on account of that right practice, achieve the skillful path. And what is right practice? It is right view,... right concentration."[14]
>
> ---
>
> "Bhikkhus, just as the Ganges River flows, inclines, and surges

> toward the sea, when a bhikkhu develops and makes much of the noble eightfold path, he is disposed, inclines, and surges toward *nibbāna*."[15]

The Path as a Principle of Social Practice

> "Ānanda, having good friendship (*kalyāṇamittatā*), good associates, and the appreciation of good people is equal to the holy life in its entirety, because one who has a good friend[16]...can expect this: to bring forth the noble eightfold path, and to make much of the noble eightfold path."[17]

This Buddhavacana acknowledges the importance of the relationship between people in the social environment as an essential factor for inducing and encouraging practice of the Dhamma. Lifestyle, ethics, or systems of conduct in Buddhism are connected to society, not separate from it.

> "Bhikkhus, just as the light of dawn is the harbinger of the rising of the sun, just so is the endowment of wise attention (*yoniso-manasikāra*) the harbinger of the arising of the noble eightfold path in a bhikkhu. Of a bhikkhu who is endowed with wise attention, it can be expected that he will grow in and make much of the noble eightfold path."[18]

This Buddhavacana points out that while social factors are important, we must not overlook the importance of factors within the individual. Both social and individual factors can be the starting point for right practice and a right way of life. In fact, they support and encourage each other. Right practice, or a wholesome life, arises from the combined effect of these two kinds of factors, social and personal, and it is through these two factors supporting each other that progress on the way to life's objective is most effectively realized.

Note, however, that special emphasis is given to social factors, in having a good friend, over and above factors within the individual, in that the Buddha praises this social factor as of equal value to the practice of Buddhism known as the holy life (*brahmacariya*) in its entirety. This is because for the majority of people, right practice, the wholesome life, or the noble way can only be established with the help of social factors. Wholesome social factors are both catalysts for the ability to think known as *yoniso-manasikāra* in the initial stages and supports, supplements, and stimuli for *yoniso-manasikāra* during the further advancement of the practice.

The Path as the Way to the Cessation of Kamma

> "This noble eightfold path is the way leading to the cessation of *kamma*; that is, right view... right concentration."[19]

Here the Middle Way has the meaning of the way leading to the cessation of *kamma*. The important point here is not to take the cessation of *kamma* as the cessation of "bad fortune"—as it is often understood—which is a narrow understanding, nor that the cessation of *kamma* is attained by inaction, as described in the chapter on *kamma*.

First, we can see that in order to quell *kamma*, or bring it to cessation, applied and earnest effort is required, but the effort in this case is made in accordance with the Middle Way, according to the proper method, giving up wrong actions.

Second, the phrase "cessation of *kamma*" does not mean giving up all activity, but rather giving up the actions of an ordinary person (*puthujjana*) and instead doing the actions of a noble one (*ariya-puggala*). Basically unenlightened people do things on the basis of desire and clinging. They cling to good and evil in terms of the self, belonging to self, and self-interests. The actions of unenlightened beings are thus technically referred to as *kamma*, divided into good and bad varieties and clung to out of desire and clinging. The cessation of *kamma* is the giving up of actions based on attachment to good and bad as they concern the self, belonging to self and self-interests. When there is no good and bad tied to oneself, actions are not referred to as *kamma*. The actions of the noble ones are thus fully attuned to their true meaning and objective, and are not concerned with any selfish desire or clinging.

Noble ones do not commit evil actions, because the causes and conditions for their arising are no longer present [there is no greed, aversion, and delusion to cause actions for self-interests]. They perform only good and beneficial actions because their actions are done with wisdom and compassion. Even though their actions are said to be "good" in conformity with worldly conventions, they do not cling to their actions as being "their own" goodness or as means of achieving something or other. When unenlightened beings do a beneficial action, there is not only the creation of benefit in accordance with the meaning and objective of that action, but also an expectation for some personal gain, if not material reward then something more subtle, such as reputation or, on a subtler level, a sense of pleasure or pride in one's own goodness. When the noble ones perform beneficial actions, there are only the actions in accordance with their objectives and reasons. Thus, their actions are not referred to as *kamma*. The path or Middle Way is a system of practice for doing away with the actions known as *kamma*. *Kamma* is ended, leaving only pure actions (*kiriyā*). This is the difference between the mundane way and the transcendent way. The Buddha and the arahants were able to travel far and wide teaching the Dhamma, but their actions were not *kamma*, even though these were actions that ordinary people would refer to as "good."

The Path as a Tool to Be Used, Not Something to Be Clung To or Carried Around

> "Bhikkhus, it is like a man going on a long journey, who comes across a great expanse of water. The hither shore is frightening and full of danger, while the further shore is clear and safe. There is no boat or bridge to take him across to the other side. That man thinks to himself, 'This expanse of water is great. The

hither shore is frightening...What if I were to collect grass, logs of wood, branches, and leaves, and bind them together to make a raft, and with that raft, using my arms and legs, safely cross over to the further shore?'

"Then he...binds his raft...and crosses safely over to the further shore. Having crossed to the further shore, he thinks to himself, 'This raft has truly been of great use to me. Using it...I have been able to safely cross over to this shore. What if I were to lift this raft onto my head or onto my shoulders and continue on my way?' Bhikkhus, what do you think? Could that man, doing so, be said to have done the right thing in terms of the raft?"

[The bhikkhus answer that he would not. The Buddha continues:]

"What should that man have done in order to be said to have done the right thing in terms of the raft? As to this, having crossed over to the further shore, that man thinks to himself, 'This raft has truly been of great use to me...What if I were to lift this raft onto the dry land, or tie it up here in the water, and then be on my way?' That man, doing so, could then be said to have done the right thing in terms of the raft.

"In the same way, the Dhamma can be compared to a raft. I give it for the objective of crossing over, not for clinging to. Therefore, once you know the Dhamma, which I have here compared to a raft, in full, you should let go of even that which is the teachings, let alone that which is not the teaching (*adhamma*)."[20]

"Bhikkhus, if you still cling to, delight in, cherish, or see as yourself the *diṭṭhi* [theory, principle, understanding of the Dhamma] that is so purified and immaculate, would you then be knowing in full the teaching compared to a raft, which I have given for the purpose of crossing over, not for clinging to?"[21]

These two Buddhavacana not only warn us not to cling to teachings (even those that are true and right) without deriving the benefit from them in accordance with their meaning, value, or objective, but, more importantly, they stress that we should look on teachings as tools or methods for attaining an objective rather than as ends in themselves. For this reason, when doing any kind of Dhamma practice, one should always be clearly aware of its objective and its relationship with other teachings in attaining that objective. This objective is not just the general objective on the ultimate level, but also specific objectives of particular teachings, understanding what things that teaching is meant to support or to lead to, where it ultimately leads, and what things carry on from it. It is like going on a long journey in many stages, which may involve changing vehicles for land, sea, and air travel. It is not enough to only roughly know the final destination; one must also know where each of the vehicles will lead one, and from that point what vehicle will be used for the next leg of the journey.[22] When Dhamma practice lacks awareness of its objectives, of its capacity as a tool and its relationship to other practices, it becomes aimless, narrow, and futile, and—what is particularly dangerous—strays from the right path and its objective. It becomes a listless, inoperative, and fruitless practice. It is due to this directionless kind of practice that deviation and undesirable results arise in relation to such major practices as contentment with little (*santosa*) and equanimity (*upekkhā*).

The Path as the Holy Life or Conduct of the Buddha

> "Bhikkhus, go forth for the benefit, the weal, and the happiness of the many, for the welfare of the world, for the benefit, the weal, and the happiness of devas and humans...Teach the Dhamma... proclaim the holy life..."[23]
>
> ---
>
> "They say 'holy life, holy life.' What is this holy life? What is its destination?
>
> "The noble way containing eight factors—that is, right view... right concentration—this is the holy life. Whoever is endowed with this noble eightfold path is a follower of the holy life

(*brahmacārī*). The cessation of desire, aversion, and delusion is the destination of the holy life."[24]

The Path as a Way for Realizing Different Objectives in Life

"As to this, Your Majesty, I said to the bhikkhu Ānanda: '... Ānanda, having good friendships, or good associates, and an appreciation of the company of good people, is equal to the whole of the holy life. A bhikkhu who has a good friend can expect to bring forth the noble eightfold path and make much of the noble eightfold path'...For that reason, Your Majesty, you should intend thus: 'I will be someone with good friends, good associates, and will have an appreciation of the company of good people'...With good friends, Your Majesty should abide with this prime quality—that is, the quality of heedfulness [non-negligence] toward skillful qualities. When Your Majesty is heedful and dwells with the quality of heedfulness, the ladies of the harem...the royal retinue...the armed forces...and even the townspeople and villagers will think to themselves: 'Our king is heedful and dwells with the quality of heedfulness. We, too, must be heedful and dwell with the quality of heedfulness.' When Your Majesty is heedful and dwells with the quality of heedfulness, Your Majesty will be protected, the ladies of the harem will be protected, and the royal granaries and treasuries will be protected.

"One who desires increase in wealth should dwell with heedfulness. The wise praise heedfulness in all meritorious actions (*puññakiriyā*). The wise are heedful, and therefore they attain these two benefits: the immediate benefit (*diṭṭhadhammikattha*) and the further benefit (*samparāyikattha*). One is called a sage, a pundit, on account of attaining benefit."[25]

Attha can mean subject, meaning, objective, benefit, goal, or destination. Here I would like to translate it freely as "benefit that is the objective," or "goal of life," referring to the goal of the holy life (*brahmacariya*), or the whole Buddhist way of life and practice. It is well known that the highest objective of Buddhism is *nibbāna*, which is also known as *paramattha*, meaning the ultimate benefit. In teaching the Dhamma, it is natural to teach and encourage practice for the highest objective, but Buddhism does not overlook lesser benefits or objectives that can be attained in accordance with people's level of development, and actually formalizes them into teachings, as can be seen in the canonical excerpt cited above.

As far as can be ascertained, it seems that in the earlier texts benefit was divided into two main levels:

1. Basic benefit, known as *diṭṭhadhammikattha*, meaning the immediate benefit, or benefit here and now
2. Profound benefit, known as *samparāyikattha*, meaning further or higher benefit

In this case, *paramattha*, the highest benefit, is included in the second level, being the culmination of the second level of benefit. However, in the later texts it was desired to give more emphasis to the *paramattha*, so it was put under its own separate heading, the benefits or objectives organized into three levels, thus:[26]

1. *Diṭṭhadhammikattha*: benefit here and now, benefits in this life or benefits in the present: these are basic or immediate goals, the benefits readily visible and easily understood concerning everyday life—such as material gain, status, happiness, praise, wealth, position, honor, friendship, and a happy married life. It includes the rightful seeking of these things and dealing with them properly, using them for the happiness of oneself and those around one, for peaceful coexistence and proper dealings among people for their mutual happiness.
2. *Samparāyikattha*: further benefit, profound benefit, benefit related to the inner life, or benefit in terms of values. These are higher objectives, the assurances for leaving this world, or guarantees for attaining higher and more profound values than are

normally attained in this world. It is growth and development of the mind/heart in virtue, predilection for morality, having confidence in virtuous qualities, peace of mind, conversance with the subtle inner rapture and happiness, and the special qualities that are the mental attainments, the *jhānas* (originally this level also included enlightenment, which is the ultimate benefit). On this level, attachment to material things is mitigated; material interests are not valued so highly that one immerses oneself in them, or that they become causes for evil actions. Instead, one places value on virtue and goodness and does things out of a predilection for Dhamma, love of goodness, a love of quality of life, and development and growth of the mind.

3. *Paramattha*: the ultimate benefit, the benefit that is the real core of life, the highest objective or final destination. It is realization of the nature of all things as they really are, being wise to the ways of formations, not falling into enslavement to the world and life, having a mind that is free and clear, not oppressed or confined by one's clinging and fears, free of the burning defilements that stain and cloud one, living without suffering, experiencing the subtle inner happiness that is utterly clean and pure and that contains the serenity, coolness, radiance, and buoyancy known as liberation and *nibbāna*.

The Buddha acknowledged the importance of all these levels of benefit, as related to different lifestyles, ways of livelihood, environments, and the readiness or maturity of the faculties of each individual. However, it should be noted that in the Buddhavacana cited above, according to the Buddhist view, all people should live their lives with the aim of achieving at least the second level of benefit: attaining the immediate benefits is well and good, but it is not yet enough. One should advance to attain, in part at least, the further benefits. The Buddha called one who realizes benefit on both levels a sage, meaning one who lives with wisdom and whose life in this world is not in vain.

The Buddha gave practical teachings for all levels of objectives, as for example, in the four principles for attaining immediate goals (*diṭṭhadhammikattha*), consisting of being diligent and organizing one's enterprises wisely (*uṭṭhānasampadā*), keeping one's wealth and the fruits of one's labors safe from danger and harm (*ārakkhasampadā*), association with good people (*kalyāṇamittatā*), and living moderately and being able to save some of one's wealth (*samajīvitā*).

The Buddha also taught four principles for attaining further benefit: endowment with faith in the Triple Gem in accordance with Buddhist principles (*saddhāsampadā*); endowment with morality, good conduct, and honest livelihood (*sīlasampadā*); endowment with self-sacrifice, knowing how to share, being ready to help people who are in need (*cāgasampadā*); and living one's life with wisdom, using discernment, being wise to the world and life (*paññāsampadā*).[27]

As for the *paramattha*, since it is the highest objective and most difficult both to understand and to practice, and also because it is the quality peculiar to Buddhism, setting it apart from any previously known teaching, the Buddha naturally gave it special emphasis, as can be seen from his teachings on this level of benefit throughout the Tipiṭaka.

In the sutta cited above, the Buddha emphasizes another principle for attaining the fulfillment of benefits, and that is *appamāda*—heedfulness, non-negligence, care, fervor, watchfulness, diligence in doing what needs to be done. This heedfulness is considered to be a fundamental quality for realizing both the immediate and further benefits. The Buddha explains heedfulness as heedfulness in regard to skillful qualities, and explains these skillful qualities as meritorious actions (*puññakiriyā*).

The provision or connection of meritorious actions is an interesting one. When the Buddha taught about the lower levels of goals or benefits, he relaxed his emphasis on the ultimate goal, and also relaxed in terms of methods for attaining them. For example, in teachings dealing with the three objectives, instead of arranging the (eightfold) path into the familiar threefold training of morality, concentration, and wisdom, where the *paramattha* is the point of focus, the Buddha arranged the path into a different form based on the general principle known as the "meritorious actions" (*puñña-kiriyā*), or bases for meritorious action (*puññakiriyā-vatthu*), which, like the threefold training, contains three factors or levels. The three bases for meritorious action are as follows:[28]

1. *Dāna:* giving, sacrifice, sharing. It is giving in order to help, such as helping those in need; giving as sympathetic action (*saṅgaha*); giving to honor something good, to extol and encourage good people; giving of material things, life's necessities, or materials and supports; giving of knowledge and learning, or instructing on a way of life or Dhamma; giving others the chance to participate in performing good deeds, and up to the "giving" of forgiveness (*abhayadāna*).[29]
2. *Sīla*: good conduct, honest livelihood, the possession of self-discipline, and good manners. The stress is particularly on *sīla* on the level of not hurting others and living peacefully in society—that is, not killing or injuring, not violating each other's property rights, not violating loved ones, not hurting each other by disparaging each other's honor or undermining each other's families or reputations, not cheating or embezzling others' interests through harmful speech, and not plying oneself with intoxicants that impair mindfulness and discernment.[30] In addition, one may try to train oneself further by abstaining from luxurious things and sensual indulgence, and training oneself to live simply by keeping the observance days (*uposatha*), observing the eight or ten precepts as occasion permits, or practice in a more positive way by making an effort to help, participate, and serve (*veyyāvacakamma*).
3. *Bhāvanā*: "cultivation," training the mind and wisdom, developing the mind to grow in virtues, to be firm and stable, and to have an understanding of the way of formations, or, in modern terminology, being wise to life and the world. *Bhāvanā* comprises both the concentration and wisdom limbs of the threefold training, being mental cultivation (*samādhi bhāvanā*) and wisdom cultivation (*paññābhāvanā*), but the two are included

> under the one heading and not given individual emphasis here. *Bhāvanā* encompasses the path factors from right effort in the concentration group down to right view and right thought, comprising goodwill (*mettā*) and compassion (*karuṇā*) that are of the wisdom group. The methods and practices stressed in this general cultivation of mind and wisdom are: seeking wisdom and purifying the mind through listening to the teaching (including reading), called *dhammassavana*, teaching and discussing the Dhamma, correcting and instilling right belief, view and understanding, cultivating goodwill and restraint and control and removal of defilements in general.

Thus, it is clear that the Buddha, having relaxed the objectives in life or Dhamma practice down to the most elementary level, also relaxed the system of conduct or methods of practice accordingly. In this more lenient system, the emphasis is on elementary practices dealing with bodily and verbal expressions and the way human beings deal with each other, or social relationships, which are actions that are concrete, readily visible, and easier to practice. They can be largely grouped under the two headings of generosity (*dāna*) and morality (*sīla*). The objective is cultivation of the inner heart/mind to greater subtlety and growth through the use of outer actions—in the language of the texts, "for the removal of coarser defilements."

The practice on the level of concentration and wisdom, the higher mentality and higher wisdom, in which the emphasis is more directly on the inner being, is more difficult and profound. Therefore they are not given separate emphasis in the practice of meritorious actions, but put together under the one heading "cultivation" (*bhāvanā*), and the intended meaning is more relaxed. In the practices of later times, it has become generally recognized that this presentation of the path in the form of the three meritorious actions is an adaptation for teaching householders. The presentation in the form of the threefold training, which will be discussed later, is the central principle for comprehensive Dhamma practice.

Thus, the bhikkhus, who are the exemplars of this comprehensive practice, are the vanguard in the practice of the threefold training.

Apart from the arrangement of the benefits into the levels given here, there is another threefold arrangement made according to the level of responsibility or relationship between people, as shown in the following canonical extracts:

> "Bhikkhus, it is like a body of water, clear and clean, not murky. A clear-sighted person standing on its banks may see within it the snails and clams, pebbles and stones, and the schools of fish swimming about and remaining still in that body of water. Why is that so? Because the water is not murky. Just so, bhikkhus, when a bhikkhu's mind is not murky, he is able to clearly see what is of benefit to himself, what is of benefit to others and what is of benefit to both sides. He will be able to experience for himself the special qualities exceeding ordinary capacity—that is, direct knowledge and vision, which transforms him into a noble one. This is a possibility. Why is that? Because his mind is not murky."[31]
>
> ---
>
> "Bhikkhus, seeing the benefit to yourself, it is fitting that you accomplish that benefit with heedfulness. Seeing the benefit to others, it is fitting that you accomplish that benefit with heedfulness. Seeing the benefit to both, it is fitting that you accomplish that benefit with heedfulness."[32]

The relevant meaning of the three benefits is as follows:[33]

1. *Attattha*: personal benefit, the attainment of the objectives of one's own life. *Attattha* refers to the three groups of benefits just mentioned (the immediate, the further, and the ultimate) as far as they concern oneself and that arise specifically for oneself. The emphasis is on self-reliance on every level, so that one is not a burden on others or an encumbrance on the group, and that one is ready to be of help to others. The core quality for

realizing one's own benefit is wisdom. The general teachings given for this objective are many, such as the ten *nāthakaraṇa-dhamma*. Broadly speaking, personal benefit is the practice of the threefold training in the sense of fully taking responsibility for oneself.

2. *Parattha*: benefit to others, helping and encouraging others to attain their own benefit or reach their goals in life on various levels. *Parattha* is guiding others to be established in self-reliance, and refers to the three benefits of the previous section as far as they concern others, and as results arising for others. The core quality for realizing the benefit of others is compassion. The general teachings used to describe it include the four bases for sympathetic action (*saṅgahavatthu*), and the work and cultivation of virtues of a good friend (*kalyāṇamitta*).
3. *Ubhayattha*: benefit to both sides, or mutual benefit. *Ubhayattha* is the three levels of benefit given previously that are results arising for both oneself and others, or for society and the community, such as benefits that arise from communal property, communal activities, and especially to environmental conditions and living conditions that aid the practice for the realization of personal benefit and the performance of communal benefits for all people. The core qualities for attaining this objective are discipline (*vinaya*) and harmony (*sāmaggī*), and the general principles that may be used to teach it are the six conditions for harmony (*sārāṇīyadhamma*) and the seven conditions for welfare (*aparihāniyadhamma*), including all behavior that is helpful, desirable, and useful for society.

The Path as the Threefold Training

> "And what, bhikkhus, is this threefold training? It is the training in higher morality, the training in higher mentality, and the training in higher wisdom.
>
> "What, bhikkhus, is the training in higher morality? A bhikkhu in this teaching and discipline is one with morality (*sīla*),

restrained in the Pāṭimokkha, perfect in conduct and resort, is one who sees the danger and the fault of even minor wrongdoings, and applies himself to the study of the training rules. This, bhikkhus, is called the training in higher morality.

"And what, bhikkhus, is the training in higher mentality? A bhikkhu in this teaching and discipline, calmed of sensual pleasures, calmed of unskillful conditions, enters the first *jhāna*, which is accompanied by initial and sustained thought, and has the rapture and well-being born of seclusion. He enters into the second *jhāna*, which comprises internal clarity of the mind, in which one-pointedness of mind arises. There is no initial or sustained thought because they are quietened, and there is rapture and well-being born of *samādhi*. Through the fading away of rapture, he dwells in equanimity, with mindfulness and clear comprehension, and experiencing happiness in the mental body he enters the third *jhāna*, of which the noble ones say, 'One who has equanimity and mindfulness dwells happily.' With the going beyond of pleasure and pain and the fading away of joy and sadness, he enters the fourth *jhāna*, which is void of happiness and suffering and has mindfulness purified by equanimity. Bhikkhus, this is called the training in higher mentality.

"And what, bhikkhus, is the training in higher wisdom? Bhikkhus, a bhikkhu in this teaching and discipline knows clearly as it is that 'this is suffering, this is the cause of suffering, this is the cessation of suffering, and this is the way leading to the cessation of suffering.' Bhikkhus, this is called the training in higher wisdom.

"Bhikkhus, this is the threefold training."[34]

The threefold training is regarded as a comprehensive system of Dhamma practice that encompasses the whole of the path. In summary, just as the path is a comprehensive system of Dhamma practice in terms of information, the threefold training is a comprehensive system of it in terms of practice, and it is the threefold training that takes the teaching of the path and synthesizes it into a vast and detailed description of practical methods. What this means, and why, we will now consider.

From the Path to the Threefold Training

The eight factors of that noble eightfold path are as follows:

1. *Sammādiṭṭhi*: right view or right understanding
2. *Sammāsaṅkappa*: right thought
3. *Sammāvācā*: right speech
4. *Sammākammanta*: right action
5. *Sammā-ājīva*: right livelihood
6. *Sammāvāyāma*: right effort
7. *Sammāsati*: right mindfulness
8. *Sammāsamādhi*: right concentration

Sometimes this path with eight factors is known simply as the eightfold path, which has led some people to mistake it for "eight paths," and therefore interpret the meaning to be eight separate or contiguous paths: once one path is traveled to completion, the next is begun, and so on until the whole eight are completed. According to this interpretation, each of the eight factors of the path is a teaching to be taken up and practiced on its own, in succession. However, this is not the case. The term "path with eight factors" clearly means one path with eight components, like a good highway that must have many components before it becomes a highway, such as earth, pebbles, sand, stones, gravel, and tar or concrete in layers up to the road's surface. Together these make up the road itself. Then there are the edges, the white lines, the rises, dips and inclinations along the curves, and the signals, traffic signs, signposts, mileage indicators, place signs, and lighting for use at night. A highway may contain all of these things, and anyone who travels on the highway must make use of all of the components simultaneously. In the same way, the path is made up of eight components, and the Dhamma practitioner must utilize all eight of them for the length of the journey.

To help clarify our understanding of the path, the eight factors are divided into different groups called *khandha*, of which there are three: the *sīlakhandha* (morality group), the *samādhikhandha* (concentration group), and the *paññākhandha* (wisdom group),[35] or simply *sīla*, *samādhi*, and *paññā* (morality, concentration, and wisdom). Right speech, right action, and right livelihood form the morality group. They are like the pounded earth, pebbles, stones, and materials that make up the road's surface. Right effort, right mindfulness, and right concentration form the concentration group. They are like the road's edges, railings, and white lines that define the road's direction. Right view and right thought form the wisdom group. They are like the road's traffic signals, signposts, and lighting. They can be represented like this:

1. Right View
2. Right Thought } 3. Wisdom
3. Right Speech
4. Right Action
5. Right Livelihood } 1. Morality
6. Right Effort
7. Right Mindfulness
8. Right Concentration } 2. Concentration

Fig. 6.1. Path factors and the threefold training.

This is a division of the path into groups of related factors. In practice, the same arrangement is used under the name of the threefold training (*tisikkhā*), using the slightly modified terms "training in higher morality" (*adhisīlasikkhā*), "training in higher mentality" (*adhicittasikkhā*), and "training in higher wisdom" (*adhipaññāsikkhā*).[36] They may be simply represented as follows:

1. *Adhisīlasikkhā*
   - Right Speech
   - Right Action
   - Right Livelihood

2. *Adhicittasikkhā*
   - Right Effort
   - Right Mindfulness
   - Right Concentration

3. *Adhipaññāsikkhā*
   - Right View
   - Right Thought

Fig. 6.2. Path factors and the higher training.

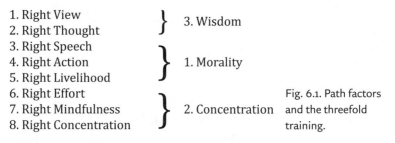

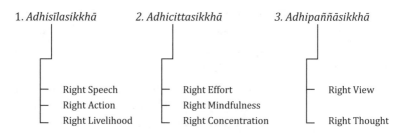

To explain the threefold training in full, it is necessary to connect the factors to their objectives. So we can say that the threefold training is the training of conduct, the training of the mind, and the training of wisdom that leads to the solving of human problems, that leads to the cessation of suffering and results in true happiness and liberation. When the definition clearly shows the objective, we can see the essential meaning of each of the parts of the threefold training as follows.

The essence of higher morality is conducting oneself well, leading a helpful life, playing a part that is conducive to a wholesome life for all, and acts as a good foundation for developing the quality of the mind and wisdom.

The essence of higher mentality is developing the mind to a higher level of quality and effectiveness, so that it supports the wholesome life and is ready to be put into action in the service of wisdom in the most effective way.

The essence of higher wisdom is the vision, knowledge, and understanding of things as they really are, the way of formations (*saṅkhārā*), which enables one to live and act with wisdom, knowing the proper outlook and practice to adopt toward life and the world in a way that increases benefit and happiness, having a mind that is clear, without suffering, free, and buoyant.

The threefold training not only expresses itself in individual practice, but also includes dealings on the communal and social levels—that is to say, in the establishment of procedures, institutions, and activities, and the arrangement of activities and methods to bring about the essence of the threefold training in the human community.

In this respect, *sīla* includes the organization of physical and social conditions to close off opportunities for bad actions and encourage opportunities for good actions. *Sīla* specifically refers to the creation of a form and social systems by imposing regulations, laws, and legislation and to conventions for controlling individual conduct, organizing communal activities, and promoting harmonious living. Together these are known by the technical term *vinaya*. *Vinaya* should be established in conformity with the objectives of each particular community or level of society. For example, the *vinaya* established by the Buddha for the orders of bhikkhus and bhikkhunis contains not only ordinances for regulating their individual conduct but also regulations for organizing the way of life of the community, for administration, for investigating and dealing with legal cases, for imposing punishments, forms and procedures for conducting formal gatherings, and even for outlining manners and techniques for receiving guests, for being a guest, and for using communal property.[37] There are also the broad principles the Buddha recommended for secular authorities to determine procedures for dealing with society on a broad scale, on the national level, as in the observances for a universal emperor (*cakkavattivatta*), in which the emperor is advised to provide rightful protection for the different groups of people in his community, to establish methods for stamping out injustice, bad actions and troubles in the land, and to see to the fair distribution of gains or proportioning of wealth so that the people are not impoverished.[38] In modern terms, the *vinaya* that supports morality (*sīla*) on a wider social scale comprises the systems of government and administration, legislation, adjudication, economic planning, procedures of tradition and culture, and other social systems, even on the reduced scale of methods for supporting or limiting breeding grounds of the "pathways to ruin" (*apāyamukha*), such as drugs and crime, and establishing standards for employment.

The higher mentality, or *samādhi*, on the highest level is the various techniques for developing calm (*samatha*) meditation, which have evolved along the course of Buddhism's history, and appearing in the standardized procedures given in the commentaries[39] and enlarged on and adapted down to the present. But on a broader scale, *samādhi* includes any techniques and devices used for inducing the mind to calm, fixing the mind in virtue and rousing it with predilection and endeavor for the greater development of goodness. It also includes any means for encouraging quality of mind. These might include places for relaxation that are calm and refreshing and that encourage wholesome thoughts, making the atmosphere in the home and the workplace cheerful, friendly, kind, and conducive to good actions and subtler states of mind, activities that arouse virtue, encouraging good actions, the pursuit of ideals, and development of the mind in stability, resilience, and higher efficiency.

Strictly speaking, the higher wisdom is the cultivation of insight (*vipassanā bhāvanā*), which, similarly to the teachings for calm meditation, has undergone an evolution in terms of practical techniques. However, in a broader sense, in terms of its essential meaning and objectives, the domain of wisdom is all of the activity of training in knowledge and thought known as education, which is dependent on a good friend, particularly a teacher, to impart *suta* (knowledge that is transmitted, or passed on by word of mouth) and skill in the arts and sciences, beginning with one's profession (which is a concern of the morality level). However, for higher wisdom mere knowledge and professional and academic skill are not enough. As a "good friend," a teacher must be able to build faith and guide the student to think for oneself, to at least be able to guide the student toward right view that accords with Dhamma and, if possible, to encourage the student to look on the world and life as they really are. The student's learning is of a type that removes defilements and frees the mind from suffering, enabling that person to serve others while also feeling happy within oneself. Training on this level is usually the responsibility of educational institutions, and normally such institutions should provide training on all three levels, not just wisdom. This is because higher wisdom is the highest level of training, and can only succeed with a foundation of the first two levels of training. Moreover, the three levels of training have factors that are mutually supportive, and only when the three are fully developed can training be said to be complete.

The way in which the factors of the threefold training influence each other can be seen most simply thus: when we live together harmoniously the mind has no need to be fearful and wary; when we do no wrongful actions (*sīla*) the mind is calm and at ease (*samādhi*); when the mind is calm and at ease, then it is able to think clearly and understand things (*paññā*).

The relationship of the threefold training to the functioning of the factors of the path may be made clearer by use of an analogy. It is like a man driving on a long journey, beginning at a small rural village on the edge of a forest on a plain, crossing through a rugged mountain range, and reaching his destination in the middle of a busy and crowded city. The journey may be divided into three legs. The first is the long but flat journey along the countryside. The middle leg is along the mountain range, the path hugging the mountain ridges, valleys, and precipices, full of frightening and dangerous bends and steep inclines. The third leg is the road to the city, full of byways and streets large and small, congested buildings, crowds of people, an easy place to get lost in and difficult for a stranger to find his way around. This man has never driven a car before. He learns to drive as he goes along the way, hoping that, the way being so long, by the time he reaches the destination he will have mastered the art of driving.

On the first leg of the journey, the man must train his hands and feet in working the mechanics and equipment of the car and become proficient in driving, being careful to avoid soft edges or holes on the road. The central concern of his task at this stage is simply to preserve normalcy: to control the movement of the car and keep it smooth. As long as the road is smooth and he uses the car's controls properly, the car will proceed smoothly.

For the second leg of the journey the man must exercise great energy and care in order to control the car while it travels along the mountain sides and steep ravines. He must be constantly decreasing and increasing speed according to the gradient of the road and maintaining the car's balance. The central concerns of his task at this stage are fortitude, control, full alertness at all times, and focus. If it were to be asked whether he no longer has to be watchful of the mechanisms of the car and be careful to avoid the road's potholes and soft edges, the answer is that care with these things must also be present, and in fact is even more necessary than in the first leg of the journey, but at this stage these qualities need no mention, because if by this stage he were not already proficient in driving, or if the road were so potholed and loose that driving was difficult, he would find it almost impossible to proceed and may even give up the journey altogether. What demands his special attention at this stage is the road's edges, the highway lines, the bends and the gradients of the road. Apart from these factors, there may be other factors that come into play. For instance, if, after finishing the first leg of the journey, he looks at the road ahead of him and becomes disheartened, he may stop right there or just turn back; or he may drive on but make a mistake and drive the car over a cliff (like some meditators who develop delusions or go completely off track), or he may become so enchanted with the beautiful views along the way that he parks his car and stays right there admiring the scenery (like those who get attached to *jhāna* attainments).

For the third leg of the journey, with streets, intersections, buildings and their adornments, traffic signals, signs, cars and people everywhere, the driver must be alert, and he must also be able to understand the signals and read the signs along the roadside, and know where to turn. He must have the acumen to make quick and correct decisions. The central concern of his task at this stage is non-delusion.

The first leg of the journey, along the flat plain, in which the main concern is maintaining regular movement, is comparable to *sīla*. The second leg of the journey, on the mountain range, in which the main concern is firmness of control, alertness, and concentration, is comparable to *samādhi*. The third stage of the journey, in the crowded city, in which the main concern is non-delusion, is comparable to wisdom. We can see that although each of the legs has different emphasis, each has the same general factors.

This is looking from the broadest perspective in order to give the overall picture. As for the actual training or practice, this sequence proceeds with minor stages embedded within the greater stages, like one long highway that has successive sections of flat road, winding mountainous roads, and busy roads within it. That the practice proceeds in this way is a confirmation of the interactive support between the external factors of the threefold training and the functioning of the internal factors of the path. When conduct is moral, the mind is concentrated; when the mind is concentrated, thinking is wise; when wisdom arises, this becomes right view, the first factor of the path. Right view leads to right thought, which leads the way to right speech, right action and livelihood in accordance with the principle of relationship between the factors of the path. This in turn helps the arising of morality once again and strengthens the quality of training and all of the other factors of the path.[40]

At a glance, this abbreviated cycle of the threefold training seems to be three parts of training undertaken simultaneously—as, for example, where the Visuddhimagga describes the development of *ānāpānasati*, mindfully attending to the in- and out-breaths. In essence, it states that while practicing the meditation technique, restraint of one's activities and modes of expression to the most skillful and appropriate states for the task at hand is the training in higher morality. The concentration of the mind (on the task, or the object of concentration) is the training in higher mentality. The use of wisdom, or the knowledge or understanding that arise during the course of practice, is the training in higher wisdom.[41]

The following Buddhavacana shows the sequential nature of the process:

> "Morality is like this; concentration is like this; wisdom is like this. Concentration tempered by morality is of great fruit, of great reward; wisdom tempered by concentration is of great fruit, of great reward; the mind tempered by wisdom is utterly released from the outflows [*āsava*]—that is to say, the outflow of sensuality, the outflow of becoming, and the outflow of ignorance."[42]

The contiguous relationship of the threefold training can be easily seen even in everyday life situations: when there is purity of conduct, confidence in one's purity, no fear of being punished, no alarm over possible retribution from enemies, no fear of criticism or social rejection, and no confusion resulting from pangs of conscience over one's wrongdoings, the mind will be clear, at ease, and concentrated on one's thoughts, words, and actions. The calmer and more concentrated the mind is, the clearer and more fluent are thinking, consideration, and cognition, and the better it is for wisdom. It is analogous to still and undisturbed water: silt and other impurities in the water settle to the bottom, and the water is no longer murky but clear. When the water is clear, everything in it can be clearly seen. For the higher stages of Dhamma practice—that is to say, the level of the arising of direct knowledge and insight in which the outflows are destroyed—there is even more need for calm, stillness, clarity, and firmness of concentration. At such levels, cognition through the senses is suppressed, and only the object of attention remains, so that the "silt" remaining on the bottom of the "pond" can be swept away and no longer have the chance to make the "water" murky.

The Buddha sometimes taught the threefold training in a simple, practical way that Buddhists often refer to. It appears in the "Ovādapāṭimokkha" (the cardinal teachings of all buddhas), which states:[43]

sabbapāpassa akaraṇaṁ	the non-doing of all evil
kusalassūpasampadā	full cultivation of the good
sacittapariyodapanaṁ	purification of the mind

The importance of right view, the wisdom factors of the path, needs to be reiterated. Be it the threefold training or the eightfold path, the Buddhist system of practice always begins and ends at wisdom. Even though morality is the first factor of the threefold training, it must actually be based on a foundation of understanding, which is right view. However, because this initial knowledge and understanding is simply an awareness of what path is to be taken and the point of departure, it is not considered to be a part of the more broadly based system of training known as the threefold training. Once the practitioner gains a foundation of initial understanding, or right belief, one begins training with bodily conduct, speech, and livelihood (*sīla*). When morality is well established, one proceeds to the subtler level of mental training (*samādhi*), and eventually arrives at the final level, which is the development of wisdom until one transcends ignorance.

In fact, wisdom is growing throughout the training process. At first, the knowledge and understanding known as right view may be simply a rational belief, but during the training this initial base of belief or understanding gradually grows and becomes clearer through wise attention, investigation, and examination, seeing clearly the results of the practice and the strengthening of the faculties, until ultimately wisdom develops to the level of understanding of things as they really are, liberation and attainment of *nibbāna*. Rational knowledge, understanding, or belief are transformed into full knowledge and understanding through one's own true wisdom, as stated in the canon: "This Middle Way leads to direct knowledge (*ñāṇakaraṇī*), to vision (*cakkhukaraṇī*), to peace, to enlightenment, to *nibbāna*."[44] Thus we find that the path finishes at wisdom, which is the factor most instrumental in attaining the objective. It is for this reason that the eightfold path is sometimes supplemented with two final factors, right direct knowledge (*sammāñāṇa*) and right liberation (*sammāvimutti*).[45] Accordingly, view is like a bridge leading from ignorance to knowledge. When there is knowledge, right direct knowledge arises, and that is followed by right liberation.

Three of the factors of the path have especially important functions, and must be involved in the practice of all the other factors. They are right view (*sammādiṭṭhi*), right effort (*sammāvāyāma*), and right mindfulness (*sammāsati*). The reason these three factors must always be practiced in conjunction with the other factors can be easily seen in our analogy of the journey. Right view is like a light or compass, enabling us to see the way and have confidence that it is the right path for the objective; right effort is like the energy expended in taking the steps; right mindfulness acts like a governor or guard, ensuring that the journey proceeds along the right path, in proper sequence and avoiding any dangers. The practice of morality, concentration, and wisdom must always incorporate these three factors.[46]

Progress along the Path

Sammādiṭṭhi means "right view." On the mundane level it means view that accords with the way of Dhamma. On the transcendent level it means seeing things as they really are, seeing the reality or causality of things.[47] The meaning of right view will be given in detail in the chapters dealing with the factors of the path, but its general meaning needs some explanation in order to clarify the subject under discussion here. In the beginning, right view, as view or belief that accords with the way of Dhamma, for example seeing that good actions bring good results and bad actions bring bad results, is enough to initiate the practice of Dhamma. Once one believes or sees in this way, one will naturally be ready to do good, and therefore enter onto the first level of training of morality in the threefold training. However, a practitioner with merely this amount of right view will usually center his or her practice around moral conduct and rarely progress to the practice of concentration or wisdom, as can be seen in the usual description of right view in this sense in the ten ways of skillful conduct (*dhammacariyā* or *kusalakammapatha*), which are a mundane level of practice of the path.

A deeper interpretation of right view is right view in the sense of understanding the nature of problems, knowing the cause that must be corrected, sufficiently knowing the objective and path of practice to serve as a base from which to make a start: knowing where one is going, knowing which path will take one there, and knowing where the path begins.

The deepest interpretation of right view is knowledge or understanding that accords with the truth, seeing things as they really are and seeing the faring of things according to their causes and conditions. This interpretation encompasses all the other interpretations. For example, it includes seeing the nature of the problem, seeing the process of causes and conditions that are its cause, seeing the path as it is, as a path, and it is the interpretation of right view that grows clearer as the practice of the path progresses: the more one practices, the more one understands, until one accomplishes the task and attains full knowledge.

However, not only does right view act as a support for the other factors: right view itself is also supported by the other factors. The more the practice progresses, the more is right view developed and tempered in strength, clarity, and purity. Ultimately, it becomes the prime factor for leading to the final destination of the way. Thus, it can be said that right view is both the beginning and the end of the way.

The fact that right view does evolve and expand in the course of the path implies that the right view arising at various stages of the practice must differ in terms of quality. Specifically, the initial kind of right view may not have comprehensive enough qualities to be considered as right view in the full sense of the term, while the final kind of right view may possess such special qualities that it deserves another name. At this stage, the use of different terms may be advisable, and since right view is one of the characteristics of wisdom, the most suitable general term here would be *wisdom*, meaning the wisdom that evolves and develops in the process of this path's development. What qualities and specialized terms wisdom takes on in the stages it passes through deserves further examination.

Speaking in terms of the Middle Way, the stages of the development of wisdom may be briefly summarized as follows:

For most people, the training process begins with belief in some form, referred to in Buddhism as *saddhā*. *Saddhā* may be a result of a predilection for the rationality of the teaching, or a belief in the rationality or trustworthy characteristics of the teacher. From there follows listening to the teaching, training and study, the arising of increased understanding, and seeing the proper rationale for oneself, which can be generally referred to as right view. As this view and understanding increase in clarity, through practical application or verification through personal experience, it becomes clear realization. This is the development of wisdom to the level known as *sammāñāṇa* (right direct knowledge), which is a level that transcends belief and is beyond any rational understanding (*diṭṭhi*). It is the end of the path and the attainment of the objective, which is liberation, known as *sammā-vimutti* (right liberation). This progression of wisdom may be represented thus:

faith → right view → right direct knowledge	→ right liberation

Fig. 6.3. Progression from faith to wisdom.

According to this progression, at the outset wisdom is there only in covert form, as a constituent of faith. It then comes gradually more into its own until, reaching the final stage, it becomes right direct knowledge, and wisdom is clear, pure and authentic. Here faith is no longer present, being entirely replaced by wisdom. Only at this stage can enlightenment or liberation take place. This process will become clearer in the chapters that follow.

One point particularly worthy of note is that the faith that becomes involved in this process is specifically the kind that is for, or leads to, wisdom, and thus must be a belief conjoined with wisdom, or belief founded on rational understanding (*ākāravatīsaddhā* or *saddhāñāṇasampayutta*), not credulous belief in which wisdom is thrown to the winds and no rational consideration exercised (*amūlikāsaddhā* or *saddhāñāṇavippayutta*).

So far the discussion has focused on the development of wisdom or growth of right view as arising from faith alone, and as such it is not comprehensive. In fact, according to the teachings, some especially gifted persons are able to develop wisdom without the need for belief in others. They rely only on their ability to think and see things as they are, according to their causes and conditions, known as wise attention (*yoniso-manasikāra*), and through that develop wisdom to penetration of the truth.[48] Even for ordinary people, who start with faith, wisdom will only grow and develop when wise attention becomes involved. Faith on its own cannot bring about the development of the ultimate level of wisdom. Wisdom on the transcendent level, which penetrates the truth and completely eliminates defilements, cannot arise without wise attention.[49] The right kind of faith is that which connects to, or initiates, the arising of wise attention. Thus, the full process should be represented like this:

Fig. 6.4. Progression from faith / wise attention to wisdom.

Summarizing, there are two factors instrumental in the arising of right view. The first is faith, referring to trust in the wisdom of others, or using the recommendations of others as a source of wisdom, which begins with external factors. The second is wise attention, referring to a person's own ability to think, or correct thinking. It begins with an internal factor.

Faith does not include the actual source of knowledge, but is simply an internal quality that connects the individual to external factors. The real external source of knowledge is another person, the person who induces one to believe, or another person's teachings. In Buddhism these external factors are called *paratoghosa*. *Paratoghosa* not only aids the arising of faith, and indirectly the creation of right view, but can also directly incite use of wise attention. For this reason, the sources or factors of right view are said to be twofold: the "voices of others," known as *paratoghosa*, as external factors, and the ability to think, known as *yoniso-manasikāra*, as an internal factor.

Buddhism gives great emphasis to the importance of right view, because most people, even Buddhists, do not give it the attention it deserves. Thus, it is necessary to caution here that while right view is important, what is of more importance is how that right view is to be brought about. Before going on to the subject of the factors of the path, I will therefore discuss the determinants of right view.

CHAPTER 7

The Precursors of Learning

Right view is one of the important factors of the path, being the first step on the Buddhist system of training. It is a factor that must be progressively developed in purity, clarity, and freedom until it ultimately becomes enlightenment.

In the Tipiṭaka the following principles are given for the cultivation of right view: "Bhikkhus, there are two factors for the arising of right view. They are *paratoghosa* and *yoniso-manasikāra.*"[1]

Paratoghosa is "the voice of others," instigation or influence from outside. These are, for example, teachings, advice, transmissions, testimonials, reports, news, writings, explanations, and learning acquired from others. Here only the wholesome and righteous kinds are intended, in particular the hearing of teachings or advice from one known as the "good friend" (*kalyāṇamitta*).

This first factor is external, being social conditions. It may be simply referred to as "the way of faith" (*saddhā*).

Yoniso-manasikāra is "wise attention," intelligent application of mind, proper use of thought, knowing how to think, being able to think, or thinking systematically. It refers to the ability to examine things and see them as they really are, through rational thinking, analytical investigation and thorough research, and in relation to the stream of causes and conditions, not conditioned by one's desires and attachments.

This second factor is an internal one. It may be simply referred to as "the way of wisdom."

There are Buddhavacana describing these two factors within the practical context of training, with emphasis on the importance of both of them as a pair, as follows:

> "For the bhikkhu who still has learning to do...I see no other external factor that is as beneficial as the presence of a good friend (*kalyāṇamitta*).
>
> "For the bhikkhu who still has learning to do...I see no other internal factor that is as beneficial as wise attention (*yoniso-manasikāra*)."[2]

The two factors are mutually supportive. For the ordinary person, with wisdom undeveloped, practice must be supported by advice from others, and it is easy to comply with skillful words of advice and encouragement, but practitioners must also train to think properly for themselves in order to proceed to the goal of the path. Those with highly developed wisdom will better know how to use *yoniso-manasikāra*; even so, they may still need to rely on the guidance of good advice as an incentive for more rapid progress along the path.

The cultivation of right view through *paratoghosa* is the method that begins with, and largely depends on, faith. In training, it is necessary to ensure that one receives the most effective advice, encouragement, and teaching: that is, there must be a teacher endowed with certain qualities and abilities, using techniques that do lead to results. Therefore, the training system specifies a focused external influence with the principle known as *kalyāṇamittatā*, having a good friend.

Paratoghosa: The Way of Faith

> "Bhikkhus, just as the light of dawn heralds the rising of the sun, just so having a good friend is the precursor, the herald, of the arising of the noble eightfold path to a bhikkhu. Of a bhikkhu who has a good friend it can be expected that he will develop and make much of the noble eightfold path."[3]

The *paratoghosa*, voice of others, which leads to right view is that "voice" which is wholesome and right, the voice that reveals the truth, is rational and beneficial. It is especially that voice that arises from love and goodwill. Such wholesome voices come from good sources—good people, wise people, virtuous people. Such people are called in Buddhism "true persons" (*sappurisa*; literally, "good men") or sages (*paṇḍita*). If such a person performs the function of helping, advising, and teaching another to develop right view, he or she is then said to be performing the duty of a good friend (*kalyāṇamitta*). However, aspirants to right view should not simply wait for good or wise people to find them. On the contrary, they must make the effort to seek out, consult, listen to, associate with, and take example from them. Doing this is called "association with true people" (*sevanāsappurisa*).[4] But regardless of whether the teacher seeks out the student or the student seeks out the teacher, once an acknowledgment of influence has been established, the student is said to have a *kalyāṇamitta* and the whole relationship is called *kalyāṇamittatā*, having a good friend.

The word *kalyāṇamitta* does not refer to a good friend in the normal sense, but to a person endowed with the ability to teach, to point out the way or act as an example for developing the proper way of training. The Visuddhimagga gives as examples the Buddha, the arahant disciples, teachers, and all who are learned and capable of teaching and serving as advisers, even if they are younger in years.[5]

Within the process of wisdom development, having a good friend is said to be on the level of developing wisdom at the stage of faith. As for the training process, the definition of a good friend should encompass all people who provide training, such as parents and teachers, the qualities of the teacher, the principles, methods, equipment, and techniques used in teaching, and all activities the person responsible for teaching sees fit to carry out to make that training effective. It also includes books, media, role models, and all social factors that are wholesome and beneficial, insofar as they are external factors in the process of wisdom development.

The Importance of Having a Good Friend

> "I see no other quality that is so much a cause for the arising of skillful qualities as yet unarisen and the decline of unskillful qualities already arisen as having a good friend. When a person has a good friend, skillful qualities as yet unarisen arise, and unskillful qualities already arisen decline.[6]
>
> "In terms of external factors, I see no other which is of such great benefit as having a good friend."[7]

This canonical passage stressing the importance of having a good friend was addressed to bhikkhus. There are numerous other teachings and sayings of the Buddha stressing the importance of approaching and associating with good people for householders. For example, having a good friend is listed as one of the factors for attaining benefits here and now (*diṭṭhadhammikattha*);[8] association with bad people is one of the pathways to ruin (*apāyamukha*);[9] meeting friends and associating with them properly is one of the principles given in the teaching on the six directions,[10] specifically knowing how to associate with people according to the teachings on true and false friends;[11] association with a true person (*sappurisa*) is one of the four "wheels" (*cakka*) to prosperity,[12] one of the four factors for growth in wisdom (*paññāvuḍḍhidhamma*),[13] and one of the four factors for stream entry (*sotāpattiyaṅga*);[14] having a good friend is one of the factors in the ten conditions leading to self-reliance (*nāthakaraṇadhamma*).[15] In the Jātaka tales, which are teachings for people of all levels, householders in particular, there are a great number of stories, sayings, and recommendations dealing with association with others. In addition to these, there are sayings on the subject scattered throughout the Sutta Piṭaka, of which the following are noteworthy:

> "Avoiding fools, associating with the wise, and honoring those worthy of honor—this is the highest blessing."[16]
>
> ---
>
> "We become like the people with whom we associate."[17]

> "One who mingles with evil persons is suspected of evil actions and one's name suffers, even if one has not committed any evil."[18]
>
> ---
>
> "Look on the wise one who points out your faults, who has critical speech, as one who points out a treasure. Such a person is a sage worthy of association. Associating with such a person, one can only get better, not worse."[19]
>
> ---
>
> "To have many friends and relatives is good, like many trees in a forest. A tree that stands alone, no matter how big and strong it is, can be easily blown down by the wind."[20]

This small sampling of sayings is enough to see that, comparing the two, the Buddhavacana on association given to bhikkhus were mostly aimed at the highest benefit (*paramattha*) and were clearly intended to create and build transcendent right view, while those given to householders stressed the immediate benefit (*diṭṭhadhammikattha*) in combination with the further benefit (*samparāyikattha*). They focused on people helping each other in daily life in conjunction with encouraging right view on the mundane level: belief in *kamma*, and responsible awareness in terms of good and evil. Transcendent right view, looking at life and the world as they really are, is not the emphasis here. Such teachings were allowed to remain implicit and brought forward from time to time as the occasion arose,[21] gradually building up a foundation, so to speak, taking into account people's different levels.

The Qualities of the Good Friend

The *sappurisa*, the truly good person, is endowed with the following seven qualities (*sappurisadhamma*).[22]

1. *Dhammaññutā*: knowing the principle and knowing the cause. One knows the basic truths of nature, knows the principles,

standards, procedures, and duties that are the causes for achieving the desired results. For example, a bhikkhu knows what teachings he is to study and practice and what they consist of.

2. *Atthaññutā*: knowing the objective and knowing the result. One knows the meaning and objective of the teachings or principles, standards, and duties; one knows the results to be expected from actions. For example, a bhikkhu knows the meaning of the teachings [Dhamma] he is studying and practicing and what they will lead to, and ultimately knows the benefit that is the objective or essence of life.
3. *Attaññutā*: knowing oneself. One knows one's status, situation, gender, strengths, knowledge, proficiencies, abilities, and virtues as they really are, so that one can act appropriately for the best possible result. For example, a bhikkhu knows how much faith, morality, learning, relinquishment, wisdom, and wit (*paṭibhāna*) he is endowed with.
4. *Mattaññutā*: knowing moderation. One knows how much is enough or appropriate. For example, one knows the right amount in eating food and using wealth. A bhikkhu knows moderation in receiving the four necessities (food, clothing, shelter, and medicine).
5. *Kālaññutā*: knowing the occasion. One knows when to do what; one knows the appropriate time for learning, for working, and for resting.
6. *Parisaññutā*: knowing one's company. One understands the locality, the community, and the people; one knows the required modes of conduct, forms and regulations, traditions, and required behavior for that community.
7. *Puggalaññutā*: knowing the person. One knows the differences between people due to their temperaments, abilities, and virtues, so that one can relate to them appropriately. One knows, for example, whether to associate with them, and how to do so effectively, to involve oneself with them, use them, praise or criticize them, and instruct them.

A sage (*paṇḍita*) is a clever person, one who conducts one's life wisely. He or she possesses qualities that are described in many ways in the texts, as in the following Buddhavacana:

> "Bhikkhus, the fool is defined by his *kamma*. The sage is defined by his *kamma*. Both are clearly shown up by their deeds."[23]
>
> ---
>
> "Bhikkhus, there are three characteristics of a sage, signs of a sage or ways of conduct of a sage. They are that one regularly has good thoughts, good speech, and good actions."[24]
>
> ---
>
> "Bhikkhus, there are two kinds of fool: the one who shoulders the burden that has not yet come, and the one who does not shoulder the burden that has come...
>
> "There are two kinds of sage: the one who shoulders the burden that has come, and the one who does not shoulder the burden that has not yet come."[25]
>
> ---
>
> "A person with little learning ages like an old bull: his meat increases, but his wisdom does not."[26]
>
> ---
>
> "Small streams bubble loudly; large rivers flow silently. Empty vessels make sound; full vessels are silent. A fool is like a half-full pot, a sage like a full-flowing river."[27]
>
> ---
>
> "The fool who knows he is a fool can be said to be wise in some respects, but the fool who thinks he is wise is truly a fool."[28]
>
> ---
>
> "Bhikkhus, relying on a good person you can expect the following four blessings (*ānisaṁsa*): growth in noble morality, growth in noble concentration, growth in noble wisdom, and growth in noble liberation."[29]

When someone approaches a good and wise person, or when such a person fulfills the function of spreading knowledge or goodness to others, or instills in them the faith to follow, whether it be by teaching, advising, or imparting knowledge and understanding in any other way, with a heart of goodwill and compassion, that person is called a good friend (*kalyāṇamitta*).

The good friend, in addition to the qualities so far described, may be examined according to the fundamental four or five qualities mentioned in the definition of a good friend. Having a good friend is defined as the association, seeking out, loyalty to or aspiration to seek out one who possesses faith, morality, learning, relinquishment and wisdom.[30] Sometimes only four of these qualities are mentioned, learning being omitted, indicating that learning is less necessary than the other four qualities. This is expanded on with the advice that whenever one becomes familiar and converses with one who is endowed with faith, morality, relinquishment, and wisdom, one should study and emulate those qualities.[31]

In terms of the duties toward others, a good friend should also have a number of special qualities for the purpose, especially the fundamental qualities known as the seven qualities of a good friend (*kalyāṇamittadhamma*):[32]

1. *Piyo*: endearing. Good friends have rapport; they create an atmosphere of familiarity and informality, encouraging students to approach them with questions.
2. *Garu*: worthy of respect. Good friends have conduct that befits their position and inspires confidence.
3. *Bhāvanīyo*: inspiring. Good friends have true knowledge, possess a real store of wisdom, and constantly train themselves, and therefore they are worthy of praise, an example to follow, inspiring their students to speak of them and think of them with profound appreciation, confidence, and pride.
4. *Vattā*: effective at speaking. Good friends can talk; they know how to explain things. They know when to say what and how, give guidance, instruction, and exhortation, and are good advisers.
5. *Vacanakkhamo*:[33] patient with words. Good friends are always ready to listen to advice and questions, even the pettiest, and

to hear offensive words and criticisms. They patiently listen to them and are neither dejected nor offended by the words of others.

6. *Gambhīrañca kathaṁ kattā*: able to explain higher teachings. Good friends can clearly explain matters that are profound and complex, and teach their students on progressively more profound subjects.
7. *No caṭṭhāne niyojaye*: not leading in wrongful ways. Good friends do not lead their followers in ways that are harmful or in things that are worthless and improper.

The following Buddhavacana, while not specifically stated to be the defining qualities of a good friend, can nevertheless be regarded as additional qualities:

> "Bhikkhus, a bhikkhu who is endowed with the following six qualities is one who is able to practice for the benefit and assistance of both himself and others. What are those six qualities? They are as follows:
>
> 1. "He is one with quick understanding of skillful qualities.
> 2. "He remembers the teachings he has heard.
> 3. "He examines the meaning of the teachings he has remembered.
> 4. "He understands the implications (*attha*), he understands the principles (*dhamma*), and practices accordingly.[34]
> 5. "He has pleasant speech, and speaks good words, words that are civil, refined, eloquent, and illuminating.
> 6. "He is able to give teachings that clarify, inspire confidence and bring forth joy, to his friends in the holy life."[35]

While in the general teachings we usually find instructions not to associate with inferior or bad people, there is an exception in cases where association is done out of compassion, out of a desire to help. Even so, one who is thinking of helping others should first carefully examine one's own ability.

Some of the teachings about the qualities of a good friend stress the benefits on the immediate level (*diṭṭhadhammikattha*), or a combination of the immediate and the further (*samparāyikattha*) benefits, as in the teachings on true and false friends in the *Siṅgālaka Sutta*,[36] which states:

> "Listen, son of householder, these four kinds of persons should be known as enemies (*amitta*), false friends: the out-and-out robber...the smooth talker...the flatterer...the leader into ruin.
>
> 1. "The enemy who is a false friend known as the out-and-out robber can be known by the following four attributes: he seeks only gain...he gives little in the hope of getting much...he only helps his friend when he himself is in danger...he associates with his friend only for [his own] benefit.
> 2. "The enemy who is a false friend known as the smooth talker can be known by the following four attributes: he is good at talking about what is done and gone...he is good at talking about what has not yet come...he helps in things that are useless...when his friend is in need, he always has an excuse [for not helping].
> 3. "The enemy who is a false friend known as the flatterer can be known by the following four attributes: he consents to his friend doing evil...he consents to his friend doing good...he praises his friend to his face...he criticizes him behind his back.
> 4. "The enemy who is a false friend known as the leader to ruin can be known by the following four attributes: he is a companion in drinking...he is a companion in night life...he is a companion in frequenting shows...he is a companion in gambling.
>
> "Listen, son of householder, these four kinds of persons should be known as true friends of good heart: the helping friend...the friend through thick and thin...the good counselor...the loving friend.

> 1. "The true friend of good heart known as the helping friend can be known by the following four attributes: when his friend is heedless, he looks out for him...when his friend is heedless, he looks out for his possessions...when his friend is in danger, he is a refuge...when his friend is in need, he gladly gives more than he is asked for.
> 2. "The true friend of good heart known as the friend through thick and thin can be known by the following four attributes: he confides in his friend...he safeguards his friend's confidences...he does not desert his friend in face of danger... he will give even his life for his friend's sake.
> 3. "The true friend of good heart known as the good counselor can be known by the following four attributes: he dissuades his friend from doing evil...he establishes his friend in goodness...he enables his friend to hear things never heard before...he points out to him the way to heaven.
> 4. "The true friend of good heart known as the loving friend can be known by the following four attributes: when his friend is unhappy he commiserates...when his friend is happy he rejoices...when others criticize his friend he stands up for him...when others praise his friend he joins in."

The principles that can be taken as the practices for friends in general are the teachings on the six directions,[37] which state:

> "Listen, son of householder, friends and associates, which are [like] the left direction, should be supported by a son of good family in these five ways:
>
> 1. "Giving (*dāna*)
> 2. "Kindly speech (*piyavācā*)
> 3. "Helpful action (*atthacariyā*)
> 4. "Solidarity (*samānattatā*)
> 5. "Truthful speech (*avisaṁvādantā*)"

Note that the first four codes of conduct are the four principles for integration (*saṅgahavatthu*), or principles for unity and social harmony. They are general principles for interpersonal relationship. Since both teachings are the same, it is the same as saying that Buddhism recommends all people be friends to each other, or relate to each other as friends.

Members of the monastic order, or recluses and religious practitioners, are to be good friends to householders as shown in the duties of bhikkhus to householders according to the principles for the "upper direction," which are exactly the same qualities of the true friend who "gives good counsel." However, the duties of the bhikkhus have two additional clauses, making six altogether:[38]

1. To forbid them [teach them to abstain] from evil.
2. [To teach them] to be established in goodness.
3. To support them with kindness [additional].
4. To enable them to hear what they have not yet heard.
5. [To explain], clarifying what they have already heard [additional].
6. To point out the way to heaven [teaching the way to lead a happy life].

However that may be, the "good friendship" of the Saṅgha must retain the special characteristic of having an independent life and the status of being recluses (*samaṇa*). It should not turn into fraternization with householders, which would lead to harmful results for both parties: impeding the bhikkhus' own progress in the Dhamma and depriving the laity of their refuge, since the bhikkhus would be just as immersed in the confusion of everyday life as householders. This mistaken kind of relationship, in which a bhikkhu falls into the same state of confusion and gets caught in the same "nets" as do householders and is no longer able to lift them to freedom, is called "being ensnared by humans," as described in the following Buddhavacana:

> "Bhikkhus, what is it to be ensnared by humans? A bhikkhu in this teaching and discipline is one who fraternizes with house-

> holders, rejoices with them and sorrows with them. When they are happy, he is also happy; when they are sad, he is also sad. When they have some business, he manages it himself (he is a busybody). This is called 'being ensnared by humans.'"[39]

A good friend who is directly engaged in teaching should be established in the following sets of principles, which stress the good friend's purity, goodwill, and integrity.

The first set of principles is called the qualities of a Dhamma teacher (*dhammadesakadhamma*). There are five of them, which can be summarized as follows:[40]

1. *Anupubbikathā*: teaching systematically and in orderly progression. The teacher explains the subject matter in order from simple to difficult, shallow to profound, in rational progression.
2. *Pariyāyadassāvī*: identifying and elaborating on the essential points. The teacher elucidates each of the aspects and points involved and illustrates their different nuances to show their rational basis.
3. *Anuddayatā*: establishing the heart in, and teaching out of, goodwill (*mettā*), aiming for the benefit of one's listeners.
4. *Anāmisantara*: not aspiring for material reward. The teacher does not teach for the purpose of gaining any reward, payment, or personal gain in exchange.
5. *Anupahacca*: being established in integrity, not upsetting oneself or others. The teacher teaches according to the teachings, according to the subject, aiming to explain the meaning of the teachings, not to exalt oneself or disparage others.

The ways in which a teacher must behave toward one's students, according to the teaching on the six directions, while not specifically stressing purity, nevertheless have a similar trend, stressing the presence of goodwill and earnest action:[41]

1. Teaching and training them to be good
2. Teaching them to clearly understand

3. Teaching the subject in full
4. Encouraging and openly praising the students' virtues and abilities
5. Providing them with a protection for all directions (that is, teaching them how to really use their knowledge to make a living)

Two final virtues of the good friend, which may be taken to be the supreme virtues, are (1) being one who has actually practiced what one teaches, or has attained the goal before teaching it to others, and (2) being free. In helping others, one does not get stuck in the same bonds as they are stuck in. The first quality is supported by many of the Buddha's statements, such as the following:

> "First establish yourself in an appropriate level of goodness before teaching others. The sage should have no blemishes.
>
> "However you teach others, that is how you should act."[42]

Such warnings refer mostly to the level of conduct—that is, good and evil. In terms of mental and intellectual attainments, finding a good friend who has attained them is the ideal, but if one cannot find such a person, one should search for one who has progressed further along the path than oneself, or at least who is on a similar standing, as in the Buddhavacana already cited. There have been teachers advanced in scriptural learning who were able to guide others all the way to enlightenment, even though they themselves were not enlightened.[43] Cases are also recorded of two people of equal spiritual maturity discussing the Dhamma together and becoming enlightened simultaneously.[44]

One of the greatest values or benefits of having a good friend is the presence of an example that instills confidence, a living proof that what one is practicing and aspiring to can actually be attained, and if one does attain it one will receive a good result. Also, a good friend's greater knowledge and experience in the practice enables him or her to provide ways or means for facilitating the practice. A good friend who has attained to the fruits of the practice for oneself will be able to provide these values or benefits to the utmost, inspiring faith and strong resolve in the practitioner. Thus, it is natural to first seek out such a fully realized good friend.

As for freedom, it can be looked at from two perspectives: first, freedom of lifestyle, and second, mental freedom. The importance of freedom has already been stated in regard to bhikkhus who fraternize with laypeople: those who are tied up in the same concerns as others cannot even help themselves. If they were stuck in the same binding social system, struggling to attain the same things in the same way as everybody else, holding to the same values, they would be oppressed by the same problems of livelihood, being the subsistence and survival of themselves and their families, as everyone else.

Finally, we have the following three characteristics of how the Buddha taught, which should be a general gauge by which a good friend can assess one's own effectiveness in teaching:[45]

1. He teaches from superior knowledge: having first known and seen the truth for himself he teaches others for the knowledge and vision of the truth that can be known and seen.

This factor takes the perspective of the teacher.

2. He teaches reasonably: he teaches and explains the reasoning in a way that the listener is able to follow and understand for oneself.

This factor takes the perspective of the student or the listener, to whom the teacher gives a teaching in a way that provides the student with freedom or the chance to reflect, to use and develop one's own wisdom and to understand or penetrate the truth for oneself. The teacher only presents the data and the rationale and inspires the listener to examine it.

3. He teaches in a way that is amazingly effective: he teaches what is true, that which an astute listener with a love of truth, having examined, will naturally accept, and he teaches what can be put into practice, through which the practitioner will attain results in conformity with the practice done.

This factor takes the perspective of what is taught, which is accurate, verifiable, meaningful, practicable, and productive of results: however much one practices, one receives results in accordance with the causes and conditions involved.

If it is not possible to find a good friend who has experienced the results for oneself, one who has really done the practice and become free, then a teacher who is learned, even one who has not attained enlightenment, is acceptable. Such a learned teacher is compared to a herdsman who tends another person's cattle, or a blind person holding a lantern:[46] when those with good sight open their eyes, they will see what there is to see. The term "those with good sight" here refers to those with *yoniso-manasikāra*. For them, not only teachings from a skilled teacher thoroughly versed in the doctrine, but even the meaningful words recited from memory by a fool or a madman can be food for thought, and one with *yoniso-manasikāra* listening to such words may even gain a penetrating understanding of the truth.[47] On this level, of course, the importance lies with the listener, the internal quality that encompasses the second factor for right view, to be described in the next section.

The Work of a Good Friend

In terms of learning or progress in Dhamma practice, the activity, cooperation, or help of friends is only an external factor. The importance here lies in their influence to encourage others in the thoughts, views, values, and understandings known collectively as *diṭṭhi*. If these thoughts, views, values, and understandings are faulty or harmful, they are known as wrong view (*micchādiṭṭhi*); if they are wholesome, right, and beneficial they are called right view (*sammādiṭṭhi*). A friend who influences the arising of wrong view is called a bad friend (*pāpamitta*), while a friend who encourages the arising of right view is a good friend (*kalyāṇamitta*).

It often happens that the "friends" within the household, the parents, or even teachers, have less influence in encouraging these views than the friends one acquaints on a casual basis, and sometimes it even happens that such friendly acquaintances have less influence than a "friend" more distant but with greater impact on the mind—the mass media, entertainment, and books. The link that enables those "friends" to influence us, or the connecting factors between these "friends" and the influence they have over our minds, is the belief, inspiration, preference, or appreciation known as faith. Once faith is implanted, even a remote "friend" can have influence. On the other hand, without faith, even a friend nearby will have no influence.

The deciding factor for whether or not the duty of a good friend has been fulfilled is whether or not such association leads to right view. Right view according to the standard scriptural explanation will be discussed later, but for the purposes of this discussion it can be summarized into two kinds:

The first type of right view is that which is wholesome, reasoned, and beneficial, consisting of beliefs, thoughts, views, and understandings in relation to good and evil, regarding good and evil actions and the good and bad results that arise in conformity with those actions: that is, "good actions bring good results, bad actions bring bad results"; belief in virtue, such as the virtues of mother and father; and beliefs and attitudes that conform with religion, such as belief in a next world. In brief, this kind of right view is a view that sees correctly in accordance with the way of Dhamma, or belief in *kamma*, which leads to a sense of responsibility for one's own actions. It is technically referred to as *kammassakatañāṇa*, the knowledge that differentiates between what is and is not one's *kamma*. This is the right view referred to as mundane right view (*lokiyasammādiṭṭhi*). It is acquired from rational understanding obtained from teachings and social conditioning, and leads to skillful moral conduct, a wholesome life, and peaceful community existence.

The second type of right view consists of knowledge and understanding of the world and life, or formations, as they really are—that is, in reality, and as faring according to causes and conditions. This view leads to an understanding of the proper relationship that should exist between oneself and the things around one, or to life and the world: knowing, for example, that things are formations, concocted of conditioning factors and faring according to a causal relationship determined by conditioning factors. Thus, they are in a state of instability, are impermanent and are constantly oppressed by contrary conditioning factors. This kind of knowledge and understanding arises from knowing how to look at, reflect on and examine things as they really are and according to their causes and conditions. It is the knowledge and understanding known as transcendent right view (*lokuttarasammādiṭṭhi*).

The first kind of right view is called right view in regard to *kamma* (*kammassakatāsammādiṭṭhi*). It is right view on the level of moral conduct or the ways of skillful action. It concerns the levels of the immediate and further benefits or goals, but is also the foundation for the ultimate goal.

The second kind of right view is classed as right view arising from insight (*vipassanāsammādiṭṭhi*), but in the canon it is known as "direct knowledge that accords with the truth," or "knowledge that is in line with the truth" (*saccānulomikañāṇa*), and this leads to subsequent enlightenment and realization of ultimate truth.[48]

The right view that leads to the ultimate goal of Buddhism is the second kind, knowledge that accords with the truth. All Buddhists, regardless of whether or not they aspire to the ultimate goal, should not content themselves with merely the first kind of right view but should aspire to the second kind, to try to cultivate this level of wisdom, at least to some extent, because it is this level of right view that helps to mitigate greed, anger, and delusion and makes the mind clear and calm, conducive to a better and happier relationship with the world. This would be a much more effective way of reducing contention, suffering, and troubles in the world than constraint through morality.

When the process is analyzed into stages, we find that having a good friend leads, both directly and indirectly, to hearing the Dhamma; when the teachings, the principles of truth or goodness, so given are true, truly good, or rationally explained, the listener experiences the arising of faith. The process may be represented thus:[49] association with the good (having a good friend) → hearing the teaching → faith.

Here we have another important juncture in the process of learning: it is the connection between external components, or social factors, and internal components, or personal factors. According to the teaching, external factors, the "sound from outside" (here meaning having a good friend) alone can lead only to faith and the attainment of mundane right view.[50] If this is all there is, it is not the whole process of training and does not reach the highest objective of Buddhism. Staying merely on the level of faith, one still has to rely on the good friend, the teacher, and conduct is still based on following or emulating. There is not yet true realization for oneself or complete liberation. The solution lies in finding a way to connect with the internal component or personal factor, *yoniso-manasikāra*, by bringing forth *yoniso-manasikāra* to take over the work, as in the teachings stating that only through *yoniso-manasikāra* can one advance to transcendent right view and attain the ultimate goal of Buddhism.

This connection to the internal factor is made with the help of the good friend. In fact, according to the teachings, it is the responsibility of the good friend to help his or her students awaken *yoniso-manasikāra*. A good friend should not simply aim for faith but also use faith as a tool to facilitate the ignition of the flame of *yoniso-manasikāra*, using the teaching of Dhamma to encourage students to think for themselves, to reflect on all things as they really are according to causes and conditions. With the arising of *yoniso-manasikāra* the process may continue to the ultimate goal. In the meantime, the good friend may help support, guide, and strengthen the student's *yoniso-manasikāra* through regular teachings. When both the internal and external factors are right—that is, when the "voice from outside" helps strengthen the arising of wise attention—a trainable human being (*veneyya*)—one who is neither a genius, who can begin one's practice directly with *yoniso-manasikāra*, nor a hopeless case (*padaparama*), who is incapable of thinking for oneself—will be able to progress properly along the training process and practice of the Dhamma.

The Buddha's Words on Faith

The *Kālāma Sutta*[51] provides principles for establishing a rational outlook that is relevant for all people, regardless of the ideas, doctrines or teachings they adhere to:

At one time, the Buddha journeyed to the town of Kesaputta, belonging to the Kālāmas in the Kosala country. There the Kālāmas, having heard his reputation, approached the Buddha, introduced themselves, and asked:

> "Revered Sir, one group of recluses and brahmins enters Kesaputta village and explains and extols their own doctrine, but they make aspersions to, disparage and belittle other teachings, encouraging us not to believe them. Another group of recluses and brahmins enters Kesaputta village, and they explain and extol their own teaching, but make aspersions to, disparage and belittle the teachings of the other group, encouraging us not to believe them. We wonder and are in doubt as to who is speaking the truth and who speaking falsely?"
>
> "Kālāmas, it is fitting that you should wonder, fitting that you should doubt. Your wondering and doubting are well founded. Kālāmas, do not adhere[52] through listening (learning) from others (*anussava*); do not adhere through tradition (*paramparā*); do not adhere on the basis of rumor (*itikirā*); do not adhere on the basis of scripture (*piṭakasampadāna*); do not adhere through logic (*takka*); do not adhere through inference

> (*naya*); do not adhere through reasoned thinking (*ākārapari-vitakka*); do not adhere because it accords with your views (*diṭṭhinijjhānakkhanti*); do not adhere because it seems plausible (*bhabbarūpatā*); do not adhere because 'this recluse is our teacher' (*samaṇo no garūti*).
>
> "But when you know for yourselves that these things are unskillful, these things are harmful, these things are censured by the wise; that these things, when adhered to and put into practice, lead not to what is of benefit, but to suffering, then you should give them up... When you know for yourselves that these things are skillful, these things are not harmful, these things are praised by the wise; that these things, when adhered to and put into practice, lead to benefit and happiness, then you should practice and cultivate (those things)."

If a listener lacked knowledge and understanding and had not yet adopted any particular belief, the Buddha did not encourage belief, but simply advised to examine and decide on the basis of one's reason. For example, in regard to ethical belief in future lives, there is a passage at the conclusion of the same sutta that states:

> "Kālāmas, the noble disciple, whose mind is so devoid of ill will, whose mind is so devoid of harmful thoughts, whose mind is thus clear and pure, acquires four assurances in the present moment:
>
> "'If there is a next world (*paraloka*) and there really are results of good and evil actions, then there is a chance that I, at the breakup of the body, will go to a good rebirth in heaven.' This is the first assurance he gains.
>
> "'But if there is no next world, and no results of good and evil actions, then at least I live without suffering, without enmity or harm, and I abide peacefully in this very life.' This is the second assurance he gains.
>
> "'And if, when a person does evil, then evil really has been done, I have not intended any evil upon anybody, so from where

> is suffering going to come for a person such as myself, who has not committed any evil?' This is the third assurance he gains.
>
> "'And if, when a person does evil, it is said to be not done, then in this case I see myself as pure in either case.' This is the fourth assurance he gains."

Properly used, faith is a good starting point for practice and causes the practice to bring speedy results. For this reason, it sometimes happens that those with more wisdom but less faith achieve results slower than those with less wisdom but strong faith.[53] If faith is in accordance with what is right, it is a great time- and energy-saver. Conversely, if faith arises in what is wrong it can cause the practice to go astray and lead to a great waste of time. In any case, faith in Buddhism is based on reason and tempered by wisdom, so it is unlikely to go astray except in exceptional circumstances, and even then can be easily corrected, not falling wholly into wrong ways, because it is always open to reason, research and experiment.

Yoniso-manasikāra: The Way of Wisdom

Yoniso-manasikāra is generally translated as "wise attention." It is thinking correctly or thinking methodically.

Looked at in terms of the process of wisdom development, *yoniso-manasikāra* is on a level just above faith, being the level on which one begins to use one's thinking independently. It is crucial in developing pure and independent wisdom, allowing one to be one's own refuge and leading to the real objective of the Buddha's teaching.

The Importance of Yoniso-manasikāra

> "Bhikkhus, just as the light of dawn is the precursor, the herald, of the rising of the sun, so the perfection of *yoniso-manasikāra* is the precursor, the herald, of the arising of the noble eightfold path in a bhikkhu. Of a bhikkhu who is endowed with *yoniso-*

> *manasikāra* it can be expected that he will develop and make much of the noble eightfold path."[54]
>
> ---
>
> "I see no other factor for the arising of as yet unarisen skillful qualities and the decline of unskillful qualities already arisen as *yoniso-manasikāra*. When there is *yoniso-manasikāra*, skillful qualities as yet unarisen arise, and unskillful qualities already arisen decline."[55]

The word *yoniso-manasikāra* is made up of two parts, *yoniso* and *manasikāra*. *Yoniso* comes from *yoni*, meaning "cause," "source," "birthplace," "wisdom," "means," "method," or "path."[56] *Manasikāra* means "attending," "thinking," "considering," "recollecting," "reflecting," "examining."[57] Together we have *yoniso-manasikāra*, which is usually translated in Thai as *kan tham ny chai doy yaap khai* (การทำในใจโดยแยบคาย; literally, "careful consideration"). The range of definitions for this "wise attention" is given in the commentarial and subcommentarial texts through a number of descriptions showing the word's various senses, as follows:

1. *Upāya-manasikāra*: thinking or considering through skillful means (*upāya*). It is thinking according to a method that leads to penetration of the truth, that is compatible with the truth and that leads to penetration of the true and universal characteristics of all things.
2. *Patha-manasikāra*: thinking along a path, or on track. It is thinking in systematic progression, methodically or in orderly progression, meaning ordered thinking that conforms with causes and results, thinking that is not confused or muddled; it is not just getting stuck on one thing in one place, then jumping off to think of something else somewhere else, or just jumping around disjointedly. It includes the ability to steer thinking along the right path.
3. *Kāraṇa-manasikāra*: thinking according to causes, delving into causes, thinking according to cause and effect, or thinking

rationally, meaning to delve back along the causal relationship, to examine causes and origins and go to the root or source of resulting events.

4. *Uppādaka-manasikāra*: thinking to produce results. It is the use of thinking to bring about a desired objective. Its focus is on thinking with a certain aim in mind, meaning thinking and examining in such a way as to give rise to skillful qualities (*kusaladhamma*), as in arousing diligent effort, thinking so as to abolish fear, to calm anger, to establish mindfulness or to make the mind firm and resolute.[58]

These four definitions are simply descriptions of different characteristics of the thought known as *yoniso-manasikāra*. Within one instance of *yoniso-manasikāra*, all of these features may be present. If we wanted to put the four characteristics in a nutshell, we could say methodical thinking, orderly thinking, rational thinking and thinking to arouse the skillful.

To summarize *yoniso-manasikāra* into a concise definition would be more difficult. Most definitions either focus on particular aspects of the meaning, and are either incomplete or are long explanations like the one given at the beginning of this section. Even so, there are some prominent features of this kind of thinking that may be taken as representative, such as the interpretive translations I have often used: thinking according to the method, knowing how to think, being able to think, thinking in accordance with reality and determinants, and delving back into roots. Once we understand the meaning, we can settle on the traditional translation, "wise attention."[59]

We can see that in the first three senses of *yoniso-manasikāra*, a good friend can help only as far as recommending or pointing out the way, but the actual reflection on, or seeing of, the truth must be achieved by each individual for oneself. Faith alone cannot produce the level of true understanding.[60] Thus, the role of faith is limited in aiding *yoniso-manasikāra* of the first three kinds.

In the fourth sense, however, faith plays a prominent role. Some people, for example, are irresolute, easily depressed or discouraged, or given to worthless or harmful thoughts. If a good friend is able to successfully instill faith, this can help such people a good deal, by, for example, inspiring them and encouraging them through various means. On the other hand, there are those who are naturally endowed with *yoniso-manasikāra*. They know how to think for themselves and, in the face of depressing, discouraging or saddening events, can think in ways that rouse their minds out of those states.

Conversely, if people have bad friends or unwise attention (*ayoniso-manasikāra*), even in good situations they can respond in a negative way and produce destructive actions. For example, a criminal may see a peaceful and secluded place as an ideal spot to do a wicked deed or plan a crime. Some people have a suspicious nature: they may interpret even a casual smile as an act of ridicule. If such thinking is allowed to flow unchecked, unwise attention becomes the nutriment for fostering such unskillful qualities to greater strengths, as can be seen in people who become so habituated to suspicious thinking that they develop paranoia and severe mental disorders.[61]

One and the same object of thought will have a different effect on the psyche and conduct depending on whether it is attended to with *yoniso-manasikāra* or *ayoniso-manasikāra*. For example, one person reflecting on death with unwise attention may experience anxiety, depression, or melancholy, while another person considering death with wise attention may experience a desire to give up evil actions, or develop calmness or heedful application to doing good actions.[62]

In terms of penetrating reality, *yoniso-manasikāra* is not in itself wisdom, but is a determinant for its arising, in that it leads to right view. The Milindapañha illustrates the difference between *yoniso-manasikāra* and wisdom thus: first, all animals, even goats, cattle, and donkeys, have *manasikāra* (although it is not *yoniso*), but they do not have wisdom. Second, *manasikāra* is of the nature to estimate and examine, while wisdom is of the nature to cut off. *Manasikāra* brings together various thoughts for wisdom (*paññā*) to work on in eliminating defilements, just as the left hand takes hold of a clump of rice plants, while the right hand, holding the scythe, cuts them.[63] Looked at in this light, *yoniso-manasikāra* is that kind of attention that instigates the use of wisdom and at the same time nourishes it to further growth.[64]

The Papañcasūdanī says of *ayoniso-manasikāra* that it is the root of the cycle of rebirth (*vaṭṭa*), and explains that when *ayoniso-manasikāra* comes to growth, it augments ignorance and desire for becoming (*bhavataṇhā*). The arising of ignorance sets in motion the *paṭiccasamuppāda* process in its entirety, beginning with "ignorance as a determinant for volitional formations (*saṅkhārā*)" down to the arising of the mass of suffering. When desire arises it also enters the *paṭiccasamuppāda* process, beginning with desire as a determinant for clinging and proceeding along the sequence to the arising of the mass of suffering. *Yoniso-manasikāra*, on the other hand, is the root of the cycle of "unwinding" (*vivaṭṭa*), because it leads to the practice of the eightfold path, which begins with right view. Right view is knowledge (*vijjā*). When knowledge arises, ignorance ceases. With the cessation of ignorance, the cessation mode of the *paṭiccasamuppāda* is activated, leading to the cessation of suffering.[65]

In terms of its extent, *yoniso-manasikāra* covers a broad area, encompassing everything from thinking along lines of moral principles, thinking according to the various principles of wholesomeness and truth that one has learned or been trained in and understands well—as in thinking with love and goodwill, thinking of giving or helping, or thinking in ways that make one strong and resolute, all of which do not require particularly profound levels of understanding—up to the levels of analyzing constituent factors and delving into determinants, which require subtle wisdom. Since *yoniso-manasikāra* encompasses such a wide range, any ordinary person can make use of it. In its simpler forms, in particular, all that is required is guidance of the stream of thought along wholesome lines that have already been learned or familiarized.

For such forms of *yoniso-manasikāra*, which are generally on the level of helping the arising of mundane right view, faith is a major influence. That is, faith is both a center of support for the mind and a ready source of inner energy: as soon as we cognize a mental object (*ārammaṇa*) or experience a situation of some kind, the thought stream is pulled along the path created by faith, as if faith had made a channel for the thought stream to follow. Thus, there is the principle that "(proper) faith is a nutriment for the growth of *yoniso-manasikāra*,"[66] because *paratoghosa* that are "good friends," through the channel of faith, are more able to increase and augment knowledge and understanding, and to advise and guide thinking through, for example, consultation and advice. When *yoniso-manasikāra* is used often and well nourished, it becomes more and more fluent and far-reaching, leading to the growth and maturation of wisdom. When one considers and sees the truth of what has been taught, that the teaching is true, wholesome and beneficial, one becomes even more confident, and faith is increased. Then *yoniso-manasikāra* becomes a determinant for faith,[67] encouraging one to learn even more, until in the end one's own *yoniso-manasikāra* leads to realization and liberation. This is the way of practice that utilizes a combination of both internal and external factors, and this is one meaning of the injunctions "Self as refuge of the self," and "having oneself as a refuge."[68]

We can clearly see that the Buddha did not deny the use of external factors, as external factors and faith are important, but the deciding factor is internal, and that is *yoniso-manasikāra*. The more efficiently one can use *yoniso-manasikāra*, the less needed are external factors, while one who does not use *yoniso-manasikāra* at all cannot be helped by a good friend of any description.

In terms of its functions, *yoniso-manasikāra* is the thinking that blocks off ignorance and desire. Whenever there is cognition of a sense object or an experience, a thought process will be set in motion. At this stage there is a struggle for supremacy: if ignorance and desire gain control of thinking, the subsequent thoughts will be a process of ignorance and desire, imbued with the embellishment of mental formations according to likes and dislikes and preconceived perceptions. But if *yoniso-manasikāra* blocks off and intercepts ignorance and desire, it leads thinking in a right direction, a thought stream free of ignorance and desire. It is instead a process of direct knowledge and vision (*ñāṇadassana*), or of knowledge and liberation (*vijjāvimutti*).

For unenlightened beings, whenever there is the cognition of a sense object, thinking tends to automatically flow along the process of desire and ignorance: people measure that object against their likes and dislikes or preconceived perceptions, and this is the base upon which subsequent mental fabrications about that object are built. This is the process of ignorance and desire, seeing things as one would either want or not want them to be, thinking according to attachment and aversion. This kind of thinking not only blinds us to things as they really are, causing us to sway according to likes and dislikes and see things distortedly, but also causes suffering.

Yoniso-manasikāra, on the other hand, is looking at things as they really are, or according to true causes, not according to ignorance and desire. In other words, it is looking at things as they are in themselves rather than as we would want or not want them to be. When the unenlightened being perceives an object, thoughts immediately race into like and dislike. *Yoniso-manasikāra* performs the function of blocking off or intercepting at this point, taking over the process, and becoming the spearhead of a purified thought process that examines realities and determinants, thinking in an ordered progression. It leads to understanding of the truth and the arising of skillful qualities. At the very least, it helps to establish the most suitable attitude and practical response at that time.

Figuratively speaking, *yoniso-manasikāra* allows people to use their thinking; that is to say, they are the masters of their thinking, and put thinking to use in solving problems. This is opposite to *ayoniso-manasikāra*, which enslaves people to their thinking. Note also that in a thinking process that contains *yoniso-manasikāra*, mindfulness and clear comprehension (*sati sampajañña*) will always be present, because *yoniso-manasikāra* is a constant nutriment for them.

Summarizing this point, *yoniso-manasikāra* is the thinking that blocks off ignorance and desire. Ignorance and desire always arise together, but sometimes ignorance plays the dominant role and desire is more covert, while at other times desire is dominant and ignorance is covert.[69] With this in mind, we may divide the meaning of *yoniso-manasikāra* into two kinds, according to the roles of ignorance and desire, and the characteristics of thought that follows ignorance and that which follows desire should be understood as follows:

1. When ignorance is the dominant factor, thinking tends to be characterized by either getting stuck on and revolving around one particular aspect of an object in a generally vague way, disjointed and lost, or otherwise confused, disorderly, fabricating irrationally, as in the images conceived by a frightened person.
2. When desire is the dominant factor, thinking tends to be characterized by inclination in the direction of delight and aversion, like and dislike, or attachment and offense, revolving around the objects of liking or aversion.

However, more profoundly speaking, in reality ignorance is the foundation for desire, and desire is a support for ignorance. Thus, in order to utterly eliminate the bad, it is necessary to eliminate ignorance.

The Yoniso-manasikāra *Techniques of Thinking*

The *yoniso-manasikāra* ways of thinking are the practical applications of *yoniso-manasikāra*. While these methods are many, in principle there are two: *yoniso-manasikāra* that aims to block off or eliminate ignorance, and *yoniso-manasikāra* that aims to block off or mitigate desire.

Yoniso-manasikāra that aims to eliminate ignorance is generally the kind that must be used in the practice of Dhamma up to the highest level, because it leads to knowledge and understanding of things as they are, an essential prerequisite of enlightenment. *Yoniso-manasikāra* for blocking off or mitigating desire tends to be more used as an interim practice, where the aim is to make a foundation for the higher levels of practice; it is merely the level of mitigating defilements. However, many methods of *yoniso-manasikāra* can be used in both capacities, both in eliminating ignorance and in mitigating desire.

The methods of *yoniso-manasikāra* to be found in the canon can be collected into the following ten main kinds: delving into determinants; breaking down into component factors; reflecting on the universal characteristics; using the noble truths; relating the teaching to the objective; reflecting on benefit, harm, and the way out; reflecting on true and false value; reflection as a means for arousing virtues; being in the present moment; and using the method of analysis (*vibhajjavāda*).

Delving into Determinants

"Delving into determinants" means examining problems and seeking ways to solve them through the determinants that produce the result. This kind of thinking may be called "thinking according to the principle of causality (*idappaccayatā*)" or "thinking according to the *paṭiccasamuppāda*." It is a fundamental kind of *yoniso-manasikāra*, as can be seen from its use in the textual descriptions of the Buddha's enlightenment. In the canon, the way to practice this method is given as follows:

- Reflecting on causal relationships, in which the noble disciple wisely attends (*yoniso-manasikāra*) to the dependent co-arising of things thus: "When there is this, then there is that; with the arising of this, that arises; when there is not this, there is not that; with the cessation of this, that ceases."[70]
- Thinking through interrogation, or posing a question, as in the Buddha's reflections: "I thought to myself, 'With what as condition does clinging exist; clinging exists on account of what?' Then, through wise attention (*yoniso-manasikāra*), I realized

> with wisdom that 'when there is desire, there is clinging; clinging exists with desire as condition.' I then thought to myself, 'With what as condition does desire exist; desire exists on account of what?' Through wise attention, I realized with wisdom that 'when there is feeling, there is desire; desire exists with feeling as condition..."[71]

Breaking Down into Component Factors

"Breaking down into component factors" is a way of thinking aimed at examining things as they really are. In the teachings it tends to be used in examining the absence of abiding essence, or true self, of things, thus removing attachment to appearances and conventions. It is specifically the examination of the person as merely a collection of component factors, known as the five *khandhas*, each of which is once again made up of smaller components. Such examination helps to see not-self (*anattā*). However, in order to see this reality clearly, it is usually required to incorporate the first kind of thinking or the third kind of thinking, to be explained next. That is, once the component factors are analyzed, one sees the reality that they are interdependent and subject to determinants. They are not truly independent. Moreover, the components and determinants are entirely subject to the laws of nature: they are constantly arising and ceasing, impermanent, unstable and ephemeral. This state of arising and inevitably ceasing, if not examined in terms of delving into determinants according to the first method, which may be difficult, can also be seen in terms of the characteristics of things, which comes into the domain of the third method of thinking. In the Tipiṭaka the second method of thinking is usually discussed in conjunction with the third method.

However, in the commentaries, which follow the later Abhidhamma style, the second method of thinking is usually taken as a separate level and included as one of the methods of analysis (*vibhajja vidhī*).[72] Moreover, the analysis is usually according to body and mind (*nāmarūpa*) rather than the five *khandhas*. This kind of thinking involves not only breaking down or dissecting, but also classifying into groups or categories. However, since the emphasis is on the function of analysis, it is said to be *vibhajja*. In modern terminology we might call it "the analytical method."

The traditional practice of insight described in the commentarial texts refers to the elementary reflection and analytical examination based on body and mind as *nāmarūpavavatthāna*, or *nāmarūpa-pariggaha*.[73] Here the being or person is not looked at in conventional terms, as "him," "her," "Mr. This" or "Ms. That," but in terms of realities, being analyzed into mere mentality and physicality (*nāmadhamma rūpadhamma*). The components are each noted—"this is physicality," "that is mentality," "physicality is of this nature," "mentality is of this nature," "this is of this nature, therefore it is physicality; that is of that nature, therefore it is mentality." When the components are broken down in this way, there are only mentality and physicality. When this kind of perception is honed and cultivated, beings and things are seen as agglomerations of mentality and physicality, merely natural realities void of being or personality.

Here are some canonical examples of this kind of thinking:

> "On account of the bringing together of components, there is the word 'cart.' In the same way, when there are the five *khandhas*, there is the concept of a being."[74]
>
> ---
>
> "Bhikkhus, this Ganges River carries along a large mass of froth. A man with clear sight looks at it, scrutinizes it and examines it wisely.[75] When he looks, scrutinizes, and examines wisely, it appears to him as void, having no essence. How can there be an essence in a mass of froth? In the same way, form, of whatever description, be it past, future or present... far or near, when looked at, scrutinized and examined wisely by a bhikkhu, appears void, without essence. How could there be an essence in form?"

From here the same is said of feeling, perception, mental formations, and consciousness, and concluded with the verse:

> "The Kinsman of the Sun [i.e., the Buddha] has taught that form is like a mass of froth on a river, feeling is like bubbles in the rain, perception is like a mirage, mental formations are like a banana tree, consciousness is like a conjurer's trick. When a bhikkhu looks into and attends wisely to the five *khandhas* in all their manifestations, they appear as void..."[76]

Reflecting on the Universal Characteristics

To "reflect on the universal characteristics" is to look on things being wise to the way they proceed, and must proceed as the natural order. This natural order is that all things that arise from the concoction of determinants, having arisen, must disintegrate; they are transient, unstable, ephemeral and impermanent. This is the characteristic of impermanence (*aniccaṁ*). All factors or determinants, both internal and external, are constantly arising, passing away and changing. Thus, their coming into contact creates conflict and fills them with stress and oppression. It is impossible for them to maintain any fixed state; they are forced to change and disintegrate, which is the characteristic of stress (*dukkha*). Being subject to determinants, things cannot be owned or controlled by anyone, just as they cannot be their own masters or have any independent existence. They cannot follow anyone's desires and no one can control them because they fare according to determinants, not people's desires. This is the characteristic of not-self (*anattā*). In summary, it is being wise to the fact that all things are nature; they possess universal characteristics as the norm, since they are all equally fabricated from determinants and subject to those determinants.

This method of thinking according to the universal characteristics can be divided into two stages.

The first stage is being aware of and accepting the truth. It is the level of adopting an attitude to things that is compatible with the truth of nature, an attitude of wisdom, an attitude of freedom. Even when we experience situations that are not to our liking, or unfavorable events occur, we are able to reflect that those things or events have proceeded according to the natural order, according to their determinants. To think in this way is to have an attitude of acceptance and detachment, relieving us of, or mitigating, suffering. Alternatively, when such events arise, simply determining to look at the situation as it really is rather than as we want or do not want it to be immediately reduces the possibility of suffering, because we have freed ourselves and do not place ourselves in an oppressive bind over it (or more accurately, we do not create a self to be oppressed by it).

The second level is correcting and responding to situations in accordance with determinants. It is the level of dealing with things in conformity with the truth of nature, practicing with wisdom, awareness and detachment. That is to say, knowing that all things naturally fare according to determinants, if we want them to be any particular way we study the determinants that will make them that way and adjust them accordingly. Having prepared the determinants for that result, whether we want the result to arise or not, it must arise. If, on the other hand, the determinants are not yet ripe, results will not arise no matter how much we want them to. In short, we solve problems with knowledge, and we solve them at their causes, not with desire.

Practicing according to this second stage of the third method of *yoniso-manasikāra* is related to the fourth method of thinking, which will be described below; that is to say, the fourth method takes over from here.

Here are a few selections from the canon illustrating the use of the second and third types of thinking in conjunction:

> "Bhikkhus, attend wisely (*yoniso-manasikāra*) to form, seeing the impermanence of form as it really is... attend wisely to feeling, seeing the impermanence of feeling as it really is... attend wisely to perception, seeing the impermanence of perception as it really is... attend wisely to mental formations, seeing the impermanence of mental formations as it really is... attend wisely to consciousness, seeing the impermanence of consciousness as it really is..."[77]

> "A bhikkhu who is learned should attend wisely to the five groups of clinging (*upādānakkhandhā*) as being impermanent, as being oppressed... as being not-self."[78]

The following Buddhavacana illustrates the type of thinking that searches out determinants and continues on with the reflection on the universal characteristics, with the objective of seeing things as they really are, liberating the mind from attachment and suffering:

> "Bhikkhus, what do sorrow, lamentation, pain, grief and despair arise from, what is their place of origin? (Understand as follows:) Unenlightened beings in this world who lack *suta* (learning), who have not met with the noble ones, are not versed in the noble teaching and untrained in the noble teaching; who have not met the true people, are not versed in the teaching of the true people (*sappurisadhamma*) and are untrained in the teaching of the true people, see form as self, see the self as having form, see form in the self or see self in form. [When] their form changes and becomes otherwise, sorrow, lamentation, pain, grief, and despair arise in them on account of that form changing and becoming otherwise. They see feeling... perception... mental formations... consciousness as self... When consciousness changes and becomes otherwise, sorrow, lamentation, pain, grief, and despair arise in them on account of that feeling... perception... mental formations... consciousness changing and becoming otherwise.
>
> "The bhikkhu who clearly knows that form... feeling... perception... mental formations... consciousness are impermanent, subject to change, subject to fading and cessation, and sees the truth with right wisdom as it is that all form... feeling... perception... mental formations... consciousness are impermanent, oppressed by determinants, subject to change, both now as in the past, casts off sorrow, lamentation, pain, grief, and despair. Having cast off sorrow, that bhikkhu has no need to fear. Being without fear, he dwells happily. A bhikkhu who dwells happily can be said to have attained the temporary (*tadaṅga*) *nibbāna*."[79]

The Method of the Noble Truths

"The method of the noble truths" can also be referred to as the method of the cessation of suffering. It is one of the fundamental ways of thinking, because it can be enlarged upon to encompass all of the other methods. A short canonical passage in support of this says:

> "That bhikkhu attends wisely (*yoniso-manasikāra*) thus: 'suffering is like this'; he attends wisely thus: 'the cause of suffering is like this'; he attends wisely thus: 'the cessation of suffering is like this'; he attends wisely thus: 'the way leading to the cessation of suffering is like this.' When he attends wisely in this way, the three fetters—attachment to self view (*sakkāya-diṭṭhi*), doubt (*vicikicchā*), and grasping at rites and observances (*sīlabbataparāmāsa*)—are given up."[80]

This method of thinking has two general characteristics:

1. It is a method that accords with cause and effect, searching back from effects to causes, and solving problems and responding through those causes. This first characteristic can be divided into two pairs, thus:
    - First pair: *Dukkha* (suffering) is the result. It is the problem, the unwanted situation. *Samudaya* (arising) is the cause. It is the source of the problem, the point that must be eliminated or adjusted before the problem can be overcome.
    - Second pair: *Nirodha* (cessation) is the result. It is the state of the ending of problems, the objective to be attained. *Magga* (the path) is the cause. It is the method, the practice to be done in correcting the cause of suffering, for attaining the objective, which is the cessation of suffering.
2. It is a way of thinking that is right on target, straightforward, and aimed directly at what needs to be done and dealt with in actual life. This second characteristic is focused on solving problems, not floating off into impractical philosophical speculations in the service of desire, pride and views.[81]

In this way of thinking, one must properly understand the task or duty to be performed for each of the noble truths. To give a general idea, I will here discuss the noble truths and their practice in brief.

The first step of the noble truths is in regard to *dukkha*, the nature of the problem—the oppression, obstruction, pressure, stress, and imperfection that arise in life or in human experience. In the broadest sense, *dukkha* refers to the state of all formations, mentality and physicality, the five *khandhas*, or life and the world, falling under the laws of the natural order, being impermanent, unstable, oppressed by conflicting conditions, subject to determinants, and void of essence or self. Our duty in relation to *dukkha* is simply to observe it, to understand it, and ascertain its extent, just as a doctor observes or diagnoses the symptoms and extent of an illness. This duty is called *pariññā* (knowing). The task in regard to suffering is not to worry about it, hate it, or be anxious over it, because such reactions only serve to increase suffering. We cannot solve it through wanting. We must solve it with knowledge and elimination of its cause.

On this level, apart from observing, we merely adopt an attitude of knowing the natural order of things as described in the first level of the third kind of thinking. Once suffering is noted and the problem understood, *pariññā* has been done, and the practice in relation to suffering has been carried out. We should then immediately proceed to the second step.

The second step of the noble truths is in regard to *samudaya*, the cause of suffering or the source of problems. *Samudaya* consists of the determinants that come together and interact with, conflict with, and affect each other to create the state of stress, frustration, and imperfection in all their variations, which must be located and dealt with in the proper way, which is *pahāna*, elimination or abandoning. The Buddha pointed out the central, core causes that form the underlying cause of human suffering, both on the level of the dominant factor, which is desire,[82] and on the level of the full process, which is the interrelated conditioning of determinants according to the *paṭiccasamuppāda*.[83]

Each time suffering or a particular problem is experienced, the relevant causes and determinants should be searched out. This is using the first method of thinking. If the problem is caused by human factors, the core or underlying causes should be considered in conjunction with the specific causes of that situation. Once the underlying causes of the problem that need to be eliminated or corrected have been searched out, analyzed, and ascertained, this is the completion of the thinking on the second level.

The third step of the noble truths is in regard to *nirodha*, the cessation of suffering, or the state free of problems. *Nirodha* is the desired objective, in relation to which our duty is *sacchikiriyā*, realization, actualization, accomplishment, or attainment. On this level we must note what our desired objective is, for what purpose our practice is intended, where it will lead us, whether it is attainable and how, what principles there are for attaining it, and what subsidiary or intermediate objectives or stages within the objective there are.

The fourth step of the noble truths is in regards to *magga*, the way to quell suffering, the practices leading to the cessation of suffering or methods for solving the problem. *Magga* refers to the methods and practical details of what is to be done to eliminate the determinants of the problem and attain the desired objective. Here our duty is *bhāvanā* (cultivation), or practical application. On the level of thinking, what needs to be done here is to note the method, the procedures and the particulars of the work to be done to redress the cause of the problem in a way that conforms with the desired objective.

Relating the Teaching to the Objective[84]

"Relating the teaching to the objective" means to contemplate and understand the relationship between Dhamma and *attha*, or principle and objective. Dhamma means "truth" or "principle"—that is to say, principles of truth, principles of goodness, or principles of practice, including teachings on how to practice and act properly. The word *attha* means "meaning," "objective," "goal," "desired benefit," or "desired meaning." In practicing Dhamma, it is essential to understand its meaning and objectives, what purposes it is to achieve, both the ultimate objective and the intermediate aims, which in turn have an effect on other teachings or principles. Correct understanding in regard to principles and objectives leads to right practice, called *dhammānudhammapaṭipatti.*

Dhammānudhammapaṭipatti has been traditionally translated as "practicing appropriately to the teachings." It means practicing the minor teachings in compliance with the major ones, or practicing the minor principles in compliance with the major ones. It may be simply rendered as "practicing properly according to the teachings."[85]

Dhammānudhammapaṭipatti may be called the deciding factor for whether or not Dhamma practice will achieve its intended purpose. Without it, Dhamma practice is distorted, aimless, deluded and fruitless. It may even have the opposite effect to what is desired and lead to harm. All teachings have an objective: teaching is for a benefit, principles are for their objectives, and every aspect of practice should be answerable to its purpose. The importance of reflecting on and understanding this matter is given great emphasis in the teachings, both in the sense of personal qualities, as in the qualities of a true person (*sappurisadhamma*) and the four kinds of analytical knowledge (*paṭisambhidā*), and in the sense of stages of practice, such as the principles for growth in wisdom (*paññāvuḍhidhamma*) and the approaches to practice presented below. To further clarify this, the following canonical passages may be helpful:

> "Bhikkhus, how is a bhikkhu one who knows the teaching (*dhammaññū*)? A bhikkhu in this teaching and discipline knows the teaching [Dhamma]—that is, the suttas, the texts (*geyya*), the expositions (*veyyākaraṇa*), the verses (*gāthā*), the utterances (*udāna*), the Itivuttaka, the Jātakas, the Abbhutadhamma, and the Vedalla…
>
> "And how is a bhikkhu one who knows the meaning (*atthaññū*)? A bhikkhu in this teaching and discipline knows

> the meaning (*attha*) of those sayings thus: This is the meaning of this statement, this is the meaning of that statement..."[86]

> "Bhikkhus, these five conditions are for the fading and the disappearance of the true teaching. They are: bhikkhus do not respectfully listen to the teaching; they do not respectfully learn the teaching; they do not respectfully commit the teaching to memory; they do not respectfully consider the meaning of the teaching memorized; and knowing the meaning and the letter, they do not respectfully practice in accordance with it (*dhammānudhammapaṭipatti*)...
>
> "Bhikkhus, these five conditions are for the firm establishment, the non-fading, and non-disappearance of the true teaching. They are: bhikkhus respectfully listen to the teaching; they respectfully learn the teaching; they respectfully commit the teaching to memory; they respectfully consider the meaning of the teaching so memorized; and knowing the meaning and the letter, they respectfully practice in accordance with it. These five conditions are for the firm establishment, the non-fading and the non-disappearance of the true teaching."[87]

Note the progression in this sutta, which may be summarized as follows:

> Hearing and studying the teaching → committing it to memory → considering the meaning → practicing accordingly (*dhammānudhammapaṭipatti*)

The same progression occurs in a great many other suttas,[88] so that it must be taken to be an important principle in Buddhist study and practice. Having established this principle, let us now compare it with the four principles for the growth of wisdom, or qualities leading to stream entry attainment, stated as follows:

> "Bhikkhus, these four conditions are for the growth of wisdom. They are: association with a true person (*sappurisa-*

> *saṁseva*); hearing the true teaching (*saddhammassavana*); wise attention (*yoniso-manasikāra*); and practice accordingly (*dhammānudhammapaṭipatti*)."[89]

Comparing the two, we see that both progressions have essentially the same meaning. Worthy of special note is that instead of *yoniso-manasikāra*, the sutta cited above uses instead the term *atthupparikkhā* (reflection on or examination of the meaning), indicating that here *yoniso-manasikāra* is intended specifically in this fifth sense. When the teaching and the meaning are clearly understood, or the principle and its objective compatible, the next step is putting the teachings into practice in the proper way.

In Buddhism the importance of such reflection and understanding needs to be given regular emphasis. Even the "middle-ness" of the Middle Way is determined by understanding and bearing in mind the objective of the practice. All of the teachings derived from or comprising the Middle Way have their own specific goals and shared objective, which must be understood and borne in mind for right practice, so that those teachings can interrelate, harmonize, and interact to bring about the desired objective. In another sense, understanding and awareness of the meaning and value of the various teachings is the determining factor for the rightness and suitability of the practice to bring about *dhammānudhammapaṭipatti.*

In terms of the ultimate benefit (*paramattha*; rather than the benefit here and now [*diṭṭhadhammikattha*], the further benefit [*samparāyikattha*], or the social benefit [*parattha*]), morality, concentration, and wisdom all have the ultimate objective of *nibbāna*, but from a more specific perspective, each has its own specific zone, which must be integrated with other factors before the ultimate objective can be attained. Any one of them on its own is incapable of bringing about a total accomplishment, but at the same time each is indispensable.

Thus, there is the principle: morality is for concentration, concentration is for wisdom, and wisdom is for liberation. If morality is practiced without awareness of its objective, it can become deluded attachment to rules and observances (*sīlabbataparāmāsa*) and encourage asceticism for its own sake (*attakilamathānuyogo*). If concentration is practiced without an awareness of its objective, it can lead to obsession with psychic powers and encourage certain kinds of wrong view or "low arts" (*tiracchānavijjā*). If wisdom is developed without the objective of liberation, it strays from the Middle Way and does not lead to the goal of Buddhism. It may get sidetracked somewhere along the way or get stuck on some form of wrong view.

In this respect, practitioners who lack *yoniso-manasikāra* can go astray at any stage along the way. For instance, in the beginning stages, with morality, it is generally held that to practice strictly and purely in conformity with rules and regulations is an important attribute, and practitioners should always give a good deal of importance to their moral conduct. However, even though a practitioner is strict in one's morality, as soon as one loses attention to "relating the teaching to the meaning," forgetting to consider the meaning and objectives of morality, mistakes in the practice can arise. The practitioner may look on morality as a complete and isolated end in itself, not as a part of an overall process.

Alternatively, lack of consideration of the meaning and objectives of morality will lead to attachment to forms and procedures, leading to the phenomenon of blindly following the practice without understanding what it is for, failing to see morality as a training. Some people get so engrossed in their moral observances that they go overboard, as if strict observance and diligence were virtues in themselves, and that simply by practicing in such a way they will be virtuous and attain the objective. Or they see that accomplishment can be achieved simply by strict observance of moral precepts, and morality and observances become ends in themselves rather than means to the end. Or they feel that simply to have morality is enough to attain the objective. They may go so far as to hold that "the stricter the better." When people reach this stage, they have totally lost their awareness of the objectives of morality.

As for those who observe precepts with an understanding of their objective, while they give due importance to strictness and orderliness, they will always bear in mind, or ask themselves, what they are for, and how they do or do not relate to other parts of the process of practice. They will be able to discern, for example, that "this is *sīla*" (central practice) and "this is *vatta*" (auxiliary practice); "this person should undertake this strict observance for such and such reasons; that person should not undertake that observance for these reasons"; "this practice should be compulsorily observed by all because of this or for this objective, and this practice should be undertaken voluntarily because of these reasons or for these objectives related to differences in individual temperaments," and so on.

In practice, it seems that the importance of this way of reflection would be reduced if the practitioner has access to the close guidance of a good friend, because one's practice is fed by trust in the wisdom of the good friend and the expectation that the good friend will not lead one astray. However, in the Tipiṭaka no exceptions are found, because one of the responsibilities of a good friend is to explain both the letter and the meaning of the teaching, or to show the way to achieve such an understanding.

Reflecting on Benefit, Harm, and the Way Out

"Reflecting on benefit, harm, and the way out" refers to examining to see the attraction (*assāda*), the danger (*ādīnava*), and the escape (*nissaraṇa*). This method of *yoniso-manasikāra* is another way of looking at things as they really are, stressing acknowledgment of the truth of things from all perspectives, both the good and the bad.

Assāda is the good part, the tasty part, the sweet part, the benefit, the value, the favorable aspect.

Ādīnava is the bad part, the flaw, the fault, the harm, the defect.

Nissaraṇa is the way out, the escape, freedom or deliverance.

This kind of thinking has two features that need to be stressed:

1. In order to be said to have "seen things as they are," one must see both the positive and the negative aspects, the benefits and the harm, of something, not just its advantages or benefits or just its harm or disadvantages. To have seen sensuality as it really is, for example, means to see both its benefit and its harm.[90]

2. When addressing a problem, or following a way out of an undesirable situation, it is not enough simply to know the benefit and harm, the advantages and disadvantages. One must also see the way out, the destination, and know what that destination is, what it is like, and how it betters the problematic state and transcends its faults, weaknesses, dangers, and disadvantages. Is it truly independent of the old benefit and harm, attributes and defects? Does the destination, objective, or state that is free of those problems really exist, and how does it come about? Although the Buddha, for example, clearly knew that sensuality was rife with disadvantages and harm, as long as he still did not know the way out of sensuality he could not guarantee that he would never return to it:[91]

> "Bhikkhus, before the enlightenment, while I was still an unenlightened *bodhisatta*, the thought arose in me, 'What is the attraction (*assāda*) of the world, what is the danger (*ādīnava*) of the world, and what is the way out (*nissaraṇa*)?' The thought arose in me, 'The pleasure and happiness contingent on whatever is in this world: this is the attraction of the world. That the world is impermanent, stressful (*dukkha*), and subject to change: this is the danger of the world. Dis-association from passion and desire (*chandarāga*): this is the way out in the world…'
>
> "Bhikkhus, I went in search of the attraction of the world. Whatever attraction there is in this world, I have experienced it. However much attraction there is in this world, I have well seen it as it is with wisdom. I went in search of the danger of the world. Whatever is the danger of this world, I have experienced that. However much danger there is in this world, I have well seen as it is with wisdom. I went in search of the escape from the world. Whatever is the escape from this world, I have experienced that. However much escape there is in this world, I have well seen as it is with wisdom.
>
> "Bhikkhus, as long as I did not clearly know as it is the attraction of this world as the attraction, the danger of this world as the danger, and the escape from this world as the escape,

I did not declare that I had attained complete and unexcelled enlightenment...

"Bhikkhus, if there were no attraction in the world, beings would not be attached to the world, but because there is attraction in this world, beings are attached. If there were no danger in the world, beings would not become disillusioned with the world; but because there is danger in this world, beings become disillusioned with it. If there were no escape in the world, beings could not break out of the world, but because there is an escape, beings can break out of the world.

"Bhikkhus, as long as beings do not see clearly as it is the attraction in the world as the attraction, the danger of the world as the danger, and the escape from the world as the escape, they will not be able to break out of, detach from, and transcend the world...or to abide with minds that are boundless. But whenever worldly beings see clearly as it is the attraction of the world as its attraction, the danger of the world as its danger, and the escape from the world as the escape, then will they be able to break out of, detach from, and transcend the world...and to abide with minds that are boundless.

"Bhikkhus, whatever recluses or brahmins there be who do not yet clearly know the attraction in the world as the attraction, the danger of the world as the danger, and the escape from the world as the escape, those recluses and brahmins cannot be called recluses among recluses or brahmins among brahmins, and they cannot be said to have realized through their own wisdom and abided within the objective (*attha*) of being a recluse or the objective of being a brahmin."[92]

"Bhikkhus, when a bhikkhu attends to (*manasikāra*) sensuality and his mind does not race toward, does not praise, does not fix onto, and does not absorb into sensuality, and when he attends to renunciation (*nekkhamma*), and his mind races toward, praises, fixes onto, and absorbs into renunciation, his mind is well conducted, well trained, well gone, well freed, unattached to

> all sensuality. Whatever outflows, oppression, and trouble that might arise on condition of sensuality, he has transcended those outflows, that oppression and that trouble. He does not experience those feelings. This is called the escape from sensuality."[93]
>
> ---
>
> "I myself, in the past, while I was still living the household life, endowed and surfeited with the five strands of sense pleasures, enjoyed myself... In time, I realized as it is the cause of the arising, the instability, the attraction, the danger and the way out of sensuality, and therefore I gave up sensual desire, soothed the agitation over sensuality, was without thirst, and abided with mind calmed. I look at other beings, still possessed of desire for sensuality, eaten up by desire, agitated by sensual burning, enjoying sensual pleasures. I am not moved to envy those beings and do not delight in those sense pleasures. Why not? Because I delight in a refreshment that requires no sensuality or unskillful qualities. For that reason, I am not moved to desire the lesser kinds of happiness, and do not delight in those lesser kinds of happiness."[94]

This sixth kind of reflection can be used with all kinds of things, even with the teachings. The Paṭisambhidāmagga describes, for instance, the attraction and the danger (*ādīnava*) of the five faculties (*indriya*). The non-appearance of restlessness (*uddhacca*), the non-appearance of distress dependent on restlessness, the courage that results from a life lived without confusion and the experience of a subtle kind of pleasant abiding are the attraction of concentration. That restlessness can still appear, that distress contingent on restlessness can still appear, and the fact that concentration is still impermanent, imperfect (*dukkha*) and not-self is the danger of concentration.[95]

An example illustrating this thinking in terms of benefit, harm, and the way out appears in the *anupubbikathā*, one of the teachings frequently given by the Buddha as a preliminary to teaching the four noble truths. That teaching first describes the wholesome, warm, and helpful life of living with good conduct known as generosity (*dāna*) and morality (*sīla*). It then describes the life of happiness, contentment, and plenty resulting from such a life, known as heaven (*sagga*). Then the teaching describes the disadvantages, the fault, the harm, the imperfection, and insufficiency of such happiness and plenty, called *kāmādīnava*. Finally, the teaching describes the way out and the good results of that way out, known as rewards of renunciation (*nekkhammānisaṁsa*). Once the listener could see the good results of the way out, the Buddha would complete the teaching with an explanation of the four noble truths.

Reflecting on True and False Value

"Reflecting on true and false value" is a way of examining our use or consumption (*paṭisevanā*) of things. It is a reflection for cutting off or reducing desire or defilements (*kilesa*). This kind of thinking is commonly used in daily life because it deals with the use and consumption of the four supports (food, clothing, shelter, and medicine) and material conveniences. The principle in brief is that people see things in terms of satisfying desires. Whatever is capable of feeding our desires we see as of value, of use. This value can be divided into two kinds, in accordance with the kind of desire, thus:

1. True value, referring to the meaning, value, or benefit of things in how they directly responding to the needs of life. This value is determined or evaluated by wisdom. It may be called the value that serves wisdom. For example, the value of food is its use in nourishing the body, allowing the body to live with good health and comfort, and providing the strength to perform its duties. A car helps us to move quickly from place to place and helps to perform our tasks and conduct our lives. It should be chosen on the basis of its convenience, safety, strength, durability, and so on.
2. Supplementary or false value, referring to the meaning, the value, or use that we affix onto things in order to cater to our search for pleasure or increase our sense of self. This kind of

> value is determined or evaluated by desire. It may be called the value that serves desire. For example, the value of food is seen in its delicious flavor, its provision of pleasure, and status appeal. A car is seen as a symbol of status, fashion, or wealth. It is chosen for its appearance and its impact on others.

This kind of thinking is used for dealing with all kinds of things, be it through consumption, use, purchase, or possession. The emphasis is on understanding and choosing things in accordance with the value that is of real benefit in life, both for oneself and others. This real value is not only of real benefit to life but also aids the growth of skillful qualities, such as mindfulness, allowing one to rise above enslavement to material things, because it is a relationship of wisdom and lies within what is appropriate and moderate. True value is in contrast to the value added on by desire, which is not particularly beneficial to life and sometimes even dangerous. False value gives rise to the growth of unskillful qualities such as greed, delusion, envy, pride, stubborn views, and self-exaltation; it has no limits and leads to contention and exploitation. For example, a meal costing ten dollars eaten with wisdom, for its true value, may be more valuable to the body than another meal costing one thousand dollars eaten out of a desire to inflate one's own value, and the latter meal may even be dangerous to health.

The following extract from the scriptures illustrates the attitude toward the four requisites that is encouraged for Buddhist bhikkhus:

> "A bhikkhu attends wisely before using a robe, as merely for elimination of cold, heat, the touch of gadflies, mosquitoes, wind, sun, and crawling creatures, and merely to cover the parts of the body that should be covered.
>
> "A bhikkhu attends wisely before eating alms food, as not for pleasure, not for intoxication, not for showing off, not for ostentation, but for the continued existence of the body, for survival, for the elimination of difficulty and supporting the

> holy life, thinking, '[With this food] I eliminate old feeling [of hunger] and do not produce new feeling [of overeating or sense pleasure], and thus there will be for me the continuation of life, blamelessness and comfort.'
>
> "A bhikkhu attends wisely before using his dwelling place, as merely for eliminating cold, heat, the touch of gadflies, mosquitoes, wind, sun, and crawling creatures, simply to minimize the dangers from the elements and to provide a shelter for living in retreat.
>
> "A bhikkhu attends wisely before using medicines and supports for times of illness, as simply for the elimination of feelings contingent on illnesses that have already arisen and for being entirely free of illness."[96]

Reflecting as a Means for Arousing Virtues

"Reflecting as a means for arousing virtues" may be simply called "the way of thinking to rouse the skillful," or "thinking as cultivation of the skillful (*kusala-bhāvanā*)." It is a technique for filtering, reducing, or training desire, and therefore is regarded as one of the elementary forms of practice for supporting the growth and fruition of skillful qualities and building and strengthening mundane right view.

The general principle behind this method of thinking is that different people may see or react to the same experience or object of cognition in different ways, depending on the context, approach, or habitual tendencies that condition the mind—the mental formations—they have accumulated, or depending on how they establish their minds at that time. One person seeing one object or gesture may think good, useful, or skillful thoughts, but another person may think bad, unwholesome, or harmful thoughts. Even the one person perceiving the same object or experience at different times may have different mental responses, at one time negative, another time positive.

Establishing the mind in a way that initiates and influences thinking to proceed in a wholesome and beneficial direction is known as *yoniso-manasikāra* for rousing the skillful. This kind of *yoniso-manasikāra* is important both in the sense that it causes the arising of wholesome thought and action, and also in that it helps to counteract accumulated bad habits and thought patterns while creating new, wholesome mental habits. Conversely, without this corrective means, a person's thoughts and actions will be led entirely by the momentum of accumulated habits, and continually strengthened in those habits.

One simple example of this kind of thinking given in the texts is reflection on death. If there is wrong attention or thinking (*ayoniso-manasikāra*), unskillful qualities will arise. Thinking about death may lead to depression, sorrow, melancholy, fear, and terror, or even pleasure at the thought of the death of someone one hates. With *yoniso-manasikāra*, however, skillful qualities will arise: feelings of alertness, urgency, heedfulness, diligent application to one's duties, performance of good actions, practice of the Dhamma, and, ultimately, being wise to the truth of the way of formations. It is said that proper reflection on death will comprise mindfulness or recollection (*sati*), a sense of urgency (*saṁvega*) and direct knowledge (*ñāṇa*). In addition, many skillful means for reflecting on death are recommended.[97]

In the Tipiṭaka the Buddha gives some simple examples of how the same event, reflected on in one way, gives rise to laziness, but reflected on in another way gives rise to diligence, as stated in the sutta:

> "Bhikkhus, there are these eight occasions for laziness (*kusīta-vatthu*). What are the eight?
>
> 1. "A bhikkhu has work to do. He thinks to himself, 'I have work to do. Doing this work will cause the body to be tired. Enough! I will lie down [and build up my strength] first.' Thinking in this way, he lies down. He does not put forth the effort to attain what is not attained, to realize what is not yet realized, to experience what is not yet experienced...

2. "Again, a bhikkhu has finished working. He thinks to himself, 'I have just finished working and, having worked, now the body is tired. Enough! I will lie down [and have a rest] first.' Thinking in this way, he lies down...
3. "Again, a bhikkhu must set out on a journey. He thinks to himself, 'I must set out on a journey. While traveling the body will be tired. Enough! I will lie down [and build up my strength] first.' Thinking in this way, he lies down...
4. "Again, a bhikkhu has just finished a journey. He thinks to himself, 'I have just completed a journey and, having traveled, the body is tired. Enough! I will lie down [and have a rest] first.' Thinking in this way, he lies down...
5. "Again, a bhikkhu goes for alms round in the surrounding villages or communities and does not obtain as much coarse or refined foods as he needed. He thinks to himself, 'I have gone for alms round in the surrounding villages or communities and have not obtained as much coarse or refined foods as I needed. My body is tired and unfit for practice. Enough! I will lie down [and have a rest] first.' Thinking in this way, he lies down...
6. "Again, a bhikkhu goes for alms round in the surrounding villages or communities and obtains as much coarse or refined foods as needed. He thinks to himself, 'I have gone for alms round in the surrounding villages or communities and obtained as much coarse or refined foods as needed. Now the body is heavy, unfit for practice, like fermented beans. Enough, I will lie down.' Thinking in this way, he lies down...
7. "Again, a bhikkhu contracts a minor illness. He thinks to himself, 'I have contracted a minor illness. This is sufficient reason to lie down. Enough! I will lie down and have a rest.' Thinking in this way, he lies down...
8. "Again, a bhikkhu has recently recovered from an illness. He thinks to himself, 'I have recently recovered from an illness. My body is still weak, not fit for practice. Enough! I will lie down.' Thinking in this way, he lies down..."

Under these very same circumstances, a different kind of reflection leads to the diligent putting forth of effort. These are called the "occasions for putting forth effort" (*ārabbhavatthu*), of which there are eight just the same:

1. "[Having some work to do]...the bhikkhu thinks, 'I have work to do. While working it will not be easy for me to attend to the Buddha's teachings. Enough! Let me first put forth diligent effort in order to attain what is not attained, to reach what is not yet reached, to realize what is not yet realized.' Thinking in this way, that bhikkhu puts forth diligent effort...
2. "[Having finished some work]...the bhikkhu thinks, 'I have finished this work. While working I was not able to attend to the Buddha's teachings. Enough! Let me put forth diligent effort'...
3. "[Having to go on a journey]...the bhikkhu thinks, 'I have to go on a journey. While traveling, it will not be easy for me to attend to the Buddha's teachings. Enough, I will put forth diligent effort'...
4. "[Having completed a journey]...the bhikkhu thinks, 'I have just completed a journey. While traveling I was not able to attend to the Buddha's teachings. Enough! Let me put forth diligent effort'...
5. "[Having gone on alms round and not obtained all the food needed]...the bhikkhu thinks, 'I have gone on alms round around the village or town and not obtained all the coarse or refined food I needed. My body is light and suitable for practice. Enough! Let me put forth diligent effort'...
6. "[Having gone for alms round and obtained all the food needed]...the bhikkhu thinks, 'I have gone on alms round around the village or town and obtained all the coarse or refined food I needed. My body is light and suitable for practice. Enough! Let me put forth diligent effort'...
7. "[Having contracted a minor illness]...the bhikkhu thinks,

> 'I have contracted this minor illness. It is possible that this illness may become more serious. Enough! Let me put forth diligent effort'...
>
> 8. "[Having recovered from an illness]...the bhikkhu thinks, 'I have only recently recovered from this illness, but it is possible that I may suffer a relapse. Enough! Let me put forth diligent effort'..."[98]

If unskillful thoughts have already arisen, techniques are recommended for correcting them, and the techniques recommended are generally the *yoniso-manasikāra* for arousing the skillful. For example, in the *Vitakkasaṇṭhāna Sutta*[99] the Buddha recommends some general principles for correcting unskillful thoughts on five levels. Basically, if unskillful, evil thoughts based on desire (*chanda*),[100] aversion or delusion arise they can be corrected in the following ways:

1. *Manasikāra*: attending to something else that is wholesome and skillful, or replacing the unskillful thoughts with something wholesome (as, for example, in thinking of something that produces goodwill (*mettā*) instead of something that produces aversion). If, after practicing in this way, the unskillful thoughts do not disappear...
2. Then examining the ill effects of those unskillful thoughts, that they are unwholesome, harmful, and cause suffering. If they still do not disappear...
3. Use the next method, which is to pay no attention, to ignore those evil, unskillful thoughts, as a man who does not want to see a certain sight might close his eyes, or look the other way. If they still do not disappear...
4. One should examine the forming base of those thoughts; that is, taking the thoughts themselves as an object of study, delving into them for the purposes of knowledge, not as a personal possession, to see what they are, what conditions or determinants they arose from. If they still do not disappear...

5. One should grit one's teeth, press the tongue firmly against the palate and make a determination; that is, resolutely force the mind to banish those thoughts.

In the texts, methods are recommended for correcting particular kinds of unskillful thoughts. In one passage, for example, the Buddha recommends a method for correcting and eliminating enmity by developing friendly thoughts (*mettā*), developing compassionate thoughts (*karuṇā*) or developing equanimous thoughts (*upekkhā*) toward our enemies, or by not thinking of or attending to them, or by reflecting on them according to the teaching that all beings have their own *kamma*, thinking "This person has his own *kamma*, is heir to his *kamma*, has *kamma* as birthplace, retinue and refuge, and whatever *kamma* he does, good or evil, he will have to inherit the fruits of that."[101]

Venerable Sāriputta recommended five further ways for correcting or eliminating enmity, or malice and rancor, by understanding the truth of the differences between individuals, thus:

1. Some people have unruly and impure bodily conduct but they have speech that is polite and pure.
2. Some people have unruly and impure speech but they have some bodily conduct that is polite and pure.
3. Some people have unruly and impure bodily conduct and unruly and impure speech, but their minds are at times clear and wholesome.
4. Some people have unruly and impure bodily conduct, unruly and impure speech, and their minds do not give rise to even a glimpse of goodness or clarity.
5. Some people have polite and pure bodily conduct, polite and pure speech, and their minds are always wholesome and clear.

For those who are defective in bodily conduct and expressions but whose verbal conduct and expression is polite and pure, to remove malice toward them one should not attend to or examine their bad bodily conduct but attend only to their good verbal conduct. It is like a bhikkhu who maintains the practice of wearing rag-robes: coming across a piece of discarded cloth along the roadside, he holds the cloth down with his left foot, and with his right foot spreads it out: whatever is good and can be used, he tears off only that part and takes it with him.

As for those who are defective in verbal conduct or expression but whose bodily conduct is polite and pure, one should not attend to their bad verbal conduct, but to their polite and pure bodily conduct. It is like a pond completely covered in duckweed: a traveler, hot, tired, and thirsty, arrives at the pond. Approaching the pond, he uses his hands to push aside the duckweed, scoops out some water, drinks his fill, and continues on his way.

As for those who are defective in both their bodily conduct and verbal expression, but whose minds are from time to time clear and wholesome, for them one should not attend to their conducting themselves badly through body and speech, but attend to their minds occasionally opening up to clarity and wholesomeness. It is like a tiny amount of water in a cow's footprint. A traveler, hot, tired, and thirsty, arrives there. He thinks, "The water in this cow's footprint is so meager, if I were to use my hand or some receptacle to scoop it out for drinking, the water would be stirred up and become muddy, and would be unfit for drinking. What if I were to get down on my knees, prop myself up with my hands, bend down and drink the water like a cow?" Thinking in this way, he gets down on his knees, props himself up with his hands, bends down, and drinks the water like a cow, and then continues on his way.

As for those who are defective in bodily conduct and verbal expression, and in whom not even a glimpse of goodness or clarity arises in the mind, for them one should adopt an attitude of goodwill and compassion, thinking: "Oh, may they give up their bad bodily conduct and develop good bodily conduct; may they give up that bad verbal conduct and develop good verbal conduct; may they give up that bad mental conduct and develop good mental conduct; may this person not die and go to the netherworlds, the woeful states, damnation, hell." It is like a sick man, suffering and gravely ill, traveling on a long journey: the village ahead is still far off, the previous village is far behind; he cannot obtain suitable food, he cannot obtain suitable medicine, he cannot find a suitable person to nurse him, nor a suitable guide to direct him to the nearest village. Another person on a long journey, seeing him, should bring forth thoughts of kindness and compassion, assistance and succor for that sick man, thinking, "Oh, may this person obtain suitable food, may he obtain suitable medicine, may he obtain a suitable person to nurse him, may he obtain a suitable guide. May this person not come to ruin at this place."

As for those who are of good bodily conduct, who have polite and pure speech, and whose minds are consistently clear, wholesome, and pure, for them one should attend to their having polite and pure bodily conduct, to their having polite and pure speech and to their having a mind that is always clear, wholesome, and pure, that they are thus worthy of faith on all counts, leading those who reflect on them also to have pure minds. It is like a pond with crystal clear water, cool and refreshing, its banks clean and clear, shady and restful, surrounded by trees of many kinds. A traveler, hot and burned from the sun, tired and thirsty, arrives there. He goes down to that pond, bathes in it, and drinks of the water and then comes up. He may then sit or lie down under the shade of a tree on the bank of that pond as he pleases.[102]

The above are illustrations of the kinds of reflecting and examining that are included in *yoniso-manasikāra* for arousing the skillful. Some are ways of examination that can be used in general, some are for use in relation to specific skillful qualities. The important point is that, once the basic principles and general approach of these methods are understood, a resourceful person may devise adaptations of this kind of thinking for creating and cultivating specific skillful qualities, and in conformity with a particular time, which makes the practice even more effective. It may be said that this thinking for arousing virtues is the method most open to extension, adaptation, and improvisation for a great variety of uses, depending on the different characters and in accordance with environments that change with time and place.

Apart from the general principles stated above, an important factor for keeping thought within the domain of *yoniso-manasikāra* is *sati* (recollection or mindfulness). *Sati* helps to put a rein on thinking that has strayed into *ayoniso-manasikāra* and helps bind it or pull it back onto *yoniso-manasikāra*. Thus, it is a factor that must always be present in *yoniso-manasikāra*.

The various kinds of *yoniso-manasikāra*, which can be summarized into two main kinds—that for seeing in accordance with reality, and that for generating and developing skillful qualities—find a parting of the ways at the initiation of thought, and *sati* may play an important role in choosing here which kind of *yoniso-manasikāra* is to follow. For example, once an object has been cognized, and *sati* notes it for the purpose of seeing its true nature, the thought process becomes *yoniso-manasikāra* for seeing the reality, but if *sati* takes some kind of skillful quality as object or recollects some kind of wholesome mental image within the mind, the thought stream becomes *yoniso-manasikāra* for generating skillful qualities. *Yoniso-manasikāra* for seeing the reality is defined by the truth, which follows the natural order, and thus it is more fixed and uniform. *Yoniso-manasikāra* for the generation of skillful qualities is still a matter of the embellishment in the mind following the nature of formations, and therefore can come in many diverse forms.

Being in the Present Moment

The kind of thinking called "being in the present moment" is simply another perspective on all the other kinds of thinking already mentioned, but it is described separately because it has some features that need to be understood in their own right, and it is an important kind of thinking in itself.

This method of thinking in the present moment is contained within the four foundations of mindfulness, which will also be dealt with in the section on the seventh factor of the noble eightfold path, but it is here discussed separately because we are considering a different perspective. In the foundations of mindfulness, the discussion focuses on establishing *sati*, recollecting on the condition that is arising, existing, being cognized, or being enacted in each present moment with full alertness. Here, the discussion will focus on the use of thinking and the subject of the thoughts being recollected.

There are many misunderstandings around the meaning of being in the present moment. Many people think that Buddhism tells us to think only of what is in front of us, happening in the present moment, and not to think of the past or the future, or even to make any plans or preparations for the future. With this kind of misconception, Dhamma practitioners stray from the true Buddhist practice, and outside observers point out all kinds of bad effects that Buddhism will have on those who practice it. In brief, the correct understanding of the present moment, the past, and the future in regard to this ninth kind of thinking, is as follows:

The important feature of thinking that is not in the present moment—thinking that is stuck on the past or floating off into the future—can be briefly stated as thought along the lines of desire, or thought under the influence of desire. In modern terminology, we might call it "falling slave to one's moods." It is characterized by pining for things that are done and gone, through attachment or some kind of yearning, and fantasizing about things that have not yet come because of dissatisfaction with what one is experiencing in the present.

The thinking of the present moment is characterized by thinking along the lines of knowledge, or powered by wisdom. If thinking is along the lines of knowledge or wisdom, regardless of whether it is in relation to something in the present, something in the past, or something of the future, it is all classed as thinking in the present moment. This can be clearly seen from the fact that knowledge and wise reflection about the past, the present, or the future is regarded as correct, and an important teaching of Buddhism on all levels, both on the level of daily life—as in teachings about learning from the lessons of the past and heedfully preparing to prevent future dangers—and on the level of truth realization and the Buddha's practice, such as *pubbenivāsānussatiñāṇa* (direct knowledge of past lives), *atītaṁsañāṇa* (direct knowledge of the past), and *anāgataṁsañāṇa* (direct knowledge of the future).

In terms of actual mental training, the words *past*, *present*, and *future* do not correspond with the general understanding. The word *present* as most people understand it tends to take in a broad and indeterminate period of time. In Buddhism, in terms of mind training, the present refers to the single instant that is arising. In this more profound meaning, "being in the present moment" means to have *sati* following what is being cognized, dealt with, or being done as it happens, each and every moment. If the mind reacts to an object of cognition with liking or disliking, and gets stuck on and revolves around an image of that object created in the mind, it has fallen into the past. It cannot follow, or has slipped away from, the present. Alternatively, when the mind floats out of the present and grasps into an image of something not yet arisen, it has "floated off" into the future. In this respect, both the past and the future of the Buddha's teaching may lie within the domain of the present as it is usually understood.

According to the above, we can see another important meaning of the term "present moment" in Buddhism, as not simply implying events arising in the outside world but applying to whatever is being related to at that moment. Thus, from another perspective, what is commonly understood to be the past or the future may be the present moment according to the Buddha's teaching, just as what most people conceive to be the present may become the past or the future in the sense of the Buddha's teaching, as already stated.

Summarizing briefly, being in the present moment is defined by a relationship to what is known or done, the mind not wandering around or straying off into objects of like or dislike, getting caught up in affection and aversion, or aimless fantasizing.

These various meanings can be seen in the various Buddhavacana presented here. Even the exhortation not to pine for the past or hope for the future are related to and focus on the performance of duties. Note, for example, the following canonical passages:

> "One should not pine for things that are done and gone, nor fantasize and hope for things not yet come. What is past is done and gone; what is future has yet to come. Those who see clearly

> what is the present at that time, not wavering or faltering, seeing clearly, should apply themselves to that.
>
> "Practice should be done today; who knows whether tomorrow will bring death? There is no bargaining with the Lord of Death, the great general.
>
> "One who abides like this, who is ardent and not slothful both day and night, is said by the Peaceful One to be one who grows day by day."[103]
>
> ---
>
> "Those who attain the truth, not sorrowing over what has passed, not dreaming about what has yet to come, abide with what is present. Thus, their features are clear.
>
> "Those who are still feeble in wisdom are always dreaming for what has not yet come and sorrowing over what has passed. Thus, they are haggard, like fresh reeds uprooted and left to wilt in the sun."[104]

Compare the attitude of mind that relates to time in a way that is not powered by desire, given in the canonical passages above, with the practice in relation to the future through wisdom in the performance of duties according to the following canonical passages, beginning with teachings dealing with the householders' life up to the bhikkhu's practice, and from personal practice to the acceptance of social responsibility:

> "Be wary of that of which one should be wary; guard against the danger that has not yet come. The brave survey both worlds, because they consider the danger yet to come."[105]
>
> ---
>
> "Accomplish what must be done [personal benefit and benefit for others] with heedfulness."[106]
>
> ---
>
> "Bhikkhus, seeing the following five future dangers, it is only fitting that you should abide with heedfulness, diligent, devoted, for the attainment of that truth not yet attained, for the reaching

of that truth not yet reached, for the realization of that truth not yet realized. What are the five?

1. "A bhikkhu in this teaching and discipline reflects thus: 'Right now, I am still young, a young man, my hair is black, and I am possessed of the vigor of youth, but there will come a time when old age will come upon this body. For an old man, overwhelmed by age, attending to the teachings of the Buddha will be no easy task, and living in a secluded dwelling in the forests will not be easy. Enough! Before that undesirable, unlikeable and unfavorable condition befalls me, let me quickly put forth effort to attain that not yet attained... after gaining which, even when old age comes upon me, I will dwell at ease...'

2. "Moreover, a bhikkhu reflects thus: 'Right now I have little illness, little pain, I am possessed of balanced powers of digestion, neither too cold nor too hot, just right for the development of the practice. But there will come a time when illness and fever will come upon this body... let me quickly put forth effort... even when I am sick I will dwell at ease...'

3. "Moreover, a bhikkhu reflects thus: 'Right now the food is good, alms food is easily come by, and I can easily maintain myself with the alms bowl, but there will come a time when food is scarce, the food is not good, alms food will be hard to find, and I will not easily be able to maintain myself with the alms bowl. Those living in areas where food is hard to find will move to other locations where food is easier to find. In those locations the monasteries will be crowded and noisy. When the monasteries are crowded and noisy, attending to the Buddha's teachings will be no easy task, and to live in a secluded dwelling in the forests will not be easy. Enough!... let me quickly put forth effort... even when food is scarce I will dwell at ease...'

4. "Moreover, a bhikkhu reflects thus: 'Right now the people are harmonious, delighting in each other's company, not contentious, mixing together like milk and water, looking on each other with friendly eyes, but there will come a time when danger will arise, there will be revolution in the land, and the village

> folk will take to their carriages and flee. When danger arises, the people flee to safer ground. The monasteries in such places will be crowded and noisy...let me quickly put forth effort...even in times of danger I will dwell at ease...'
>
> 5. "Moreover, a bhikkhu reflects thus: 'Right now the order is harmonious, delighting in each other's company, not given to contention. There is the recitation of the Pāṭimokkha together and the bhikkhus live in comfort. But a time will come when the order is divided. When the order is divided, attending to the Buddha's teaching will be no easy task, and to enter into and live in a secluded dwelling in the forests will not be easy. Enough!... let me quickly put forth effort...Even when the order is divided, I will dwell at ease...'"[107]

The Method of Analysis (*Vibhajjavāda*)

A final method of *yoniso-manasikāra* is "the method of analysis," or *vibhajjavāda*. The term *vibhajjavāda* actually refers to a way of speaking. However, thinking and speaking are closely related. Before speaking there must be thought, and all spoken words are results of thought. In the Buddha's teachings it is said that initial and sustained thought (*vitakka* and *vicāra*) are the forming factors of speech (*vacīsaṅkhāra*).[108] Thus it is possible to speak of *vibhajjavāda* as a kind of thinking, the word *vāda* being synonymous with *diṭṭhi*, theory or view.

Vibhajjavāda is one of the words used to describe the Buddhist system of thought, and the Buddha called himself an advocate of analysis (*vibhajjavādī*).[109]

The word *vibhajjavāda* comes from *vibhajja*, meaning to analyze, to separate, to break down or to classify, and *vāda*, meaning speech or teaching. *Vibhajjavāda* therefore means speaking analytically, or an analytical system of teaching. The important feature of this kind of thinking and speaking is looking at and expressing truth by analysis into all of its different perspectives, rather than focusing only on one aspect, or analyzing only a few of the perspectives and making from that an all-encompassing statement. The opposite of *vibhajjavāda* is *ekaṁsavāda*, "stating only one aspect," making a universal judgment or categorical statement based on only one aspect, side or part of something.

To more clearly understand the meaning of *vibhajjavāda*, we may divide this way of thinking into seven different kinds showing its different features, as follows:

1. Breaking something down according to different aspects of truth, which can be divided into two kinds

First, breaking down according to the different aspects of something as they actually are: that is, looking on or reporting the truth as it actually is according to the context within which it is perceived, rather than making a blanket statement from piecemeal truths or from only one aspect or another of something. This would mean, for example, that when saying a person is good or bad, one points out the truth in accordance with those aspects or perspectives, such as saying that that person is good or bad in that respect, that context, or that situation, rather than making a simple, overall statement. When evaluating, we must stipulate which aspects or perspectives we are talking from and examine each separately, then evaluate on a proportional basis. An example of this kind of analysis is the teachings on the ten kinds of householder (*kāmabhogī*), which will be discussed below.

Second, breaking down by looking at or expressing the truth of something in all its aspects or perspectives: that is, when looking at or examining any condition, one does not look narrowly, fixing on only one part or aspect of it, but looks from many perspectives. For example, in saying something is good or bad, we might say it is good in that respect, that context, or that situation, but bad in that respect, in that context, in that situation. This kind of analytical thinking seems similar to the first kind, but it amplifies the first kind. Examples are the ten kinds of householders and the kinds of forest bhikkhus and city bhikkhus worthy of praise and worthy of censure.

2. Breaking something down into components

Analyzing and breaking down to become aware of the actuality of something as arisen from the coming together of subsidiary components, not getting stuck on externals or being deceived by the overall appearance. For example, breaking a person or being down into mentality (*nāma*) and physicality (*rūpa*), or the five *khandhas*, and breaking each of these down again until one can clearly see that they are not-self. This aspect of *vibhajjavāda* corresponds with the second method of thinking (breaking down into component factors) described above, so it need not be gone into again. In earlier texts, *vibhajjavāda* was not intended to include this sense, but it is included in later texts, so I have included it here.[110]

3. Breaking something down into a sequence of moments

Breaking events down into a series of successive causes and effects on a moment-to-moment basis is another way to see the actual determinants involved. This kind of thinking is an aspect of the methods of breaking down into component factors and breaking down according to causal relationships, but it has its own special features and functions, and therefore is mentioned here as another kind of thinking. It is a method often used in the Abhidhamma.

As an example, if a burglar breaks into a house and kills the owner, many people would say that he had killed out of greed: his desire to steal was the cause for him killing the owner. This statement can only be used as a manner of speaking, but when the actual mental process is analyzed, it is inaccurate. Greed cannot be a cause for killing; only hatred or anger can be a cause for killing. When the sequence of moments is analyzed more carefully we see that the burglar wanted the money, but the owner was an obstacle to obtaining it. Greed for the money was thus a cause for the burglar being angry at the owner, so he killed the owner as a result of that anger. The burglar's greed was for the money, not for the owner. The real cause for the killing was aversion, not greed. Greed was merely the cause for stealing the money, but it was also a determinant for the arising of aversion toward something that obstructed or was not helpful to the gaining of its objective. Even so, in everyday speech we can say that the burglar killed the man out of greed, as long as we are aware and understand the truth of the stages in the process just described, that greed simply initiated the process. This tendency to analyze things in terms of moments in later times led to Buddhism being known as *khaṇikavāda* (the teaching of moments).

4. Breaking something down according to causal relationships
This is delving back along the determinants that come together in a sequential process to produce phenomena, revealing the truth that things are not isolated entities, randomly arisen independent of other things, and they do not have intrinsic entity in themselves, but arise dependent on determinants. They can cease, and will cease, through the cessation of those determinants. This important kind of analysis corresponds with the first method described above, the method of delving into determinants, or thinking in terms of conditionality (*idappaccayatā*), which has not only been covered in the discussion of the first method of thinking, but also explained extensively in the chapter dealing with the *paṭiccasamuppāda*.

5. Conditional analysis
Conditional analysis refers to looking at or expressing the truth via a conditional examination, a kind of *vibhajjavāda* that is very often found. For example, if asked whether a certain person should be associated with, or a certain place frequented, a bhikkhu may answer according to the canon that if that association leads to the growth of unskillful qualities and the decline of skillful qualities, then it should not be done, but if it leads to the growth of skillful qualities and the decline of unskillful qualities, then it should be done.[111] If we were asked whether the Buddha was an advocate of annihilation (*ucchedavāda*), we might answer conditionally, as the Buddha did, that if the term is used in one sense, then he was, but if it is used in another sense, then he was not.[112] Similarly, if asked whether a bhikkhu who lives and travels alone can be said to be practicing according to the Buddha's teaching, we must also give a conditional answer.

6. Breaking down options or alternative possibilities
In practicing toward any goal, the thinker should consider the following in order to break down options or alternative possibilities:

1. There may be many paths, methods or possibilities.
2. Among those paths, methods, or possibilities, some may be better and more efficacious than others.
3. Among those many possibilities, some may be more suitable or beneficial for some people or in some situations than others.
4. There may be one or more options or possibilities that are not really options—that is, they are not options or possibilities as you understand them.

Considering like this is beneficial in many ways. For example, it causes us not to just agree to and get trapped in practices or ideas that are unproductive, wrong, or inappropriate, and therefore become discouraged and give up the practice when something proves unsuccessful. Most important, it enables us to search for and find more appropriate and direct methods or options that give the best results.

An example of this kind of thinking can be seen in the Buddha's own life, when he experimented with ascetic practices, which were held to be the ideal at that time, to the limit of his abilities, and found them to be unproductive. Instead of getting stuck and giving up hope, he deduced that it was not the correct path leading to the goal, and considered further, as shown in the Buddhavacana:

> "I have not attained the direct knowledge and vision of the noble ones, the superhuman knowledge through these harsh ascetic practices"[113]

Having reflected in this way, he reflected further and discovered the Middle Way, and followed that practice until he eventually gained enlightenment.

7. *Vibhajjavāda* as a way of answering questions

Vibhajjavāda appears often in the form of answers to questions and is classed as one of the four ways of answering questions (*pañhābyākaraṇa*):

1. *Ekaṁsabyākaraṇa*: answering from one perspective with one categorical answer
2. *Vibhajjabyākaraṇa*: answering by analysis
3. *Paṭipucchābyākaraṇa*: answering with a counterquestion
4. *Ṭhapana*: setting aside or putting away the question; not answering it

These four ways of answering are classed according to the different kinds of questions. Here are examples of them as given in some of the later texts:[114]

1. *Ekaṁsabyākaraṇīyapañhā*: questions that should be answered categorically, such as "Is the eye impermanent?" which can be answered quite definitely, "Yes."
2. *Vibhajjabyākaraṇīyapañhā*: questions requiring analysis or breaking down. For example, "Is that which is impermanent the eye?" The answer should be broken down, thus, "Not only eye, but ear, nose, and so on, are also impermanent."
3. *Paṭipucchābyākaraṇīyapañhā*: questions that should be answered with a counterquestion, such as "As is the eye, so is the ear; as is the ear, so is the eye: is this so?" This should be countered with "In what way do you mean this? If you mean that they both perform the function of seeing, then the answer is 'no,' but if you mean they are both impermanent, then the answer is 'yes.'"
4. *Ṭhapanīyapañhā*: questions that should be shut down, put away, not answered, such as "Are the soul and the body one and the same thing?" This question should be cut off, not answered.

In essence, the first kind of question is one that has no special perspectives to be explained or hidden catches, and therefore it can be immediately answered quite definitely. Another example of this kind of question is "Do all people have to die?" which can be immediately answered, "Yes." The second kind of question is one that contains perspectives requiring some explanation using the various methods of analysis already discussed. For the third kind of question, a counterquestion should be posed in order to clarify the issue. This method may be used in conjunction with the second kind of answer with *vibhajjabyākaraṇa* questions. In the Tipiṭaka the Buddha is recorded using this method often, and he was able, through his counterquestions, to lead the questioners to better understand the question, or help them to answer their own question, the Buddha merely suggesting lines of investigation.

The fourth kind of question, which should be suppressed and not answered, comprises worthless questions void of any meaning such as "turtle's beard" or "rabbit horns" questions, questions the questioner is not yet capable of understanding, which were suppressed, and another matter explained as a way of preparing the listener's understanding before continuing the discussion, or leaving the listener to form his or her own understanding. On a deeper level are questions that are wrongly asked, based on a misunderstanding, not in accordance with reality, or having no basis in reality.[115] Canonical examples are "Who makes contact (*phassa*), whose contact, or to whom does contact belong? Who experiences the object, whose feeling is it?" which cannot be answered in a way that will satisfy the questioner, and therefore must be suppressed or put away. The reason for not answering may be given,[116] or the questioner may be asked to rephrase the question in accordance with the way things are.[117]

Following are some excerpts from the canon giving examples of *vibhajjavāda*:

> "Bhikkhus, robes I say are of two kinds: those that should be made use of and those that should not be made use of. On account of what do I say this? Any robe of which a bhikkhu knows that when used, unskillful qualities will increase and skillful qualities will decline, that robe should not be made use of. Any robe of which a bhikkhu knows that when used, skillful qualities will increase and unskillful qualities will decline, that robe should be made use of...

"Bhikkhus, alms food...dwelling places...villages and public places...localities...people I say are of two kinds: those that should be made use of and those that should not be made use of..."[118]

The Buddha: "Ānanda! Moral observances (*sīlavatta*), undertaking difficult practices, the holy life and reverential offerings—are they all of benefit?"

Ānanda: "Revered Sir, as to this, it is not possible to answer definitely one way or the other."

The Buddha: "If that is so, then break it down."

Ānanda: "In whatever kind of moral observance, ascetic practice, holy life or reverential offering unskillful qualities come to growth and skillful qualities decline, such moral observance, ascetic practice, holy life or reverential offering is of no fruit. In whatever kind of moral observance, ascetic practice, holy life or reverential offering skillful qualities come to growth and unskillful qualities decline, such moral observance, ascetic practice, holy life or reverential offering is of fruit."[119]

The Buddha approved of Ānanda's answer.

The Buddha divided householders (*kāmabhogī*; literally, "those who partake of sense pleasures") into ten groups, with their respective good aspects and bad aspects, as follows (divided into four goups, including one special group):

Group 1: Seeking in Wrongful Ways

1. One kind of person seeks wealth in wrongful ways. Having obtained wealth, he does not support himself comfortably, nor does he share it with others or use it for good works—censurable on three counts.
2. One kind of person seeks wealth in wrongful ways. Having obtained wealth, he supports himself comfortably, but he does not share it with others or use it for good works—censurable on two counts, praiseworthy on one.
3. One kind of person seeks wealth in wrongful ways. Having

obtained wealth, he supports himself comfortably and shares it with others and uses it for good works—censurable on one count, praiseworthy on two.

Group 2: Seeking in Ways That Are Both Right and Wrong

4. One kind of person seeks wealth in ways that are partly right, partly wrong. Having obtained wealth, he does not support himself comfortably, nor does he share it with others or use it for good works—censurable on three counts, praiseworthy on one.
5. One kind of person seeks wealth in ways that are partly right, partly wrong. Having obtained wealth, he supports himself comfortably, but he does not share it with others or use it for good works—censurable on two counts, praiseworthy on two.
6. One kind of person seeks wealth in ways that are partly right, partly wrong. Having obtained wealth, he supports himself comfortably, shares it with others, and uses it for good works—censurable on one count, praiseworthy on three.

Group 3: Seeking in Rightful Ways

7. One kind of person seeks wealth in rightful ways. Having obtained wealth, he does not support himself comfortably, nor does he share it with others or use it for good works—censurable on two counts, praiseworthy on one.
8. One kind of person seeks wealth in rightful ways. Having obtained wealth, he supports himself comfortably, but he does not share it with others or use it for good works—censurable on one count, praiseworthy on two.
9. One kind of person seeks wealth in rightful ways. Having obtained wealth, he supports himself comfortably, shares it with others and uses it for good works. But he is still attached to and deluded by his wealth; he uses it oblivious of its harm and does not have the wisdom that would free him and make him master over his wealth—praiseworthy on three counts, censurable on one.

Special Group: Seeking Rightfully and Using Wealth Mindfully with a Mind Detached

10. One kind of person seeks wealth in rightful ways. Having obtained wealth, he supports himself comfortably and also shares it with others and uses it for good works. He is not attached to or deluded by his wealth, but uses it heedfully, seeing its benefit and its harm, its merits and its demerits, and has the wisdom that frees him and makes him master over his wealth. He is the most excellent and highest of householders, praiseworthy on four counts.[120]

This kind of *vibhajjavāda* thinking makes the examination of things clear according to the truth and to the extent of the truth, so that things are not confused. A simple example in everyday life is the statement "She is a candid person; she is outspoken and speaks bluntly; she can't speak nicely." In this appraisal, the characteristic of being candid is thrown in together with the characteristics of bluntness and speaking badly. If we were to analyze the statement according to the method of *vibhajjavāda*, the quality of being candid is an asset of that person, while her offensiveness and speaking badly are faults. One who has the asset of straightforwardness must also accept one's failings in the direction of speaking badly; the two qualities should not be put together as one.

The *vibhajjavāda* presented in these canonical passages prompts the further consideration that a selection of short passages from the Tipiṭaka to support views on the Buddha's teachings can sometimes give the reader only a partial, incomplete impression of the teaching, and lead to a mistaken understanding of it. Teachers of Buddhism should be careful in their selection of Buddhist texts, knowing how to choose teachings that illustrate the broad, general principles of Buddhism. Any teaching that illustrates the teaching only from a particular perspective, angle or situation, or is conditional, should be presented together with other perspectives to show the complete picture, or the cases and provisions that apply should be given so that readers obtain an accurate impression of Buddhism.

Summary

In this presentation of the methods of *yoniso-manasikāra*, I have tried to preserve the original format appearing in the Buddhist texts, but the student should not merely attach to the forms or words but strive to grasp the essential meaning. It should also be stressed that *yoniso-manasikāra* is a practical teaching that can be used at all times. It shouldn't be saved for use when you have something to sit down and think about, or practiced only when you can be alone to reflect. It should rather be incorporated into our everyday lives, at all times and all places, beginning with adopting an attitude to the people and events we come into contact with, establishing an approach to thinking and examining whenever we cognize an experience, so as not to cause suffering, create problems or harm, but instead lead to benefit and happiness both for oneself and for others, for the growth and development of wisdom and skillful qualities, for the strengthening of good character and virtues, for knowledge of the truth, for self-training in a way that leads to transcendence and liberation.

From the discussion so far, all of the methods of *yoniso-manasikāra* can be summarized into two main varieties:

1. *Yoniso-manasikāra* for instilling wisdom: it aims at developing knowledge of the reality, focusing on the elimination of ignorance. It is insight (*vipassanā*). Its characteristic is that of shining a light into darkness or cleaning up something that is dirty. Its result is not limited in time and is absolute, leading to transcendent right view.
2. *Yoniso-manasikāra* for improving mental health: it aims at arousing other skillful qualities, focusing on the interception or suppression of desire. It is calm (*samatha*). Its characteristic is enhancing the power of the good and suppressing or hiding away the bad. Its result is dependent on time, temporal; it is a preparation and creation of good habits, leading to mundane right view.

In essence, for most people, with wisdom still weak, it is necessary to rely on teachings and encouragement from others. Their development of wisdom can be said to begin with external factors, having good friends to instill faith. From there, it proceeds to the level of internal factors, beginning with the application of the understanding obtained through faith as a foundation for independent thinking through *yoniso-manasikāra*. This in turn leads to right view and the further development of wisdom, until it ultimately becomes direct knowledge and vision of reality (*ñāṇadassana*).[121]

CHAPTER 8

The Wisdom Factors of the Middle Way

Right View and Right Thought

As already stated, Buddhism looks on ethics from the perspective of making use of the laws of nature, or putting the laws of nature to use in a way that is to our benefit. Therefore, the correct conduct is a life lived with a thorough knowledge of the principles of nature, practicing in such a way as to influence and build various factors to create a beneficial result, as can be seen in the teachings on the law of *kamma*.

In this sense, if we were to use Dhamma terminology, we can see that the important principles of conduct (*cariya*) can be divided into three stages, as follows:

First stage: understanding the truth of the natural laws, being wise to the principle that all things fare according to determinants.

Second stage: putting that knowledge to use—that is, practicing in conformity with the norm or natural laws using actions that cause the factors to proceed in a beneficial way.

Third stage: having acted correctly in terms of the determinants, allowing those determinants to proceed as per the norm or natural laws, with a free mind, looking on with awareness and not attaching oneself to it.

According to these principles, knowledge and understanding are the core factors of practice, which must always be used from beginning to end. Simply speaking, we can call this way of conduct living with wisdom, and call those who have this way of conduct sages (*paṇḍita*), meaning those who live with wisdom.

Because wisdom needs to be used right from the outset, the way of conduct known as the path (*magga*), or Middle Way, thus has right view (*sammādiṭṭhi*) as its first factor.

Right View

The most commonly found definition of right view is knowledge of the four noble truths, as in the following Buddhavacana:

> "What, bhikkhus, is right view? Knowing suffering, knowing the cause of suffering, knowing the cessation of suffering, knowing the practice leading to the cessation of suffering: this is right view."[1]

Right view is also defined as knowing the unskillful and the skillful, seeing the three characteristics, and seeing the *paṭiccasamuppāda*:

> "When a noble disciple clearly knows the unskillful...the roots of the unskillful...the skillful...and the roots of the skillful, on account of this he is said to have right view, to have straight view, to be endowed with unshakable faith in the Dhamma and to have penetrated this true teaching."[2]
>
> ———
>
> "A bhikkhu sees form...feeling...perception...volitional formations...consciousness, which are impermanent as impermanent. Such seeing by him is right view. Seeing rightly, he is disenchanted. Being no longer enamored he is no longer captivated; being no longer captivated he is no longer enamored; being no longer enamored and captivated, his mind is liberated, and has completely transcended."[3]
>
> ———

> "A bhikkhu sees eye...ear...nose...tongue...body...mind... forms...sounds...smells...tastes...tangibles...mind objects which are impermanent as impermanent. Such seeing by him is called right view..."[4]

> "Whoever sees the *paṭiccasamuppāda* sees the Dhamma; whoever sees the Dhamma sees the *paṭiccasamuppāda*."[5]

> "Truly, bhikkhus, a learned noble disciple has direct knowledge for himself, without having to believe others, that 'When there is this, then there is that; with the arising of this, that arises...'"[6]

In the following Buddhavacana right view is divided into two levels, that which contains outflows (*āsava*) and that which is transcendent:

> "Bhikkhus, what is right view? I say that right view is of two kinds: the right view that still has outflows, which is classed as meritorious, and brings *kamma* results on the *khandhas*, and the right view that is noble (*ariya*), without outflows, transcendent, a factor of the path.
>
> "And what is the right view that still has outflows, which is classed as meritorious, and brings *kamma* results on the *khandhas*? It is view that offerings bear fruit; the practice of generosity bears fruit; worship bears fruit; good and evil deeds done bear fruit; there is this world; there is a next world; there is mother; there is father; there are spontaneously arisen beings; there are recluses and brahmins who practice well, who declare clearly this world and the next through their own super knowledge. This is the right view that still has outflows, which is classed as meritorious, and brings *kamma* results on the *khandhas*.
>
> "And what is the right view that is noble, without outflows, transcendent, a factor of the path? It is the path factor of right view, which is wisdom, the faculty of wisdom (*paññindriya*), the power of wisdom (*paññābala*), the investigation of *dhammas* enlightenment factor (*bojjhaṅga*), of one whose mind is noble,

whose mind is without outflows, who has converged in the noble path (*maggasamaṅgi*), who is maintaining the noble path. This is the right view that is noble, without outflows, transcendent, a factor of the path."[7]

The Importance of Right View

"Bhikkhus, just as the light of dawn is the precursor, the herald, of the rising of the sun, so is right view the precursor, the herald of enlightenment to the four noble truths. Of a bhikkhu who is endowed with right view it can be expected that he will see, as it is, that suffering is like this...the cause of suffering is like this...the cessation of suffering is like this...the way leading to the cessation of suffering is like this."[8]

"Bhikkhus, of the factors of the path, right view is the leader. And how is right view the leader? It is through right view that one knows wrong view as wrong view and knows right view as right view; knows wrong thought as wrong thought and right thought as right thought; knows wrong speech...right speech; knows wrong action...right action;..."[9]

"And how, bhikkhus, is right view the leader? With right view, thinking can be right; with right thinking, speech can be right; with right speech, action can be right; with right action, livelihood can be right; with right livelihood, effort can be right; with right effort, mindfulness can be right; with right mindfulness, concentration can be right; with right concentration, direct knowledge can be right; with right direct knowledge, liberation can be right. In this way, the learner (*sekha*) who is endowed with eight factors becomes an arahant endowed with ten factors."[10]

"I see no other factor that is so much a cause for the arising of skillful qualities as yet unarisen, or for the increase and fulfillment of skillful qualities already arisen, as right view."[11]

Salient Features of Right View

The Pali word *diṭṭhi* translates as "view." It includes beliefs, doctrines, theories, rational beliefs, points that accord with one's own beliefs, principles one agrees with, compatible ideas, ideas upheld, preferences, or—as we would say nowadays—values, and even ideals, world- and life- outlooks, and fundamental attitudes derived from those views, understandings, and preferences.[12] If we were to divide *diṭṭhi* into groups, there would be two kinds: views and beliefs in relation to values—as in good and bad, should and shouldn't—and views and beliefs about the truth—as in what is it, how is it, for what reason, and so on, as in the two kinds of right view.

Views, understandings, and preferences have an overwhelming influence on, and play a major role in determining, people's ways of life and the nature of human society. In the ten courses of action (*kammapatha*), view is included as one of the mental deeds (*manokamma*), which is an important kind of *kamma* with more far-reaching and significant effects than bodily or verbal *kamma*,[13] because it is the covert creator of those other kinds of *kamma*. It is capable of guiding lives, society, or the entire human race to growth, prosperity, and liberation or guiding them to decline and destruction.

This capacity can be seen in the life of the individual: view is the driving and determining factor of the way of life, both in terms of receiving and in terms of expressing—that is, how life and the world are perceived, and how they are responded to—beginning with the way new experiences are interpreted, how they are evaluated and decided upon—and then instigating approaches in thought, speech, and actions in response to those experiences. Briefly, in Buddhist terms, views condition and lead the various factors of the path, starting from *sammāsaṅkappa*, right thought or aspiration, to be either wrong or right.

In practice, the importance of views is not hard to see: when people favor wealth and hold the view that abundance of material things is the goal of life, the gauge of personal success, and a source of pride, they will naturally struggle and strive to seek an abundance of material wealth, and all their study and labor will be to this end. When they look at others, they will assess and evaluate them on the basis of the amount of wealth they have. If they lack a predilection for virtuous conduct, moreover, they will search for wealth with no interest in whether the methods they use are honest or not, and they will look on honest but poor people as fools, simpletons or non-entities. If children see the possession of power as an accomplishment or virtue, they will tend to throw their weight around, act tough, and bully others. If people believe that there are no such things as good and evil, that they are merely words used to scare people into doing good, they will not devote themselves to the things said to be good or be heedful nor restrain themselves in regard to the things said to be bad. When people do not fully understand the nature of life and the world as naturally impermanent and unstable, they will naturally be extremely attached to life, to their bodies, to their wealth, and to the people around them, and this will lead to insecurity, fear, and actions and behavior that reflect the suffering resulting from that clinging, insecurity, and fear. On the positive side, with right view the effects should be understood as just the opposite.

Wrong view is called *micchādiṭṭhi*, while right view is called *sammādiṭṭhi*. We have already seen that the factors that condition wrong view are detrimental social surroundings (bad *paratoghosa*), particularly bad friends (*pāpamitta*), and unwise attention (*ayoniso-manasikāra*). The conditioning factors of right view are wholesome *paratoghosa*, benign formulating influences from the social environment, especially good friends (*kalyāṇamitta*), and wise attention (*yoniso-manasikāra*). In the following discussion I will address mainly right view, dealing with wrong view intermittently.

Right view can be divided into two kinds or levels: mundane right view and transcendent right view.

Mundane Right View

Lokiyasammādiṭṭhi is right view on the mundane level—that is, still connected to the world and subject to the world. It is view, belief, or understanding in relation to the world and life that is right according to the principles of goodness, that accords with the Dhamma, or that is compatible with morality (*sīladhamma*), as shown in the Buddhavacana cited earlier.

Generally, this kind of right view arises from external or social factors, with faith the connecting or driving force.[14] It arises especially from the formulating influences of society, such as moral teachings and cultural transmission. Even when it is related to *yoniso-manasikāra*, it tends to be *yoniso-manasikāra* for rousing the skillful (rather than *yoniso-manasikāra* on the way things are). Views on this level are related to values such as good and evil, right and wrong, better and worse, should and shouldn't, up to and including all principles of belief and views that serve to preserve such wholesome values.

Because this kind of view arises from the formulating social influences and is transmitted via external influences, it comes in the form of human-made principles, regulations, standards, and beliefs. They are supplementary to, or separate from, the normal laws of nature, and as such are said to be mundane: they are subject to variation according to time and place, and they can change according to social influences and events.

Favored ideas, preferences, and values are all included under mundane views. However, even though the finer details of this kind of view may vary and change in accordance with locality and occasion, there is a central principle by which a view can be gauged as right: its conformity with the law of *kamma*. The law of *kamma* is a principle or truth that underlies all human behavior. In this respect, mundane right view is supported by natural laws, or conforms with the truths of nature, and for this reason it is sometimes defined more specifically as *kammassakatañāṇa*:[15] the knowledge that life proceeds according to the law of *kamma*—or in other words, the knowledge or belief that human behavior and its results proceed according to the natural law of the causal relationship of determinants.

Mundane right view thus points to a number of fundamental values, such as responsibility for personal actions, aspiring to achievements through one's own actions, efforts, abilities, and intelligence, being self-reliant, and being mutually helpful via human effort. Note also that knowledge of *kamma* on this level is simply a belief that accords with the law of *kamma*. It is not yet true knowledge or understanding of that law or direct penetration into the causal process, because knowledge that directly penetrates the law or the determinants is classed as the transcendent kind of right view, which will be described next.

In addition, mundane right view can be described in other ways, such as view that leads to benefit and happiness in life and society, or view that causes advancement along the path, affecting the other factors of the path, beginning with its helping to cause the arising of right thought. And because mundane right view is a knowledge and understanding that conforms with the ordinary truths of nature, it can also lead on to transcendent right view.

Transcendent Right View

Lokuttarasammādiṭṭhi, right view on the transcendent level, is proper knowledge and understanding of life and the natural world as they really are, or understanding the reality of nature. Simply speaking, it is understanding nature.

This kind of right view arises from *yoniso-manasikāra*, which is an internal factor. Beneficial external influences (*paratoghosa*) or good friends can help only in inciting the use of *yoniso-manasikāra* for subsequent personal realization, meaning that this level of right view cannot be obtained by merely listening and believing what others say; it must be a direct knowledge of the reality. Nature itself is the point of examination, and for this reason this kind of right view does not come in the form of a principle, regulation, or tenet created or pasted over the norms of nature, and therefore it is free of social conditioning and not subject to changing environmental influences. It is a direct relationship with nature itself, which has the same reality and norms in all times and in all places. In this respect, this kind of right view is transcendent—not subject to time, not limited to occasion. It is a universal kind of understanding, necessary for wisdom and liberation in all times and in all places.

Right view in this second sense is specifically the clear and certain knowledge on the level of noble path and fruit, which makes one a noble one. Even so, that enlightened right view is a continuation of the same kind of right view of the unenlightened being. For this reason, I would like to suggest that this second right view on the level of an unenlightened being be called "transcendent-type right view."[16]

The significance of the transcendent, or transcendent-type, right view is that its effect is much more profound than mundane right view. It is capable of causing profound changes to character on the roots level. Only this kind of right view eliminates defilements (*kilesa*), rather than just suppressing them or covering them over, and leads to true assurance of virtue that does not waver in the face of social values. This is because it sees reality on a level that penetrates the social level. Thus, it does not race around after the conditioned appearances of the social level. This point has an important meaning in an educational sense, because it is a point of consideration in individual development as to how to relate to society and to nature, and how much influence or benefit should be obtained from society and from nature.

As we know, transcendent right view arises from wise attention. Thus wise attention plays an important role in its development, in regard to which it should be reiterated that, for the most part, the conduct of unenlightened beings follows the influences of social values and social conditioning, as in refraining from certain bad acts and conducting oneself in obedience to teachings, hearsay, ideas handed down, or remembered modes of behavior. Whenever the unenlightened being is not under the influence of these values, one is most likely to fall into the power of desire or, as we say nowadays, to follow one's own moods.[17]

Wise attention helps to transcend both the influence of social values and enslavement to desire or personal moods and defilements, leading to independent conduct guided by wisdom. Thus, it may be concluded that whatever an unenlightened being may say or do, if it lacks wise attention it will fall either under the influence of values obtained from outside or desires. Only when there is transcendent right view can people be truly freed from the influence of social conditioning.

When view becomes right view, it is classed as wisdom,[18] even though in its initial stages it is simply a view or belief, because this view or belief accords with the truth. It is based on an understanding in accordance with reality or determinants, and has begun to go beyond the domination of ignorance and desire. From that point on, even though such view or belief may evolve into the clear and true realization known as direct knowledge (*ñāṇa*), it is always known by the original term, right view, in order to show the consistency of its growth or fruition. In this respect, right view has a broad meaning, ranging from views and beliefs that are correct up to knowledge and understanding of reality itself.

Right View and Learning

In terms of learning, it can be said that people begin to learn only when they have right view. Some teachers may approach learning from the outside inward according to the method of the threefold training (*tisikkhā*), taking morality as the beginning and saying that learning begins with good conduct,[19] but this statement does not get to the essence of learning: training on the level of morality is for the purpose of accumulating wholesome character or habits, as a way by which trainable beings can be led to an appreciation of the value of such moral conduct. (This is the sense in which conduct, like other social factors, can condition mental values.) When there is appreciation, understanding, and predilection for goodness—that is, when there is right view—then morality or good conduct can become stable and assured (here, mental values define conduct), and only then can one truly be said to be "one who has learning."

To put it another way, practicing the threefold training, beginning with morality, is for the purpose of nurturing all the factors of the path, beginning with right view, to arise. It is only when the factors of the path, with right view at the lead, arise in a person that that person can be said to have learning, because it is only from that moment on that the factors begin to take their stations and work together. Right view not only makes morality or good conduct truly stable and genuine, but also helps the practice of morality to proceed sincerely, without guile, and is a guarantee that conduct is in conformity with the meaning and objectives of *sīla*, rather than falling into deluded fumbling with rites and observances (*sīlabbata-parāmāsa*) or blind observance. When there is right view, then one can be confident of moral practice, but without right view one cannot be assured of morality.

If we were to define learning (or training) in a more relaxed sense, based on the factors of right view, we might say that training begins when people begin to know how to think (*yoniso-manasikāra*). This definition can be regarded as correct in that it draws things together, because when there is wise attention it can be expected that right view will follow.

It can be seen that even in the practice of morality, only when it is guided by wise attention can conduct be expected to proceed correctly and appropriately, and be such that it has a beneficial objective, by which one can gain understanding, be confident, and have a clear and wholesome mind. For example, in regard to dress and neatness, *yoniso-manasikāra* not only considers the value of dressing in terms of covering the body to protect it from cold and heat and in the interests of decency, but also considers in ways that benefit others and society. For instance, one may have in mind dressing neatly and tidily for the orderliness of the community or society, dressing in a way that is not offensive to others, that is neat and pleasant to the eye, so that one helps to keep the mental state of those one meets wholesome, not stained or defiled, so as to encourage an atmosphere that helps others to have clear minds, inclined to wholesome thoughts. But if we dress in order to show off, to flaunt wealth, to draw attention to ourselves, to belittle others or to incite others to thoughts of lust and attachment, or simply with the thought of pleasing ourselves with no consideration of others' feelings, this becomes unwise attention (*ayoniso-manasikāra*). Unskillful qualities dominate the mind, the mind walls itself in and our conduct in regard to dress is immediately ready to exceed what is balanced and appropriate.

When they think of learning, most people tend to think of studying to acquire the knowledge to make a living, which is a matter of livelihood and lies on the level of morality (*sīla*). Learning that aims solely to create a livelihood with no consideration of whether that livelihood is right or wrong is not condoned by good people anywhere. However, learning that emphasizes the development of right livelihood alone while ignoring the development of right view cannot be called right learning, and is not likely to achieve its objectives, even in terms of right livelihood, because it has not yet become true learning. It may lead to right livelihood only in name, but not in essence, because it is a training of conduct without development of the factors of the path, and as such is superficial and not firmly founded. The proper way is to instill right view as a foundation of right livelihood. Simply speaking, to have people practice morality without an appreciation of its value, or to practice honestly without an appreciation for honesty, is not enough.

There is, for example, the phenomenon of the widespread predilection for dishonesty, where a large number of people believe that achieving success or obtaining wealth in dishonest ways, through deceiving, cheating, dishonesty, and exploitation, is a kind of daring and cleverness. Societies where this attitude prevails may be generally affluent, but they will be full of dishonesty and crime. On the other hand, another society that is generally much poorer may have comparatively little crime; even the poorest people in that society would prefer to beg rather than steal.

The subject under discussion here has a bearing on the relationship between the path and the threefold training, because right view and training in morality are the first factors respectively in these two groups of *dhammas*.

Regarding the conditional relationship between morality and

right view, when people are living together harmoniously and peacefully their minds need not be preoccupied with fear and suspicion. When conduct is good and moral there is no distress and confusion, which allows the mind to become calm and concentrated (*samādhi*). When the mind is calm, resolute, and clear, this state helps thinking to be fluent: whatever one looks at one sees clearly, without bias and with understanding, and wisdom arises. If that wisdom realizes and appreciates the value of good conduct and morality, it is right view. With right view or right understanding, one again speaks, acts, and practices correctly and morally.

It is said that training in morality or conduct can only be called learning (*sikkhā*) when it is capable of leading to right view, at the very least on the level of appreciating the value of morality or having a predilection for goodness. Here I will mention two kinds of moral training that produce such results:

The first of the two is moral training through familiarization and faith (*saddhā*). This method emphasizes form and discipline. It is the organization of environmental factors into a framework for regulating conduct, and "tightening up" the way of life, with routines, for example, to which the practitioner is accustomed and habituated, and at the same time creating and fostering faith by having a good friend, such as a teacher, to instruct and guide the practitioner to see the benefit of that good conduct. The teacher may also act as an example of someone who has such wholesome, inspiring conduct, who has happiness and success in the practice. Through this method, profound appreciation of the value of good conduct, a love of discipline, and a predilection for morality can arise. Even without the presence of a good friend or many examples to follow, if the form and discipline or framework of conduct are such that the practitioner can adapt himself or herself to them and become habituated to them, or receives sufficient results from them to see their benefit, that person will conceive a predilection for the practice and find his or her own reasons for that good conduct, form, and discipline. Having gone beyond the level of practicing according to the framework or the enforced regulation, and arrived at the level of seeing the value and having a predilection for practice for his or her own self, a practitioner arrives at the level of right view and can be considered to have begun training (*sikkhā*), even though it is only a weak degree of mundane right view and not particularly stable, and still capable of turning into practice out of deluded mishandling of rites and observances (*sīlabbataparāmāsa*).

The second method is moral training controlled by wise attention. Here the emphasis is on understanding the meaning of one's practice—that is, practicing with wise attention. According to this method, a good friend such as a teacher can be of help by initially guiding a practitioner's thoughts to a line of investigation and understanding of that kind of conduct, but when it comes to actually doing the practice the student or practitioner must in every instance form his or her own reflections. As an example of this kind of reflection: a person bowing to members of the Saṅgha or showing respect to an elder may bring the mind in line with the correct and wholesome meaning of that action, as in thinking, "I bow in order to train myself to be humble and not stubborn or arrogant"; "I bow to uphold a graceful social form"; "I bow as a symbol of reverence for the teaching that this person represents"; "I bow out of goodwill (*mettā*) and desire for benefit for this person, as an instrument by which this person may maintain himself in the position and standing that are good and proper"; or, at the very least, "I bow as a personal practice, in order to do what is best for me."

As for the bhikkhus, elders, or teachers, who are the receivers of such forms of reverence, they may reflect that being bowed to is an opportunity to survey themselves to see whether they still have the virtue or conduct worthy of such reverence. Or they may reflect, "This person is one who can be taught. Is he or she bowing in the proper way? Here is a chance for me to observe and perhaps give a teaching." Or they may rejoice at that person's virtues, at their knowing how to respect good social forms or revere the Dhamma. They may even reflect, "Well, this is a worldly convention. Whatever is of benefit to the world, let it be done."

A practioner who has brought wise attention into the mind in this way can then be confident of his or her actions, and unskillful thoughts will not dominate the mind. The person doing the bowing, for example, will not have to get caught up in conceited evaluations of relative status such as "What's so good about him that I should bow to him? I'm better than he is, why should I bow to him?" The person receiving the reverence does not have to get caught up in suspicion, aversion, or umbrage with such thoughts as "Why isn't that person paying respect to me?" "Why is that person paying respect to me in such a way?" or fall into delusions with such thoughts as "I am a special being; everyone is bowing to me."

The examples given here are all of wise attention for arousing skillful qualities and developing mundane right view only. It can be seen, however, that the second way of training is more profound than the first, capable of preventing the harmful effect of hidden unskillful qualities arising, which the first method cannot do. It is a practice that carries the assurance of wisdom, leading to the steady increase of right view in conjunction with the development of morality, preventing the practice of morality from becoming the blind kind known as *sīlabbataparāmāsa*.

The way of practice that is truly correct in accordance with the path is the second. If the first method is used in conjunction, the result is likely to be even better, but to use the first method on its own is not considered sufficient to be real learning, because correct learning requires wise attention to create wisdom and bring about right view right from the outset.

When this is done, it is using wise attention in a practical way, which can be applied at all times in daily life, not simply when investigating one's thoughts. Wise attention must be incorporated not just on the level of morality, but also on the levels of concentration and wisdom itself, in order for right view and the other inner factors of the path to become strong and mature.

In summary, the correct way to practice is, externally, practicing the threefold training, and internally, to follow the path. This is the meaning of the statement "a balance between the system of personal training from the outer level, and the system of development of the factors of the path, which are internal."

Looking deeper down to the development of the individual, when considered according to the principles just mentioned, we can see that if people are left to develop on their own according to nature, entirely without any help from social factors, only a few exceptionally gifted beings would be able to use wise attention alone to lead them to a life of the highest good. Conversely, allowing people to develop entirely through the molding of social factors would not be enough to enable them to achieve the highest good. In this respect, it may be said that the following two approaches to human development are mistaken extremes:

1. Development by leaving people to fare freely according to nature
2. Development according to the conditioning and demands of society

Developing according to nature alone is not enough. Development must proceed with an understanding of the reality of nature that will enable us to look on and relate to nature properly and beneficially. Similarly, developing exclusively according to social demands is not enough: there must be development with a comprehension that also allows freedom from the power of social conditioning.

Comprehensive development should involve both nature and society. It may be said of proper personal development that it is done with an understanding that causes one to grow in such a way that is of benefit to society and is at ease with nature, and at the same time is nourished by nature and society for a life that is satisfying, wholesome, and secure.

For even only two people to live together in harmony there must be some restrictions and a willingness to control and constrain behavior. When many people live together, it is necessary to have regulations or agreements as to what behavior is to be avoided, what to be done, when and where, so that things can proceed smoothly and everyone benefits (even within one individual there will be contradicting personal desires, necessitating some kind of personal regulation or discipline to guide one's conduct in a way that is fruitful). For example, many people are driving toward an intersection from all directions: each of them accelerates to get there first, and so they all get stuck and none of them can move. But by agreeing to some kind of intelligent and rational form, all may proceed in safety.

It is for such reasons that a community or society must have order. Over and above the actual order there must be procedures, customs and traditions, culture and social institutions, including arts and sciences handed down from previous generations, all of which give the society its particular structure.

The various factors in society condition it and also condition the individual to have qualities that are compatible with that society. At the same time, however, individuals are factors that condition other factors in society. Society and the individual condition each other. However, since society has a clear structure, it is relatively fixed and definite. This means that the individual tends to be the side that is conditioned by society to serve its interests.

But an individual does not only exist for society. Society is also for the individual, and in fact society is basically there to enable individual lives to proceed well and more beneficially. Looking from this perspective, society is simply one supporting factor, but is not enough to lead human beings to the attainment of a good life. Societies begin with, or arise from, the need for order to allow people to live together in harmony. Once people are living together harmoniously, however, there is something wholesome over and above that which their lives should aspire to. Over and above society is nature, and life will only attain the highest good when it penetrates to nature. This is because in reality nature is the foundation of life, society being merely a fostering component that may either help to bring life closer to nature or alienate it from nature.

Be that as it may, even though society has such a clear and fixed form, it is not always the side that conditions and molds the individual. A person who uses wise attention can transcend the conditioning influence of society. Wise attention enables us to see through society to the timeless truths of nature that lie behind it. With wise attention, we can also transcend the conditioning of society and attain to the higher good, and then turn back to mindfully help shape society.

The point here is that human beings must have order to be able to live together harmoniously. Society must have a code of discipline (*vinaya*) and encourage the individuals within it to have the moral restraint to follow that social discipline. However, order and discipline can become constraints on people's freedom, or may even be tools for enslaving people to the system, if they are simply prohibitions and rules that are blindly followed. On the other hand, the expressions known as "free action" may simply be outward expressions of a mind that is enslaved by defilements and pent-up suffering. It may be called the freedom to express one's enslavement, freedom to be enslaved, or freely allowing people to be slaves.

Conversely, for those whose minds are freed from the domination of defilements and suffering, who have the opportunity and freedom to use their intelligence purely, without hidden agendas—living with wisdom, as it is called—regulations of order and discipline are not necessary, because these people already have order and discipline within them. Even so, they are ready and willing to practice in accordance with any order and discipline that they see are for the common good and the benefit of humanity.

When right view arises, it leads to the objective via the support of various factors as shown in this Buddhavacana:

> "Bhikkhus, right view, supported by five factors, has liberation of mind (*cetovimutti*) and liberation through wisdom (*paññāvimutti*) as its fruit, as its reward. Those five factors are as follows:
>
> 1. "Having good, honest conduct, being disciplined (*sīla*)
> 2. "Learning obtained from hearing, studying, and further instruction (*suta*)
> 3. "Conversation, debate, discussion, exchange of views, inquiry (*sākacchā*)
> 4. "Calm, making the mind calm, having no mental distraction and confusion (*samatha*)

> 5. "Seeing things as they really are, as they are in truth (*vipassanā*)"[20]

In summary, right view is view that accords with reality, seeing things as they really are. For right view to grow requires constant wise attention, which helps to prevent seeing things superficially and instead see things both in terms of their constituent factors and in terms of their causal relationship. It prevents us from being fooled by appearances or becoming puppets roused, prodded, and pulled about by visual, audible, gustatory, olfactory, tangible, and mental phenomena to the extent that problems arise for ourselves and for others. Instead we have mindfulness and comprehension, are free and independent, and think, decide, and act with wisdom.

Right Thought

Sammāsaṅkappa, the second factor of the path, is generally glossed in the texts in this way:

> "Bhikkhus, what is right thought? Thoughts of renunciation (*nekkhammasaṅkappa*), thoughts of non-enmity (*abyāpādasaṅkappa*), thoughts of non-aggression (*avihiṁsāsaṅkappa*). This is right thought."[21]

In addition, there is the definition that divides right thought into the mundane and transcendent levels, thus:

> "Bhikkhus, what is right thought? I say that there are two levels of right thought: the right thought that still has outflows, which is classed as meritorious, and brings *kamma* results to the *khandhas*, and the right thought that is noble, without outflows, transcendent, a factor of the path.
>
> "Right thought that still has outflows... is thoughts of renunciation, thoughts of non-enmity, thoughts of non-aggression...
>
> "Right thought that is noble, without outflows, transcendent, a factor of the path, is that cogitation, deliberation, thought,

> fixing of the mind, resolve, focus, and speech formations (*vacīsaṅkhāra*) of one whose mind is noble, whose mind is without outflows, who has converged with the path (*maggasamaṅgī*), who is maintaining the noble path..."[22]

The following explanation is limited to the general definition of right thought, called the mundane level. According to this definition, right thought is deliberation or thought in the right way, diametrically opposed to the wrong ways of thinking (*micchāsaṅkappa*), of which there are three:

1. *Kāmasaṅkappa*, or *kāmavitakka*: thoughts that revolve around sensuality, thoughts of seeking or indulging in the objects of desire through the five sense doors, or various objects of desire and attachment; selfish thoughts. They are thoughts of passion (*rāga*) or greed (*lobha*).
2. *Byāpādasaṅkappa*, or *byāpādavitakka*: thoughts containing hatred, anger, or resentment; thinking and seeing things negatively, seeing others as enemies, opponents, seeing everything as an affront. It is thoughts of aversion in the passive sense (its opposite being *mettā*).
3. *Vihiṁsāsaṅkappa*, or *vihiṁsāvitakka*: thoughts of hurting, damaging, cutting down, destroying; wanting to hurt others, wanting others to suffer and be miserable. It is thoughts of aversion in the aggressive sense (its opposite being *karuṇā*).

These thoughts or approaches to thought are normal for the majority of people. When an unenlightened person cognizes a sense object, be it through seeing, hearing, or feeling, for example, one of two reactions will usually arise. If the experience is agreeable, they like it, want it, get attached to it, and follow after it; if it is not agreeable, they don't like it, are offended by it, angered by it, and want to push it away. From there, subsequent thoughts will proceed under the influence of that like and dislike. For this reason, the normal thinking of unenlightened beings tends to incline to one direction or another, insidiously pulled along by either likes or dislikes, and this causes them to fail to see things as they actually are. The thoughts that proceed from pleasure and liking lead to conflict, attachment, and attraction, and this becomes *kāmavitakka*; those that proceed from displeasure or dislike, lead to aversion, hatred, hostility, seeing things negatively, and this becomes *byāpādavitakka*; those thoughts that surge outward into aggressiveness, thoughts of hurting and destroying, become *vihiṁsāvitakka*. These three kinds of thinking lead to an incorrect attitude to the things of the world.

These biased kinds of thought arise as a result of lacking wise attention at the outset: looking at things superficially, cognizing objects at their face value, without mindfulness (*sati*) and comprehension (*sampajañña*). Thoughts are left to run as they will after feelings or the rationalizations of like and dislike. There is no analytical reflection on component factors or delving into determinants according to the principles of wise attention (*yoniso-manasikāra*).

In this respect, wrong view is mistaken understanding, not seeing things as they really are, and that causes the arising of wrong thought, a mistaken and distorted thought, deliberation and attitude toward things. This wrong thought in turn reflects back to give rise to increased wrong view. So wrong view and wrong thought reinforce each other.

In order to look at things as they actually are in themselves, wise attention must be employed, which means that at that time, thinking and deliberation must be clear, independent and free of either like, attachment, and involvement, or dislike, repulsion, and hostility. This means that there must be both right view and right thought, and the two must support and reinforce each other.

In other words, by having wise attention one has right view, and sees things according to the truth. When things are seen according to the truth, there is right thought. When there is this kind of impartial[23] thought and deliberation, independent of like and dislike, then things can be seen as they really are, and right view is reinforced and augmented. From there both factors continue to reinforce and influence each other.

In the mind containing wise attention there is clear and independent thinking that is free of bias, either of the kind that attaches and attracts, or the kind that repulses. In opposition to wrong thought (*micchāsaṅkappa*), it is called right thought (*sammāsaṅkappa*), and is also said to be of three kinds:

1. *Nekkhammasaṅkappa* or *nekkhammavitakka*: thoughts that are free of greed and sensual desire, not immersed or caught up in trying to satisfy desires; thoughts that are without selfishness; thoughts of renunciation and all thoughts that are virtuous and skillful.[24] It is classed as thought free of passion (*rāga*) or greed (*lobha*).
2. *Abyāpādasaṅkappa* or *abyāpādavitakka*: thoughts that are free of aversion, resentment, or various kinds of negativity. It particularly focuses on the opposite quality, which is *mettā*—goodwill, friendliness, the desire for others to be happy. It is classed as thought free of aversion (*dosa*).
3. *Avihiṁsāsaṅkappa* or *avihiṁsāvitakka*: thoughts that are free of hurtfulness, thoughts of damaging or destroying. It particularly focuses on the opposite quality, which is *karuṇā*, compassionate thoughts of helping others to be free of suffering. This is also classed as a kind of thinking free of aversion.

Note that in Buddhism, when talking of good or skillful conditions as opposites of unskillful conditions, instead of using an antonym, or opposite term, the same term is often simply phrased in the negative. This causes people to feel that Buddhism is a negative and passive teaching—that simply giving up evil actions and doing nothing is already a virtue. For instance, in this case wrong thought is described as thoughts of enmity, while right thought, instead of being described as thoughts of goodwill, is simply said to be non-enmity, merely negating the wrong quality. The mistake of this understanding will be discussed later, but at this point I would like to briefly offer three arguments for countering these wrong ideas:

1. The path is a practical teaching that aims specifically at a result

in terms of wisdom, and its objective is realization of the truth, not simply to develop ethical values or morality. It must be especially borne in mind that right thought is a wisdom path factor, not a morality factor. Thus, the teaching of right thought, to abstain from thoughts of enmity and to have thoughts of love and goodwill, is not geared only toward making people moral, to refrain from killing and hurting each other and to be helpful to each other, but to train them to have thoughts that do not incline toward hatred, for example, so that thought is lucid and independent, and accords with the truth. In this way, a correct and undistorted understanding of the truth is obtained. In this respect, a negatively constructed definition of right thought as "thinking that is free of greed, without enmity, and without aggression" is in fact the most suitable. This means that when one thinks of something, if one does not side with oneself, and does not think with hatred, aggression, and the intention to destroy, that thinking will be pure and it can be expected that it will be accurate in accord with the truth.

2. From an etymological perspective, Pali words with the negative prefix *a-* do not merely mean "not" that thing but can also mean opposition, or both negation and opposition together. For instance, the word *akusala* does not mean "not skillful" (which technically may include *abyākata*—neutral, neither bad nor good), but actually means the evil that is opposite to *kusala*. The word *amitta* ("non-friend") does not refer to neutral people, those who are not friends (*mitta*), but actual enemies. But in *sammāsaṅkappa*, the prefix *a-*carries a meaning that negates in a broad sense—that is, meaning both that which is diametrically opposed to the condition concerned and also that which is not it. For example, *abyāpādasaṅkappa* means the goodwill (*mettā*) that is opposite to enmity (*byāpāda*), and also pure impartial thoughts that are clear and free of enmity. Thus, positive qualities such as *mettā* are included in this path factor.

3. The negative prefix *a-* not only gives words a broad meaning, but also a firm and absolute one; it is more than simply an opposite, because the use of the negative in this case aims to specify the

utter absence of that thing—the complete absence of any trace of it. For example, *abyāpādasaṅkappa* here refers to thought in which there is no remaining trace of enmity of any description, a perfect goodwill, without boundaries. It emphasizes the absolute level.

From the discussion so far, it may be summarized that in general, when unenlightened beings think of something, they do so in response to desire in some form or other. If their thinking is not in accordance with views, such as a personal value, formed by desire based on ignorance, then it is under the influence of fresh desire arising at that time, which may take the form of wanting, which still goes by the name of desire (*taṇhā*), or in the form of pride and attachment to station, known as *māna*. Thus it is said that the thinking of unenlightened beings contains *ahaṁkāra* ("I-making"), *mamaṁkāra* ("mine-making"), and *mānānusaya* (the conceit "I am"), or in short, their thoughts are connected and manipulated by desire, conceit and views. It would not be wrong to say that the thinking of unenlightened beings is a service rendered by the mind to desire.

The ways thinking in the service of desire manifest can be both positive and negative. On the positive side it manifests as *kāmasaṅkappa*, thinking to obtain, thinking to serve the self. On the negative side it manifests as *byāpādasaṅkappa*, thinking obstructively or in negative ways, thinking as an adversary (afraid others will contend with or oppose one), thinking offensively, unfavorably, hatefully; and *vihiṁsāsaṅkappa*, thinking aggressively and destructively.

Thoughts that serve desire can be countered with wise attention (*yoniso-manasikāra*) on realities.[25] Such thinking has no sensual desire, enmity or aggression, and thus it is pure and in accordance with the truth. It does not incline or veer off to one side, and thus it is thinking that has a broad range. We may define right thought in this sense as "Any thought that is not for the purpose of indulging selfish desires, that is not malicious, and that is not aimed at hurting or harming." This is countering desirous thoughts as a function of wisdom, which directly supports right view.

Alternatively, thoughts that serve desire may be countered by *yoniso-manasikāra* for arousing the skillful. Thoughts that contain this kind of *yoniso-manasikāra* are the opposite kinds of thought to sensuality, enmity, and aggression: altruistic thoughts, thoughts with goodwill, and thoughts with compassion, which bring forth specific kinds of skillful qualities. While right thought in this sense is helpful to right view, it is more directly related to morality, leading directly to right speech, right action, and right livelihood.

It may be represented graphically as in figure 8.1 on page 499.

Note that this kind of classification is not an absolute division but simply a way of showing the results that are predominant in each case. In addition to this, I would like to submit figure 8.2 (see page 499), showing the relationship between right thought and two of the morality factors of the path, right speech and right action, which are the channels through which the divine abidings (*brahma-vihāra*) find practical expression, and also the bases for integration (*saṅgahavatthu*).[26]

There is another noteworthy point regarding the relationship between right view and right thought, and that is that, in terms of the three roots of unskillfulness—greed, hatred, and delusion—right view eliminates the most rudimentary defilement, delusion, whereas right thought eliminates secondary or derivative defilements: *nekkhammasaṅkappa* counters desire or greed, while *abyāpādasaṅkappa* and *avihiṁsāsaṅkappa* counter hatred.

However, progress in merely these two factors of the path is still only the beginning. The development of wisdom has not yet reached the full level that is the goal of practice. In fact, the practice of any one factor of the path alone cannot bring about the consummation of that factor; all factors must grow and be developed in step with each other. Thus, at this point we must understand that of the three aspects of right thought, *nekkhammasaṅkappa* sometimes refers merely to the physical act of going forth (*pabbajā*) as a bhikkhu or bhikkhuni, or going to live in seclusion from household life; *abyāpādasaṅkappa* focuses on the development of goodwill, and *avihiṁsāsaṅkappa* focuses on the development of compassion.

The wisdom arising on this level, while it may be right view and sees things as they are, is not pure or full liberating realization until it reaches the level in which there is equanimity, which requires a foundation of *samādhi*.

Even *mettā* (goodwill), a quality that can be developed right from the very beginning stages of Dhamma practice, is not as simple a quality as its usual superficial understanding would indicate, because the *mettā* that people speak of everywhere is rarely true *mettā*. For that reason, in order to prevent any misunderstandings, a number of elementary points should be first understood.

Mettā means friendliness, love, goodwill, sympathy, and understanding—the predilection or desire to create and foster benefit for all beings, both human and animal.[27] *Mettā* is a universal condition, both from the perspective of those who should have it and from the perspective of those who should receive it. Thus, it should be used both by the poor to the rich, and by the rich to the poor; by people of low standing to people of high standing and by people of high standing to people of low standing; by householders to bhikkhus (Saṅgha) and by bhikkhus to householders. *Mettā* is the fundamental quality of the heart in building human relations, causing people to look at each other in positive ways, to have goodwill toward each other, and to be ready to listen to and reason with each other rather than adhering to selfishness or aversion.

An important observation in regard to *mettā* is its success (*sampatti*) and failure (*vipatti*). The "success" refers to the successful result desired from *mettā*. "Failure" is the failure, or mistaken practice, of *mettā*. According to the teachings, the success of *mettā* is the suppression of enmity (*byāpādupasamo etissā sampatti*),[28] and its failure is the arising of infatuation (*sinehasambhavo vipatti*).[29]

There are no special points for consideration on the success of goodwill, but in terms of its failure there are some important points that need to be borne in mind. *Sineha* means love, desire, and attachment for a particular person—personal affection, such as love for a child or one's partner. *Sineha* can be a cause for bias and helping others in the wrong way, known as *chandāgati* (biased action based on affection). When we hear it said, "He was especially

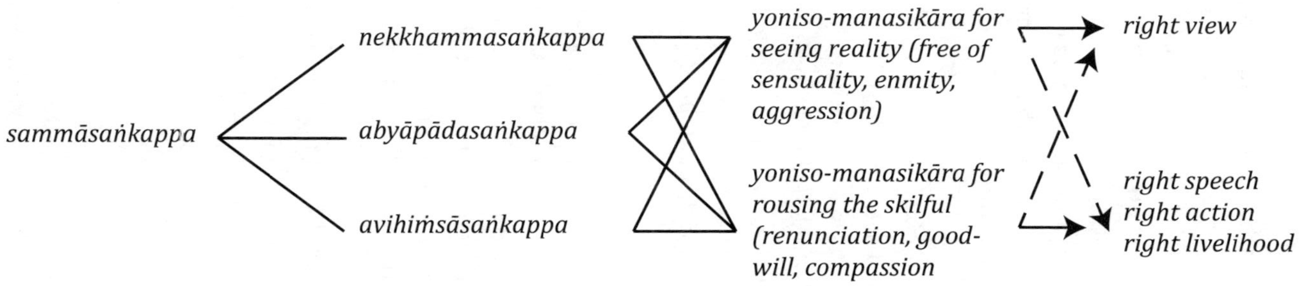

Fig. 8.1. From right thought to right view, right speech, right action, and right livelihood.

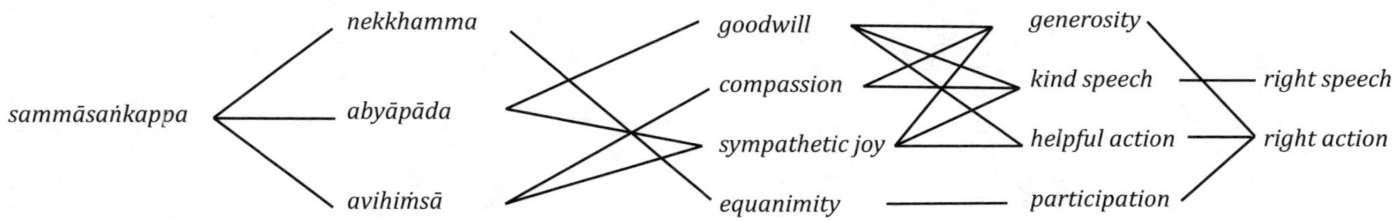

Fig. 8.2. From right thought to right speech and right action.

kind (*mettā*) to me," "The boss was really kind (*mettā*) to her," these are rather examples of affection (*sineha*), which are a failure of *mettā*. True *mettā* is a quality that supports fairness, because it is a neutral quality leading to a state of mind that is free of both selfish impulses to lean toward something and aversion and hostility to destroy it. There is friendliness, a desire for the benefit of all, equally. One considers, judges, and acts on the basis of reason, aiming for true benefit and happiness for all, not just aiming for what one or someone else likes or wants. True *mettā* is like this:

> "The Blessed One has a heart that is equally disposed toward the archer Khamaṅdhanū [who was hired to kill the Buddha], Devadatta [who tried to kill the Buddha and caused a split in the order of bhikkhus], the bandit Aṅgulimāla [who killed many people and even tried to kill the Buddha before he became converted to Buddhism], the elephant Dhanapāla [which was released by Devadatta in the hope of killing the Buddha], and Rāhula [the Buddha's own son]."[30]

The benefit of goodwill can be seen, for example, in an argument or debate. It causes each of the sides to listen to the other's arguments and helps both sides to attain the proper understanding. For example, when one of the Nigaṇṭhas in conversation with the Buddha used harsh speech and reviled the Buddha, the Buddha responded with reasoned speech, moving the Nigaṇṭha to exclaim:

> "In that case, I am inspired by the Revered Gotama. It is true, the Revered Gotama is one who is trained in body and in mind.
>
> "It is marvelous! It is unheard of! Even though the Revered Gotama has been so confronted and harassed by me, his features are still clear, his face is radiant, as is fitting for an arahant, a fully enlightened Buddha."[31]

In the event of wrong thought arising, to correct it with the wisdom method, one must not fall into thoughts that are agitated, scattered, or depressed, but use *yoniso-manasikāra*, delving into the causes of that thinking and reflecting on its benefits and defects, as in this Buddhavacana:

> "Bhikkhus, before the enlightenment, when I was still an unenlightened *bodhisatta*, the following thought arose in me: 'What if I were to divide my thinking into two sides?' Then I put sensual thoughts (*kāmavitakka*), thoughts of enmity (*byāpādavitakka*), and thoughts of aggression (*vihiṁsāvitakka*) on one side, and put thoughts of renunciation, thoughts of non-enmity, and thoughts of non-aggression on the other.
>
> "When I, heedful, ardent, and resolved, experienced sensual thoughts, I knew clearly that 'Sensual thoughts have arisen in me. This sensual thought is harmful to myself, is harmful to others, and is harmful to both myself and others. It stifles wisdom, is an oppression, and does not lead to *nibbāna*.'
>
> "When I reflected that it harmed myself, sensual thought disappeared. When I reflected that it harmed others...that it harmed myself and others...that it stifled wisdom...was an oppression...that it did not lead to *nibbāna*, that sensual thought disappeared. Thus did I relinquish and reduce sensual thoughts that arose, and do away with them.
>
> "When I, heedful...experienced thoughts of enmity... thoughts of aggression...I knew clearly...Thus did I relinquish and reduce all thoughts of enmity...aggression that arose, and eliminate them all.
>
> "Bhikkhus, the more you consider, the more you mull over any particular thought, the more your mind will be inclined to that thought. If a bhikkhu considers and mulls over sensual thoughts, he discards thoughts of renunciation and thinks only sensual thoughts. His mind inclines toward sensual thoughts... If a bhikkhu considers and mulls over thoughts of renunciation, he thereby gives up sensual thoughts and thinks only thoughts of renunciation. His mind will be inclined toward thoughts of renunciation..."[32]

The initial practice of Dhamma according to these first two factors of the path can be summarized in the following Buddhavacana:

> "Bhikkhus, a bhikkhu who possesses four qualities can be said to be one who is maintaining the practice that is not wrong, and to have planted the beginnings of the destruction of the outflows. Those four qualities are thoughts of renunciation, thoughts of non-enmity, thoughts of non-aggression, and right view."[33]

CHAPTER 9

The Morality Factors of the Middle Way

Right Speech, Right Action, and Right Livelihood

Right speech, right action, and right livelihood are all on the level of morality (*sīla*), so they will here be dealt with together. According to evidence in the texts, definitions appear along the lines of the following example:

1. "What, bhikkhus, is right speech? Just this is right speech:
   - *Musāvādā veramaṇī*: intentionally refraining from false speech.
   - *Pisuṇāya vācāya veramaṇī*: intentionally refraining from malicious tale-bearing.
   - *Pharusāya vācāya veramaṇī*: intentionally refraining from coarse speech.
   - *Samphappalāpā veramaṇī*: intentionally refraining from frivolous chatter."
2. "What, bhikkhus, is right action? Just this is right action:
   - *Pāṇātipāta veramaṇī*: intentionally refraining from taking life.
   - *Adinnādānā veramaṇī*: intentionally refraining from taking things not given.
   - *Kāmesumicchācārā veramaṇī*: intentionally refraining from sexual misconduct."

3. "What, bhikkhus, is right livelihood? Just this is right livelihood: A noble disciple gives up wrong livelihood[1] and lives by right livelihood."[2]

In addition, there are definitions that distinguish into the mundane and transcendent levels. The mundane level is defined in the same way as given above. The transcendent level is explained as follows:

1. Right speech that is transcendent: "The ceasing, the refraining, the total abstention, the intention to abstain from the four forms of verbal misconduct by one whose mind is noble, whose mind is free of outflows, in whom the path has converged, who is developing the path."
2. Right action that is transcendent: "The ceasing, the refraining, the total abstention, intentionally abstaining from the three forms of bodily misconduct, by one whose mind is noble..."
3. Right livelihood that is transcendent: "The ceasing, the refraining, the total abstention, intentionally abstaining from wrong livelihood, of one whose mind is noble..."[3]

Sīla as Core Tenets for Basic Conduct

From these main definitions as given by the Buddha, which is the central core of the system of moral training known as the training in higher conduct (*adhisīlasikkhā*), the Buddhadhamma enlarges on the teaching with practices and principles of conduct to produce practical results on the individual and social levels. These begin with teaching a line of conduct that corresponds with these factors of the path, known as the *kammapatha* (courses of action), and the code of basic moral conduct for all people known as the five precepts.

For practical implementation the teachings can be expanded on indefinitely to suit specific people, times, places, and other environmental factors. Here, however, it is sufficient to simply show the central principles to give an overall understanding. As for the various practical applications, these must be left up to each individual to seek out for him- or herself according to character, form of livelihood, and needs.

In regard to the practical application of the teachings, apart from considerations of character, time, place, and specific occasion, the main principle is status or form of livelihood. In this respect, different precepts or systems of practice have been laid down for householders and for renunciants. Students of *sīla* should therefore understand the principles, essential meaning, and, most importantly, objectives, of those precepts, both in terms of practical details, which differ, and the overall, highest level, which is one and the same, before they can be said to have correct understanding and practice.

These morality path factors are broken down into principles of conduct leading to results on the practical level. The following example has corresponding factors and expands on each of the factors of the path, except that it places bodily deeds (*kāyakamma*; corresponding to right action) before verbal deeds (*vacīkamma*; corresponding to right speech). It is known variously as the courses of skillful action (*kusalakammapatha*), types of good conduct (*sucarita*), cleanliness of body and speech (and mind), and the qualities of action. The illustrating story goes:

When the Buddha was staying at the town of Pāvā, in the mango grove of Cunda Kammāraputta, Cunda approached him to discuss the purification rituals (*soceyya kamma*). Cunda stated that he was an adherent of the teaching on the purification rituals of the Pacchābhūmi brahmins, who carried a gourd, wore wreaths of flowers and seaweed, worshipped fire, and observed the ritual of going down to the river. The teaching of these brahmins was that every day in the early morning, on rising from one's bed, one was to touch the earth. If one did not touch the earth, one was to touch fresh cow dung, or green grass, or worship the fire, or raise one's hands in salutation to the sun, or, failing that, to go down to the water a full three times in the evening.[4]

The Buddha answered that while the methods for purification stipulated by these brahmins was one way of purification, purification in the noble discipline was different. He went on to say that one who was endowed with the ten courses of unskillful action (killing living beings, stealing, sexual misconduct, lying, malicious tale-bearing, abusive speech, frivolous speech, harboring greed, enmity, and wrong view) had impurities in body, in speech, and in mind. Whether such a person, arising early in the morning, were to touch the earth or not, to touch cow dung or not, to worship the fire or salute the sun or not, that person was still impure, because the courses of unskillful actions are impure in themselves and also are causes for impurity. Then the Buddha taught the ten courses of purifying skillful action, grouped as three purifiers of the body, four purifiers of speech, and three purifiers of the mind.

The three purifiers of the body are as follows:

1. Totally abstaining from taking life (*pāṇātipāta*), laying down the rod, laying down the weapon, being possessed of shame, possessed of goodwill, disposed to helping all beings.
2. Totally abstaining from taking things not given (*adinnādānā*), not taking any possession or object belonging to another, be it in the town or in the forest, which the owner has not given, with the action of a thief.
3. Totally abstaining from sexual misconduct (*kāmesumicchācārā*), not violating women under the protection, for example, of their mothers, under the protection of their fathers, under the protection of their older or younger brothers, under the protection of their older and younger sisters, under the protection of relatives, under the protection of *dhamma* (protected by law, for example), or women who are married or who are off-limits,[5] including those who are engaged.

The four purifiers of speech have the following requirements:

1. Totally abstaining from false speech (*musāvāda*): when, in a council, at a meeting, among a circle of relatives, in an assembly, or in the presence of the royal family, if someone is called to witness with the invitation, "Please, sir, tell us what you know,"

not knowing, he says he does not know; not having seen, he says he did not see; knowing, he says he knows; having seen, he says he saw. Such practitioners are not intentional speakers of falsehood, either on their own account, on the account of others, or on account of any material gain whatsoever.

2. Totally abstaining from malicious tale-bearing (*pisuṇāvācā*). Such practitioners are not the kind to listen to this person's words and then inform that person in order to hurt this person, or to listen to that person's words and then inform this person in order to hurt that person. They are conciliators of the discordant; they encourage harmony, they like harmony, they delight in harmony, they are content with harmony, and they like to speak words that are conducive to harmony.
3. Totally abstaining from coarse speech (*pharusavācā*), speaking only speech that is not harmful, is pleasant to the ear, endearing, engaging, polite, pleasing to the many, praised by the many.
4. Totally abstaining from frivolous speech (*samphappalāpā*), speaking at the right time, speaking the truth, speaking meaningfully (*attha*), speaking with principle (*dhamma*), speaking with discipline (*vinaya*). They say things that are well founded, authenticated, within reason, and useful at the appropriate time.

Finally, the three purifiers of the mind consist of non-covetousness (*anabhijjhā*), non-enmity (*abyāpāda*), and right view (*sammādiṭṭhi*). These three factors are gleaned from the first two factors of the path, right view and right thought, so the passages dealing with them are not discussed here.

> "If one who is endowed with these ten courses of skillful action, having arisen in the morning, touches the earth, one is pure; if one does not touch the earth, one is pure...if one raises one's hands in salutation to the sun one is pure, and if one does not raise one's hands in salutation to the sun, one is pure...because these ten courses of skillful action are in themselves pure and conducive to purity..."[6]

I would like to give an example of how the meaning of *sīla* in practical form may differ in accordance with different situations. When talking of a man who has gone forth as a Buddhist bhikkhu, not only are some of the precepts changed and others added, but some of those precepts that are held in common are also interpreted differently. Compare the abstention from stealing (*adinnādānā*) and lying (*musāvādā*) described below for bhikkhus with the ones given in the ten courses of skillful action give above:

> "He gives up *adinnādānā*, totally abstaining from taking things that are not given, taking only those things that are given, aspiring only to those things that are given. He is not a thief; he is pure."
>
> ---
>
> "He gives up *musāvādā*, totally abstaining from false speech, speaking only the truth, maintaining truth. He is honest, trustworthy, and does not deceive the world."[7]

An important observation to be made here is that the expanded explanations of these morality path factors usually come in two parts, the first part dealing with abstention from bad actions, and the second dealing with performance of the good actions. In brief, the beginning part is in negative form ("abstaining from taking things not given"), while the second part is in positive form ("taking only what is given"). This is a general characteristic of Buddhist teachings, which tend to use paired instructions containing both negative and positive statements together, as in the principle "Give up evil, practice the good." Taking the giving up of evil as the starting point, the continued cultivation of the good can be expanded on indefinitely, and is not limited to the examples given in the explanations of the factors of the path. For example, in the precept of abstaining from taken what is not given, the explanation of the practice of the cultivational aspect is not expanded upon, but there are already clear teachings on giving (*dāna*), which is one of Buddhism's core teachings.

Theistic and Natural-Order Forms of *Sīla*

Some Western scholars have criticized Buddhism as being negative, a teaching that aims only for the renunciation of evil actions but not encouraging Buddhists to make any effort with cultivating goodness (positive). Some see Buddhist teachings as subjective, "an ethic of thoughts," a reclusive and passive teaching, making Buddhists content with simply giving up evil actions and being careful to avoid situations that might lead to "sin," and not taking any interest in helping other people through dedicated action to free them from suffering and create true benefit and happiness.

These scholars state that even in teaching goodwill (*mettā*) and compassion (*karuṇā*), Buddhism merely supports the mental activity of establishing an attitude of goodwill and spreading it outward. They cite sections of the Tipiṭaka to support their view, such as the following definition of the right action factor of the path (the cited passage is of Venerable Sāriputta):

> "And what, Revered Sirs, is right action? Giving up killing, giving up taking what is not given, giving up sexual misconduct. This, Revered Sirs, is right action."[8]

Students who understand the practical meaning of these path factors as explained so far will immediately see that if the writers of these criticisms were acting with good intentions, then their conclusions must have been based on an incomplete understanding of Buddhism. It can clearly be seen that the system of morality in the path is not merely negative, passive, subjective, or an ethic of thoughts.

The reasons that the definitions of the morality path factors are presented in a negative form can be briefly stated in eight points as follows:

1. Morality as part of the Buddhadhamma is not divine commandment laid down to force followers to practice a certain way out of blind faith. In Buddhism, morality is formulated according to the

natural principle of cause and effect, within which the practitioner must see the system of interconnected relationship. Even though he or she may not yet have true realization, only faith (*saddhā*), that faith must be rooted in understanding (*ākāravatīsaddhā*), in which there is enough initial rational understanding to serve as a base for the subsequent cultivation of wisdom and clear knowledge.

2. Considering the process of Dhamma practice or self-development in terms of an increasingly refined graduated system, it must begin with abandoning or eliminating bad actions before proceeding on to the perfection of the good, and thence ultimately to purity and liberation. It is like planting a garden: at first the earth must be cleared, eliminating those things that are harmful (such as weeds, rocks, and snails). Then the plants are sown and tended until they give the desired fruit.

In the Buddhist system, morality is the most elementary level of practice. It focuses on basic conduct, and therefore it emphasizes giving up various kinds of bad actions as the starting point. It reiterates and clarifies what must be eliminated. This is expanded on with higher levels of cultivating goodness through further practice in the progressively higher levels of *samādhi* and wisdom.

3. Within the system of the threefold training, morality is not in itself a practice for reaching the ultimate objective but is simply a means to reach the next level, which is concentration (*samādhi*). Concentration is therefore the immediate objective of morality. In this respect the mental aspect of morality is important. The mental aspect of morality is the intention to refrain from, or absence of any thoughts to do, a bad action of any kind, which renders the mind pure and clear, untroubled by confusion or worry. Thus, the mind is easily calmed and concentrated. When the mind is calm and concentrated (*samādhi*), fluency arises in the use of wisdom, rational thought, and the search for more effective ways to create the good.

4. Buddhism holds that the mind is of utmost importance. Its system of conduct must therefore always involve an interaction between the mind and external expressions of action and speech. Holding the mind to be the starting point, intention is the funda-

mental principle for ensuring that the development of good actions proceeds with assured sincerity—it is not simply not deceiving others, but also not deceiving oneself, eliminating the chances for mental problems arising from contradictions in conduct.

5. The path factors of morality teach us that the most fundamental level of personal responsibility is toward oneself, by ensuring that no thoughts of harming or exploiting others exist in the mind. With this initial support of purity, responsibility expands outward to the level of maintaining and promoting the growth of personal virtue, by making an effort with good actions, and creating benefit and happiness for others. In short, it is to have responsibility to oneself in giving up bad actions, and have responsibility to others in doing good things for them.

6. To define moral training as the abandoning of bad actions is to give the practice the broadest possible scope, by focusing on bad actions and emphasizing an intention that harbors not even a trace of evil. As for goodness, it is something that can be expanded on indefinitely, thus it is not specified. And in fact, goodness is an infinitely broad subject, its particulars and methods varying greatly according to place and time. The evil that must be refrained from is fixed and definite. For example, both the monastic order and householders are required to give up lying, but the ways in which they can accomplish the virtue that is void of false speech are different. Thus, in establishing the principle, the abandoning of evil actions is the standard. As for the particulars and methods of practice on the level of practicing goodness, these are practical affairs to be determined in conformity with the situation, time and way of life of each individual.

7. The practice of all the factors of the path is considered essential for attaining the Buddhist objective. Thus, each of the path factors must be a central principle that all people can practice, regardless of status, time, locality, or environment. Accordingly, we can see a direct relationship on the level of *sīla*: refraining from stealing, for instance, is a practice that all people can observe, but the practice of generosity (*dāna*) is dependent on other factors, such as having

something to give, the presence of someone to receive, and whether the receiver is worthy of receiving. In situations where one is not in a position to give, an intention that is free of taking what is not given is a quality that purifies the mind and can form a foundation for concentration. However, in situations where one is in a position to give, being disinterested or miserly will be a defilement of the mind, while giving is a condition for preserving or enhancing one's virtue. In this respect the basic definition is in the form of negation—abstaining from or being free of the bad—while the expanded definition is in the form of developing goodness, and therefore is a matter of practical application as already stated.

8. In the practice of Dhamma, at any particular time the practitioner will be practicing one particular quality, or kind of quality. At such times the practitioner's interest and attention will be focused on what he or she is practicing at the time. In this case, the responsibility to other aspects of the practice will be secondary—that is, merely seeing to it that no kind of badness arises. The value of morality in this case is in protecting one's conduct in other areas, safeguarding it from going astray and falling into evil of some kind, thus ensuring a solid foundation from which to fully develop the particular kind of goodness being practiced at that time.

Since the natural order-based system for life development is systematized as morality-mind-wisdom, scholars who are coming from a theistic kind of morality tend to be unable to make sense of it. A number of observations should be noted concerning the difference between morality in Buddhism, which is natural order-based, and morality in theistic religions (including the matter of *kamma*, good and evil):

1. In the natural order-based method, morality consists of principles of conduct determined according to the natural principle of cause and effect. In the theistic teachings, morality is divine decree, determined by the divine will.

2. Natural order-based morality consists of principles for training the self to refrain from bad actions. Thus, the formalized morality is in the form of "training rules" (*sikkhāpada*). Morality in theistic religions is in the form of prohibitions or divine commandments.

3. The required motivation for the practice of natural order-based morality is *ākāravatīsaddhā*, confidence in the law of *kamma*, with a fundamental understanding that sees behavior and results of behavior as related on a cause-and-effect basis. The required motivation for the practice of theistic morality is faith: belief, acceptance, and obedience to whatever is defined as the will of God. Trust is unconditionally granted without any need for explanation.

4. In the natural-order system, observance of morality consists of training one's conduct, beginning with the intention to give up bad actions and continuing up to developing the various kinds of good that are their opposites (that is, it is a personal commitment). In the theistic teachings, the observance of morality is strict obedience and conformity to the divine commandments (that is, it is an obligation).

5. In the natural-order system, practice on the level of morality has the specific objective of forming a foundation for concentration (*samādhi*), to most effectively prepare the mind for creating wisdom and ultimately attaining liberation or perfect freedom. As regards rebirth in heaven, it is considered one of the general byproducts of the practice. In the theistic religions, however, observance of morality according to the divine commandments is the cause for being blessed from above; it is conduct that is pleasing to God, as a result of which God grants the reward of rebirth in heaven.

6. In the natural-order system, the good and bad results of behaving morally or immorally are natural consequences, the unwavering and impartial operation of the natural law known as the law of *kamma*. This expression of results manifests initially in the mind, and spreads outward to a person's character and way of life, be it in this life or the next. In the theistic religions, the good and bad results of conduct conforming to or infringing on morality (divine commandments) are in the form of retribution. Good results, rebirth in heaven, are rewards. Bad results, rebirth in hell, are punishments. The receiving of either good or bad results is subject to the judgment from on high.

7. In terms of understanding good and evil, the natural-order system teaches that goodness is the quality that preserves and promotes the quality of the mind, making the mind clean and pure,

or lifting it to a higher level. Thus, it is said to be *puñña* (good, moral, or meritorious). It is something that brings growth and benefit to the mind, leading to liberation or freedom of the mind and intelligence. It is clever action, conducted according to the way of wisdom, and conducive to mental health, thus it is called *kusala* (skillful or wholesome). Evil is what causes the quality of the mind to decline. Thus, it is said to be *pāpa* (sin). It causes deterioration in the mind, does not lead to liberation, and is unintelligent action, not conducive to mental health. So it is said to be *akusala* (unskillful or unwholesome). In the theistic religions, good and evil are defined by faith in the deity, holding belief, acceptance, and obedience to the divine will and the divine command or otherwise as the standard. Evil, in particular, is wrong, an infringement of the god (sin) in some form or other.

8. Because of these fundamental differences, at least two further distinctions can be seen:

First, morality in the natural-order system must be taught with a rational connection. The practitioner can only practice correctly when he or she understands that system and the reasons behind it. Morality or ethical conduct in the theistic teachings comes in the form of divine decree or pronouncements of the will of God, as individual decrees or prohibitions. Even when these pronouncements are brought together, they are a compilation, not a system, because, at most, all the practitioner is required to understand is the meaning of the various commandments. It is not necessary to understand the system or the reasons behind them, since the system and all of its reasons are entirely at the discretion of the will of God. The practitioner cannot doubt, only obey unquestioningly, and that is enough.

Second, morality or ethics based on the natural-order system is neutral and universal, determined by the facts of the natural laws (that is, the essential meaning of morality in terms of the teaching on good and evil, not the meaning in terms of *vinaya*—codes of conduct—which concerns the meting out of punishments in society). For example, it examines the results or reactions that arise within the mental processes, the effects on behavior, on character, and on personality. Thus, it is not possible to make distinctions in the interests of one particular group or based on personal preference. It cannot be said, for instance, that only compassionate people in this religion are good, while compassionate people of other religions are not good; or that only to kill people of this religion is sin, but to kill people of other religions is not; or that only people in this religion who make offerings will go to heaven, but those of other religions, if they do not believe in God, will all fall into hell; or that killing animals (even when it is not for food) is not sin because animals are food for human beings (while human beings are not the food of tigers, lions, etc.).[9] Any distinction that is made, such as cases that are of greater or lesser evil, is in accordance with the facts of the natural law: for example, examining the results and reactions that arise within the mental processes, as already explained.

In theistic teachings, these precepts can be determined or defined in any way that accords with the divine will, like legislation, because the divine being is both the legislator and the judge.

Third, since morality consists of general principles determined by the facts of the natural laws, a practitioner of the Buddhadhamma must dare to acknowledge that truth. Whatever the facts of good, evil, right, and wrong, one must face up to them. Whether or not, or to what extent, one can practice accordingly is another matter. We must also dare to accept our good and bad actions as they are, rather than saying that something is not an evil just because we want to do it. The natural facts are not subject to evaluation by our wanting or not wanting to do them. If it happens that we are forced to do something for which we must go to hell, it is still better to accept the truth, tell ourselves that the action is not good, and accept the consequences, than to deceive ourselves that the action was not bad.

There are some advantages of morality by divine commandment:

It dispenses with any need to examine right and wrong, true and false. It might be said that when there is belief through faith, practical results are quicker, more fervent, and more intense. However, problems follow, especially in more rational times, of how to maintain belief, and long-term problems concerning safety in living with people of other faiths, concerning the stability of the faith, and the lack of opportunity to attain intellectual freedom.

For ordinary people it is much easier to understand morality simply through faith, and such morality controls their conduct much more effectively. Thus, we find that even among many Buddhists the understanding of morality, good and evil is in some ways similar to that of people who follow theistic religions. They see moral precepts, for example, as prohibitions (although it is not clear who has done the prohibiting), and see the results of good and evil actions as rewards and punishment. The problem here is the same as in the first point: how can such faith be maintained?

Decreeing that certain bad actions, which are deemed necessary for one's own interests, are not bad *kamma*, is one way of inducement. According to the principles of cause and effect, it can be acknowledged that methods for inducement are effective because they are an additional determinant that enters into the picture. For example, decreeing that to kill animals is not wrong allows one to be at ease and untroubled in killing animals. However, such inducement leads to harmful results in other areas, and it is not the way of wisdom. For human beings to develop, it must be with full and clear cognition of the truth at all times and knowing how to make decisions for oneself. It may be acceptable to use some methods of inducement, but those inducements must be in forms that are not harmful, and are used only in cases that help propel the effectiveness of other kinds of good actions.

Morality for the People

Before expanding on the subject of the principles of practice on the level of ordinary people or householders, it would be appropriate to emphasize the broad principles that should be kept in mind and that help the practice of morality on all levels to be correct and in accordance with the objective, to be *dhammānudhammapaṭipadā*.

The practitioner of morality should from the outset clearly see the meaning of that practice and bear in mind its objective. The practitioner should also see the practice of morality within the system of development, how the growth in morality is related to the development of the mind and wisdom, supporting *samādhi* and direct knowledge and vision (*ñāṇadassana*), leading to freedom from suffering and the accomplishment of benefit and happiness.

As we know, the path, or as it is fully known, the noble eightfold path, is a compilation of all the practices of Buddhism, and those eight factors can be arranged into three groups—morality, concentration, and wisdom. When it comes to actual practice, the training of these is referred to as the threefold training (*tisikkhā*): the training in higher morality (*adhisīlasikkhā*), the training in higher mentality (*adhicittasikkhā*), and the training in higher wisdom (*adhipaññāsikkhā*). The entire practice leading to *nibbāna* lies within these three groups, which are derived from the eight factors of the path.

Having established this, when speaking of morality, we must say that the true, real, and comprehensive morality is that which is derived from the eightfold path. The path factors within the morality group are right speech, right action, and right livelihood. This is the true, real, and comprehensive morality.

The Buddhavacana at the beginning of this chapter describe the meaning of right speech, right action, and right livelihood individually and in detail, showing what the essence of *sīla* is, and the extent of morality as a path factor, or that is essential for a good life. The ancient masters referred to these eight subfactors of *sīla* in the path as the *ājīvaṭṭhamakasīla*, meaning the factors of morality that have right livelihood as the eighth.

This is all there is to true, real morality. This central basis is further subdivided, as organized training for specific groups of people appropriate to their livelihood, objectives, or emphasis, as morality of bhikkhus or of novices or of householders. It goes on to include systems established for clarity in society for attaining specific and clear goals, called *vinaya*, which entails control of activities, and affixing of penalties and punishments for transgressions.

Having established this principle, in order to more clearly see the salient points, let us consider some noteworthy features of morality, starting with the observation that it is not just for bhikkhus. The Buddhavacana describing the *sīla* path factor indicates that the path is not directed solely at bhikkhus, otherwise the definition of morality would be the 227 precepts (of the Pāṭimokkha code of discipline), the renunciants' morality (*pabbajitasīla*), the morality of restraint in the Pāṭimokkha (*pāṭimokkhasaṁvarasīla*), or something along those lines. This shows that the Buddha described the essence of morality in a form that is flexible and covers many subsidiary models of morality that can be broken down into different sets of factors; it was not required to specify any particular name or group, such as the five precepts, eight precepts, or ten precepts.

Another feature of morality is that it includes livelihood. The point needs to be emphasized, because it is often forgotten that morality means not only good and wholesome conduct in body and speech, but also honest livelihood. How we make a living has moral significance.

Morality also includes the positive and the negative. To repeat the point made earlier, *sīla* is usually described only in the form of brief injunctions, such as abstaining from killing living beings or abstaining from stealing, and appears to contain only negative aspects. If we want to see it more clearly and comprehensively, we should refer to the Buddhavacana expanding on the meaning, such as the ten bases for skillful action (*kusalakammapatha*), where all of the factors of *sīla* are defined in two aspects: that which is abstained from, and that which is cultivated (the negative followed by the positive).

Morality must incorporate other path factors. Within the path there are moral factors, mental factors, and wisdom factors, which must all be there together in order to form the path and produce the result. Even though at this time we are discussing the level of *sīla*, we must bear in mind that we are on a path. In order to walk forward, we must bring together the other two sectors in order to achieve the result.

The Buddha laid down a standard incorporating the mentality and wisdom factors of the path into *sīla* for householders. Usually there are four groups of factors (in some places another is added to make it five). In the Tipiṭaka it is discussed often, so I would like to repeat it here in brief.

After teaching about preparing for victory in this world (that is, looking after the home and one's dependents and assets), which are the immediate benefits (*diṭṭhadhammikattha*), the Buddha taught about preparing for victory in the next world, the further benefit (*samparāyikattha*), as follows:

> "Herein, Visākhā, a woman endowed with these four qualities can be said to be practicing for victory in the next world, to have prepared for the next world. What are the four?
>
> "... And how is a woman endowed with faith? ... A woman is endowed with faith. She believes the wisdom and enlightenment of the Tathāgata (*tathāgatabodhisaddhā*), that because of this, the Blessed One is an arahant...
>
> "... And how is a woman endowed with morality (*sīla*)? ... A woman is one abstaining from killing living beings, from taking what is not given, from sexual misconduct, from lying, and from taking intoxicants that are a cause of heedlessness...
>
> "... And how is a woman endowed with generosity (*cāga*)? ... A woman lives the household life without the stains of stinginess; she is kind and giving, open-handed, delighting in giving, someone who is approachable for requests, who delights in sharing...
>
> "... And how is a woman endowed with wisdom (*paññā*)? ... A woman is endowed with wisdom—that is, she has the noble wisdom that penetrates arising and ceasing, that penetrates the matter and attains the correct ending of suffering."

Another less crucial factor that is sometimes added is *suta*, having learned, having heard, or acquiring information—ideally, becoming a learned person (*bahussuta*).

Another feature of morality is that it includes *vinaya*. The word *sīla* has a broad meaning and is used in both very strict and very loose senses. In the Thai language, in particular, it has become distorted and is often confused with the word *vinaya* (discipline). Even though we must move with the times, we should use the words with full knowledge and at least be able to distinguish their fundamental meanings.

In essence, morality can be divided into two levels:

1. Morality on the level of Dhamma: this refers to the principles of conduct of body, speech, and livelihood that are taught as something that should be maintained according to nature, and whoever abides by or violates this type of morality receives results, good or bad, directly according to the normal laws of nature. It includes the practice on the level of morality and maintenance of *vinaya* that has become one's regular practice or quality.
2. Morality on the level of *vinaya*: this refers to the specific orders and regulations laid down as social dictates for defining and controlling individual behavior in conformity with the specific objective of that group or community. These dictates are mostly designed to support and fortify the practice of Dhamma, and any violation incurs the consequences in terms of responsibility to the group, over and above the mental repercussions that will arise in accordance with the natural law. It also refers to the methods used to train people to have morality.

Strictly speaking, *vinaya* is not *sīla*, but it is an adjunct of *sīla*, being the systems and methods used to organize society, to train people to have *sīla*.

Finally, the essence of morality is intention, not thinking of transgressing. In one sense, the word *transgress* means to transgress the established order, to transgress regulations and precepts, to transgress the established discipline. In another sense, it is to transgress other people, meaning to intentionally harm them. *Sīla* therefore means not to intentionally transgress the order and discipline and not to intentionally transgress or harm others. In terms of action, *sīla* is not transgressing and not harming.

From another angle, *sīla* resides in composure or restraint; that is, it is composing and restraining the mind to prevent and steer clear of bad states. If we look on the most profound level, the mental state of one who does not think of transgressing and does not think of harming others is *sīla*.[10]

Now I will summarize the general principles or fundamental level of morality and present Buddhavacana and statements from the canon dealing with morality for ordinary people.

Basic Morality

Basic morality encompasses the general principles of morality that constitute the path factors of right speech, right action, and right livelihood—namely, speech, action, and livelihood that contain an intention that is void of dishonesty (*ducarita*) or harmful thoughts. It encompasses the forms of good conduct (*sucarita*) that are their opposites.

Right Speech (*Sammāvācā*)

- Giving up false speech (*musāvāda*); incorporates true speech (*saccavācā*)
- Giving up malicious tale-bearing (*pisuṇāvācā*); incorporates harmonious speech (*samaggivācā*)
- Giving up harsh speech (*pharusavācā*); incorporates gentle and polite speech (*saṇhavācā*)
- Giving up frivolous chatter (*samphappalāpā*); incorporates useful, meaningful speech (*atthasaṁhitāvācā*)[11]

Right Action (*Sammākammanta*)

- Giving up the taking of life (*pāṇātipāta*): incorporates helpful and compassionate action
- Giving up taking what is not given (*adinnādānā*); its opposite lies in right livelihood, or giving (*dāna*)

· Giving up sexual misconduct (*kāmesumicchācāra*); incorporates contentment with one's own spouse (*sadārasantosa*)

Right Livelihood (*Sammā-ājīva*)

Steering clear of wrong livelihood and making a living with right livelihood; this incorporates diligent application to honest livelihood—for example, not leaving work unfinished (not allowing things to pile up, procrastinating, or working haphazardly or in a confused manner).[12]

The Five Precepts

For ordinary people the standards of Buddhist morality are relaxed, and the essence of this fundamental level of morality is presented as the minimal standards of conduct by which human society can proceed smoothly and the individual can have a blameless and harm-free life. These standards are called the five training rules (*sikkhāpada*), or, as they later became known, the five precepts (*sīla*), as follows:[13]

1. Refraining from killing (*pāṇātipāta*). In essence this is conduct that does not harm others physically.
2. Refraining from stealing (*adinnādānā*). In essence this is conduct that does not harm others in terms of wealth and property.
3. Refraining from sexual misconduct (*kāmesumicchācāra*). In essence this is conduct that does not harm others in terms of their spouses or loved ones, that does not involve breaking sexual customs or committing adultery, that does not have the outcome of damaging other families.
4. Refraining from false speech (*musāvāda*). In essence this is conduct that does not harm others with false, deceiving, extorting, or intentionally destructive speech.
5. Refraining from liquor and intoxicants that are bases for heedlessness (*surāmerayamajjapamādatthānā*). In essence this is conduct that is free of heedlessness, mistakes, and delusion resulting from the use of addictive substances that cause one to lose mindfulness and comprehension.

The meanings and boundaries of the precepts tend to be stated according to the explanations that have been handed down in later times. Here I would like to present the Buddhavacana for consideration:

> "Householders, I will give a discourse for inner reflection.
>
> "A noble disciple reasons thus: 'I desire to live, I do not want to die; I love happiness and I abhor suffering. If someone were to deprive me, who desires life, not death, who loves happiness and abhors suffering, of life, that would not be pleasing to me. And if I were to deprive of life another, who wanted to live, not to die, who loved happiness and abhorred suffering, that would not be pleasing to that person. Whatever is displeasing to me, that is not pleasing to others. Why, then, should I inflict that which is not pleasing onto others?' That noble disciple, reasoning in this way, himself abstains from taking life, encourages others to abstain from taking life, and speaks in praise of abstaining from taking life. The bodily conduct (*kāyasamācāra*) of that noble disciple is thus pure on these three counts.
>
> "Moreover, a noble disciple reasons thus: 'If someone were to take something that I had not given, with the action of a thief, that would not be pleasing to me. If I were to take something not given from another, that would not be pleasing to that person…'
>
> "Moreover, a noble disciple reasons thus: 'If someone were to misbehave with my wife, that would not be pleasing to me. And if I were to misbehave with someone else's wife, that would not be pleasing to that person…'
>
> "Moreover, a noble disciple reasons thus: 'If someone were to harm my interests through false speech, that would not be pleasing to me. If I were to harm the interests of another through false speech, that would not be pleasing to that person…'
>
> "Moreover, a noble disciple reasons thus: 'If someone were to provoke me to fall out with a friend with malicious tale-bearing, that would not be pleasing to me. If I were to provoke another person to fall out with a friend with malicious tale-bearing, that would not be pleasing to that person…'

"Moreover, a noble disciple reasons thus: 'If someone were to address me with harsh speech, that would not be pleasing to me. If I were to address another with harsh speech, that would not be pleasing to that person...'

"Moreover, a noble disciple reasons thus: 'If someone were to address me with frivolous words, that would not be pleasing to me. If I were to address another with frivolous words, that would not be pleasing to that person. Whatever is displeasing to me, that is not pleasing to others. Why, then, should I inflict that which is not pleasing onto others?' That noble disciple, reflecting in this way, himself abstains from speaking frivolously, encourages others to abstain from speaking frivolously, and speaks in praise of abstaining from speaking frivolously. The verbal conduct (*vacīsamācāra*) of that noble disciple is thus pure on these three counts..."[14]

"Bhikkhus, how do you consider this? Have you ever seen or heard that a certain man has given up taking life and is one who totally abstains from taking life, and on this account is taken by the king and executed, imprisoned, banished, or dealt with in some way?"

"No, Lord, never."

"That is so, bhikkhus. I myself have also never seen or heard such a thing...only that they announce evil acts, saying, 'Such and such a person has killed a woman or a man, and he has been taken by the king and executed, imprisoned, banished, or dealt with because of that taking of life.' Have you ever seen or heard this?"

"Yes, Lord, we have seen it and heard it, and we will hear of it again in the future."

"Bhikkhus, how do you understand this? Have you ever seen or heard that [this man has given up taking what is not given, is one who totally abstains from taking what is not given...from sexual misconduct...from lying...from taking intoxicants that are a cause for heedlessness] and is taken by the king and exe-

> cuted, imprisoned, banished, or dealt with in some other way on account of his giving up taking what is not given...sexual misconduct...lying...intoxicants leading to heedlessness?"
>
> "No, Lord, never."
>
> "That is so, bhikkhus. I, too, have never seen or heard such a thing...only that they announce evil acts, saying, 'This person has stolen from a village or forest...this person has violated this woman or daughter...this person has harmed the interests of the village folk or their children through lying...this person has become drunk and killed this man or woman...this person has become drunk and stolen from the village or the forest...this person has become drunk and violated the woman or daughter...this person has become drunk and damaged the interests of the village folk or their children through lying...and on account of that stealing...sexual misconduct...lying...taking intoxicants has been taken by the king's men and executed, imprisoned, banished, or punished.' Have you ever seen or heard of this?"
>
> "Yes, Lord, we have seen it and heard it, and we will hear of it again in the future."[15]

Almost all severe criminal offenses are violations of the five precepts. In any society where murder, killing, aggression, violence, theft, or sexual misconduct are rife, or where cases of murder, theft, rape, extortion, or partaking of intoxicants and addictive substances and their resulting problems and accidents are rampant, life and possessions are endangered. Wherever people live or go, they have no security and their minds are full of worry. Their minds are fearful, and they look on each other with mistrust and fear rather than warmth. They do not live contentedly, their mental health declines, and it is hard to improve the quality and efficiency of their minds. Such a society is not an environment conducive to the creation of higher kinds of goodness, because it is embroiled in trying to solve its problems, and full of destructive activities that contribute to society's deterioration. Lack of the five precepts, for whatever reason, is one good gauge for measuring social decline. The conduct and life that are opposite to this constitutes having the five precepts. Thus, the five precepts are the minimum standard of human behavior required to maintain a social environment that is conducive to and supportive of a wholesome life.

The commentators have compiled certain criteria for defining violation of each of the five precepts. These criteria are arranged as factors of transgression, called *sambhāra*. A person is said to have transgressed (or, simply, broken) one of the precepts when his or her actions contain the factors of transgression in full, as follows:[16]

The first precept, against killing (*pāṇātipāta*), has five factors: (1) a living being; (2) one knows it is a living being; (3) there is intention to kill; (4) effort; (5) the being dies as a result of that effort.

The second precept, against stealing (*adinnādānā*), has five factors: (1) something valued by another person; (2) one knows that person values it; (3) intention to steal; (4) effort; (5) the object is stolen through that effort.

The third precept, against sexual misconduct (*kāmesumicchācāra*), has four factors: (1) a male or female who should not be violated (*agamanīyavatthu*); (2) intention to have intercourse; (3) effort to have intercourse; (4) contact of sexual organs.

The fourth precept, against lying (*musāvāda*), has four factors: (1) a matter that is not true; (2) intention to speak falsely; (3) effort based on that intention to speak falsely; (4) another person understands what has been said.

The fifth precept, against taking intoxicants (*surāmeraya*), has four factors: (1) a substance that is intoxicating; (2) desire to drink that substance; (3) effort as a result of that desire to drink; (4) the substance passes the throat [is ingested].

Regarding the first precept, even though "killing living beings" basically intends human beings, as in the Buddhavacana already cited, animals generally referred to as "dumb" (*tiracchāna*) also love life, love pleasure, and abhor pain, and are our companions in the world, in birth, aging, sickness, and death. We should also not hurt them. This precept is therefore also meant to include dumb animals, but it is conceded that killing animals is less blameworthy than killing human beings. The commentators have given the following principles for ascertaining which kinds of killing carry little fault and which carry much fault, thus:

1. Worthiness: to kill beings with much worth carries more fault, while to kill beings with little or no worth carries less fault. For example, to kill an arahant is more blameworthy than to kill an unenlightened being; to kill a work animal is more blameworthy than to kill a wild animal.
2. Physical size: among dumb animals that are equally without worthiness, to kill a larger animal carries more fault than to kill a smaller one.
3. Effort expended: if much effort is expended in the killing, there is more fault; if only little effort is expended, the fault is less.
4. Defilement (*kilesa*) or intention: a strong defilement or intention carries great fault, while a weak defilement or intention carries little fault. For example, to kill out of anger or malicious intent will carry more fault than to kill out of self-defense.

The levels of greater and lesser fault of the other precepts are discussed along similar lines. For example, stealing has greater or lesser fault according to the value of the object stolen, the virtue of its owner, and the effort expended in the theft. Sexual misconduct has greater or lesser fault depending on the virtue of the person violated, the intensity of the defilement, and the effort expended. The fault of lying is dependent on whether the damage resulting from it is major or minor and dependent also on the speaker; for example, a householder who does not want to give a certain thing away, and who lies that he does not have it, incurs little fault, while a witness who gives false testimony in a trial brings on more fault. If a bhikkhu speaks in fun, the fault is little, but if he intentionally says he has seen something that he hasn't, there is much fault. As for taking intoxicants, it has more or less fault depending on the unskillful mental state or defilement in the drinking, the amount imbibed, and the results the intoxication has in terms of leading to mistaken or evil actions.[17]

Later teachers compiled certain qualities into a group paired with the five training rules, or precepts, to be practiced by laypeople in conjunction with the five precepts, called the five good *dhammas* (*pañca kalyāṇadhamma*). Those qualities follow the same lines as the ten courses of skillful conduct, but the choice of factors to be included differs somewhat, especially in terms of their breadth of scope. The factors of the five good *dhammas* are arranged to match the five precepts, thus: (1) goodwill and compassion; (2) right livelihood (sometimes generosity is included here); (3) *kāmasaṁvara*, control and restraint in regard to sensual objects or matters of desire so as not to transgress social mores (some teachers give *sadārasantosa*, contentment with one's own partner, here); (4) truthfulness (*sacca*); and (5) mindfulness and comprehension (*sati sampajañña*; some teachers give "heedfulness" (*appamāda*) here, which carries a similar meaning).

As to the word *sadārasantosa*, which is the practice opposite to sexual misconduct, it translates literally as "contentment with one's own wife," but it means essentially to limit oneself to one's partner. The texts leave the matter of how many partners open, not stipulating only having one or any definite number but leaving it entirely up to the agreement in accordance with established custom and social convention. The essence is taken to be not transgressing another's spouse, or having sexual contact with someone who is forbidden or who is committed to someone else, nor to override the feelings of the other person or deceive one's own partner. When partners are open and fully consenting, neither infringing on or deceiving each other, this is not regarded as wrong. Even so, in terms of preferred practice, the teachings praise monogamous marriages that are loving, faithful, and long-lasting, a stable family, and security and warmth for the children, as in the life of the noble couple known as Nakulapitā and Nakulamātā (literally, "father and mother of Nakula"), the model couple recorded in the suttas. This married couple were both noble disciples, stream enterers, and were foremost of the Buddha's disciples (*etadagga*) in being close to and familiar with the Buddha. Both were bound by mutual love, loyalty, and truthfulness, and this led to their being so harmonious in virtues that they desired to be together both in this life and the next, as recorded in Nakulapitā's statement to the Buddha:

> "Lord, from the time when her family brought the young maiden Nakulamātā Gahapatānī to me as a young man, I have never been inclined to go to another woman, even in my thoughts, let alone in my actions. We two aspire to be together both in this life and the next."

The same sentiments were expressed by Nakulamātā.[18]

Sadārasantosa is classed as one kind of celibacy (*brahmacariya*) and is a way of life highly praised in Buddhism. It is said to be one of the factors for preventing death at an early age, as implied in the passage: "We do not commit adultery against our wives, and our wives do not commit adultery against us. We practice celibacy (*brahmacariya*) toward women other than our wives. For that reason, we do not die young."[19]

The essence of *sīla* is summarized in the following statement:

> "Whoever is restrained in body, speech, and mind, who does not commit evil deeds, who does not speak ambiguously for self-interests, is one who has morality."[20]

And this Buddhavacana can be taken to be the essence of *sīla*:

> "Create security (*khema*) for all beings."[21]

Morality for Enhancing Virtue in Life and Society

The teachings contained within the *Siṅgālaka Sutta*[22] are described by the commentators as the Buddha's declaration of the householders' discipline (*gihivinaya*),[23] or morality for ordinary people. The teachings given in this sutta can be summarized thus:

Group 1: Being Free of Fourteen Kinds of Evil

Abandoning the four pollutants of behavior:

1. Killing
2. Stealing
3. Sexual misconduct
4. Lying

Not committing bad actions on the basis of four biases—that is, not committing evil deeds by giving in to:

1. Bias on account of affection (*chandāgati*)
2. Bias on account of aversion (*dosāgati*)
3. Bias on account of foolishness (*mohāgati*)
4. Bias on account of fear (*bhayāgati*)

Not associating with the six pathways to decline of wealth:[24]

1. Addiction to liquor and intoxicants
2. Addiction to night life
3. Addiction to shows
4. Addiction to gambling
5. Addiction to association with bad friends
6. Laziness

Group 2 : Preparing Investment for Life on Two Sides

Knowing real friends and false friends, those who should be associated with and those who should be avoided, as follows:[25]

Four kinds of false friends:

1. The swindler
2. The good talker
3. The flatterer
4. The leader into trouble

Four kinds of real friends:

1. The helping friend
2. The friend through thick and thin
3. The good adviser
4. The loving friend

Knowing how to obtain, preserve, and amass wealth—like the honeybee, which collects pollen to feed the hive, or like ants and termites building their nests—one should organize one's wealth, use it, and cement friendships by dividing it into four portions: one portion for personal use, two portions for investment, and one portion to be put aside for emergencies.

Group 3: Protecting the Six Directions

Carrying out one's duties correctly toward those one relates to according to the six stations:

1. Children ↔ Parents

   Sons and daughters support their parents, who are like the forward (east) direction, by
   - having been cared for by them, caring for them in return
   - helping with their business or work
   - continuing the family line
   - behaving as is fitting for an heir
   - making offerings in their parents' names when the parents have passed away

   Parents assist their children by
   - cautioning them from evil
   - training them in goodness
   - seeing to their education
   - finding a partner for them
   - bequeathing their inheritance to them at the proper time

2. Pupil ↔ Teacher

   Pupils support their teachers, who are like the right (south) direction, in these ways:

   · standing to receive them and showing respect
   · approaching them (for example, by doing things for them, seeking advice, receiving instruction)
   · paying attention to the teachings
   · serving them
   · studying the teachings earnestly, giving them their due importance

   Teachers assist their pupils as follows:

   · teaching them to be good
   · teaching them to understand clearly
   · teaching the subject in full (not teaching "with a closed fist" by keeping a little bit aside)
   · praising pupils in front of others
   · providing a protection for all directions (teaching them things that can actually be used to make a living)

3. Husband↔ Wife

   A husband supports his wife, as the rearward (west) direction, by

   · praising his wife in accordance with her position as wife
   · not disparaging her
   · not committing adultery
   · giving her the authority of the household
   · providing her with gifts of clothing and jewelry when the occasion arises

   A wife assists her husband in the following ways:

   · keeping the house in order
   · supporting the families on both sides
   · not committing adultery
   · protecting the wealth obtained
   · being diligent in her work

4. Friends ↔ Friends
   Friends, as the left (north) direction, should be supported in the following ways:
   · sharing with them
   · speaking to them affectionately
   · helping them
   · being faithful to them through times good and bad
   · being sincere to them
   Friends should respond by assisting in the following ways:
   · when their friend is heedless, helping to protect him
   · when their friend is heedless, helping to protect his wealth
   · being a support to him when he is in danger
   · not deserting him when he is in difficulty
   · respecting his relatives
5. Master ↔ Servants and employees
   A master should support his servants and employees, who are like the nadir, by
   · giving work that is commensurate with their strength, sex, age, and abilities
   · paying a wage that is appropriate for the work and their needs
   · providing sufficient benefits, such as medical support in times of sickness
   · sharing with them any special gains that arise
   · providing holidays and days of rest from time to time
   Servants and employees should assist their masters as follows:
   · starting work before them
   · finishing work after them
   · taking only what their master gives them
   · working well and constantly striving to improve their work
   · spreading a good word about their masters and their work
6. Householders ↔ Members of the order
   Householders should support the order, who are like the zenith, by
   · when acting, doing so with goodwill

- when speaking, doing so with goodwill
- when thinking, doing so with goodwill
- receiving them gladly
- providing them with the four supports

Members of the order assist the laity as follows:

- enjoining them from evil actions
- instructing them in goodness
- assisting them with kindness
- causing them to hear what they have not before heard
- clarifying those things that they have already heard
- pointing out the way to heaven (teaching the way to happiness)
- practicing the *saṅgahavatthu*, the four principles for unity and for harmonizing society: (1) giving and sharing (*dāna*); (2) kindly speech (*piyavācā*); (3) helpful action (*atthacariyā*); and (4) impartiality (*samānattatā*)

General Principles of Right Livelihood

In terms of its general principles, the subject of livelihood holds much that is worthy of examination and explanation, deserving a separate chapter in its own right, but rather than discussing them in detail, I will offer only a few observations.

The Minimum Standard of Livelihood

Buddhism looks on the aim of livelihood in terms of the minimum standard defined by the needs of human life, aiming for a sufficiency of the four supports (*paccayā*: food, clothing, shelter, and medicine) for all people to live on. People are the basis. Buddhism does not set its aim on abundance of material wealth, which is a standard based on material objects.

This principle can be seen in the teachings dealing with government: among the duties of a universal emperor (*cakkavatti*), for example, there is one enjoining such a person to apportion wealth to the poor,[26] to see to it that abject poverty does not arise in the kingdom. In other words, a ruler's success in terms of livelihood or the economy should be gauged by the absence of poverty rather than by wealth filling the royal coffers. Once this basic standard is met, there are no indications that the teaching has any objections to the amount of wealth that does exist, or stipulate that it should be distributed equally, because there are also other factors involved, such as those discussed in the following point.

The Higher Objective

Having enough of the four supports to live on, or, for that matter, a surfeit of material possessions, is not an objective in itself, because it exists merely on the level of *sīla*; it is a method or stage to help proceed to a higher objective. That is, material possessions are a foundation for the development of mental virtue and wisdom, for a wholesome life and the attainment of a higher kind of happiness. Some people are able to concentrate on mental and intellectual development with minimal material possessions, with just enough to live on. Others, however, are not ready for that: their lives are more dependent on material things. Even so, as long as their livelihood does not exploit others, this is acceptable. Furthermore, there are people who have a tendency, talent or ability to help others: the possession of great wealth by such people enables them to create great benefit for their fellows.

Livelihood That Is Proper

The term *sammā-ājīva* (right livelihood) in Buddhism does not refer simply to righteously using one's labor to create products, and receiving in exchange the supports for life. It also refers to the proper performance of duty and conduct, or a way of life that makes one worthy of the supports. For example, that Buddhist bhikkhus live devoted to their "duties of a renunciant" (*samaṇa dhamma*), in return receiving the four supports offered by the laity, is right livelihood for bhikkhus. When a child behaves well as befitting the care received from parents, this is right livelihood for the child.

Again, rather than gauging the value of labor in terms of its productivity and how it fulfils a human demand, which may either be the demand of desire (*taṇhā*) or a true life need, Buddhism gauges the value of labor in terms of its benefit or non-benefit to life, society or the well-being of humanity.

This leads to two further considerations. In Buddhism, the relationship between labor and livelihood and reward can be divided into two kinds:

1. For most people, labor expended in the performance of duty is strictly a matter of livelihood; that is, it is done for the sake of the readily visible supports of life.
2. For a *samaṇa*, one who has renounced the world, labor expended in the course of duties is not a concern of livelihood: it has no objective in terms of making a living. That is, its objective is not material rewards in the supports of life, but realizing the Dhamma and maintaining the Dhamma in the world. If renunciants do use their labor for the purposes of seeking material supports, this becomes wrong livelihood for them. Moreover, if they use the labor that is for the purpose of their duties for the sake of some reward, or they demand supports that are not voluntarily given, this is considered impure livelihood.

In this respect, not only clear forms of wrong livelihood, such as deceiving, cajoling, hinting, threatening, or exchanging,[27] but also maintaining a livelihood by serving others, as in acting as a messenger, or practicing various arts and professions such as fortune-telling or healing, are all considered to be wrong livelihood for a bhikkhu.[28]

For a bhikkhu who is not sick to ask for fine foods (*bhojana*), or even curries or cooked rice, for himself and eat them is said to be a failure (*vipatti*) of livelihood.[29] Using the Dhamma as an object of commerce is said to contravene the ethic of a renunciant,[30] and even a Dhamma teaching given in the hope of gaining the affection of listeners and receiving something in return is said to be an impure teaching.[31] Giving something as a way of payment is improper for a bhikkhu.

At one time the Buddha was going on alms round and stopped to stand in the vicinity of a field of a certain brahmin. The brahmin addressed the Buddha: "I till and sow the field before I get my meal. You, too, should till and sow the field for your food." The Buddha answered that he also tilled and sowed his field before eating. When the brahmin asked for an explanation, the Buddha answered that his tilling and sowing resulted in deathlessness. The brahmin was impressed by his answer and brought him an offering of food. However, the Buddha refused to accept it, saying that it was improper to accept food that had been obtained by a performance (literally, "singing for your supper").[32]

The truly right and pure source of supports for a Buddhist bhikkhu is when householders recognize the value of the Dhamma, and the necessity of helping those responsible for its preservation to live and fulfill their duties, so that when they become aware of the bhikkhus' need for food expressed by their serene alms round, they voluntarily bring food to offer them. The people who make these offerings receive in return the cleansing and purifying of the mind and its elevation through the realization that they have done a good deed and have had a share in preserving the Dhamma. This is called, in brief, "making merit" (*puñña*) or "getting merit."

The bhikkhus who receive these supports are constrained by the teachings on the four supports to be frugal and to know moderation in receiving them, which is in exact opposition to their work, such as teaching and explaining the Dhamma, of which they are expected to do as much as possible for the benefit of others. In this respect, the principle of eating as little as possible for as much work as possible is feasible for a renunciant, in that labor expended in the performance of duty and livelihood occupy such separate positions that there is no connection by which work performed by a bhikkhu can be raised as a justification for a demand of rights in terms of livelihood, and as long as renunciants are practicing according to this teaching the social system likewise cannot dominate them.

All of the principles mentioned here have the main objective of creating the kind of life that is free of all social systems, an independent community to perform the work of Dhamma, which requires utter purity, in the world.

From the perspective of the Dhamma, a lot of production labor, be it for goods or services, is spent in ways that are not beneficial to life or society. Apart from industries that are directly destructive, such as manufacture of weapons and addictive drugs, there are others that damage the environment, those that are destructive to human dignity, and those that are destructive to virtues and mental quality. And then there is all the labor expended in solving the destructive results of those kinds of production. Such labor can be taken as mostly wasteful, and the value of its products destructive. Growth in this kind of production tends to force humanity to expend an ever-increasing amount of money and labor in preventing and correcting the destructive results that have arisen from their own doing. Labor that is beneficial to life and society need not be economically productive—as, for example, the ideal of life according to the Dhamma, which encourages wisdom and virtue in people.

Even in terms of production, virtue can be more valuable than labor in achieving it. For example, a Buddhist bhikkhu practicing the Dhamma in a forest, while not expending any labor at all to look after the forest, may be considered by forestry officials to attain better results in conservation of the forest than they do, in spite of those officials using the labor of many people expressly for that purpose.

If true benefit and well-being of humanity are the focus, it is not enough to simply look at the value of production and consumption. We must also look at the value of not producing and not consuming. In terms of the Dhamma, a person who is not economically productive but whose consumption of the world's resources leads to the least wastage, and who leads a life that is sufficiently beneficial to the environment, is better than one who diligently manufactures goods that are harmful to life and society and at the same time consumes large amounts of the world's resources. However, it seems that modern economic teachings would praise the latter rather than the former.

One may question whether it is fair to talk of people's duty to produce without considering the perspective of consumption, how much they have contributed to the wastage of the world's resources, and whether such an emphasis on the duty to produce is truly beneficial to life and society. If economics focuses solely on measurable quantities and the increase of material things, holding itself to be a science, then economics and current economic doctrines must accept their narrowness and deficiency. Acknowledging these truths would be more beneficial and lead to a more holistic economics.

The Limitations of Wealth

As has been mentioned, in terms of Dhamma, how much wealth a person has is not of great interest. The Dhamma does not hold possession of material wealth as a gauge for measuring good and evil, but sees it as merely a means to an end. Whether material wealth is commendable or not depends on the objectives to which it is applied. The focus of interest for Buddhism is twofold: first is the methods through which wealth is obtained, and second is the uses to which it is put. Briefly, the emphasis is not on the possession of wealth but on the seeking and use of wealth. Obtaining or having wealth and then simply hoarding it is said to be a great evil, just like obtaining wealth wrongly or using it harmfully.

In this respect, there are initially three kinds of bad actions in relation to wealth: seeking it wrongfully, hoarding it and not putting it to use, and using it in ways that are harmful.

However, even when wealth is obtained honestly and spent usefully, this cannot yet be called dealing correctly with wealth according to the Dhamma. In the Dhamma there is also an emphasis on quality of mind and wisdom, in the attitude adopted to wealth, which must incorporate *nissaraṇapaññā*—comprehending the true value or benefit of wealth and the limitations of that value and those benefits, so that the mind is free, not enslaved by wealth but master of it. Wealth is there to serve us, a tool to create benefit and goodness, to help relieve suffering and bring about well-being, not to become a cause for increased suffering, damaging the quality of mind, destroying human dignity, or causing people to drift apart. For this reason, in his tenfold classification of householders, the Buddha describes the tenth kind of householder as the superior kind. In the qualities of this superior kind of householder we can see the principles for the proper relationship to wealth according to the Dhamma, summarized as follows:[33]

1. *Seeking*: seeking wealth in rightful ways, not through exploitation
2. *Using:* planning the use of wealth, which includes saving and living moderately
   - Supporting oneself (and one's dependents) comfortably
   - Sharing
   - Using some wealth for doing meritorious deeds (including using some for the spread and promotion of the Dhamma)
3. *Possessing the wisdom that liberates*: not being engrossed with or captivated by wealth, but using it with awareness, seeing its benefits and liabilities, and having a mind made free by *nissaraṇapaññā*, and, by means of that wealth, further developing the mind and understanding.

The following Buddhavacana explains the practice in relation to wealth:

> "Bhikkhus, there are these three groups of people in the world. What are the three? They are the blind, the one-eyed, and the two-eyed.
>
> "What is the blind person? Some people in this world do not have the vision that leads to acquisition of new wealth or to the increase of wealth already gained. Moreover, they do not have the vision that enables them to know the qualities that are skillful and unskillful...what is harmful and what is not... what is coarse and what is refined...the qualities that are white or black. This is called a blind person.
>
> "And what is the one-eyed person? Some people in this world have the vision that leads to the acquisition of new wealth, and to

> the increase of wealth already obtained, but they do not have the vision that enables them to know the qualities that are skillful and unskillful...what is harmful and what is not...what is coarse and what is refined...the qualities that are white or black. This is called a one-eyed person.
>
> "And what is the two-eyed person? Some people in this world have the vision that enables them to acquire new wealth and to increase the wealth already obtained, and they have the vision that enables them to know the qualities that are skillful and unskillful...what is harmful and what is not...what is coarse and what is refined...the qualities that are white or black. This is called a two-eyed person...
>
> "One who is blind, whose vision is gone, is hounded by misfortune on two counts: wealth is not gained, and merit is not performed.
>
> "The person known as the one-eyed goes about seeking wealth, taking it rightfully or wrongfully, be it stealing, cheating, or fraud. That person is an enjoyer of sense pleasures who is clever at acquiring wealth, but from there goes to hell. The one-eyed person suffers in due course.
>
> "The person known as the two-eyed is the excellent one: that person shares a portion of wealth obtained through diligent labor from the wealth that is rightfully gained. That person has noble thoughts, a resolute mind, and attains to a good bourn, free of sorrow.
>
> "One should steer clear of the blind and the one-eyed, and associate with the two-eyed, the excellent ones."[34]

An example of a teaching that condemns the hoarding of wealth and putting it to no use is illustrated in the following story. One day King Pasenadi of Kosala paid a visit to the Buddha. When the Buddha asked him where he had come from at such a time, the king informed him that a rich householder in the city had just passed away, and he was on his way back from collecting all the remaining wealth, for which there was no heir, to be taken to the palace.

King Pasenadi informed the Buddha that the amount of wealth

that had to be carted away consisted of eight million gold coins and countless other coins such as silver. When he was alive, that householder had lived on broken rice and vinegar, dressed in three coarse cloths sewn together, used an old chariot, and shaded himself with a sunshade of leaves.

The Buddha remarked:

> "That is how it is, Your Majesty. The foolish man (*asappurisa*), obtaining wealth in great measure, does not support himself in comfort, does not support his father and mother... his wife and children... his servants and employees... his friends and associates in comfort. He does not place offerings of high result, which are conducive to wholesome mental states, result in happiness and lead to heaven, to recluses and brahmins.
>
> "That wealth unconsumed and unused by him is confiscated by the king, stolen by thieves, burned by fire, swept away by floods, or appropriated by wicked heirs. That wealth of his, not rightfully used, disappears to no purpose and is not put to use.
>
> "It is like a pool in a place inhabited by demons: even though its water is clear, cool, fresh, and limpid, and it has good approaches and shady setting, no one can take, drink, bathe in, or make use of that water...
>
> "As for the wise man (*sappurisa*), obtaining wealth in great measure, he supports himself in comfort, supports his mother and father... his wife and children... his servants and employees... and his friends and associates in comfort. He places offerings of high result, which are conducive to wholesome mental states, result in happiness and lead to heaven, to recluses and brahmins.
>
> "The wealth that is rightly consumed and used by him is not confiscated by kings, thieves cannot steal it, fire cannot burn it, floods cannot sweep it away, wicked heirs cannot appropriate it. That wealth of his, rightly used by him, is put to use, it does not disappear in vain.
>
> "It is like a pool not far from a village or town, its water cool,

clear, fresh, and limpid, with good approaches and shady setting: people can take it, drink it, bathe in it, or use it as they please...

"The evil person, obtaining wealth, does not use it himself and does not share it, like water in a forest of demons: it cannot be used for drinking, and people cannot use it.

"As for the wise, obtaining wealth, they use it and do their duty [both their own work and work for helping others]. They are supreme. Having supported their relatives, they are beyond reproach and attain to heaven."[35]

"Your Majesty, those people who, having obtained wealth in great measure, are not intoxicated by it, not heedless, do not become deluded by sense pleasures, and who do not endanger other beings, are rare in this world. Those beings who, having obtained wealth in great measure, are intoxicated by it, heedless, deluded by sense pleasures, and who endanger other beings, are truly of far greater number."[36]

People who hoard wealth without putting it to use or sharing it are likened to a certain bird called the *mayhaka* bird, which watches over the fig tree laden with ripe fruits calling out *mayhaṁ mayhaṁ* ("mine, mine"). While other birds flock to the tree, eat its fruits, and fly off, the *mayhaka* bird just stands there calling out *mayhaṁ, mayhaṁ.*[37]

In the texts there are many stories reproving misers who hoarded wealth and did not use it for themselves or to help others, especially dealing with how rich merchants who had such behavior were taught to change their ways, a good indication of the Buddhist perspective on possession of wealth and its use.[38]

Sīla and Economic Prosperity

In Thailand there is a well-known tradition of "requesting" precepts (*sīla*), "giving" precepts, and "receiving" precepts. When precepts are "received," the bhikkhu who is giving the precepts recites the benefits of *sīla* as follows: *sīlena sugatiṁ yanti* and so on, meaning through *sīla* one will go to a happy place (*sugati*), will attain endowment of wealth (*bhogasampadā*), and will attain *nibbāna*.

Significantly, this states that *sīla* will lead to endowment of wealth, or, simply speaking, to a good economy. Even though these verses on the benefits of *sīla* are later compositions and are not found in the Tipiṭaka or the commentaries, occurring only in the Thai Buddhist model, it is appropriate to discuss them here as a brief aside.

The major principle of *sīla* is the creation of a firm foundation in the environment for important work to proceed. From the economic perspective, it is clear that when people live with *sīla*, when there is no crime or danger to life and property, when travel is safe and convenient, when employers and employees have good relations and are helpful to each other, when government systems are honest and effective, businesses are trustworthy, and people both far and near can communicate and travel conveniently, then manufacture and commerce flow freely. This is a simple illustration of how *sīla* helps establish an economic foundation for society to ready it for advancement to prosperity.

Once the country is stable and prosperous, and the people have a high level of confidence, we can then take a look at the individual. In short, let's put aside the negative repercussions of lacking morality, such as delinquency, theft, fraud, laziness, and drunkenness, and look only at the results of having morality. When householders who are making a living decide to live morally (to live with *sīla*), if they are confident in their honest livelihood, having made this intention, thoughts of seeking this or that or looking for ways to do this or that wrong action or dishonest behavior, even looking for incidental gain, do not arise. There are no external issues to vie for one's thoughts.

When one is content to focus on one's work and livelihood as they are, this is to enter the path of *samādhi*. When the mind is focused on making a living, concentrated on really doing the work, thoughts become focused on the work, on how to make a start, how to carry it out, how to do it most effectively, identifying obstacles and solutions, knowing where to make contacts and open up work opportunities, who to meet, who to consult, who to work with and how. This is how *sīla* has an effect on thinking, with concentration and wisdom following on. From there the four bases for success (*iddhipāda*) can follow on, and success can be expected to follow.

I would like to clarify that the duty of *sīla* is to create a foundation and a stable environment for further work. If there is no *sīla*, the foundation is faulty, the base is crumbly and full of gaps and the environment is not conducive. If there is no *sīla* you cannot make a start. If you do make a start it is unstable and wobbly. When the environment is conducive and the foundation stable, then one can start on the method—that is, make a start on the work. In the language of bhikkhus we say there is the *samādhi* to carry out the task.

At this point I would briefly like to refer to a fragment of a verse that the Buddha uttered as a general guideline. It is a sentence used at the beginning of verses summarizing the teachings for householders, as follows:[39]

> *uṭṭhātā kammadheyyesu appamatto vidhānavā*

This translates as "diligent in work, not being heedless, clever in management." We could briefly render it as "diligent, heedful, clever in management."

The content of this Buddhavacana may be taken as a principle for work in general. Certainly, work must begin with diligence (the Pali word *uṭṭhāna* can mean to get up, not waste one's time lying down, or increasing in wealth or prosperity). When one is diligent, work progresses toward completion and success.

The Buddha stressed diligent effort, not only as a factor for success, but also as something to reflect on for instilling pride and happiness in one's work life, as was regularly stressed in his teaching to householders: "With wealth that has been obtained through one's own efforts, collected by the strength of one's own arms and the sweat of one's brow, that is rightful, rightfully gained."[40]

Apart from this, by way of this diligent effort, a person can develop himself or herself, since progress in work is one kind of personal development, a condition that requires one to develop oneself in all areas that lead to progress and success.

Even so, diligence on its own is not enough. There must also be heedfulness. If one is diligent in a misguided way, at the wrong time, in the wrong place or situation, not being diligent with what requires diligence and being diligent in what one should not be diligent, the work may be ruined. Heedfulness is mindfulness acting in conjunction with effort—that is, being alert, in step with events, able to grasp the essence of matters, not wavering in the face of bad events, not hesitating when the time comes for action, not leaving loopholes, being ready to rise to the occasion, not missing an opportunity or occasion, not neglecting, by adhering to the principle "Prepare and be ready for tasks in the future. Do not allow those tasks to put pressure on you when the time comes for action."[41]

Briefly, heedfulness aids effort on four fronts: (1) the effort to close off and prevent decline, (2) the effort to solve problems and destroy dangers, (3) the effort to create and fulfill good actions, and (4) the effort to maintain good qualities and to promote their growth to fruition.

The third principle, being clever in management, is particularly important. It is the factor of wisdom. It causes us to use diligence for the correct matter, at the correct time, for example, and it maximizes heedfulness' effectiveness. We can briefly say that one must act with wisdom of the principles, especially the seven qualities of a true person (*sappurisadhamma*): knowing the cause, knowing the objective and the result, knowing oneself, knowing moderation, knowing occasion, knowing the person, and knowing the assembly—for example, knowing how to utilize people appropriate to the task, and knowing the needs of the community with its particular culture.[42]

Being clever in management is a quality that was frequently emphasized or taught for both the Saṅgha and of course for householders, who are responsible for various businesses. For instance, the Buddha talked about the principles for one who is responsible in the household thus: "A householder...should be one who shares and knows how to manage things (*vidhānavanta*)."[43]

He gave many teachings for those who are in government service that illustrated these principles, including "One who has circumspection, who is endowed with intelligence, who is clever in management, who knows the time and place—such a one is capable of serving the government. Those who are diligent, not heedless, who are discerning and can manage tasks well, are capable of serving the government."[44]

Summarizing, *sīla* encompasses things that are related to business and communal living. In one sense, *sīla* is about organizing one's life, having a good society and environment, in order to be able to proceed to development of the mind and wisdom.

The following suttas illustrate the principles of livelihood for a householder, dealing with procurement of wealth, use of wealth, and the happiness to be expected from a right livelihood.

Seeking and Protecting Wealth

> At one time, the brahmin Ujjaya went to visit the Buddha. Informing the Buddha that he was going to live in a different locality, he requested a teaching on the conditions for benefit and happiness in the present and the conditions for benefit and happiness in the future. The Buddha answered:
>
> "Brahmin, these four conditions are for benefit and happiness in the present. They are *uṭṭhānasampadā*, *ārakkhasampadā*, *kalyāṇamittatā*, and *samajīvitā*.
>
> 1. "And what is *uṭṭhānasampadā*? A son of good family supports himself through diligent effort. Whether it be farming, commerce, animal husbandry, military service, civil service, or the arts, he is diligent, skilled, and not lazy in that work. He examines and considers things with wisdom. He knows the method in that matter, he is capable in work and is clever in management: this is called *uṭṭhānasampadā*.
>
> 2. "And what is *ārakkhasampadā*? A son of good family has

wealth obtained from his own labor, from the strength of his own arms and the sweat of his own brow, rightfully acquired, rightfully gained. He arranges protection for that wealth, thinking, 'What can I do so that kings will not confiscate this wealth, thieves will not steal it, fire will not burn it, floods will not sweep it away, and wicked heirs will not appropriate it?' This is called *ārakkhasampadā*.

3. "And what is *kalyāṇamittatā*? Herein, a son of good family, residing in a town or market town, befriends and has discourse and discussion with those householders, sons of householders, young people who have the conduct of elders, and people advanced in years who have the conduct of elders, who are possessed of faith, possessed of morality, possessed of generosity, and possessed of wisdom. He studies and emulates the endowment of faith of those endowed with faith; he studies and emulates the endowment of morality of those endowed with morality; he studies and emulates the endowment of generosity of those endowed with generosity; he studies and emulates the endowment of wisdom of those endowed with wisdom. This is *kalyāṇamittatā*.

4. "And what is *samajīvitā*? A son of good family supports himself in moderation, neither extravagantly nor stingily, knowing the ways of increase and decrease of wealth, knowing which undertakings will yield an income higher than the outlay rather than the outlay exceeding the income. It is like a weighman or a weighman's apprentice: once he lifts the scale, he knows the balance either way... If this son of good family had only a small income, but lived extravagantly, it could be said of him that he consumed his wealth as if it were peanuts. If this young man had a large income, but used it stingily, it could be said of him that he will die like a pauper. But because this young man supports himself in moderation... this is *samajīvitā*.

"Brahmin, the wealth so rightfully gained has four pathways of decline (*apāyamukha*). They are to be a womanizer, to be a drunkard, to be a gambler, and to have bad friends, to be drawn

> to bad people. It is like a large reservoir with four channels going into it and four channels going out. If the channels going inward are closed off, and the channels going out are opened up, and the rain does not fall in due season, it can be expected that for that large reservoir there will be only decrease, not increase...
>
> "Brahmin, wealth so rightfully gained has four pathways of growth (*āyamukha*). They are not to be a womanizer, not to be a drunkard, not to be a gambler, and to have good friends, good associates, to be drawn to good people. It is like a large reservoir with four channels leading into it and four channels leading out. If the channels leading into it are opened up, and the channels leading out are closed off, and rain falls in due season, it can be expected that for that large reservoir there will be only increase, not decrease... Brahmin, these four conditions are for the benefit and happiness of a young man in the present moment."

From there, the Buddha goes on to describe four conditions that lead to benefit and happiness in the future (*samparāyikattha*), which are endowment with faith (*saddhāsampadā*), endowment with morality (*sīlasampadā*), endowment with generosity (*cāgasampadā*), and endowment with wisdom (*paññāsampadā*).[45]

The Happiness to Be Rightly Expected for a Householder

The following teachings, given to the householder Anāthapiṇḍika, are called the four kinds of happiness for a householder:

> "Herein, householder, these four kinds of happiness are things that a householder, a partaker of sense pleasures (*kāmabhogī*), should obtain and achieve at the proper times. They are *atthisukha*, *bhogasukha*, *anaṇasukha*, and *anavajjasukha*.
>
> 1. "What is *atthisukha* (the happiness arising from possessions)? A son of good family has wealth obtained by his own diligent labor, acquired through the strength of his own arms and the sweat of his own brow, rightfully acquired, rightfully gained.

He experiences happiness, he experiences gladness, thinking, 'I have wealth that has been obtained through my own diligent labor, amassed through the strength of my own arms and the sweat of my brow, rightfully acquired, rightfully gained.' This is called *atthisukha*.

2. "And what is *bhogasukha* (the happiness arising from using wealth)? Herein, a son of good family makes use of and does good deeds that are meritorious with the wealth that has been obtained by his own diligent labor, through the strength of his own arms and the sweat of his own brow, rightfully acquired, rightfully gained. He experiences happiness, he experiences gladness, reflecting, 'Through this wealth obtained through my own diligent labor... rightfully gained, I make use of it and can also do good deeds that are meritorious.' This is called *bhogasukha*.

3. "And what is *anaṇasukha* (the happiness of being without debt)? Herein, a son of good family is not in debt, be it small or great, to anyone. He experiences happiness and gladness, thinking, 'I owe no debts, be they small or great, to anyone at all.' This is called *anaṇasukha*.

4. "And what is *anavajjasukha* (the happiness arising from blameless conduct)? Herein, a noble disciple is possessed of blameless bodily conduct, blameless verbal conduct, and blameless mental conduct. He experiences happiness and gladness, thinking, 'I am one possessed of blameless bodily conduct, possessed of blameless verbal conduct, possessed of blameless mental conduct.' This is called *anavajjasukha*.

"Considering the happiness of being free from debt, one reflects on the happiness of having possessions. Using possessions, one sees clearly with wisdom the happiness of using wealth. Clearly seeing, one has wisdom, and understands that the two are comparable, (seeing that) the first three kinds of happiness are not worth a sixteenth part of the happiness that arises from good and blameless conduct."[46]

Using Wealth

At one time, the Buddha explained to the merchant Anāthapiṇḍika the benefit to be obtained from wealth. The teaching was given in accordance with social conditions at the time, so the reader is advised to glean the gist of the matter.

> "Herein, householder, there are these five benefits to be obtained from wealth, as follows:
>
> 1. "With the wealth that has been obtained by his own diligent labor, acquired through the strength of his own arms and the sweat of his own brow, rightfully acquired, rightfully gained, the noble disciple supports himself in comfort, in sufficiency, seeing to his own needs and comfort appropriately. He supports his father and mother...wife and children, servants and employees in comfort, in sufficiency, seeing to their needs and their comfort appropriately. This is the first benefit to be obtained from wealth.
>
> 2. "Moreover, with the wealth that has been obtained by his own diligent labor...rightfully gained, the noble disciple supports his friends and associates in comfort, in sufficiency, seeing to their needs and comfort appropriately. This is the second benefit to be derived from wealth.
>
> 3. "Moreover, with the wealth that has been obtained by his own diligent labor...rightfully gained, the noble disciple protects his wealth from the dangers arising from fire, water, kings, thieves, and wicked heirs. He sees to his own security. This is the third benefit to be derived from wealth.
>
> 4. "Moreover, with the wealth that has been obtained by his own diligent labor...rightfully gained, the noble disciple makes five offerings: offerings to relatives (*ñātibali*), offerings to visitors (*atithi-bli*), offerings to ancestors (*pubbepeta-bali*); offerings to the king (*rājabali*; supporting the government), and offerings to the gods (*devatābali*; supporting religion). This is the fourth benefit to be derived from wealth.
>
> 5. "Moreover, with the wealth that has been obtained by his

> own diligent labor... rightfully gained, the noble disciple places offerings that are of high result, conducive to wholesome mental states, resulting in happiness, and leading to heaven, in recluses and brahmins who refrain from heedlessness, are established in patience and gentleness (*khanti-soracca*), who train themselves, calm themselves, and cool themselves of the heat of defilements. This is the fifth benefit to be obtained from wealth.
>
> "Householder, there are these five benefits to be obtained from wealth.
>
> "If, when a noble disciple obtains these five benefits to be obtained from wealth, wealth should become spent, he thinks thus: 'Whatever are the benefits to be obtained from this wealth, those I have obtained and my wealth is spent.' On this count, that noble disciple is untroubled.
>
> "And if, when a noble disciple obtains these five benefits to be obtained from wealth, wealth increases, he thinks thus: 'Whatever are the benefits to be obtained from this wealth, those I have obtained and now my wealth has increased.' On this count, that noble disciple is not troubled, and therefore he is not troubled in both cases."[47]

When a householder has sufficient for his own use, it is said to be important that one shares with others, and doing this is said to be following the path of the noble ones, as in the saying:

> "If you have little, give little; if you have a middling amount, give a middling amount; if you have much, give much. It is not fitting not to give at all. Kosiya, I say to you, 'Share your wealth, use it. Enter the way of the noble ones. One who eats alone eats not happily.'"[48]

Training oneself in generosity can be done through observances, which are special practices that are regularly followed. For example, one may determine a fixed percentage of one's income for giving to others, or determine to donate a certain amount each month or year to charitable causes. Some people make it a practice not to eat until they have given something to others, such as a reformed miser in the time of the Buddha, who said:

> "If I have not first shared with others I will not even drink water."[49]

Preparing Wisdom: Even If Wealth Is Gained, Independence Is Not Lost

Not only do we need to reflect that wealth is not in itself the goal, we must also know the limitations of the value of wealth, and the necessity of seeking out that which is of higher value, as for example:

> "Work, knowledge, truth, morality, and a full life: all beings are purified by these things, not through family name or wealth."[50]
>
> ———
>
> "I see people in the world who have wealth, having obtained wealth, not sharing it because of their attachment to wealth. They only amass it and desire more and more sensual pleasures.
>
> "A king who invades and conquers a land, who has power over the land, is not content with only this side of the ocean. He wants to obtain the far side of the ocean as well. The king and many other people, who have not yet done with ambition, reach their deaths. Still feeling unsatisfied, they discard their bodies. There is no satisfaction on account of sense pleasures in this world.
>
> "The relatives let down their hair and wail for that person, saying, 'Oh, our dear one has departed,' and they wrap the body in white and throw it on the pyre and burn it, to be poked with sharp sticks by the funerary attendants until it is all burned. The deceased are left with only one piece of cloth, and discard all their wealth.

> "When one dies, no relatives, friends, or associates can prevent it. That person's wealth is carried away by the heirs. Beings fare according to their *kamma*. At death, not even a little of the wealth can be taken with them. It's the same for children, wives, wealth, and property. One does not live long on account of wealth. One cannot destroy old age with wealth. The wise say of this life that it is little, not lasting, and subject to change.
>
> "Both those who have and those who have not experience contact (*phassa*). Both fools and the wise are affected just the same. But the fool, because of lack of wisdom, sleeps in fear. The wise person, even though affected by contact, does not tremble. For that reason, wisdom is more excellent than wealth, because it is a cause for attaining the highest goal in this world."[51]

An important tool for conducting a right livelihood is education, or *sippa* (professional knowledge, skills, work ability). We are cautioned to put effort into education, and parents are instructed to see it as their duty to allow their children to obtain an education. Even so, having professional knowledge or work skills alone is not enough. We are therefore instructed to have *bāhusacca*, being one who has heard much or who has broad learning, to help expand the range of application of one's education, so that we can develop a broad understanding that allows us to see things in a more profound way, in particular having the knowledge of things that lead to right view, which is the real source of learning.

At the same time, we should train in discipline in order to be ready to use education (*sippa*) in an honest manner and have good general behavior that is conducive to living with others, and train ourselves to be able to talk and consult effectively so as to broaden the avenues for our lives.

This principle is illustrated in the Buddha's statements:

> "Being one who has heard much (*bāhusacca*), professionalism or vocational ability (*sippa*), good discipline (*vinaya*), well-spoken

> words, these are supreme blessings...Having no unfinished business, this is a supreme blessing...Blameless endeavors, this is a supreme blessing."[52]
>
> ---
>
> "See to your children's education."[53]
>
> ---
>
> "Learn what should be learned."[54]
>
> ---
>
> "You should learn and study everything, be it low, high or middling. Know and understand the meaning of it all. You may not have to use all of it, but one day the time will come when that knowledge will be useful."[55]

In regard to the "supreme blessings" cited above, broad learning (*bāhusacca*) should be coupled with practical skill (*sippa*)—that is, to be good in terms of both knowledge and ability. When these two qualities are present, excellence in work can be expected. Success is even more assured if one is endowed with good discipline and is skilled in speech, knowing how to speak effectively. When augmented by good and efficient work practices, not leaving things unfinished, and by doing useful activities, there is even more guarantee of success and fulfillment in one's working life.

In order to prevent the loophole of merely reveling in one's knowledge and work to the extent that one forgets one's obligations to one's dependents, two further "blessings" are added—namely, supporting one's parents and taking care of one's wife and children.

Once personal obligations are taken care of, the noble disciple considers further the obligations one has to helping others, ultimately to all human beings. Therefore three more "blessings" are added in the gap afterward—namely, *ñātisaṅgaha*, supporting one's relatives; *dāna*, giving, sharing outwardly; and *dhammacariyā*, principled conduct. By having such conduct, this is sufficient for one to be called one who is leading a good life in this world.

In regard to livelihood, it would be useful to summarize once again that Buddhism accepts and asserts the necessity of material things, in particular the four necessities, as illustrated in the words often spoken by the Buddha:

> *Sabbe sattā āhāraṭṭhitikā*
> "All beings are sustained by food."[56]

Even so, the real necessity lies within the boundaries of what is required to maintain the physical body in a condition that is suitable for its normal functioning—that is, free of harm resulting from lack and excess, free of disease, safe from dangers, and faring in comfort.

The value and importance of material things are flexible, being related to social conditions and individual factors, such as wisdom of the benefits and harm and limitations of material things, and the ability to experience a more refined kind of happiness than material happiness.

For this reason, Buddhism is not interested in regulating an equal amount of material things for all people. Buddhism is rather more interested in laying down a minimum standard, which is that all people should have a sufficiency of the four necessities to survive comfortably. Over and above that, Buddhism allows the use of material things as per their availability and people's level of intelligence, within the bounds of what does not harm oneself or others. This means that to have a happy life, people with lower mental development may desire more material things, or their lives will be more dependent on having material pleasures, than those who have a higher level of mental development.

Having a life that is free, not overly dependent on material things, one that is based on wisdom of the harm or faults or material things, is called *ādīnavadassārī*, and the wisdom that frees one is called *nissaraṇapaññā*.

One who has wisdom knows the various kinds of harm in material wealth and sensual pleasures. By their very nature, these things lack any perfection that would be capable of really fulfilling our desires, because they have the nature of impermanence, instability, and changeableness. No one is able to truly own them; they do not truly lie within anyone's power and ultimately must disappear.

With this understanding, one can make use of material things according to their real use or value to life, using wealth so that it is beneficial to life and other people, and practicing the four principles for integration (*saṅgahavatthu*). It is not wealth for the sake of ever greater wealth, for increased enjoyment or personal pleasure.

Householders who are industrious in livelihood and obtain wealth honestly, using their wealth generously, taking responsibility for others and using their wealth beneficially are highly praised in Buddhism. They are said to have been victorious both in this world and the next.[57] The more they possess the wisdom that liberates them, the more they are regarded as excellent, as truly free persons.

These people, even if they are noble ones of the level of stream enterer or even once-returner, make a living, attending to their responsibilities. It does not appear that householders are encouraged to just live day by day, neglecting their livelihood and responsibilities, which may be called "being attached to non-attachment."

The Saṅgha as the Community of the Free, Both in Life and in Mind

The Saṅgha is a community that exemplifies a life lived with minimal material possessions, utilizing specific social conditions so that bhikkhus can live a lifestyle that allows them to devote their time and energy fully to activities related to the Dhamma. They do not need to worry about looking for material things, and make themselves easy for householders to support, and thereby maintain the free community that transcends as much as possible the influence of social systems. All bhikkhus, be they arahants or unenlightened beings, live a life based on the principle of minimal material supports, for a maximum gain in terms of Dhamma. Nowhere is it said that the Buddha wished laypeople to live like bhikkhus, or that all people should become renunciants. The facts of nature clearly show that at any one time people live in various levels of development and therefore have different needs. Many stream enterers lived household lives.

The essence of this principle would seem to be having a free community within the wider society as a force for Dhamma, to nourish

Dhamma within society and to be a source for encouraging freedom from the influence of social factors to those who desire it and are ready to seek liberation.

This community consists of both a formal community and an abstract community.

- The formal free community is the bhikkhu Saṅgha, known in the Pali language as *sammatisaṅgha* (conventional Saṅgha), which is embedded within, yet removed from, the wider community of householders.
- The abstract free community is the *sāvaka saṅgha*, or the *ariya-saṅgha*, which is made up of the noble ones, both householders and renunciants, who are embedded within, yet removed from, the wider society of unenlightened beings.

This is tantamount to saying that the ideal society is not one in which all people are the same, and such a society cannot exist. The ideal society is one in which people, with their differing levels of intellectual development, are advancing toward the same goal and can live together in harmony even with their differences. It is also a society in which there is a suitable alternative if they do not wish to live in that broader society.

With the bhikkhu Saṅgha, being able to maintain material freedom requires a lifestyle that is supported by few material things, which must be coupled with mental virtues that enable one to live within such a lifestyle. The important quality that is evident in such a lifestyle is contentment with little (*santosa*). This is a quality that the Buddha emphasized for all bhikkhus or renunciants. With *santosa* in terms of material things, bhikkhus can fully focus their time, energy, and thought on practicing for mental liberation, as is shown in the important teaching given by the Buddha called the four traditions of the noble ones (*ariyavaṁsa*):

> 1. "Bhikkhus, a bhikkhu in this teaching and discipline is one content with whatever robes he is given and is one who praises contentment with whatever robes are given. He is not given to

seeking in wrongful ways (*anesanā*) on account of robes. If he does not obtain a robe, he is not troubled; if he obtains a robe, he is not attached, deluded or engrossed by it. He uses that robe heedful of its dangers and has the wisdom that liberates him. Moreover, he does not exalt himself or disparage others on account of his contentment with whatever robes are offered. Any bhikkhu who is clever, not lazy, who is fully aware and of firm mindfulness in contentment with robes, is said to be one who is established in the ancient noble lineage.

2. "Moreover, a bhikkhu is one content with whatever alms food he is given...

3. "Moreover, a bhikkhu is one content with whatever dwellings he is given...

4. "Moreover, a bhikkhu is one who delights in developing skillful qualities and is one who praises the development of skillful qualities; he delights in abandoning unskillful qualities and is one who praises the abandoning of unskillful qualities. Moreover, he does not exalt himself nor disparage others on account of his delighting in the development of skillful qualities, on account of his being one who praises skillful qualities, on account of his delighting in the abandoning of unskillful qualities and on account of his being one who praises the abandoning of unskillful qualities. Any bhikkhu who is clever, not lazy, who is fully aware and of firm mindfulness in such cultivation (*bhāvanā*) and cutting off (*pahāna*) is said to be one who is established in the ancient noble lineage..."[58]

To summarize here, the commentators have collated and classified the *sīla* for bhikkhus into four types, called the four *pārisuddhisīla* (the purifying *sīla*, or four kinds of pure conduct that can be classified as *sīla*):

1. *Pāṭimokkhasaṁvarasīla*: the *sīla* of restraint in the Pāṭimokkha (the code of monastic discipline), refraining from the injunctions and following the allowances, strictly following the rules. This kind of *sīla* is said to be accomplished through faith (*saddhā*).

2. *Indriyasaṁvarasīla*: the *sīla* of restraint of the faculties, being

careful to prevent unskillful qualities such as like, hatred, attachment, or aversion to overwhelm the mind when becoming aware of sense impressions via the six senses: eye seeing forms, ear hearing sounds, nose sensing odors, tongue tasting flavors, body sensing bodily contact, and mind sensing thoughts. This kind of *sīla* is said to be accomplished through mindfulness (*sati*).

3. *Ājīvapārisuddhisīla*: the *sīla* of purity of livelihood. This is maintaining a livelihood in proper ways, not engaging in wrongful ways of seeking, such as not falsely bragging of superhuman attainments (such as *jhāna*, *vimokkha*, *samādhi*, *samāpatti*, path, fruit, and *nibbāna*) that one does not possess; not requesting foods that one likes if one is not sick; not engaging in deception, such as putting on a show of strict practice in order to inspire people to make offerings; not engaging in ingratiating oneself to householders for livelihood; not engaging in employing various devious approaches to obtain offerings; not engaging in threatening or hounding for offerings; and not engaging in exchange, such as in giving something small in the hope of getting many offerings. This kind of *sīla* is said to be accomplished through effort (*viriya*).

4. *Paccayasannisitasīla*: the *sīla* in relation to the four supports—namely, *paccayapaccavekkhaṇa*: accompanying the use of the four supports with contemplation of their meaning and benefit, or their true value, not using them out of desire. This means eating food to nourish the body, for good health, for comfort and convenient performance of one's duties, enabling one to progress in the threefold training. This kind of *sīla* is said to be accomplished through wisdom (*paññā*).

Some Final Observations

Returning to the subject of householders, it may be useful to summarize here with some of the practices in relation to wealth.

From the Individual Perspective

From the individual perspective, one should practice according to the Buddha's practice of praising those wealthy people who have accrued their wealth as a result of their own honest and diligent efforts, and who use their wealth in wholesome and useful ways. That is, he gave praise for being a good person rather than having wealth.

The tendency to praise people merely because they are rich, seeing them as having merit (*puñña*) accumulated through past actions (in previous lives), and not looking at the causes of their wealth in the present life, is wrong application of Buddhist teachings on two fronts: It is not following the Buddha's way as described above, and it is not using wisdom to consider the entire stream of factors. The factors of the present life, in particular, are more closely related, so they must be given more consideration and more importance. As for previous *kamma*, it helps only in terms of the previous supporting foundation, such as physical attributes, aptitudes, intellect, and character.

The point that the Buddha praised in terms of the individual is good *kamma*, which is a cause for desirable results. When someone is born into wealth and abundance, that person has received the results of their good *kamma* already. They do not need to be praised for it. In the Buddhist view this is considered to be "capital," a good foundation that provides that person with opportunity, or you could say it provides them with an advantage for progress in this life. The results of old *kamma* are done and a new beginning is made. The point that is criticized or praised by the Buddha for this kind of person is how they deal with that capital or good foundation.

In other words, it is not wealth or being rich that the Buddha praised or criticized, but the actions of wealthy people.

From the Social Perspective

According to Buddhism, wealth is a tool or a factor for supporting life, not the goal of life. From the social perspective, therefore, wealth should be a tool for greater human convenience and readiness to lead a good life and do good actions, in order to attain a greater good.

Wherever wealth arises, for whatever person, it should arise for the welfare of all people, becoming a factor for supporting people to be able to lead good lives and be ready to do greater good.

According to this principle, when wealth arises for one person, it means wealth has arisen for humanity, or for society. When one person becomes wealthier, society grows in prosperity. Therefore, wealth arising for one person is equal to it arising for society. A good person who becomes wealthy is like a good field in which the rice grows beautifully for the benefit of all.[59]

A wealthy person according to this principle should be glad and content that one has been able to act as an agent, or to have received the honor of being entrusted by society to supply wealth to help and support one's fellows.[60]

Conversely, if any person gains wealth but as a result society deteriorates and fellow humans are in greater suffering, this indicates a wrong application of wealth. Wealth does not become a helping factor according to its objectives. In no long time that society will become disorderly. In the end, either the wealthy will not be able to live in it, or society will be unsustainable, or both. The society may strip them from power and establish another system to procure wealth, and appoint new custodians of the wealth, for better or for worse.

From a Government Perspective

From a government perspective, Buddhism acknowledges the importance of wealth in worldly society, because poverty is one kind of suffering in the world.[61] Hardship and destitution are significant causes for crime and various kinds of social evils,[62] and Buddhism considers it the duty of the government or rulers of the land to see that wealth is distributed to those in need, so that there is no poverty.[63] This requires various methods as appropriate to the situation.

In particular, it requires creating opportunities for the common people to make a good honest living: supporting vocations, managing capital and equipment in accordance with the four bases for unity (*saṅgahavatthu*),[64] and preventing injustice—that is, all kinds of actions and methods that are immoral, unjust, and exploitative. The state should hold to the principle that reduction and elimination of poverty are better measures of progress than the increase of wealthy persons, and that reduction of hardship comes from social administration that does not neglect human development.

From the Economic and Political Perspectives

It is often asked which economic or political systems are correct or incorrect according to Buddhism. This is not something that Buddhism is obliged to answer. We could say that whatever system is practiced according to Buddhist principles is the correct one according to Buddhism. The various economic systems are matters of methodology. Buddhism recognizes that methodologies can vary according to environmental or temporal factors. What must first be addressed are the principles and objectives.

The essence of wealth and possessions is that they are tools or supporting factors to assist people to organize their lives so that they are convenient and conducive to harmony, and to have greater preparedness for doing good actions and attaining good objectives. Wherever or to whomever wealth arises, it is the arising of a supporting factor in society, enabling all people to be able to lead better and more fruitful lives. Whatever economic or political system is able to bring about the successful attainment of results as per these principles and objectives is in accordance with Buddhism.

It is easy to understand how methodologies are subject to environmental and temporal factors. For example, in the Buddha's time, when the Buddha was establishing the Saṅgha as a community with specialized duties and specialized objectives, he established the rule that bhikkhus were not to have any personal wealth apart from the eight accessories,[65] but he allowed wealth for the Saṅgha community, as communal or shared assets. At the same time, in worldly society—which at that time in the Jambudvīpa region consisted of states that were ruled by two forms of government—he taught the conditions for welfare (*aparihāniyadhamma*) for those states governed by solidarity, or republics, and the duties of a great king (*cakkavattivatta*) for states ruled by monarchs.

This also illustrates another feature of Buddhism: it is not merely a philosophy or a matter of thought. The Buddha had to give teachings that the people in that time could put to use and benefit from in the present time. If we had to wait until we had first created an ideal system, which in effect would only be a system that was hoped to be the best, before using that ideal system to create happiness for the people, how could it escape being an abstract and credulous kind of practice?

Since there were both republics and kingdoms at that time, the Buddha had to help people to live happily under both systems:

- For the system of republics, he emphasized that those in governance should see their rank and power as tools for creating benefit and happiness for the people, not as tools for procuring personal gratification.
- For kingdoms in a monarchical system, he recommended principles and methodologies for carrying out duties with strength, stability, and effectiveness.

During a time when a monarchical system was developing to its highest form, this kind of Buddhist approach became a principle of government of Ashoka the Great, as shown in one of his edicts:

> "His Royal Majesty Piyadassi, beloved of the devas, does not hold much value in glory or fame, except where that glory and fame are held for this objective: that both in the present and in the future, may the people heed my teachings and practice in accordance with the Dhamma."[66]

CHAPTER 10

The Concentration Factors of the Middle Way

Right Effort, Right Mindfulness, and Right Concentration

Right Effort

Right effort is the first path factor in the concentration group, also known as the training in higher mentality (*adhicittasikkhā*). The sutta definition is as follows:

> "What, bhikkhus, is right effort? This is right effort: a bhikkhu in this teaching and discipline
>
> 1. "Arouses zeal (*chanda*), makes an effort, puts forth energy, arouses and applies himself to (preventing) the arising of unskillful conditions that have not yet arisen.
> 2. "Arouses zeal, makes an effort, puts forth energy, arouses and applies himself to abandoning unskillful conditions that have already arisen.
> 3. "Arouses zeal, makes an effort, puts forth energy, arouses and applies himself to generating skillful conditions that have not yet arisen.
> 4. "Arouses zeal, makes an effort, puts forth energy, arouses and applies himself to the maintenance, non-fading, increase,

> perfection, growth, and fulfillment of skillful conditions already arisen."[1]

In the Abhidhamma a further definition is given:

> "What is right effort? It is the bringing forth of effort (*viriyārambha*) in the mind, the going forward, the striving, the diligence, the effort, the industry, the tenacity, the firmness, the steadfastness, the unrelenting persistence, the non-abandoning of zeal, the non-abandoning of responsibility, the shouldering of responsibility, effort (*viriya*), the faculty of effort (*viriyindriya*), the power of effort (*viriyabala*), right effort (*sammāvāyāma*), the effort enlightenment factor (*viriyasambojjhaṅga*), which are factors of the path, and which are included in the path—this is called right effort."[2]

Right effort presented in four divisions, as in the sutta definition above, is also called the four *sammappadhāna*[3] or *padhāna*,[4] right efforts, and each of the four divisions is given its own specific name, as follows:

1. *Saṁvarapadhāna*: effort to prevent or to prepare against (unskillful conditions that have not yet arisen).
2. *Pahānapadhāna*: effort to abandon or eliminate (unskillful conditions already arisen).
3. *Bhāvanāpadhāna*: effort to develop or generate (skillful conditions as yet unarisen).
4. *Anurakkhanāpadhāna*: effort to preserve, protect, or promote (skillful conditions already arisen).

In some places the following explanation of the four efforts, incorporating examples, is given:[5]

1. *Saṁvarapadhāna*: When a bhikkhu perceives form with the eye, he does not adhere to its image (*nimitta*; he does not fantasize

about or attach to the general characteristics), and he does not adhere to its details (*anubyañjana*; he does not fantasize about or attach to the details). He practices for the restraint of the senses, which if unrestrained would be a cause for the arising of evil, unskillful conditions, such as covetousness (*abhijjhā*) and grief (*domanassa*), to overwhelm him. He guards the eye faculty and is composed in the eye. When hearing a sound with the ear, smelling an odor with the nose, tasting a flavor with the tongue, touching a tangible with the body, cognizing a mental object with the mind... (as before).

2. *Pahānapadhāna*: A bhikkhu does not allow sensual thoughts (*kāmavitakka*), hostile thoughts (*byāpādavitakka*), aggressive thoughts (*vihiṁsāvitakka*), and evil, unskillful conditions that have arisen to become established. He abandons them, calms them, banishes them, and allows none to remain.
3. *Bhāvanāpadhāna*: A bhikkhu develops the seven enlightenment factors, which are dependent on seclusion, dispassion and cessation, and incline to liberation.
4. *Anurakkhanāpadhāna*: A bhikkhu cherishes and safeguards good concentration images (*samādhi nimitta*), which are the six perceptions, already arisen.

Effort is a vital quality in Buddhism, as can be seen from the inclusion of right effort as one of the three factors of the path (right view, right effort, and right mindfulness) that must always support all other factors, as stated above,[6] and also its inclusion, under one name or another, within almost all of the other groups of factors concerning Dhamma practice. Its importance can be gleaned from the following Buddhavacana:

> "This teaching [Dhamma] is for the diligent, not for the indolent."[7]
>
> "Bhikkhus, I perceive clearly the value of these two qualities:
>
> 1. "Being one who knows no contentment with skillful qualities
> 2. "Being one who knows no relenting in practice.

> "...So reflect to yourselves thus: 'I will establish unrelenting effort. Though I waste away to mere skin and bones, and the blood in this body may dry up, if I have not attained the fruit that is attainable through a man's strength, a man's effort, and a man's striving, there will be no abandoning of the practice for me.' Thus should you reflect."[8]

Apart from other considerations, the reason for the emphasis on the importance of effort is derived from the fundamental Buddhist principle that truth (*saccadhamma*) is a natural law or principle that exists as a norm, and the position of the Buddha or a teacher is merely of one who discovers that law and announces it to others. Attainment of results in the practice is subject to the unbending process of determinants in nature, not the teacher. Since this is so, everybody must strive to bring about the achievement of results through their own efforts, and not expect results without doing the work. Thus, the Buddhist teaching in this regard is as follows:

> "Effort is your own responsibility. The Tathāgata only points out [the way]."[9]

Even so, like all other factors of the path, the putting forth of effort must first take form properly in the mind, and from there expand out to practical application accordingly. It is not a matter of thinking of applying effort and then simply throwing in a great deal of physical energy, which can easily turn into self-mortification and lead to harmful results. Application of effort must be harmonious with other factors, especially mindfulness (*sati*) and comprehension (*sampajañña*), incorporating wisdom and understanding, applying effort with wisdom so that it is suitable, neither too tense not too slack, as illustrated in the story:

> At that time, the Venerable Soṇa was staying in the Sītavana forest, near the city of Rājagaha, and devoting himself to zealous exertion, walking meditation until both feet were cut, but to no avail. While in seclusion, he thought to himself, "Of those

disciples of the Blessed One who have put forth diligent effort, I surely am one. In spite of that, my mind is still not liberated from the outflows or done with clinging. But my family is well-off. I can spend my wealth and do good deeds at the same time. Enough! I will take leave of the training, use my wealth and perform good deeds."

The Buddha, knowing of his thoughts, went to see Venerable Soṇa.

The Buddha: "Soṇa, has [that thought described above] arisen in you?"

Soṇa: "Yes, Lord."

The Buddha: "How do you consider this? Previously, when you were a householder, you were skilled at playing the lute, were you not?"

Soṇa: "Yes, Lord."

The Buddha: "How do you consider this? When the strings of your lute were too taut, was your lute sweet-sounding and fit for playing?"

Soṇa: "No, Lord."

The Buddha: "How do you consider this? When the strings of your lute were too slack, was your lute sweet-sounding and fit for playing?"

Soṇa: "No, Lord."

The Buddha: "But when the strings of your lute were neither too taut nor too slack, but tuned just right, then your lute was sweet-sounding and fit for playing, was it not?"

Soṇa: "Yes, Lord, it was."

The Buddha: "In the same way, Soṇa, exertion that is overzealous leads to distraction, while exertion that is too slack leads to indolence. Therefore you should determine the proper amount of exertion, understand the balance of the faculties,[10] and devote yourself to that proper amount."[11]

While right effort itself, as a path factor, is an internal quality of the individual mind, it can only function and come to growth through interaction with the external world—that is, through attitudes adopted, responses, and dealings with sense objects (*ārammaṇa*) cognized through eye, ear, nose, tongue, and body, through the external application of that internal effort to actions, conduct, daily living, and the carrying out of activities, through conducive or obstructive surroundings and their helpful or obstructive influence on the putting forth of effort and the growth and development of inner qualities.

Effort in the practice of Dhamma, of the kind that is expressed outwardly in physical actions and applied in the form known as *padhāna*, must involve and be supported by many external factors, including physical surroundings, natural surroundings, and social surroundings.

It is at this point that the Buddhadhamma discusses the role and importance of those external factors in the creation of a good life and attaining Buddhism's highest goal.

As examples of this kind of idea, I present some Buddhavacana on the subject for extra consideration.

> "Bhikkhus, there are these five qualities of one who is endowed with effort (*padhāniyaṅga*). What are the five? [Herein,] a bhikkhu in this teaching and discipline:
>
> 1. "Is one possessed of faith (*saddhā*); he believes in the Tathāgata's awakening, that for such and such reason the Blessed One is an arahant, a fully enlightened Buddha... a proclaimer of truth.
> 2. "Is one with few illnesses, few diseases; he has a stable digestive system, neither too cool nor too hot, just right for putting forth effort.
> 3. "Is not a braggart, not a deceiver. He is candid, both to the Teacher (*satthā*) and to those of his fellow practitioners (*sabrahmacārī*) who are wise.
> 4. "Is one who puts forth effort for abandoning unskillful qualities and bringing skillful qualities to fruition. He is resolute, a striver, constant, and does not neglect skillful qualities.

5. "Is one with wisdom, possessed of the wisdom of the noble ones, which penetrates to arising and cessation, scatters defilements, and leads to the rightful cessation of suffering."[12]

"Bhikkhus, there are five occasions not suitable for the putting forth of effort. What are the five? [They are when] a bhikkhu in this teaching and discipline:

1. "Is old and overwhelmed by aging.
2. "Is sick and overwhelmed by illness.
3. "Is in a time of famine, when food is hard to come by and it is not easy to maintain oneself on the alms round.
4. "Is in a time of danger, when there is trouble and attacks by bandits from the forests, and the countryfolk take to their carriages and flee.
5. "Is in a time when there is schism in the Saṅgha. When there is schism in the Saṅgha, there is abuse, slander, accusation, and abandoning of each other. Non-believers are not moved to believe, and some of those who previously believed become otherwise.

"Bhikkhus, there are five occasions suitable for the putting forth of effort. What are the five?

1. "A bhikkhu is still young, in his youth, black-haired, endowed with the vigor of youth, in the prime of manhood.
2. "A bhikkhu is of few illnesses, of few diseases.
3. "The time is one in which food is plentiful, food is easy to come by, and it is easy to maintain oneself on the alms round.
4. "The time is one in which the people are harmonious, friendly to each other, and not contentious; they are like milk and water, looking on each other with kindly eyes.
5. "The time is one in which the Saṅgha is harmonious, friendly to each other, not contentious, of unified view. When the bhikkhus are in harmony, they do not abuse each other, they

> do not slander each other, they do not accuse each other, they do not abandon each other, and non-believers are moved to believe, while believers find their belief even stronger."[13]

Right Mindfulness

Right mindfulness is the second factor in the concentration group. Its sutta definition is as follows:

> "Bhikkhus, what is right mindfulness? This is right mindfulness: a bhikkhu in this teaching and discipline:
>
> 1. "Contemplates the body in the body, ardent, comprehending, mindful, eliminating covetousness (*abhijjhā*) and grief (*domanassa*) toward the world.
> 2. "Contemplates feelings in feelings, ardent, comprehending, mindful, eliminating covetousness and grief toward the world.
> 3. "Contemplates the mind in the mind, ardent, comprehending, mindful, eliminating covetousness and grief toward the world.
> 4. "Contemplates *dhammas* in *dhammas*, ardent, comprehending, mindful, eliminating covetousness and grief toward the world."[14]

Another definition appearing in the Abhidhamma states:

> What is right mindfulness? Continuous recollection, reflecting back on; the *sati* that is the state of recollecting, the state of remembrance, the state of non-fading, the state of non-forgetting; the *sati* that is a faculty, the *sati* that is a power; right mindfulness and the mindfulness enlightenment factor, that are factors of the path, that are included in the path: this is right mindfulness.[15]

According to the sutta definition, right mindfulness is the teaching known as the four foundations of mindfulness (*satipaṭṭhāna*). The foundations are, in brief,

1. Contemplation of the body, being fully aware of the body (*kāyānupassanā*).
2. Contemplation of feelings, being fully aware of feelings (*vedanānupassanā*).
3. Contemplation of the mind, being fully aware of the mind (*cittānupassanā*).
4. Contemplation of *dhammas*, being fully aware of *dhammas* (*dhammānupassanā*).

Before examining the meaning of right mindfulness according to the four foundations of mindfulness, it would be appropriate to give a general explanation of the term *sati*.

Sati *as Heedfulness (*Appamāda*)*[16]

The word *sati* translates most simply as "recollection." This rendering makes us think of the perspective of memory, which is correct in one sense, but it may not convey the full objective of the word, for in a negative sense, *sati* not only means "not-forgetting" but also refers to "non-distraction," "non-neglect," and "non-confusion and fuzziness." Simply speaking, it is the mind being here and now, not going away or floating off.

These negative senses point to the positive senses of "care," "attention," a state of readiness to cognize whatever is being dealt with and recognizing how to deal with it, which can become caring and protection.

The functioning of *sati* is compared to a gatekeeper who keeps watch over the people passing through the gate, allowing only those people to enter and leave as are appropriate to enter and leave, and forbidding access and egress to those who should not be allowed to enter or leave. *Sati* is thus an important quality in conduct, being the quality that governs how we carry out our activities and that protects and restrains us, neither allowing the mind to wander into evil states nor allowing evil to infiltrate into the mind. Simply speaking, it exhorts us into performing good actions and blocks off the chance to perform bad ones.

The Buddhadhamma gives great emphasis to the importance of *sati* in all levels of conduct. Living or practicing under the constant control of *sati* is known by the specialized term of *appamāda* (heedfulness). *Appamāda* is a vital factor for progress in the Buddhist system of conduct. It is usually defined as living with unbroken *sati*, which can be further defined as continuous carefulness, not allowing oneself to slide into decline or miss a chance for development; being well aware of what should be done and not done; constantly reflecting on one's duty, not neglecting it; doing things earnestly and striving for advancement at all times. It could be said that *appamāda* is the Buddhist sense of responsibility.

Appamāda is an internal factor, like wise attention (*yoniso-manasikāra*), which is coupled with the external factor of the good friend (*kalyāṇamitta*). Sometimes the Buddhavacana dealing with the importance of *appamāda* duplicate those dealing with wise attention. The reason for this is that both qualities are equally important, but in different ways: *yoniso-manasikāra* is a wisdom factor, a tool to be implemented in practice, whereas *appamāda* is a factor of concentration; it is that which controls and inspires the use of those tools and the advancement of the practice.

The importance and extent of the use of *appamāda* in various levels of practice can be seen from the following Buddhavacana:

> "Bhikkhus, the footprints of all kinds of land animals can be fit into the elephant's footprint; the elephant's footprint is the greatest of all in terms of size. In the same way, all skillful qualities have heedfulness as source, and all can be included within heedfulness. Heedfulness can be said to be the greatest of all those qualities."[17]
>
> ———

"I see no other quality that is so much a cause for the arising of skillful qualities as yet unarisen and the decline of unskillful qualities already arisen as heedfulness. When there is heedfulness, skillful qualities yet unarisen arise, and unskillful qualities already arisen decline."[18]

"I see no other quality that is for such great benefit[19]...for the firm establishment, non-decline, and non-disappearance of the true teaching (*saddhamma*) as heedfulness."[20]

"Among internal qualities, I see no other factor that is for such great benefit as heedfulness."[21]

"All things that are fabricated by determinants are subject to decline and cessation. Strive on to realize your objective with heedfulness."[22]

"Just as the rising of the sun is heralded by the light of dawn, endowment with heedfulness leads to and heralds the arising of the noble eightfold path in a bhikkhu...The prime factor of great benefit in the arising of the noble eightfold path is endowment with heedfulness...I see no other quality that is so much a cause for the arising of the noble eightfold path as yet unarisen or the growth and fulfillment of the noble eightfold path already arisen as endowment with heedfulness. A bhikkhu who is heedful may be expected to develop and make much of the noble eightfold path."[23]

"Bhikkhus. Cultivate heedfulness in four areas:

1. "Give up bodily misconduct, cultivate good bodily conduct, and be heedful therein.
2. "Give up verbal misconduct, cultivate good verbal conduct, and be heedful therein.

3. "Give up mental misconduct, cultivate good mental conduct, and be heedful therein.
4. "Give up wrong view, cultivate right view, and be heedful therein.

"When a bhikkhu gives up wrong bodily conduct and cultivates good bodily conduct...gives up wrong view and cultivates right view, he will not be afraid even in the face of death."[24]

"Bhikkhus, a bhikkhu should cultivate heedfulness—that is, govern the mind with mindfulness—these four areas:

1. "My mind will not be attached to those qualities that incite attachment.
2. "My mind will not be averse to those qualities that incite aversion.
3. "My mind will not be deluded by those qualities that incite delusion.
4. "My mind will not be intoxicated by those qualities that incite intoxication.

"When a bhikkhu's mind does not attach to those qualities that incite attachment, because it is free of desire; is not averse... not deluded...not intoxicated, he does not tremble, waver, feel dread or alarm, and he does not (have to) believe even in the words of a teacher (*samaṇa*)."[25]

"Your Majesty, the teachings well expounded by me are for those with good friends, good companions, who keep company with good people, not for those with bad friends, bad companions, or who keep company with bad people...Having good friends is equal to the whole of the holy life.

"For that reason, Your Majesty, you should reflect to yourself, 'I will be one with good friends, good companions, who keeps company with good people.' Your Majesty, when you have good

> friends, you must conduct yourself with this quality: heedfulness in regard to all skillful qualities.
>
> "When Your Majesty is heedful and conducts himself with heedfulness, the royal retainers...the nobles...the soldiers...the town and village dwellers will think, 'Our king is heedful and conducts himself with heedfulness. We too will be heedful and conduct ourselves with heedfulness.'
>
> "Your Majesty, in being heedful and conducting yourself with heedfulness, Your Majesty will be protected, the royal retainers will be protected...the treasuries and granaries will be protected."[26]

The Social Value of Sati

The Buddhavacana describing the value of *sati* in the *Sedaka Sutta* is a good example of the similarity of meaning and practical value of heedfulness and *sati*. It helps to understand both of those qualities more clearly and at the same time shows the attitude of the Buddhadhamma to life in society, proving that Buddhism sees the inner, personal life of each individual in relation to outer, social values, and holds these two values to be inextricably connected, compatible and one and the same, not separate:

> "Bhikkhus, there was once an acrobat who stood a bamboo pole on its end and called his apprentice, saying, 'Come, my boy, climb this bamboo pole [and balance yourself] on my shoulders.' The apprentice assented, climbed the pole, and stood [balancing] there on his master's shoulders.
>
> "Then the acrobat said to his apprentice, 'Come, you keep an eye on me, and I'll keep an eye on you, and we, each keeping an eye on the other, shall perform our feat, earn our fee, and come down safely from the pole.'
>
> "When the master had said this, the apprentice said, 'Master, we cannot do it that way. You, Master, should keep an eye on yourself, while I keep an eye on myself, and we, each watching

over himself, shall perform our feat, earn our fee, and come down safely from the pole.'"

The Blessed One said, "This was the right course of action in that case. Just as the apprentice said to his master, with the thought, 'I will protect myself,' you must practice the foundations of mindfulness [maintain mindfulness]; with the thought, 'I will protect others,' you must practice the foundations of mindfulness.

"Bhikkhus, in protecting yourself, you protect others; in protecting others, you protect yourself.

"How does one protect others by protecting oneself? By ardent practice, by cultivation, by making much of the practice. In this way, in protecting yourself, you protect others.

"How does one protect oneself by protecting others? By forbearance (*khanti*), by non-aggression (*avihiṁsā*), by friendliness, by kindness and compassion. In this way, protecting others, you protect yourself.

"Bhikkhus, with the thought, 'I will protect myself,' you must practice the foundations of mindfulness; with the thought 'I will protect others,' you must practice the foundations of mindfulness. In protecting yourself you protect others; in protecting others, you protect yourself."[27]

The Role of Sati *in Wisdom Development*

Being heedful means living with unbroken *sati*, or using *sati* at all times in one's life. It is the agent that makes us watchful, protects us from mistakenly falling into bad or corrupt ways, restrains and warns us against preoccupation and delusion in pleasure, stirs us out of stagnation and incites us into ardent pursuit of advancement, causes us to be heedful of our duties by considering what should be done and what should not be done, what has been done and what remains to be done, and helps to ensure that our actions are circumspect. Thus, as already stated, it is a principal factor in the Buddhist system of conduct.

However, it can be seen that the importance of heedfulness is in terms of conduct. It can be roughly determined as covering the area from morality to concentration. On this level, *sati* mostly works in conjunction with many other factors. Effort (*vāyāma*), in particular, will always be involved. When our field of examination is narrowed down to the workings of the mind within the process of wisdom development, or the use of wisdom for cleansing the mind, heedfulness manifests as an instigating agent. On this level, our range of investigation narrows down to the mental processes, and is broken down to a discrete moment-to-moment analysis. It is on this level that *sati* performs its function in full and comes into its own, becoming a factor with its own specific role and its own specific name.

The real, specific meaning of *sati* can be gleaned from considering its function when it has a distinct role, as in the practice known as the four foundations of mindfulness. In this case, the function of *sati* can be summarized as follows:

The general characteristic of the functioning of *sati* is not allowing the mind to wander, not allowing mental objects (*ārammaṇa*) to pass by unheeded, or not allowing thinking to become distracted by mental objects, but rather carefully watching over, as if taking note of each object that passes through awareness, deliberately focusing on it. Whatever object is to be noted, *sati* fixes on that and does not allow the mind to wander. It recollects that object and does not allow it to be forgotten.[28] *Sati* is compared to a foundation post, because it is firmly fixed to the object, or to a gate keeper, because it guards over the different sense doors through which objects appear, inspecting the objects that arise in awareness. The proximate causes (*padaṭṭhāna*) for the arising of *sati* are firm *saññā* (perception and interpretation), or the various foundations of mindfulness, which will be discussed shortly.

In terms of conduct, the functioning of *sati* can be seen from both negative and positive perspectives. From the negative perspective, *sati* is a guard, preventing the mind from distraction and error, preventing it from falling into undesirable states, not allowing evil to arise in the mind or thinking to be used in wrongful ways. In a positive sense, *sati* is a controller and inspector of the streams of cognition, thinking and conduct so that they are all along acceptable lines. It keeps the mind with the desired object of awareness, and therefore it is the tool for holding or fixing on to the mind's object, laying it before the mind, so to speak, for examination and response.

The importance of *sati* is given great emphasis in Buddhist practice, in regard to which it is said that *sati* is desirable (i.e., must be used) in all situations. It is compared to salt, which must be used in all foods, or like a prime minister, who is involved in all government business. It is the quality that both constrains the mind and supports it, depending on the circumstance.[29]

When these characteristics of the functioning of *sati* are taken into consideration, the benefits of practicing *sati* can be seen as follows:

1. To control the mental state by examining the cognitive and thought processes, selecting what is wanted and rejecting what is not wanted, stilling the thought processes and thus facilitating the concentration of the mind.
2. To put the body and mind into a state that can be said to be more independent, because they have lightness, relaxation, and well-being in themselves, and are ready to encounter and respond effectively to things in the world.
3. In the concentrated mind, *sati* may be used to constrain and direct the cognitive and thought processes, to expand the scope of cognition and thought into different dimensions or into different states.
4. To hold the object that is the point of investigation to awareness, thus enabling the work of examining and investigating to proceed with greater clarity, and thereby acting as a foundation for the development of wisdom.
5. To cleanse all facets of conduct (physical, verbal, and mental) and make them pure, free of the influence of desire and clinging

and, together with comprehension (*sampajañña*), to cause that conduct to proceed with wisdom or pure reason.

The fourth and fifth benefits of sati are high-level objectives. They can only be attained through the special practice of the four foundations of mindfulness.

The Foundations of Mindfulness as Right Mindfulness

Satipaṭṭhāna is translated as the bases for *sati*, or as the establishment of *sati*—that is, being under the control of *sati*. In principle it is the method of practice for putting *sati* to the most effective use, as stated in the Buddhavacana in the *Mahāsatipaṭṭhāna Sutta*: "Bhikkhus, this is the supreme way for the purification of beings, for the transcendence of sorrow and lamentation, for the extinguishing of suffering and grief, for the attainment of the transcendent path, for the realization of *nibbāna*: that is, the four foundations of mindfulness."[30]

The development of the foundations of mindfulness is a popular and highly acclaimed method of practice. It is said to comprise both calm (*samatha*) and insight (*vipassanā*) development. A practitioner may develop calm as far as the absorptions (*jhāna*), as will be described in the section on the eighth factor of the path (right concentration), and then develop insight through the foundations of mindfulness to reach the goal, or develop only the initial stages of concentration, only as much as required, and reach the goal by practicing insight as the main factor of practice according to the foundations of mindfulness.

Insight (*vipassanā*) is an important part of Buddhist practice that is often heard about, but often misunderstood. Thus it deserves some clarification. The following brief examination of the foundations of mindfulness may help to clarify the meaning of insight, in terms of its essential meaning, its scope, and the variations of its practice. Be that as it may, here it is not my intention to examine insight as such, but simply to convey the general idea through the foundations of mindfulness.

The foundations of mindfulness are essentially as follows:

1. *Kāyānupassanā*: examining the body, or being fully aware of the body
   - *Ānāpānasati*: going to a secluded place, sitting cross-legged, establishing *sati* on the in- and out-breathing in various manifestations.
   - *Iriyāpatha*: clearly noting each posture as it is when the body is standing, walking, sitting, reclining or in other postures.
   - *Sampajañña*: developing clear comprehension in all activities and in all movements, such as stepping, turning the head, stretching out the hand, dressing, eating, drinking, chewing, defecating, urinating, waking, sleeping, talking, and being silent.
   - *Paṭikūlamanasikāra*: examining one's own body, from the top of the head down to the tips of the feet, as containing a mass of numerous unclean component parts.
   - *Dhātumanasikāra*: examining one's own body broken down into each of the four elements.
   - *Navasīvathikā*: gazing on corpses in nine different states, from a fresh corpse to brittle bones, and in each case turning the reflection back on oneself, that one's own body will one day have to be in that state.
2. *Vedanānupassanā*: being fully aware of feelings, noting clearly as they are in the present moment when feelings of pleasure, pain, or indifference arise, be they with material base (*sāmisa*) or without material base (*nirāmisa*).
3. *Cittānupassanā*: being fully aware of the mind, how the mind is at that time. Knowing, for instance, whether the mind has desire, is without desire, has aversion, is without aversion, has delusion, is without delusion, is distracted, is concentrated, is liberated or not yet liberated—knowing the mind clearly as it is at the time.

4. *Dhammānupassanā*: being fully aware of phenomena (*dhammas*):
   - *Nīvaraṇa*:[31] knowing clearly in each moment whether or not any of the five hindrances (*nīvaraṇa*) are present within one; how those as yet unarisen come to arise, how those already arisen are done away with, and how those given up can be made not to arise again.
   - *Khandhas*: noting what the five *khandhas* are, how they arise, how they cease.
   - *Āyatana*: knowing clearly the internal and external sense bases; knowing clearly the fetters (*saṁyojana*) that arise on account of each sense base; knowing clearly how fetters as yet unarisen come to arise; how those already arisen are done away with; how those already done away with are made not to arise again.
   - *Bojjhaṅga*:[32] knowing clearly in the present whether each of the seven enlightenment factors is there in the mind or not; how those as yet unarisen are made to arise; how those already arisen are made to develop and come to fulfillment.
   - *Ariyasacca*: knowing and understanding clearly each of the four noble truths.

Each of the groups above contains the same passage:

> "A bhikkhu examines the body in the body internally [= his own]; he examines the body in the body externally [= belonging to other people]; he examines the body in the body both internally and externally. He examines the truth of the arising in the body; he examines the truth of decline and cessation in the body; he examines the truth of arising and cessation in the body.
>
> "And he has the clear recollection 'there is the body,' just as an object of awareness, and just enough for recollection, and he abides not dependent on or attaching to anything in the world."[33]

Essential Meaning of the Foundations of Mindfulness

From the brief summary of the foundations of mindfulness it can be seen that they (and indeed the practice of insight) are not a teaching that necessitates physical seclusion, being away from society, or being in a particular time or occasion. For this reason, many teachers recommend practicing them in ordinary everyday life.

In essence, the teaching of the four foundations of mindfulness tells us that our lives have merely four areas that require the attention of *sati*. They are the body and its conduct; *vedanā*, feelings of pleasure and pain; the various states of mind; and thought and reflection. If we live with *sati* guarding these four areas, this will help us to live in safety, free of suffering, and with well-being. It is the practice that is conducive to realization of the four noble truths.

From the passages describing each of the foundations of mindfulness it can be seen that the practice makes use of not only *sati* but also other factors. One that is not specifically mentioned is concentration (*samādhi*), which must always be present, at least in sufficient measure for the purpose.[34] Qualities specifically mentioned are as follows:

1. *Ātāpī*: there is effort (that is, the sixth factor of the path, right effort, which is the effort to guard against and give up evil, and the effort to generate and maintain goodness).
2. *Sampajāno*: there is comprehension (the wisdom factor).
3. *Satimā*: there is *sati* (that is, *sati* itself).

Worth noting is *sampajāno*, meaning "there is *sampajañña*." The word *sampajañña* is often coupled with *sati*. It is a factor of wisdom, so training in *sati* is also part of the process of wisdom development. *Sampajañña* is comprehension and clear awareness of the object that *sati* is attending to, or the action being done at any given time, as to its objectives and what to do about it, and not giving way to delusion or misunderstanding about the situation.

The next phrase, "eliminating covetousness and grief toward the world" indicates the mental outlook that results from having *sati* and clear comprehension, as impartial, free, not bound by defilements, either of attachment and desire or aversion and sorrow, in that situation.

The final phrase, the same for each of the foundations, "seeing arising and cessation," shows the examination of things in terms of the three characteristics, leading to the resultant outlook of seeing and perceiving things as they really are, as in "there is the body." This refers to bare awareness of things as they are, stripped of conventional concepts and attachments such as "person," "self," "him," "her," or "my body." This outlook is one of freedom and independence, not subject to external conditions and not attached to the world through craving and clinging.

In order to show the meaning more clearly, I would like to translate some of the Pali terms used in the teaching of the foundations of mindfulness and give their meanings in brief.

Kāye kāyānupassī: "examines the body in the body." This is looking at the body as just the body, seeing the body according to its reality of a collection or assemblage of component parts, the large and small organs, rather than seeing the body as me or them, "John Smith" or "Jane Jones," as "mine" or "belonging to others." It is to see things as they really are, according to their reality. What is looked at is what is seen: when looking at a body, one sees a body, not John, or Jane, or someone we dislike or we admire. This accords with the old saying: "What is looked at is not seen; what is seen is not what is looked at. Not seeing, one falls into the trap; trapped, there is no liberation."[35]

Ātāpī sampajāno satimā: "there is effort, there is comprehension, there is mindfulness." That is, there is right effort, right view, and right mindfulness, which are the factors of the path that must always be used in conjunction with the development of all other path factors.[36] Effort arouses the mind and prevents it from becoming discouraged, procrastinating, or regressing, and therefore gives no opportunity for the arising of unskillful qualities but rather urges the mind to keep going forward with the development of skillful qualities. *Sampajañña* is the wisdom faculty, which examines and comprehends the objects noted by *sati*. *Sati* is the factor that attends to and holds on to objects, making it possible for the mind to follow them as they arise rather than becoming forgetful, distracted or confused.

Vineyya loke abhijjhādomanassaṁ: "eliminating covetousness and grief in the world." This means that when the practice of *satipaṭṭhāna* is maintained, the mind is clear and buoyant, free of domination or disturbance by attachment and desire, aversion and sorrow.

Atthi kāyoti vā panassa sati paccupaṭṭhitā hoti yāvadeva ñāṇamattāya paṭissatimattāya: "having the clear recollection 'there is the body,' just as an object of awareness, and just enough for recollection." That is, *sati* clearly notes things as they are—there is only the body, not a being, a person, a man or a woman, a self, things belonging to the self, things belonging to others, or whatever—simply for awareness and for recollection, for the development of *sati* and comprehension, or for the increase of *sati* and wisdom, not for distracted thinking and daydreams, or for excessive cogitation. The same applies to feelings, mind, and *dhammas*.

Anissito ca viharati: "and he dwells independent..." The mind is free, not subject to anything else. One does not have to place one's mind in this or that thing or this or that person. Technically, this means that the meditator does not take shelter in desire and views and is not subject to them. For example, when one cognizes experiences, one cognizes them as they actually are; desire and views do not come in and create images around them or color and embellish them.

Na ca kiñci loke upādiyati: "and he clings to nothing in the world." One does not attach to anything, be it form, feeling, perception, mental formations or consciousness, as self (*attā*) or belonging to self (*attanīyā*).

Ajjhattaṁ vā... bahiddhā vā: "internally... externally." This passage has been interpreted in different ways by different teachers, but the consensus of the commentaries is that "internally" means "one's own," while "externally" means "belonging to others."[37] This view accords with the Abhidhamma Piṭaka, which explains the matter clearly:

> "How does a bhikkhu dwell observing the mind in the mind externally? As to this, when another person's mind is desirous, a bhikkhu knows that that person's mind is desirous..."[38]

The question arises whether it is appropriate to go around looking into what is happening in the bodies and minds of other people, and how it is possible to do so. In this regard, we must simply understand that the commentators want us to use *sati* in relation to all things we come into contact with, knowing them merely as they are. In our daily lives we must inevitably come into contact with other people. When we do so, we must deal with them mindfully, knowing them as they really are and according to what actually appears to us; that is, knowing only as much as directly appears to our senses (if we do happen to have direct knowledge [*ñāṇa*] of the mental states of others, we know according to what the direct knowledge tells us; if we do not have such direct knowledge, we need not go prying), so that we are not led into confused ideation about other people, and the subsequent desire or aversion to which that leads. If we do not see or have to deal with others, that is the end of the matter. It does not mean that we must go out of our way to look into the mental and physical behavior of others.

We may summarize here that the practice of the foundations of mindfulness is dwelling with *sati* and clear understanding that cut off self-images concocted by ignorance.

Some Western scholars have compared the practice of the foundations of mindfulness with modern psychoanalysis, and evaluated the foundations of mindfulness as being more effective and more broadly applicable, because it can be practiced by all people, in normal situations, to obtain a healthy mind.[39] However, I will not go into the subject here, but instead summarize once more the essential points of the practice of the foundations of mindfulness according to modern thinking.

The Process of Practice

1. The factors or components involved in this process of practice are on two sides: the active side (the agent that notes, observes, or examines) and the passive side (the objects that are noted, observed, or examined).

2. The factors on the passive side, which are noted and examined, are the ordinary, natural phenomena that lie within all people, such as the body, the movements of the body, the feelings and thoughts that arise in the present moment.

3. The factors on the active side, the noting and examination, are the essential agents of the foundations of mindfulness—*sati* and *sampajañña*. *Sati* is what fixes onto the object of examination; *sampajañña* is the wisdom factor, which attends to and knows the condition or manifestation that is being examined—what it is and what its objectives are. For instance, while observing the movements of the body, such as walking, one knows why one is walking and in order to go where, and one understands that action as it actually is, without pasting one's feeling over it.

There is a certain misunderstanding that may cause the practice to go astray, and that is the misinterpretation of the translations of *sati* and *sampajañña* as self-awareness,[40] taking recollection to be observing and recollecting the self, as in the feeling "I am doing this." This is creating an image of self that the mind proceeds to fix onto. To counter this, the meaning of *sati* should be understood in its sense of "applying consideration," "keeping the mind on its object," "holding the mind to the task at hand," or "holding the mind to the stream of activity," and *sampajañña* as "clearly comprehending what is being considered," or "clearly comprehending what is being done." That is, it is not applying *sati* to the self (as doing this or that); it is recollecting the task (what is being done), not recollecting the self (the doer). *Sati* attends to what is being done or what is happening so closely that there is no chance to think of a self or a doer. The mind is so "with" the task being done that there is no room for a notion of self to arise.

4. The action of observing and examining is essentially seeing

things as they are at that time. It is facing up to, cognizing, examining, and understanding things, keeping abreast of them every step of the way, not building reactions in the mind. There is no evaluation or speculation as "good," "bad," "right," or "wrong." The mind does not add its feelings, biases, inclinations, or attachments as "agreeable," "disagreeable," "liked," or "disliked," for example. It sees that thing, manifestation, or perspective only as it is and does not add on the idea "mine," "theirs," "me," "them," "Jane," or "John." For instance, in examining the feelings in one's own mind, when an unpleasant feeling arises, one knows that an unpleasant feeling has arisen, how it has arisen, and how it passes away. If one is examining mental objects (*dhammārammaṇa*), such as when worry or depression arise, one takes that very worry or depression and examines them to see how they arise, and how they proceed. When anger arises in the mind, as soon as one realizes that anger has arisen, the anger disappears. One takes up the anger itself to examine its benefits and its harm, the causes of its arising and the way it ceases, so that it can even be pleasant to study and analyze one's suffering, and that suffering is stripped of its sting for the person analyzing it. It is purely suffering, a feeling that arises and passes away. It is not "my suffering." No matter what good and bad states may arise or appear in the mind, we face up to them and do not turn away from them. We direct our attention right onto them and see them as they are, from the moment they arise to the moment they naturally pass away. Then we look at something else. It is like watching a play, or being an onlooker of some scene. It is the attitude of a doctor dissecting a corpse or a scientist examining a specimen rather than a judge presiding over a case. It is an objective rather than a subjective position.

Living with such continuous *sati* and clear comprehension requires one important factor, known as "being in the present moment." That is to say, *sati* observes things at the very time they arise, occur, or are being done, not allowing them to slip away, and not allowing the mind to get stuck on or linger over objects that have passed away or drift ahead in search of things that have not yet come. The mind neither slides back into the past nor floats off into the future. If one does consider past events or future tasks, *sati* takes hold of those things so that wisdom can examine them meaningfully, and therefore those matters become present objects of the mind. There is none of the aimless drifting, yearning, or pining that characterize thoughts that are stuck in the past or the future.

Living in the present moment in this way means to be not enslaved or seduced by desire. It is rather to live with wisdom, which frees the mind of symptoms of suffering such as sorrow, grief, guilt, and worry, and leads to knowledge, clarity, and well-being.

The Fruits of the Practice

1. In terms of purity, when *sati* fixes solely on the object of attention and comprehension understands it as it is, the streams of cognition and thought are kept pure and there is no chance for defilements to arise. When a condition is analyzed and seen just as it is, not added to with the subjectivity of personal feelings, thoughts, biases and predilections, there is no clinging and there are no channels through which defilements such as anger could arise. It is a method of eliminating old outflows (*āsava*) already arisen and preventing new outflows from arising.

2. In terms of freedom, once there is the pure mind as just described, there is also freedom. The mind does not waver in the face of the objects that arise in awareness, because those objects are all used as subjects of study and objective examination. When objects are not interpreted according to the outflows, which are subjective, they no longer have any subjective influence over one. One's actions are freed of the compulsion of defilements, subconscious drives or motivations. Such a person lives independently (that is, not subject to desire and views) and attaches to nothing in the world.

3. In terms of wisdom, within such a mental process, wisdom is able to function most effectively, because it is not coated over or diverted by feelings, biases, and prejudices, and things are seen as they are: one knows according to the truth.

4. In terms of freedom from suffering, when the mind is in a state of alertness and comprehension of how things are, and this kind of attitude is maintained, positively or negatively biased feelings that are not a result of pure reason cannot arise. Thus, there are no feelings of covetousness (*abhijjhā*) or grief (*domanassa*). The mind is free of anxiety. It is the mind that is said to be free of suffering: clear, light, relaxed, calm and independent.

These fruits of the practice are actually all related and are different perspectives of the same thing. When summarized in terms of the *paṭiccasamuppāda* and the three characteristics, the picture that emerges is that people do not know that the self they cling to does not really exist, that there is only a stream of countless interrelated and interdependent subsidiary mental and material conditions. These are constantly arising, dissolving, and changing. Not knowing this, people cling onto their feelings, thoughts, desires, habits, attitudes, views, and perceptions at each moment as the self, and that self is constantly changing. They think, "I am this," "I am that," "I feel like this," "I feel like that," and so on. The feeling that the self is various things is merely a deception created by the thoughts and feelings that are the subsidiary mental constituents of the moment. This deception is the beginning of wrong thinking, and so the mind is drawn into thoughts, feelings, and actions under the influence of whatever is held to as self at the time. By practicing according to the foundations of mindfulness, the physical and mental qualities that constitute the stream of experience are seen in a state of constant arising and ceasing. When the components of the stream are analyzed and seen as separate constituents or moments of time, and as a causally dependent process, we are no longer deceived into clinging onto those things as a self or belonging to self. Those things lose their power to control us.

If this kind of perception is sufficiently profound and complete it is the state known as "liberation." The mind is established in a new form, a purified, clear, and free mental process, free of inner biases, attachments, and complexes. A new character arises.

In other words, it is the state of perfect mental health, like the physical body that is said to be in perfect health when all of its organs are in perfect functioning order and it is not marred by illnesses. In this respect, practicing according to the foundations of mindfulness is a method of cleansing the mind of symptoms and illnesses and eliminating the complexes and obstacles that impair and obstruct its functioning. The mind is rendered clear and ready to live, to face up to and deal with the things in the world with strength and cheerfulness.

This may be best summarized in the Buddhavacana:

> "Bhikkhus, there are two kinds of illness: physical illnesses and mental illnesses. Beings who can declare that they have been free of physical illness for a whole year can be found. Beings who can declare that they have been free of physical illness for two years... three years... four years... five years... ten years... twenty years... thirty years... forty years... fifty years... one hundred years can be found, but beings who can declare that they have been free of mental illnesses, even for a moment, are hard to find in this world, except among those who have destroyed the outflows (*khīṇāsava*)."[41]
>
> ---
>
> Sāriputta: "Householder, your features are clear, your face pure and radiant. Could it be that today you have listened to a Dhamma teaching in the presence of the Blessed One?"
>
> Nakulapitā: "Venerable Sir, what else? Today I have been anointed with the nectar of a Dhamma teaching from the Blessed One."
>
> Sāriputta: "With the nectar of what teaching did the Blessed One anoint you?"
>
> Nakulapitā: "Venerable Sir, I approached the Blessed One, saluted and sat down respectfully to one side, and said, 'Revered Sir, I am aged, an old man, wizened in years, my body beset by illnesses, visited frequently by sickness. Moreover, I do not [have the chance to] see the Blessed One and the bhikkhus, who fill me with inspiration, regularly. May the Blessed One please grant

me some teaching that will be for my benefit and happiness for a long time to come.'

"The Buddha answered, 'It is true, householder, that is how it is. This body is beset by illness, like an egg enveloped in its shell: who but a fool among those with such bodies would say that he has no illnesses, even for a moment? Thus should you, householder, consider to yourself: 'Even though my body be beset with illness, my mind will not be beset by illness.'"

"Venerable Sir, it is with the nectar of this teaching that the Blessed One anointed me."[42]

Importance of Sati *in the Present Moment in Insight Practice*

The most mundane activity, which is occurring throughout our daily lives, is the cognition of sense objects though eye, ear, nose, tongue, body, and mind. When there is cognition it is accompanied by feelings—pleasurable and comfortable, unpleasant or painful, or indifferent. When pleasant or unpleasant feelings arise, there is a mental reaction. If pleasure arises in regard to something, we like it and attach to it; if displeasure or suffering arises in regard to something, we are averse to it and don't like it. When we like something, we want to experience it again, or possess it; when we do not like something, we want to run away from it, or eliminate it. This process is occurring all the time, both on subtle levels that we hardly notice, and on more obvious levels that have a clear and lasting effect on the mind. Those parts of the process that are particularly extreme or unusual tend to lead to extended thought and cogitation. If they do not cease in the mind, they push outward into major and minor verbal and physical expressions. Our lives, the roles we play in the world and the interaction we have with each other are largely a result of these small, momentary processes.

In terms of wisdom, allowing the mind to follow the process outlined above—cognizing an object, feeling pleasant, liking it and attaching to it, or cognizing an object, feeling unpleasant, feeling averse to it and disliking it—is an obstacle to clear awareness of things as they really are, because such a mind has the following characteristics:

- It is preoccupied with likes and dislikes; it falls under the power of attachments and aversion and is blinded by those attachments and aversions, and therefore sees things in a biased way, not as they really are.
- It falls into the past or the future. That is, once cognition arises and like or dislike follow, the mind becomes obsessed with or offended by the part, point, or aspect of that object that it likes or dislikes, and holds onto a mental image of that part, point, or aspect, which it fixes onto and cogitates about to the point of fantasizing. Fixing onto one liked or disliked part and holding onto the image that appears in the mind is sliding into the past. The mental cogitation around the image that follows is floating off into the future. Any knowledge or understanding that may arise regarding that object is only knowledge of that part of the object that the mind likes or dislikes, which has already been embellished in the mind; it is not the thing itself as it actually is at that time.
- It falls under the power of mental embellishment and subsequently translates the meaning of sense objects or experiences according to background, or accumulated habits, such as values, attitudes, or views that one upholds and esteems. The mind is in an embellished state, and is unable to look impartially and see experiences as they actually are.
- Apart from being embellished, the mind also uses the embellished images of new experiences to create new embellishments, promoting and strengthening the accumulated habits of the mind.

This process not only involves the coarse and superficial affairs of our everyday lives and activities but also the subtle and profound levels of mental processes, which cause unenlightened beings to perceive things as lasting, solid entities, endowed with beauty or ugliness, and to hold fast to conventional realities, failing to see the process as faring according to constantly operating causes and conditions.

Be that as it may, these processes are acquired tendencies or habits of the mind that we have accumulated virtually since the day we were born—twenty, thirty, forty, fifty years or more—and we have never trained to cut the cycle of the process. Thus, correcting it is no easy matter. As soon as a sense object or experience is cognized, the mind runs along its well-worn pathways before we even have a chance to prepare ourselves. In order to correct this, it is necessary not only to cut off the cycle and purify the process, but also to correct the forceful habits of the mind.

An important factor for use in paving the way, one that is a gathering point in both cases, is *sati*, and this is the goal of the practice of the foundations of mindfulness. When *sati* is abreast of the present moment and continuously sees things as they really are, we are able to cut the cycle, destroy the unskillful process, and gradually correct old habits, at the same time creating new habits in the mind. The mind that has *sati* to help keep it in the present moment will have the opposite characteristics of one that follows the process of unskillful qualities described above—namely:

- Like and aversion are unable to arise within it, because in order to like or dislike something the mind must affix and dwell on one particular part or aspect of it—that is, fall into the past.
- It does not slide into the past or float off into the future. Like, dislike, and falling into the past go together. When the mind is not caught up in or lingering over something, but seeing its reality as it is, there is no falling into the past or floating off into the future.
- It is not led by excessive cogitation based on accumulated histories into interpreting experiences or objects of cognition in a biased, distorted, or tainted way, and thus is ready to see things according to their reality.

- It does not embellish, add to, or reinforce the wrong habits it has accumulated.
- Being aware of all things as they are in the present moment, we also see the habitual mental states that are undesirable, or normally not acknowledged, coming out into the open. This enables us to become aware of and face up to our true condition rather than trying to run away from it or deceive ourselves, and allows us to eradicate those defilements and solve our problems.

In addition, in terms of the quality of the mind, it will be pure, clear, unhindered, buoyant, and free, not constricted or obscured.

All things are established according to their nature and fare according to the natural order. Truth is always revealing itself, but people either hide themselves away from it, distort it, or deceive themselves about it. That which does the concealing, distortion, or deceiving is the mind falling into the stream of the process described above. The concealing, distorting, or deceiving factor is already there: add to this the misleading influence of accumulated habits and there is almost no chance of seeing the truth. Since these tendencies or habits have been continuously accumulated over a long period of time, it naturally requires time to change them and create new habits.

When *sati* is aware of things as they arise, functioning consistently and skillfully, and we do not block ourselves off or distort the images we perceive, and are freed from our accumulated mental habits, then we are ready to see things according to their reality and see the truth. At this stage, if other faculties, especially wisdom, are sufficiently strong and primed, they work hand in hand with *sati*, or have the way prepared for them by *sati*, to function fully, leading to direct knowledge and vision (*ñāṇadassana*), to penetration into the truth, which is the objective of insight practice (*vipassanā*).

Whether or not the wisdom faculty is sufficiently strong or primed depends on progressive training, together with a basis of learning and conversance with the teachings. Thus learning, listening, and reasoned reflection are aids to realizing the truth.

The Foundations of Mindfulness as Nutriment for the Factors of Enlightenment

Sati is not in itself insight. Wisdom, or the use of wisdom, is insight, but wisdom only gets the chance to function, and can only function fluently and fully, when it is controlled and supported by *sati*, as explained above. Thus, the development of *sati* is important in insight practice. In other words, we practice *sati* in order to make full utilization of wisdom. In the terminology of Dhamma practice, when we talk of *sati*, we tend to include *sampajañña*, which is wisdom, and *sati* is made stronger, more fluent and more skillful when used in conjunction with wisdom.[43] On this level, wisdom seems to be almost a supporting factor, working hand in hand with *sati*, and here it is usually *sati* that is spoken of as the important factor, but on levels in which wisdom is working more intensively, the emphasis is given to wisdom and *sati* is like an accessory to wisdom. The wisdom that functions on this level is *dhammavicaya*, one of the seven enlightenment factors.

The Buddha stated that the four foundations of mindfulness are a nutriment for the seven enlightenment factors (*bojjhaṅga*), and the enlightenment factors are nutriments for knowledge and liberation (*vijjāvimutti*):

> "Bhikkhus, I say that knowledge and liberation have nutriment; they are not without nutriment. What is the nutriment for knowledge and liberation? The seven enlightenment factors are the nutriment of knowledge and liberation. The seven enlightenment factors have nutriment; they are not without nutriment. And what is the nutriment for the seven enlightenment factors? The four foundations of mindfulness...
>
> "The four foundations of mindfulness that are fully developed lead to the full development of the seven enlightenment factors. The seven enlightenment factors that are fully developed lead to the fulfillment of knowledge and liberation. Knowledge and liberation have nutriments and come to fulfillment in this way."[44]

Sampajañña, *dhammavicaya*, or *paññā* under any of its other names, which works for realization and understanding of things as they really are, for liberation of the mind, is insight.[45]

Sati plays an important role in both calm (*samatha*) and insight (*vipassanā*) meditation. A discussion of the comparative roles of *sati* in *samatha* and in *vipassanā* practice may help to clarify this. In *samatha* meditation, *sati* holds the mind to its object, or holds the object to the mind, just in order to allow the mind to fix unwaveringly onto or become at one with it, to become still and unmoving. When the mind is resolutely fixed on and at one with the object for a sustained period of time, this is called *samādhi* (concentration), and with just this, *samatha* is achieved.

In *vipassanā* practice, *sati* also holds the object to the mind, or holds the mind to its object, but the emphasis is on using the mind as a platform on which to "place" objects for examination by the wisdom faculty; that is, objects are held up on the "platform" of the firmly concentrated mind for wisdom's examination and analysis.[46] To use a simile, *samatha* meditation is like tying an unruly calf to a stake with a rope so that it cannot wander off, but only walk around the vicinity of the stake. Eventually, losing its unruliness, the calf lies down quietly at the stake. Here, the mind is like the unruly calf, the meditation object (*ārammaṇa*) is the stake, and *sati* the rope. *Vipassanā* meditation is like tying an animal or object onto a bench or bed in order to examine it or perform some kind of task, such as an operation. The rope or binding is *sati*; the animal or thing is the object; the bench or bed is the concentrated mind; and the examination or operation is wisdom.

There are a few minor observations that should be further mentioned. One is that in *samatha* meditation the objective is calming the mind. Thus, whenever *sati* is noting an object, it holds and fastens the mind onto that alone, and does not allow it to wander, until eventually the mind is resolutely absorbed on a sign (*nimitta*) or mental image of the object of contemplation. In *vipassanā* the objective is understanding reality. Thus, *sati* attends only to the object as it actually is, and in order to allow the wisdom faculty to fully and clearly comprehend its true nature, it follows the object through all its manifestations, such as its arising and its transmutations up to its passing away. Moreover, it must also note all objects that come into or become involved in awareness, and that must be understood with wisdom in order to have full comprehension of the truth. Thus, the object of attention is always changing, and in order to comprehend it as it actually is, it is necessary to keep abreast of its changes in each and every moment, not allowing the mind to dwell on any particular object or aspect of an object.

In addition, in *samatha* meditation *sati* attends to an object that is either fixed and unmoving or is moving repeatedly in a formalized way within fixed limitations. In *vipassanā* meditation *sati* attends to objects that are moving or that may be in any state whatsoever, without limitation. In *samatha* meditation it is preferred to choose for attention only certain objects from among those specified techniques for helping the mind to become calm and concentrated. In *vipassanā* meditation, all objects without limitation can be attended to, depending on what comes up for examination and can enable one to see the truth (which can be summarized as body, feelings, mind, and *dhammas*, or mentality and physicality).

Another important component that helps to clarify the distinction between *vipassanā* and *samatha* is wise attention (*yoniso-manasikāra*). Wise attention is a factor that aids in the arising of wisdom, and therefore holds much importance for *vipassanā* practice. In *samatha* meditation, while wise attention may be an aid in some cases, its necessity is less, and in some cases it may not be required at all, with mere attention (*manasikāra*) being sufficient. Enlarging on this, in the practice of *samatha* meditation the essential factor is to use *sati* to hold the mind on the object, or recollect that object, so that the mind becomes resolutely fixed on it. In this case, if the results arise according to plan there is no need for wise attention at all. However, in cases where the mind refuses to take an interest in the object, cannot be held to it and is always floating off, or in some kinds of meditation in which discursive thinking is required, such as meditation on goodwill (*mettā*), it may be necessary to use techniques to help bring the mind to its objective. In such cases it may be necessary to use the help of *yoniso-manasikāra*—that is, attention with skillful means (*upāya-manasikāra*)—thinking, for example, via a means that suppresses aversion and instead initiates goodwill. But in any case, in *samatha* meditation, any *yoniso-manasikāra* that may be required is only the kind for arousing skillful qualities,[47] not the kind that initiates insight into reality.

In *vipassanā* practice, wise attention is an extremely important stage in the development of wisdom, and therefore is an essential factor. Wise attention is contingent on wisdom, being the agent that paves the way for wisdom to operate[48] or widens the channels for wisdom's growth and maturity. Its features or functions are so similar to that of wisdom that the two are often used ambiguously, or in talking of one, the other is also implied. Thus, students often cannot distinguish between them.

It may be said that wise attention functions as a connection between *sati* and wisdom, being the guide or director of the thought process in ways that allow wisdom to operate effectively. In other words, it is what gives wisdom its techniques, or the skillful means by which wisdom gains effect.

Moreover, as long as *yoniso-manasikāra* is functioning, *sati* will be present and will not stray. Thus *sati* and *yoniso-manasikāra* are mutually helpful in the practice of *vipassanā*.

Right Concentration

Right concentration (*sammāsamādhi*) is the last factor of the path, and it is the factor with the most material for study, since it deals with the training of the mind on a profound level. It is subtle and detailed, both in the sense that the mind is a subtle condition, and in the sense that the practice contains such a wide-ranging and complex body of instruction. It is the summation or coming together of the practice.

Samādhi is usually translated as "firm establishment of mind," or the state in which the mind is resolutely fixed on its object. A common definition of *samādhi* is *cittassekaggatā*, or simply *ekaggatā*, meaning one-pointedness of mind, the state in which the mind is resolutely fixed on something and does not wander or waver.

Commentarial texts further define the meaning as the state of one-pointedness of a skillful mind, and explain that this means successfully maintaining the mind and its concomitants evenly and continuously with one object.[49]

The usual definition of right concentration in the suttas is specifically the concentration of the four absorptions (*jhānas*).

> "Bhikkhus, what is right concentration? [Herein,] a bhikkhu in this teaching and discipline:
>
> "Secluded from sensuality, secluded from unskillful conditions, attains the first *jhāna*, which has initial application of mind (*vitakka*), sustained application of mind (*vicāra*), and the rapture and well-being born of seclusion.
>
> "He attains the second *jhāna*, which has inner clarity and a state of one-ness. It has no initial or sustained application of mind because they have ceased, and contains only rapture and well-being born of concentration.
>
> "Because of the fading out of rapture, dwelling with equanimity, with mindfulness and comprehension (*sati sampajañña*), and experiencing well-being in the body, he attains the third *jhāna*, of which the noble ones say, 'One who has equanimity and mindfulness indeed dwells happily.'
>
> "By giving up pleasant and unpleasant feeling, through the cessation of pleasure (*somanassa*) and woe (*domanassa*), he attains the fourth *jhāna*, in which there is neither suffering nor happiness, but only mindfulness purified by equanimity."[50]

The above passage may be taken as a description of right concentration in its fullest sense. In some places *cittassekaggatā* is described as the concentration faculty (*samādhindriya*), as in the following passage:

> "Bhikkhus, what is the faculty of concentration (*samādhindriya*)? [Herein,] a noble disciple in this teaching and discipline, attending to detachment, attains to concentration and one-pointedness of mind [*cittassekaggatā*]. This is called the faculty of concentration."[51]

The Abhidhamma definition is as follows:

> What is right concentration? Any establishment of the mind, resolute establishment of the mind, firmness of mind, non-wavering, non-wandering of mind, non-digression of mind, calmness (*samatha*), *samādhi* faculty, *samādhi* power, right concentration, or *samādhi* enlightenment factor, which is a factor of the path, which is related to the path, this is called right concentration.[52]

In essence, any concentration that is rightly used, for the objective of liberation, for the wisdom that understands things according to the truth and not in response to selfish desires, such as desires to display psychic powers or special abilities, is right concentration.[53] This is supported by the teaching that it is possible to practice insight (*vipassanā*) even from the elementary level of concentration known as *vipassanā samādhi*, the concentration used with insight for the development of wisdom, which is a level of concentration found between the *khaṇika* and *upacārasamādhi*[54] (described below).

The Levels of Samādhi

In commentarial literature *samādhi* is divided into three main levels:[55]

1. Momentary concentration (*khaṇika-samādhi*): this is the basic level of *samādhi* that ordinary people can effectively make use of in the performance of their everyday duties and that can be used as the starting point for the practice of insight.

2. Access concentration (*upacārasamādhi*): close concentration or concentration that is almost firm. It is concentration on a level in which the hindrances have been suppressed before entering the state of absorption (*jhāna*), or the concentration that is the precursor to attainment concentration.
3. Attainment concentration (*appanāsamādhi*): resolute or fixed concentration. This is the highest level of concentration, found in all the *jhānas*, and considered to be the desired result of concentration practice.

The second and third kinds of *samādhi* are often mentioned in explanations of meditation practice, and are fairly clearly defined: *upacārasamādhi* is the concentration when the mind is firm through having abandoned the five hindrances. In terms of the object of attention, it is the stage in which there arises a *paṭibhāganimitta*—an image of the meditation object in the mind's eye, more subtle and profound than a remembered visual object. *Paṭibhāganimitta* is a product of pure perception, is free of color or defect, and can be expanded or contracted at will.[56] This kind of *samādhi* is almost fully concentrated, almost *jhāna*. Once this level is mastered and familiarized, it firms up to the one-pointedness of *appanāsamādhi* and the factors of *jhāna*.[57] However, the first level of concentration, *khaṇika-samādhi*, does not seem to have such clearly defined parameters. Therefore I would like to embark on an examination of it here in order to give a general idea of its form and its extent.

In the Paramatthamañjusā[58] it is said that *mūlasamādhi* (rudimentary concentration) and *parikamma-samādhi* (preparatory concentration), mentioned in the Visuddhimagga,[59] are both varieties of *khaṇika-samādhi*.

Mūlasamādhi is illustrated with the following passages:

> "Therefore, bhikkhus, train yourselves thus: 'My mind will be firmly established and well concentrated within, and bad, unskillful qualities will find no footing in my mind.' This, bhikkhus, is how you should train yourselves.

> "When your minds are thus firmly established and well concentrated, and the bad, unskillful qualities cannot find footing in your mind, train yourselves thus: 'I will develop and make much of the mind deliverance of goodwill (*mettācetovimutti*). I will make of it a vehicle, a foundation; I will make it firm, build on it, and bring it to fruition.' This, bhikkhus, is how you should train yourselves.
>
> "When this kind of concentration is developed and made much of by you, then should you practice this concentration that has both initial and sustained application of mind, has sustained but no initial application of mind, has neither initial nor sustained application of mind, has rapture, has no rapture, has pleasant feeling, has equanimity..."[60]

It is explained that the state of mind that is centered on an object in a state of inner independence, as described in the first paragraph of the passage above—"My mind will be firmly established and well concentrated within, and bad, unskillful qualities will find no footing in my mind"—is rudimentary concentration (*mūlasamādhi*). The passage following in the second paragraph describes the stage of development, the further strengthening of that rudimentary concentration through the practice of goodwill (*mettā*). Rudimentary concentration is compared to the fire resulting from rubbing two sticks together, or striking a flint, while the development of that rudimentary concentration through meditation on goodwill, for example, is like adding fuel to that fire to keep it burning. The third paragraph describes the level in which rudimentary or momentary *samādhi* is developed into *appanāsamādhi* (via *upacārasamādhi*) in the *jhānas* by concentrating on an object, such as a *kasiṇa* device.

Further examples can be found in the Buddha's accounts of his own practice:

> "I, bhikkhus, while living heedfully, ardent and resolved, had thoughts of renunciation... thoughts of non-enmity... thoughts of non-aggression arise. I knew clearly that, 'Thoughts of renun-

> ciation...thoughts of non-enmity...thoughts of non-aggression have arisen within me. Such thoughts are not harmful to me, nor are they harmful to others, nor are they harmful to both sides. They augment wisdom, do not encourage distress, and incline to *nibbāna*. Even were I to dwell devoted to thinking such thoughts for an entire night, I foresee no danger resulting thereof. Even were I to dwell devoted to thinking such thoughts for an entire day...for an entire night and day, I foresee no danger resulting thereof. However, if I were to dwell devoted to such thoughts for too long my body would become wearied. If the body were weary, the mind would become distracted. If the mind were distracted, it would stray far from concentration.' Then I, bhikkhus, directed my mind inward, calmed it, made it one-pointed and firm. For what reason? With the intention of not letting my mind become distracted...
>
> "Bhikkhus, having exerted diligent effort, unrelenting, [with mind] controlled unwaveringly by mindfulness and the body relaxed and not restless, my mind was firmly established in one-pointedness.
>
> "Bhikkhus, I, secluded from sensuality, secluded from unskillful qualities, attained the first *jhāna*..."[61]

It is explained that the passage in the first paragraph, "directed my mind inward, calmed it, made it one-pointed and firm," and the passage in the second paragraph, "my mind was firmly established in one-pointedness," are referring to rudimentary concentration (or momentary concentration) that arose prior to the attainment of *appanāsamādhi* in the *jhānas* described in the third paragraph.

As an example of *parikamma-samādhi*, one who wants to develop the divine ear (*dibbasota*), after leaving *jhāna*, inclines the mind to observing sounds, beginning with the sounds that are loud but distant, such as a tiger roaring, or traffic noises, and proceeds to notice progressively softer sounds—the sound of drums, bells, music, chanting, people talking, birds, the breeze in the trees, insects, rustling leaves, and so on. Sounds that are audible to ordinary perception will be much clearer for one who has *parikamma-samādhi* or *khaṇika-samādhi*.

Some texts also add *vipassanā samādhi* between momentary (*khaṇika*) and access (*upacāra*) concentration.[62] This is simply momentary concentration applied to the development of insight.

Obstacles to Samādhi

The matter to be dealt with now is not *samādhi* but its adversaries, the things that must be eliminated before *samādhi* can arise—or we may say they must be eliminated by *samādhi*. They are called *nīvaraṇa*.

The word *nīvaraṇa* means "impediment" "or hindrance." It is technically defined as that which impedes the functioning of the mind, that which hinders the wholesomeness of the mind or debilitates wisdom. To give a more technical definition, they are that which prevents advancement in skillful qualities, or the unskillful qualities that defile the mind and weaken wisdom.

For an explanation of the characteristics of the hindrances there is this Buddhavacana:

> "Bhikkhus, these five things are obstacles [to skillful qualities], hindrances [to growth]. They constrict the mind and weaken wisdom."[63]
>
> "[. . .] They are *upakkilesa* (stains or defilements of the mind) which weaken wisdom."[64]
>
> "These five things are hindrances: they make one blind, deprive one of sight, create lack of direct knowledge (they create unknowing), crush wisdom, encourage distress, and do not lead to *nibbāna*."[65]

One must be careful not to confuse the five hindrances with calm (*samatha*) or *samādhi*. The five hindrances are as follows:[66]

1. *Kāmachanda*: wanting to obtain things [literally, predilection

for sensuality], or *abhijjhā*, covetousness. It is desire for the five desirable, attractive, and pleasing sense pleasures: visual forms, sounds, tastes, smells, and tangibles. It refers to defilements of the greed group. The mind seduced by various objects is always wanting this and that, getting attached to this and that, and being drawn outward to other objects. Being caught up in them, the mind does not become firm, does not flow smoothly, and cannot attain *samādhi*.

2. *Byāpāda*: resentment and aversion. It is pique, aversion, hatred, resentment, negativity, aggressive thoughts, enmity, and the many forms that aversion may take. The mind that is getting upset and clashing with things does not flow smoothly and cannot attain *samādhi*.
3. *Thīnamiddha*: depression and lethargy, or boredom and melancholy. It is divided into *thīna*—depression, despair, dullness, or listlessness, which are mental conditions—and *middha*—lethargy, laziness, sloth, drowsiness, lassitude, and torpidity, which are physical conditions. The mind dominated by these physical and mental conditions is not strong, fluent, or functional and therefore cannot attain *samādhi*.
4. *Uddhaccakukkucca*: distraction and worry. It is divided into *uddhacca*—distraction, unease, agitation, or restlessness—and *kukkucca*—confusion, irritation, anxiety, vexation, and worry. The mind dominated by *uddhaccakukkucca* is stirred up, agitated, and cannot settle down into *samādhi*.
5. *Vicikicchā*: doubt. This refers to perplexity, uncertainty, and doubt regarding the Teacher (*satthā*), the teaching (Dhamma), the order (Saṅgha), or the training (*sikkhā*). In brief it is doubt in regard to skillful qualities, being undecided as to whether a certain practice (such as meditation) is really valuable, beneficial, and worth practicing, whether it can really lead to results. Thought becomes divided into two forks and cannot be settled. The mind disturbed, held down, and misled by doubts through *vicikicchā* cannot become firmly one-pointed in *samādhi*.

The Attributes of the Concentrated Mind

The training in higher mentality (*adhicittasikkhā*) is the training for developing the quality and efficiency of the mind. Thus *samādhi*, which is the objective of this training, refers to a mental state of optimum quality and efficiency. The mind with *samādhi* contains the following main attributes:

1. Strong and vigorous. It is compared to a stream of water channeled into one direction, which has greater power than water that has been allowed to flow about without direction.
2. Calm and serene, still and deep. It is like a pool or lake of still water, the surface untouched by wind and unbroken by waves.
3. Clear, lucid, transparent. It is like still water, without ripples, in which any dust has settled to the bottom.
4. Pliant and malleable, or fit for work, because it is not tense, not willful, not confused, not dull, not agitated.

The synonym for *samādhi* previously mentioned—*ekaggatā*—is usually translated as one-pointedness of mind. However, analyzing the word, we find the mental state similar to the attribute of "strong and vigorous" described in the list above. *Ekaggatā* comes from the roots *eka* + *agga* + *tā* (state). The word *agga* is here rendered as "object" (*ārammaṇa*), but its original meaning is "point" or "tip." In this respect, the mind with *samādhi* is one that has a single point or tip—that has the quality of sharpness and is capable of cutting through things with ease.

The mind that is fully concentrated, particularly *samādhi* on the level of *jhāna*, is said in the commentaries to be endowed with the following eight attributes, as gleaned from statements made by the Buddha: (1) concentrated, (2) pure, (3) cleansed, (4) blemish free, (5) free of defilements, (6) malleable, (7) fit for work, and (8) unmoving. It is said that a mind with these attributes is in an ideal state for any undertaking, be it in the use of wisdom to examine and produce real, clear understanding or in the use of creating psychic power and the superknowledges (*abhiññā*) or attainments (*samāpatti*).[67]

In this regard, it must be stressed that the most prominent attribute of the mind in *samādhi*, which is also related to the objectives of *samādhi*, is functionality or fitness for work (*kammaniya*), and the right kind of work according to Buddhism is work in relation to wisdom (*pañña*). It is the use of the mind that has been prepared as a field of operations for *paññā* to examine realities and develop realization of the truth. And in this respect, it should be added that the right kind of *samādhi* is not a state of unconsciousness in which one disappears into something but instead is a state of bright-mindedness, clarity; a state transcending obstructions and impediments; a state that is free, independent, alert, buoyant, and ready for the use of wisdom.

Consider the following Buddhavacana:

> "Bhikkhus, these five things are obstacles, hindrances, oppressions on the mind, which weaken wisdom. The five are sensual desire... aversion... sloth and torpor... restlessness and worry... doubt... That a bhikkhu who has not thrown off these five things that are obstacles, hindrances, oppressions on the mind, which weaken wisdom, will know his own benefit, the benefit of others, the benefit of both sides, or will experience and realize the immaculate direct knowledge and vision that make one a noble one, that are beyond the ken of ordinary beings with ineffective and weak wisdom, is not possible. It is like a river that springs from a mountain and flows for a great distance, its current strong enough to cast movable objects before it. But a man comes along and breaks down the banks on both sides of that river. Then the current in that river is dispersed and flows aimlessly about. It flows neither far nor strong, and cannot cast movable things before it..."[68]
>
> ---
>
> The brahmin Saṅgārava asked the Buddha:
>
> "Revered Gotama, what is the cause, what is the reason, that

sometimes even those verses that have long been recited are not clear, let alone those that have not been recited at all? And what is the cause, what is the reason, that sometimes even those verses that have not been long recited are clear, let alone those that have been recited regularly?"

The Buddha answered: "Brahmin, at any time that a person has a mind overcome with sensual desire, dominated by sensual desire, and does not clearly know as it is the way out of sensual desire already arisen, at such times that person does not see clearly, as it is, what is of benefit to oneself, what is of benefit to others, and what is of benefit to both sides. Even those verses that have long been recited will not be clear, let alone those that have not been recited at all."

[The same is said for a person whose mind is overcome with aversion, sloth and torpor, restlessness and worry, and doubt, and the mind dominated by each of the hindrances is illustrated as follows:]

1. "[The mind overcome by sensual desire] is like a vessel of water into which lac, turmeric, or green or red dye has been mixed. A clear-sighted man, looking at the reflection of his face in that vessel, could not see it as it really is.

2. "[The mind overcome by aversion] is like a vessel containing water that has been heated, which is bubbling and steaming. A clear-sighted man, looking at the reflection of his face in that vessel, could not see it as it really is.

3. "[The mind overcome by sloth and torpor] is like a vessel of water covered in slime and duckweed. A clear-sighted man, looking at the reflection of his face in that vessel, could not see it as it really is.

4. "[The mind overcome by restlessness and worry] is like a vessel of water over which a wind blows, causing the water to wave and ripple. A clear-sighted man, looking at the reflection of his face in that vessel, could not see it as it really is.

5. "[The mind overcome by doubt] is like a vessel of murky, muddy water standing in a darkened place. A clear-sighted man,

looking at the reflection of his face in that vessel, could not see it as it really is.

"As for one whose mind is not dominated by the five hindrances, and who knows the way out of the five hindrances already arisen, that person will know as it is what is of benefit to oneself, of benefit to others, and of benefit to both sides. Even verses that have not been long recited are clear to that person, let alone those that have been long recited." The similes given above are repeated in opposite form for the mind free of hindrances.[69]

"Bhikkhus, when gold is tainted with the following five contaminants (*upakkilesa*) of gold, it is not pliant, not malleable, not lustrous, but brittle and unfit for use. What are the five? They are iron, other metals, tin, lead and silver...

"When gold is free of these five contaminants it becomes pliant, malleable, lustrous, not brittle, and fit for use. Whatever jewelry a goldsmith wished to make, be it a ring, earrings, a necklace, or a tiara, could be made as that goldsmith wished.

"In the same way, when the mind is tainted with the following five contaminants it is not pliant, not malleable, not clear; it is fragile and not firmly established [it is not *sammāsamādhi*] on the cessation of the outflows. What are the five? They are sensual desire, aversion, sloth and torpor, restlessness and worry, and doubt...Whenever the mind transcends these five contaminants it is pliant, malleable, bright, strong, and firmly established [it is *sammāsamādhi*] on the cessation of the outflows. Moreover, whatever truths realizable through superknowledge one inclines the mind to experiencing and realizing, one is in a position to witness them for oneself when the conditions are there..."[70]

"If a bhikkhu is free from these five hindrances and has brought forth unrelenting effort, is controlled by unfailing mindfulness, his body relaxed and tranquil, not tense or agitated, his mind firm and one-pointed, whether that bhikkhu goes, stands, sits, or reclines with alertness, he is said to be possessed of effort,

> to have moral dread (*ottappa*), to have brought forth constant effort and dedicated himself wholly to the practice."[71]

These analogies for *samādhi* from the commentators are worthy of note. It is said that *samādhi* establishes the mind steadily on its object, causing the factors that arise with it to be harmonious, undistorted, and collected, just as water cements flour into dough, and it allows the mind to proceed strongly and unwaveringly, like a candle flame in a windless place: its flame is still and constant and casts an even light.[72]

The Objectives and Benefits of Samādhi

The objective of *samādhi* (or to use the technical term, *sammāsamādhi*), properly used, is quite clear, as often stated: to prepare the mind for the effective use of wisdom. Simply speaking, *samādhi* is for the purpose of wisdom, as stated in the canonical passages already cited: "*Samādhi* is for the objective of direct knowledge and vision of reality (*yathābhūtañāṇadassana*),"[73] "*Samādhi* has direct knowledge and vision of reality as its objective and reward,"[74] "Purity of mind (*cittavisuddhi*) is simply for the objective of purity of view (*diṭṭhi*) [the cultivation of *samādhi* to purify the mind has as its objective correcting and purifying views]."[75] The following Buddhavacana may also be cited:

> "*Samādhi* well matured by morality is of great fruit, of great reward; wisdom that is well matured by *samādhi* is of great fruit, of great reward; the mind that is well matured by wisdom rightly transcends the outflows, which are the outflow of sensuality (*kāmāsava*), the outflow of becoming (*bhavāsava*), and the outflow of ignorance (*avijjāsava*)."[76]

Although *samādhi* has this goal, it also has other uses and benefits. Some of these are byproducts obtained in the process of practicing toward the goal, some are special benefits requiring express development, and some are benefits that are helpful even to those who have already attained the goal of *samādhi*.

In brief, the benefits of *samādhi* can be compiled as follows.

The Benefit That Is the Goal of Buddhism

The benefit that is the real goal of *samādhi* in Buddhism is that it is an integral part of the practice for attaining the ultimate goal, which is liberation from all defilements and suffering.

1. The benefit that directly corresponds with this point is preparation of the mind for the application of wisdom to examine and realize realities as they truly are. Technically speaking, it is a base for insight, or direct knowledge and vision into reality, as already stated, which eventually leads to knowledge (*vijjā*) and liberation.
2. A secondary objective along the same lines, while not considered to be the real objective, is the attainment of the temporary escape from defilements known as provisional liberation of mind (*cetovimutti*). That is, it is transcendence of defilements via the power of concentration, especially the power of *jhāna*. Defilements are suppressed by the power of concentration for the duration of the state of *samādhi*. This is technically called *vikkhambhanavimutti*.

The Benefit in Creating Extraordinary Abilities

Another benefit of *samādhi*, the benefit in creating extraordinary abilities—that is, special extraordinary mental accomplishments—may be simply called the benefit of superknowledges (*abhiññā*). This benefit involves using *samādhi* on the level of *jhāna* attainment to produce powers (*iddhi*) and other kinds of mundane superknowledge, such as the divine eye, the divine ear, the ability to read other people's minds and to recollect past lives, which nowadays are referred to as extrasensory perception.

The Benefit to Mental Health and Character Development

The benefit of *samādhi* to mental health and character development appears, for example, in the way *samādhi* makes the mind and character strong, stable, calm, gentle, cheerful, clear, and compassionate, and enables one to see oneself and others as they really are (as opposed to the features of someone who is enveloped in hindrances, such as being moody, easily deluded, easily angered, distracted, depressed, or fearful). *Samādhi* puts the mind in a state that is conducive to the implanting of virtues and encourages good character. In modern terms, it is having mental stability and a protection against mental illness.

This benefit is even greater when the concentrated mind is used as a base for the practice of the foundations of mindfulness, living with mindfulness of all activities through body and speech, as well as one's fluctuating mental states, and seeing them as objects of awareness to be utilized, not giving those experiences and events the opportunity to endanger one's mental well-being. This benefit also functions in everyday life.

The Benefit in Daily Life

The benefits of *samādhi* in daily life are as follows:

1. It helps to relax the mind and relieve tension, inducing calm, getting rid of confusion, and putting a stop to worry and anxiety. It is a technique for resting the body and producing mental well-being. Some people, for instance, practice mindfulness of the breathing (*ānāpānasati*) in their spare moments, such as when sitting on a bus in a traffic jam or between bouts of heavy mental activity. In its fullest sense, *samadhi* is synonymous with the absorption attainments that the Buddha and the arahants used to rest body and mind in a pleasant state when they were unoccupied with other matters, a practice known by the special term *diṭṭhadhammasukhavihāra*.

2. It supports efficiency in work, study, and other activities. A mind that has *samādhi* is focused on the task at hand, not distracted, scattered, or wandering about. This helps study, thought, and work to be more effective—more meticulous and less prone to

mistakes—and gives a good protection against accidents, because where there is *samādhi* there is mindfulness. As it is said, the mind is *kammaniya*—fit for work or suitable for the job. When the inducement of mental well-being outlined in point 1 is incorporated, this second benefit regarding work, study, and other activities is even more effective.

3. It promotes health and cures illnesses. Body and mind are interrelated and have an influence on each other. Ordinarily, when the body is not well, people let their minds become weak and depressed. Once the mind is sad and despondent, bodily illnesses can be aggravated even further. Even when the body is in normal condition, illnesses can result when a person encounters life experiences that cause intense sorrow. For those whose minds are strong and whole (especially those whose minds are liberated), times of illness are simply discomfort of the body—the mind is not affected. Moreover, such people can use that healthy and strong mind to exert an influence on relieving or reducing physical illnesses, or even to allow them to be cured more quickly, or they may use the power of *samādhi* to suppress unpleasant bodily feeling.[77] On the good side, a person's clear and buoyant mind will help to give the body a pleasant appearance, radiant complexion, and good health, which are themselves protections against illness. This relationship has an effect on the amount of energy required and expended by the body. A comfortable, clear, cheerful, and buoyant mind, for example, needs less food to make the body comfortable. When one is happy or excited about something, one may not feel hungry. A bhikkhu who is enlightened has rapture as a nutriment. He may eat only one meal a day but have a radiant complexion, because he does not hanker for the past or dream about the future.[78]

A healthy mind not only helps the body to be healthy. Many kinds of physical illnesses are products of mind-body interaction, arising from vicissitudes of the mind such as tendencies toward anger, depression, or worry, which can cause headaches or contribute to gastric ulcers. Improving the mental state through some means or other can help to alleviate such illnesses. This benefit is perfected when wisdom of the true nature of things is incorporated.[79]

Objectives and Benefits of *Samādhi* by Meditation Type

Summarizing according to the canon, the training or practice of *samādhi* has the objective of leading to the following benefits:

> "Bhikkhus, there are four kinds of *samādhi* development (*samādhi bhāvanā*), as follows:
>
> 1. "The *samādhi* development that, when well developed and made much of, leads to a pleasant abiding in the here and now (*diṭṭhadhammasukhavihāra*).
> 2. "The *samādhi* development that, when well developed and made much of, leads to direct knowledge and vision (*ñāṇadassana*).
> 3. "The *samādhi* development that, when well developed and made much of, leads to mindfulness and comprehension (*sati sampajañña*).
> 4. "The *samādhi* development that, when well developed and made much of, leads to the cessation of the outflows (*āsava*)."[80]

The texts define the first kind of *samādhi* as consisting of the four *jhānas*. This kind of *samādhi* is specifically the practice of *jhāna* as a means for seeking one of ten progressively higher levels of happiness,[81] which are sensual happiness, happiness in each of the four *jhānas* of form, happiness in each of the formless *jhānas*, and the happiness of cessation attainment (*nirodhasamāpatti*). The Buddha and the arahants tended to practice the *jhānas* in their spare moments as the pleasant form of rest known as *diṭṭhadhammasukhavihāra*.

The texts explain that the second kind of *samādhi* refers to the attention to a perception of light (*ālokasaññā*) and to determining a perception of daytime (*adhiṭṭhāna divāsaññā*) throughout night and day; having a mind that is open, clear, and unenveloped (by hindrances); and training to make the mind bright. The commentaries explain that the gaining of direct knowledge and vision (*ñāṇadassana*) here refers to the divine eye, which is said to be the culmination of the five mundane superknowledges (the other four being psychic powers, the divine ear, the ability to read minds, and recollection of past lives). Sometimes *ñāṇadassana* is said to encompass all five of the mundane superknowledges. This benefit refers to the employment of *samādhi* to gain mental attainments: special abilities such as superknowledges and psychic powers (*pāṭihāriya*).

The third kind of *samādhi* is the practice of mindfully following feelings and thoughts that arise and pass away in one's everyday life, as explained in the Pali: "feelings, perceptions, and thoughts arise, are established, and cease with clear awareness."

The Pali explains the fourth kind of *samādhi* as abiding with wisdom—examining the arising and passing away of the five aggregates of clinging (*upādānakkhandha*), such as reflecting "Form is like this, the arising of form is like this, the cessation of form is like this; feeling, perception, mental formations, and consciousness are like this; they arise like this; they pass away like this." Broadly speaking, it is the use of *samādhi* for the purposes of wisdom, as a tool for developing insight, as it is said: as a foundation for insight, for attaining the highest objective, which is direct knowledge of the cessation of the outflows (*āsavakkhayañāṇa*), or knowledge and liberation (*vijjāvimutti*).[82]

According to the explanations of the commentaries it seems that the first and second benefits of *samādhi* are aspects of calm (*samatha*), while the third and fourth are aspects of insight (*vipassanā*). The other benefits of *samādhi*, which I have described earlier, although they are not specifically mentioned in the Pali, should be understood as either byproducts obtained in the process of practicing for the other four benefits or other unspecified practices.

The rewards of *samādhi* development are also summarized in commentarial literature. For example, the Visuddhimagga lists five of these:[83]

1. *Samādhi* is a means of resting comfortably in the present moment (*diṭṭhadhammasukhavihāra*). This is a reward of *samādhi* on the level of attainment concentration (i.e., *jhāna*)

experienced by the arahants, those who have completed the task in relation to liberation and do not need to use *jhāna* to attain any further states. It cites the Buddhavacana, "These *jhāna*s are referred to in the discipline of the noble ones as a pleasant abiding in the here and now."[84]

2. *Samādhi* is a base or proximate cause (*padaṭṭhāna*) for insight: this can be a benefit of both the attainment and access concentration levels of *samādhi*, although the latter not so clearly. This benefit applies to learners (*sekha*) and ordinary people (*puthujjana*) and is based on the Buddhavacana: "Bhikkhus, develop *samādhi*. A bhikkhu whose mind is firmly established will see the truth."[85]
3. *Samādhi* is a base or proximate cause for superknowledges (*abhiññā*): this is a reward of *samādhi* on the level of attainment concentration for those who have gained the eight attainments (*samāpatti*): if they wish to produce superknowledge they may do so. The Buddhavacana is cited: "The mind malleable and fit for work . . . inclining the mind for the realization through superknowledge of whatever *dhamma* can be realized through superknowledge, he becomes witness to that *dhamma*, when the conditions for it are there."[86]
4. *Samādhi* leads to special planes of existence—that is, being born in favorable and high spheres of existence. This is a reward of *samādhi* on the level of attainment concentration in unenlightened beings who have gained *jhāna*, and that *jhāna* does not regress, leading to rebirth into the Brahma realms. The Buddhavacana is cited: "Having developed the first *jhāna* to a moderate level of skill (*parittakusala*), where is one reborn? One is reborn in the realm of Brahma's Assembly."[87] However, even *samādhi* on the level of access concentration may lead to rebirth in special states in any of the six sensual heavens (*kāmāvacara*).
5. *Samādhi* allows access to cessation attainment (*nirodhasamāpatti*). This is a reward of *samādhi* on the level of attainment concentration attained by those arahants and non-returners who have gained the eight attainments (*samāpatti*), allowing them to experience well-being without mental activity for up to

seven days. Here direct knowledge (*ñāṇa*) of *nirodhasamāpatti* in the Paṭisambhidāmagga is cited.[88]

Correct Understanding of the Objectives and Benefits of *Samādhi*

An understanding of the benefits or objectives of developing *samādhi* can help avoid and eliminate misunderstandings concerning meditation practice and the life of Buddhist bhikkhus, such as that meditation practice entails seclusion or turning one's back on social activities, or that the monastic life is a cop-out from social responsibility. The following considerations may be useful in preventing and eliminating some of these misunderstandings:

- *Samādhi* is simply a means to an end, not an objective. A person just beginning the practice may have to go into seclusion and reduce dealings with social concerns for a special period of training, then return to a more active role, according to one's situation. Moreover, the practice of *samādhi* in general does not require sitting all day and all night, and there are many methods of practice to choose from for application to different dispositions (*cariyā*).
- In the Buddha's teaching of the four foundations of mindfulness, it is stated that one may practice the four foundations of mindfulness ardently and consistently for only seven days and attain arahantship. For those who receive such results, any subsequent practice of *samādhi* will usually be for the benefit of well-being in the present moment. The time remaining in life can be devoted to following the Buddha's exhortation to the bhikkhus, which has been a fundamental principle of the teaching from the outset: *caratha bhikkhave cārikaṁ bahujana-hitāya bahujana-sukhāya*—"Go forth, bhikkhus, for the welfare and the happiness of the many."
- The practice of the bhikkhus is dependent on personal abilities, conformity with temperament, and personal preferences. Some bhikkhus may prefer and be suited to living in the forest; some may wish to live in the forest but not be suited to it. There

are examples of the Buddha refusing to allow certain bhikkhus to live in the forests,[89] and those bhikkhus who do live in the forest are not allowed by the bhikkhus' discipline (Vinaya) to cut themselves off completely from all social contact like hermits.[90]

- The benefits of *samādhi* and *jhāna* that are required in the Buddhadhamma are the mental states of "malleability" and "fitness for work," which are used as wisdom's field of operations. The use of *samādhi* and *jhāna* for benefits other than these is regarded as a byproduct, and in some cases was regarded as undesirable, not encouraged by the Buddha. For example, those who develop *samādhi* for the purpose of attaining psychic powers (*iddhi pāṭihāriya*) are said to have established their intentions wrongly. Psychic powers can lead to many kinds of harmful consequences, they can degenerate, and they do not lead to the objective of Buddhadhamma.[91] If one were to develop *samādhi* for the objective of wisdom, and in the process gain psychic powers, this is considered to be possession of special abilities. However, even when practicing with a proper intention, as long as the objective has not been reached, the attainment of psychic powers can be dangerous,[92] because such powers are a cause of delusion and attachment, both for oneself and for others, and can cause such an increase in defilements that one cannot continue with the practice. Although the Buddha possessed numerous psychic powers, he did not encourage their use because they are not the way of wisdom and liberation. In the accounts of the Buddha's life we find that the Buddha only used psychic powers to put an end to psychic powers, or to put an end to a desire for psychic powers.
- For those who have trained and made progress in the path or attained the goal, *samādhi* on the level of *jhāna* tends to be used as a means for resting comfortably in their spare time. Although the Buddha himself, for example, traveled all over the countryside teaching a great number of people of all castes, and administered a great company of bhikkhus, he had a certain quality known as a *jhāyī*, or *jhānasīlī*,[93] meaning he had a predilection for *jhāna* and preferred to dwell in *jhāna* in his spare

> moments instead of resting in the normal way, and so did many of his disciples. This is what is known as the pleasant abiding in the here and now. It is recorded that the Buddha even went into seclusion for long periods of up to three months to abide in *samādhi*.[94]

The amount of time and the level of *samādhi* used in enjoying this form of well-being is up to each individual, but if the preference and attachment to it become so much that they are causes for neglecting communal responsibilities, this would be censurable, even though it is a subtle level of attachment and delusion. Moreover, the life style of bhikkhus in Buddhism, according to the stipulations of the Vinaya, places importance on communal responsibility. The prosperity and decline, and viability and nonviability, of the order are essentially dependent on responsibility to community concerns.

Ultimately, it is clear to see that for the Buddha and those who practice properly, *samādhi* was an aid in the practice for the benefit of the many.

Methods for Developing Samādhi

It has been mentioned that a meditator may use the elementary level of *samādhi*, momentary concentration, as a starting point from which to examine natural states according to the teachings on insight, and such *samādhi* will develop in conjunction with the development of insight. However, even though *samādhi* developed in this way will eventually have sufficient force to enable the meditator to attain the desired objective of insight—liberation from the defilements and suffering, and realization of *nibbāna*—it is not strong enough to lead to the special mental achievements, the mundane superknowledges such as psychic powers. Moreover, beginning the practice with a weak level of *samādhi* is like a man setting out on a journey in a weak and sickly condition: his fitness for the journey is naturally impaired. Even though he may hope to gradually build up his stamina as he goes along, this is not as good as one who is fully prepared for the journey right from the outset, and begins the journey with full confidence and no anxieties. The practice will be even more difficult if wisdom is not keen. Conversely, if wisdom is too strong it may lead to distraction.[95] Thus it has become the preference to develop a foundation through dedicated *samādhi* practice, not necessarily enough to attain mental attainments and superknowledges, but at least enough to provide a firm base for the development of wisdom.

This matter can be more clearly seen in real-life situations. Some people, if they find themselves in places where there is even only a little disturbing sound, or there are people walking about, find it impossible to do anything that requires concentration, let alone matters that require profound examination with wisdom. Others have stronger and more stable minds: they are able to think and do intellectual work as normal even when there are disturbing noises or people milling around. Some people have exceptionally strong minds: they are not shaken even in exciting or fearful situations, and can use their reasoning powers effectively. It is said, for example, that Emperor Napoleon I of France had great mental powers and could think of anything he wanted to whenever he wished to, and not think of what he did not want to think about. He compared his brain to a chest of drawers in which all the information he needed was neatly stored away in batches, and he could open any drawer he wished to. Even in the middle of the battlefield, surrounded by the retorts of cannon and gunfire and the cacophony of horses and shouting men, he remained composed and could make plans as clearly as in any other situation. When he wanted to rest, he could lie down and go to sleep then and there. Most people in such a situation would be unable to keep their minds from running wild, let alone make plans about anything.

The story of Napoleon pales in comparison to some of the stories from the texts. It is said, for instance, that the ascetic Āḷāra Kālāma,[96] while in the middle of a long journey, stopped to rest under a certain tree when a caravan of five hundred ox carts passed close by. He neither saw nor heard them. The Buddha was once resting near the city of Ātumā. Near where the Buddha was staying, there was a great thunderstorm during which a lightning bolt struck and killed two farmers and four oxen. The Buddha was dwelling in deep meditation and did not hear the sound at all.[97]

There is a Buddhavacana stating: "Of those who are not shaken by a lightning bolt, there are only an arahant vanquisher of the outflows, a well-trained elephant, a well-trained horse, and a lion."[98]

Among ordinary people, mental strength, intelligence, and mental stability vary greatly. For most people, whose mental stability is not great and intelligence not keen, it is considered that if they do not first make their minds a field of operations for wisdom, there is little chance of successfully penetrating the truth with transcendent wisdom. It is thus recommended to train the mind through the process of *samādhi* cultivation to make of it a proper foundation for wisdom development.

While in principle the development of *samādhi* can be expressed in few words, the details of its practical techniques are exhaustive; if the discussion extends to the use of *samādhi* as a field of operations for wisdom for attaining the highest goal of Buddhism, the subject becomes even larger, with a broad range that encompasses both calm and insight meditation, a subject that deserves a book in its own right. Here I will merely describe some of the main principles of meditation practice to convey the general idea.

Developing *Samādhi* according to the Natural Method

Samādhi development of this kind involves practicing along a process that occurs naturally and is described in many Buddhavacana. The essential factors of the process begin with doing a good action and having gladness (*pāmojja*) at that action. Then rapture (*pīti*) arises, which in turn is followed by tranquility (*passaddhi*), then well-being (*sukha*), and finally *samādhi*. It can be represented like this: *pāmojja* → *pīti* → *passaddhi* → *sukha* → *samādhi*.

The general principle is that in order for this process to arise there must normally be a supporting foundation of morality. For ordinary people, this morality means simply not having harmed or infringed on others, which would be a cause for confusion, suspicion, or remorse—that is, it means having good conduct, which is a comfort to the mind and produces confidence.

The actions that can lead to gladness can be of many kinds. For example, one may reflect on one's own good conduct and feel a sense of gladness, or recollect on one's useful actions, the Triple Gem or other wholesome themes, or take up a theme from the teachings for examination and experience understanding of its meaning, and all of these can lead to feelings of gladness.[99] The important factor, the criterion or proximate cause, for the arising of *samādhi* is well-being (*sukha*), as in the often-cited Buddhavacana: *sukhino cittaṁ samādhiyati*—"The mind that is happy is easily concentrated." A relevant Buddhavacana describes the process this way:

> "...[When he knows in full the meaning and the letter], gladness arises. When there is gladness, rapture arises; when there is rapture the body is relaxed; one whose body is relaxed has well-being; the mind of one who has well-being becomes concentrated."[100]

Developing *Samādhi* through the Pathways to Success (*Iddhipāda*)

Iddhipāda translates as the "conditions leading to accomplishment or achievement"—that is, the conditions causing success, or simply, pathways to success. There are four of them—namely, zeal (*chanda*), effort (*viriya*), application of mind (*citta*), and analytical reflection (*vīmaṁsā*).

The Buddha talked of the *iddhipāda* in connection with *samādhi* because they are practices that lead to the development and the achievement of the goal of *samādhi*. The *samādhi* is named according to the *iddhipāda* from which it arises. Therefore there are four kinds of *samādhi*:[101]

1. *Chandasamādhi*: concentration arisen from zeal, or in which zeal is predominant
2. *Viriyasamādhi*: concentration arisen from effort, or in which effort is predominant

3. *Cittasamādhi*: concentration arisen from mental application, or in which mental application is predominant
4. *Vīmaṁsāsamādhi*: concentration arisen from analytical reflection, or in which analytical reflection is predominant

These kinds of *samādhi* arise in conjunction with the effort known as *padhāna saṅkhāra*, which translates as "effort formations," but which I would translate simply as "constructive effort."

How *samādhi* arises from the four pathways of zeal, effort, mental application, and analytical reflection, is explained thus:

Chanda (zeal) This refers to a love of what one is doing and a predilection for its objectives, wanting to see it through to completion or to see the objective reached. Simply speaking, it is love of the work and love of the work's objectives. More profoundly, in terms of the Dhamma, it is predilection and desire for the state of wholesomeness, fullness, and completion, which result from or can be achieved by what one is doing, wanting that thing to reach its ideal and most perfect state, or wanting the wholesomeness, completion, and perfection of that work to come about, to see it achieve its results according to its wholesome objective.

The wanting that is *chanda* is quite different from the desire to obtain objects to enjoy or to keep as personal possessions, which is called *taṇhā*. The desire of *chanda* leads to well-being, or a delight when a thing or task is seen attaining success and completion. It may be analyzed thus: while that task is proceeding toward its goal there is joy and satisfaction, and when it reaches its goal there is pleasure (*somanassa*), delight, and feelings of ease, clarity, and buoyancy. The wanting of *taṇhā* leads to happiness and pleasure only when desirable objects are obtained or when the sense of self-importance is served. It is a stained and tainted kind of joy, which confines one and tends to be followed by possessiveness, worry, regret, fear, and suspicion.[102]

If *chanda* is strongly evoked in the mind, when there is an appreciation of the value of something, people will devote themselves to that. If they truly love it, they may even give their lives for it. In the time of the Buddha, princes, nobles, merchants, brahmins, and young men and women of great number gave up their palaces, their wealth, and their worldly possessions in order to "go forth" as bhikkhus and bhikkhunis with the Buddha out of zeal for the Buddha's teaching. Similarly, people who love their work, who have *chanda*, will want to do the best they can, to see the work to its completion in the best possible way. They will not be concerned over external temptations or rewards: their minds are unwaveringly fixed on seeing the work through to its objective. They work steadfastly. *Chanda samādhi* arises in this way, and it arises together with constructive effort (*padhāna saṅkhāra*).

Viriya (effort). This refers to daring, boldness, striving, advancement, tenacity, and resilience in the face of obstacles and hardship. When we know that something has value and is worth attaining, once effort is aroused, we will not be discouraged even if we hear that the objective is difficult to attain, that there are many obstacles, or that we will have to strive for it for months or years. We will see it as a challenge, something we have to rise to, to achieve. In the Buddha's time, for example, followers of other sects who were inspired enough by the Buddha's teaching to seek ordination as bhikkhus, on being informed that people who had previously been members of other sects were required to undergo a period of probation (*titthiya parivāsa*) of four months, would not be discouraged but instead volunteer to undergo the probation for four years.[103] People who lack effort, while they too may want to attain the Dhamma, are disheartened and give up as soon as they hear that the practice may take years. During the practice their minds are distracted and confused, and it is difficult for them to attain results. People who have effort will have a storehouse of energy, and when they work or practice the Dhamma their minds will be resolute, stable, and focused on the goal, and so *samādhi* arises for them. This is called *viriyasamādhi*, and it arises together with constructive effort.

Citta (applied thought, or application of mind). This refers to having a mind that is committed to, focused on, and attentive to the matter at hand. The mind is bent on its task. If *citta* is especially strong in one particular matter or task, we will not be distracted by other concerns. When people talk of other things, we will not be interested, but if they speak about that task our interest is immediately sparked. We may even devote ourselves to and immerse ourselves in that task day and night, taking little heed of the body or matters of dress. We are not interested in other things, and sometimes things may occur very close by but we are not even aware of them. We apply ourselves to the task until we forget night and day, and forget to eat and sleep. This kind of single-minded application naturally leads to *samādhi*. The mind becomes firm, absorbed on its task, and has its energies concentrated on that task. This is called *cittasamādhi*, and it arises together with constructive effort.

Vīmaṁsā (analytical reflection). This refers to the use of wisdom to examine and look into causes and results, to survey the strengths and weaknesses, excesses and shortcomings, of the task at hand, being able to experiment and seek ways for correction and improvement. This point deals with the use of wisdom to lead *samādhi*, which is not difficult to see: people with *vīmaṁsā* like to think of causes and conditions, to examine and experiment. Whatever they do, they will reflect on it and experiment. They may consider, for example, what cause has led to a particular result, why such a result has arisen. Or they may inquire, since a certain result has arisen one time from particular constituent factors, how the result will vary if a certain factor is removed, and how it will vary if another factor is added, or why the expected result does not arise when a certain factor is changed, and what factor should be corrected. Or, in the practice of Dhamma, they will tend to examine and inquire, asking themselves, for example, the meaning of a certain teaching, what its objective is, when it should be used, what factors it should be used in conjunction with, why a certain practice does not progress, which faculties (*indriya*) are weak and which are in excess, what particular qualities (*dhamma*) people in the present age are lacking, how certain teachings (*dhamma*) should be implemented, and which aspects, for example, should be emphasized. Such rational inquiry and experimentation help to bring the mind together, to observe and reflect keenly and consistently on the subject of examination, thereby helping it to become resolute and absorbed on the subject of examination, not distracted or scattered, but strong. This is called *vīmaṁsā samādhi*, and it arises together with constructive effort.

The four pathways to success are mutually supportive and tend to arise together. For example, when *chanda* arises and there is zeal in the mind, that produces effort (*viriya*). When there is effort, one applies the mind consistently (*citta*) and therefore paves the way for the use of wisdom to examine and inquire (*vīmaṁsā*). These pathways are examined separately point by point insofar as their being predominant or the leaders of other factors in the practice in different situations.

For example, among a group of people listening to a teaching, some people may like the teaching. Those people listen with love and zeal for the teaching, looking to increase their knowledge and understanding of it (or they may simply like the particular teaching being given at the time, or the teacher), so they listen with undivided attention. *Chanda* is the predominant factor leading *samādhi* and other skillful qualities.

Other people may be of the character to think, or the feeling arises at that time, that whenever they have a task to be done they should apply themselves to it and master it, face up to it, and accomplish it, and therefore they see listening to the talk as a challenge, something to be understood at all costs. *Viriya* is the predominant factor here.

Another group of people may be of the character to be conscientious and take responsibility. Whatever they become involved with, they will take heed and apply their full attention. So they listen with full attention, taking in the subject of the talk. *Citta* is the predominant factor here.

Others may want to examine whether the teaching being given is true or not, whether it is good or not, or to examine the line of reasoning of the teaching. While listening to the teaching, they inquire into and examine it. Their minds are thus concentrated on the teaching to which they are listening. *Vīmaṁsā* is the predominant factor here.

For this reason, the four pathways to success are sometimes also called the four governors (*adhipati*) or four sovereign principles (*ādhipateyya*),[104] in the sense of their being predominant, the leaders, in those situations.

The essential point of building *samādhi* through the four pathways to success is taking on the job, the task or the objective required as the mind's object, and then arousing *chanda*, *viriya*, *citta*, or *vīmaṁsā* to help. *Samādhi* arises and is strong and powerful, and helps to do the task happily and to see it through to completion.

In this respect, be it in the practice of Dhamma, in study, or in other forms of work, whenever concentration is required, at least one of the four pathways to success should be aroused and put into effect in order to ensure that the undertaking proceeds smoothly. Then it is to be expected that *samādhi*, well-being, and success in the task will follow. The development of *samādhi*, or Dhamma practice, will then arise in the school room, the home, the field, the work place, and in all places.

Here I would like to present some passages from the canon to review what we have dealt with so far, beginning with the meaning of the word *iddhi* itself.

> "The word *iddhi* means success, accomplishment, completion, completing well, obtaining, obtaining specifically, attaining, advantage, attainment, realization, the full endowment of that condition."[105]
>
> ---
>
> "Bhikkhus, what is *iddhi*? [Herein,] a bhikkhu in this teaching and discipline performs many kinds of powers: from one he becomes many, from being many he becomes one; he can appear, he can disappear; he can easily pass through walls, ramparts, and mountains as if they were thin air; he can rise up from and plunge into the earth as if it were water; he can walk on water as if it were land; he can fly in the air like a bird; he can touch with his bare hands the sun and the moon with all their power; he can physically travel to the Brahma realms. This is called *iddhi*."[106]
>
> ---
>
> "Bhikkhus, what are the pathways to success? Whatever way

or practice leads to the gaining of *iddhi*, the experience of *iddhi*, that way or practice is called *iddhipāda*.

"What is the cultivation of *iddhipāda*? A bhikkhu in this teaching and discipline develops the pathway to success comprising *chanda samādhi* and constructive effort; he develops the pathway to success comprising *viriyasamādhi* and constructive effort; he develops the pathway to success comprising *cittasamādhi* and constructive effort; he develops the pathway to success comprising *vīmaṁsā samādhi* and constructive effort. This is called the cultivation of *iddhipāda*."[107]

"Bhikkhus, if a bhikkhu, through zeal, attains *samādhi*, attains one-pointedness of mind, this is called *chanda samādhi*. That bhikkhu brings forth zeal, he strives, puts forth effort, raises and fixes the mind for the non-arising of bad, unskillful qualities as yet unarisen...for the abandoning of bad, unskillful qualities already arisen...for the arising of skillful qualities as yet unarisen...for the establishment, the non-fading, the increase, the abundance, the growth, and the fulfillment of those skillful qualities already arisen. These are called constructive effort. This zeal, this *samādhi* that arises from it, and this constructive effort are together called the pathway to success (*iddhipāda*) that contains *chanda samādhi* and constructive effort.

"If a bhikkhu, through effort, attains *samādhi*, attains one-pointedness of mind, this is called *viriyasamādhi*...This effort, this *viriyasamādhi*, and this constructive effort are together called the pathway to success that contains *viriyasamādhi* and constructive effort.

"If a bhikkhu, through application of mind, attains *samādhi*, attains one-pointedness of mind, this is called *cittasamādhi*... This application of mind, *cittasamādhi*, and this constructive effort are together called the pathway to success that contains *cittasamādhi* and constructive effort.

"If a bhikkhu, through analytical reflection, attains *samādhi*, attains one-pointedness of mind, this is called *vīmaṁsā*

> *samādhi*...This analytical reflection, this *vīmaṁsā samādhi*, and this constructive effort are together called the pathway to success that contains *vīmaṁsā samādhi* and constructive effort."[108]
>
> ---
>
> "What is the practice that leads to development of the pathways to success? This very noble eightfold path—that is, right view... right concentration. This is the practice that leads to the development of the pathways to success."[109]
>
> ---
>
> "Bhikkhus, these four pathways to success, developed and made much of, are for the transition from that which is not the shore [not the destination] to that which is the shore [the destination]."[110]

Developing *Samādhi* in Everyday Life, or under the Direction of *Sati*

The development of *samādhi* with the four *iddhipāda*, in terms of everyday life, can be used with tasks such as study or any activities where the progress or accomplishment of that task provides a goal for the *iddhipāda*, leading to the constructive effort known as *padhāna saṅkhāra* and from there causing the arising of *samādhi*; that is, it helps the mind to be firmly established and undivided. But in leading our everyday lives, when we are dealing with mental objects (*ārammaṇa*) that are simply passing by and are involved with things that are static or things that are just there in the natural course of things, there is no base upon which the *iddhipāda* can establish themselves. In such a case, the factor to be used in inducing or developing *samādhi* is the fundamental quality known as *sati*, because *sati* is what brings the mind to its object and holds it there—that is, to what is being dealt with and done at that time.

The development of *samādhi* through *sati* can be divided into two main methods. The first method involves training for use with wisdom (*paññā*), or for the specific purpose of wisdom. It is the use of *sati* to pave the way for, or work in conjunction with, wisdom, by holding objects for submission to wisdom's examination. (To put it another way, *sati* pulls or holds the mind to its object and wisdom examines or understands it.) According to this method of training, *samādhi* is not the point of emphasis but is gained and developed in the process, promoting the use of wisdom and making it more effective. This way of training consists of most of the methods of the foundations of mindfulness, the general principles of which have already been explained, and it is known as the development of *samādhi* in everyday life.

The second method is that of training for the express development of *samādhi* itself, or focusing on *samādhi* alone. This is the use of *sati* to hold the object or to hold the mind continuously to its object of attention. It is a method that gives direct emphasis to *samādhi*. Even though wisdom may be used to some extent, it is minimal, only a supporting element—as, for example, reflecting on and comprehending what one has remembered, not trying to penetrate to the reality. This kind of training is the essential factor of the fourth method for developing *samādhi*, the traditional development of *samādhi*, which is discussed next.

Systematic (or Traditional) Development of *Samādhi*

The phrase "systematic development of *samādhi*" here refers to a method of developing *samādhi* that has been practiced over time in the Theravada Buddhist tradition, as written and explained in commentarial literature, especially the Visuddhimagga.[111] It is a method of dedicated and earnest practice focusing on development of *samādhi* itself, within a context that is entirely on the mundane level.[112] It is laid out in a systematic, graded path, beginning with initial preparations and proceeding to methods of practicing with each of the kinds of meditation object (*kammaṭṭhāna*) and the progress of the practice up to the *jhāna* attainments and mundane superknowledges.

The text given for the systematic development of *samādhi* can be summarized into the main steps as follows: first, once morality is pure or one's morality has been purified:[113]

1. Cut off the ten impediments or causes of concern (*palibodha*).

2. Approach a good friend, a teacher who is endowed with suitable qualities to give a meditation object.
3. Receive one of the forty meditation objects that is suitable to one's disposition (*cariyā*).
4. Enter a monastery, a dwelling, or any other area that is suitable for meditation practice. Eliminate minor impediments (*palibodha*).
5. Cultivate *samādhi* according to the method of *samādhi* cultivation.

The particulars of practice of these main headings are described in the context of a bhikkhu entering into an intensive program of *samādhi* development, which could take many months or years. For householders, or for anyone who wants to practice for only a short time, the basic principles suitable to one's situation should be applied.

Step one: Remove the impediments

Palibodha means a bond or encumbrance that causes the mind to have worry and concern and thus not be clear. It can be simply translated as "worry." When there are *palibodha*, the practice will proceed with difficulty and will not be conducive to the arising of *samādhi*. Therefore these worries must be eliminated. Ten *palibodha* are detailed:

1. Abode or monastery: one has amassed many belongings, or has unfinished work that causes one to worry. However, if the mind is not encumbered by them, then it is all right.
2. Clan (*kula*): this can refer to a clan of relatives or a clan of supporters, which one is close to and will be a cause of worry if one leaves them. One must completely focus on developing the mind.
3. Wealth (*lābha*): faithful lay supporters come and make offerings and one is caught up in them and cannot practice. One should go off and find seclusion.
4. The group (*gaṇa*): one has a group of students to whom one is

obliged to give instruction and is caught up in the work of teaching and answering questions. One should finish off what is still unfinished or find a replacement and take leave of the group.

5. Work (*kamma*), especially construction work. This should be completed or delegated to others.
6. Travel (*addhāna*): long journeys undertaken for some business or other, such as ordaining novices or bhikkhus. Such responsibilities should be completed so that one does not have to worry about them.
7. Relatives (*ñāti*): both relatives from home and "relatives" from the monastery (preceptor, teachers, students, and their friends). When they are sick one must make an effort to treat them and therefore relieve oneself of that worry.
8. Illness (*ābādha*): one is ill. One should quickly treat the illness. If it seems that the illness will not abate, then one should arouse a stout-hearted attitude thinking, "I will not be enslaved by you; I will practice."
9. Books (*gantha*): study. This is an encumbrance for one who is caught up in trying to memorize what one has learned, as by reciting. If one is not caught up in it, it presents no problem.
10. Psychic powers (*iddhi*): the powers of an unenlightened being are a burden to maintain. However, they are an encumbrance only for those who are developing insight, not for the direct development of *samādhi*, because one who is still developing *samādhi* does not yet have any powers to worry about.

Step two: seek out a good friend

Having severed the encumbrances and having nothing weighing down on one's mind, one must then approach someone who is capable of teaching meditation, who is endowed with wholesome qualities and truly moved to help others, known as the good friend (*kalyāṇamitta*), and who is endowed with the following seven qualities of a good friend: endearing, worthy of respect, inspiring, eloquent, open to criticism, capable of expounding on the profound, and not leading in wrongful ways.[114] The ideal good friend is the

Buddha. Failing that, in descending order, the ideal good friend is an arahant, one of the lower levels of noble one, one who has gained the *jhānas*, one who has memorized the Tipiṭaka, or one who is conversant with the teachings (*bahussuta*).

It is said that an unenlightened bhikkhu who is learned may sometimes be a better teacher than an arahant who is not so learned, because the arahant may be conversant only with the style of practice that he himself has used and only be able to teach that way, and some arahants may not be gifted at teaching. A learned bhikkhu, on the other hand, has done much research and questioned many teachers. He can teach a way that is broad and knows many techniques to adapt the teaching as needed. A learned bhikkhu who is also an arahant is, of course, so much the better. Having found a good friend, one should approach him or her, conduct the appropriate duties toward that person, and request instruction on meditation.

Step three: receive or learn a suitable meditation object (*kammaṭṭhāna*)

One should receive a meditation object (*kammaṭṭhāna*) suitable to one's disposition (*cariyā*). *Kammaṭṭhāna* literally means "the location of the mind's work," or "the mind's working place." Its official meaning is the object used for developing *samādhi*, a device used for training the mind, a technique or strategy for holding the mind in *samādhi*. Simply speaking it is the meditation object, giving the mind something to work with, a subject upon which it can settle and not wander. In this case, *kammaṭṭhāna* is anything taken as an object of concentration to induce the mind to *samādhi*, or anything that, once the mind has taken as object, induces the mind to have undivided attention and to become concentrated. Forty of these meditation objects (*kammaṭṭhāna*) are described by the commentators as follows:

1. The ten *kasiṇas*: A *kasiṇa* is a device for inducing the mind to concentration, a device to concentrate on and lead the mind to

samādhi. This method makes use of external objects to concentrate and center the mind in one-pointedness. The ten *kasiṇas* can be either natural objects or devices made especially for concentration. Mostly the latter is preferred. There are ten kinds of *kasiṇa*, as follows:

- Four great elements (*bhūtakasiṇa*): earth (*paṭhavī*), water (*āpo*), fire (*tejo*), and wind (*vāyo*)
- Four colored devices (*vaṇṇakasiṇa*): blue, yellow, red, and white
- Two miscellaneous *kasiṇas*: light (*āloka*) and space (*paricchinnākāsa*)[115]

2. The ten unattractive objects (*asubha*): This category of meditation involves the contemplation of dead bodies in ten different stages of decomposition, from a body just starting to fester to a skeleton.[116]
3. The ten recollections (*anussati*): This meditation relies on wholesome objects for regular recollection—namely: [117]
   - *buddhānussati*: recollection on the Buddha and examination of his qualities
   - *dhammānussati*: recollection on the teaching and examination of its qualities
   - *saṅghānussati*: recollection on the order and examination of its qualities
   - *sīlānussati*: recollection on morality, examining one's own purely maintained morality
   - *cāgānussati*: recollection on giving, on the things one has given, and examination of the virtue of generosity and sacrifice within one
   - *devatānussati*: recollection on devas (meaning devas that one has seen and heard of) and also examination of the virtues within oneself that lead to being a deva
   - *maraṇasati*: recollection on the inevitability of one's own death, examining it so as to bring forth heedfulness (*appamāda*)
   - *kāyagatāsati*: mindfulness of the body, or recollection of the

body, examination of it as containing thirty-two unclean, unattractive, and repulsive parts (this is a way of comprehending the reality of the body and thus preventing delusion or infatuation in regard to it)

- *ānāpānasati*: mindfulness of the in- and out-breathing
- *upasamānussati*: recollection on that which is peaceful, which is *nibbāna*; examining the virtue of *nibbāna*, which is the calming of all defilements and suffering

4. The four limitless abidings (*appamaññā*): qualities that are to be spread toward all beings with impartiality, without limit or distinction. Often referred to as the four *brahmavihāra* (the "holy abidings"—the principles for divine abiding, or that make the mind excellent, or the virtues of a great being),[118] these qualities are as follows:
   - *mettā*: love, goodwill, friendliness, the desire to see all people and beings happy
   - *karuṇā*: compassion, wanting to help all beings be free of suffering
   - *muditā*: sympathetic joy, feeling glad when others are happy, prospering, and experiencing good fortune
   - *upekkhā*: equanimity, establishing the mind in serenity, constancy, and equilibrium, like a scale; seeing all beings receive the good and bad fruits of their actions according to determinants; not inclining toward like or dislike
5. *Āhāre paṭikūlasaññā*: reflection on the loathsomeness of food[119]
6. *Catudhātuvavaṭṭhāna*: reflection on the four elements (earth, water, wind, and fire), examining one's own body as merely the four elements one by one[120]
7. The four formless meditations (*arūpa*): attending to formless qualities as a meditation subject. These four can be accessed only by those who have attended to any of the first nine *kasiṇa* objects until fourth *jhāna* is attained.[121]
   - *akāsānañcāyatana*: attending to limitless space (which arises from removing the *kasiṇa* object) as object
   - *viññāṇañcāyatana*: attending to limitless consciousness

(ceasing to attend to limitless space and attending instead to the consciousness that spreads to emptiness) as object
- *ākiñcaññāyatana*: (ceasing to attend to consciousness and so) attending to the state of nothingness as object
- *nevasaññānāsaññāyatana*: (ceasing to attend even to the state of nothingness and) entering the state that is neither with nor without perception

All of these meditation objects are sometimes divided into two categories.[122] One category is *sabbatthaka-kammaṭṭhāna*, or meditation objects that are of benefit or should be used in all situations; that is, they can be practiced by anybody at any time. These are the meditation on goodwill (*mettā*) and recollection on death. The other is *pārihāriya-kammaṭṭhāna*, or meditation objects that require management. These are meditation objects that are suitable for individual dispositions (*cariyā*), and that, once taken on for practice, must be constantly managed in order to be a foundation for higher practice.

It is said that these forty meditation themes differ in their suitability for individual practitioners. They must be carefully chosen in accordance with the temperaments and inclinations of each individual, which in Pali are called *cariyā*. If the right meditation subject is chosen, the practice will yield results quickly, but if the choice is wrong, the practice may be slowed or even fail.

The word *cariyā* translates as "regular behavior," and it refers to the basic dispositions of the mind, underlying temperament, or features of behavior that incline one way or another according to a person's regular state of mind. The behavior or temperament is referred to as *cariyā*, while the people who have such tendencies are known as *carita*. For example, a person with *rāgacariyā* (greedy behavior) is known as *rāgacarita* (a greedy temperament). There are six main *carita*, as follows:[123]

1. *Rāgacarita*: those who have greed as tendency. Their disposition is toward desire, and their conduct tends toward love of

beauty and refinement. They should use the meditation subject for countering that tendency, which is contemplation of the unattractive (and recollection on the body).

2. *Dosacarita*: those who have aversion as tendency. Their disposition is toward aversion, and their conduct tends toward impatience, irritation, and being hot-tempered. The appropriate meditation subject for these is *mettā* (including the other divine abidings), as well as some of the *kasiṇas*, especially the colored ones.
3. *Mohacarita*: those who have delusion as tendency. Their disposition is toward delusion, and their conduct tends toward low intelligence, dullness, confusion, or gullibility. This should be countered by learning, inquiring into, or listening to the teachings, discussing the Dhamma, or living with a teacher. (A helpful meditation subject is mindfulness of the breathing.)
4. *Saddhācarita*: those who have faith as tendency. Their disposition is toward belief, and their conduct tends toward faith, inspiration, humility. and being easily moved to acceptance. They should be guided toward something that is worthy of faith and a belief that is rational, as in recollecting on the virtues of the Triple Gem or recollecting their own moral conduct. (Any of the first six recollections are appropriate.)
5. *Buddhicarita* or *ñāṇacarita*: those who have knowledge as tendency. Their disposition and tendency are toward thinking and examining and seeing things as they really are. They should be encouraged to examine realities (*sabhāvadhamma*) and skillful conditions that are conducive to wisdom, such as the three characteristics. (The appropriate meditation subjects are recollection on death, recollection on peace, analysis on the four elements, and reflection on the loathsomeness of food.)
6. *Vitakkacarita*: those who have thinking as tendency. Their disposition and tendency are toward thinking exhaustively, toward scattered thinking. This tendency should be countered with something that focuses the attention, such as mindfulness of breathing (or concentration on a *kasiṇa*, for example).

These personalities have predictable behavioral expressions: for example, when people with *rāgacarita* see something, if it has any pleasant aspects, they will focus on those. They will become attached to those and dwell on them, paying no attention to the object's bad aspects. If that object has any bad aspects, those with *dosacarita* will be affronted by those, even if the object has many positive aspects—before they see those, they have already focused on the bad aspects. *Buddhicarita* people are similar in some ways to those with *dosacarita*, in that they do not easily attach to things, but they differ in that the *dosacarita* will search for flaws and find them even where there are none, and fall into aversion, while the *buddhicarita* will search for negative aspects and flaws that actually exist, and simply not attach to them and pass them by. People with *mohacarita* will not be able to decide clearly on the object. They tend toward indifference: if others say it's good, they tend to agree; if they say it's bad, they'll agree with that too. The *vitakkacarita* types think aimlessly, thinking of a thing's good points and bad points in a generally confused manner, and can't decide whether to like it or not. The *saddhācarita* types are similar in some ways to the *rāgacarita*: they have a tendency to look at the good aspects of things, but they differ in that they may be inspired by something, but they do not attach to and yearn for it like the *rāgacarita*.

Even so, people tend to have mixtures of these different temperments, such as a mixture of *rāga* and *vitakka*, or *dosa* mixed with *buddhi*. In the practice of *samādhi* development, apart from choosing a suitable meditation subject, choosing other factors that are helpful and appropriate (*sappāya*)—such as living place, atmosphere, ease of access, requisites, and food—is also advised.

The forty meditation themes differ not only in terms of suitability to different personalities but also in the different level of results to which they lead. Each has a different capacity to produce the various levels of *samādhi*. The table below briefly outlines the relationship between the meditation objects and the relevant suitable dispositions and levels of *samādhi* they can achieve.

Table 1. Summary of Meditation Techniques

Meditation technique	Appropriate disposition						Highest level attainable						
	rāgacarita	*dosacarita*	*mohacarita*	*saddhācarita*	*buddhicarita*	*vitakkacarita*	*paṭibhāganimitta*	*upacārasamādhi*	first *jhāna*	second *jhāna*	third *jhāna*	fourth *jhāna*	formless *jhānas*
Ten *kasiṇas*:													
Four colored *kasiṇas*		x					o	o	o	o	o	o	
Other *kasiṇas*	x	x	x	x	x	x	o	o	o	o	o	o	
Ten unattractive objects	x						o	o	o				
Ten recollections:													
-first six				x				o					
-recollection on peace					x			o					
-recollection on death					x			o					
-recollection on body	x						o	o	o				
-recollection of breath			x			x	o	o	o	o	o	o	
Four limitless abidings:													
-first three		x						o	o	o	o		
-equanimity		x						o				o	
Loathsomeness of food					x			o					
Four elements					x			o					
Four formless:													
-infinite space	x	x	x	x	x	x		o				o	1
-infinite consciousness	x	x	x	x	x	x		o				o	2
-nothingness	x	x	x	x	x	x		o				o	3
-neither perception nor non-perception	x	x	x	x	x	x		o				o	4

Ideally, when receiving the meditation subject, the following small ceremony should be performed: Having approached the teacher, one should declare one's commitment to the Buddha, along these lines: "Blessed One, I give up this body to you."[124] Or one can offer oneself to the teacher, saying, "Venerable Sir, I give up this body to you."[125]

Offering oneself to the teacher is a skillful means for developing a desire to practice resolutely and fearlessly, helping to eliminate fear and encourage obedience. It creates a bond between the teacher and student and opens the way for the teacher to give instruction and help the student in the training. During the ceremony the student should instill in his or her mind non-greed, non-hatred, non-delusion, renunciation, and predilection for seclusion and liberation; incline his or her mind to *samādhi* and *nibbāna*; then ask for the meditation subject.

If the teacher is able to ascertain the temperament of the student through direct knowledge, he or she should take note of that disposition. Otherwise the teacher should find out by asking, for example, "What kind of personality do you have?" "What are your usual thoughts and feelings?" "What things make your mind comfortable?" "Which meditation subject is your mind inclined to?" Then the teacher assigns a meditation object to the student in accordance with the student's disposition, explaining how to begin the practice and how to attend to and develop the meditation object, as well as explaining about *nimitta*s and the levels of *samādhi*, and how to maintain, nurture, and strengthen the *samādhi*.[126]

Step four: taking up a residence

Enter a monastery that is suitable for the development of meditation. Preferably it is the monastery of the teacher, but if that is not conducive, one should go to a temple that is suitable (*sappāya*). The essential point is to find a place that is suitable and conducive to the practice of meditation.

It is recommended to avoid monasteries that have the following eighteen faults: large monasteries (that have many bhikkhus, many opinions, many concerns, and are not very peaceful); new monasteries (one has to join in with the building); very old monasteries (which require a lot of maintenance); monasteries fronting onto roads (which have many visitors); monasteries that have rock ponds (where people like to gather); monasteries that have vegetable gardens; monasteries that have flowers; monasteries that have fruit trees (to which people will always be coming, to gather flowers, ask for fruit, and so on); monasteries that are highly venerated (as having gifted bhikkhus, for example); monasteries adjacent to towns; monasteries adjacent to forests; monasteries adjacent to fields; monasteries with people who do not get along; monasteries adjacent to boat landings; remote monasteries (located in areas where people do not uphold the religion); frontier monasteries (located at the border between two countries, which could be dangerous); monasteries that are not comfortable (which bring up disturbances); and monasteries with no access to a good friend. Dwellings or monasteries that are suitable are dwellings that have the following five qualities: (1) not too far, not too near, with ease of access; (2) not crowded in daytime, not noisy at night; (3) free of disturbance from gnats, mosquitoes, sun, wind, and crawling creatures; (4) where the four supports are available; and (5) where there is a resident learned elder (*bahussuta*) who is available for questioning and is capable of relieving doubts.[127]

Upon entering a monastery, eliminate remaining minor encumbrances, such as worries concerning the body and personal belongings, so that they do not disturb one. This is done, for example, by cutting and shaving one's hair, beard, and nails; sewing, dyeing, and arranging one's robes; and cleaning out one's residence.

Step five: Developing *samādhi*: general principles

It should be known that each of the meditation objects has its own discrete methods, but all of them can be generally summarized into broad general principles, as some of the texts have described them, in terms of the three levels of cultivation (*bhāvanā*): preparatory cultivation (*parikammabhāvanā*), access cultivation (*upacārabhāvana*), and attainment cultivation (*appanābhāvanā*).[128] Before explaining these three kinds of cultivation, there is one term that needs to be explained first: *nimitta*.

A *nimitta* is a sign to which the mind attends or a mental image that stands in place of the meditation subject. There are three kinds of *nimitta*, presented here in order of stages of development:

1. *Parikamma-nimitta*: the *nimitta* of the preparatory or initial stage. This is any object that is attended to as the subject of meditation practice, such as a colored disk, the breath, or the qualities of the Buddha.
2. *Uggahanimitta*: the "learned *nimitta*," or the "fixed *nimitta*." This is a *parikamma-nimitta* that has been gazed on or attended to until it is clearly seen as a fixed mental image, such as a colored disk that is concentrated on until it is seen even when the eyes are closed.
3. *Paṭibhāganimitta* : the "replica nimitta," or counterpart *nimitta*. This is an image that is a copy of the *uggahanimitta* but is more deeply fixed, until it becomes a creation of the meditator's own perception (*saññā*), for which reason it is pure, colorless, and free of contamination and can be expanded or contracted at will.

The first two kinds of *nimitta*, the preparatory and learned *nimittas*, can arise in all of the meditation subjects, but the *paṭibhāganimitta* can only arise in the twenty-two subjects that contain a concrete object of concentration: the ten *kasiṇas*, the ten unattractive reflections, the reflection on the body, and mindfulness of the breath (see table 1 on page 641). Now I will explain the three levels of cultivation (*bhāvanā*).

1. *Parikammabhāvanā*: development of initial concentration. This level involves attending to an image of the meditation object, such as gazing on a colored disk, noting the sensations of the in- and out-breath at the nose tip, or recollecting or mentally intoning the virtues of the Buddha. Simply speaking, it is noting the preparatory *nimitta*. When the meditation subject (the *parikamma-nimitta*) is attended to until an image of that sign arises and is fixed accurately in the mind, the *uggahanimitta*

arises. The mind is then in the initial level of *samādhi* known as *parikamma-samādhi* (that is, *khaṇika-samādhi*).

2. *Upacārabhāvanā*: development of access concentration. Here the concentration on the *uggahanimitta* in *parikamma-samādhi* is continued until it becomes undivided and firm in the mind, and a *paṭibhāganimitta* arises. The hindrances are suppressed. (In those meditation objects that do not have a concrete object of concentration, but rely on discursive reflection, there is no *paṭibhāganimitta*. The *uggahanimitta* is observed with undivided attention and the hindrances are suppressed.) The mind becomes firm in access concentration. This is the highest level of *samādhi* on the sensual realm (*kāmāvacara-samādhi*).
3. *Appanābhāvanā*: development of attainment concentration. This level consists of the unwavering experience of the *paṭibhāganimitta* in *upacārasamādhi*, which is maintained and not allowed to decline by avoiding those places, people, or foods that are not conducive and associating with only those things that are conducive (*sappāya*),[129] as well as by following a suitable method, as in maintaining the mind appropriately[130] until eventually the mind attains *appanāsamādhi* and enters the first *jhāna*—the first level of *samādhi* on the material sphere (*rūpāvacarasamādhi*).

Many meditation subjects are subtle and profound—they have no visible or tangible object, so they are not clear enough for the mind to absorb into for long periods of time. Therefore, they have no *paṭibhāganimitta* and can lead only to the stage of *upacārasamādhi*. More tangible meditation subjects that can be seen and felt are more clearly noted. The mind can absorb into these for long periods, and therefore a *paṭibhāganimitta* can arise and *appanāsamādhi* be achieved. The only exception here is in the limitless abidings (*brahmavihāra*), which, although possessing no *paṭibhāganimitta* because they have no concrete object, do have sentient beings as object, and as such are sufficiently clear and can lead to *appanāsamādhi*.[131]

Once the first *jhāna* is attained, the practice consists of developing proficiency[132] in it and attaining the successively higher *jhānas* as far as can be done with that particular meditation subject. This is the achievement of calm (*samatha*).

*An Example of Meditation Practice (*Ānāpānasati*)*

Having explained the general principles of the methods for developing *samādhi*, it would be appropriate to give an example of how meditation practice is developed. From among the forty meditation subjects, I will describe the method for mindfulness of the breathing (*ānāpānasati*).

There are many reasons that I have chosen mindfulness of the breathing. Since it makes use of the breath, which is within everyone, it is one of the most convenient techniques to practice. It can be used in all times and all places, whenever one wishes to use it, and does not require the preparation of devices as do other techniques, such as the *kasiṇas*. At the same time, it is a concrete object, something that is fairly easy to concentrate on, not overly subtle and profound (such as the abstract meditation subjects that rely on thinking from memory). Moreover, if one wishes to practice this technique very simply, one need not think at all, but just apply mindfulness to the natural breathing that is already there. There is no need to analyze or contemplate its reality, such as in the attention to the elements. It can be practiced even when one is tired.

Results and benefits appear as soon as one starts the practice, and they continue to arise. It is not necessary to wait until the attainment of any specific level of *samādhi*. That is to say, the body and mind become relaxed and rested, and the mind becomes increasingly calm and more profound, causing unskillful qualities to be suppressed and skillful ones to grow.

It does not have a bad effect on health, as the Buddha said of his own experience: "Even after dwelling much in this abiding [concentration based on mindfulness of the breathing], the body was not tired, the eyes were not strained."[133] It is not like some meditation techniques that require prolonged periods of standing, walking, or fixed staring. On the contrary, mindfulness of the breathing meditation is actually good for the health and helps the body to obtain good rest. The respiratory system that has been regulated and refined by the practice of this kind of meditation is beneficial to health. Consider, for example, a person who has just run for some distance, or is tired from a steep climb, or is excited, furious, or frightened: the breath is much heavier than for a person in a rested state. The nasal passages may not be sufficient for the strong passage of air required, and the person has to gasp for air through the mouth. On the other hand, the breathing of one whose body is relaxed and whose mind is calm will be subtler than normal. The practice of mindfulness of the breathing helps to calm the body and mind, so that the breath becomes increasingly subtle until it may be hard to tell if there is any breathing at all. At that time the body is functioning smoothly on a minimum of energy, saving its energy for undertaking later activities and thereby helping to slow down the aging process or helping to do more work for less amount of rest.

Mindfulness of the breathing is one of only twelve meditation techniques that are capable of achieving the highest level of calm (*samatha*), which is fourth *jhāna*. It also has an influence on the formless *jhānas* and even cessation attainment (*nirodhasamāpatti*). It can therefore be used as a fundamental practice from the very beginning onward, with no need to concern oneself with other meditation subjects. This is supported by the Buddhavacana: "Therefore, if a bhikkhu thinks, 'I will enter the fourth *jhāna*...' he should attend well to the *samādhi* based on mindfulness of the breath... If a bhikkhu thinks, 'I will totally go beyond the sphere of nothingness (*ākiñcaññāyatana*) and enter into to the sphere of neither perception nor non-perception... I will totally transcend the sphere of neither perception nor non-perception and enter to the state of cessation of perception and feeling,' he should attend well to the *samādhi* based on mindfulness of the breathing."[134]

Mindfulness of the breathing practice can be used for both calm (*samatha*) and insight (*vipassanā*)—that is, either for the exclusive development of *samādhi* or as a basis for the practice of all four of the foundations of mindfulness, using the concentrated mind as a field of operations for wisdom.[135]

Mindfulness of the breathing is the method of cultivating *samādhi* most praised by the Buddha, the one that on many occasions he encouraged the bhikkhus to practice. The Buddha himself used the technique as a place of rest, both before and after the enlightenment, as shown in the Buddhavacana:

> "Bhikkhus, *samādhi* based on mindfulness of the breathing, developed and made much of, is calming, subtle, and refreshing. It is a pleasant abiding, and it quickly eliminates and suppresses bad, unskillful conditions that have arisen, just as an unseasonable torrent of rain quickly and effectively eliminates and suppresses the dust of the last month of summer."[136]
>
> ---
>
> "Bhikkhus... correctly speaking, *samādhi* based on mindfulness of the breathing must be called a noble abiding (*ariyavihāra*), a holy abiding (*brahmavihāra*), a *tathāgata*'s abiding (*tathāgatavihāra*). The *samādhi* based on mindfulness of breathing, developed and made much of by bhikkhus who are learners (*sekha*), who have not yet attained arahantship, who aspire to the matchless secure release from all bonds, leads to the cessation of the outflows. The *samādhi* based on mindfulness of breathing, developed and made much of by a bhikkhu who is an arahant, a destroyer of the outflows, leads to a pleasant abiding in the present moment, and to *sati* and clear comprehension."[137]
>
> ---
>
> "Bhikkhus, it so happened that I, before the enlightenment, while still unenlightened, still a *bodhisatta*, dwelled mostly in this abiding [*samādhi* based on mindfulness of the breathing]. Dwelling mostly in this abiding, my body was not tired, my eyes were not strained and my mind was delivered from all the outflows through non-clinging. For that reason, bhikkhus, should any bhikkhu think, 'May my body be not tired, my eyes not

strained, and my mind delivered from all the outflows through non-clinging,' he should attend carefully to this *samādhi* based on mindfulness of the breathing."[138]

At one time, the Blessed One was dwelling at the forest grove known as Icchānaṅgala, near the city of Icchānaṅgala. There, the Blessed One addressed the bhikkhus thus, "Bhikkhus, I wish to go into seclusion for three months. No one is to come to see me except the bhikkhu who brings me my food"...Then, at the end of the three months, the Blessed One came out of his retreat and said to the bhikkhus, "Bhikkhus, if any adherent of another sect or wanderer should ask of you, 'In which abiding did the recluse Gotama spend most of his time during the rains retreat?' you should, on being so asked, explain to that adherent of another sect or wanderer thus: 'Venerable Sir, the Blessed One spent most of his rains retreat in the *samādhi* based on mindfulness of the breathing.'"[139]

"Ānanda, one condition, *samādhi* based on mindfulness of the breathing, developed and made much of, brings about the perfection of the four foundations of mindfulness. The four foundations of mindfulness, developed and made much of by a bhikkhu, bring about the perfection of the seven enlightenment factors. The seven enlightenment factors, developed and made much of by a bhikkhu, bring about the perfection of knowledge and deliverance."[140]

"Rāhula, when mindfulness of the breathing is developed and made much of in this way, even the last breaths are extinguished with knowing, not with unknowing."[141]

The Buddha's Words on the Technique

"And how, bhikkhus, is mindfulness of the breathing to be developed and made much of, so that it leads to great benefit and great reward?

> "A bhikkhu in this teaching and discipline, (1) gone to a forest, the foot of a tree, or to an empty building,[142] (2) sits cross-legged, body erect, maintaining *sati* before him [= directing *sati* to the meditation subject, the breath]. (3) He is mindful while breathing in, mindful while breathing out."[143]

First group of four: can be used for developing mindfulness of the body (*kāyānupassanā satipaṭṭhāna*):

1. Breathing out a long breath, he knows clearly that he is breathing out a long breath. Breathing in a long breath, he knows clearly that he is breathing in a long breath.
2. Breathing out a short breath, he knows clearly that he is breathing out a short breath. Breathing in a short breath, he knows clearly that he is breathing in a short breath.
3. He reflects thus: "I will be one who is aware of the entire body on the out-breath." He reflects thus: "I will be one who is aware of the entire body on the in-breath."
4. He reflects thus: "I will be one who calms bodily formations (*kāyasaṅkhārā*) on the out-breath." He reflects thus: "I will be one who calms bodily formations on the in-breath."

Second group of four: can be used for developing mindfulness of the feelings (*vedanānupassanā satipaṭṭhāna*).

1. He reflects thus: "I will be one who clearly notes rapture (*pīti*) on the out-breath." He reflects thus: "I will be one who clearly notes rapture on the in-breath."
2. He reflects thus: "I will be one who clearly notes well-being (*sukha*) on the out-breath. He reflects thus: "I will be one who clearly notes well-being on the in-breath."
3. He reflects thus: "I will be one who clearly notes mental formations (*cittasaṅkhāra*) on the out-breath." He reflects thus: "I will be one who clearly notes mental formations on the in-breath."
4. He reflects thus: "I will be one who calms mental formations on the out-breath." He reflects thus: "I will be one who calms mental formations on the in-breath."

Third group of four: can be used for developing mindfulness of the mind (*cittānupassanā satipaṭṭhāna*).

1. He reflects thus: "I will be one who clearly notes the mind on the out-breath." He reflects thus: "I will be one who clearly notes the mind on the in-breath."
2. He reflects thus: "I will be one who gladdens the mind on the out-breath." He reflects thus: "I will be one who gladdens the mind on the in-breath."
3. He reflects thus: "I will be one who makes the mind firm on the out-breath." He reflects thus: "I will be one who makes the mind firm on the in-breath."
4. He reflects thus: "I will be one who releases the mind on the out-breath." He reflects thus: "I will be one who releases the mind on the in-breath."

Fourth group of four: can be used to develop mindfulness of phenomena (*dhammānupassanā satipaṭṭhāna*).

1. He reflects thus: "I will be one who contemplates impermanence on the out-breath." He reflects thus: "I will be one who contemplates impermanence on the in-breath."
2. He reflects thus: "I will be one who contemplates dispassion on the out-breath." He reflects thus: "I will be one who contemplates dispassion on the in-breath."
3. He reflects thus: "I will be one who contemplates cessation on the out-breath." He reflects thus: "I will be one who contemplates cessation on the in-breath."
4. He reflects thus: "I will be one who contemplates relinquishment on the out-breath." He reflects thus: "I will be one who contemplates relinquishment on the in-breath."[144]

Now I will give a brief explanation of the development of calm in the first group of four.[145]

1. Preparation

Place

In the beginning, if one wishes to practice earnestly, one should find a secluded place,[146] where there are no sounds or other external disturbances, so that one's surroundings are conducive to the practice, just as a child learning to swim needs the support of water wings or should start off by swimming in still water. However, if there are obstacles, or one is practicing for an objective in a specific situation, one must accept what is available.

Sitting posture

The main point is that any position that makes the body most comfortable, without producing pain even during long periods of practice, and that is conducive to comfortable breathing, is appropriate. The posture that has been verified by innumerable successful meditators since ancient times as being most effective is the lotus or half-lotus sitting posture, or the cross-legged posture. The upper half of the body is straight, the eighteen vertebrae lined up end to end. It is said that in this posture the skin, flesh, and ligaments are not cramped, and respiration is convenient. It is a stable posture, in which one is extremely well balanced. The body will be light and not feel burdensome, and one can sit for long periods of time without physical torment. This helps the mind to be concentrated and the meditation practice does not regress, but advances smoothly. According to the traditional teaching, it is added that the soles of the feet should be pressed to the lower abdomen. If the legs are not interlocked (as in full lotus), then the right leg may be rested on the left leg. The hands should be resting on the lap against the belly (palms raised upward), right hand on the left hand, thumbs lightly touching, or the right forefinger lightly touching the left thumb.

However, these minor details depend on each individual's physical condition. Those who have never sat in this way may train to do so if they have the patience, but if they cannot do so it is acceptable to sit in a straight-backed chair or even to use a different physical posture. There is the additional injunction that if the body is not yet comfortable, if it is rigid and tense, then the posture is not correct, and it should be corrected before resuming the practice. The eyes can be either closed or opened, as long as the posture is comfortable and the mind not distracted. If the eyes are opened, they can be cast down or the gaze can be rested comfortably on the nose tip.[147]

Having seated oneself comfortably, before beginning the meditation practice, some teachers recommend taking two or three deep, slow breaths to lighten oneself and clear the mind, then to breathe and note according to the technique.

2. Beginning practice: noting the breaths

The commentators have devised further techniques to supplement the Buddha's instructions given above, which are explained as follows:

Counting (*gaṇanā*)

In the beginning, when noting the long and short in- and out-breaths, it is recommended to also count the breaths, as this is a good technique for concentrating the mind. The counting can be divided into two stages:

The first stage consists of slow counting. The counting should be up to no less than five and no more than ten. It should be in numerical order, and none of the numbers skipped. If the number is less than five, the mind will feel cramped; if the number is more than ten, the mind will be more concerned with the counting than the meditation object, the breaths. If the counting is incomplete or numbers skipped, the mind has become distracted.

One should count the in- and out-breaths in a relaxed manner in pairs: on the out-breath, count "one," then on the in-breath, count "one"; on the out-breath, count "two," then on the in-breath count "two," up until "five, five." Then one begins again at "one, one," going up to "six, six." Then one goes back and begins counting again, up to five. This process can be written as follows:[148]

1,1	2,2	3,3	4,4	5,5					
1,1	2,2	3,3	4,4	5,5	6,6				
1,1	2,2	3,3	4,4	5,5	6,6	7,7			
1,1	2,2	3,3	4,4	5,5	6,6	7,7	8,8		
1,1	2,2	3,3	4,4	5,5	6,6	7,7	8,8	9,9	
1,1	2,2	3,3	4,4	5,5	6,6	7,7	8,8	9,9	10,10
1,1	2,2	3,3	4,4	5,5	and so on.				

The second stage involves fast counting. When the in- and out-breathing is clear in the mind—that is, the mind stays on the breaths, and the breaths hold the mind still so that it does not wander to other objects—one can stop counting by the slow method and begin counting in a quicker way.

Here it is no longer necessary to be concerned whether the breath is going in or out; the practice is one of noting only the contact of the breath at the nasal passage. One counts quickly from one to five, then from one to six, increasing one at a time up to ten, then beginning at one to five again. The mind becomes firm and one-pointed on the counting, just as a boat maintains its stability in a swiftly flowing river through skillful punting.

Counting quickly in this way, the meditation subject will appear continuously, with no gaps. The rapid counting should be continued in this way without noting whether the breath is coming in or going out, but simply putting mindfulness at the point of the breath's contact as it passes in and out, at the nose tip or the upper lip (wherever it is more apparent).[149]

This technique can be written thus:

1	2	3	4	5					
1	2	3	4	5	6				
1	2	3	4	5	6	7			
1	2	3	4	5	6	7	8		
1	2	3	4	5	6	7	8	9	
1	2	3	4	5	6	7	8	9	10
1	2	3	4	5	and so on.				

The counting should be continued until such time as even when the counting has been discarded mindfulness can be fixed unwaveringly on the object, the in- and out-breath. The objective of the counting is the undivided fixing of *sati* on the meditation object, by cutting off any external distractions.

Following (*anubandhanā*)

When *sati* is established and the mind is focused on the breathing, the counting can be abandoned and mindfulness fixed uninterruptedly on the breathing. The term "following" does not mean following the breath inward through the nose, to the chest, and down to the abdomen, then following the breath from the abdomen up to the chest and out to the nose, noting the beginning, middle, and end of each breath. Such a practice would disturb and distract both body and mind and spoil any results. The proper way to follow is to mindfully follow the breath at the point where it makes contact (the nose tip or upper lip). It is likened to a man sawing wood, who puts his attention on the point where the teeth of the saw contact the wood, not on the saw teeth that have passed by or are coming to that point, or following the top of the saw, the middle of the saw, and the end of the saw. However, even though he concentrates only on the point of contact between the saw's teeth and the wood, he is still aware of the saw's teeth passing by that point. In this way his work is completed successfully. It is the same for the meditator: having fixed mindfulness at the point where the breath makes contact and not following the coming and going of the breath, he is aware of the breath coming and going, and in this way his practice is successful.

At this stage some meditators may experience *nimittas* (signs or images) and quickly enter attainment concentration (*appanāsamādhi*), but others will proceed more gradually. From the initial counting of the breaths, the breathing becomes more and more subtle, and the body more and more relaxed. The body and mind feel light, as if one were floating on air. When the coarser breath is gone, there will be a *nimitta* of the breath remaining in the mind as a subtle object. When that *nimitta* disappears, there will be an even subtler *nimitta* of the breath. It is compared to the sound of a struck gong or bell: there will be a *nimitta* of the sound echoing in the mind long afterward, at first quite coarse but becoming progressively subtler and fainter.

At this stage a problem arises that is specific to the breath as meditation object: instead of the object becoming clearer and clearer the longer the meditation continues, as with other meditation objects, the object becomes more and more subtle, fainter and fainter, until it can no longer be felt, leaving the meditator without an object of meditation. When this happens, we are advised not to become discouraged or rise from the meditation but instead to reestablish the breath. This is easily done by simply establishing the mind at the point where the breath usually makes contact, and attending to the thought that this is where the breath makes contact. In no long time the breath will appear again. As one continues to concentrate on the meditation object, the *nimitta* will again arise.[150]

Nimittas appear to meditators in different ways. Some of them appear as a ball of kapok or cotton wool; some as a breeze; some as like a star, a jewel, a pearl, a cotton seed, or a splinter, with rough texture. Sometimes they are like a sash or a garland, or like a flame or smoke; like a spider's web, or clouds; a lotus flower, or a wheel; and some are like the moon or the sun. The reason for these different forms is that *nimittas* arise from *saññā* (memory, accumulated perceptions), which varies from person to person.

Once a *nimitta* appears, the teacher should be informed (checking for misunderstandings). Then the mind should be firmly established on that *nimitta*. When this *nimitta* (*paṭibhāganimitta*) appears, the hindrances will be suppressed, *sati* will become firm and the mind single-pointed in *upacārasamādhi*. The meditator must try to maintain the *nimitta* (that is, to maintain the *samādhi*) by avoiding what is unconducive, associating with the seven conducive things (*sappāya*), and attending to the *nimitta* often so that it develops and grows, by practicing the methods helpful to attaining *appanāsamādhi* (the ten *appanākosalla*), such as exerting even effort, until eventually *appanāsamādhi* arises and the first *jhāna* is attained.

The Highest Benefits of Samādhi *and Accomplishments beyond* Samādhi

The practice of *samādhi* gets gradually more and more subtle. The state of mind in *appanāsamādhi* is called *jhāna*, absorption.[151] There are many levels of *jhāna*, and the higher it gets the fewer factors it has. In general, *jhāna* can be divided into two main levels, each further divided into four sublevels, giving altogether eight levels of absorption, known as the eight *jhāna*s, or eight attainments (*samāpatti*), as follows:

Absorptions of Form (*Rūpajhāna*)

1. First absorption (*paṭhama-jhāna*) has five factors: initial application of mind (*vitakka*), sustained application of mind (*vicāra*), rapture (*pīti*), well-being (*sukha*), and one-pointedness (*ekaggatā*).
2. Second absorption (*dutiya-jhāna*) has three factors: rapture, well-being, and one-pointedness.
3. Third absorption (*tatiya-jhāna*) has two factors: well-being and one-pointedness.
4. Fourth absorption (*catuttha-jhāna*) has two factors: equanimity and one-pointedness.

Formless Absorptions (*Arūpajhāna*)

1. Absorption of attention to limitless space (*ākāsānañcāyatana*).
2. Absorption of attention to limitless consciousness (*viññāṇañcāyatana*).
3. Absorption of attention to the state of nothingness (*ākiñcaññāyatana*).
4. Absorption in which attention is totally given up, and the mind enters a state that is neither with nor without perception (*nevasaññānāsaññāyatana*).

In the Abhidhamma, especially the later Abhidhamma of commentarial and subcommentarial times, the *jhāna*s of form tend to be divided into five levels, called the fivefold division of *jhāna*.[152] This is a finer breakdown of the four (form) *jhānas*, in which a second *jhāna* is inserted between the first and original second *jhāna*, containing four factors: sustained application of mind (*vicāra*), rapture (*pīti*), well-being (*sukha*), and one-pointedness (*ekaggatā*). In other words, it is *jhāna* without initial application of mind, only sustained application of mind. From there the original second *jhāna* is moved to third place, the third *jhāna* becomes the fourth, and the fourth becomes the fifth.

Effort to cultivate *samādhi*, through whatever strategy to achieve those results, is called *samatha*. Unenlightened people, no matter how much effort they put into cultivation of *samādhi*, can achieve only this at most. That is to say, *samatha* on its own can lead at most to the sphere of neither perception nor non-perception.

However, those who have attained the fruit of both *samatha* and *vipassanā*, who are either non-returners (*anāgāmī*) or arahants, are able to enter a higher state, which may be called a ninth level, called the cessation of perception and feeling (*saññāvedayitanirodha*),[153] or cessation attainment (*nirodhasamāpatti*), a state in which perception and feeling cease to function; this state is the highest level of happiness.

Although *samādhi* is a vital factor in Dhamma practice, its importance has limitations, and it should also be borne in mind just to what extent it is necessary within the process of practice for the attainment of liberation, which is the objective of the Buddhadhamma. These limitations may be summarized as follows:

1. The benefit of *samādhi* within the context of reaching the goal of Buddhadhamma lies in its use as a place in which wisdom can operate effectively, and *samādhi* used to this end does not have to be on the highest levels. *Samādhi* on its own, even developed to the highest levels of *jhāna*, is not capable of leading to the goal of Buddhadhamma if it does not advance to the use of wisdom.

2. As long as they are simply fruits of the practice known as *samatha*, all eight levels of *jhāna*, although very profound, are mundane, and should not be confused with the goal of Buddhadhamma.

3. In the state of *jhāna*, which is the accomplishment of *samādhi*,

the defilements are suppressed, and therefore this state is also regarded as a kind of liberation. However, it is a temporary liberation, lasting only as long as the *jhāna* lasts, and the mind can regress to its former state. This kind of liberation is called mundane liberation (*lokiyavimokkha*), reversible liberation (*kuppa-vimokkha*),[154] and liberation through suppression (*vikkhambhanavimutti*; that is, defilements are suppressed through the power of *samādhi*, like covering grass with a rock: whenever the rock is taken off, the grass grows again).[155]

Ultimately the critical factor is wisdom, and the wisdom used in this sense carries the specialized name *vipassanā*. Thus, practice should always advance to the level of *vipassanā*. As for *samādhi*, while it is required for preparing the mind for work, it may be used selectively, beginning with the lower levels, known as *vipassanā samādhi*, which lies on the same level as momentary concentration and access concentration. In this respect, although the practice for attaining the goal of the Buddhadhamma essentially entails the even development of the eight factors of the path, in terms of the strategies used to develop *samādhi*, these may be divided into two main methods:

1. The *vipassanāyaka* method: the first method, already described to some extent on the section on right mindfulness, is that in which *sati* plays the important role. Here, only an elementary level of *samādhi*, just as much as is necessary, is used; *samādhi* plays strictly a supporting role and *sati* is the main factor for holding or tying the object for investigation in mind so that the wisdom faculty can examine it. This method of practice is called *vipassanā* (in fact it does contain a degree of *samatha*, but that is not emphasized).

2. The *samatha-yānika* method: this method emphasizes the use of *samādhi*. Here *samādhi* is developed so that the mind is firm and undivided, first entering the state known as *jhāna*. This allows the mind to be firmly absorbed on the object of attention until it is ready for work—malleable and fit for work, as it is said—well primed for any function that may be required of it. In this state the mental defilements and outflows, which usually rise up

and interfere with the mind, forcing it into turmoil, are contained and stilled within a limited area, just as silt settles to the bottom of still water, leaving the water above clear and clean. The mind is in the best possible condition for advancing to the use of wisdom to utterly eliminate whatever "silt" may be remaining. This is the kind of practice usually called *samatha*. If the meditator does not stop here, he or she will continue on to the level of using wisdom to eliminate the defilements and outflows—that is, the level of *vipassanā*, just as in the first method, but it is said to be easier because the mind is then fully primed. This kind of practice makes use of both *samatha* and *vipassanā*.

In terms of the people who have experienced the accomplishment of the practice, those who are accomplished through the first method are known as liberated through wisdom (*paññāvimutta*). Those who are accomplished through the second method are known as liberated in both ways (*ubhatobhāgavimutta*)[156]—that is, liberated through the mental attainments and through the noble path.

A number of points should be emphasized regarding the second method—that of developing *samatha* completely before going on to practice *vipassanā*, resulting in attainment of *ubhatobhāgavimutti*—as follows:

One who practices this method may gain special abilities of various kinds, which result from the *jhāna* attainments, especially those abilities known as the superknowledges (*abhiññā*), of which there are six:[157]

1. *Iddhividhi*—psychic powers, being able to perform various feats
2. *Dibbasota*—the divine ear, clairaudience
3. *Cetopariñāṇa*—the ability to read the minds of others
4. *Dibbacakkhu* or *cutūpapātañāṇa*—the divine eye or clairvoyance, the knowledge of the passing away and rebirth of beings in accordance with their *kamma*
5. *Pubbenivāsānussatiñāṇa*—the ability to recall past lives
6. *Āsavakkhayañāṇa*—direct knowledge of the extinction of the outflows

One who is accomplished through the first method of practice gains only the sixth ability, but none of the other special abilities, which are products of *jhāna*.

One who practices the second method must complete the two stages of the process. Practicing *samatha* on its own, even if it leads to the *jhānas*, without practicing *vipassanā*, cannot lead to the goal of the Buddhadhamma.

Factors That Support, Aid, and Augment the Benefits of Samādhi

Many factors are involved in the development of *samādhi*. Some of them are supports and aids for the arising of *samādhi*, while some of them both support its arising and help it to achieve higher goals, as in *vipassanā* practice.

Some of these factors are frequently encountered in different teachings. For example, *viriya*, effort, is counted as one of the pathways to success (*iddhipāda*), one of the powers (*bala*), one of the faculties (*indriya*), and one of the enlightenment factors (*bojjhaṅga*). It seems to be repetitive, but the different classifications are based on the different qualities and functions each factor takes on in different contexts. For instance, effort is a pathway to success when it is the main strength in achieving success; it is a power when it is used as a power or protection against domination by adverse qualities; it is a faculty when it is the prominent agent in eliminating unskillful qualities, such as laziness, despair, or despondency, and readying the mind for work; and it is an enlightenment factor when it is one of the factors that go together, interact, and interrelate with other factors to lead to the goal of enlightenment.

The Foundation, Proximate Cause, and Target of *Samādhi*

It may be said that morality is the foundation of *samādhi*, the support upon which the various practices for developing *samādhi* rest, as brought out in the Buddhavacana, which Ācariya Buddhaghosa used as the theme for composing the entire Visuddhimagga:

> "A bhikkhu who is clever, established in morality, and trained in mind and wisdom, who is diligent and protected by wisdom, will be able to unravel this tangle."[158]

There are other Buddhavacana asserting that the various methods of practice, such as the eightfold path, the enlightenment factors, the foundations of mindfulness, or the right efforts, can only be effectively developed by one who is established in morality, just as a man who wishes to perform some physical task relies on the earth to stand on, or when land animals stand, walk, or lie down, it is always on the support of the earth.[159]

For ordinary people, morality refers to good conduct and avoiding actions that are hurtful and troublesome to others, which would be a cause for remorse and confusion and would destroy one's self-confidence. Bad actions are like thorns that prick and aggravate the mind, or impede it, oppose it, and prevent it from becoming calm and serene. Morality over and above that is dependent on the *vinaya* governing the way of life that one has taken on. The bhikkhus, for example, must practice according to the principle of restraint within the bhikkhus' code of discipline (the Pāṭimokkha). Over and above morality, the important supporting factors in the practice that were often emphaszied by the Buddha are heedfulness (*appamāda*), having a good friend (*kalyāṇamitta*), and wise attention (*yoniso-manasikāra*).[160]

Morality is the foundation for the practice for *samādhi*; it serves as a base and effects results indirectly, so to speak.[161]

The immediate supporting factor for the arising of *samādhi*, however, is said to be well-being (*sukha*). Thus, it is said that "well-being is the proximate cause (*padaṭṭhāna*) of *samādhi*,"[162] and it is to be noted, in order to avoid any misunderstandings, that what is known as *samādhi* must, at least in the early stages, arise in conjunction with well-being.

The objective of *samādhi* has already been stated many times. Here I will only mention, for the purposes of revision and summary, that it is knowledge and vision of reality (*yathābhūtañāṇadas-*

sana),[163] or we may cite the Buddhavacana and say it is *samāhito… yathābhūtaṁ pajānāti*—"one whose mind is firm sees in accordance with the truth."[164]

In explanation, *samādhi* serves as a field of operations for wisdom, allowing wisdom to develop and to attain its objectives. Even so, it must be remembered that according to the principle of interrelationship within the factors of the path, wisdom, as right view, is the compass needle or lantern that shows the way for all the other factors to proceed in the right direction. Thus, the growth of wisdom also supports the growth of *samādhi*: the more clearly one sees, the firmer the mind becomes and the stronger *samādhi* is. The development of these two major path factors is interdependent and mutually supportive, as shown in two often-cited Buddhist proverbs: *natthi jhānaṁ apaññassa*—"There is no *jhāna* for one without wisdom"—and *natthi paññā ajhāyino*—"There is no wisdom for one without *jhāna*." This is concluded with, *yamhi jhānañca paññañca sa ve nibbānasantike*—"One who has both *jhāna* and wisdom is close to *nibbāna*."[165]

The commentaries, when dealing with the various factors of Dhamma practice, tend to explain them from certain perspectives, such as their characteristics (*lakkhaṇa*), their function (*rasa*), their manifestation (*paccupaṭṭhāna*), and their proximate cause (*padaṭṭhāna*). Having discussed the proximate causes of *samādhi*, it would be appropriate to also discuss the salient features of *samādhi* according to this commentarial exegesis in full, thus: the characteristic of *samādhi* is non-vacillation; the function of *samādhi* is to eliminate vacillation, or to bring together the concomitant factors (*sahajātadhamma*); the manifestation of *samādhi* is non-wavering, calm, or direct knowledge, knowledge in accordance with the truth; and the proximate cause of *samādhi* is well-being (*sukha*).[166]

The Component Factors of *Samādhi*

As already stated, the *samādhi* that is undivided and firm is called "attainment concentration" (*appanāsamādhi*). When the mind attains *samādhi* on this level, it enters the state known as *jhāna*.

In the *jhānas*, *samādhi* will always be composed of a number of concurrent factors.

There are many levels of *jhāna*, either four according to the earlier sutta definition or five according to the Abhidhamma definition. The higher the level of *jhāna*, the finer it becomes, and the finer it becomes the fewer the number of concomitant factors will be involved. The concomitant factors of *jhāna* are called simply "factors of *jhāna*" (*jhānaṅga*). There are six altogether—namely, *vitakka*, *vicāra*, *pīti*, *sukha*, *upekkhā*, and *ekaggatā*.[167] In brief, their definitions are as follows:[168]

1. *Vitakka*: initial application of mind. It is the connection or implanting of the mind on an object, or lifting the mind to its object. It is present in the first *jhāna*.
2. *Vicāra*: sustained application of mind. It is the "massaging," "hovering around," or bonding of the mind with its object. It is present in the first *jhāna* (and in the second *jhāna* according to the fivefold system).

These two factors are connected: *vitakka* connects the mind with its object, and *vicāra* holds the mind to it. It is like cleaning a bronze dish that has become corroded—*vitakka* is like one hand that holds the dish, and *vicāra* is like the other hand that rubs the scouring cloth over the dish. Or it is like a potter—*vitakka* is like one hand that holds the clay down, while *vicāra* is like the other hand that molds it.

3. *Pīti*: rapture, profound satisfaction. It is specifically the rapture that infuses the whole body known as *pharaṇāpīti*.[169] It is present in both the first and second *jhānas* (first, second, and third in the fivefold division).
4. *Sukha*: well-being. It is the ease, refreshment, and fluency, the freedom from stress or disturbance, that is present in the first three *jhānas* (and the fourth in the fivefold division).

The difference between *pīti* and *sukha* may be difficult to discern. *Pīti* refers to gladness at obtaining a desired object, while *sukha* refers to the pleasure at experiencing that desired object. For example, a man is traveling through a desert, tired, hot, and thirsty. Eventually he sees an oasis ahead, or he meets someone who tells him that there is an oasis not far away. In time, he reaches the oasis, rests there, and drinks there under the shade of the trees to his heart's content. The feeling of gladness he experiences on seeing or hearing of the oasis is *pīti*, while the refreshment he experiences on resting at the oasis and drinking the water there is *sukha*.

5. *Upekkhā*: equanimity or impartiality. In full, it might be glossed as detached observation, meaning to be calmly looking on without taking sides. In the *jhānas*, this means not attaching even to the *jhānas* that are endowed with such lofty happiness. On a higher level, it also means detached observation when everything is going smoothly, when the task has been accomplished and there is no need to get involved or make an effort. Fourth *jhāna*, especially, is pure and free of adverse qualities, so there is no longer any need to struggle to eliminate them. *Upekkhā* is thus said to be a factor exclusively of the fourth *jhāna* (or the fifth in the fivefold division).

Upekkhā is present in all levels of *jhāna*, but in the lower levels it is not prominent because it is overshadowed by competing qualities, such as *vitakka*, *vicāra*, and *sukhavedanā*. It is said to be like the moon during broad daylight—it is not bright or radiant because the sun's light overwhelms it. On the attainment of fourth *jhāna*, all of the competing qualities are suppressed, and the "night" is attained; one is supported by equanimity (neither happiness nor unhappiness);[170] the mind becomes pure, clear, and bright, making other factors such as *sati* clear and pure in the process.

6. *Ekaggatā*: one-pointedness of mind. This is *samādhi* itself. It is present in all of the *jhānas*.

It needs to be reiterated that "factors of *jhāna*" refers to those factors that are generally present in each of the *jhānas* and that are criteria by which one level of *jhāna* is distinguished from the others. It does not mean that in each of the *jhānas* these will be the only factors present. In fact, there are many other factors involved, associated qualities, but some are regular, some irregular, and they are not defining factors of the different levels of *jhāna*. They include perception (*saññā*), intention (*cetanā*), zeal (*chanda*), effort (*viriya*), mindfulness (*sati*), and attention (*manasikāra*).[171]

In the descriptions of *jhāna* given in the suttas certain other qualities are given special mention. For instance, in third *jhāna*, *sati* and comprehension (*sampajañña*) are said to play a more prominent role than in the first two *jhānas*, which also have those qualities. In the fourth *jhāna*, it is said that *sati* is more purified and clearer than in all of the previous *jhānas*, because it is supported by clear and pure equanimity. Not only *sati*, but also other associated qualities are clearer.[172] This helps to prevent confusion between *jhāna* and states in which the mind forgets itself, feels nothing and slips into some state or other.

The Visuddhimagga, citing the Peṭakopadesa,[173] states that the five factors that arise on the attainment of first *jhāna* are correspondingly antithetical to the five hindrances that have been given up. Specifically, initial application of mind is the adversary of sloth and torpor; sustained application of mind is the adversary of doubt; rapture is the adversary of enmity; well-being is the adversary of restlessness and worry; one-pointedness is the adversary of sensual desire.

When the five factors of *jhāna* arise, they automatically eliminate the hindrances, and as long as they are present the hindrances cannot arise. Conversely, as long as the hindrances are dominating the mind, the factors of *jhāna* cannot function. The enlightenment factors are also said to be directly opposed to the hindrances according to the Buddhavacana, which will be cited shortly.

The Gauges of Readiness

The five factors that are gauges of maturity and indicators of the speed or tardiness of progress in Dhamma practice are known as the five faculties (*indriya*)—faith, effort, mindfulness, concentration, and wisdom. These qualities can be used not only in the development of concentration but in all forms of Dhamma practice, from the beginning stages up to the highest.

Indriya means "the state that takes priority," the factor that directs a certain function. Here it means the director in the function of sweeping away opposing unskillful qualities, as, for example, when effort removes laziness. The meaning of the five faculties is given in brief thus:[174]

1. *Saddhā* (known in full as *saddhindriya*—the faculty of faith). *Saddhā* can be seen in the four factors of stream entry (*sotāpattiyaṅga*). Essentially, it is faith in the Buddha's enlightenment (*tathāgatabodhisaddhā*). The duty or function of *saddhā* is inclining or conviction (*adhimokkha*). Its general meaning is rational belief, confidence in the truth and in the goodness of what one practices.

2. *Viriya* (known in full as *viriyindriya*—the faculty of effort). *Viriya* can be seen in the four right efforts (*sammappadhāna*). In some places it is said to be the effort obtained from raising up the four right efforts, or the four right efforts themselves; sometimes it is more briefly described as the effort to remove unskillful qualities and develop skillful ones, having resolution, striving, steadfastness, and non-neglect of skillful qualities. The function of *viriya* is to raise the mind up (*paggaha*). Its general meaning is effort, motivation, striving forward and not retreating.

3. *Sati* (known in full as *satindriya*—the faculty of mindfulness). *Sati* can be seen in the four foundations of mindfulness. In some places it is said to be the mindfulness obtained from bringing forth the four foundations of mindfulness, or the four foundations of mindfulness themselves; sometimes it is more simply rendered as "having mindfulness," being protected by supreme *sati*, being able to recollect things done or words spoken even long ago. The function of *sati* is to oversee or govern the mind (*upaṭṭhāna*). Its general meaning is recollection, application of the mind to its task, mindfulness of what needs to be done.

4. *Samādhi* (known in full as *samādhindriya*—the faculty of concentration). *Samādhi* can be seen in the four *jhānas*. Sometimes

it is said to be the four *jhāna*s themselves. Simply speaking, it is taking letting go as mental object, thereby gaining concentration and one-pointedness. The function of *samādhi* is to make the mind steady and unwavering (*avikkhepa*). Its general meaning is firmness of mind—resolution in the task, in the object of attention.

5. *Paññā* (known in full as *paññindriya*—the faculty of wisdom). *Paññā* can be seen in the four noble truths. It is knowing the four noble truths as they really are. To put it another way, it is having wisdom, being endowed with the wisdom that penetrates into arising and cessation that is noble (*ariya*), that destroys defilements and leads to the rightful cessation of suffering. The function of wisdom is seeing the truth (*dassana*). Its general meaning is comprehension in accordance with reality, knowing what needs to be done, knowing clearly, penetrating or comprehending the truth.

There is a Buddhavacana endorsing a statement made by Sāriputta that the five faculties have a contiguous relationship: faith leads to effort; effort helps to make mindfulness firm; when mindfulness is firmly established on the object, *samādhi* arises; when *samādhi* is well established, understanding arises and one sees clearly the harm of ignorance and desire—which are the causes of the wheel of rebirth—and the value of *nibbāna*. Once one clearly understands for oneself, then the faith that is supreme, or that is beyond faith, arises; that in turn supports the faculty of faith, as the final passage of this Buddhavacana states:

> "Sāriputta, a noble disciple puts forth effort in this way. Having put forth effort, he recollects in this way. Having recollected, his mind is firmly established in this way. When his mind is firmly established he knows clearly in this way. Knowing clearly, he is beyond faith, thus: 'All those teachings I had previously only heard about are just like this, as I now experience for myself and penetrate with wisdom in this very moment.'"[175]

In the Buddhavacana on the four different ways of practice for four different kinds of person—some practicing with great difficulty and attaining knowledge slowly; some practicing with great difficulty and attaining knowledge quickly; some practicing with ease and attaining knowledge slowly; some practicing with ease and attaining knowledge quickly—the Buddha revealed that the deciding factor for whether knowledge came quickly or slowly was the presence of the five faculties. If the five faculties are weak, knowledge will come slowly; if the five faculties are strong, knowledge will come quickly.[176] The division of individuals who have attained the state of non-returner into different types is also determined by the five faculties.[177]

More broadly speaking, the maturity or weakness of the five faculties is usually the gauge for achievement of all the levels of enlightenment. That is, through perfection of the faculties one is an arahant; with weaker faculties is the non-returner; weaker again is the once-returner; weaker than that is a "truth follower" (*dhammānusārī*) stream enterer; weaker than that, a "belief follower" (*saddhānusārī*) stream enterer, and so on down to one in whom the five faculties are totally lacking, who is a *puthujjana*, an outsider. The conclusion is given that differences in the faculties define differences in results; differences in results cause differences in individual persons.[178]

The Paṭisambhidāmagga lists the unskillful qualities together with the five faculties that eliminate them in pairs. I present them here, together with a reiteration of the functions of each of the faculties:[179]

1. Faith is responsible for inclining or guiding the mind to conviction, eliminating the unskillful quality of disbelief.
2. Effort is responsible for supporting or rousing the mind, eliminating the unskillful quality of laziness.
3. Mindfulness is responsible for protecting or watching over the mind, eliminating the unskillful quality of heedlessness.
4. Concentration is responsible for making the mind firm and unwavering, eliminating the unskillful quality of restlessness.
5. Wisdom is responsible for looking into reality, eliminating the unskillful quality of ignorance.

The Visuddhimagga discusses the importance of balancing the five faculties, stressing that if any one of them is too strong, and others too weak, those other faculties will lose their ability to function. For example, if faith is too strong, effort will be unable to raise the mind up, mindfulness will be unable to watch over the mind, concentration will be unable to make the mind firm, and wisdom will be unable to see according to the truth. Faith must be tempered by the use of wisdom to examine the reality of things or by attending in such a way that does not add fuel to faith.

Generally, it is said that the faculties should be balanced in pairs, faith balanced with wisdom and concentration balanced with effort. If faith is strong and wisdom weak, one may have faith in things that are not worthy; if wisdom is strong but faith weak, one may be inclined to arrogance and become impossible to teach. It is like an illness caused by medicine.

If concentration is strong and effort weak, indolence may dominate, because *samādhi* shares attributes with indolence, while if effort is strong and *samādhi* weak, it may lead to restlessness (*uddhacca*), because effort shares attributes with restlessness. When these two pairs of faculties are balanced, the practice proceeds smoothly and effectively.

This principle is also applied to the development of *samādhi*. However, it is said that if *samādhi* is developed exclusively—that is, if only *samatha* is cultivated—even if faith is very strong it is possible to attain very strong concentration to the level of *appanā*, and therefore faith is suitable for the development of *samādhi*. In the development of *vipassanā*, on the other hand, the stronger wisdom is, all the more rapidly will the practice progress. These, however, are special circumstances, and in general the two pairs of faculties must be balanced for good results.

Sati is the exception. It is said that the more mindfulness there is the better, as mindfulness can help other factors to be more effective. It helps prevent the mind from falling either into restlessness or indolence. Lifting and suppression of the mind require mindfulness, and for this the Buddhavacana is cited: "*Sati* should be used in all situations,"[180] and "*Sati* is the refuge of the mind."[181]

When some of the faculties are too strong and some too weak, it is generally necessary to adjust them by developing the appropriate enlightenment factor. For instance, if effort is too strong, it can be moderated by practicing the tranquility (*passaddhi*) enlightenment factor, as will be explained later in the discussion on the enlightenment factors.[182]

According to these general principles, one needs to develop all five faculties for the practice to make progress. However, there are exceptions where not all of the faculties are developed, or only certain or essential ones are developed. This is possible, as supported by Buddhavacana, especially in the practice for penetrating the truth, which is the highest objective. It is possible to develop only four of the faculties and, in that case, faith is the first faculty that can be put aside and not further cultivated:

> "Bhikkhus, through developing and making much of four faculties, a bhikkhu can extinguish the outflows and declare arahantship...What are the four? They are the faculty of effort, the faculty of mindfulness, the faculty of concentration and the faculty of wisdom."[183]

The next faculty that may be put aside from the training is effort:

> "Bhikkhus, through developing and making much of three faculties, the bhikkhu known as Piṇḍolabhāradvāja has declared arahantship...What are the three? They are the faculty of mindfulness, the faculty of concentration and the faculty of wisdom."[184]

If it is necessary to reduce this again, the next factor that may be reduced is *sati*:

> "Bhikkhus, having developed and made much of two faculties, a bhikkhu may destroy the outflows and declare arahantship... What are the two? They are noble wisdom (*ariyapaññā*) and noble liberation (*ariyavimutti*). His noble wisdom is simply that

> bhikkhu's faculty of wisdom, and his noble liberation is simply his faculty of concentration."[185]

The last, most essential faculty, which cannot be done away with and with which, if it is of sufficient quality, it is possible to attain the goal of Buddhism, is wisdom:

> "Bhikkhus, through developing and making much of just one faculty, a bhikkhu may destroy the outflows and declare arahantship...What is that faculty? It is the faculty of wisdom."[186]

When it is said that only four, three, two, or one of the faculties may be developed, this does not mean that the other faculties are not needed. In fact, they are there and are made use of, but they are secondary and arise as a result of the development of the main faculty, and are there only as much as is required. They are not consciously developed in themselves, as can be seen from the Buddhavacana concerning wisdom:

> "For a noble disciple who has wisdom, faith that arises in the wake of wisdom becomes balanced. Effort...mindfulness...concentration that arises in its wake becomes balanced."[187]

These exceptions apply only to certain individuals with exceptional abilities. For most people it is more fitting to develop the faculties evenly, as mentioned above.

There are Buddhavacana illustrating the importance of the wisdom faculty that could be cited to illustrate the Buddhist attitude to wisdom:

> "Bhikkhus, of all the beasts there are in the world, worldly beings say the lion, the king of beasts, is greatest in strength, speed, and courage. In the same way, of all the factors supporting or aiding enlightenment (*bodhipakkhiyadhamma*) there are, the faculty of wisdom is greatest in effecting enlightenment (*bodhi*)."[188]

> "Bhikkhus, it is like a building with a peaked roof—as long as the ridge beam has not been placed, the rafters will not yet be in place, are not yet firm. Once the ridge beam has been placed, the rafters fall into place and are firm. In the same way, as long as noble direct knowledge (*ariyañāṇa*) has not arisen for a noble disciple, the four faculties do not fall into place and are not yet firm. When noble direct knowledge arises in a noble disciple, the four faculties fall into place and become firm. What are the four faculties? They are the faculty of faith, the faculty of effort, the faculty of mindfulness, and the faculty of concentration. For a noble disciple with wisdom, faith...effort...mindfulness... concentration that arises in its wake can sustain itself."[189]

Wisdom's Work Force

The term "work force" refers to the enlightenment factors (*bojjhaṅga*). The enlightenment factors both aid the development of *samādhi* and are what puts it to use for a higher objective, ultimately attaining knowledge and liberation (*vijjāvimutti*). There are seven enlightenment factors: mindfulness (*sati*), investigation of *dhammas* (*dhammavicaya*), effort (*viriya*), rapture (*pīti*), tranquility (*passaddhi*), concentration (*samādhi*), and equanimity (*upekkhā*).

One Buddhavacana briefly defines the enlightenment factors thus: "Because they are for enlightenment (*bodha*), they are called 'enlightenment factors.'"[190] The commentators, interpreting the term literally, translate *bojjhaṅga* as "qualities of one who is enlightened," "qualities of one about to be enlightened," and "qualities of enlightenment."[191]

In principle, the enlightenment factors are directly opposed to the five hindrances, and in the texts we find that the Buddha mostly mentioned the enlightenment factors together with the five hindrances, as performing opposing functions.[192] In fact, the descriptions of the qualities of the enlightenment factors are coined in terms of opposing the five hindrances. For example:

> "Bhikkhus, these seven enlightenment factors are not obstacles, they are not hindrances, they are not contaminants of the

> mind. When developed and made much of, they bring about the realization of knowledge and deliverance (*vijjāvimutti*)."[193]
>
> ---
>
> "Bhikkhus, these seven enlightenment factors are qualities that lead to vision and direct knowledge; they promote the development of wisdom, are not among the oppressions, and lead to *nibbāna*."[194]

The discussions above show clearly that the hindrances destroy or impair the quality of the mind, and this feature could be used as a gauge for decline of mental health. In the same way, the enlightenment factors, which are opposite to the hindrances, support the quality of the mind and lead to good mental health, being supports for and gauges of quality of mind.

The meaning of each of the enlightenment factors is as follows:

1. *Sati*, recollection: this refers to the ability to recall, or to apply the mind to whatever it is involved with or needs to be done at the moment. In the enlightenment factors, the meaning of *sati* ranges from having *sati* as a control, and being aware of the object of attention in the present moment,[195] to the systematic recollection of memorized teachings, or what is being attended to at the moment, for examination by the wisdom faculty.[196]
2. *Dhammavicaya*, investigation of *dhammas*: this refers to using wisdom to examine the things noted by *sati* as they are, as in examining and understanding the meaning; ascertaining the essence of what is being attended to; investigating and selecting a teaching (*dhamma*) or something supportive to the psyche, or that is most efficacious at that time; or seeing the characteristics of arising, duration, and cessation of what is being attended to according to the three characteristics—and ultimately seeing the four noble truths with wisdom.[197]
3. *Viriya*, effort: this refers to resilience, fortitude, enthusiastic application to the truth or the object of investigation; boldness in the performance of good actions; drive, tenacity, striving,

going forward, uplifting the mind, resistance to depression or despondency.

4. *Pīti*, rapture: this refers to a sense of fullness, bliss, delight, absorption, profound appreciation, thrill, elation.
5. *Passaddhi*, physical and mental tranquility: this refers to relaxation of body and mind, peace, serenity, lack of stress or agitation, comfort.
6. *Samādhi*, firmness of mind: this refers to one-pointedness, undivided attention on the object, stability, steadfastness, attention to the task; non-vacillation, non-wavering, non-distraction.
7. *Upekkhā*, equanimity: this refers to impartiality, being able to detach and watch when the mind is resolute on its task and things are going smoothly; not meddling or interfering.

Each of the hindrances and the enlightenment factors can be divided into pairs, giving ten hindrances and fourteen enlightenment factors, thus:[198]

Five Hindrances Divided into Ten:

1. Internal sensual desire (based on one's own *khandhas*) and external sensual desire (based on other people's *khandhas*)
2. Internal enmity and external enmity
3. Dullness (*thīna*) and torpor (*middha*)
4. Restlessness (*uddhacca*) and worry (*kukkucca*)
5. Doubt about internal things and doubt about external things

Seven Enlightenment Factors Divided into Fourteen:

1. Mindfulness of internal conditions and mindfulness of external conditions
2. Investigation of internal things and investigation of external things
3. Physical effort and mental effort
4. Rapture with *vitakka* and *vicāra* and rapture without *vitakka* and *vicāra*
5. Bodily tranquility and mental tranquility

6. Concentration with *vitakka* and *vicāra* and concentration without *vitakka* and *vicāra*
7. Equanimity toward internal conditions and equanimity toward external conditions

The nutriment (*āhāra*) and "antinutriment" (*anāhāra*) of the hindrances and the enlightenment factors are also discussed. The nutriments are those conditions that nourish and enhance, which cause the arising of hindrances or enlightenment factors not yet arisen, and the growth and fulfillment of those already arisen. The antinutriments are those conditions that do not support or enhance them. The nutriment of the hindrances is unwise attention (*ayoniso-manasikāra*). The antinutriment is wise attention (*yoniso-manasikāra*). The nutriment of the enlightenment factors is wise attention, while the antinutriment is lack of wise attention.[199]

The Nutriments and Antinutriments of the Five Hindrances:

1. Sensual desire has the nutriment of unwise attention to attractive objects (*subhanimitta*).[200] Its antinutriment is wise attention to unattractive objects (*asubhanimitta*).
2. Enmity has the nutriment of unwise attention to offending objects (*paṭighanimitta*).[201] Its antinutriment is wise attention to mental deliverance.[202]
3. Sloth and torpor have the nutriment of unwise attention to boredom, melancholy, sloth, depression. Their antinutriment is wise attention to initiating, advancing, and striving.
4. Restlessness and worry have the nutriment of unwise attention to a state or matter with which the mind is not peaceful. Their antinutriment is wise attention to something with which the mind is peaceful.
5. Doubt has the nutriment of unwise attention to something that is a basis for doubt. Its antinutriment is wise attention to what is skillful and unskillful, harmful and beneficial.

The Nutriments of the Seven Enlightenment Factors:

1. Mindfulness has as nutriment wise attention to states that are a basis for mindfulness.
2. Investigation of *dhammas* has as nutriment wise attention to skillful and unskillful, harmful and non-harmful, conditions, and so on.
3. Effort has as nutriment wise attention to initiating, advancing, striving.
4. Rapture has as nutriment wise attention to conditions that are a basis for rapture.
5. Tranquility has as nutriment wise attention to bodily and mental tranquility.
6. Concentration has as nutriment wise attention to concentration images (*samādhi-nimitta*), or on whatever does not cause the mind to wander or be confused.
7. Equanimity has as nutriment wise attention to the conditions that are a basis for equanimity.

The antinutriments of the enlightenment factors are lack of attention to the conditions that lead to the arising of each enlightenment factor.

Conditions that are a basis for sati: These are the objects of *sati*. In one of the commentaries it is said to be the thirty-seven requisites of enlightenment (*bodhipakkhiyadhamma*) and the nine transcendent conditions (*lokuttara dhamma*),[203] but broadly speaking it is practicing according to the four foundations of mindfulness. The Visuddhimagga and the Sammohavinodanī[204] give another four conditions that help in the arising of *sati*: *sati* and clear comprehension, avoidance of people with scattered mindfulness, association with people who are well-controlled by mindfulness, and inclining the mind to the mindfulness enlightenment factor.

Conditions that aid the arising of investigation of dhammas: Seven of these are given: being inquisitive, making things clean and tidy,[205] balancing the faculties (*indriya*), avoiding foolish people, associating with wise people, contemplating profound subjects, and inclining the mind to investigation of *dhammas*.

Conditions that aid the arising of effort: Eleven of these are given: reflecting and seeing dangers such as the nether realms (*apāya*: arousing the mind with the thought that if one does not bring forth effort one will meet with such and such dangers); seeing rewards, that if one strives one will receive special results, both mundane and transcendent; reflecting that the path of practice is one followed by great beings, such as the Buddha and the great disciples, and that if one is indolent one will have no chance of succeeding; respecting the alms food, resolving to make it bring great fruit to those who have given it; examining the greatness of the Teacher, who praised diligent effort, and resolving to honor him by following his teachings; examining one's status, that one should make oneself worthy of the great bequest of the Buddha's teachings; countering sleepiness by various methods, such as changing posture or bringing forth the perception of light; avoiding indolent people; associating with diligent people; reflecting on the right efforts (*sammappadhāna*); and inclining the mind to effort.

Conditions that aid the arising of rapture: Eleven of these are given: recollecting the qualities of the Buddha; recollecting the qualities of the Dhamma; recollecting the qualities of the Saṅgha; reflecting on one's own virtuous conduct; reflecting on one's past acts of generosity; reflecting on the devas and the *devadhamma* (conditions leading to rebirth in a deva realm); reflecting on peace, or *nibbāna*; avoiding depressing people; associating with cheerful people; reflecting on inspiring suttas; and inclining the mind to rapture.

Conditions that aid the arising of tranquility: Seven of these are given: partaking of fine foods; living in pleasant surrounds; abiding in a comfortable posture; exerting moderate effort; avoiding tense and restless people; associating with relaxed, peaceful people; and inclining the mind to tranquility.

Conditions that aid the arising of concentration: Eleven of these are given: making things clean and tidy; being skilled in meditation signs (*nimitta*); balancing the faculties; subduing the mind when it requires subduing; lifting the mind when it requires lifting; energizing the mind when it is cheerless with faith and a sense of urgency (*saṁvega*);[206] watching the mind impartially (*upekkhā*) when it is proceeding properly; avoiding people whose minds are not concentrated; associating with those whose minds are concentrated; examining the release of *jhāna*; and inclining the mind to *samādhi*.

Conditions that aid the arising of equanimity: Five of these are given: making the mind impartial to all beings (both bhikkhus and householders); making the mind impartial to all formations (including one's own bodily organs and material possessions); avoiding people who are concerned with and worried about beings and formations; associating with those who are impartial to beings and formations; and inclining the mind to equanimity.

The seven enlightenment factors affect each other as shown in the practice described by the Buddha,[207] which can be essentially summarized thus: a bhikkhu learns or hears a teaching from a learned being, withdraws himself physically, and withdraws himself mentally. The enlightenment factors then follow:

1. The bhikkhu brings the teaching he has heard or learned to mind for review, for reflection, and for cogitation. This is developing the mindfulness enlightenment factor.
2. With this recollection by *sati*, he then uses wisdom to sift through it, ponder it, question and examine it. This is developing the investigation of *dhammas* enlightenment factor.
3. Using wisdom to sift through, ponder, question and examine, he exerts effort. The more he sifts through and begins to understand and obtain results, the more inspired he becomes, and he is zealous, determined, energetic, unrelenting. Thus he develops the effort enlightenment factor.
4. While putting forth effort and applying himself, zealous, determined, and unrelenting, spiritual rapture arises, and he develops the rapture enlightenment factor.
5. When the mind is rapt, both body and mind are relaxed and

calm, bodily and mental tranquility ensue, and he develops the tranquility enlightenment factor.

6. When the body is relaxed and calm, the mind becomes concentrated (*samādhi*), and he develops the concentration enlightenment factor.
7. When the mind is firmly established on its task, it settles down and watches over things with detachment. Practicing in this way, he develops the equanimity enlightenment factor.

The Buddha taught that when the four foundations of mindfulness are developed and made much of, the seven enlightenment factors are perfected; when the seven enlightenment factors are developed and made much of, knowledge and deliverance are perfected.[208]

The way to practice the four foundations of mindfulness for the perfection of the enlightenment factors is as follows: whenever the practitioner is practicing contemplation of the body (*kāyānupassanā*), contemplation of the feelings (*vedanānupassanā*), contemplation of the mind (*cittānupassanā*), or contemplation of *dhammas* (*dhammānupassanā*), at that time he or she is possessed of steady, unremitting *sati.* With steady *sati*, the practitioner uses wisdom to contemplate and sift through the teachings according to the principle of *dhammavicaya.* From there the practice proceeds according to the other enlightenment factors outlined above, leading ultimately to knowledge and liberation.

Even when listening to a Dhamma teaching, if one establishes the mind, pays full attention, and listens well, at that time the five hindrances are absent and the seven enlightenment factors can develop to perfection.[209]

The seven enlightenment factors can be developed or practiced in conjunction with other practices, such as mindfulness of the breathing, meditation on the boundless abidings or four divine abidings, and various reflections such as the reflection on impermanence, the reflection on the unattractive, the reflection on dispassion, and the reflection on cessation, and will cause those practices to bring great results, great assurance, and safety, leading to a sense of urgency in the development of skillful qualities and to a pleasant abiding.[210]

The enlightenment factors are recommended for practicing with the changing mind and can be used to support a mind that is still new to *samādhi*, to make that *samādhi* stronger,[211] as is shown in the following Buddhavacana:

> "Bhikkhus, when the mind is depressed, that is not the time to develop the tranquility enlightenment factor...the concentration enlightenment factor...the equanimity enlightenment factor. Why is this? Because the depressed mind is not easily uplifted by these conditions. It is like a man who wishes to stoke a small fire and make it blaze: he puts green grass, fresh manure, and fresh wood onto the fire, and splashes it with water and smothers it with dust. Will that man be able to stoke the small fire and make it blaze?" [The bhikkhus answer, "No, not at all."] "It is the same when the mind is depressed...
>
> "When the mind is depressed, that is the time to develop the investigation of *dhammas* enlightenment factor...the effort enlightenment factor...the rapture enlightenment factor. Why is this? Because the depressed mind is easily uplifted by such conditions. It is like a man who wishes to stoke a small fire and make it blaze: he puts onto it dried grass, dried manure, dead wood, and fans it and does not smother it with dust. Will he be able to stoke the small fire and make it blaze?" [The bhikkhus answer, "Yes, he will."] "It is the same when the mind is depressed...
>
> "Bhikkhus, when the mind is scattered, that is not the time to develop the investigation of *dhammas* enlightenment factor... the effort enlightenment factor...the rapture enlightenment factor. Why is that? Because the scattered mind is not easily calmed by those conditions. It is like a man who wishes to douse a large fire: he puts onto it dried grass, dried manure, dead wood, and fans it and does not smother it with dust. Will that man be able to douse that fire?" [Answer, "No he will not."] "It is the same when the mind is scattered...

> "When the mind is scattered, that is the time to develop the tranquility enlightenment factor... the concentration enlightenment factor... the equanimity enlightenment factor. Why is this? Because the scattered mind is easily calmed by these conditions. It is like a man who wishes to douse a fire: he puts onto it green grass, fresh manure, fresh wood, sprinkles it with water, and smothers it with dust. Will that man be able to douse the fire?" [Answer, "Yes, he will."] "It is the same when the mind is scattered...
>
> "As for mindfulness, I say that it is beneficial in all situations."[212]

In the Pali canon the seven enlightenment factors are described as the effort to cultivate skillful qualities (*bhāvanāpadhāna*),[213] which is said to be the supreme effort;[214] as the power of cultivation (*bhāvanābala*);[215] as the method for eliminating outflows through cultivation;[216] as the *kamma* that is neither black nor white, which leads to the cessation of *kamma*;[217] as the conditions leading only to progress, never to regress (*aparihāniyadhamma*);[218] and, along with the other requisites of enlightenment (*bodhipakkhiyadhamma*), as the way to the unconditioned (*asaṅkhata*), *nibbāna*.[219]

The Convergence of the Path Factors

The objective of right concentration, as already stated, is to create a field of operations for wisdom—or, to put it broadly, to put the mind in the most suitable condition for the combined functioning of the factors of the path to achieve their purpose, which is the realization of truth, the elimination of defilements, and the cessation of problems and suffering. It has also been stated that the eight factors of the path work together and in harmony, with right view leading the way. Thus we can state here that the other seven factors of the path are supports for *samādhi*, helping to bring about the arising and establishment of *samādhi* as *sammāsamādhi*, by eventually giving rise to two further path factors, right direct knowledge (*sammāñāṇa*) and right liberation (*sammāvimutti*). In this respect, the other seven factors of the path are said to be accessories of *samādhi* (*samādhi-parikkhāra*); that is, they are associated or supporting factors of *samādhi*. *Samādhi* that is combined with these accessories is called *ariyasammāsamādhi*, and leads to the goal, as is stated in the Pali canon:

> "These seven accessories of *samādhi* have been well expounded by the Blessed One who knows, who sees, the arahant and fully enlightened Buddha, for the cultivation and development of right concentration, for the perfection of right concentration. What are the seven? They are right view, right thought, right speech, right action, right livelihood, right effort, and right mindfulness. The one-pointed mind that is accompanied by these seven factors is called right concentration that is noble, which has an *upanissaya* [a support, base, or foundation] or has accessories [it has components or aids].
>
> "When there is right view, right thought is ready for work; when there is right thought, right speech is ready for work; when there is right speech, right action is ready for work; when there is right action, right livelihood is ready for work; when there is right livelihood, right effort is ready for work; when there is right effort, right mindfulness is ready for work; when there is right mindfulness, right concentration is ready for work; when there is right concentration, right direct knowledge is ready for work; and when there is right direct knowledge, right liberation is ready for work."[220]

When the eightfold path is fully developed, there comes a point and a moment when all the factors converge and function collectively to produce a strong direct knowledge (*ñāṇa*) that penetrates the truth and utterly eliminates the defilements that bind and oppress the mind. The point at which the factors of the path function in unison in this way is technically called *magga* (path), because that is the instant at which all the factors truly function as one path. When the path has so functioned, the state of fruition follows, which is the knowledge and understanding of reality and liberation from defilements, a state that is without oppression and is free. This is called *phala* (fruition).

If everything follows the usual order, this strong or absolute functioning of the path will occur altogether four times, or on four levels, called the four paths. The state of fruition also has four. Together they are called the four paths and the four fruits, or the four noble paths and the four noble fruits: stream entry path (*sotāpattimagga*) and stream entry fruit (*sotāpattiphala*); once-returner path (*sakadāgāmimagga*) and once-returner fruit (*sakadāgāmīphala*); non-returner path (*anāgāmimagga*) and non-returner fruit (*anāgāmiphala*); and arahant path (*arahattamagga*) and arahant fruit (*arahattaphala*).

Thus, in terms of component factors, the noble path has eight, and therefore it is known as the eightfold path (*aṭṭhaṅgikamagga*), but in terms of its operation or function there are four, known as the four paths (*catumagga*).[221]

The action of the factors of the path functioning in unison in one mind moment to produce the achievement of the goal is called *dhammasāmaggī*,[222] and *dhammasāmaggī* is enlightenment (*bodhi*).[223] At the moment of path attainment, it is not just the eight factors of the path that function in unison in the one mind moment, but the whole thirty-seven requisites of enlightenment (*bodhipakkayadhamma*).[224] However, the thirty-seven requisites of enlightenment can be summarized as the eightfold path.[225] Thus, when talking of the path, all those other factors are also implied.

It may be asked how so many factors of the path can manage to function all in the same moment, as some of the factors, especially the morality factors such as right speech and right action, do not seem to be involved at all on that level. This question may be better understood through the simple example of a skilled shooter or archer. On the day of a competition, we see a woman shooting and hitting the target, and winning first prize. She hits the target with a shot that takes only an instant. Looking superficially, we might simply say that she had a firm hand and good aim and that is the end of the matter. But if we were to examine the factors involved more closely, behind her firm hand and good aim, and that good shot that took only an instant, we would find a long process of training that led up to the event. She may have invested a great deal of time and effort in training her physical posture, her standing position, the position of her legs, shoulders, and arms, the way she held the bow and fixed the arrow, her aim and judgment of the distance, and the decision-making and concentration that led to the fluency and dexterity that enabled her to do all these things in a seemingly effortless instant. When the time came for her to perform, when she shot the arrow and hit the target, it is undeniable that this instantaneous shot was a product of the holding, balancing, poise, and balanced effort of her body along with the confidence, concentration, and judgment that together form the determinants behind that shot. In other words, all the movements and poise of the body, the primed and fluent state of the mind, and the wisdom or comprehension that caused her to make good decisions worked together in that one moment of shooting, and the readiness of the body, the readiness of the mind, and the readiness of her wisdom at that time were products of months or years of training. Thus, it can be said that her shooting the target in that instant was the result of months and years of training.

It is at this point that the question of individual differences comes in, particularly the maturity or strength of the faculties. Some people may train only a little and achieve results easily; others may train for a long time but nevertheless attain results with ease. Some have a lot of difficulty in the practice and take a long time to achieve results, while others may experience difficulty in the practice and achieve no results no matter how hard they try. Apart from the factor of individual differences, the results and speed or slowness of the practice are also dependent on other factors, particularly the correctness of the practice, the availability of a teacher or instructor—the good friend—and also physical health and environmental conditions.

In this respect the commentators have divided the successful practice into four kinds, called the four *paṭipadā*:[226]

dukkhā paṭipadā dandhābhiññā	Difficult practice, slow realization (*abhiññā*)
dukkhā paṭipadā khippābhiññā	Difficult practice, fast realization
sukhā paṭipadā dandhābhiññā	Comfortable practice, slow realization
sukhā paṭipadā khippābhiññā	Comfortable practice, fast realization

Among the many factors making the practice difficult or easy, and realization fast or slow, one is *samādhi.* It has been said that it is possible to begin practicing insight meditation immediately, using only an elementary level of *samādhi*, and to thereby attain direct knowledge of the cessation of the outflows (*āsavakkhayañāṇa*), which is the goal of the practice. But one can also first cultivate *samatha* and gain a firm foundation of *jhāna* for the practice of insight. This point becomes clearer in the four ways of practice: that is, it is said that those who gain the four *jhānas* will have *sukhā paṭipadā*, or comfortable practice, while those who develop the reflection on unattractiveness, the reflection on the repulsiveness of food, and the reflection on death (which, according to the teachings already discussed, lead only to access concentration, or at most first *jhāna*) will have *dukkhā paṭipadā*, or difficult and uncomfortable practice.

Following is a Buddhavacana describing a kind of practice that shows how all of the requisites of enlightenment (*bodhipakkhiyadhamma*) are contingent on the eightfold path. It is a kind of practice that on the surface may seem simple, but it is only easy for those whose practice is ripe; for those who are not yet ready, it may be difficult and may necessitate preparation by undertaking many other practices.

> "Bhikkhus, one knows and sees as it is eye... forms... eye consciousness... eye contact... feeling, be it pleasant, unpleasant or neither pleasant nor unpleasant, contingent on eye contact, and does not attach [to eye, etc.]. Not attaching, one is not entan-

gled, one is not enamored, one sees the harm therein. The five *khandhas* of clinging do not come to growth; the desire that leads to rebirth, contains lust, and delights in objects (*ārammaṇa*) is given up. Agitation of body, agitation of mind, burning of body and burning of mind, turmoil of body and turmoil of mind are given up. One experiences bodily pleasure and mental pleasure.

"Whatever views such a one has will be right views, one's thoughts will be right thoughts, one's effort will be right effort, one's mindfulness will be right mindfulness, and one's concentration will be right concentration. One's bodily actions, verbal actions, and livelihood are purified from the first. Thus is the noble eightfold path of that person developed and fulfilled.

"While practicing the noble eightfold path in this way, the four foundations of mindfulness are fully developed. The four right efforts...the four pathways to success...the five faculties...the five powers...the seven enlightenment factors are fully developed. One is possessed of two qualities—calm and insight—working hand in hand.

"Whatever conditions there are to be noted with superknowledge (*abhiññā*),[227] one notes those conditions with superknowledge; whatever conditions are to be given up with superknowledge, one gives up those conditions with superknowledge; whatever conditions there are to be brought about with superknowledge, one brings those conditions about with superknowledge; whatever conditions are to be realized through superknowledge, one realizes those conditions through superknowledge.

"Bhikkhus, what are the conditions to be noted through superknowledge? They are the things known as the five *khandhas* of clinging: the clung-to group of form, the clung-to group of feelings, the clung-to group of perceptions, the clung-to group of mental formations, the clung-to group of consciousness...

"Bhikkhus, what are the conditions to be given up through superknowledge? They are ignorance and desire for becoming (*bhavataṇhā*)...

"Bhikkhus, what are the conditions to be brought about [developed] through superknowledge? They are calm and insight.

"What are the conditions to be realized through superknowledge? They are knowledge and liberation."[228]

The Buddha once summarized all things as follows:[229]

"Bhikkhus, if you are asked in this way, you should answer those members of other sects and wanderers, 'Venerable Sirs,

1. "All things (*dhammas*) have desire as root (*chandamūlakā*).
2. "All things have attention as origin (*manasikāra sambhavā*).
3. "All things have contact as birthplace (*phassa samudayā*).
4. "All things have feeling as meeting point (*vedanā samosaraṇā*).
5. "All things have concentration as leader (*samādhi pamukhā*).
6. "All things have mindfulness as sovereign (*satādhipateyyā*).
7. "All things have wisdom as apex (*paññuttarā*).
8. "All things have liberation as essence (*vimuttisārā*).
9. "All things have the deathless as merging point (*amatogadhā*).
10. "All things have *nibbāna* as end (*nibbāna pariyosānā*).'"

The Buddha also said:

"Bhikkhus, a bhikkhu leads the holy life (*brahmacariya*), which is blessed by the training rules, culminates in wisdom, has liberation as its core, and is governed by mindfulness.

"How is the holy life blessed by the training rules? Those rules for higher conduct that I have laid down for the disciples of this teaching and discipline, for the faith of those yet without faith and for the further development of those with faith, those rules for higher conduct I have laid down... in whatever way, are followed and practiced by a disciple in that way, not allowed to falter, not allowed to be broken, not allowed to become soiled or stained. Moreover, those rules of higher training that I have laid down for disciples, for the total and proper cessation of suffering, those rules of higher training laid down by me...in whatever way, are followed and practiced by a disciple in that way, not allowed to falter, not allowed to be broken, not allowed to become soiled or stained. Thus is the holy life blessed by the training rules.

"How does the holy life culminate in wisdom? Those teachings that I have given to disciples in this teaching and discipline for the total and proper cessation of suffering, those teachings given by me...in whatever form are seen clearly in that way with wisdom by those disciples. Thus does the holy life culminate in wisdom.

"How does the holy life have liberation as its core? Those teachings that I have given to disciples in this teaching and discipline for the total and proper cessation of suffering, those teachings given by me...in whatever form are experienced by those disciples through liberation. Thus does the holy life have liberation as its core.

"Bhikkhus, how is the holy life governed by mindfulness? A disciple is well-controlled internally by mindfulness, reflecting, 'I will perfect the training rules of higher conduct that are not yet perfected, and I will promote with wisdom the training rules in higher conduct that are already perfected...I will perfect the training rules of the higher training that are not yet perfected, and I will promote with wisdom the training rules in the higher training that are already perfected...I will survey and see in full those teachings that I have not yet seen in full with wisdom, while those teachings that I have seen in full with wisdom I will promote with wisdom...I will experience those truths that I have not yet experienced through liberation, while those truths that I have already experienced, I will promote with wisdom.' Thus does the holy life have mindfulness as sovereign."[230]

Conclusion

The Four Noble Truths as a Summary of the Buddhadhamma

The four noble truths are an important teaching that encompasses all the other teachings of Buddhism. The entire subject matter of this book can be included within the four noble truths, and therefore I have used the four noble truths as its summary. Some noteworthy Buddhavacana about the four noble truths are as follows:

> "Venerable Ones, just as the footprints of all animals that roam over this great earth can be contained within the footprint of the elephant, and the elephant's footprint is the greatest of all in terms of size, so all skillful qualities can be contained within the four noble truths."[1]
>
> ---
>
> "Bhikkhus, as long as my knowledge and vision of things as they are, including the three cycles (*parivaṭṭa*) and twelve facets of the four noble truths, was not yet pure and clear, I did not declare myself to have attained the complete, unexcelled enlightenment..."[2]
>
> ---
>
> "Bhikkhus, it is through not being enlightened to and not understanding the four noble truths that both you and I have raced around aimlessly (through various births) for such a long time."[3]
>
> ---

> Then the Blessed One gave the graded instruction to the householder Upālī—that is, instruction on generosity, morality, heaven, the harm, fault and defilement of sensuality, and the blessings of renunciation. When the Blessed One sensed that the householder Upālī's mind was ripe, malleable, free of hindrances, gladdened, and inspired, he declared the teaching that is specific to all the buddhas, which is suffering, the cause[4] of suffering, the cessation of suffering, and the way leading to the cessation of suffering.[5]
>
> ---
>
> "The holy life (*brahmacariya*) with the Blessed One is led for the purpose of knowing, seeing, attaining, realizing, and penetrating the things as yet unknown, unseen, unattained, unrealized and unpenetrated, [that is, the realization that] 'this is suffering,' 'this is the cause of suffering,' 'this is the cessation of suffering,' and 'this is the way leading to the cessation of suffering.'"[6]

One feature of Buddhism is that it teaches those truths that are useful—that is, those truths that can be put to benefit in life. The Buddha did not teach things that are not useful, even though they may be true, and it is the noble truths that fit the description of "things that are useful." For this reason, the Buddha was not interested in and refused to waste his time on arguing about metaphysical questions, as is brought out in the well-known Buddhavacana:

> "Even were someone to say, 'As long as the Blessed One does not make a statement (*byākaraṇa*) [answer my questions] as to whether the world is eternal or not eternal, whether the world is finite or infinite, whether life (*jīva*) and the body are one and the same, or whether life is one thing and the body another, whether a being exists after death or does not exist after death, or both exists and does not exist after death, or neither exists nor does not exist after death, I will not lead the holy life under him,' the Tathāgata would not make a statement on those matters, and that person would die in vain. It is like a man who has been shot

by a poisoned arrow, steeped in poison. His friends and blood relatives bring a skilled surgeon to take out the arrowhead, but the wounded man says, 'As long as I do not yet know of the man who shot me whether he was a noble, a brahmin, a merchant, or a tradesman, or his name and clan, whether he was tall, short, or of medium height, of dark, light, or medium complexion, and which village, market town, or city he came from, I will not allow you to take out this poisoned arrow. As long as I do not know whether the bow used to shoot me was a bow or a crossbow, whether its string was of hemp, bamboo fiber, gut, cord, or wood fiber; whether the arrow was made of forest wood or cultivated wood; whether the end of the arrow was affixed with a vulture feather, a heron feather, a hawk feather, a peacock feather, or a stork feather; whether the shaft was wound with cow gut or buffalo gut, with langur gut or the gut of some other monkey, and what kind of arrow was used to shoot me, I will not consent to having this arrow taken out.' That man would surely die before he found out all he wanted to know. It is the same [for one who demands such answers from the Tathāgata].

"Māluṅkyaputta, when there is the view 'the world is eternal,' there can be no living of the holy life. When there is the view 'the world is not eternal,' there can be no living of the holy life. Whether there is the view 'the world is eternal' or 'the world is not eternal,' there will still be birth, there will still be aging, there will still be death, there will still be sorrow, lamentation, pain, grief, and despair, and these [kinds of suffering] are what I teach the elimination of in this very moment..."

"Therefore, understand those things that I do not state as being unstated by me, and remember those things that I do state as being stated by me. And what are the things I do not state? The views that the world is eternal, the world is not eternal... And why do I not state these? Because those matters are not useful, they are not initiators of the holy life, they are not conducive to disenchantment, to dispassion, to cessation, to peace, to superknowledge, to *nibbāna*. And what are the things that I do state?

> I state: 'This is suffering, this is the cause of suffering, this is the cessation of suffering, and this is the way leading to the cessation of suffering.' And why do I state this? Because it is useful, it is the initiator of the holy life, it leads to disenchantment, to dispassion, to cessation, to peace, to superknowledge, to *nibbāna*."[7]

Elsewhere the Buddha stated that his knowledge was vast, but what he taught was only a small fraction of that. Why he did so was because he taught that which was beneficial, which could be used to solve problems, and that which is beneficial and can be used to solve problems is this teaching of the four noble truths, just as in the previous Buddhavacana, as stated in the canon:

> At one time, the Blessed One was staying at the Sīṁsapā forest, near the city of Kosambī. At that time, the Blessed One took up a handful of rosewood leaves and held them in his hand, then said to the bhikkhus:
>
> "Bhikkhus, which do you think is greater: this small amount of rosewood leaves in my hand, or the number of leaves in the trees in the whole of this Sīṁsapā forest?"
>
> "Revered Sir, the small amount of rosewood leaves in your hand is trifling; the leaves on the trees of the Sīṁsapā forest are far greater in number."
>
> "In the same way, bhikkhus, the things that I have realized and not told you are of far greater number. Why have I not told you? Because those things are not beneficial, they are not initiators of the holy life, they are not conducive to disenchantment, to dispassion, to cessation, to calming, to superknowledge, to *nibbāna*.
>
> "And what, bhikkhus, are the things I tell you? I say 'this is suffering'; I say 'this is the cause of suffering'; I say 'this is the cessation of suffering'; and I say 'this is the way leading to the cessation of suffering.' And why do I tell you this? Because these things are beneficial, they are initiators of the holy life, they are conducive to disenchantment, to dispassion, to cessation, to calming, to superknowledge, to *nibbāna*. That is why I tell you these things. Therefore, bhikkhus, exert yourselves to realize

> as it is that this is suffering, this is the cause of suffering, this is the cessation of suffering, and this is the way leading to the cessation of suffering."[8]

Because the four noble truths are teachings necessary for both renunciants and householders, the Buddha exhorted the bhikkhus to teach the four noble truths to householders:

> "Bhikkhus, whatever groups of people should be assisted by you, whatever groups of people are capable of receiving the teachings, be they friends, associates, relatives, or blood relations, you should encourage them, teach them to maintain and be established in enlightenment to the truth of the four noble truths."[9]

The Meaning of the Noble Truths

> "Bhikkhus, these four noble truths are real, unvarying, and never become otherwise. For this reason, they are called 'noble truths'. . .
>
> "Bhikkhus, the Tathāgata is noble in this world with its devas, *māras*, *brahmās*, human beings, recluses, and holy men, with its devas and humans. For that reason, they are called noble truths [because they are truths that the Tathāgata, a noble one, has become enlightened to and taught]."[10]
>
> ---
>
> "Through having realized as they are these four noble truths, bhikkhus, the Tathāgata, Arahant, and Fully Self-Enlightened Buddha, is called a noble one (*ariya*)."[11]

The Visuddhimagga, citing references in the Pali canon, gives four senses of meaning for the term "noble truths":[12]

1. The truths that are realized by a noble one
2. The truths of a noble one (second sense in the canon)
3. The truths that make one noble (third sense in the canon)

4. The truths that are real (*ariya*)—that is, unequivocally true (first sense in the canon)

The meaning of each of the four noble truths should be understood according to these canonical passages:

> "Bhikkhus, this is the noble truth of suffering: birth is suffering, aging is suffering, sickness is suffering, death is suffering, association with what is unloved is suffering, separation from what is loved is suffering, desiring that which cannot be obtained is suffering; in short, the five clung-to *khandhas* are suffering.
>
> "Bhikkhus, this is the noble truth of the cause of suffering: it is that desire that leads to renewed becoming, consisting of delight and attachment, and the seeking out of sense objects—specifically, sense desire, desire for becoming, and desire for annihilation.
>
> "Bhikkhus, this is the noble truth of the cessation of suffering: it is the cessation of that desire, through its complete and utter rejection, abandonment, giving up, and non-association.
>
> "Bhikkhus, this is the noble truth of the way leading to the cessation of suffering: it is the noble eightfold path—that is, right view, right thought, right speech, right action, right livelihood, right effort, right mindfulness, and right concentration."[13]

These basic definitions can be expanded on as follows:

1. *Dukkha* means "suffering," that which is hard to endure. It refers to all the problems that human beings experience. On a more profound level, it is the state of all things that are subject to the natural laws of impermanence, stressfulness (*dukkha*), and not-self, and that have in them the states of stress, conflict, opposition, lack, and imperfection; it is the characteristic of things lacking a permanent core, unable to provide true fulfillment and always ready to cause problems and suffering, both now and in the future, at some time or other, in some form or other, for those who cling to them.

2. *Dukkhasamudaya*, briefly referred to as *samudaya*, means the cause for the arising of suffering. It is the wanting based on self, which manifests as a self who experiences, who attains, who becomes or does not become this or that, oppressing life with constant agitation, greed, confusion, avarice, hatred, fear, suspicion, boredom, and other forms of mental oppression, so that the mind is incapable of being truly clear, light, free, and buoyant and does not experience the happiness that is boundless and void of blemishes.
3. *Dukkhanirodha*, briefly referred to as *nirodha*, means the cessation of suffering. It is the state that is reached when ignorance is eliminated and desire utterly expelled. The mind, not being colored or pulled about by desire, is no longer oppressed by feelings of agitation, boredom, or any other negative mental states. It is free and independent, and it experiences pure happiness, which is peaceful, lucid, unbounded, clear, and buoyant. In brief, this is *nibbāna*.
4. *Dukkhanirodhagāminīpaṭipadā*, briefly referred to as *magga*, means the way of practice leading to the cessation of suffering. It is the noble eightfold path—that is, right view, right thought, right speech, right action, right livelihood, right effort, right mindfulness, and right concentration, known as the Middle Way (*majjhimā paṭipadā*) that proceeds just right for the attainment of cessation, not fixing onto or inclining toward the two extremes of indulgence in sense pleasures (*kāmasukhallikānuyoga*) and self-mortification (*attakilamathānuyoga*).

The Noble Truths and Dependent Arising

In this book I have discussed the principle of dependent arising (*paṭiccasamuppāda*) at length and in many places. Both the four noble truths and the principle of dependent arising are cardinal Buddhist teachings. When asked, "What did the Buddha become enlightened to?" we could equally answer that he was enlightened to the four noble truths or that he was enlightened to the principle of dependent arising. Both answers can be backed up by

Buddhavacana. What must be understood is that both answers are in fact correct, and the meaning of the two is in agreement: the principle of dependent arising is the essence of the noble truths, and the meaning of the noble truths encompasses the principle of dependent arising. We can begin to examine this from textual sources.

The Vinaya Piṭaka[14] discusses events of the Buddha's enlightenment. At first, just after the enlightenment, the Buddha is said to have been savoring the bliss of liberation and examining the principle of dependent arising, in both forward mode (the process of the arising of suffering) and reverse mode (the process of the cessation of suffering) for one whole week. After savoring the bliss of liberation for a total of seven weeks, when he considered going out to teach the truth he had realized to others, he had the following thought:

> "This Dhamma that I have attained is profound, hard to see, difficult to comprehend... For people who delight and revel in attachment, this is a difficult thing to see; that is, the principle of conditionality (*idappaccayatā*), the dependent arising (*paṭiccasamuppāda*). This also is a difficult thing to see—that is to say... *nibbāna*."[15]

In the suttas, the treatment of the Buddha's life story at this point is much the same, beginning with his reflections before leaving home and going forth to homelessness, his practice under the ascetics Āḷāra and Uddaka, his adoption and subsequent renunciation of rigorous austerities and his return, and his attainment of the *jhānas* and realization of the three knowledges. Concerning the enlightenment, the Buddha relates:

> "When I had eaten and felt stronger, I, secluded from sensual pleasures and secluded from unskillful qualities, attained the first *jhāna*... the second *jhāna*... the third *jhāna*... the fourth *jhāna*, which is without suffering and happiness... accompanied by mindfulness purified by equanimity.

> "When my mind was concentrated, pure, bright, without defilements, free of blemishes, malleable, fit for work, firm and unshaken in this way, I inclined it to *pubbenivāsānussatiñāṇa* and recollected many previous lives [the first knowledge]... I inclined my mind to *cutūpapātañāṇa*, seeing the arising [birth] and passing away [dying] of beings [the second knowledge]... I inclined my mind to *āsavakkhayañāṇa*, knowing clearly as it is that 'This is suffering, this is the cause of suffering, this is the cessation of suffering, this is the way leading to the cessation of suffering; these are the outflows, this is the cause of the outflows, this is the cessation of the outflows, and this is the way leading to the cessation of the outflows.' Seeing this, my mind was liberated from the outflow of sensual desire (*kāmāsava*), the outflow of becoming (*bhavāsava*), and the outflow of ignorance (*avijjāsava*) (the third knowledge)..."[16]

From here, there is a description of the Buddha's deliberations on teaching the Dhamma, which follows the excerpt from the Vinaya Piṭaka given above.

Notice that the Vinaya Piṭaka recounts the events following the enlightenment and the time spent enjoying the bliss of liberation (which, according to the commentaries, was a period of seven weeks), beginning with reviewing of the principle of dependent arising up until the Buddha's disinclination to teach the Dhamma because of the profundity of dependent arising and *nibbāna* that he had become enlightened to. The suttas record the events before the enlightenment up until the enlightenment to the three knowledges, and then skip the entire period of savoring the bliss of liberation, rejoining the story at the Buddha's disinclination to teach the Dhamma, just as in the Vinaya Piṭaka.

Those who follow the account of the Buddha's contemplation of dependent origination given in the Vinaya Piṭaka, and his deliberations about not teaching given in both the Vinaya Piṭaka and the Sutta Piṭaka, can state that the Buddha was enlightened to the principle of dependent arising. Those who base their conclusions on the Sutta Piṭaka, especially the events of the enlightenment to the three knowledges, and in particular the third knowledge, which is the actual enlightenment (the other two are neither considered to be enlightenment nor essential for *nibbāna*), might decide that the Buddha was enlightened to the four noble truths.

However that may be, both answers, although correct, entail meanings that have their own specific nuances and encompass different areas, and this should be understood in order to see why they are treated as two different teachings.

The senses of these two teachings that correspond are easily seen. The following is a brief comparison of the four noble truths and the principle of dependent origination:

1. *Samudayavāra*: ignorance arises → mental formations arise→... birth → aging and death, sorrow...despair arise.
2. *Nirodhavāra*: ignorance ceases → mental formations cease →... birth ceases → aging and death, sorrow...despair cease.

No. 1. The origination mode (*samudayavāra*) of the dependent-arising process shows it as the arising of suffering. It corresponds to the first two noble truths—suffering and the cause of suffering. In the noble truths this is divided into two in order to put the end section (birth, aging, death, sorrow...), which is resultant, separately as the first truth, as the problem to be dealt with. From there, it goes on to the entire process, which is the second noble truth, tracing back to the original cause of the problem.

No. 2. The cessation mode (*nirodhavāra*) of dependent origination shows the process of the cessation of suffering. It corresponds to the third noble truth, since it shows how the problem ceases in accordance with determinants. While, strictly speaking, this mode of dependent arising corresponds with the third noble truth, it is also considered to include the fourth noble truth, because the process of dissolution of problems in itself necessitates the required method—that is to say, what needs to be done and where.

Condensing the noble truths down, there are only two—suffering (first and second truths) and suffering's cessation (third and fourth truths).

These two modes of dependent arising are sometimes used as definitions of the second and third noble truths respectively. The origination mode is used as a definition of the second noble truth (cause) and the cessation mode as a definition of the third noble truth (cessation).[17] However, in the definition given above, desire (*taṇhā*) alone is said to be the cause, and desire's cessation is said to be cessation. This is because desire is the prominent defilement, the one that is most openly expressed on the level of active expression, and therefore it is the focus of interest. Even so, the entire process, including behind the scenes, fares according to the whole of the dependent-arising process.

The ways in which the principle of dependent arising and the four noble truths differ can be summarized as follows.

The two teachings are expressions of truth in different forms, with different objectives. The principle of dependent arising shows truth according to its processes, as they occur in nature, while the teaching of the noble truths is truth presented in a form that is suitable for examining, investigating and effectuating practical results. In this respect, the noble truths are a teaching that conforms with the story of the Buddha's own search for truth, beginning with his encounter with suffering, which manifests as the problem, his search for its cause, his discovery that there is a way to correct it, his determining the details or points to be corrected and defining the goal, and his proceeding to correct the problem according to that method and attaining the desired goal.

By the same token, it is the principle taught to give students a systematic understanding, aimed at efficacy for those giving the teaching and those receiving the teaching. Dependent arising, on the other hand, is the core process of the noble truths and the academic substance to be studied in order to understand the noble truths most clearly, and this is why it is the teaching that the Buddha examined and reviewed immediately after his enlightenment.

An important distinction or disparity between the two teachings lies in the cessation mode of dependent arising, which corresponds with the third and fourth noble truths. Namely, in contrast with the third noble truth (*nirodha*), while the cessation mode of the dependent-arising principle deals with cessation, it seeks to describe only the process that leads to it, not the state of cessation, or *nibbāna*, itself. For this reason, in the Buddha's reflections before he began to spread the teaching, he distinguishes his points of reflection into two parts, the first mentioning the principle of dependent arising, as above, and then continuing, "Moreover, this is also a difficult thing to see: that is, the calming of all formations, the rejection of all clinging (*upadhi*), the ending of desire, dispassion, cessation, *nibbāna*." This indicates that the Buddha wished to divide what he had become enlightened to into two: the principle of dependent arising and cessation (*nibbāna*). The third noble truth, on the other hand, aims specifically to describe the state of cessation itself, although implicit in its meaning is also the process leading to it.

Even though the cessation mode of dependent arising encompasses the fourth noble truth, *magga*, it does not give any clear practical application. This is because the dependent-arising principle is intended to show a purely natural process and is not concerned with specifying the practicalities: it does not lay down a system of practice for bringing about results. It is like a doctor who knows how to treat an illness but does not prescribe any medication or a course of treatment to cure it. In the noble truths, however, the fourth noble truth is formulated for this very purpose as a separate truth, as a practice that has been verified as leading to the goal.

The fourth noble truth shows the principles of practice comprehensively and in detail. It is a practical teaching, the entire system of practice in Buddhism known as the Middle Way (*majjhimā paṭipadā*). In comparison with the noble truths, the principle of dependent arising is the *majjhena dhammadesanā*, the teaching given impartially, or Middle Teaching of the nature of things. It encompasses the first three noble truths. The fourth noble truth, the path, is the Middle Way of practice (*majjhimā paṭipadā*). It is for human application, to bring about results in accordance with that nature.

Summarizing this point, the Buddha spoke of what he had become enlightened to in two main teachings: the principle of dependent arising and *nibbāna*, on one hand, and the four noble truths, on the other. Both of these teachings are essentially the same, but they examine different perspectives, thus:

1. The Buddha spoke of the principle of dependent arising and *nibbāna* when he said, in the process of deliberating on whether to declare the Dhamma, that what he had realized was profound and extremely difficult to understand. His talking of it in this sense indicates that dependent arising and *nibbāna* are the actual essence of the Buddha's enlightenment, or, to put it in relation to the second perspective, they are the essence of the noble truths, the essence of what it is that is so hard to understand.
2. The Buddha spoke of the four noble truths both when he was recounting the stages of his own practice for enlightenment and when he was teaching others, beginning with the first sermon (*paṭhamadesanā*). His talking of it in this sense indicates that the four noble truths are the totality of what he became enlightened to, in a systematic formulation made with ease of comprehension and practice in mind.

In other words, the principle of dependent arising and *nibbāna* are the pure substance of the Dhamma, while the four noble truths are the Dhamma in a form that human beings can relate to. It can be said that the four noble truths are the totality of the Dhamma, at the heart of which lie the most profound and abstruse principles of dependent arising and *nibbāna*: if the principle of dependent arising and *nibbāna* are understood, then the whole of the Buddhadhamma is understood.

The Tasks in Relation to the Noble Truths

An important aspect of the noble truths is knowing and dealing with each of them correctly. Whether in terms of teaching or practice, each of the truths must be related to its appropriate duty or task before that teaching or practice can be said to be right, otherwise misunderstandings can arise. Some misunderstandings of Buddhism, such as the view that Buddhism is a pessimistic religion, stem from misunderstanding the tasks in the noble truths.

The "tasks" of the noble truths are the duties that must be carried out in relation to, or responsibilities toward, each of the four noble truths:[18]

1. *Dukkhaṁ ariyasaccaṁ pariññeyyaṁ*: (the noble truth of) suffering is to be known.
2. *Dukkhasamudaya ariyasaccaṁ pahātabbaṁ*: (the noble truth of) the cause of suffering is to be eliminated.
3. *Dukkhanirodho ariyasaccaṁ sacchikātabbaṁ*: (the noble truth of) the cessation of suffering is to be realized.
4. *Dukkhanirodhagāminīpaṭipadā ariyasaccaṁ bhāvetabbaṁ*: (the noble truth of) the way leading to the cessation of suffering is to be cultivated.

These tasks can be simply arranged as follows:

1. *Pariññā*, noting, is the task in relation to suffering. It refers to studying and understanding the state that is suffering as it actually is. Simply speaking, it is understanding the problem and clearly recognizing its scope. It is a first step that ensures that any subsequent steps taken are in conformity with the problem.
2. *Pahāna*, eliminating, is the task in relation to the cause of suffering. It refers to eliminating the cause of suffering, removing the conditions for its arising. Simply speaking, it is treating and removing the source of the problem.
3. *Sacchikiriyā*, realization, is the task in relation to cessation. It refers to the realization or attainment of the cessation of suffering. Simply speaking, it is entering the state in which problems are wholly corrected and the desired objective attained.
4. *Bhāvanā*, cultivation, is the task in relation to the way. Liter-

ally, *bhāvanā* means "to bring forth and to develop." It refers to training in accordance with the practices of the path, putting into practice the method for eliminating the cause of suffering. Simply speaking, it is following the method that leads to the objective, or determining the particulars of the practice and then setting to solving the problem.

Each of these tasks for its respective noble truth must be observed properly and comprehensively. In practice, there must be some knowledge, or direct knowledge (*ñāṇa*), before it is possible to perform the tasks properly. Knowing the tasks of the noble truths is called *kiccañāṇa*. When this direct knowledge is used to connect each of the noble truths to its respective task, a practice of successive stages for solving problems on all levels is revealed:

1. *Kiccañāṇa* in suffering (knowing that suffering must be known): this is knowing the state that is suffering, which must be clearly seen as it really is (that is, not as one would want it to be or according to one's aversion). This is the stage of noting or surveying the problem, which must be understood and the extent ascertained.
2. *Kiccañāṇa* in the cause (knowing that the cause of suffering must be eliminated): this is the stage of researching, analyzing, and diagnosing the cause of the problem that must be corrected and eliminated.
3. *Kiccañāṇa* in cessation (knowing that the cessation of suffering must be realized): this is knowing the state of cessation of suffering that must be realized. This stage is focusing on the state of no problems as the goal, seeing that the correction of problems is a possibility and is worth attaining, and must be attained, and knowing how the attainment of the objective can be done.
4. *Kiccañāṇa* in the way (knowing that the path must be cultivated): this is knowing *magga*, the practices leading to the cessation of suffering, which must be cultivated and practiced. This stage is carefully determining or taking note of the methods of

practice, the stages, and the particulars involved in correcting and eliminating the causes of the problem, which must be put into practice.

Simply speaking, it is knowing what suffering is, knowing what causes it, knowing what we want or should want in relation to it, and knowing how to bring about the desired result.

This direct knowledge into tasks is one of three kinds of direct knowledge concerning the four noble truths that are used as criteria for gauging enlightenment. That is, when there is knowledge of each of the four noble truths through all three kinds of direct knowledge (making altogether twelve facets), then one can be said to really know the four noble truths, or be enlightened.

Those three kinds of direct knowledge are called in full "direct knowledge and vision (*ñāṇadassana*) in three cycles (*parivaṭṭa*)," or the three rounds of direct knowledge and vision, as follows:[19]

1. *Saccañāṇa*: direct knowledge of truth. *Saccañāṇa* is direct knowledge into each the four noble truths as they are; knowing this is suffering, this is the cause of suffering, this is the cessation of suffering, and this is the way leading to the cessation of suffering; or, knowing suffering is like this, the cause of suffering is like this, the cessation of suffering is like this, and the way leading to the cessation of suffering is like this. *Saccañāṇa* in all four noble truths is one cycle (one *parivaṭṭa*).
2. *Kiccañāṇa*: direct knowledge of the task, direct knowledge into the duties to be done for each of the truths. *Kiccañāṇa* is knowing that suffering is to be seen, the cause is to be given up, the end to be realized, and the way to be cultivated. *Kiccañāṇa* in all four noble truths is one cycle (one *parivaṭṭa*).
3. *Katañāṇa*, direct knowledge into accomplishment, direct knowledge that the task for each of the noble truths has been completed. *Katañāṇa* is knowing that the suffering that should be seen has been seen; that the cause that should be given up has been given up; that the cessation that should be realized

has been realized; that the way that should be practiced has been practiced. *Katañāṇa* in all four noble truths is one cycle (one *parivaṭṭa*).

These three kinds of direct knowledge occur in each of the four noble truths, one cycle for each kind of direct knowledge, making three cycles, known in full as cycles of direct knowledge and vision (*ñāṇadassana*). The three cycles for all of the four noble truths makes altogether twelve, called the twelve facets (*ākāra*). It was only when the Buddha had direct knowledge and vision into the four noble truths in all three rounds, with the full twelve facets, that he declared his attainment of complete, unexcelled enlightenment.

The principle of the twelve-faceted direct knowledge and vision is used as a criterion for measuring success in addressing problems of every description. It can be simply represented as follows:

1. Suffering is like this. → Suffering is to be seen. → Suffering has been seen.
2. The cause of suffering is like this. → The cause is to be abandoned. → The cause has been abandoned.
3. The cessation of suffering is like this. → Cessation is to be realized. → Cessation has been realized.
4. The way to cessation is like this. → The way is to be cultivated. → The way has been cultivated.

It can also be represented as shown in Table 2 (see next page).

In order to gain a broader picture, the following points should be noted:

1. Suffering is paired with *pariññā*, meaning that it is something to be seen. Thus, suffering and all the conditions that fall into the category of "problems" are together called *pariññeyyadhamma* (conditions to be noted).
2. The cause of suffering is paired with *pahāna*, meaning that it

Table 2. Summary of the Noble Truths and Their Tasks

Four truths (*sacca*)	Three direct knowledges (*ñāṇa*)		
	Saccañāṇa	*Kiccañāṇa*	*Katañāṇa*
Dukkha	Knowing suffering = knowing what the problem is, where the problem lies	Knowing that suffering should be known = knowing that the nature and extent of the problem must be understood	Knowing that suffering has been known = knowing that the nature and extent of the problem have been understood
Samudaya	Knowing that the cause of suffering (desire) is like this = knowing what the cause of the problem is	Knowing that the cause (desire) should be given up = knowing that that cause must be rectified	Knowing that the cause (desire) has been given up = knowing that that cause has been rectified and destroyed
Nirodha	Knowing that cessation is like this (knowing that *nibbāna* is the state of cessation of suffering) = knowing the state of cessation of problems that one aspires to	Knowing that cessation should be realized (knowing that *nibbāna* should be attained) = knowing that that state is the goal that should be attained	Knowing that cessation has been realized (knowing that *nibbāna* has been attained) = knowing that the goal has been attained
Magga	Knowing that the path is like this (knowing that the eightfold path is the way to the cessation of suffering) = knowing the way to solve the problem	Knowing that the path should be developed (knowing that the eightfold path should be practiced) = knowing that that method must be put into practice or carried out	Knowing that this path has been developed (knowing that the eightfold path has been practiced) = knowing that the practice has been completed in accordance with that path

is something to be given up or eliminated. Thus, desire and all conditions that cause problems and are causes of suffering, such as ignorance, greed, hatred, and clinging, are together called *pahātabbadhamma* (conditions to be eliminated).

3. Cessation is paired with *sacchikiriyā*, meaning that it is something to be realized or attained. Thus, *nibbāna* and those conditions that are the objective, or the solution of problems, are together called *sacchikātabbadhamma* (conditions to be realized).
4. The path is paired with *bhāvanā*, meaning that it is something to be cultivated or put into practice. Thus, the eightfold path and all conditions that fall into the category of practices for attaining the goal are together called *bhāvetabbadhamma* (conditions to be cultivated).

All things that exist can be classed into one or another of these four groups. Within the way leading to the cessation of suffering, from the coarse level to the refined, from external conditions to the profound and internal, a student may note and place all the conditions one deals with into these four kinds. For example, the Buddha described the appropriate teachings for practicing on the core level as follows:[20]

1. *Dukkha*: The *pariññeyyadhamma* are the grasped-at *khandhas*.
2. *Samudaya*: The *pahātabbadhamma* are ignorance (*avijjā*) and desire for becoming (*bhavataṇhā*).
3. *Nirodha*: The *sacchikātabbadhamma* are knowledge (*vijjā*) and liberation (*vimutti*).
4. *Magga*: The *bhāvetabbadhamma* are calm (*samatha*) and insight (*vipassanā*).

Explaining the Four Noble Truths in Brief

The commentarial texts already cited give various analogies for the four noble truths, some of which are of interest here. For example:[21]

Dukkha is a disease.	*Samudaya* is the cause of the disease.
Nirodha is the cure of the disease	*Magga* is the medicine.
Dukkha is a famine.	*Samudaya* is lack of rain.
Nirodha is abundance.	*Magga* is good rainfall.
Dukkha is danger.	*Samudaya* is the cause of danger.
Nirodha is freedom from danger.	*Magga* is the way for escaping the danger.
Dukkha is a heavy burden.	*Samudaya* is carrying the burden.
Nirodha is releasing the burden.	*Magga* is the way to release the burden.

These analogies are explanations of the noble truths that are easy to understand, and we could say that just this is enough, but there are some points that may help to increase our understanding.

The Visuddhimagga, the Sammohavinodanī, and the Saddhammapakāsinī[22] each give an interesting explanation of why the Buddha taught the noble truths in the order that we now see them. The discussion, while brief, is significant, so it is presented here as an outline and summary of the four noble truths.

Dukkha *Is Posited First*

Dukkha refers to all the problems that human beings have, the things that oppress life and the mind. It is present everywhere in all beings, in all people. Whenever and for whomever it arises, it is a focus of interest, a prominent reality for that person at that time. From a broader perspective, life naturally contains problems, and is a problem, all the time. For that reason, suffering is a clear and relevant point of focus in everyone's life. It is obvious, demands our attention, and as such is a point suitable for raising—that is, it is a good point from which to begin a Dhamma teaching.

Moreover, suffering is an object of abhorrence and fear for most people. Even though it is impossible to avoid, people do not want to hear about it. Those who are abandoning themselves to pleasure do not realize that they are experiencing and creating problems. When someone comes along and points this out to them, it upsets them. For people in this situation, the Buddha gave the teaching of suffering in order to provoke them into thinking about something that they normally avoid thinking about. It is the first step to examining and resolving problems and overcoming suffering.

Beginning the teaching at suffering is starting the teaching at the problem, at that point which is most apparent and easily understood, at that which is of interest. Most importantly, it is teaching what is truly relevant. It is not abstract, imaginary, or mere empty rhetoric. When addressed to a particular person it is relevant to that person, and when it is stated in general it concerns everyone.

The Buddha did not teach suffering in order to cause suffering but in order to provide a starting point for quelling it. He knew that suffering or problems are things that can be dealt with and ended. They are not permanent conditions. Life is problematic because there is still suffering; the problem is still unresolved. If one can quell suffering and solve problems, or develop the ability to quell suffering and solve problems, life will become secure and untroubled, and one finds true happiness.

The cessation of suffering or solving of problems cannot be achieved by avoiding problems or closing our eyes to suffering. On the contrary, we must use the method of acknowledging and confronting suffering. Acknowledging and confronting does not mean carrying suffering around or bringing it on oneself but simply to comprehend it so that one can correct it and eliminate it. To comprehend suffering is to deal with it properly, which is *pariññā*, observing, comprehending the nature of suffering or problems, knowing what suffering or problems actually are and where they lie, and how far it extends. Noting suffering in this way is like a doctor examining an illness and ascertaining where it lies.

This is all that has to be done in relation to suffering. It is not our duty to eliminate or abandon suffering, because suffering cannot be given up directly—it must be dealt with at its cause. Trying to give up suffering itself is like trying to cure an illness by suppressing the symptoms—it does not really cure the illness. We must look for the cause.

To study illnesses a doctor must study the body, which is the seat of illness. In the same way, if we want to quell suffering we must study suffering and learn about life, which is the seat of suffering, and the nature of the world of formations it involves.

The essential point of the first noble truth is to accept the truth of suffering as it is and to look at life and the world as they really are.

Searching for the Factors with Wisdom

Samudaya is the cause of suffering, the cause of the problem. In order to quell suffering, it is necessary to eliminate its cause. Thus, once we have ascertained what suffering or the problem is, and where it lies, we must delve back for the cause so that we can perform the task of *pahāna*, giving up or eliminating. However, even in searching for the cause, people again tend to evade the truth, looking outside, away from themselves and the present moment, and put the blame for their suffering on external conditions. Even when the cause is seen as associated with themselves, it is usually seen as being far away and beyond one's field of responsibility. The things that are blamed as being the reasons [for suffering] usually find expression in these three mistaken doctrines:[23]

1. The "old *kamma*" school (*pubbekatavāda*): the belief that all happiness and suffering experienced in the present are a result of *kamma* committed in previous times.
2. The "God" school (*issaranimittavāda*): the belief that all happiness and suffering experienced in the present are a result of the commands of an Almighty God.
3. The "blind chance" school (*ahetukavāda*): the belief that all happiness and suffering experienced in the present happen by themselves, are random and causeless.

The Dhamma refutes these schools of thought because they conflict with the natural law of causality. We are taught to look for the cause of suffering in accordance with that natural law, seeing the determinants for suffering, beginning with those that arise at and within ourselves. These are *kamma*—the deeds, speech, and thoughts, both good and bad, that we have committed and are committing, and that we have accumulated as habitual tendencies, including the way we look on things and relate, rightly and wrongly, to the determinants around us.

Fundamentally, the commentators say that on the deeper level, desire (*taṇhā*)—which causes us to look on, express ourselves within, and deal with our lives and the world wrongly, so that our lives are not conducted with knowledge of the truth but through delight and aversion—is the source of human problems and suffering. There are three kinds of desire: desire for sense objects (*kāmataṇhā*); desire for becoming, wanting to maintain existence (*bhavataṇhā*); and desire for annihilation (*vibhavataṇhā*). On a deeper level, the commentators cite the dependent-arising process, rooted in ignorance, as the source from which all problems spring.

When the ignorance and desire, which are the sources of problems and the causes of suffering, have been eliminated, we no longer fall into the power of the defilements of self-preservation. Then we will be able to deal with life and relate to the world, other people, other beings, and nature with the wisdom that understands reality and knows the determinants of things as they are, enabling us to truly solve problems to the full extent of our abilities and intelligence. While there still may be suffering, it is only the natural reality of suffering, and it has no power to dominate our minds. When desire is no longer dominating us internally, the only task that remains is to wisely study the situations and concerns of life to see their reality and their determinants as they really are, and then to deal with them with that wisdom in a way that is beneficial and favorable. But as long as the dominating influence of defilements is oppressing us, we will be unable to truly solve problems and destroy suffering, either external problems or internal suffering. For the most part, rather than solving problems, we tend to aggravate them, either in the same form or in the form of new problems. When oppressed by inner suffering, instead of quelling it or being able to reduce its power through wisdom, we are forced by desire into replacing it with even greater internal suffering or else venting it outward to harm other people and society.

Thus the suffering and problems of human beings have been, and are in the present moment, always under the control of desire supported by ignorance.

The Life Lived with Wisdom, Happiness, Freedom, and Compassionate Action

Nirodha is the quelling of suffering or the state without problems. Having discussed suffering, or problems, together with their causes, which are undesirable qualities, the Buddha anointed the hearts of his listeners with relief and hope with his teaching of the third noble truth, cessation. He showed that the suffering that oppresses us can be quelled, the problems that press on us can be resolved, and there is a desirable way out. This is because the cause of problems or suffering can be eliminated. Suffering exists because of a cause. When the cause is eliminated, the suffering dependent on it comes to an end. When suffering ceases, problems are done with, leaving a state free of problems and void of suffering. In this respect, the noble truth of cessation is placed third, both because it follows this order in natural progression and because of its suitability in the process of a teaching that arouses one's interest, aids in understanding, leads to good results, and encourages advancement to the level of practice for truly attaining and realizing the result.

When desire is eliminated, together with the defilements that are its offshoots, the mind no longer has to be tortured by agitation, greed, confusion, fear, and depression. It no longer has to seek happiness merely by running away from these states, by covering them up or substituting them for something else, or by finding a channel to release them externally to gain temporary relief. By correcting these factors, the mind is free, independent, clear, and tranquil. It has a happiness that is buoyant in that it is not held down by worries and doubts. It is calm, cheerful, and clear at all times and attains inner perfection. This is the completion of the task of *sacchikiriyā*, the realization of the goal.

From another perspective, when the mind has been liberated from the domination and deception of the defilements and inner complexes, no longer influenced and controlled by ignorance, this means that wisdom is liberated from the blinding, distorting, or tainting influence of defilements. It is pure and liberated, enabling the mind to consider and examine things as they really are, seeing them according to their reality and according to determinants. Without ignorance and desire to lead the mind astray, wisdom becomes the director of behavior, allowing us to evaluate, conduct, and express ourselves in the world—and relate to the world and life—with a comprehension of how things are. Not only is wisdom the root of purity and freedom on the internal level, but externally it also causes one's knowledge and abilities to be used in a way that resolves problems and truly promotes benefit and happiness. Intelligence and abilities are fully utilized for benefit without any constraining or distorting influence, so that they lead only to what is wholesome. This is called living with wisdom.

Moreover, when the mind is free, clear, and naturally happy within itself, no longer obsessed with self-interests, no longer having to spend time searching for objects of enjoyment or to protect and promote the strength and greatness of the self it carries around with it, the mind opens out; it spreads its feeling of freedom outward and is ready to open up to the sufferings of fellow beings and find ways to help them.

In this respect, wisdom is aided by compassion to influence and guide conduct, causing us to live our lives fully for the benefit of others. When there is no longer any clinging to anything through defilements or binding things to oneself for personal gain, we are able to perform truly wholesome actions, to practice for the benefit of others in the most undivided and resolute manner. Internally, the mind is free, happy, clear, and buoyant; this attainment of personal benefit is known in Pali as *attahitasampatti*. Externally, there is conduct for the benefit of other beings, called *parahitapaṭipatti*, as its pair, completing the characteristics of one who has attained to the highest meaning of the word of *cessation*.

Be that as it may, those following the way of the noble ones need not necessarily wait for the attainment of *nibbāna*, which is the highest sense of the term cessation, to experience this wholesome and salutary state. Even during the practice of the right path, it is possible to continuously experience the fruits of the practice as appropriate to one's level, since the meaning of *nirodha* can be expanded to include the following five different levels:[24]

1. *Vikkhambhananirodha*: cessation of defilements and suffering through suppression; calming the mind; making it serene, relaxed, tranquil, and clear, relieved of defilement, heat, and agitation through the development of *samādhi*. It refers particularly to the *samādhi* of the *jhāna*s, where the defilements are subdued and the happiness that is independent of material things (*nirāmisasukha*) is experienced for the duration of the *jhāna* state.
2. *Tadaṅganirodha*: cessation of defilements and suffering through a competing factor or opposite quality. This refers especially to wise attention (*yoniso-manasikāra*), having the wisdom to comprehend the truths that are the natural order of things as faring according to determinants. One assumes a proper outlook on things and deals with them through an attitude of knowledge, with understanding, goodwill, kindness, and detachment. When this kind of wisdom is clear and in accordance with the reality, it is called insight wisdom (*vipassanā-paññā*), and it causes defilements and suffering to cease for the duration of that time, rendering the mind calm, pure, happy, clear, and buoyant. It also makes the mind subtle and contributes to the growth of wisdom.
3. *Samucchedanirodha*: the utter cessation of defilements and suffering, which is the attainment of the transcendent paths

(*lokuttaramagga*), from the stream entry path (*sotāpattimagga*) upward. Defilements and suffering are utterly severed according to the level of path attained.

4. *Paṭipassaddhinirodha*: cessation of defilements and suffering through calming, which is attainment of the transcendent fruits (*phala*), becoming one of the noble ones from stream enterer upward. The defilements are extinguished and there is purity, clarity, and freedom in the mind, according to the level of noble one attained.
5. *Nissaraṇanirodha*: cessation of defilements through relinquishing. This refers to the state of perfect freedom and clarity of *nibbāna*.

Reaching the Triple Gem

Magga is the way to the cessation of suffering, or the method of practice for eliminating the causes of problems. Once one knows the problem, the cause of the problem, and the objective that is the state free of problems, one is then ready and it is time to get down to the actual practice. The important point is that, once we know what the desired objective is, and know that it is possible to attain, then the practice to attain it is feasible. If we do not know what the objective is or where we are going, then we do not know how to practice or make the journey. Thus, in terms of the relationship between the noble truths, it is fitting that *magga* comes last.

Moreover, in terms of teaching, practice is a task that usually depends on energy and effort. If practitioners could not see the value or benefit of the goal, they would have no energy to practice. They may become discouraged or even refuse to practice, and if they were to practice it would be only out of compulsion, simply going through the motions, and the practice would not fare well. Conversely, if they can see the value or benefit of the goal, they will practice gladly. The better the goal is, and the more they want it, the more inspired and energetic will their practice be. If they really aspire to it, they will persevere and succeed no matter how difficult it is.

This is another reason why the Buddha placed cessation before the path: to give listeners hope and show them the value of cessation, which is the goal—to arouse their interest and enthusiasm and therefore be prepared to get down to practice. Once the Buddha had stated that cessation is truly worth attaining, his listeners were willing to give full attention to the path with a strong resolve to follow it, and they were glad to face any difficulties its practice might entail.

When looking for the cause of suffering, people tend to look externally for somewhere to put the blame, or they look beyond their own areas of responsibility. In the same way, when it comes to resolving suffering, people tend to look outward, looking for something that will protect them and lead them from danger or help relieve the suffering for them. Both of these reactions are the same: they are evasions of the truth, not daring to look at suffering and avoiding facing up to one's responsibilities, like the cartoon of the ostrich hiding its head in a hole for safety when the rest of its body is in full view.

This kind of attitude leads to the tendency to place one's hopes in external factors, such as by praying to supernatural forces, making oblations and sacrifices, waiting for an act of God, or simply waiting on luck. Buddhism teaches that taking refuge in these kinds of things, or just waiting on luck, is not the way to assurance or safety; these approaches do not lead to the true transcendence of suffering. The proper way to remove suffering is to have confidence in the Triple Gem (the Buddha, the Dhamma, and the Saṅgha), to make the mind calm and strong, and to use wisdom to consider problems impartially, seeing them according to their reality and finding a way to deal with them according to their determinants. In other words, it is knowing how to go about solving problems with the four noble truths: noting suffering, delving back into its cause, taking note of the state of cessation of suffering to be attained, and practicing the method for addressing the problem at its cause, using a path that is just right for achieving the goal, known as the noble eightfold path. This is the real way to transcend suffering, as stated in the Buddhavacana:

> "Many people, threatened by danger, take refuge in mountains, forests, parks, and sacred trees. These are not sure refuges, they are not the highest refuge. Holding to these refuges, they cannot transcend all suffering.
>
> "As for those who go to the Buddha, the Dhamma, and the Saṅgha for refuge, seeing with real wisdom suffering, the cause of suffering, the transcendence of suffering, and the noble eightfold path leading to the cessation of suffering, they attain a sure refuge, the highest refuge. Holding to these refuges, people can transcend all suffering."[25]

"Buddha" is the recollection that assures us that human beings, all of us, have the intelligence and the potential to train to perfection, to penetrate to the truth and attain liberation from suffering, thereby becoming completely independent of worldly conditions, and to possess a glory that is revered even by the devas, as exemplified by the Buddha. All those people who put faith in deities and occult objects, if they bothered to develop themselves, would find that there is nothing those devas and occult objects could do for them that their own good *kamma* and human wisdom could not do better.

"Dhamma" is the recollection that assures us that truth is the natural way of things. All things fare according to determinants. If we know how to look on and understand things as they really are, putting our knowledge of Dhamma, of the truth, to use, dealing with things with comprehension of their reality and acting on the determinants, we can resolve problems, attain the Dhamma and have the best possible life.

"Saṅgha" is the recollection that assures us that the wholesome community has Dhamma as its foundation, and is composed of members whose minds are free of, or far from, suffering, and who are free and independent. While they may be on different levels of intellectual development, they can live together in harmony and are compatible and equal in the Dhamma. All human beings can play an active role in creating this kind of society by knowing the Dhamma and practicing accordingly.

Without confidence in the Triple Gem we must continue to cling to external factors—performing ceremonies to supplicate occult forces, for example, or praying to the devas. With firm confidence in the Triple Gem, we study the principles for eliminating suffering and solving problems in accordance with the noble truths, and we practice according to the method of human development in the way of Buddhism.

The Way of the Noble Ones

Those who have perfectly firm faith (*saddhā*) in the Triple Gem are not shaken or moved by opinions from outside, or even by the vicissitudes of life known as the worldly conditions (*lokadhamma*), which ordinary people call "bad luck." Their minds are like healthy people, who are strong and can always help themselves.[26] They do not have to resort to external powers but aspire only to the fruits of *kamma*—that is, their own efforts made in accordance with determinants—and their wisdom has developed to the level of clearly comprehending the principles for solving problems and quelling suffering in accordance with the four noble truths. They resolutely put the method for solving problems and quelling suffering into practice with the way known as the noble eightfold path. Such people are said to be "enterers of the stream" to the cessation of suffering and true freedom, and they are said to have entered the clan of the noble ones, to be "learners" (*sekha*). They are called noble ones of the first level, or "stream enterers" (*sotāpanna*).

As for those who are still running around dominated by worldly conditions, and wavering in the face of worldly vicissitudes, their faith is shaky. They do not have confidence in themselves based on the qualities of the Triple Gem. Their minds are like sickly people, who cannot help themselves and must always rely on others. During good times they may feel strong, but as soon as life starts getting difficult they collapse. Their only options are to either endure intense suffering, to lose themselves in the pursuit of ever more intense sense pleasures or intoxicants, or to take refuge in occult forces and seek help from divine intervention, from auspicious objects, or from luck, to cover over, compensate for, or comfort them in their suffering. They have not yet seen and understood things as they are with the wisdom that comprehends the reality and determinants, and therefore cannot free their minds from the stream of the world. In their daily lives, they lean to either one of two extremes: if not heedless indulgence in sense pleasures, then to placing rigorous strictures on themselves with systems or methods they blindly cling to. They do not practice the Middle Way.

Such people are called *puthujjana*. Those who live far from noble teachings, who are completely blind, ignorant of good and evil, and live their lives as desire leads them without using any intelligent reflection, and are thus ready to exploit anybody in pursuit of their own interests, are called *andhabālaputhujjana* (literally, "a foolish ordinary person").

Those who have heard the noble teaching and have heard the call of the noble ones, who have begun to lead a wholesome life, who are moral and observe the ten bases of skillful action, or who at least are established in the five precepts, are called *kalyāṇaputhujjana*, "good people," or *sutavanta-ariyasāvakā*, those who have heard the teaching of the noble ones and have begun to approach the noble way.

The practice for eliminating the cause of suffering, or the methods for solving problems, is called *magga* because it is like a pathway leading to the destination. It is said to have eight factors because it is only one path with eight components. To reach the destination it is necessary to have all eight factors functioning interactively, harmoniously, and in proper balance. Such balance and direction are guided by wisdom—seeing properly or understanding rightly—illuminating and pointing out the way. Right view is thus the first factor of the path. And because the practice is balanced and attuned to the objective, the path is called *majjhimā paṭipadā*, the Middle Way. It is easily distinguished by the characteristic of avoiding the two extremes: seeking only happiness through indulging in sensual pleasures, and turning to the opposite extreme of seeking only to be strict with oneself and put oneself through all kinds of suffering, as if one hated oneself.

For the practice of the path to begin and to proceed, there must be the help of two factors, which are its spark and its nourishment. They are called the determinants of right view. The first is an external or social factor: good *paratoghosa*, voices, encouragement, instigation, and influence from others. It refers especially to a *kalyāṇamitta*, a good friend, who may be a parent, a teacher, a bhikkhu, someone who has achieved fame and success through good actions, or anyone else who is endowed with suitable qualities to serve as a good example or inspiration, both far and near. A good friend helps instruct, teach, advise, or inspire one to a predilection for the good, and he or she imparts true knowledge, working through the medium of *saddhā*, faith and respect; a good friend helps to arouse one and encourage one to examine for oneself things as they really are.

The second determinant of right view is an internal factor. It is *yoniso-manasikāra*, wise attention, or reflecting intelligently, knowing how to think, or thinking properly. It is knowing how to examine things according to their reality and according to their determinants.

When these two factors are inspiring and promoting right view, practice or life is more assured of being along the proper lines, and the skillful qualities that are the other factors of the path will grow in combination with wisdom, leading to benefit for oneself and for others, and bringing one closer to the objective of Buddhist practice.

In this respect, unshakable belief in the Triple Gem, knowledge of the noble truths, and practice according to the Middle Way, or the eightfold path, are buffers against wrong ways of living or wrong responses to suffering, be it allowing oneself to fall into the power of suffering, trying to deceive oneself into forgetting about suffering by sinking even deeper into sensual indulgence, resorting to occult forces, praying for divine intervention, waiting for one's lucky day, venting one's suffering onto others, or turning to self-torment and self-punishment.

The path that is supported by this right kind of belief causes us to have good conduct (*sucarita*), to perform helpful actions that are of benefit both to oneself and to others, enabling us to face up to situations with strength and steadiness, with a calm mind, so that we are able to conduct our lives, solve problems, and quell suffering with mindfulness and wisdom, and strive to do things according to the ways of determinants.

On the weakest level, if we are not in a position to help ourselves, we know how to seek the help of a good friend, who will inspire us to be bold in cultivation of skillful qualities and will teach us to develop the wisdom to understand determinants so that we can solve problems properly.

The task in relation to the path is cultivation or development (*bhāvanā*). But to call the path "practices" or "the practice of Dhamma" sometimes gives too narrow an impression of what the path really is. In fact, the path encompasses the entire practical side of the Dhamma in Buddhism, encompassing all of what conduct entails, including all of the actions carried out for a wholesome life, as implied by the name often used to refer to the path: *brahmacariya*, meaning the holy life.

All eight factors of the path can be further analyzed and reorganized into different sets of factors, with different points of emphasis in accordance with different levels of practice. Clear examples are the organization of the path into a form that is suitable for ordinary people, stressing external expressions over internal mental states, in the teaching called the ten courses of skillful action (*kusalakammapatha*), as opposed to the arrangement into a practice that is aimed specifically at Buddhism's highest objective, stressing teachings on the level of insight wisdom, such as the seven levels of purity (*visuddhi*).

The Triple Gem and Progress in the Threefold Training

Among the numerous collections or sets of teachings or systems of practice that are based on these eight factors of the path, the central, fundamental, or all-encompassing system is that known as the threefold training (*tisikkhā*). To illustrate, we might place the threefold training side by side with the path, in which case we would see that the latter is a way or a system for conducting a good life—or, to be more precise, the essentials of leading a good life—while the threefold training represents a system of study or training. The two are interconnected, since when there is study or training, the well-conducted life can come about. Thus, practicing according to the threefold training leads to the arising of the path, which essentially means that the development of the threefold training is *for* the arising of the path. In fact the substance of the path and the threefold training are one. When one is developed, the other is attained. That training or learning is not separate from the conduct of everyday life, but part of it.

Once begun and well established, faith in the Triple Gem supports progress in the threefold training and development of the factors of the path until the goal is reached.

The threefold training is the training in higher conduct (*adhisīlasikkhā*), the training in higher mentality (*adhicittasikkhā*), and the training in higher wisdom (*adhipaññāsikkhā*)—or, simply speaking, morality, concentration, and wisdom.

1. *Adhisīlasikkhā* is the training of good conduct in body, speech, and livelihood. It includes three factors of the path—right speech, right action, and right livelihood. In essence, it is conducting oneself well in society, observing rules and regulations, fulfilling one's social obligations, having good, helpful, and beneficial social relations, and helping to keep one's surroundings, especially one's social surroundings, in a state that is conducive to everyone being able to live a wholesome life or practice the path.[27]

Morality (*sīla*) is the most elementary level of training, and therefore its scope is very broad. It can be divided into many levels, encompassing the entire extent of external expression and self-discipline, and the relationship to one's surroundings, both social and natural. The basic standard of *sīla* is "not harming others" (just as one does not harm oneself), not destroying those aspects of the social environment that are conducive to a good life or to the path. From there, *sīla* is training within the discipline (*vinaya*) for higher levels of goodness. If one is able, one can advance to actions that are helpful to others, promoting a positive environment that blocks off the chances for bad actions and increases opportunities for a way of life and practice that lead to higher levels of virtue.

2. *Adhicittasikkhā* is the training of the quality and efficiency of the mind. It combines the three factors of the path known as right effort, right mindfulness, and right concentration. In essence, it is training the mind to be strong, stable, undivided, well-controlled, concentrated, and energized so that it is most fit for work—in particular, the work of utilizing profound wisdom in accordance with the truth.

3. *Adhipaññāsikkhā* is the training of wisdom to bring about comprehension of all things as they really are, leading ultimately to liberation. This combines the first two factors of the path: right view and right thought. In essence, it is the training and cultivation of the pure wisdom that knows clearly in accordance with reality. It is not knowledge or thought that is distorted, blinding, tainted, or obscured through the influence of the defilements, led by ignorance and desire. This training of wisdom must be based on a prior development of mental firmness and clarity. Once the pure wisdom that understands the truth arises, it in turn helps the mind to become more firmly peaceful, pure, and clear, and it has an effect on everyday conduct, leading to a correct outlook, attitude, and relationship with things. One's wisdom is used purely and is not biased or permeated with defilements. One examines and deals with problems and performs one's tasks in a way that leads to real benefit and happiness.

To put it into the modern academic terminology of Western educational research, *adhisīlasikkhā*, *adhicittasikkhā*, and *adhipaññāsikkhā* constitute social development, emotional development, and intellectual development, respectively. They differ only in the extent of their meanings, and in that the threefold training has a clearly Buddhist objective. However, at least initially, we can see that they are quite compatible: they both state fundamentally the same thing, in pointing out the necessity of training the individual to have discipline (*vinaya*) (including personal responsibility and wholesome social relations), to grow emotionally (the Buddhist teaching would say to make the mind strong and subtle, so that it has good quality and efficiency), and to grow in terms of intelligence.

The factors of this threefold training are contiguous and mutually enhancing. According to the modern principles of human development, it cannot be denied, for example, that rational knowledge will naturally support emotional development and promote an observance of discipline, as well as personal responsibility and social relationships. Thus, training in the threefold training, or the three kinds of development, must proceed in unison.

In summary, the threefold training is a graded system of training from the outside inward, from the coarser level to the finer, and from the simple to the complex and profound. In the beginning, training depends on only a small amount of the right view or correct understanding, known as *sammādiṭṭhi*, to act as a spark or serve as a rough outline, sufficient to know where one is going, where the path lies, and where to begin. Understanding the problem and looking on one's life and the world as they really are is the proper starting point and is the fundamental meaning of right view.

During the actual training, practice on the coarse external level of morality serves as the foundation for the more subtle inner practice, preparing and priming the practitioner to train the mind and wisdom more effectively. When the subtle, inner levels of meditation and wisdom have been developed, they in turn help to support external life conduct, to have, for example, stable good conduct and morality that is natural and automatic, no longer requiring force or a dedicated effort to observe, or to be able to examine and solve problems and perform one's tasks with pure wisdom, as already discussed. When the threefold training has been developed in full, one's entire way of life becomes the path, harmonious on both the internal and external levels.

The Buddhist Way to Solve Problems

It is sometimes stated that Buddhism teaches the resolving of all problems, even economic and social ones, in the mind. This would not seem to be an adequate or effective solution. To respond to this, we must reach an understanding on two fronts: (1) in terms of principles and (2) in terms of the teaching's emphasis.

In terms of principles, the Buddhist way to solve problems has two important characteristics. First, it solves problems at their determinants; and second, it solves human problems through human means. Incorporating both of these characteristics, it can be defined as solving human problems through human means that accord with their determinants. The phrase "accord with their determinants," is said very generally, referring to neither exclusively external nor exclusively internal determinants. The phrase "addressing human problems through human means" is based in the Buddha's pointing out that human beings should look at their problems within themselves; not looking for the causes and solutions in the sky or placing it all on luck, but solving problems through personal, rational effort.

In terms of the teaching's emphasis, or the relative proportion of the teaching, it must be first stressed that Buddhism teaches the solution of all problems, both internal and external, both social and within the individual mind. There are teachings on morality, which is external, and also on the level of the mind and wisdom, which are internal. Then it must be further understood that in terms of the emphasis in the teachings that do exist, of the teachings recorded in the texts, the portion dealing with solving internal problems, in the mind, is greater than the portion of teachings dealing with solving external problems or social problems. In other words, the teachings emphasize solving mental problems more than social or other kinds of external problems. That this is so is reasonable and proper. Here are some reasons why.

Because of the Consistency of Human Nature

Problems of the inner life or mind are matters that concern human nature more than anything else. People in all locations and all times have the same nature of mental problems. Even though they may live in different societies or in different ages, the nature of their minds remains the same. Human beings will always be human beings, subject to greed, aversion, and delusion, loving happiness and hating suffering.

External problems concerning society, on the other hand, are in part due to human nature—as long as one is a human being one will have this nature—but are also due to other factors specific to the environment, the particulars of which vary greatly from place to place and time to time. Because of this truth, it is only natural and fitting that the Buddha taught fundamentally about solving inner problems concerning the mind and wisdom, and his teachings on this subject were numerous. As for dealing with external problems, the teachings on the level of morality consisted only of general principles based on human nature, such as prescriptions about not violating the physical being, wealth, or possessions of others through body and speech and about helping each other. The practical details of these moral guidelines may differ according to time and place. It is up to those people who understand the general principles to determine standards and methods for solving the problems in accordance with those principles, rather than laying down fixed precepts for all people in all situations.

There is, in fact, a practical precedent of the Buddha proclaiming a specific system for solving problems externally—that is, for a community—and that system was for the community or Saṅgha of bhikkhus that he himself founded. The Buddha laid down the bhikkhus' Vinaya, a system for solving external problems of a social nature, in great detail, in accordance with the specific objectives of the Saṅgha community as appropriate for the well-being of the Saṅgha within the situation of that particular locality and time. Modern students of Buddhism tend to overlook the Vinaya, but by understanding the essence of Vinaya it is possible to understand the Buddhist approach to solving external problems in society. Without studying the Vinaya Piṭaka (in particular, that part which lies outside the Pāṭimokkha), it is not possible to understand Buddhist social thought.

It is not reasonable to expect the Buddha to have set down a detailed system of practice for other communities without consideration of the variables of time and place. But by understanding the essence of the principles, it is possible to organize a system for solving problems and dealing with the various concerns of society of a particular time and place. An example is the reign of Emperor Asoka. When he instituted the policy of "victory by righteousness" (*dhammavijaya*) in his empire, it was not necessary for him to make any changes at all to the teachings on inner problems of the mind and wisdom, only to promote the propagation of the true teachings through methods that were appropriate to the time and place.

However, in relation to external, social matters, Asoka took only the general principles of the teaching, which he used as his fundamental antecedents, and from there devised a new system of procedures and methods of administration and implementation appropriate for that time.

In present-day Thailand, the tradition of royal administration is based on the Buddha's teachings on the duties and virtues of kings: the ten royal precepts (*dasabidharājadhamma*), the twelve tenets of a universal emperor (*cakkavattivatta*), the four bases for royal benefaction (*rājasaṅgahavatthu*), and the five powers of a king are the established principles, which are interpreted in terms of time and place. The system of civil administration is organized in accordance with each particular time and place.

Buddhism's Field of Expertise

The solving of external or social problems is not only subject to environmental factors, which vary with time and place, but is also dealt with by other fields and systems. Conversely, internal problems of the mind and wisdom are given less attention by the arts and sciences. Buddhism sees these problems as requiring earnest attention, even more so since other disciplines fail to give them the attention they deserve. It is also the field in which Buddhism is especially proficient.

Buddhism's Profundity and Difficulty, and the Real Core of Life

The problems of the mind and wisdom are profound and subtle, much harder to understand than external problems. If it took one hour to explain and analyze an external problem, it may take ten hours to explain one on the level of the mind, and even then, there would have to be much reiteration and clarification. It is therefore natural that teachings that deal with internal problems will have to be of higher proportion than those dealing with external problems. Moreover, the Buddha held that mental and intellectual benefit is the true core of human life. Being born into this world we must strive to achieve those benefits and not allow our lives to pass in vain. In addition, people tend not to see these kinds of problems, and therefore it is natural that the Buddha would emphasize them. As for external benefits, most people are already striving for these, so there is little need for further encouragement.

Buddhism and the Interconnection between All Facets of Life

All human problems, whether internal or external, have an effect on each other, and in solving a problem, be it external or internal, all aspects of humanity must be involved. This is particularly so when we consider that the internal life is our base, the deep-seated foundation, which has enormous influence on the way external problems are dealt with. For example, if the mind is deluded and heedless, it does not see problems as they really are. When the streams of thought and wisdom are dominated by the influence of ignorance, or distorted by desire, conceit, and views, they are biased and cannot examine problems properly. Problems are not only dealt with wrongly but are sometimes even aggravated or increased. Therefore, cleansing the mind and making wisdom pure, undistorted, and unbiased are necessary prerequisites for effectively dealing with problems of all kinds, both internal and external, in all times and in all places. If people cannot solve problems on this level, there is no way that problems on the social or external level can be resolved successfully. When the fundamental problems on the level of the mind and wisdom are solved, problems on all levels become easier to deal with, and human beings will be much better equipped to solve problems. Buddhism emphasizes the solving of problems on the fundamental level—that is, the level of the mind and wisdom.

Buddhism and the Disparity of Levels of Lifestyle

Buddhism recognizes that society is made up of individuals with different levels of mental and intellectual development. Furthermore, there are subsocieties or communities nestled within each society, which give the opportunity for those who volunteer to enter them to live different kinds of lifestyles. For example, there is the community of laypeople and the community of monastics. Life in lay society emphasizes social interaction and working for a living. Life in the monastic community emphasizes a focus on the mind and on intellectual understanding. Looking at monastic society, even though it does possess a discipline that addresses problems from the social perspective, in comparison with lay society, monastacism gives more emphasis to the mental and intellectual perspective and less emphasis to external concerns. In this respect, it is a mistake to cite the teachings for bhikkhus as the standard for gauging Buddhism's teachings on solving problems.

Buddhism and the Nature of All Beings

Buddhism sees humans as beings that can be developed and trained, and naturally at any given time human beings are at different levels of development physically, socially, mentally, and intellectually. Therefore, what they desire in life differs, materially and mentally, including their desires for happiness.

This truth of disparity must be accepted, as also must the societies and the world containing these people with their disparate levels of development. Stubbornly expecting the people of the world or society all to live in exactly the same way is not correct, is not useful for anyone, and cannot come to pass.

Those in positions of responsibility must organize material things, society, and intellectual life so as to be appropriate and helpful in answering to the needs of people of different levels of development, fairly and in sufficiency such that those people can live together happily. At the same time, what cannot be neglected in responding to the needs of humanity, since they are beings that can be trained, is that life, society, and the world should be organized in a way that aids and inspires the development of all, in order to give them the chance to attain the highest goal of life development, culminating in the fully developed mind and wisdom. If all of this is present, that is consistent with the Buddhist teaching.

Buddhism's Emphasis on Solving through Determinants

Finally, we return to the principle that Buddhism teaches the human resolution of human problems in accordance with determinants. This is spoken in a general sense, specifying neither internal nor external problems. It should be repeated that the sciences and the arts tend to emphasize the resolution of problems solely on the external level, totally overlooking the resolution of problems internally, which must be counted as an incomplete resolution of problems.

The Buddhist way to solve problems is neither exclusively internal nor exclusively external, but from the internal outward, meaning that problems should not be solved only internally, but also externally—that is, solved completely, solved at determinants, be they internal or external.

The Main Value of the Noble Truths

The teaching of the noble truths not only encompasses all of the teachings of Buddhism, both theoretical and practical, but also has many outstanding benefits that are worthy of note, which may be summarized as follows:

1. It is a method based on wisdom, in which problems are solved according to a rational system. It is the prototypical method for solving problems: any method of solving problems that is to be effective and reasonable must follow this approach.
2. It is a method of solving problems and organizing life through human intelligence, by utilizing the truths that naturally exist, without having to resort to intervention from any higher or supernatural power or occult force.
3. It contains truths that concern the lives of all people. No matter how far people may stray, and no matter how remote and broad the things they deal with, if they are to conduct a worthwhile life and effectively deal with those external things, they will always have to deal with and utilize these truths.
4. They are neutral truths that are contingent on life or deal with life itself. No matter how much in the way of the arts and sciences humanity may create, or whatever undertakings they engage in for addressing problems and improving the quality of life, and no matter how those arts and sciences or undertakings may prosper, decline, disappear, or be replaced, the teaching of the noble truths is constant, always new and always applicable.

Summarizing *Buddhadhamma* into the Noble Truths

While the content and structure of this book may seem different in many parts and in many ways from existing Buddhist literature, in effect it follows the original principle used by the Buddha to present his teachings: the four noble truths. To show how this is so, I have arranged the content of the book into the four noble truths, as follows.

Book One: The Middle Teaching
Truth One: Suffering
Part One, Chapter 1: What Is Life? The Five *Khandhas* and the Six Sense Bases
Part Two, Chapter 2: What Is Life Like? The Three Characteristics
Truth Two: The Cause of Suffering
Part Three, Chapter 3: How Does Life Work? *Paṭiccasamuppāda*
Part Three, Chapter 4: How Does Life Work? *Kamma*
Truth Three: The Cessation of Suffering
Part Four, Chapter 5: How Should Life Be? *Nibbāna*

Book Two: The Middle Way
Truth Four: The Way Leading to the Cessation of Suffering
Part Five, Chapter 6: How Should Life Be Lived? Introduction to the Middle Way
Part Five, Chapter 7: How Should Life Be Lived? The Precursors of Learning
Part Five, Chapter 8: How Should Life Be Lived? The Wisdom Factors of the Middle Way
Part Five, Chapter 9: How Should Life Be Lived? The Morality Factors of the Middle Way
Part Five, Chapter 10: How Should Life Be Lived? The Concentration Factors of the Middle Way

Those parts of the book that seem unfamiliar, such as discussions of *paratoghosa*, *kalyāṇamitta*, and *yoniso-manasikāra*, and the various unfamiliar perspectives given on those teachings that are already well known and that are given special treatment in this book, even though they may be little mentioned in other Dhamma books, should be understood as occurring frequently in the Tipiṭaka, but in certain times and situations there is no reason to give them particular emphasis and therefore they have faded and become unfamiliar. The reason they are included in this book is that it is considered the appropriate time to give them special attention. Similarly, some readers may notice that some subjects or perspectives of the teachings that have elsewhere been given special emphasis are not points of emphasis in this book. However that may be, the author is confident that the relative proportions given to different subjects and perspectives on the teachings in this book are very close to the proportions given to them in the Pali canon, the Tipiṭaka, which is the source material of the original teaching.

Glossary

This brief glossary contains only those Pali terms that are used frequently in the book, sometimes without definition. All other Pali terms in the text are translated as they appear. The definitions provided here are not comprehensive and are meant to serve merely as a quick reference.

Abhidhamma: The third "basket" of the Pali Tipiṭaka, containing the "higher teachings" of Buddhism and generally regarded as a later addition to the Pali canon.
akusala: Unskillful, unwholesome.
anatta: Not-self.
anicca: Impermanent, impermanence.
appamāda: Heedfulness.
ārammaṇa: Mental object.
ariyasacca: Noble truth.
avijjā: Ignorance.

bhāvanā: (Mental) cultivation, meditation.
bhikkhu: A Buddhist monk.
bhikkhuni: A female Buddhist monk.
bojjhaṅga: The (seven) enlightenment factors.
brahma: A god.
brahmacariya: The holy life, or higher life.
brahmin: A member of the highest caste.
Buddha: The historical Buddha; the first arm of the Triple Gem.
Buddhadhamma: The teaching of the Buddha.
Buddhavacana: "Words of the Buddha," quotes attributed to the Buddha from the Tipiṭaka.

cittānupassanā: Mindfulness of the mind or mental objects.
commentaries: Secondary texts of the Pali canon consisting of the Aṭṭhakathā and Ṭīkā collections.

deva: A celestial being.
Dhamma: The Buddha's teaching; the second arm of the Triple Gem.
dhamma(s): Thing(s).
dukkha: Suffering, stress, unsatisfactoriness.

idappaccayatā: The principle of conditionality.

jhāna(s): Absorption, the state of absolutely firm concentration.

kalyāṇamitta: A good friend.
kasiṇa(s): Objects used for developing concentration, such as a colored disk.
khandha(s): The five groups that make up existence: form, feeling, perception, volitional formations, and consciousness.
kilesa: (Mental) stain, defilement.
kusala: Skillful, wholesome.

magga: The path, more specifically the noble eightfold path.
Māra: The Evil One, similar to Satan, a personification of evil.

nimitta(s): "Signs," images that arise in meditation practice.

Pali: The language believed to have been spoken at the time of the Buddha, and the language used to preserve the Theravada Tipiṭaka.
paññā: Wisdom.
paratoghosa: "Sounds from outside"; external influences, more specifically the influence of the good friend.
paṭiccasamuppāda: The principle of dependent arising.
Pāṭimokkha: The Buddhist monastic code, traditionally recited every fortnight in Buddhist monasteries.
puthujjana: An ordinary unenlightened person.

rūpa: The body, form.

saddhā: Faith, belief.
samādhi: Concentration, meditation.
samaṇa: A recluse, a wandering ascetic.
samatha: Calm, calm meditation (as opposed to insight meditation).
saṁsāravaṭṭa: The wheel of rebirth.
saṁyojana: The (ten) fetters.
Saṅgha: The Buddhist monastic order, or the "order" of persons who have attained at least the first stage of enlightenment, stream entry; the third arm of the Triple Gem.

saṅkhāra(s): Formations, all things formed from determinants, which means all things apart from *nibbāna*.
saññā: Perception.
sati: Mindfulness.
sīla: Morality, virtue.
sīlabbataparāmāsa: Blind grasping at rites and observances.
sutta: The teachings of the Buddha as recorded in the Sutta Piṭaka.

Tathāgata: The "Thus Gone One," an epithet of the Buddha.
Tipiṭaka: The Three Baskets, the collected scriptures of the Buddha, consisting of the Vinaya Piṭaka (monastic code), the Sutta Piṭaka (recorded teachings of the Buddha and disciples), and the Abhidhamma Piṭaka (the "higher teachings," a collection of later philosophical works).
Triple Gem: The Buddha, the Dhamma, and the Saṅgha.

vedanā: Feeling.
Vinaya: The Buddhist monastic discipline; also *vinaya*, meaning discipline in general.
viññāṇa: Consciousness.
vipassanā: Insight, insight meditation.
yoniso-manasikāra: Wise attention.

Abbreviations of Sources

Unless otherwise indicated in the text, all references are to the Pali language versions of the Pali Tipiṭaka and commentaries, published by the Pali Text Society.

A.	Aṅguttaranikāya (5 vols.)
AA.	Aṅguttaranikāya Aṭṭhakathā (also known by the title *Manorathapūraṇī*)
Ap.	Apadāna (from the Khuddakanikāya)
ApA.	Apadāna Aṭṭhakathā (also known by the title *Visuddhajanavilāsinī*)
Bv.	Buddhavaṁsa (from the Khuddakanikāya)
BvA.	Buddhavaṁsa Aṭṭhakathā (also known by the title *Madhuratthavilāsinī*)
Comp.	Compendium of Philosophy (*Abhidhammaṭṭhasaṅgaha*)
CompṬ.	Abhidhammaṭṭhasaṅgaha Ṭīkā (also known by the title *Abhidhammatthavibhāvinī*)
Cp.	Cariyāpiṭaka (from the Khuddakanikāya)
CpA.	Cariyāpiṭaka Aṭṭhakathā (from the *Paramatthadīpanī*)
D.	Dīghanikāya (3 vols.)
DA.	Dīghanikāya Aṭṭhakathā (also known by the title *Sumaṅgalavilāsinī*)
DAṬ.	Dīghanikāya Aṭṭhakathā Ṭīkā (also known by the title *Līnatthapakāsinī*)
Dh.	Dhammapada (from the Khuddakanikāya)
DhA.	Dhammapada Aṭṭhakathā
Dhtk.	Dhātukathā (from the Abhidhamma)
DhtkA.	Dhātukathā Aṭṭhakathā (from the *Paramatthadīpanī*)
Dhs.	Dhammasaṅganī (from the Abhidhamma)
DhsA.	Dhammasaṅganī Aṭṭhakathā (also known by the title Aṭṭhasālinī)
It.	Itivuttaka (from the Khuddakanikāya)
ItA.	Itivuttaka Aṭṭhakathā (from the *Paramatthadīpanī*)
J.	Jātaka
JA.	Jātaka Aṭṭhakathā
Kh.	Khuddakapāṭha (from the Khuddakanikāya)
KhA.	Khuddakapāṭha Aṭṭhakathā (from the *Paramatthajotikā*)

Kvu.	Kathāvatthu (from the Abhidhamma)
KvuA.	Kathāvatthu Aṭṭhakathā (from the *Paramatthadīpanī*)
M.	Majjhima Nikāya (3 vols.)
MA.	Majjhima Nikāya Aṭṭhakathā (also known by the title *Papañcasudanī*)
Miln.	*Milindapañha*
Nd. I	Mahāniddesa (from the Khuddakanikāya)
Nd. II	Cūḷaniddesa (from the Khuddakanikāya)
Nd1A.	Niddesa Aṭṭhakathā—Mahāniddesavaṇṇanā (also known by the title *Saddhamapajjotikā*)
Nd2A.	Niddesa Aṭṭhakathā—Cūḷaniddesavaṇṇanā (also known by the title *Saddhamapajjotikā*)
Nett.	Nettipakaraṇa
NettA.	Nettipakaraṇa Aṭṭhakathā
PañcA.	Pañcapakaraṇa Aṭṭhakathā
Paṭ.	Paṭṭhāna (from the Abhidhamma)
PatA.	Paṭṭhāna Aṭṭhakathā (known by the title *Paramatthadīpanī*)
Ps.	Paṭisambhidāmagga (from the Khuddakanikāya)
PsA.	Paṭisambhidāmagga Aṭṭhakathā (also known by the title *Saddhammapakāsinī*)
Ptk.	Peṭakopadesa
Pug.	Puggalapaññatti (from the Abhidhamma)
PugA.	Puggalapaññatti Aṭṭhakathā (from the *Paramatthadīpanī*)
Pv.	Petavatthu (from the Khuddakanikāya)
PvA.	Petavatthu Aṭṭhakathā (from the *Paramatthadīpanī*)
S.	Saṁyutta Nikāya (5 vols.)
SA.	Saṁyutta Nikāya Aṭṭhakathā (also known by the title *Saratthapakāsinī*)
Sn.	Suttanipāta (from the Khuddakanikāya)
SnA.	Suttanipāta Aṭṭhakathā (from the *Paramatthajotikā*)
Thag.	Theragāthā (from the Khuddakanikāya)
ThagA.	Theragāthā Aṭṭhakathā (from the *Paramatthadīpanī*)
Thig.	Therīgāthā (Khuddakanikāya)
ThigA.	Therīgāthā Aṭṭhakathā (from the *Paramatthadīpanī*)
Ud.	Udāna (from the Khuddakanikāya)
UdA.	Udāna Aṭṭhakathā (from the *Paramatthadīpanī*)
Vbh.	Vibhaṅga (from the Abhidhamma)
VbhA.	Vibhaṅga Aṭṭhakathā (also known by the title *Sammohavinodanī*)
Vin.	Vinaya Piṭaka (5 vols.)
VinA.	Vinaya Aṭṭhakathā (also known by the title *Samantapāsādikā*)
VinṬ.	Vinaya Aṭṭhakathā Ṭīkā (also known by the title *Saratthadīpanī*)
Vism.	Visuddhimagga
VismṬ.	Visuddhimagga Mahāṭīkā (also known by the title *Paramatthamañjusā*)

Vv.	Vimānavatthu (from the Khuddakanikāya)
VvA.	Vimānavatthu Aṭṭhakathā (from the *Paramatthadīpanī*)
Yam.	Yamaka (from the Abhidhamma)
YamA.	Yamaka Aṭṭhakathā (from the *Paramatthadīpanī*)

Notes

Introduction

1. The original version of this book was written in much shorter form in response to an invitation to compile the Buddhist teachings as part of a collection of works on philosophy.
2. See for example *Vāseṭṭha Sutta* (Sn. 115-16) and *Brahmaṇadhammika Sutta* (Sn. 52-55).
3. According to the Pali canon, the teachings of these recluses and brahmins could be divided into sixty-two different views or theories (D. I. 13-45).
4. For a description of the situation in Jambudvīpa at this time, see G. C. Pande, *Studies in the Origins of Buddhism* (Allahabad: University of Allahabad, 1957), 310-68.
5. For this portion of the Buddha's life, see, e.g. *Sagārava Sutta* (M. II. 209-13).
6. Vin. I. 20-1.
7. See *Pāsādika Sutta* (D. III. 122-25). Note that the meaning of "holy life" includes householders.
8. As in A. I. 286-87.
9. As in S. V. 386.
10. See for example A. IV. 202-3; D. III. 97-98.
11. See for example P. V. Bapat, *2,500 Years of Buddhism* (Delhi: Ministry of Information and Broadcasting, 1959), 355, and Sukumar Dutt, *Buddhist Monks and Monasteries of India* (London: Allen & Unwin, 1962), 210.
12. See Vin. II. 139.
13. See for example A. V. 193-98; M. I. 426-32.
14. See A. IV. 41; A. V. 190-91; Sn. 51-3; see also the following sections.
15. See the sequence of teaching at MA. II. 219 (explaining M. I. 184-91).

Chapter 1. The Five *Khandhas* and the Six Sense Bases

1. S. I. 135.
2. A very broad analysis is into mind (*nāma*) and matter (*rūpa*), or the mental

(*nāmadhamma*) and the physical (*rūpadhamma*), but in the Abhidhamma the preferred analysis is into three: mind (*citta*), mental concomitants (*cetasika*), and matter (*rūpa*). According to the Abhidhamma analysis, the five *khandhas* discussed here can be grouped thus: *citta* = *viññāṇa-khandha*; *cetasika* = *vedanā- saññā-*, and *saṅkhārakhandha*; *rūpa* = *rūpa khandha*.

3. In terms of the Abhidhamma, *rūpa* is analyzed into twenty-eight categories: four *mahābhūtarūpa* (great elements; simply called the four *dhātu*, elements) and twenty-four *upādāyarūpa* (dependent forms or forms derived from the four great elements).
4. The three kinds of *vedanā* are *sukha* (pleasant, either bodily or mental), *dukkha* (unpleasant, either bodily or mental), and *adukkhamasukha* (neither pleasant nor unpleasant, indifferent; sometimes called *upekkhā*). *Vedanā* can also be divided into five kinds—*sukha* (pleasant bodily feeling), *dukkha* (unpleasant bodily feeling), *somanassa* (pleasant mental feeling), *domanassa* (unpleasant mental feeling), and *upekkhā* (neutral feeling)—and six kinds according to the sources of its arising, through eye, ear, nose, tongue, body, and mind.
5. *Saññā* is divided into six kinds according to the sense door through which consciousness arises: through the eye, ear, nose, tongue, body, and mind.
6. *Saṅkhāra*: according to the Abhidhamma, mental concomitants (*cetasika*) are divided into fifty-two kinds. In terms of the classification of the five *khandhas*, the *cetasika* correspond to all *vedanā*, *saññā*, and *saṅkhārā*. *Vedanā* and *saññā* are two of these *cetasika*. The remaining fifty are all *saṅkhārā*. Thus, the *saṅkhārakhandha* is equal to fifty *cetasika*.
7. *Upekkhā* is an important quality and is often misunderstood, so it is worthy of close attention. We should be able to distinguish between *upekkhā* as one of the *saṅkhārakhandha*, which corresponds with *tatramajjhattatā* (equanimity or equilibrium) and *upekkhā* in the *vedanā-khandha*, which corresponds with *adukkhamasukha*, indifferent feeling. This will be discussed in detail later.
8. *Viññāṇa* is divided into six according to the channels of its arising: *cakkhuviññāṇa* (eye consciousness), *sotaviññāṇa* (ear consciousness), *ghānaviññāṇa* (nose consciousness), *jivhāviññāṇa* (tongue consciousness), *kāyaviññāṇa* (body consciousness), and *manoviññāṇa* (mind consciousness). According to the Abhidhamma, all kinds of *viññāṇa khandha* are called *citta*, and are divided into 89 or 121 kinds.
9. The explanations that follow are based on the Pali canon (Tipiṭaka) and commentaries (Aṭṭhakathā), especially M. I. 292–93; S. III. 87; MA. II. 462; SA. II. 291; Vism. 436, 452–53.
10. The commentaries describe the characteristics, functions, and so on of

saññā thus: it has the characteristic of *sañjānana* (recognizing); it has the task of marking an object of consciousness, becoming a condition for future remembering that "this is that," just as a carpenter marks timber; it has the manifestation of regarding the object in terms of the quality so given, like the blind men groping the elephant; and it has as its proximate cause the object as it appears to the perceiver, just as when a fawn sees a scarecrow and perceives it as a person (Vism. 462).

11. See the section on dependent arising in chapter 3.
12. *Vedanā* is classified as *vipāka*, resultant condition, and is thus neither good nor evil in itself (see the chapter on dependent arising).
13. According to the teaching of the three *vaṭṭa*, or cycles of *saṁsāra* (in the *paṭiccasamuppāda*), *vedanā*, *saññā*, and *viññāṇa* are *kamma* results (*vipāka*), while *saṅkhāra* is *kamma*. However, *saṅkhāra* is classified as *kamma* only when it is led by intention into active function. On the other hand, *saṅkhāra* as mind conditioner (such as greed, hatred, and delusion) is regarded as *kilesa*, or defilement.
14. A. I. 24–25.
15. M. I. 111–12. The full process referred to in this passage is given in the section on the six sense bases.
16. In the Visuddhimagga, these analogies are given: *rūpa* is like a dish, *vedanā* is food, *saññā* is the condiments, *saṅkhāra* is the cook, and *viññāṇa* is the eater of the food; *rūpa* is like a prison, *vedanā* the punishment, *saññā* the form of punishment, *saṅkhāra* the punisher, and *viññāṇa* the prisoner. Vism. 479; also CompṬ. (Samuccayaparicchedavaṇṇanā, Sabbasaṅgahavaṇṇanā).
17. M. III. 203.
18. Sn. 118–19.
19. E.g., Vin. I. 10.
20. S. III. 47–48.
21. S. III. 167.
22. Note the Buddhavacana: "Bhikkhus! It would be better for an unlearned one to adhere to the body containing the four great elements (earth, water, wind, and fire) as being the self, rather than to adhere to the mind. The body made up of the four elements can be seen to exist for two years; three, four, five years; ten, twenty, thirty, forty, or fifty years; or even one hundred years or more—but the condition known as 'mind,' or consciousness, is constantly arising and ceasing, day and night" (S. II. 94–95).
23. See S. III. 3–5, 16–18, 110–15, and so on.
24. D. III. 243–44.
25. The preferred term is *dhammārammaṇa*, to avoid confusion with *dhamma* as it is generally used, which has a very broad range of meanings.

26. M. I. 258–59.
27. M. I. 190.
28. The six feelings are as follows: (1) *cakkhusamphassajā vedanā*, feelings arising from visual contact; (2) *sotasamphassajā vedanā*, feelings arising from auditory contact; (3) *ghānasamphassajā vedanā*, feelings arising from olfactory contact; (4) *jivhāsamphassajā vedanā*, feelings arising from gustatory contact; (5) *kāyasamphassajā vedanā*, feelings arising from tactile contact; (6) *manosamphassajā vedanā*, feelings arising from mental contact. S. IV. 232.
29. The meaning of *upekkhā* as a kind of *vedanā* here differs from its meaning in the sense of a *saṅkhāra*, as in *upekkhā* as a divine abiding (*brahmavihāra*) or as an enlightenment factor (*sambojjhaṅga*).
30. In full, *papañcasaññā saṅkhā*.
31. M. I. 111–12.
32. See D. II. 277–78.
33. The idea of two truths or realities (*sacca*) was first expressed in the Kathāvatthu, though not specifically in those words. Reference is made to *sammatisacca* in Kvu. 311 and to *sacchikatthaparamattha* and *paramattha* in Kvu. 1–69. Clear reference (to the two levels of reality) is made in PañcA. 12, 84. There are also many references to the subject and mention of it in explaining other topics, such as MA. I. 217 = SA. II. 13; DhA. III. 403; [Saṅganī Mūlaṭīkā 165, 280]; [Saṅganī Anuṭīkā 328]; VismṬ. (Brahmavihāraniddesavaṇṇanā, Pakiṇṇakakathāvaṇṇanā); UdA. 396; and CompṬ. (Paccayaparicchedavaṇṇanā, Paññattibhedavaṇṇanā)
34. S. I. 135; cited in Kvu. 86–87.
35. S. I. 14.
36. D. I. 202.
37. VinA. I. 21; DA. I. 19; DhsA. 21, 56; MA. I. 217 = SA. 13.
38. A. II. 52; Ps. II. 80. *Vipallāsa* is called in the Abhidhamma *vipariyesa* (Vbh. 376); indications in the suttas at S. I. 188–89. See also SA. I. 271; Nd1A. I. 163; DhsA. 253. VinṬ. (Dutiyapārājikaṁ, Verañjakaṇḍavaṇṇanā) states that these three kinds of *vipallāsa* are arranged in order of intensity.
39. See chapter 7, "The Precursors of Learning."
40. S. IV. 15.
41. S. IV. 39–40.
42. S. IV. 95.
43. S. IV. 87.
44. S. IV. 38–39.
45. S. IV. 123–24.
46. S. IV. 195–96.
47. S. IV. 70.

48. S. IV. 162–65.
49. S. IV. 119–20; elsewhere it is written: "What is lack of restraint? What is restraint?" The answer is the same as given above (S. IV. 198–200).
50. A. I. 258–86.
51. M. III. 288–89.
52. In terms of biased or distorted knowledge and ideas, *indriyabhāvanā* provides safety from new causes, not causes already accumulated—i.e., *taṇhā*, *māna*, and *diṭṭhi*, which are already there; this is another stage of the process.

Chapter 2. The Three Characteristics: The Natural Characteristics of All Things

1. A. I. 286.
2. S. III. 66–68.
3. See Dhs. II. 193; DhA. III. 128. *Saṅkhatadhamma* is defined in the Abhidhamma as skillful conditions in the four realms, unskillful conditions and results in the four realms, neutral actions (*kiriyā*) in the three realms, and all material things.
4. A. I. 152.
5. Vin. VI. (Parivāra) 86. In the commentaries, it is said that "the deathless (*amatapata= nibbāna*) is empty of self" (*attasuññamapadaṁ*; Vism. 513) and "*nibbāna* is empty of self, because there is no self" (*nibbānadhammo attassave abhāvato attasuñño*; PsA. III. 638–39).
6. Vism. 640; VbhA. 50; VismṬ. Paṭipadañāṇadassanavisuddhiniddesavaṇṇanā.
7. Ps. I. 37; referred to at Vism. 610.
8. Vism. 611.
9. As in Vism. 628.
10. Vism. 640.
11. Vism. 618; MA. II. 113; VbhA. 48; VismṬ. (Maggāmaggañāṇadassanavisuddhiniddesavaṇṇanā and Rūpasattakasammasanakathāvaṇṇanā) state that these four reasons apply only to the nature of physical conditions, but in the Vibhaṅga commentary it is shown that it can be used with all kinds of *saṅkhārā*; see also VinṬ. (Mahākhandhakaṁ and Anattalakkhaṇasuttavaṇṇanā).
12. Ps. I. 37; referred to at Vism. 610.
13. Vism. 628.
14. Vism. 611.
15. VismṬ. Maggāmaggañāṇadassanavisuddhiniddesavaṇṇanā, Cattārisākāra Anupassanakathāvaṇṇanā.
16. Vism. 611.

17. As in Vism. 502.
18. Vism. 618; MA. II. 113 (the first one is *santāpa*); VbhA. 48.
19. See the explanation of the three *dukkhatā* on page 77.
20. As in VinṬ. Mahākhandhakaṁ, Anattalakkhaṇasuttavaṇṇanā; VismṬ. Maggāmaggañāṇadassanavisuddhiniddesavaṇṇanā (Cattārisākāra Anupassanakathāvaṇṇanā and Rūpasattakasammasanakathāvaṇṇanā).
21. Ps. I. 19; Ps. II. 108; referred to at Vism. 494; VbhA. 83. At MA. II. 113 *santāpa* is placed first among these four definitions.
22. This is the author's definition; for commentarial definitions see PsA. I. 100, 102; VismṬ. Indriyasaccaniddesavaṇṇanā, Saccavitthārakathāvaṇṇanā.
23. Important source materials are Yam. I. 174–75; PañcA. 167; Vism. 510–13; VismṬ. Indriyasaccaniddesavaṇṇanā, Magganiddesakathāvaṇṇanā.
24. D. III. 216; S. IV. 259; S. V. 56; Vism. 499; VbhA. 93; VinṬ. Dhammacakkappavattanasuttavaṇṇanā; VismṬ. Indriyasaccaniddesavaṇṇanā, Dukkhaniddesakathāvaṇṇanā.
25. As in D. II. 305; S. V. 421; Vism. 498-501; VismṬ. Indriyasaccaniddesavaṇṇanā (from Saccavitthārakathāvaṇṇanā to Pañcupādānakkhandhaniddesavaṇṇanā). The various ways in which birth is said to be suffering, listed under item 1 (*jāti*), are from the commentaries.
26. Note that sickness (*byādhi*), which normally follows from aging, is not included in this list. This is because sickness is an uncertain kind of suffering; many people may have it, but some don't, and in any case it can be included in bodily suffering (VismṬ. Indriyasaccaniddesavaṇṇanā, Saccavitthārakathāvaṇṇanā). However, in some textual references it seems that *byādhi* is included. In such cases, see the explanation at VinṬ. Dhammacakkappavattanasuttavaṇṇanā.
27. Vism. 499; VbhA. 93; PañcA. 167; VinṬ. Dhammacakkappavattanasuttavaṇṇanā; VismṬ. Indriyasaccaniddesavaṇṇanā, Dukkhaniddesakathāvaṇṇanā.
28. Vism. 499; VbhA. 93; PañcA. 167; VinṬ. Dhammacakkappavattanasuttavaṇṇanā; VismṬ. Indriyasaccaniddesavaṇṇanā, Dukkhaniddesakathāvaṇṇanā
29. M. I. 83–90, 91–95.
30. As in Vism. 531; VbhA. 145, 149. In some parts of the Thai-script Cūḷaniddesa, such as Nd. II. 7, there is *saṁsāra-dukkha*, but this is a misprint. It should read *saṅkhāradukkha*.
31. These three kinds of suffering are mentioned frequently in regard to the eight *saṁvegavatthu* (the subjects that prompt a sense of urgency), as in Vism. 135; DA. III. 795; MA. I. 298; SA. III. 163; *āhārapariyeṭṭhidukkha* (the suffering of searching for food or making a living) corresponds with *gabbhavipattimūlaka dukkha* above. The other kinds of suffering are included either directly or indirectly in those already mentioned.

32. Ps. I. 37, 53; Ps. II. 200; referred to at Vism. 610.
33. Vism. 610.
34. Vism. 628, 640.
35. Vism. 618; VinṬ. Mahākhandhakaṁ Anattalakkhaṇasuttavaṇṇanā.
36. VbhA. 49; VinṬ. Mahākhandhakaṁ Anattalakkhaṇasuttavaṇṇanā; refers to the Buddha's words in the *Anattalakkhaṇa Sutta*.
37. M. I. 190.
38. S. I. 135.
39. See Vism. 593–95.
40. Vism. 618; MA. II. 113; VbhA. 48. See also VinṬ. Mahākhandhakaṁ Anattalakkhaṇasuttavaṇṇanā; VismṬ. Maggāmaggañāṇadassanavisuddhiniddesavaṇṇanā, Rūpasattakasammasanakathāvaṇṇanā.
41. "Cogito, ergo sum": René Descartes, 1596–1650.
42. S. II. 13–14.
43. M. I. 8.
44. Vism. 595.
45. Vism. 513.
46. Vism. 602–3.
47. VismṬ. Paññabhūminiddesavaṇṇanā, Bhavacakkakathāvaṇṇanā.
48. As in S. IV. 1.
49. The Thai version of the Tipiṭaka uses *attā* and *nirattaṁ*, and in some places *attaṁ* and *nirattaṁ* (See Sn. 154, 168, 180; see also Sn. 157, 213). Other versions of the Tipiṭaka consistently use *attā* and *nirattā*.
50. See Nd. I. 82, 247, 352–53; see related passages at Nd. I. 90–91, 107–8; Nd. II. 35.
51. Sn. 180; explained at Nd. I. 352–53.
52. VbhA. 48–49; and some passages in MA. II. 113; VinṬ. Mahākhandhakaṁ, Anattalakkhaṇasuttavaṇṇanā.
53. Referring to M. III. 282.
54. Referring to S. III. 66.
55. As in S. III. 22.
56. D. II. 199; S. II. 193; spoken by others at D. II. 157; S. I. 6, 158; Ap. 385.
57. The Buddha's last words. D. II. 120, 156; S. I. 157–58. There are similar passages by Venerables Revata and Sāriputta at Thag. 67, 91.
58. S. II. 29; A. IV. 134–35.
59. S. I. 86–87; see also S. I. 89; A. III. 48–49; It. 16–17.
60. A. III. 253; see also D. II. 86; D. III. 236; Ud. 87.
61. A. I. 50.
62. *Kusalo dhammo akusalassa dhammassa ārammaṇapaccayena paccayo* (Paṭ. 154); *adhipatipaccayena* (Paṭ. 158); *upanissayapaccayena* (Paṭ. 166). See also full discussion on page 221.
63. S. V. 398.

64. In fact, the contemplation of each of the three chracteristics affects the others. Thus, contemplation of any of them may lead to liberation. However, the most important of the characteristics in this respect is not-self, as can be seen from the Buddha's statement: "Develop perception of impermanence (*aniccasaññā*) in order to uproot the conceit 'I am' (*asmimāna*). In fact, Meghiya, when there is perception of impermanence, perception of not-self will arise. One who has perception of not-self will be able to uproot the conceit 'I am' and attain *nibbāna* in the present moment." Ud. 37; see also A. IV. 353, 358).
65. M. III. 18-19.
66. D. II. 156.
67. As in S. III. 22.
68. S. III. 23-24 (translated in brief).
69. S. III. 114-15 (words of Venerable Sāriputta, translated in brief). The statements "not seeing form as self, not seeing self as having form, not seeing form in self, not seeing self in form" are rendered even more briefly in the Visuddhimagga: *na attā* (not-self), *na attano* (not belonging to self), *na attani* (not in the self), *na attavadī* (not having self). See Vism. 578. The Visuddhimagga (653-56) lists many different ways to contemplate not-self, such as seeing that form is not a being, a life, a *nara*, a *māṇava*; it is neither woman nor man, neither self nor connected to self; it is not us, not ours, not belonging to others; it belongs to no one—and so on.
70. S. III. 3-5 (spoken by Venerable Sāriputta).
71. S. III. 17-18.
72. S. III. 43.
73. M. I. 7-9; similar passages concerning the six views are at Vbh. 382.
74. S. III. 142-43.
75. Nd. I 44, 119-20 (occurs in part at D. II. 246; S. I. 108-9; Thag. 20).
76. S. I. 102.
77. Thag. verses 447-525 (words of Venerable Sirimaṇḍa Thera).
78. J. VI. 25-28.
79. J. III. 164-66.
80. A. III. 54-56, 60-62.
81. J. IV. 127.
82. Dh. verses 286-89.
83. Bv. 97-98.
84. S. II. 29; A. IV. 134-35.
85. Dh. verses 21 and 27.
86. A. V. 88.
87. Sn. 58.
88. Dh. verse 280.

89. Dh. verse 152.
90. Dh. verses 155–56.
91. J. V. 116 (two kinds of heedfulness: creating benefit and looking after it).
92. A. II. 249.
93. A. I. 50.
94. Dh. verses 271–72 (*nekkhamma sukha* is said by the commentators to be the happiness of a non-returner [*anāgāmī*].)
95. Translator's note: = the bhikkhus' training rules.
96. Vin. III. 8.
97. Vin. II. 283–84.
98. D. II. 73–79. It is said that the training requires noting all things as impermanent and of the nature to decline, but this passage states that if tasks are done with heedfulness there will be no declining, only prosperity—a perspective that should be borne in mind in order to maintain balanced practice. Note also that heedfulness in self-development should be maintained in conjunction with heedfulness in social development.

Chapter 3. *Paṭiccasamuppāda*: The Principle of Dependent Arising

1. Another name for the *paṭiccasamuppāda*. Literally, it means "the converging of conditions" or "the state in which such and such is condition." In the Abhidhamma the preferred term is *paccayākāra*, meaning "mode of conditionality."
2. S. II. 25.
3. M. I. 191.
4. S. II. 79.
5. S. II. 15, 45, 129.
6. S. II. 92.
7. Vin. I. 4; M. I. 167.
8. S. II. 28, 65.
9. Translator's note: This section could also be written as "Conditioned by ignorance are volitional formations," and so on.
10. Vin. I. 1–3; S. II. 1, 65.
11. S. II. 73.
12. S. II. 78.
13. M. I. 55.
14. See S. II. 5–11, 81.
15. As in S. II. 52.
16. As in M. I. 266.
17. As in S. II. 77.

18. As in S. II. 11, 101.
19. In the Abhidhamma texts conditionality is presented in twenty-four different modes (see Paṭṭhāna). In the example of the tree, the various conditions—such as moisture, temperature, soil, and so on—must exist together, not sequentially, for the tree to benefit. Moreover, some kinds of conditions are interdependent, each conditioning the existence of the other—as, for example, an egg is a condition for a chicken, while a chicken is a condition for an egg.
20. As in S. II. 73.
21. S. II. 65.
22. S. II. 72–73.
23. S. II. 73.
24. Abhidhammabhājanīya of the Paccayākāra Vibhaṅga: Vbh. 138ff.
25. Some of those who interpret it in this way translate *avijjā* as the state that has no knowing, and go on to say that matter is the fundamental source of existence; others define *avijjā* as "the Unknowable," saying *avijjā* is God, and then going on to translate *saṅkhārā* as "all conditioned things."
26. See Vism. 517–86; VbhA. 130–213 (in particular, pp. 199–213 describe the process occurring in one mind moment).
27. D. III. 216; S. IV. 259; S. V. 56.
28. Vism. 499; VbhA. 93.
29. The meaning of *dukkha* in *saṅkhārādukkha* can be viewed in light of some English definitions: first section is often explained as conflict, oppression, unrest, imperfection; second section as unsatisfactoriness; third section as the state of being liable to suffering.
30. *Kāmupādāna* = clinging to sensuality.
31. *Diṭṭhupādāna* = clinging to views.
32. *Sīlabbatupādāna* = clinging to rites and rituals.
33. *Attavādupādāna* = clinging to self.
34. *Kāmasukha* = the pleasure of gratifying desires through the five senses, such as, on the coarse level, gambling, drinking, and amusements.
35. S. IV. 207–10.
36. See Paccayākāra Vibhaṅga, Vbh. 135ff.; Vism. 517–86; VbhA. 130–213; Abhidhammatthasaṅgaha, chapter 8.
37. For these definitions, see S. II. 2–4; Vbh. 135. For commentary, see Vism. 517–86; VbhA. 130–213 as referred to above.
38. *Pubbanta, aparanta, pubbantāparanta* (the past, the future, both the past and future). See Dhs. 195–96.
39. This latter interpretation is used to explain the dependent-arising cycle in one mind-moment, as explained in Vbh. 145, 159, 191.
40. Vism. 576.

41. Vism. 577.
42. Vism. 529.
43. M. I. 54.
44. The three *vaṭṭa* are a commentarial idea, which may be considered a layman's picture of the wheel of rebirth.
45. The commentarial texts state that putting *avijjā* and *taṇhā* as the two sources reflects different objectives. *Avijjā* is targeted at people with tendencies to attachment to views (*diṭṭhi carita*), while *taṇhā* is targeted at people with tendencies to greed (*taṇhā carita*). Also, *avijjā* is explained as the source for removing the annihilationist view (*ucchedadiṭṭhi*); *taṇhā* is explained as the source for removing the eternalist view (*sassatadiṭṭhi*). Alternatively, the *avijjā* section is said to be intended for *gabbhasayakasatta* (beings born from a womb), while the *taṇhā* section is intended for *opapātikasatta* (beings who are spontaneously arisen). See Vism. 578.
46. *Jhāna* = absorptions, higher states of concentration encountered in meditation.
47. A. V. 113; Vism. 525; according to this sutta, ignorance has the five hindrances as nutriment.
48. A. V. 116; Vism. 525; the nutriment of *vibhavataṇhā* is *avijjā*.
49. S. II. 23.
50. Abhidhamma, Mahāpaṭṭhāna, vols. 40–45.
51. *Pubbanta.*
52. *Aparanta.*
53. M. II. 31.
54. S. IV. 327.
55. *Pubbekatahetu.*
56. S. IV. 230.
57. S. II. 65.
58. Translator's note: In this section, English definitions in parentheses are those of P. A. Payutto.
59. *Upapattibhava* is an Abhidhamma term (see Vbh. 137). In later suttas it is referred to as *paṭisandhipunabbhava* (linking to renewed being; see Nd. II. 569).
60. S. II. 114.
61. Translator's note: These are the four bases of clinging.
62. The four *āsava* (*kāmāsava*, *bhavāsava*, *diṭṭhāsava*, *avijjāsava*) are given according to the Abhidhamma. See Vbh. 373. In the suttas the preferred analysis is into three *āsava*, *diṭṭhāsava* being omitted. See D. II. 81; S. IV. 256. This can be explained as follows: in the suttas only the *āsava* that have the most prominent roles are mentioned. *Diṭṭhāsava* is not specified as it lies between *avijjāsava* and *bhavāsava*; that is, *diṭṭhāsava* is founded on

avijjāsava and expresses itself through *bhavāsava*. In the Abhidhamma, a more detailed analysis is sought, hence the four *āsava*.

63. *Sassatadiṭṭhi* = the belief in things as permanent, as fixed and enduring.
64. *Ucchedadiṭṭhi* = the belief in things as subject to annihilation, extinction. *Sassatadiṭṭhi* and *ucchedadiṭṭhi* are both forms of the misconception of self. The first is quite clear, but the second can be explained briefly thus: through perceiving things to have selves or entities, one believes that they can disappear or become annihilated. See the section titled "*Paṭiccasamuppāda* as a Middle Teaching," below.
65. *Kāma* = desire objects appearing through the five senses and the desire for those objects.
66. The most fundamental views for supporting *taṇhā* are *sassatadiṭṭhi* and *ucchedadiṭṭhi* and similar views.
67. Phra Ariyanandamuni (Buddhadāsa), *Luk Phra Buddhasāsanā* (Suvijahn, 1956), p. 60 (in Thai).
68. The four kinds of clinging occur in D. III.230; Vbh. 375, and elsewhere. *Attavādupādāna*, in particular, when analyzed, can be seen to be essentially clinging to one or another of the five *khandhas*, as said in the canon: "The unenlightened being...perceives that form [body] is self, or that self has form, or that form is within self, or that self is within form. One perceives that feeling...perception...volitional impulses...consciousness is the self, or that self has consciousness, or that consciousness is within the self or that self is within consciousness."
69. A. II. 145.
70. Coined following the Buddhavacana "*majjhena dhammaṁ deseti,*" but SA. II. 36 explains that the Buddha established himself in the middle practice (*majjhimā paṭipadā*) before giving it; Vism. 522 refers to it as *majjhimā paṭipadā*. It seems that the name taken from the original Tipiṭaka reference is preferable.
71. In reference to these doctrines, the word *vāda* in every instance can be replaced with *diṭṭhi*. Thus, these two *vāda* and those that follow can be alternatively referred to as *atthikadiṭṭhi*, *natthikadiṭṭhi*, *sassatadiṭṭhi*, *ucchedadiṭṭhi*, and so on. *Atthikavāda* is also known as *sabbatthikavāda*.
72. S. II. 16–17, 76; S. III. 134.
73. S. II. 77.
74. S. II. 19.
75. S. II. 39; for more detail, see D. I. 53; S. I. 134; D. III. 137, A. III. 336–37, 440; Ud. 69–70; Vbh. 376–77.
76. These two terms are more recently coined. They are both forms of *sassatadiṭṭhi* and *ucchedadiṭṭhi* respectively.
77. S. II. 75.

78. S. II. 61.
79. S. II. 64.
80. S. II. 26.
81. The word for *being* in the Pali is *tathāgato.* It is translated here according to the commentary (MA. III. 142). According to SA. III. 113 the term refers to the Buddha. At UdA. 339, 430 it is said to refer to a self (*attā* or *ātman*).
82. S. IV. 395: The reasons that the Buddha refused to answer questions dealing with metaphysics (*abhiprajñā*) are many. Importantly, such questions are founded on wrong understandings. The questioner conceives the question out of one's own wrong views, understanding, for example, that there is a self. The questions do not correlate with reality; as the Buddha states, "You have asked the question wrongly." The truths these questions seek to answer are not accessible to logic. There is no way that logical explanations could reveal them. It would be like trying to look at a visual object with one's ears—a waste of time. Contingent on the last rationale: since they are inaccessible to rational thinking, debating these questions would yield no practical results. The Buddha was interested in the things that were problems and related to real life in a practical way, things that could be put to use, so he swept aside the questions of metaphysics and pulled his questioners right back to the problems related to real life. If these truths were such that a person really could attain to them, the Buddha would explain how the questioner could experience it personally, rather than leaving him to his conjecture, like a blind man groping an elephant.

    The Buddha was born at a time when people had a high level of interest in these questions, and thinkers were debating them all over the country. It could be said that such questioning was a characteristic of the people of those times, who were so obsessed with these questions that they had drifted from the truth of life. Entering into the discussion by giving answers would serve no purpose, so the Buddha abstained from answering altogether. His silence was not only a check on such debate but also a powerful jolt to the listener to take heed of what the Buddha did have to teach, which was the truths of real life, an effective psychological method. For references to the practical reasons for not answering these questions, see M. I. 426, 484; S. II. 222-23; S. IV. 375; A. IV. 68; A. V. 193.
83. D. II. 55-71. (Note that in this sutta, in explaining conditionality within the mind, *taṇhā* is explained as the six desires—desire for sights, sounds, smells, tastes, and so on—whereas in the conditionality within society, *taṇhā* is explained as *kāmataṇhā, bhavataṇhā, and vibhavataṇhā.*)
84. D. II. 58. These nine conditions, from *taṇhā* onwards, occur in many other places and are known as the nine things rooted in desire (*taṇhāmūḷaka-dhamma*), such as in D. III. 289; A. IV. 400; Vbh. 390.

85. D. III. 289; Ps. I. 187. The word "elements" (*dhātu*) here refers to the eighteen elements involved in sense contact: six internal sense bases, six cognitive objects, and six consciousnesses.
86. S. II. 140–49.
87. D. III. 80–98.
88. D. III. 58–79.
89. M. II. 196; Sn. 115–23.
90. VbhA. 1 (approx.).
91. Vism. 522; identical to VbhA. 130 (approx.).
92. The explanation of the Visuddhimagga covers one hundred pages; that of the Sammohavinodanī ninety-two pages.
93. VbhA. 199 (approx.).
94. VbhA. 200 (approx.).
95. VbhA. 208 (approx.).
96. Suttantabhājanīya Vbh. 135-38; Abhidhammabhājanīya Vbh. 138–91.
97. Suttantabhājanīya VbhA. 130–98 (approx.); Abhidhammabhājanīya VbhA. 199-213 (approx.)

Chapter 4. *Kamma* as a Principle Contingent on the *Paṭiccasamuppāda*

1. Meaning all *saṅkhatadhamma.*
2. Compare the English translations often given for *niyāma*, as "orderliness of nature"; "the five aspects of natural law." Sources: DA. II. 439; DhsA. 272.
3. Also translated as "law of energy," "law of physical phenomena," "physical inorganic order," or just "physical laws."
4. Also translated as "law of heredity," "physical organic order," "biological laws."
5. Also translated as "psychic law," "psychological laws."
6. Also translated as "law of karma," "order of act and result," "karmic laws," "moral laws."
7. Also translated as "the general law of cause and effect," "order of the norm." *Dhammaniyāma* is also explained by the commentators with examples of events considered to be the "norm" from the Buddha's life story, such as when the Bodhisatta took conception, and was born, enlightened, and so on, it is "the norm" that the ten-thousand-fold world system should quake.
8. M. II. 196; Sn. 123.
9. Students of Abhidhamma can tell us that while life, made up of the five *khandhas*, may fare entirely according to the natural laws, it is only some

parts of the five *khandhas* that are direct results of *kamma* and directly fare according to *kamma*. For example, the corporeal properties in our body are analyzed by the Abhidhamma as arising from *kamma*, from mind (*citta*), from temperature (*utu*), and from nutriment (*āhāra*).

10. *Sangkhom* ("society," from the Pali *saṅgama*) is a Thai word. The original Pali term did not have the same meaning as it does in Thai. Here I use it in the Thai sense. As for the word *niyom/niyamana*, etymologically it means the same as *niyāma*, or *niyom* in Thai. However, I have avoided using *niyama* here to avoid confusion with the original five *niyāma*, which are true natural laws. On the other hand, the term *sangkhom niyom* [using a slightly differently spelling in Thai] is already in use (meaning "socialism"), thus I have taken the risk of coining a slightly different word to indicate the difference.
11. Translator's note: In earlier editions of *Buddhadhamma*, only the term "social preference" was used in this section. "Conventional laws" was introduced in a later edition, so I have revised the text accordingly.
12. A. III. 415.
13. S. III. 63-64; see also Vism. 526-27, 530-31.
14. See It. 25.
15. Sn. 612-54.
16. See A. I. 104, 263; It. 25-26, 54-55. *Akusalamūla* and *kusalamūla*, see D. III. 275; A. I. 201-2; Dhs. 180.
17. Note that in the three *kusalamūla*, non-greed (*alobha*) refers to the qualities that are opposites of greed, including relinquishment (*cāga*); non-aversion (*adosa*) refers also to the qualities that are opposite to aversion, especially goodwill (*mettā*); non-delusion (*amoha*) refers to the qualities that are the opposite of delusion, especially wisdom (*paññā*). See Dhs. 188-89; Majjhima Nikāya Ṭīkā, Burmese edition, 1.56.
18. M. I. 373; A. I. 104; Dhs. 180.
19. A. I. 104, 292.
20. These four kinds of *kamma* are explained in many different ways. See D. III. 230; M. I. 389-90; A. II. 230-37.
21. See chapter 9, "The Morality Factors of the Middle Way."
22. M. I. 373.
23. For *sammādiṭṭhi* and *micchādiṭṭhi* as mental kamma, see A. V. 296-98.
24. A. I. 30.
25. A. I. 32; see also A. V. 212.
26. A. I. 33. On the importance of right and wrong view in relation to achieving enlightenment, see S. V. 10-11, 48-49.
27. M. III. 72.
28. Dh. 1-3.

29. If we were to use the term "value," it would mean "real value" rather than "given value."
30. Translator's note: the difference between *kusalachanda* and *kāmachanda* or *lobha* is expanded on in the chapter "The Problem of Motivation" in the unabridged version of *Buddhadhamma*.
31. Instead of *rāga* (desire) here, *lobha* (greed) could have been used, and that would better fit Thai people's perceptions, but here I have used the original term given in the Paṭṭhāna (Paṭ. 154-55, 168-69, etc.). I have also used *rāga* to broaden the narrow understanding the term has gained in the Thai language [where it means "lust"].
32. Here we are looking on a simple level. In some cases, the matter may be more complicated than this, involving other factors—for example, the wisdom of whether or not to accept the convention and how, which has an effect on intention (determining whether it will be an intention to violate or not, whether it is strong or weak, and so on), which must be investigated as another level. But regardless of how it is, when thinking arises, there must always be an intention of some kind and it will always have some effect on the psyche.
33. Dhs. 181. (Neutral conditions [*abyākata dhamma*] are also dealt with, but not included here.)
34. Nd. I. 12, 360, 467; Nd. II. 199.
35. S. I. 98.
36. A. I. 201. (An explanation is also given in this text for the *kusalamūla* but it can be deduced from what has already been given here.)
37. A. I. 263.
38. A. I. 189 (Following this the Buddha goes on to deal with skillful qualities, with a similar kind formula). Suttas with similar content can be found at A. I. 193-94; A. II. 190-91.
39. *Sabyāpajjhaṁ* is a term we usually translate as "hurtful" or "comprising hurtfulness," but almost all the commentaries translate it, both here and in other places, as "painful," or "comprising suffering." "Having obstruction" would seem to be a good translation (*abyāpajjhaṁ*, the opposite, can be translated in the same manner). See MA. III. 104, 347, 360.
40. M. II. 114.
41. A. I. 216. The first part of the passage can also be found at A. I. 156-58.
42. J. II. 202.
43. Dh. 71.
44. Dh. 172.
45. S. I. 37.
46. "Blameworthy" is translated from *upavadati*, which can also be translated as "to criticize" or "find fault with."

47. A. I. 57.
48. A. I. 58.
49. A. V. 39.
50. S. I. 227; J. II. 199, III. 158 The accompanying story occurs in A. II. 202; JA. III. 158. The full words in each source are more detailed than this. The accompanying Jātaka story seems to emphasize the kinds of results that are overt events. The second line of the Jātaka verse is variously *tādisaṁ ruhate phalaṁ*, or *tādisaṁ harate phalaṁ*, meaning, "Whatever seed is planted, that kind of fruit grows therefrom," or "Whatever kind of seed is planted, that kind of fruit is derived thereof."
51. Vbh. 338. Commentarial explanation at AA. II. 218–21; VbhA. 439–54.
52. *Gatisampatti* and *gativipatti* are explained in the commentaries specifically in the sense of spheres of existence in which beings take birth.
53. Note also the principle of "making *kamma* cease" or "wiping out *kamma* through the practice of mental liberation based on goodwill (*mettācetovimutti*)" described in the Buddhavacana quoted later in this chapter.
54. There are four *acinteyya*: *buddhavisaya* (the capacity of a Buddha), *jhānavisaya* (the capacity of *jhāna* absorption), *kammavipāka* (the fruits of *kamma*), and *lokacintā* (metaphysical questions about the origin or creation of the world). See A. II. 80.
55. See Moore, trans., *Buddhadhamma: The Laws of Nature and Their Benefits to Life*, by P. A. Payutto: chapter 10, "Buddhist Teachings on Desire."
56. For example, Egerton C. Baptist, *A Glimpse into the Supreme Science of the Buddha* (Colombo: Colombo Apothecaries' Co., 1958), 44ff.; K. N. Jayatilleke, *Survival and Karma in Buddhist Perspective* (Kandy: Buddhist Publication Society, 1969), 35–93.
57. For example, Ian Stevenson, *Twenty Cases Suggestive of Reincarnation* (Charlottesville: Virginia UP, 1966), passim; A. R. Martin, *Researches in Reincarnation and Beyond* (self-published, 1942), passim; C. J. Ducasse, *A Critical Examination of the Belief in a Life after Death* (Springfield, IL: Charles C. Thomas, 1961), passim.
58. Also called the *Subha Sutta*. M. III. 203.
59. The content of this sutta is an answer to the young man Subha, who was of the brahmin caste. Looking in terms of the Brahmanist religion, we may make at least two observations about the Buddha's answer: first, it is a challenge to the Brahmanist teaching that Brahma is the creator and director of all beings, encouraging the fresh perspective that people's actions are what create and condition their lives. Second, according to the traditions of Brahmanism, whoever sponsors ceremonies such as sacrifices and gives offerings (*dakkhiṇā*) to the brahmin receives immense benefits far outweighing any perceivable causal connection to the action.

In describing the results of actions according to this sutta, the Buddha was also creating a new understanding in this respect.

60. D. I. 230; M. I. 389; A. II. 230–37.
61. M. II. 214; M. I. 93; A. I. 220–21.
62. A. III. 415.
63. S. II. 64.
64. A. I. 134.
65. A. II. 233.
66. S. V. 86.
67. *Kāyasaṅkhāra*, volitional acts of the body.
68. *Vacīsaṅkhāra*, volitional acts of speech.
69. *Manosaṅkhāra*, volitional acts of the mind.
70. S. II. 40–41.
71. See the section on *attakāravāda* and *parakāravāda* in "The *Paṭiccasamuppāda* as a Middle Teaching" [chapter 3].
72. A. I. 173; cf. Vbh. 367; M. II. 214.
73. S. IV. 230.
74. S. IV. 319.
75. M. III. 19; S. III. 104.
76. A. III. 415.
77. M. III. 203.
78. S. I. 227.
79. Thig. 240–41, 243.
80. J. I. 374.
81. J. I. 258.
82. M. III. 187.
83. A. III. 47–48.
84. S. III. 153.
85. The *bho* formality: the brahmin tradition of addressing their peers as *bho* ("friend").
86. *Kamma* translates as "action" but in some cases it carries the narrower meaning of "occupation" or "profession."
87. M. II. 196; Sn. 119–23.
88. Sn. 23–24.
89. A. IV. 202.
90. D. III. 97.
91. Dh. 276.
92. Dh. 160.
93. Dh. 165.
94. D. II. 100; D. III. 77; S. III. 42.
95. A. III. 71–72.

96. Ud. 51.
97. S. I. 93.

Chapter 5. *Nibbāna*

1. The words *saṁsāra* (or *saṁsāravaṭṭa*) and *vivaṭṭa* are here coined according to a usage that has evolved over time, not according to their original forms. *Saṁsāravaṭṭa* is rendered in the canon simply as *saṁsāra* (as in S. II. 178; A. II. 12) or simply *vaṭṭa* (as in S. III. 64; S. IV. 52; Ud. 75). In later texts the two words are used together, as in Nd. I. 343; Nd. II. 17; *vivaṭṭa* is not used in this sense in any canonical text other than the Paṭisambhidāmagga (for example, Ps. I. 2, 1-7-11). It is used more frequently in the commentarial and subcommentarial texts (Vism. 694; VinA. [Pācittayakhandhaṁ, Musāvādavaggo, Padasodhammasikkhāpadavaṇṇanā]; AA. III. 337; VismṬ. [Paṭhamo Bhāgo, Sīlaniddesavaṇṇanā, Dutiyasīlapañcakavaṇṇanā]).
2. A. I. 158-59; Note that these five qualities of *nibbāna* are identical to the last five qualities of the Dhamma (which are recited frequently in Buddhist morning and evening chanting). This is in keeping with the explanation that the first quality of the Dhamma (*svākkhāto*) is a quality of the Dhamma in its capacity as teaching, later known as *pariyattidhamma*, that which is to be studied, while qualities 2 to 6 (*sandiṭṭhiko*, *akāliko*, *ehipassiko*, *opanayiko*, *paccattaṁ veditabbo viññūhi*) are qualities specifically of the transcendent Dhamma (*lokuttara dhamma*; Vism. 215-18).
3. Vin. I. 5; M. I. 168.
4. Ibid.
5. S. IV. 251, 261.
6. S. II. 117.
7. S. III. 190.
8. This is an indirect description, not a direct definition. See, for example, S. IV. 43; Ud. 80; It. 47.
9. M. I. 226.
10. S. IV. 157, 174.
11. M. I. 486-87; S. IV. 399.
12. S. III. 108-9.
13. S. IV. 174.
14. S. IV. 195.
15. Ap. 530 (*puramuttamaṁ*).
16. Miln., book 4, Atthamavaggo, no. 5, "The Gift of Vessantara (Dilemma 71)
17. Ud. 80-81.
18. Ud. 80-81.
19. Ud. 80-81.

20. *Anidassana*: can also be translated as "incomparable."
21. *Sabbatopabha*: can also be rendered as "accessible from every direction"; that is, the state can be attained by all methods of meditation.
22. D. I. 215–23.
23. DA. II. 393; MA. II. 412.
24. M. II. 201–2.
25. Ud. 67–68.
26. See the Buddha's principles for speaking at A. II. 172–73; D. III. 134–35; M. I. 395.
27. *Saṁyojana*, described in detail later in this chapter.
28. Some of these terms occur often and are familiar; some occur rarely. See, for example M. I. 235, 280, 446–47; M. II. 29; S. III. 61–62; A. V. 16, 221–22; Nd. II. 10. The last few words, in particular, are based on ancient terms used in Brahmanism, but are given different meanings in accordance with Buddhist principles. For instance, *brahmin* originally meant one who casts off evil through bathing in holy rivers, such as the Ganges, but in Buddhism it came to mean one who casts off evil by renouncing it through practice of the eightfold path, or, to retain the analogy, "bathing in the Dhamma."
29. D. II. 135.
30. It. 78–79. (Note that the second type of person, the noble disciple (*ariyasāvaka*) who is a learner and is still practicing, is not yet a *bhāvitatta*.)
31. M. I. 237. The commentaries explain that here *kāyabhāvanā* is *vipassanā* (insight) and *cittabhāvanā* is *samādhi*, that is, *samatha* (calm) meditation—MA. II. 285.
32. D. I. 70.
33. S. V. 74. An explanation of a more profound restraint of the sense doors can be found at S. IV. 120–21.
34. M. III. 298. The word *paṭikūla* should not be interpreted in the narrower and more common sense, as it is normally understood in Thai, as "filth." Examples used are looking on a person who has unpleasant facial features or ungraceful movements with *mettā*, or looking on something that is not beautiful, in terms of the elements, to see that it is pleasing or comfortable to the eye. This is called "perceiving that which is abhorrent as not abhorrent." Looking on an object that is beautiful in light of impermanence, or in terms of the elements, so that it is seen as not beautiful, is called "perceiving that which is not abhorrent as abhorrent" (see the explanation at Ps. II. 212).
35. As in A. IV. 380; Pug. 37.
36. A. V. 139–40.
37. Following S. IV. 132–33 (cf. A. I. 263–64; A. III. 415–16).
38. Following D. III. 230; A. II. 231.

39. As in Dhs. 180-81.
40. See also book 2, on *majjhimā paṭipadā*.
41. A detailed explanation of the five hindrances can be found in chapter 10.
42. A. I. 9, 216; S. V. 121; A. III. 63-64, 230.
43. Vin. I. 20-21; S. I. 105-6.
44. Thag. verse 648.
45. Vin. I. 20-21; S. I. 105.
46. D. II. 119-20; D. III. 211-12.
47. A. III. 114-15, 355-56.
48. The Buddha: D. II. 211-12, 222; M. I. 21, 83; S. II. 275; A. I. 22; the Buddha, the arahants, and the learners (*sekha*): It. 78-79; the Buddha and the Universal Emperor (*cakkavatti*): A. I. 76; virtuous recluses and holy men possessed of the *kalyāṇadhamma*: D. II. 331-32.
49. See D. I. 228-29.
50. A. I. 60-61.
51. S. II. 203.
52. As an example for later generations: A. I. 71, 242-43; A. II. 147; A. III. 105-6, 178-79, 255-56; Vin. V. 132; as a model for others in general: A. I. 127, 239, 246-47; A. III. 114-15, 422.
53. Vin. II. 108, 128-29; Vin. III. 42; A. III. 251; M. II. 92-93.
54. A. I. 23.
55. The list of foremost bhikkhu disciples (there are also lists for bhikkunis, laymen, and laywomen) given at A. I. 23 is extensive, and includes many well-known disciples and accomplishments, such as Venerable Sāriputta (foremost of those with much wisdom), Venerable Mahāmoggallāna (foremost of those with psychic powers), Venerable Mahā Kassapa (foremost of those who observe the ascetic practices), and Venerable Ānanda (foremost of those with good memory), as well as some more obscure ones, such as Venerable Kāḷudāyī (foremost of those who inspire families) and Venerable Bakkula (foremost of those with few illnesses). See the full list at Moore, trans., *Buddhadhamma: The Laws of Nature and Their Benefits to Life*, by P. A. Payutto: chapter 7.
56. Such as Venerables Sāriputta and Moggallāna: M. I. 456-57; Venerable Mahā Kassapa: D. II. 162; and Venerable Yasoja: Ud. 24-25.
57. D. II. 76; A. IV. 21.
58. M. III. 8-13; D. II. 154.
59. See the Vinaya Piṭaka, vols. 1 and 2.
60. Vin. I. 105.
61. Vin. II. 74-76.
62. Vin. II. 284-85.
63. Vin. II. 297-300.

64. Vin. II. 288–89.
65. VinA. I. 36; Mahāvaṁsa V. 101.
66. Miln. 7–8.
67. See Paṭhamasambodhikathā, Mārabandhaparivatta, Pariccheda #28.
68. D. II. 81, 91, 123.
69. For example, Vin. III. 5; D. I. 84; M. I. 23, 183–84; A. I. 165; A. IV. 174–75.
70. A. II. 120; It. 83.
71. A. II. 120; It. 83.
72. M. III. 300–1.
73. Sn. 65, 95; Dh. verses 321–23.
74. Dh. verses 103–5.
75. A. III. 378.
76. Dh. verse 95; A. IV. 374–75 (as a training: M. I. 127, 423).
77. Sn. 101, 160; Dh. verse 401; A. II. 39.
78. S. I. 5.
79. D. III. 275.
80. S. I. 12, 23, 141; Sn. 201, 208; this word *nirāsa* is preferred for use in verses. Like *assaddha* (faithless) in the area of wisdom, it is a play on words, parodying the speech of unenlightened people. In prose form, another word, *vigatāsa*, is used to distinguish the meaning from hopeless or disappointed. It means to have completed that which is hoped for, or to no longer have need of hope (A. I. 107).
81. As in S. I. 55; A. I. 137–8; A. II. 208; Ud. 19–20; Sn. 119–20, 185.
82. M. I. 174.
83. M. I. 509; Dh. verses 202–4.
84. A. I. 138.
85. Dh. verses 200–204.
86. A. III. 422–23; note that *anulomikā khanti* is here translated as "thoughts conducive to seeing the truth." *Khanti* is used here as an attribute of wisdom, and does not merely refer to patience as normally understood. Compare this sense with Ps. I. 123–24; Ps. II. 324–25, 340. (VbhA. 411 states that *khanti* is a synonym for *paññā* and VbhA. 459 states that *anulomikā khanti* is *vipassanā-ñāṇa*; *khanti* in this sense is sometimes translated as *khanti-ñāṇa*.)
87. M I. 4–5.
88. S. II. 82–83; S. V. 205–10; M. III. 285–86; A. II. 198–99.
89. S. IV. 236–37.
90. S. IV. 127.
91. S. III. 7.
92. S. III. 42.
93. M. I. 509; Dh. verse 204; Sn. 146.
94. S. III. 1.

95. A. II. 143-44.
96. See M. I. 506-9.
97. See A. V. 202.
98. For this perspective, see S. IV. 124-25, 120-21; M. III. 299-300.
99. S. III. 69.
100. A. III. 411.
101. See M. I. 85-90; S. III. 27-31; A. I. 259-60.
102. S. I. 14.
103. S. II. 64.
104. A. IV. 67-68.
105. Nd. I. 235; see also Sn. 167 and Dh. verse 97.
106. S. V. 221.
107. *Vijjā:* MA. II. 348; MA. V. 100; SA. II. 270, 366; AA. I. 55; AA. II. 264; AA. III. 175; AA. IV. 90; *vimutti:* MA. II. 281; MA. V. 59; AA. II. 263. AA. III. 217, 227, 378, 416; ItA. I. 170; *vijjā* and *vimutti:* MA. V. 104; AA. I. 120; AA. II. 79, 154; AA. III. 220; AA. V. 43; VismṬ.: Anussatikammaṭṭhānaniddesavaṇṇanā, Ānāpānassatikathāvaṇṇanā (some of the explanations are contradictory).
108. VismṬ.: Cha-anussatiniddesavaṇṇanā.
109. It. 38 states that in the ultimate sense (*paramattha*) *nibbāna* cannot be divided into different kinds, and the twofold classification is only a relative one (*pariyāya*), not absolute (*nippariyāya*).
110. When used in this sense, the usage is more often in the form of the verb or epithet *nibbuta*, as in A. I. 162, 197; A. II. 212; Sn. 153; AA. II. 259, 307; AA. III. 184; Nd1A. I. 199; and especially DhA. I. 85; JA. I. 60; BvA. 280.
111. There are many passages analyzing the word *nibbāna* in the texts, such as Nd. II 33; VinA: Pārājikakaṇḍaṁ, Pathamapārājikaṁ, Sudinnabhāvanāravaṇṇanā; DA. II. 464; AA. II. 283; KhA. 151; ItA. I. 165; SnA. I. 253, 299; Nd1A. I. 82, 104; DhsA. 409; Vism. 293-94; VinṬ.: Paṭhamo Bhāgo, Verañjakaṇḍavaṇṇanā, Vinayapaññattiyācanakathā; VismṬ.: Paṭhamo Bhāgo, Samādhiniddesavaṇṇanā, Samādhi-ānisaṁsakathāvaṇṇanā; CompṬ: Abhidhammatthāvibhāvinīṭikā, Paramatthadhammavaṇṇanā. However, most of the references are repetitions of each other or similar.
112. It. 38; The Abhidhammatthasaṅgaha calls this kind of analysis "the analysis in terms of cause" (*kāraṇapariyāya*) and presents another way of analysis in terms of qualities with three kinds of *nibbāna*, thus: *suññatanibbāna*, *animittanibbāna*, and *appaṇihitanibbāna* (Comp.: Rūpaparicchedo, Nibbānabhedo).
113. As in ItA. I. 164; SnA. II. 410; Nd1A. I 6; PsA. I. 323; VinṬ.: Paṭhamo Bhāgo, Paṭhamamahāsaṅgītikathāvaṇṇanā; VismṬ.: Dutiyo Bhāgo, Dukkhaniddesakathāvaṇṇanā, Ekavidhādivinicchayakathāvaṇṇanā; CompṬ.: Rūpaparicchedavaṇṇanā, Nibbānabhedavaṇṇanā.
114. It. 38-39.

115. *Kilesaparinibbāna*, as in DA. II. 565; DA. III. 842, 872, 1046; MA. II. 282; SA. I. 20, 315; SA. II. 391; AA. II. 128, 174; AA. III. 4, 373; AA. IV. 52, 116, 159, 207; SnA. I. 365; SnA. II. 506; *khandhaparinibbāna*, as in: SA. I. 224; SnA. I. 364; where both are mentioned together: UdA. 407; DA. III. 899; MA. IV. 116; VbhA. 433; VinṬ.: Paṭhamo Bhāgo, Acariyaparamparakathāvaṇṇanā.
116. ItA. I. 164.
117. This presentation of *sa-upādisesanibbāna* and *anupādisesanibbāna* as a pair to analyze different kinds of *nibbāna* appears only once in the Tipiṭaka in the source already cited. Apart from that there are only references to the *sa-upādisesapuggala* and *anupādisesapuggala* (which will be discussed below), or simply the *anupādisesanibbāna* on its own in reference to the end of an arahant's life (as in the examples that will be given below). Note also that the usage, only recently adopted, of the words *nibbāna*, for the Buddha and an arahant disciple who is still alive, and *parinibbāna*, for the passing away of a Buddha and the arahants, conflicts with the textual usage.
118. May also be rendered "looking as though they do not wish to see anybody."
119. Or "practicing [in a way that is] worthy of the offerings given to them" (*paradavuttā*).
120. M. II. 121.
121. Sn. 185.
122. Ud. 20.
123. A. II. 36. (*Mahāpurisa* in this passage seems to mean the Buddha, but in other passages it is used to mean all those who have vanquished defilements (*khīṇāsava*). See M. I. 121–22, 214–15; AA. III. 5.)
124. Ud. 46.
125. Thag. verses 1002–3; cf. Thag. verses 654–55, 685–86.
126. S. IV. 40–41.
127. S. II. 274.
128. M. I. 186.
129. Kh. 8; Sn. 26. (This extract and also M. I. 185–86 are teachings for those practicing for *nibbāna*. They are regarded as already perfected by the arahants.)
130. S. I. 110–11.
131. As in M. II. 138; S. I. 219–20.
132. Vism. 634–35; VbhA. 489.
133. These nine states are collectively referred to as the nine *anupubbavihāra*, meaning "successive subtle abodes," or the *anupubbavihārasamāpatti*, "the abodes that have to be entered successively."
134. However, to maintain that the attainment of *jhāna* is attainment of *nibbāna* is wrong view (M. II. 228, 237); see also D. I. 36–7; Vbh. 379–80.

135. See A. V. 410–14, 453–55.
136. S. III. 43.
137. A. I. 158–59.
138. Ps. II. 221 (In PsA. I. 323 *nibbāna* is called according to this style *vikkhambhanaparinibbāna*, *tadaṅgaparinibbāna*, and *samucchedaparinibbāna*.)
139. *Nibbedhabhāgiyasamādhi* = *vipassanā samādhi* (*nibbedhabhāgiyasamādhi* is *samādhi* that is part of the penetration of truth; *vipassanā samādhi* is *samādhi* that contains, leads to, or is used in conjunction with insight. See VismṬ. 88–89; VismṬ.: Paṭhamo Bhāgo, Kammaṭṭhānaggahaṇaniddesavaṇṇanā, Samādhicatukkavaṇṇanā; Dutiyo Bhāgo, Ñāṇadassanavisuddhiniddesavaṇṇanā, Pariññādippabhedakathāvaṇṇanā).
140. The attainment of enlightenment is often referred to as attainment of *magga* (the path) and *phala* (the fruit). A more detailed discussion of the distinction between attainment of the various "paths" and "fruits" can be found in the expanded version of *Buddhadhamma*, in particular in the special note at the end of chapter 8, appendix 4, of the English translation. The Abhidhamma contains a description of the procession of mind moments at the attainment of enlightenment (*magga-phala*) of the *vipassanāyānika* at UdA. 33; PsA. I. 29; DhsA. 231; Vism. 669–70; and Comp.: Vīthiparicchedo, Apannājavanavāro. Translator's note: As for the distinction between *magga* and *phala* at the time of enlightenment, the venerable author explained in an email to the translator that, "in brief, *magga* and *phala* arise in consecutive mind moments (similar to when listening to someone talking: at one moment one hears the sound, and at the next moment one understands what is being said)."
141. Ps I. 26–27; Ps. II. 220–22.
142. As in Vism. 410; DA. II. 427; SA. III. 209; MA. IV. 168; DhA. I. 158, 433; UdA. 32. See also the explanation at Vism. 693–4 and VismṬ: Dutiyo Bhāgo Ñāṇadassanavisuddhiniddesavaṇṇanā, Pariññādippabhedakathāvaṇṇanā.
143. MA. I. 73; DhsA. 356; Vism. 697; VismṬ.: Ñāṇadassanavisuddhiniddesavaṇṇanā, Pariññādippabhedakathāvaṇṇanā
144. The first use of the word *ariyapuggala* as a specialized term seems to be in the Puggalapaññatti of the Abhidhamma Piṭaka. (See Pug. 11–12, 14. See also Vin. V. 117; Nd. I. 232; Ps. I. 167).
145. See Monier Monier-Williams, "Ārya," in *A Sanskrit-English Dictionary* (London; Oxford University Press, 1964), 152.
146. S. V. 433 (cited in Vism. 495; in the canon the word *ariyoti* is lost; see also ItA. I. 85; PsA. I. 62) cf. S. V. 435.
147. From *dakkhiṇā* + the suffix *ṇeyya* = *dakkhiṇeyya*.
148. The commentaries state that it is "things offered through belief in kamma and the results of kamma, not with the thought that 'this person will cure

my illness,' or '[this person] will serve me or complete my business for me'" (see KhA. 200). In some places it is described as "things given by those who believe in the next world (*paraloka*)" (as in Vism. 220; ItA. I. 88; VinṬ.: Pārājikakaṇḍaṁ, Sikkhāpaccakkhānavibhaṅgavaṇṇanā).

149. *Anuttaraṁ puññakkhettaṁ lokassa.*

150. See also DA. III. 996; AA. IV. 29; VinṬ.: Pārājikaṇḍaṁ, Sikkhāpaccakkhānavibhaṅgavaṇṇanā for example.

151. S. II. 221.

152. VinṬ.: Nissaggiyakaṇḍam, Kosiyavaggo, Rūpiyasikkhāpadavaṇṇanā; MA. III. 343; SA. II. 199; AA. I. 72; Vism. 43; VismṬ.: Sīlaniddesavaṇṇanā, Catupārisuddhisampādanavidhi-vaṇṇanā.

153. See Dh. verse 49.

154. See *Cakkavatti Sutta*, D. III. 61.

155. As in S. V. 61; A. V. 17; Vbh. 377; DA. I. 312 (note that generally in the canon the fourth and fifth fetters are *kāmachanda* and *byāpāda*, but at A. I. 242 they are *abhijjhā* and *byāpāda*. However, they are usually taught as *kāmarāga* and *paṭigha* following the commentaries and subcommentaries, such as Ps. 2.94; Vism. 683; Comp.: Samuccayaparicchedo, Akusalasaṅgaho).

156. The standard words used to describe this are "seeing form, feeling, perception, volitional impulses, or consciousness as self; seeing self as having form, feeling, perception, volitional impulses or consciousness; seeing form, feeling, perception, volitional impulses or consciousness in the self; seeing self in form, feeling, perception, volitional impulses or consciousness" (see M. I. 300; S. IV. 287; Dhs. 182–83; Vbh. 364).

157. Two *dakkhiṇeyyapuggala*, the *sekha* and the *asekha*, are given in A. I. 63, 231–32; four *dakkhiṇeyya* or *ariyapuggala* (sometimes referred to by other names or not specifically named at all) as in D. I. 156; D. II. 251–2; D. III. 107, 132; M. III. 80–81; Pug. 63. In A. IV. 279–80 stream enterers are classified into three kinds and non-returners into five, together with one kind of once-returner giving nine kinds of *sa-upādisesapuggala*.

158. See S. V. 347–48.

159. A. III. 438 states that they also give up the (stronger) forms of desire, aversion, and delusion, which would be a cause for going to the nether realms.

160. Ps. II. 94–95 states that a once-returner also gives up (a further) two fetters of grosser sensual desire and hatred (while a non-returner gives up the subtler forms of sensual desire and hatred); the Visuddhimagga (Vism. 676–77) states that a once-returner mitigates the power of sensual desire and aversion. However, all of these mean the same.

161. Translated after the commentaries, such as AA. IV. 40, 174.

162. D. II. 314; M. I. 62, 481; S. V. 129, 237, 285; A. III. 81-82, 143; A. V. 108; It. 39; Sn. 140, 148 (Explained in commentaries such as ItA. I. 169; SnA. II. 503.)
163. D. III. 255; A. IV. 292; in the Abhidhamma there are said to be two kinds: *maggasamaṅgī*, one who is endowed with the four paths; and *phalasamaṅgī*, one who is endowed with the four fruits (Pug. 73).
164. In later times these terms were sometimes essentially defined as "one established in the path of stream entry," "one established in the path of once-returner," "one established in the path of non-returner," and "one established in the path of arahantship" (while *sotāpanna* was translated as "one established in the fruit of stream entry," *sakadāgāmī* as "one established in the fruit of once-returner," etc.). This kind of translation follows the wording that arose in the time of the commentaries (see Nd1A. II. 254; Nd2A. 15; KhA. 183; DhA. I. 334; VinṬ.: Pārājikakaṇḍaṁ, Bhikkhupadabhājanīyavaṇṇanā; DA. II. 515 = AA. IV. 3 = PañcA. 191; MA. II. 120; UdA. 306), but it should be noted that the words *sotāpattimagga*, *sakadāgāmimagga*, and *anāgāmimagga* are not used anywhere in the early Tipiṭaka. They begin to appear in the Niddesas, the Paṭisambhidāmagga, and the Abhidhamma. The word *arahattamagga* is found only in the passages *arahā vā assasi arahattamaggaṁ vā samāpanno* and *arahanto vā arahattamaggaṁ vā samāpannā* (Vin. I. 32, 39; D. I. 144; S. I. 78; A. II. 42; A. III. 391; Ud. 7, 65). Apart from these sources, *arahattamagga* also became more frequently used in the Niddesas, the Paṭisambhidāmagga, and the Abhidhamma.
165. As in M. I. 37; A. III. 286.
166. Except for the last, eighth, *vimokkha* (*saññāvedayitanirodha*), which is only possible for the non-returners and arahants, who are already liberated according to their respective attainments.
167. *Vimokkha* is also called *vimutti* in the term *cetovimutti*, transcendence through the power of *samādhi*.
168. As in D. III. 262; A. IV. 306-7 (explained after Ps. II. 38-40; DA. II. 513; MA. III. 255; AA. IV. 146).
169. D. III. 105, 253-54; A. IV. 10-11, 76-77; Ps. II. 53-54. Here the meaning is explained following the Puggalapaññatti. In the suttas the explanatory passage is different, so I present that explanation in this footnote below (from M. I. 477-78). Note also that some of the words in this passage differ from version to version of the Tipiṭaka (such as the Thai-script and roman-script versions).

    1. *Saddhānusārī puggala*: one who has not directly experienced the subtle escapes, which go beyond the attainments of form (*rūpa samāpatti*) to the formless attainments, but some of the outflows (*āsava*) have ceased

through seeing (the noble truths) with wisdom, and one has faith and devotion in the Tathāgata. In addition, one is endowed with these qualities: the faith faculty, the effort faculty, the mindfulness faculty, the concentration faculty, and the wisdom faculty.

2. *Dhammānusārī puggala*: one who has not directly experienced the subtle escapes, which go beyond the attainments of form to the formless attainments, but some of the outflows have ceased through seeing (the noble truths) with wisdom, and one's own wise reflection is in accord with the Dhamma taught by the Tathāgata. In addition, one is endowed with these qualities: the faith faculty, the effort faculty, the mindfulness faculty, the concentration faculty, and the wisdom faculty.

3. *Saddhāvimutta puggala*: one who has not directly experienced the subtle escapes, which go beyond the attainments of form to the formless attainments, but some of the outflows have ceased through seeing (the noble truths) with wisdom, and one has firm and deep-rooted faith in the Tathāgata.

4. *Diṭṭhippatta puggala*: one who has not directly experienced the subtle escapes, which go beyond the attainments of form to the formless attainments, but some of the outflows have ceased through seeing (the noble truths) with wisdom, and one sees the truths taught by the Tathāgata clearly, and practices well and properly with wisdom.

5. *Kāyasakkhī puggala*: one who has directly experienced the subtle escapes, which go beyond the attainments of form to the formless attainments, and some of the outflows have ceased through seeing (the noble truths) with wisdom.

6. *Paññāvimutta puggala*: one who has not directly experienced the subtle escapes, which go beyond the attainments of form to the formless attainments, but all of the outflows have ceased through seeing (the noble truths) with wisdom.

7. *Ubhatobhāgavimutta puggala*: one who has directly experienced the subtle escapes, which go beyond the attainments of form to the formless attainments, and all of the outflows have ceased through seeing (the noble truths) with wisdom.

170. *Kāyasakkhī* may be simply translated as "one who experiences *jhāna* first before attaining *nibbāna*" (Ps. II. 52).

171. It should be stressed once more that among these six types of arahants, the *sukkhavipassaka* is a commentarial term. The other five occur in the canon. The Visuddhimagga (Vism. 710) also gives six kinds of arahants, but the first kind is called *saddhāvimutta* instead of *sukkhavipassaka*. Otherwise it is the same. (*Saddhāvimutta* is one who attains stream entry on the strength of a dominant faith faculty, and the term is applied all the

way up to the attainment of arahantship following Ps. II. 53–54, where it is written *saddhādhimutta*; but in Vism. 659 it is written *saddhāvimutta*.)

172. S. V. 364–65. "Qualities of a stream enterer" comes from *sotāpattiyaṅga*. Literally, it translates as "the factors for attainment of stream entry." Sometimes it refers to the factors that lead to the attainment of stream entry, sometimes to the qualities of a stream enterer.

173. Such as the Lady Visākhā in Ud. 91–92; UdA. 417; DhA. III. 278.

174. Important sources: Vin. I. 35–39; PvA. 209. Translator's note: The *uposatha* precepts are the eight precepts, consisting of the core five precepts as well as supplementary precepts such as not eating after noon, not indulging in entertainments, and not sleeping in luxurious beds. They are traditionally held on observance days.

175. Important sources: Vin. II. 154–59; A. I. 25–26; AA. I. 384.

176. Important sources: Vin. I. 290–94; A. I. 26; AA. I. 404; DhA. I. 384, among others.

177. Important sources: Vin. I. 71–2, 267–82; Vin. II. 119; A. I. 25–26; AA. I. 398.

178. Important sources: A. I. 25–26; A. II. 61–62; A. III. 295–96; A. IV. 268–69; S. III. 1; S. IV. 116; AA. I. 399.

179. The qualities acquired are presented before those given up in accordance with current preference, which differs from the preference of the scriptures, where the qualities given up are put before the qualities acquired. In any case, both kinds of qualities are related and interconnected.

180. The Buddha, the Dhamma (teaching), and the Saṅgha (the order).

181. Moral conduct that is free and not enslaved by desire is morality that is observed not for some expected reward, such as worldly happiness, or rebirth in heaven. Bear in mind that morality always includes right livelihood (see VbhA. 88 = Vism. 511).

182. A. III. 272–73 (as long as one has the five *macchariya* one will not be able to achieve even first *jhāna*); Vism. 683, 685.

183. Vin. II. 285; Vism. 683, 685.

184. S. III. 225; A. III. 438.

185. S. II. 133–40; S. V. 388, 441–42, 457–65.

186. Dh. verse 178.

187. As in MA. I. 74; SA. III. 55; KhA. 188; SnA. I. 193; PsA. I. 282; DhsA. 43 (*sotāpattimagga* is called "seeing": see, for example, M. I. 7–8; Dhs. 182, 220).

188. The word *kalyāṇaputhujjana* is used frequently in the commentaries contrasting *andhabālaputhujjana* (an ignorant and foolish person). In the canon, it occurs at Nd. I. 131, 138, 232, 313–14, 477–78. Sometimes the term is rendered *puthujjanakalyāṇaka*, as in Ps. I. 176; Ps. II. 190, 193 (*andhabālaputhujjana* is found in the canon at S. III. 140 and Thag. verse

575. Generally [such a person] is referred to as *assutvā puthujjana*, an unlearned ordinary person, as in M. I. 1; Nd. II. 44; Ps. I. 149; Dhs. 182; Vbh. 364, 368, 375; paired with *sutvā ariyasāvaka* it occurs in many other places). The *kalyāṇaputhujjana* (especially one who practices earnestly and is endowed with qualities that assure one's imminent attainment of stream entry) is classed by the commentaries as a *sekha*, together with the first seven other kinds of noble ones, counting from the *saddhānusārī* and *dhammānusārī* onwards. See VinA. I. 242; MA. I. 40; VbhA. 329; AA. II. 147; ItA. I. 60; VinṬ.: Pārājikakaṇḍaṁ, Bhikkhupadabhājanīyavaṇṇanā.

189. A. I. 74.

190. For *sutvā ariyasāvaka* on the level of *kalyāṇaputhujjana*, see M. I. 8; MA. I. 72.

191. Considered in terms of the two conditions for right view to be discussed later in the section dealing with the path [external influences (*paratoghosa*) and wise attention (*yoniso-manasikāra*)], *suta* is *paratoghosa* that comes from a good friend or association with the wise, which leads to faith and helps produce wise attention.

192. A. III. 53.

193. A. III. 53; these five treasures are also classed as a group of noble treasures, but the most well-known set of noble treasures is the sevenfold one, containing the further factors of shame (*hiri*) and fear of wrongdoing (*ottappa*), as in D. III. 251; A. IV. 5-6.

194. S. V. 347-48.

195. S. II. 45, 58, 79-80. The words *diṭṭhisampanna* and *dassanasampanna* are often used in place of the word *sotāpanna*. For *diṭṭhisampanna*, see M. I. 322-25; M. III. 64-65; S. II. 80, 133-39; S. V. 441-42, 457-65; A. I. 26-27; A. III. 373, 438-40; A. V. 119-20; Ps. I. 161; Vbh. 335-36 (commentary on: SA. II. 59; MA. IV. 107; AA. III. 387; AA. IV. 185); *dassanasampanna* is found only in verses, such as A. I. 151; A. III. 34; Thag. verses 45, 174 (commentary on: AA. III. 244); "a noble one with the wisdom to penetrate the truth" is translated from *ariyo nibbedhikapañño*, which may be rendered "a noble one with wisdom to penetrate or pierce [defilements]," or "one with the wisdom to correct or free oneself," or "with unattached wisdom"; see Ps. II. 201-2; DA. III. 1029; MA. III. 31, 326; MA. IV. 85; SA. I. 122; AA. II. 86; AA. III. 223, 258, 406; Nd1A. II. 285, 353, 359; Vism. 88; VismṬ.: Kammaṭṭhānaggahaṇaniddesavaṇṇanā, Samādhicatukkavaṇṇanā.

196. As in M. I. 8, 135, 300, 310, 433; M. III. 17-18. 188-89; S. III. 3-4, 16-17, 42-46, 96, 102, 113-14, 137-38, 151, 164-65; S. IV. 287.

197. Often stated after the description of the person obtaining the "Dhamma eye," as in Vin. I. 12, 16, 19, 20, 23, 37, 181, 225-26, 242, 248; Vin. II. 157, 192; D. I. 110, 148. D. II. 41; M. I. 379-80, 501; M. II. 145; A. IV. 186-87,

209–10; Ud. 49. "Has no need to rely on others" is literally rendered as "not dependent on others" (*aparappaccaya*).

198. M. I. 234, 491 (also includes the once-returner).
199. Vin. III. 189; A. III. 284 (the part in square brackets occurs only in the Vinaya source).
200. A. III. 451 (twenty-one lay followers are named, including some who were non-returners).
201. As in Vin. III. 10; D. II. 92–93, 155; M. I. 34; S. V. 193; A. I. 231–32.

Chapter 6. Introduction to the Middle Way

1. For a detailed discussion of the four noble truths, see the conclusion to this book.
2. The phrase *majjhena dhammadesanā* comes from the Pali *majjhena dhammaṁ deseti*, which occurs throughout the Nidānavagga of the Saṁyutta Nikāya, S. II. 17–77.
3. S. II. 105–6.
4. *Sammādiṭṭhi* = right view; *sammāsaṅkappa* = right thought; *sammāvācā* = right speech; *sammākammanta* = right action; *sammā-ājīva* = right livelihood; *sammāvāyāma* = right effort; *sammāsati* = right mindfulness; *sammāsamādhi* = right concentration.
5. S. II. 4–5.
6. S. V. 18–19.
7. See SA. II. 18.
8. S. II. 31.
9. Bhikkhu Ñanamoli, trans., *The Guide* (London: Pali Text Society, 1962).
10. A. V. 311. At A. V. 1–2 the same passage occurs, with the exception that *nibbidā* and *virāga* (disenchantment and dispassion) are included under the one heading. Compare also A. III. 19–20.
11. D. III. 288.
12. Vin. I. 10; S. V. 421.
13. The Buddhavacana at A. I. 295–96 and Ud. 71 may help to further clarify the meaning of the two extremes. In the first passage the Buddha states that *kāmasukhallikānuyogo* is the "coarse" way (*āgāḷhapaṭipadā*), referring to that group of people who see sensual pleasures as blameless and indulge in them to the full, and refers to *attakilamathānuyogo* as the "burnt" way (*nijjhāmapaṭipadā*), referring to the observances of the naked ascetics (we take it that the Buddha was citing them as an example).
14. S. V. 18–19; "skillful *ñāyadhamma*" may also be translated as "skillful qualities that lead to transcendence" (*ñāya* or *ñāyadhamma* refers to the transcendent path, the truth, or *nibbāna*).

15. S. V. 41.
16. The term "good friend" (*kalyāṇamitta*) does not refer to a good friend in the normal sense, but to anyone or anything, from the Buddha down to a teacher or a friend, books, or mass media, that helps with instruction, teaching, reflections, and practical guidance.
17. S. V. 2–3.
18. Eg. S. V. 31.
19. A. III. 414–15; S. IV. 133.
20. M. I. 134–35.
21. M. I. 260–61.
22. A sutta that gives emphasis to this idea is the *Rathavinīta Sutta*, M. I. 145–51, which describes the general and specific objectives of each of the *dhammas* in the seven stages of purification (*visuddhi*).
23. Vin. I. 20–21.
24. S. V. 7–8, 16–17, 26–27.
25. *Appamāda Sutta* S. I. 87–89; see also A. III. 364.
26. As in Nd. II. 57, 66, 72 (See also SnA. I. 74; Nd1A. II. 296; VismṬ. Cha-anussatiniddesavaṇṇanā, Buddhānussatikathāvaṇṇanā).
27. A. IV. 281–84.
28. See the teaching and accompanying explanation at D. III. 218; A. IV. 241–42; It. 15, 51–52; DA. III. 999; ItA. I. 78; ItA. II. 23.
29. Translator's note: Technically, this is the giving of "safety" or "fearlessness," meaning others need not be afraid. In Thailand it is often rendered as "forgiveness," absolving others of wrongdoing.
30. Translator's note: These are the five precepts.
31. A. I. 9.
32. S. II. 29.
33. Found in all the same places as for the first three benefits and the cited Buddhavacana. See also on the two qualities of the Buddha (*buddhaguṇa*) in VismṬ. Cha-anussatiniddesavaṇṇanā, Buddhānussatikathāvaṇṇanā and VinṬ.: Paṭhamo Bhāgo, Verañjakaṇḍavaṇṇanā, pointing out the connection between one's own benefit (*attattha*) and wisdom, and the benefit to others (*parattha*) and compassion.
34. A. I. 235–36.
35. See M. I. 300–1. See also A. I. 124–25, 295; A. III. 15–16; A. V. 326–27 and a division into five *dhammakkhanda* (that is, including factors over and above morality, concentration, and wisdom) at D. III. 279; A. III. 134–35, 271; AA. V. 4; Nd1A. I. 90.
36. Note that referring to the threefold training simply as morality (*sīla*), concentration (*samādhi*), and wisdom (*paññā*) is informal terminology. The terms *sīlasikkhā*, *samādhisikkhā*, and *paññāsikkhā* do not occur at all in

the Tipiṭaka. In some texts the three *dhammakkhandha* and the three *sikkhā* are given sequentially, but the original terms (*adhisīlasikkhā*, etc.) are preserved, as in VbhA. 122; PsA. 196.

37. The word *vinaya* is often looked at as merely the conventions relating to personal conduct, and this has caused the understanding of the term to become very narrow.
38. See the *Cakkavatti Sutta* (D. III. 61) and the *rājasaṅgahavatthu* according to the *Kūṭadanta Sutta* (D. I. 135), also SA. I. 144 and ItA. I. 93. The administrative system of the Emperor Asoka (reigned approx. B.E. 218-60 or 270-312) would be an outstanding example of an arrangement of a social *vinaya* on the national scale according to this teaching.
39. As in Vism. 84-228.
40. See additional explanation in the section "Right View and Learning" in chapter 8, "The Wisdom Factors of the Middle Way."
41. See Vism. 274.
42. D. II. 123.
43. D. II. 49-50; Dh. verses 183-85; for the organization into the threefold training, see DA. II. 479 and DhA. III. 237. The Sumaṅgalavilāsinī states that the first clause (the non-doing of all evil) is moral restraint (*sīlasaṁvara*); the second clause is calm and insight meditation—that is, concentration and wisdom; and the third is arahantship, but the Dhammapadaṭṭhakathā interprets this last clause to be simply cleansing the mind of the five hindrances. If we follow these two interpretations, the first clause is morality (with grounds for a higher interpretation), the second is concentration and wisdom, and the third is [also] concentration and wisdom (can also be classed as liberation). However, Vism. 4-5 interprets them quite simply as 1 = morality, 2 = concentration, and 3 = wisdom.
44. See *Dhammacakkappavattana Sutta* already cited (Vin. I. 10; S. V. 421).
45. When these last two factors (*sammāñāṇa* and *sammāvimutti*) are added on to the eight factors of the path, making ten, they are known as the ten *sammatta* or *asekhadhamma* (qualities of one who has finished the training). See D. III. 271, 292. (The commentaries state that *sammāñāṇa* refers to *phalañāṇa* (direct knowledge of fruition) and *paccavekkhaṇañāṇa* (direct knowledge of reviewing). See MA. I. 189; AA. II. 382. For *sammāñāṇa* as the final level of right view, see MA. IV. 135; AA. V. 70).
46. Regarding the three path factors arising in conjunction with other factors of the path, see *Mahācattārīsaka Sutta*, M. III. 71-78.
47. See the definitions of mundane and transcendent right view in chapter 8, "The Wisdom Factors of the Middle Way."
48. MA. II. 346 states that the buddhas and silent buddhas are enlightened through the sole use of *yoniso-manasikāra* as a determinant for right view.

49. UdA. 107 states that *paratoghosa* (literally, "the voice of others"—that is, the way of faith) is a factor for the arising of mundane right view, while *yoniso-manasikāra* is a factor for the arising of transcendent right view.

Chapter 7. The Precursors of Learning

1. A. I. 87. See also M. I. 294. There are also two conditions for the arising of wrong view, being the opposites to the above: *paratoghosa* (that are wrong) and *ayoniso-manasikāra* (unwise attention); A. V. 187-88.
2. It. 9-10: cf. S. V. 101-2.
3. S. V. 29-30.
4. In the Pali this can be rendered as *sappurisasaṁseva*, *sappurisūpasaṁseva*, *sappurisūpassaya*, *sappurisūpanissaya*, *sappurisasevanā*, or *paṇḍitasevanā*.
5. See Vism. 97-101. (This text gives these examples in the context of cultivating meditation practice.)
6. A. I. 14.
7. A. I. 17; cf. S. V. 102
8. A. IV. 281.
9. D. III. 184; A. IV. 283-84.
10. D. III. 190-91.
11. D. III. 185-86.
12. Also called *bahukāradhamma* (qualities of great benefit); D. III. 276; A. II. 32.
13. A. II. 245-46; "of great benefit to all people": A. II. 246.
14. S. V. 347.
15. This teaching was given to bhikkhus, as in D. III. 266-67; A. V. 23-24.
16. Kh. 3; Sn. 46-47.
17. It. 67-69; J. IV. 435; J. VI. 235.
18. It. 67-69.
19. Dh. verses 76-77.
20. J. I. 329.
21. The teachings for ordinary people in this regard emphasize, for example, knowing how to relate to death by contemplating the truth of formations as impermanent and unstable, and not being deluded by wealth, status, happiness, and praise.
22. D. III. 252, 283; A. IV. 113-14. Another group of *sappurisadhamma* contains eight factors; see M. III. 23. *Dhammacariyā* (righteous conduct), or the ten *kusalakammapatha*, can also be called *sappurisadhamma* (A. V. 279), and in some passages the *asekhadhamma*, or ten *sammatta*, are referred to

as *sappurisadhamma* (A. V. 245). One who is endowed with the eightfold path is called *sappurisa* (S. V. 19-20). The Buddha's words dealing with *sappurisa* and *asappurisa* are too numerous to include in full.

23. The canon states *apadāne sobhati paññā*. Translation follows AA. II. 169.
24. A. I. 102-3; M. III. 163.
25. A. I. 84.
26. Dh. verse 152.
27. Sn. 138-39.
28. Dh. verse 63.
29. A. II. 239.
30. See Dhs. 228.
31. See, for example, A. IV. 281-82.
32. A. IV. 32. The commentaries (UdA. 221; ItA. I. 65) describe eight qualities of the good friend, known as the *kalyāṇamittalakkhaṇa*, as follows: *saddhā*, *sīla*, *suta*, *cāga*, *viriya*, *sati*, *samādhi*, and *paññā*.
33. The quality known as *vacanakkhamo* refers in the canon to one who can endure the speech of others—one who is open to censure and criticism and is ready to correct oneself. In the canon, Venerable Sāriputta is praised in this connection (S. I. 64, for example). In the commentaries (SA. I. 123) it is related that some people are able to give instruction to others, but they become angry as soon as they are criticized; by contrast, Sāriputta not only taught others but humbly took heed when criticized by others. It is related that one day a seven-year-old novice pointed out to Sāriputta that he was wearing his robes unevenly, and Sāriputta took heed and went to adjust them accordingly.
34. *Dhammānudhammapaṭipanno* = "he practices the minor teachings in conformity with the major teachings"—that is, he practices *dhamma*s properly, according to their principles and objectives.
35. A. IV. 296, 328.
36. D. III. 185-88 (loose translation).
37. D. III. 190 (*piyavācā* is here written *piyavajja* and *peyyavajja*, but the meaning is the same).
38. D. III. 191.
39. S. IV. 180-81. It is sometimes called "fraternization in the household" (S. III. 11; Nd. I. 198-99), sometimes called "being stuck in the household" (Nd. I. 3878). It is one of the worries (*vitakka*) related to caring for others (Vbh. 356-57).
40. See A. III. 184 (free translation with some additional explanation).
41. D. III. 189-90.
42. Dh. verses 158-59.
43. Such scholars (*bahussuta*) are likened to herdsmen who tend others' cattle:

all they can do is count the cattle, but they do not partake of the five dairy products. See Dh. verse 19; DhA. I. 155.

44. As in S. III. 126–32.
45. M. II. 9–10; A. I. 276; Nd. I. 271–72. These Buddhavacana have been translated in contradictory ways, even in different volumes of the Thai-translated Tipiṭaka. The meaning should be compared with D. I. 193, 198–99, 239; M. II. 33; DA. II. 379, 555; MA. III. 273; SA. III. 254; UdA. 326; Nd1A. II. 355.
46. See Thag. verses 1024–33.
47. As in the story at SA. I. 273; SnA. II. 398.
48. For the Buddhavacana dealing with mundane and transcendent right view, see the later chapters dealing with the factors of the Middle Way. Commentaries such as AA. II. 24, 162; AA. III. 281 divide right view more finely into five kinds: *kammassakatāsammādiṭṭhi*, *jhānasammādiṭṭhi*, *vipassanāsammādiṭṭhi*, *maggasammādiṭṭhi*, and *phalasammādiṭṭhi*. The first three kinds are mundane right view; the last two transcendent.

    The first kind of right view above is *kammassakatāsammādiṭṭhi*, the second is classed as *vipassanāsammādiṭṭhi*. Both are therefore mundane, but they differ in that *vipassanāsammādiṭṭhi* paves the way for *magga-* and *phalasammādiṭṭhi*, which are transcendent; therefore it is referred to as "transcendent type" right view.
49. Part of a sequence given in A. V. 114. (In Pali: *sappurisasaṁseva → saddhammassavana → saddhā*). A. V. 145–49 shows a sequence of conditions that are abandoned, at one point stating that "with a good friend, it is possible to eliminate lack of faith, intolerance, and laziness." Later texts such as the Visuddhimagga use this principle to explain faith, saying "*saddhā* can have the factors of stream entry (*sotāpattiyaṅga*), such as listening to the true teaching, as its proximate cause (*padaṭṭhāna*)" (Vism. 464; DhsA. 119; Nd1A. I. 55).
50. Citing UdA. 107 (The same source may be referred to for *yoniso-manasikāra* and transcendent right view.)
51. In the canon it is called the *Kesaputtiya Sutta*, A. I. 188. The sutta that follows is very similar. See also A. II. 190–91.
52. The phrase "[do not] adhere" here should be understood to mean not deciding on or adopting a fixed view about something simply for these reasons. It corresponds with "make up one's mind." It should not be misconstrued as meaning that the Buddha was advocating not believing in things or other people. Rather it means that even for the most credible of things, the Buddha warned us not to simply place our belief in them, or make hasty judgments on them, as they still may be mistaken, but to first give them wise examination. When even the most credible things are to

be critically examined, how much more so should we exercise care and critical reflection with things or people that are not so credible?

53. Such as Venerable Sāriputta, who, despite his great wisdom, took longer to become enlightened than many of the Buddha's other disciples.
54. S. V. 31.
55. A. I. 13.
56. In the source texts it is usually rendered as *upāya* (means), as in MA. V. 81; SA. I. 88; AA. I. 51; AA. II. 38; AA. IV. 1; KhA. 229; Nd1A. II. 343; DhsA. 402; VismṬ.: Sīlaniddesavaṇṇanā, Paccayannissitasīlavaṇṇanā; VismṬ.: Anussatikammaṭṭhānaniddesavaṇṇanā, Maraṇassatikathāvaṇṇanā. It is glossed as both *upāya* and *patha* (way) at AA. II. 157; AA. III. 394; ItA. I. 62; Nd1A. II. 463; Vism. 30; glossed as *upāya*, *patha*, and *kāraṇa* (causes) at DA. II. 643; glossed as *kāraṇa* at SA. II. 268, 321; and glossed as *paññā* in Nettipakaraṇa. See also later texts such as the Abhidhānappadīpikā, verse 153.
57. Synonyms for *manasikāra* are *āvajjanā*, *ābhoga*, *samannāhāra*, and *paccavekkhaṇa* (See DA. II. 643; MA. I. 64; ItA. I. 62; Vism. 274).
58. Glossed as *upāya-manasikāra*, *patha-manasikāra*, *uppādaka-manasikāra* at SA. III. 165; as *upāya-manasikāra* and *patha-manasikāra* at DA. II. 459, 643; DA. III. 777 = VbhA. 270 = MA. I. 64, 281; ItA. I. 62; SA. II. 21; as *upāya-manasikāra* alone at MA. II. 346; SA. I. 171; SA. III. 133; AA. I. 46; AA. II. 23; VinṬ.: Mahāvaggaṭīkā, Mahākhandhakaṁ, Aññatitthiyapubbavatthukathāvaṇṇanā, Dutiyamārakathāvaṇṇanā; as *uppādaka-manasikāra* at MA. I. 296; as *kāraṇa-manasikāra* in the subcommentary to the Dīghanikāya (in explanation of the definition as *pātha-manasikāra*).
59. Many other English translations for the term have been used, some of which may help to further clarify its meaning: proper mind-work, proper attention, systematic attention, reasoned attention, attentive consideration, reasoned consideration, considered attention, careful consideration, careful attention, ordered thinking, orderly reasoning, genetical reflection, critical reflection, analytical reflection.
60. This is the more profound meaning of the adage: *attā hi attano nātho*, "Self is the mainstay of self."
61. This is known as *ayoniso-manasikāra bahula*. It is a nutriment of the hindrances. Conversely, *yoniso-manasikāra bahula* is nutriment for the enlightenment factors (sources already cited—e.g., S. V. 64–67).
62. See Vism. 230; VismṬ.: Anussatikammaṭṭhānaniddesavaṇṇanā, Maraṇassatikathāvaṇṇanā.
63. Miln.: Manasikāralakkhaṇapañho aṭṭhamo.
64. Examples of the use of *yoniso-manasikāra* and *ayoniso-manasikāra* may make the subject clearer: when a dispute arises within a group, those with

yoniso-manasikāra will stop arguing and look for a way to bring the dispute to an end (VinA. V. 1151; MA. IV. 205; JA. III. 489; DhA. I. 65); enmity overcome through *yoniso-manasikāra* (DhA. I. 51); grasping the meaning of terms used in the suttas, such as *sambhavesī*, with *ayoniso-manasikāra* and coming to the conclusion that the Buddha taught of a "between world" (UdA. 93); (*yoniso-manasikāra*) enables trainable individuals to realize the Dhamma (SA. III. 6) and benefit from listening to *dhamma* discourses (ItA. II. 25; Nd1A. I. 8—based on A. III. 174-75). *Yoniso-manasikāra* is often used in the sense of *vipassanā*, or in place of the phrase "to practice *vipassanā*," as in MA. I. 72 = ItA. I. 62; AA. I. 214, 380; cf. [AA. I. 215]; UdA. 354. In addition, see MA. I. 195; SA. III. 111; AA. III. 266; KhA. 232; DhA. I. 157; ItA. II. 150; PsA. I. 302.

65. MA. I. 65.
66. A. V. 115, 118.
67. *Yoniso-manasikāra* as a root (*mūla*) of faith: ItA. II. 79.
68. See D. II. 100-101. Having oneself as refuge is having the Dhamma as refuge, meaning to live one's life with effort, mindfulness, and clear comprehension (*sati sampajañña*) and being wise to the body, feelings, mind, and *dhammas* according to the four foundations of mindfulness, which are the factors for nourishing mindfulness and determinants for wisdom—that is, *yoniso-manasikāra* (A. I. 87-88; A. V. 115, 118, all already cited).
69. Taking ignorance and desire as the prime agents and roots of the cycle of rebirth (*vaṭṭa*): in addition to MA. I. 65, cited above, see also the sources in the canon at A.V. 113, 116-17, and the explanations of later texts at Vism. 524-25, 577-78.
70. As in S. II. 65, 70, 95-97; S. V. 389; Nd. II. 43.
71. S. II. 10, 104. The same is said of the thoughts of the Buddha Vipassī and the seven buddhas at D. II. 31; S. II. 5-9.
72. See VismṬ.: Khandhaniddesavaṇṇanā, Rūpakkhandhakathāvaṇṇanā; VismṬ.: Diṭṭhivisuddhiniddesavaṇṇanā, Nāmarūpapariggahakathāvaṇṇanā; VismṬ.: Paññabhūminiddesavaṇṇanā, Saṅkhārapaccayāviññāṇapadavitthārakathāvaṇṇanā; VismṬ.: Maggāmaggañāṇadassanavisuddhiniddesavaṇṇanā, Maggāmaggavavatthānakathāvaṇṇanā. The analysis of things and consideration of their determinants according to the *paṭiccasamuppāda* is also a kind of *vibhajjavāda*: (Vism. 523-24; VbhA. 129; VismṬ.: Paññābhūminiddesavaṇṇanā, Paṭiccasamuppādakathāvaṇṇanā).
73. See Vism. 587; Comp.: Kammaṭṭhānaparicchedo, Vipassanākammaṭṭhānaṁ, Visuddhibhedo. Sometimes called *nāmarūpapariccheda* (separation of mentality and physicality) and *saṅkhārapariccheda* (separation of formations).
74. S. I. 135.

75. In the sutta the term *yoniso-upparikkhā* (thorough examination) is used instead of *yoniso-manasikāra*.
76. S. III. 140–43.
77. S. III. 52.
78. S. III. 169. This method of examination is dealt with in almost the whole of the Khandhavagga of the Saṁyutta Nikāya of the Pali canon, and is also frequently found in other volumes.
79. S. III. 42–43 (*tadaṅganibbāna* = momentary *nibbāna*).
80. M. I. 9.
81. See *Cūḷamāluṅkyovāda Sutta*, M. I. 426–32.
82. Showing desire as the cause of suffering: Vin. I. 10; D. II. 308; S. V. 421–22.
83. Showing the *paṭiccasamuppāda* process as the cause of suffering: A. I. 177, as well as all the Buddhavacana describing the *paṭiccasamuppāda*, which conclude with the words *evametassa dukkhakkhandhassa samudayo hoti* ["Thus is the arising of this whole mass of suffering"].
84. *Atthadhamma*: this is not the original wording but a later-coined term based on the essential meaning. Correctly speaking it should be *dhammattha*, but it is rendered *atthadhamma* as a matter of style, and even in the texts the two words are also paired as *atthadhamma*; as in D. III. 155; J. VI. 222; JA. VI. 223; Ps. II. 194.
85. Examples of different meanings of *dhammānudhammapaṭipatti* from the canon and commentaries: practicing rightly, practicing harmoniously, practicing without obstruction, practicing in accordance with the objective (Nd. II. 46). Other meanings: practicing the initial practices, which are the teachings that accord with the nine *lokuttara dhamma* (DA. II. 578; DA. III. 1020; SA. II. 267; AA. IV. 57); practicing the initial practices together with morality, which are the teachings that accord with the nine *lokuttara dhamma* (AA. II. 203; AA. III. 6, 118, 164)—that is, practicing the initial practices together with morality for the objective of the nine *lokuttara dhammas* (AA. III. 290); practicing the insight teachings, which are teachings that conform to the noble Dhamma (DA. II. 555; SA. III. 254; UdA. 126); practicing the way of *vipassanā*, which is the pathway to the noble Dhamma (AA. IV. 151); maintaining the practice, which is conducive to *nibbāna*, the transcendent (SA. II. 34); practicing insight meditation that inclines to the transcendent (SnA. I. 329); *dhammānudhamma* is Dhamma plus the minor *dhammas* (*anudhamma*; DA. III. 929); *dhammānudhamma* glossed as *anudhamma*, the practice that fits the Dhamma (MA. III. 220); the nine transcendent *dhammas* are Dhamma, while *vipassanā* and so on is *anudhamma*. The way of practice appropriate to the *dhamma* is called *dhammānudhammapaṭipadā* (Nd1A. I. 65).
86. A. IV. 113–14. In reference to a king, the word *dhamma* in *dhammaññutā*

refers to principles of governance and royal customs for governing (see A. III. 148–49; AA. III. 283).

87. A. III. 176–77. The word "respectfully" (*sakkaccaṁ*) means to apply oneself earnestly, to give importance to, or do wholeheartedly, as in *vacchakaṁ sakkaccaṁ upanijjhāyati*—"watching over her calf with earnest interest" (Vin. I. 193).
88. See A. I. 35–36; A. II. 97; A. IV. 116, 220–23, 296, 337–38, 391–92; A. V. 126–27, 154–55.
89. E.g., A. II. 246 and other places already cited.
90. It must be emphasized again that the term *kāma* (sensuality) should not be understood in the narrow sense it has in Thai usage. Its meaning may be illustrated with an example. A bhikkhu greets a householder and asks after his health and that of his family: if he does so not out of goodwill (*mettā*) but out of an expectation that the householder will like him and invite him to receive offerings, this is said to be speaking out of sensual desire (See DhA. II. 156).
91. *Nissaraṇa* here refers to rapture and well-being independent of sensuality (see following Buddhavacana).
92. A. I. 258–61.
93. D. III. 239–40; A. III. 245; the sutta continues on to describe the escape from enmity (*byāpāda*) and aggression (*vihiṁsā*). At It. 61 renunciation (*nekkhamma*) is said to be the escape from sensuality.
94. M. I. 505.
95. Ps. II. 8–10.
96. See M. I. 10; Nd. I. 496; cf. D. III. 130. The most commonly found of these reflections is that on food, and practicing accordingly is said to comprise knowing moderation in food (*bhojane mattaññutā*), as in M. I. 273; M. III. 2–3; S. IV. 104, 176–77; A. II. 39–40; A. IV. 167–68. It is a curb on desire for tastes at Nd. I. 240–41. Note that for "attends wisely" in this case the Pali is *yoniso-paṭisaṅkhā*, but the meaning comes within the domain of *yoniso-manasikāra* according to M. I. 7. Clear examples of the interchangeable use of *yoniso-paṭisaṅkhā* and *yoniso-manasikāra* occur at M. I. 11 and S. V. 79. (The *Sabbāsavasaṁvara Sutta*, M. I. 6–12, is a good example of the extent of *yoniso-manasikāra*'s meaning. A similar sutta occurs at A. III. 387–88).
97. See Vism. 229–39.
98. The *kusītavatthu* and *ārabbhavatthu* occur at D. III. 255–58, 287; A. IV. 332–35.
99. M. I. 118–22. (The passage given here also includes the views of the commentaries and the author's own explanation.)
100. Here *chanda* refers to *taṇhāchanda* (desire), specifically *rāga* (passion) or *lobha* (greed).

101. A. III. 185-86.

102. A. III. 186-91 (loose translation). See also the nine *āghātavatthu* (conditions bringing on enmity) and nine *āghātapaṭivinaya* (methods for eliminating enmity) at D. III. 262-63, 289; A. IV. 408-9; and the ten *āghātavatthu* and ten *āghātapaṭivinaya* at A. V. 150-51 (the *āghātavatthu* alone occur at Vin. V. 168; Vbh. 389, 391).

103. *Bhaddekaratta Sutta*, M. III. 187-89. See also the following suttas at M. III. 189-202. (The phrase "one who grows day by day" is translated from *bhaddekaratta*, literally meaning "one who progresses for one night." It might be rendered "one for whom each night brings good fortune.")

104. S. I. 5.

105. J. III. 35, 399.

106. The Buddha's last words: D. II. 156.

107. A. III. 102-3.

108. M. I. 301; S. IV. 293.

109. As in M. II. 197-98; A. V. 190-91, which will be discussed below.

110. As in VismṬ.: Khandhaniddesavaṇṇanā, Rūpakkhandhakathāvaṇṇanā; VismṬ.: Paññābhūminiddesavaṇṇanā, Saṅkhārapaccayaviññāṇapadavitthārakathāvaṇṇanā; VismṬ.: Diṭṭhivisuddhiniddesavaṇṇanā, Nāmarūpapariggahakathāvaṇṇanā. (The original term used for this meaning was *vibhaṅga*, as in *dhātuvibhaṅga*, *khandhavibhaṅga*, and so on.)

111. See M. III. 45-61; A. IV. 305-6; A. V. 100.

112. See Vin. I., Verañjakaṇḍa.

113. M. I. 246.

114. The four kinds of questions occur at D. III. 229; A. I. 197; A. II. 46. Examples are given at Miln. 144; DA. II. 567; AA. II. 308.

115. It is said that the view or understanding that leads to such questions arises from *ayoniso-manasikāra* or from bad external influences (see A. V. 186-87; Miln. Abhejjavaggo, Abyākaraṇīyapañho; AA. II. 308).

116. As in M. I. 428-32; S. IV. 374-403.

117. As in S. II. 13-14, 60-62.

118. A. V. 100 (also occurs in the *Sevitabbāsevitabba Sutta*). There are similar passages, but explaining in more detail, about people in relation to bhikkhus at A. IV. 365.

119. A. I. 225. "Difficult practices" is from *jīvita*; "reverential offerings" is from *upaṭṭhānasāra*. (See also the definitions in the commentary.)

120. S. IV. 331-37; A. V. 177.

121. Those who are going to impart knowledge and ideas to others may use the following three kinds of *yoniso-manasikāra* as fundamental criteria for gauging their intellectual capacity:

    1. Thinking according to determinants: seeing whether or not they have

rational thought, know how to think rationally, or are rational people who know how to delve into determinants.

2. Thinking analytically: seeing whether they know how to look at things or matters from different perspectives and know how to analyze their different perspectives rather than just looking at one perspective or thinking very fuzzily.

3. Thinking by relating the meaning to the letter: seeing whether they have the ability to grasp the essential meaning of the things they say, hear, or read (*dhamma*) and understand their meaning, objectives, or value (*attha*).

Chapter 8. The Wisdom Factors of the Middle Way

1. For example, D. II 311–12; M. I. 48–49, 62; S. V. 8–9; Vbh. 104, 235.
2. M. I. 46–47 (the three roots of unskillfulness = greed, aversion, and delusion; the three roots of skillfulness = non-greed, non-aversion, and non-delusion).
3. S. III. 51.
4. S. IV. 142.
5. M. I. 190–91.
6. S. II. 78–79.
7. M. III. 72.
8. S. V. 442.
9. M. III. 71–77.
10. M. III. 76. In addition, there are similar passages at D. II. 216–17; A. V. 236–37. The phrase "can be right" is a translation of *pahoti*, which can also be translated as "sufficient for the purpose" or "workable." Passages at S. V. 1–2; A. V. 214 go a little deeper, showing that while right view is the leader of the factors of the path, knowledge (*vijjā*) is the leader in producing all skillful qualities and is also the source of right view (similarly, ignorance is the leader of unskillful qualities and the source of wrong view).
11. A. I. 30–31.
12. In the canon, the synonyms usually given together with *diṭṭhi* are *khanti* (ideas that accord with one's understanding) and *ruci* (ideas that are compatible or preferred), as in Vin. I. 69–70; Nd. I. 40; Ps. I. 176; Vbh. 245, 324–25. The word *diṭṭhi* is said to encompass the English words "belief," "view," "value," and even "attitude," although the last word also encroaches on the domain of *saṅkappa*, the second factor of the path.
13. As mental *kamma* in the *kammapatha*: see A. V. 264–68, 292. Its importance: see M. I. 373; A. V. 212.
14. Here we may cite *saddhāmūlikā ca sammādiṭṭhi* (right view, which has *saddhā* as root) at DA. I. 231; MA. I. 132; AA. II. 109; ItA. II. 45.

15. As in Vbh. 328.
16. Referred to in the commentaries as *vipassanāsammādiṭṭhi*; in the canon, *saccānulomikañāṇa* (in commentarial texts, *saccānulomikañāṇa* is used to refer specifically to the highest of the nine levels of insight).
17. In fact, both wrong values and emotion are a result of desire, but they differ in that the former is desire that is modified, while the latter is raw.
18. As in Nd. I. 44–45; Vbh. 237.
19. *Sucarita*: here the word *sucarita* is used in the normal Thai sense, referring specifically to good conduct in body, speech, and livelihood, and excluding good mental conduct (*mano sucarita*), which also encompasses right view.
20. Translated and condensed from A. III. 20–21. This can be supported by the Buddhavacana: "Listening well, inquiring, and researching are the nutriments of wisdom." (A. V. 136.)
21. D. II. 311–12; M. III. 251; Vbh. 104, 235.
22. M. III. 73; Vbh. 110, 237.
23. This attitude of mind developed to a higher level becomes equanimity (*upekkhā*), which is a crucial factor in the effective use of thought. It does not mean indifference or inaction as is commonly misunderstood. This point will be discussed later.
24. *Nekkhamma* = non-greed; *nekkhamma dhātu* (the *nekkhamma* element) = all skillful qualities; *abyāpādadhātu* = goodwill; *avihiṁsādhātu* = compassion (Vbh. 86; VbhA. 74; PsA. I. 68).
25. See this approach at VbhA. 91; Vism. 515.
26. *Upekkhā*, equanimity, is included in *nekkhamma*, in the phrase "liberation of mind through equanimity (*upekkhācetovimutti*) is the escape (*nissaraṇa*) from passion (*rāga*)" (D. III. 248–49).
27. At Nd. I. 488 it is defined as *mettāti yā sattesu metti mettāyanā mettāyitattaṁ andā anudāyanā anudāyitattaṁ hitesitā anukampā abyāpādo abyāpajjho adoso kusalamūlaṁ*. At SnA. I. 128 it is defined as *hitasukhūpanayanakāmatā mettā*.
28. Vism. 318.
29. Vism. 318.
30. Ap. 47–48; DhA. I. 145 (for an example of the Buddha spreading goodwill, see Vin. II. 195; JA. VIII. 215).
31. M. I. 239–40, 250.
32. M. I. 114–16.
33. A. II. 76–77.

Chapter 9. The Morality Factors of the Middle Way

1. Wrong livelihood (*micchā-ājīva*) is given as fraud (or deception), currying favor, trickery, extortion, and bribery: M. III. 75.

2. D. II. 311–12; M. I. 62; M. III. 251; Vbh. 105, 235.
3. M. III. 74–75; cf. Vbh. 106–7, 237.
4. This kind of deluded grasping at rites and observances (*sīlabbataparāmāsa*) was very widespread in India from ancient times before the Buddha and has not diminished even now. The attempt to overthrow this kind of belief was one of the most prominent features of the Buddha's work, along with doing away with the caste system and pulling people away from questions of metaphysics and back to the problems of real life.
5. Translator's note: In keeping with modern understanding, this could be extrapolated as also including people who do not give consent.
6. A. V. 263. These definitions of the ten factors occur in many other places, such as A. V. 283, 288–89, 292, 297–98, 301–2.
7. D. I. 4–5, 63–64, 100–101, and so on; M. I. 267–68, 345; A. V. 204–5.
8. It is cited in Albert Schweitzer, *Indian Thought and Its Development* (New York: Henry Holt, 1936), 112, which in turn is cited in Joseph L. Sutton, *Problems of Politics and Administration in Thailand* (Bloomington, IN: Institute of Training for Public Service, Department of Government, Indiana University, 1962). In his book (pp. 2–8), Sutton also quotes other Buddhist teachings to support his views, such as the law of *kamma*, belief in rebirth, and escaping from *saṁsāra*. As for the law of *kamma*, Sutton's view can be countered with the explanations given earlier, in chapter 4. In answer to his allegation that the teaching of rebirth gives people a chance to procrastinate and not apply themselves to the doing of good (in contrast to the Christian ethic that there is only one life), it can be easily explained that in Buddhism a human rebirth is said to be extremely difficult to come by, as difficult as the chances of a turtle randomly popping its head through a single life preserver floating in the middle of the ocean. Also, bad *kamma* cannot be removed simply by absolution or confession. Regarding his view on withdrawing and having nothing to do with worldly activities, Sutton cites the Buddhavacana, "Those who love nothing in this world are rich in joy and free from pain" (Ud. 92), which is a translation of the Pali *tasmā hi te sukhino vītasokā yesaṁ piyaṁ natthi kuhiñci loke*. The word translated as "love" is *piya*, here meaning "objects of fond attachment," which are causes for personal clinging and attachment. This passage describes the qualities of one who is liberated, in whom fond love no longer remains, only goodwill (*mettā*). Thus, in this case, we are talking about the liberated being, who acts out of *mettā* and has no attachment or personal bias that could cause trouble for oneself or others through selfishness.
9. The attitude in regard to food that is truly in accordance with nature is to accept the truth that because we have not yet finished the practice, we must do things we do not want to do, but for which there is no choice; we

might consider the meat of living beings eaten in the same way as would a father and mother who were forced to eat the flesh of their own deceased child in order to cross a desert (see S. II. 98–99).

10. *Sīla* is intention, which is mental concomitants (*cetasikā*), which is non-transgression (*avītikkama*) (Ps. I. 44–45; explained at Vism. 6–7).

11. In A. II. 141, there is a Buddhavacana describing the four kinds of good speech (*vacīsucarita*) as truthful speech (*saccavācā*), not backbiting (*apisuṇavācā*), gentle speech (*saṇhavācā*), and thoughtful speech (*mantābhāsā*). In regard to *mantābhāsā*, the commentaries state that it means speaking with wisdom (AA. III. 134). It is sometimes translated as "speaking in moderation." However, essentially the meaning is the same as given above.

12. At A. III. 209 there is a Buddhavacana about *akaraṇīyavaṇijjā*, the five trades a Buddhist (*upāsaka/upāsikā*) should not undertake. These are (1) *satthavaṇijjā*: trade in weapons (instruments of destruction); (2) *sattavaṇijjā*: trade in people; (3) *maṁsavaṇijja*: trade in meat (commentaries = raising animals for sale); (4) *majjavaṇijjā*; trade in liquor (including addictive substances); (5) *visavaṇijjā*: trade in poisons. In the commentaries these five kinds of trade are known as *micchāvaṇijjā* = wrong trading (DA. I. 235; MA. I. 136), or *adhammavaṇijjā* = unrighteous trading (SnA. I. 379).

13. The five precepts are often referred to in the commentaries as *niccasīla* (regular morality, or morality that should be observed regularly), as in SnA. I. 377, 379; Vism. 15.

14. S. V. 353–55.

15. A. III. 208–9 (translated in brief).

16. The full five precepts occur at ItA. II. 49–54. Only the first four, followed by other courses of action (*kammapatha*), are at MA. I. 200–201; Nd. I. 115–18; DhsA. 97–101. These are cited by later texts, such as Maṅgalatthadīpanī (I. 210–19). The factors for transgressing the precepts on backbiting (*pisuṇāvācā*) and so on are not included here because the intention is to explain the five precepts. Those who wish to know them can refer to the references given here. Regarding the fifth precept, nowadays there are addictive substances that can be taken by means other than drinking, in which case the essential principle should be taken.

17. The source here is the same as for transgressing precepts, and also VbhA. 383.

18. A. II. 61–62.

19. See DA. I. 178; MA. II. 42; ItA. I. 108; SnA. I. 43; referred to in J. IV. 53; explained at JA. IV. 53. Prince Vessantara also asked to be blessed with *sadārasantosa* (see J. VI. 572; JA. VI. 572).

20. J. V. 146.
21. M. I. 39. (The commentators explain that *khema* means "freedom from danger, helpfulness, goodwill," and they go on to note that this statement refers to purity of the mind door (*manodvāra*—MA. I. 178).
22. D. III. 180–93.
23. DA. III. 943.
24. In this sutta, the harmful results of these pathways to ruin are also explained (but not included in the list here).
25. The qualities of real friends and false friends were discussed in chapter 7.
26. *Adhanānaṁ dhanānupadānaṁ*, or in full, *ye ca te tāta vijite adhanā tesañca dhānaṁ anuppadajjeyyāsi* (D. III. 61).
27. M. III. 75.
28. As in S. III. 240; Nd. I. 372, 495; Nd. II. 61. A fairly detailed list occurs in the short, middle, and greater sections on morality, as in D. I. 8, 67.
29. Vin. 99 (already cited).
30. Ud. 66 (already cited).
31. S. II. 199 (already cited).
32. Sn. 13.
33. A. V. 181–82.
34. A. I. 128–29.
35. S. I. 89–91.
36. S. I. 74.
37. J. III. 301.
38. There is another account of a rich man's wealth being appropriated at S. I. 89–91. More is related in the Mayhakasakuṇa Jātaka, (JA. III. 298). See also Sudhābhojana Jātaka (JA. V. 382); the story of Macchariyakosiya (Kosiya the Miser; DhA. I. 366); the Illīsa Jātaka (JA. I. 345); and the story of Biḷārapādaka the rich man (DhA. III. 16).
39. A. IV. 284, 289, 322, 324–25 (four occurrences in the same volume, two uttered to householders, two to bhikkhus).
40. This is a commonly found idiom, occurring, for example, at A. II. 69; A. III. 45 (the full passage is quoted elsewhere in this book).
41. See J. IV. 166.
42. The seven *sappurisadhamma* are discussed in detail in chapter 7.
43. J. VI. 287.
44. J. VI. 296–97.
45. A. IV. 285–89 and similar at A. IV. 281, 322, 323. The qualities for further benefit have been discussed in the section dealing with the stream enterer (chapter 5).
46. A. II. 69.
47. A. III. 45. Similar passages occur at A. II. 67.

48. J. V. 387.
49. J. V. 391, 397.
50. M. III. 262; S. I. 33–34, 55. It is explained that "work" = right action; "knowledge" = right view and right thought; "truth" (Dhamma) = the *samādhi* group of factors (instilling and training qualities and the quality of the mind); "morality" (*sīla*) = right speech and right livelihood; "a full life" = the noble path or right livelihood. (See other explanations at MA. V. 81; SA. I. 88; VismṬ.: Paṭhamo Bhāgo, Nidānādikathāvaṇṇanā).
51. M. II. 72–73; Thag. 776–84.
52. Kh. 2; Sn. 46. (Blameless endeavors are activities that are good, that are not harmful—especially carrying out useful works, such as being helpful or creating gardens, building bridges, or taking the eight precepts; see KhA. 141.)
53. J. IV. 429.
54. J. I. 421.
55. J. III. 218.
56. D. III. 211, 273; S. V. 64; A. V. 55–56; Ps. I. 5, 122.
57. As in D. III. 181.
58. A. II. 27–28. (The omitted passages are the same as in the first paragraph. Similar passages occur at D. III. 224–25; Nd. II. 59.)
59. Refer to the Buddha's statement that a true person (*sappurisa*) arises for the benefit of the many (A. IV. 244–45) and that wealth in the hands of a true person is like a cool pond near a village, which everyone can drink from; but wealth arising for a bad person is like a pond in a land of demons: no matter how clear and cool it may be, it leads to no benefit (S. I. 90–91).
60. This can be compared to the arising of power and governance according to Buddhist thought in the *Aggañña Sutta* (D. III. 92–93). Wealthy Buddhists such as Anāthapiṇḍika followed this practice, sharing his wealth with the Saṅgha and the poor for many years until it was all gone, but he had no regrets.
61. A. III. 352.
62. D. III. 65–66, 70–71.
63. As in D. I. 135; D. III. 61; the aim is to help and support effort, not to encourage poverty resulting from laziness.
64. As in A. IV. 151; It. 22.
65. Translator's note: The eight accessories or tools of a Buddhist monk are the alms bowl, the upper robe, the lower robe, the outer robe, a razor, a needle, a belt, and a water filter.
66. Tenth inscription of Asoka's edicts on stone.

Chapter 10. The Concentration Factors of the Middle Way

1. D. II. 31; M. I. 62; M. III. 252-52; Vbh. 105, 235.
2. Vbh. 107, 237.
3. A. II. 15; also translated simply as right or perfect effort.
4. A. II. 74.
5. See A. II. 16.
6. See M. III. 72-75.
7. A. IV. 233.
8. A. I. 50.
9. Dh. verse 276: *tumhehi kiccaṁ ātappaṁ akkhātāro tathāgata.*
10. The five faculties are faith (*saddhā*), effort (*viriya*), mindfulness (*sati*), concentration (*samādhi*), and wisdom (*paññā*).
11. The story occurs at Vin. I. 181-82; A. III. 374-75.
12. D. III. 277; M. II. 95; A. III. 65; A. V. 15.
13. A. III. 66.
14. D. II. 312-13; M. I. 62; M. III. 251-52; Vbh. 105, 236.
15. Vbh. 107, 237.
16. Compare the commonly used English terms for *sati*: mindfulness, attentiveness, or detached watching. There are many terms for *appamāda*, including heedfulness, watchfulness, earnestness, diligence, zeal, and carefulness, or, in negative terms, such as "non-neglect of mindfulness."
17. S. V. 43; A. V. 21-22.
18. A. I. 11.
19. A. I. 16.
20. A. I. 16-17.
21. A. I. 17-18.
22. D. II. 155-56. The Buddha's last words.
23. S. V. 30, 32-33, 35-37, 41-45.
24. A. II. 119-20.
25. A. II. 120.
26. S. I. 87-89.
27. S. V. 168-69.
28. Obviously *sati* does not correspond exactly with memory. However, recollection or remembrance, which are expressions of memory, do convey different senses of the word *sati*, and the word is commonly encountered in this sense, such as in *buddhānussati* (recollection on the Buddha). But in its real sense, as discussed here, the desired meaning is that given above and is similar to the English word "mindfulness."
29. See Vism. 130, 162-63, 464; VbhA. 311; DA. III. 787 = MA. I. 291.
30. D. II. 290; M. I. 55-56; see also Vbh. 193-207.

31. *Nīvaraṇa* (obstructions to the working of the mind) are sensual desire (*kāmachanda*), enmity (*byāpāda*), depression and sloth (*thīnamiddha*), distraction and worry (*uddhaccakukkucca*), and doubt and uncertainty (*vicikicchā*). See further in the section "Right Concentration."
32. *Bojjhaṅga* (enlightenment factors) are mindfulness (*sati*), investigation of Dhamma (*dhammavicaya*), effort (*viriya*), rapture (*pīti*), tranquility (*passaddhi*), concentration (*samādhi*), and equanimity (*upekkhā*) [see further in the section "Right Concentration"].
33. The word "body" is changed to feeling, mind, and *dhamma* according to each of the foundations of mindfulness.
34. It is known as *vipassanā samādhi*, a level between momentary (*khaṇika*) and access (*upacāra*) concentration.
35. DA. III. 756; MA. I. 241; VbhA. 217. The phrase "body in the body" is glossed in several different ways by the commentaries, with an overall emphasis on the aim of the contemplation. One interpretation, for example, takes it as focusing on the body without muddle, attending, in the body, only to the body—not to feelings, mind-states, or *dhammas* in the body. Another takes it to mean attending to the smaller parts that comprise the body as a unit, distinguishing the different components and looking at them individually, until one sees that the whole body is nothing other than an aggregation of smaller constituents, that there is nobody there, no "Mr. A.," or "Ms. B." It thus implies the analysis of a composite unit, the dismantling of a complex structure, and is an endeavor comparable to that of removing all the leaves and the spadix of a banana tree and finding no heart wood, no essential tree. (The phrases "feelings in feelings," "mind in mind," and "*dhammas* in *dhammas*" should be understood in the same way.)
36. This corresponds with the teaching given in the *Mahācattārīsaka Sutta*, M. III. 72-75. As for the equivalence of *ātāpī* with *sammāvāyāma*, see Vbh. 194-95.
37. As in DA. III. 776; MA. I. 280; VbhA. 217, 268.
38. As in VbhA. 197-98. Note that in the canonical description of knowing the mind state of another person through psychic power (*cetopariyañāṇa*) there is a description of the mental state that corresponds with the case given in the teaching on the *satipaṭṭhāna* (as in D. I. 79-80).
39. See, for example, N. P. Jacobson: *Buddhism: The Religion of Analysis* (Carbondale: Southern Illinois University Press, 1970), 93-123.
40. This is a literal translation of the common Thai translation of *sampajañña*, ความรู้ตัว.
41. A. II. 143.
42. S. III. 2.
43. *Sati* arising in conjunction with *paññā* is strong, lacking *paññā* is

weak (MA. III. 30; VbhA. 312); there is no *paññā* without *sati* (VismṬ.: Asubhakammaṭṭhānaniddesavaṇṇanā, Vinicchayakathāvaṇṇanā); one lacking in *sati* cannot recollect (*anupassanā*; as in DA. III. 758; SA. III. 180); speaking of *sati* alone, *paññā* is implied (as in AA. III. 360, commenting on A. III. 324-25; see also the explanations of the term *satokārī* in Ps. I. 176-77, cited at Vism. 271).

44. A. V. 114; see also S. V. 329; M. III. 82.
45. See, for example, Vbh. 250.
46. *Sati* is used for attention, *paññā* for examination, analysis, and deduction (see VismṬ.: Asubhakammaṭṭhananiddesa-vaṇṇanā, Vinicchayakathāvaṇṇanā).
47. See chapter 7 on *yoniso-manasikāra*.
48. Note here the different results on wisdom that faith (*saddhā*) and *yoniso-manasikāra* have: *saddhā* makes, as it were, a fixed channel along which thinking follows; *yoniso-manasikāra* makes expedient paths for the working of wisdom according to circumstance. In Buddhism the *saddhā* that is encouraged is that which connects to wisdom—that is, *saddhā* that opens the way for wise attention. An example of the kind of faith that cuts a fixed channel is the belief that whatever happens does so at the will of God or fate. Thinking stops right there. An example of the *saddhā* that leads to wise attention is the belief of Buddhists who, even though they have not yet realized the truth for themselves, have faith in the Buddha's teaching that all things fare according to determinants. Thus, whenever they experience any particular event, this kind of faith will lead to the use of wise attention, delving into the determinants that have led to it.
49. Vism. 84-85; Nd1A. II. 388; PsA. I. 17. *Ekaggatā* or *samādhi* can also arise in unskillful states of mind. For example, in Dhs. 75-87 it is shown how one-pointedness, the faculty of *samādhi* (*samādhindriya*), and wrong *samādhi* (*micchāsamādhi*) are involved in the unskillful mind, and the commentaries give examples of this, such as people having undivided attention while unerringly striking the body of an animal with a weapon, when intentionally stealing, and when committing sexual misconduct. However, one-pointedness in unskillful mental states is not strong or resilient as it is in skillful mental states. It is compared to sprinkling water on parched earth—the dust is kept down for only a short time, and the earth quickly becomes dry and dusty again (see DhsA. 144, 248, 251).
50. As in D. II. 312-13; M. I. 62; M. III. 252; Vbh. 105.
51. S. V. 198, 200. The commentaries assert that attending to the state of detachment means taking *nibbāna* as object of attention (SA. III. 234).
52. Vbh. 107, 238.
53. Note the definition given elsewhere by the commentaries of *sam-*

māsamādhi as *yāthāva-samādhi* ("real concentration," or concentration that accords with reality), *niyyānaka-samādhi* (concentration that leads out of the cycle (*vaṭṭa*), leading to transcendence of suffering and liberation), and *kusala-samādhi* (skillful concentration), as in DhsA. 144.

54. PsA. I. 125. Note that the word *samādhi* is sometimes used to refer to *vipassanā*, especially in the sense of the three *samādhi* known as *suññata-samādhi* (emptiness concentration), *animittasamādhi* (sign-less concentration), and *appaṇihitasamādhi* (desireless concentration). See D. III. 219-20; A. I. 299; Ps. I. 48-49; AA. II. 386; PsA. I. 102. However, such definitions should be taken as exceptions rather than the norm.
55. Nd1A. I. 129; PsA. I. 183; DhsA. 117; Vism. 144.
56. Vism. 86, 126-27, 137-38, 146-47; VinA. II. 428.
57. In access concentration, the hindrances are suppressed and the factors of *jhāna* begin to manifest. It is similar to attainment concentration but differs in that the factors of *jhāna* are not sufficiently strong. The meditation sign (*nimitta*) is gained, and then the mind falls into subconsciousness (*bhavaṅga*) and is always coming up and going down, like a baby learning to stand—a parent holds the baby up and it falls over again. In attainment concentration, the factors of *jhāna* are strong. The mind falls into *bhavaṅga* only once and then can maintain itself all day and all night, like a strong adult. It is like an adult who can rise from his seat and can stand, walk, and work all day long. See Vism. 126-27, 146-47.
58. Vism.Ṭ.: Brahmavihāraniddesavaṇṇanā, Pakiṇṇakakathāvaṇṇanā and Abhiññāniddesavaṇṇanā, Dibbasotadhātukathāvaṇṇanā.
59. Vism. 323, 404.
60. A. IV. 299-300. I surmise that this sutta is one of the sources of the Abhidhamma concept of five *jhānas*.
61. M. I. 115-17. The text given in the second and third paragraphs is also found elsewhere, such as M. I. 21-22. Etymologically, the term *samādahati* ("firm" or "concentrated") can also be translated as "composed." Such a translation would seem to convey a more dynamic state. It is like translating it as "proceeding unflinchingly," as a well-concentrated acrobat might walk a high tightrope. The word *asāraddho*, translated here as "not restless," may also be rendered "free from stress."
62. As in PsA. I. 175.
63. As in S. V. 96.
64. As in S. V. 94.
65. As in S. V. 97.
66. The five hindrances with *abhijjhā* as the first tend to be used before descriptions of the attainment of *jhāna*, such as at D. I. 71, 207; D. III. 48-49; M. I. 181; M. III. 134; A. II. 210-11; A. III. 92-93; A. V. 206-7; Vbh. 244-45.

The five hindrances with *kāmachanda* as the first are usually described independently and given only in name without descriptions, as in D. I. 246; D. III. 234, 278; M. I. 144; S. V. 60, 97; A. III. 64; Vbh. 378. See an explanation of six hindrances (with *avijjā* added) at Dhs. 204–5; Vism. 146. *Abhijjhā* = *kāmachanda*: see PsA. I. 176. *Abhijjhā* = *lobha* as in Dhs. 190. The word "physical conditions" in the third hindrance refers to "mental body" (*nāmakāya*)—that is, the group of mental concomitants (*cetasikā*); see DhsA. 377.

67. In Pali the eight attributes are (1) *samāhita*, (2) *parisuddha*, (3) *pariyodāta*, (4) *anaṅgaṇa*, (5) *vigatūpakkilesa*, (6) *mudubhūta*, (7) *kammaniya*, and (8) *ṭhita āneñjappatta* (occurring frequently, such as in D. I. 76–77; M. I. 22; A. I. 164–65. The following commentarial references enumerate the factors: Nd. II. 357; Vism. 376–78; VismṬ. Iddhividhaniddesavaṇṇanā, Abhiññākathāvaṇṇanā. See also A. IV. 421).
68. A. III. 63–64.
69. S. V. 121–26; A. III. 230 ("will not be clear" means they cannot be recollected or brought to mind). Elsewhere (A. I. 9) the Buddha talks of the mind that is not dull as being like an expanse of limpid water in which stones, pebbles, snails, and swimming fish can be seen, while the dull mind is like an expanse of murky water.
70. A. III. 16–17; cf.: S.V. 92.
71. A. II. 14–15; It. 118–19. The effort to clear the mind of hindrances is one definition of the teaching known as devotion to wakefulness (*jāgariyānuyoga*). See A. I. 113–14; VismṬ.: Āruppaniddesavaṇṇanā, Nevasaññānāsaññāyatanakathāvaṇṇanā, referring to M. I. 346–47.
72. See DhsA. 118; Vism. 464; VismṬ.: Kammaṭṭhānaggahaṇaniddesavaṇṇanā; VismṬ.: Khandhaniddesavaṇṇanā, Saṅkhārakkhandhakathāvaṇṇanā.
73. Vin. V. 164.
74. A. V. 1–2.
75. M. I. 149.
76. D. II. 84.
77. As in D. II. 98–99; S. I. 27–29; S. V. 152–53.
78. S. I. 5.
79. The body-mind relationship may be divided into three levels according to mental development. On the lowest level, physical symptoms affect the mind—when the body suffers, the mind also suffers and adds to the suffering. On the middle level the extent of interaction is more limited—however much suffering the body may experience, the mind is mindfully aware and does not attach, so suffering does not overwhelm it. On the highest level, the mind actually helps the body—when the body is in discomfort or ill, not only does the mind not make suffering over it, but it

can also make use of its strong mental efficiency and its good quality to help improve the body's condition.

80. A. II. 44–45; D. III. 222–23.
81. M. I. 398; S. IV. 225.
82. See the explanation of the commentaries at DA. III. 1006; AA. III. 84; MA. II. 232. See also A. I. 43; A. III. 323.
83. Vism. 371–72.
84. M. I. 40–41.
85. S. III. 13.
86. A. I. 258.
87. Vbh. 424. Brahma's Assembly = Brahmapārisajjā.
88. Ps. I. 99–100.
89. See A. V. 202; M. I. 104–7; M. III. 59.
90. See, for example, the Vinaya rules dealing with the relationship between bhikkhus and laity regarding livelihood, and the injunction that all bhikkhus have a role and should participate in acts of the order (*saṅghakamma*) concerning administration and activities of the community.
91. Consider the case of Devadatta and ascetics before the Buddha's time.
92. They are a worry, a cause of concern (*palibodha*), an obstacle to insight (Vism. 97).
93. As in M. I. 34; M. III. 13–14. (Note that in later texts, mention is made of recluses before the Buddha's time who were said to have attained such high degrees of mastery over the *jhānas* that they used them as a kind of sport. Thus the word *jhānakīḷā* is coined—*jhāna* as a game or hobby of the recluses (as in Ap. 18; AA. I. 304; DhA. IV. 55; JA. II.55, 139, 272, 379). It is said that *paccekabuddhas* (SA. II. 190; AA. I. 173) and disciples of the Buddha who had yet to attain arahantship (DhA. III. 427; SnA. I. 15) sometimes played with the *jhānas*, but no mention of the Buddha or the arahants indulging in *jhānakīḷā* can be found.
94. See S. V. 325–26.
95. See Vism. 130 (in reference to Vin. I. 182–83; A. III. 375).
96. Translator's note: One of the Buddha's former teachers.
97. D. II. 130–31.
98. A. I. 77.
99. Recollecting on one's own good actions: Vin. I. 293–94; M. I. 37–38; A. III. 284–85; A. V. 328–29; contemplating the teachings and experiencing understanding: D. III. 241–42, 288; A. III. 21; Ps. I. 86; seeing one's own purity: D. I. 73–74, 249–50; M. I. 283; as a result of virtuous conduct: S. IV. 78–79, 353; A. V. 312–13; as a result of heedfulness: S. V. 398; as in the enlightenment factors: M. III. 85; S. V. 67–69; Vbh. 227; through a sign (*nimitta*): S. V. 156.

100. D. III. 241–42; A. III. 21. (The section in parentheses shows the causes for the arising of gladness in this case, which may vary. The part outside the parentheses constitutes the general principles.)
101. As in S. V. 268; cited at Vism. 88–89.
102. A detailed discussion of this theme appears in the unabridged version of *Buddhadhamma*, chapter 10: "Buddhist Teachings on Desire" (*Buddhadhamma: The Laws of Nature and their Benefits to Life*, Bhikkhu P. A. Payutto, translated by Robin Philip Moore, Buddhadhamma Foundation, 2017).
103. See the stories of the Ascetic Kassapa, (D. I. 176–77; S. II. 21); Subhadda the Wanderer (D. II. 152–53); the Ascetic Seniya (M. I. 191–92); Vacchagotta the Wanderer (M. I. 493–94); and Māgaṇḍiya the Wanderer (M. I. 512–13). The origin story for this rule occurs at V. I. 69.
104. See Dhs. 56–57; Vbh. 288.
105. Vbh. 217.
106. S. V. 276. The Paṭisambhidāmagga mentions ten kinds of *iddhi*. The powers mentioned in this Buddhavacana are one kind. The tenth kind of power in the list is described as success as a result of proper application, the final example of which is the power of having completely removed *kilesa* through arahantship (Ps. II. 205–14). The explanation of the Visuddhimagga leans to the aspect of psychic powers (Vism. 385–406), but it does cite other aspects of meaning, such as success arising from the arts of warfare or even in tilling a field, as *iddhi* of the tenth kind (Vism. 383–84). Thus, the *iddhipāda* can be used in the sense of accomplishment in all undertakings.
107. S. V. 276.
108. S. V. 268–69. In the Abhidhamma the definitions for *chanda samādhi* and so on are slightly different. For instance, "A bhikkhu makes zeal dominant and so gains *samādhi*, and so gains one-pointedness of mind. This is called *chanda samādhi*." (See Vbh. 216–26.)
109. S. V. 276.
110. S. V. 254.
111. Vism. 84–435; also mentioned in part in VinA. II. 414.
112. The *samādhi* that is transcendent is that which is part of the noble path, and it is called "path-*samādhi*" (*maggasamādhi*). Transcendent *samādhi* is developed automatically with wisdom. *Maggasamādhi* arises automatically when wisdom is perfected, so it is not discussed separately (Vism. 89).
113. Translator's note: According to the five or eight precepts for a layperson, the ten precepts for a novice, or the Pāṭimokkha precepts for a bhikkhu or bhikkhuni.

114. The seven *kalyāṇadhamma* are discussed in chapter 7, "The Precursors of Learning."

115. The ten *kasiṇas* are mentioned in the Visuddhimagga as already cited. Note, however, that in the Pali canon *viññāṇakasiṇa* (consciousness) replaces *ālokakasiṇa* in tenth place and the space (*ākāsa*) *kasiṇa* is moved to ninth position (see D. III. 268, 290; M. II. 14–15; A. I. 41–42; A. V. 46, 60–61; Ps. I. 95).

116. Nowadays it would be difficult to have a chance to contemplate the ten *asubha*, so I have summarized their essential content. In full, they are a bloated corpse (*uddhumātaka*), a livid corpse (*vinīlaka*), a festering corpse (*vipubbaka*), a corpse severed in two (*vicchiddaka*), a corpse gnawed by animals (*vikkhāyitaka*), a dismembered corpse (*vikkhittaka*), a corpse hacked up and scattered about (*hatavikkhittaka*), a bloody corpse (*lohitaka*), a worm-infested corpse (*puḷuvaka*), and a skeleton (*aṭṭhika*). In the Pali canon they are classified into various objects of reflection, as at Ps. I. 95; Dhs. 55. In the suttas only six are mentioned at most (as at D. III. 226; A. II. 16–17), and sometimes five (combined with other factors, as at S. V. 131; A. I. 41–42; A. V. 106–7). The closest to that given here is the summary of the nine corpse reflections (*navasīvathikāpabba*) in the teachings on the foundations of mindfulness regarding recollection on the body (*kāyagatāsati*), as at D. II. 295–96; M. I. 58; M. III. 91; A. III. 324.

117. Sources in the canon are found at A. I. 30, 41–42; Nd. I. 6–7, 9–10, 491–92; Ps. I. 95. Apart from these, there are many other references that do not include the whole set. Factors that are often found in different sets are *kāyagatāsati*, recollection on the body, and *ānāpānasati*, mindfulness of the breath, which is the most commonly found of all the recollections.

118. References to the *appamaññā* are so frequent in the canon it is almost unnecessary to cite them. See, for example, D. I. 250–51; D. III. 223–24. Referred to as the *brahmavihāra* at D. II. 195–96; M. II. 82.

119. In the suttas this is included with the five unattractive objects (*asubha*) in the set of ten recollections, as in A. I. 41–42.

120. Sometimes referred to simply as analysis of the elements (*dhātuvavaṭṭhāna*), attention to the elements (*dhātumanasikāra*), or meditation on the elements (*dhātukammaṭṭhāna*). Canonical references are at D. II. 294; M. I. 57–58 (occurs in the *kāyānupassanā* foundation of mindfulness).

121. Canonical sources are, for example, D. III. 224; S. IV. 266. For the last of these, the Visuddhimagga explains that *nevasaññānāsaññāyatana* is attained by attending to the sphere of nothingness (*ākiñcaññāyatana*)—not in order to enter it but in order to go beyond it (see Vism. 335, 337–38).

122. Vism. 97; VinA. II. 416; SnA. I. 53. The Visuddhimagga states that some teachers also classify reflections of the unattractive (*asubhasaññā*) as *sabbatthaka-kammaṭṭhāna*.

123. Canonical references are at Nd. I. 359-60; Nd. II. 42. In the canon the order is thus: *rāgacarita*, *dosacarita*, *mohacarita*, *vitakkacarita*, *saddhācarita*, and *ñāṇacarita*. Note also that in this section the final text in parentheses for each *carita* is additional material based on the commentaries. For more detail, see Vism. 101-10.
124. In Pali, *imāhaṁ bhagavā attabhāvaṁ tumhākaṁ pariccajāmi*. It can also be translated as "I give up this life to The Blessed One."
125. In Pali, *imāhaṁ bhante attabhāvaṁ tumhākaṁ pariccajāmi*. It can also be translated as "I give up this life to you."
126. According to the explanation of the practice of mindfulness of breathing, one should study the meditation that has five connected sectors (*sandhi*). They are (1) *uggaha*: learning the principles of meditation according to the texts; (2) *paripucchā*: asking about the meaning and clearing up any doubts; (3) *upaṭṭhāna*: the appearance of the meditation sign (*nimitta*); (4) *appanā*: the meditation becoming undivided and reaching the level of *jhāna*; and (5) *lakkhaṇa*: identifying the meditation states as having such and such characteristics and being achieved in such and such ways (see Vism. 277-78; Vism.T. Anussatikammaṭṭhānaniddesavaṇṇanā, Ānāpānassatikathāvaṇṇanā).
127. See full text at A. V. 15-16. (The canon mentions five qualities within a practitioner that will ensure attainment of liberation in no long time: [1] belief in the Buddha's enlightenment [*tathāgatabodhisaddhā*]; [2] good health, few illnesses, and a good digestive system [fire element]; [3] candidness and sincerity in regard to the teacher and one's fellow followers of the holy life; [4] earnestness and willingness to strive; and [5] wisdom that scatters defilements.)
128. On the three *bhāvanā* and the three *nimitta*, see Comp.: Kammaṭṭhāna-paricchedo, Gocarabhedo.
129. There are seven *sappāya* ("that which is suitable, helpful, or conducive"). They are dwelling place (*āvāsa*), sources of food (*gocara*), conversation (*bhassa*), people (*puggala*), food (*bhojana*), weather and natural surroundings (*utu*), and posture (*iriyāpatha*), when those conditions are agreeable or supportive. Factors that are not conducive (*asappāya*) are the same seven conditions when they are not conducive or suitable (Vism. 127-28; VinA. II. 429; MA. IV. 161).
130. Known as the ten kinds of attainment skill, *appanākosalla* (Vism. 128-37).
131. It is said that although the limitless abidings have no *paṭibhāganimitta* as do the *kasiṇas*, they do have as *nimitta* "dissolution of barriers" (*sīmasambheda*), the state in which the mind of goodwill, for example, developed fully, is spread to all beings equally without discrimination, and such a *nimitta* can be developed to the attainment of *appanāsamādhi* (see Vism. 307).

132. Such proficiency is called *vasī*. There are said to be five kinds: (1) proficiency in analyzing the factors of the *jhāna* just left (*āvajjanavasī*); (2) proficiency in entering a *jhāna* at will speedily and whenever one wishes (*samāpajjanavasī*); (3) proficiency in determining to stay in the *jhāna* for as long as desired and not allowing the *jhāna* to fall into subconsciousness (*adhiṭṭhānavasī*); (4) proficiency in leaving *jhāna*, ability to leave whenever one wishes according to a predetermined time (*vuṭṭhānavasī*); (5) proficiency in examining and reviewing the factors of *jhāna*—that is, doing the same as *āvajjanavasī* but in retrospect (*paccavekkhaṇavasī*): Ps. I. 99-100; cited and explained in Vism. 154; PsA. I. 316; CompṬ.: Manodvāravithī, Javananiyamavaṇṇanā and Kammaṭṭhānaparicchedavaṇṇanā, Gocarabhedavaṇṇanā. It is said that if one does not yet have proficiency in the lower *jhānas*, one should not attempt to cultivate the higher ones, otherwise one may lose both the *jhāna* already gained and those yet to be attained. Here the commentators cite the Pali canon at A. IV. 418.

133. S. V. 317.

134. See full details at S. V. 318-19. See also the table of *samādhi* states and meditation objects at page 641. Note also that according to the consensus of the commentators, *ānāpānasati* cannot be used to achieve formless *jhāna* because formless *jhāna* is dependent on a *kasiṇa* device (as in Vism. 324-25).

135. Classified as part of the body foundation of mindfulness (*kāyānupassanā satipaṭṭhāna*): D. II. 293; M. I. 56; stated to be a practice incorporating all four of the foundations of mindfulness in the *Ānāpānasati Sutta*: M. III. 83-84; S. V. 323-40; mention of the whole sixteen stages of its practice in other passages: Vin. III. 70; M. I. 425; S. V. 311-23; A. V. 111-12. Apart from these sources, it is also included in the recollections (*anussati*) and many other teachings.

136. Vin. III. 70; S. V. 321-22.

137. S. V. 326. Note that the word *brahmavihāra* (holy abiding) does not always refer specifically to goodwill (*mettā*), compassion (*karuṇā*), gladness (*muditā*), and equanimity (*upekkhā*). (The specific term for these conditions is *appamaññā*—"boundless abidings.")

138. S. V. 317. When the Buddha attained the first *jhāna* as a young prince sitting in the shade of a jambolan tree while his father was conducting the annual plowing ceremony, as recorded in M. I. 246; MA. II. 290; J. I. 58, it is said that it was through mindfulness of the breathing.

139. S. V. 328.

140. S. V. 329; M. III. 82.

141. M. I. 425-26. The Visuddhimagga explains that at the moment of death it is possible to observe one's last in- and out-breaths from beginning to final cessation, together with the final thought moment (*cuticitta*). It is

also explained that only some bhikkhus who have attained arahantship through other meditation techniques may be able to foresee the end of their life span, but those who have attained arahantship through practice of the entire process of mindfulness of the breathing will definitely be able to do so (i.e., know how much more time they have to live, or when they will die). See Vism. 292.

142. "Empty building" is translated from *suññāgāra*. But Vism. 271 gives the translation as "empty place" (= empty of buildings), referring to any of the seven kinds of dwellings (*senāsana*) other than a forest and the foot of a tree.

143. The commentary to the Vinaya translates *assāsa* as "out-breath" and *passāsa* as "in-breath," while the commentary to the suttas translates these words the other way round, with *assāsa* meaning "in-breath" and *passāsa* meaning "out-breath" (see Vism. 271). Here it is translated according to the Thai tradition, which follows the commentary on the Vinaya. Those who prefer the sutta commentary interpretation should exchange "in-breath" with "out-breath" and vice versa.

144. See M. III. 82–3; S. V. 311–12, for example. How mindfulness of the breathing is used to develop the four foundations of mindfulness is further explained at M. III. 83–84; S. V. 323–25. *Ānāpānasati* in this full form is called by the commentaries the sixteen-step meditation on the breath (*soḷasavatthu-ānāpānasati-kammaṭṭhāna*). It is divided into four groups of four (*catukka*), as shown here, at Vism. 266–67.

Some scholars have commented on the difference between *ānāpānasati* and breathing techniques of other traditions, such as the breath control of yoga known as *prāṇayāma*, pointing out that they are entirely different matters. *Ānāpānasati* is a method of training mindfulness, not the breath. It sees the breath simply as a tool for training the mind. Some yogic techniques of breath control, on the other hand, are included among the austerities which the Buddha experimented with and discarded. See P. Vajirañāṇa Mahāthera, *Buddhist Meditation in Theory and Practice* (Colombo: M. D. Gunasena, 1962), 235–36; Nyanaponika Thera, *The Heart of Buddhist Meditation* (London, Rider, 1962), 61.

145. The consensus of the commentators is that a beginner should practice only the first group of four, with the remaining groups to be practiced once *jhāna* is attained. The first three groups of four can be used for both *samatha* and *vipassanā*, while the last group can be used only for *vipassanā* (Vism. 275–76, 290).

146. The commentators state that mindfulness of the breathing is a heavy meditation technique, hard to practice, and they emphasize its importance as the supreme meditation technique, the exclusive sphere of attention of the Buddhas, silent Buddhas (*paccekabuddhas*), and great disciples. It

is not a trifling matter, not for lesser beings to experience. If one cannot relinquish noisy places, it is very difficult to cultivate it, because sound is an adversary of *jhāna*. In the subsequent objects of attention, keen wisdom must be used. The commentators cite the Buddhavacana at M. III.83-84 in support of this: "Bhikkhus, I do not say that there can be mindfulness of the breathing for those of confused mindfulness and no comprehension" (see Vism. 268-69, 284). However, since this technique is said to be so great and so difficult, why is it said to be the meditation subject most suited to those of delusional disposition (*mohacarita*)?

147. Mindfulness of the breathing is the only one of the many meditation techniques mentioned in the *Mahāsatipaṭṭhāna Sutta*, which specifies this physical posture (see also the *Kāyagatāsati Sutta*, M. III. 88-99; the *Girimānanda Sutta*: A. V. 108-12). Other meditation techniques are practiced in whatever posture is suitable. If there is sitting, it is only because it is a useful expedient. That is, when any meditation subject can be well noted in the sitting posture, and when sitting in this way is the best posture, then it is natural to sit in this way—as, for example, when gazing on a *kasiṇa* device or examining some mental concept for prolonged periods. It is like when someone is writing: the sitting posture is more convenient than standing or reclining. The sitting posture should be understood in this way, rather than seeing sitting itself as *samādhi*. In other words, the cross-legged sitting posture is the best sitting posture for both health and the work of meditation. Thus, when sitting, or in the event that one wishes to do something requiring sitting, it is recommended to sit in this way (even when simply sitting thinking, resting, having a conversation, or collecting oneself, as for example at M. II. 139-40; M. III. 238; A. II. 38; Ud. 21), just as it is recommended to lie in the "lion's posture" (lying on the right side) when sleeping, or when walking to walk as in walking meditation.

148. The Visuddhimagga's explanation here may be too brief, as readers interpret the text in different ways. The Thai, Roman, and Sri Lankan recensions are not quite the same. For convenience I have used the version studied in Thailand (the counting may be begun on an in-breath or an out-breath, depending on which is clearer). Again, note that the example of practice described here follows the Visuddhimagga in order to show the original procedure. It can be adapted to other ways by meditators—as, for example, some of the schools in Thailand who use the "bud-dho" and other techniques in conjunction with the in- and out-breaths instead of counting (essentially the meditation object is only a technique for concentrating the mind).

149. It is said that for those with longer noses the air strikes more clearly at the nose tip, while for those with flatter noses it is clearer at the upper lip. It is also said that if the mind is allowed to follow the breath inward,

tension in the chest will result, while if the mind is allowed to follow the breath outward, the result will be distraction.

150. In the practice according to the commentaries, another two stages can be discerned between following (*anubandhanā*) and the arising of the *nimitta*: they are *phusanā* (the observation of the sensation of the breath of one who is following the breath with mindfulness, who is about to enter *appanā* and is fixing attention on the tip of the nose) and *ṭhapanā* (fixing undivided attention on an object until it is *appanā*). The stages mentioned from here on—that is, establishing the mind on the *nimitta*, maintenance of the *nimitta*, and management of the *nimitta* until *appanāsamādhi* is attained—are all counted as *ṭhapanā*. After *jhāna* has been gained, if this meditation subject is subsequently used to develop insight, it is known as *sallakkhaṇā* ("observing"; i.e., observing and examining the three characteristics), from where it goes on to reach *magga*, where it is known as *vivaṭṭhaṇā* (unraveling), and then fruit, where it is called *pārisuddhi* (purification from defilements), ultimately culminating in *paṭipassanā* (reviewing)—that is, reviewing the path and fruit attained (which is *paccavekkhaṇa*). From beginning to end there are seven stages.
151. The word *jhāna* as it is generally used, without any qualifying terms, usually refers to the *rūpajhāna*, material absorption.
152. Original sources: Dhs. 42–43, 236; for later texts, see the arrangement of the four and five *jhānas* in Vism. 89; Comp.: Cittaparicchedo, Rūpāvacaracittaṁ.
153. Meaning the cessation of ideation and feeling.
154. That is, it is changeable: Ps. II. 40–41.
155. Occurs in many commentarial texts, such as DA. II. 426; MA. IV. 167; SA. III. 209; Vism. 410 (cf. the term used in the Tipiṭaka, *vikkhambhana-nirodha*: Ps. II. 220).
156. See the discussion of *cetovimutti* and *paññāvimutti* in the chapter on *nibbāna* (chapter 5).
157. See Vism. 373–435.
158. Vism. I. Original quote at S. I. 13.
159. See S. V. 45, 63, 78, 143, 246.
160. For example, S. V. 91, 101. These references cite specifically the enlightenment factors. See also the earlier references.
161. As for example: morality (*sīla*) → remorselessness (*avipaṭisāra*) → gladness (*pāmojja*) → rapture (*pīti*) → tranquility (*passaddhi*) → well-being (*sukha*) → *samādhi*. See A. V. 1–3.
162. Vism. 85; occurs often in the canon. See the discussion of the natural way of developing *samādhi* earlier in this chapter.
163. As in A. V. 1–3.

164. S. V. 414.

165. Dh. 372. *Jhāna* here can be interpreted as meaning either *ārammaṇūpanijjhāna*, attending to an object, or *lakkhaṇūpanijjhāna*, attending to the three characteristics.

166. Vism. 85; Nd1A. II. 388; PsA. I. 17; DhsA. 118. In the Paṭisambhidāmagga, *avikkhepa*, non-vacillation or non-distraction, is said to be the purpose (*attha*) of *samādhi* and *sammāsamādhi* (as in Ps. I. 21, 30, 73-74).

167. The original Abhidhamma texts collectively name the factors of *jhāna* and describe them in full, as far as can be discerned in the sutta descriptions of each of the *jhānas*, as follows: first *jhāna* = *vitakka*, *vicāra*, *pīti*, *sukha*, (*cittassa*) *ekaggatā*; second *jhāna* = *sampasāda* (*saddhā*), *pīti*, *sukha*, (*cittassa*) *ekaggatā*; third *jhāna* = *upekkhā*, *sati*, *sampajañña*, *sukha*, (*cittassa*) *ekaggatā*; fourth *jhāna* = *upekkhā*, *sati*, (*cittassa*) *ekaggatā* (Vbh. 257-58, 260-61).

Upacārasamādhi also dispels with the five hindrances and has five factors, but they are weaker than in *appanāsamādhi* (Vism. 146-47). However, in some instances *upacāra-samādhi* may contain *upekkhā* instead of *pīti* and *sukha*, at which times it will have only four factors: *vitakka*, *vicāra*, *upekkhā*, and *ekaggatā* (Vism. 85-86).

168. See Vism. 141-69; VinA. I. 144-56; PsA. I. 181-93; DhsA. 114-18. In the Abhidhammatthasaṅgaha, Comp.: Samuccayaparicchedo, Missakasaṅgaho seven factors of *jhāna* are given, replacing *sukha* with *somanassa* and *domanassa* (mental happiness and unhappiness).

169. It is said that *pīti* is of five kinds: (1) *khuddakāpīti*: a little rapture, enough to produce goose bumps or tears; (2) *khaṇikāpīti*: momentary rapture, causing momentary sensations like flashes of lightning; (3) *okkantikāpīti*: rapture that comes in waves, or in spells, thrills that sweep over the body like waves lapping on a shore; (4) *ubbeṅgāpīti*: untethered rapture, causing floating sensations and spontaneous, involuntary actions such as utterances, or feelings of floating up into the air; (5) *pharaṇāpīti*: infusing rapture, manifesting as feelings of refreshing coolness infusing the entire body (Vism. 143-44).

170. Again, the *upekkhā* that is a factor of *jhāna*, which is a state of impartiality (*tatramajjhattatā*) and a skillful quality classified in the *saṅkhārakhandha*, should not be confused with *upekkhā*, which is simply a feeling of indifference, also called *adukkhamasukhavedanā*, classified in the *vedanakhandha*, which is neither good nor bad. In fourth *jhāna* the equanimity that is a factor of *jhāna* also contains equanimous feeling (*upekkhāvedanā*), and so contains both kinds of *upekkhā*.

171. See M. III. 25-28.

172. See Vism. 162-63, 167-68.

173. Vism. 141. For the source of the fourth and fifth *jhānas* and the factors of *jhāna* according to the Abhidhamma, see Vbh. 263-68.
174. See S. V. 196-201. The tasks or functions of the *indriya* are not given in Buddhavacana as such, but in the Visuddhimagga (Vism. 129-30), which is in turn gleaned from the canon at Ps. I. 16, 180, Ps. II. 21-22.
175. S. V. 225-27.
176. See A. II. 149-52.
177. A. II. 155-56.
178. See S. V. 200-205. See also Ps. II. 48-57, dealing with the doorways to liberation (*vimokkha mukha*) and how the faculties define different kinds of noble ones.
179. See Ps. II. 2, 21-22.
180. This Buddhavacana occurs in the section on the enlightenment factors; S. V. 114-15.
181. S. V. 218.
182. The section on the balancing of the faculties has been gleaned from Vism. 129-30. I understand that the basis of the teaching is the Buddha's teaching on recognizing the appropriateness and balance of the faculties, at Vin. I. 182-3; A. III. 375.
183. S. V. 223.
184. S. V. 224.
185. S. V. 222-23.
186. S. V. 222.
187. S. V. 222.
188. S. V. 227. *Bodhipakkhiyadhamma* here refers to the five faculties. There are further analogies for wisdom of a similar vein, such as the elephant's footprint, which is the greatest footprint of all land animals; sandalwood, the most fragrant of woods; the jambolan tree and the *pārichattaka* tree. See S. V. 231-32; 237-39. In the Maṅgalaṭṭhadīpanī, the importance of wisdom is eloquently stated: "In truth, of all the qualities that aid the attainment of *nibbāna*, wisdom is foremost, and all other qualities are merely its retinue."
189. S. V. 228-29.
190. S. V. 72, 83.
191. See Vism. 678; SA. III. 138.
192. See S. V. 91-128; Vbh. 199-201.
193. S. V. 93. At S. V. 97, the phrase "are not contaminants of the mind" becomes "do not suppress the mind."
194. S. V. 97-98.
195. That is, the use of *sati* in the foundations of mindfulness. See M. III. 85; S. V. 331.
196. S. V. 67-68.

197. MA. IV. 142 and SA. III. 274 give a broader description: *dhammavicaya* is direct knowledge (*ñāṇa*), profound penetration, in conjunction with *sati*.
198. S. V. 110-11.
199. See S. V. 102-7.
200. *Subhanimitta* = things taken to be attractive. Once seen, the mind fixes onto those aspects it likes and perceives or imagines them as attractive images in the mind.
201. *Paṭighanimitta* = things taken to be offensive. Once seen, the mind fixes onto those aspects it does not like and perceives or imagines them as offensive images in the mind.
202. *Cetovimutti* = that which frees the mind, making the mind clear and free of oppression. Usually, in the case of enmity, the appropriate condition would be goodwill (*mettā*), but any of the other boundless abidings (*appamaññā*: compassion, sympathetic joy, or equanimity) could be used.
203. SA. III. 154.
204. The text from here is based on Vism. 133-35; VbhA. 275-88.
205. "Making things clean and tidy," or making them pure and graceful: for example, cutting one's hair and nails, bathing, keeping one's clothes clean and neat, keeping one's dwelling tidy.
206. The word *saṁvega* should not be understood as being depressed or despondent, but as the state of being prodded into thinking or obtaining an incentive to exert oneself in doing good things (it corresponds with the word *samuttejana*, meaning "to rouse to courage," and is opposite to lethargy, as in Vism. 657-58).
207. S. V. 67-69. The commentaries state that in this case the seven enlightenment factors occur in one mind moment (VbhA. 313).
208. Usually stated at the end of a description of the development of *samādhi* based on mindfulness of the breathing: see M. III. 82; S. V. 329, 334.
209. S. V. 95-96
210. S. V. 130-34.
211. See Vism. 133-34.
212. S. V. 112-15.
213. D. III. 226; A. II. 16-17.
214. D. III. 106.
215. A. I. 52-53.
216. M. I. 11.
217. A. II. 237.
218. D. II. 78-9; A. IV. 23.
219. S. IV. 367. Note that the investigation of *dhammas* enlightenment factor is said to be one definition of transcendent right view (M. III. 72) and enlightenment (*bodhi*; Nd. I 331).
220. D. II. 216-17. Similar in parts to M. III. 72 and A. IV. 40. Said in relation

to the accessories of *samādhi* at D. III. 252. At M. I. 301 there is mention of only the most immediate accessory, right effort. In the Nettipakaraṇa (Nett. 125) the relaxed body that is without tension or restlessness is said to be an accessory of *samādhi*. The phrase "ready for work" is a translation of *pahoti*, which can also be translated as "can be suitable."

221. This collective term of *catumagga* (four paths) arose in commentarial literature, and was usually used as a compound with other words. See SA. I. 206; SA. II. 384; SnA. I. 6; PsA. I. 171; Vism. 688–89.

222. As far as I can ascertain, the term *dhammasāmaggī* was first used at Nd. I. 132. Later uses are at Nd1A. I. 66 and VbhA. 310. It is worth noting that this word is often confused with *maggasāmaggī*, which refers to a person who is endowed with one of the four stages of the noble path, as in Pug. 72. At M. III. 9 there is yet another usage of the term *dhammasāmaggī*.

223. MA. I. 83; KhA. 84.

224. For the source of this explanation of the factors of the path and other factors arising at the moment of path attainment in one mind moment, see Ps. II. 82–85, and in the commentarial literature, see Vism. 509–10; VbhA. 121, 320.

225. The thirty-seven requisites of enlightenment are the four foundations of mindfulness (*satipaṭṭhāna*), the four right efforts (*sammappadhāna*), the four pathways to success (*iddhipāda*), the five faculties (*indriya*), the five powers (*bala*), the seven enlightenment factors (*bojjhaṅga*), and the eightfold path (*aṭṭhaṅgikamagga*). For the classification of the *bodhipakkhiyadhamma* into the path, see Vism. 511–12; VbhA. 88.

226. A. II. 149–52; D. III. 106, 229; A. V. 63; Vbh. 331–32. Canonical examples from the Aṅguttara Nikāya: Venerable Sāriputta was *sukhāpaṭipadā khippābhiññā*, while Venerable Mahāmoggallāna was *dukkhāpaṭipadā khippābhiññā*. Notably, in Vism. 688, the description of the practice of Mahāmoggallāna does not accord with the description in the Pali canon.

227. The word *abhiññā* is well worth studying. It is usually translated as "supreme wisdom" or "great knowledge" (= *uttamapaññā* at VinA. I. 125 and *adhikañāṇa* at VinA. I. 125; DA. I. 175; PsA. I. 136). It can also be translated, on the basis of its lexical roots, as referring to penetrating knowledge, specific knowledge, knowledge that is beyond (experiences through the five senses). In the Aṭṭhasālinī and the Visuddhimagga it is explained that the wisdom that functions from the level of *upacārasamādhi* up to *appanāsamādhi* is *abhiññā* (DhsA. 182; Vism. 86–87). In the Paramatthamañjusā it is further explained that *abhiññā* is *appanā paññā* (wisdom that arises when the mind has entered attainment concentration: VismṬ. Kammaṭṭhānaggahananiddesavaṇṇanā, Samādhicatukkavaṇṇanā). It is

sometimes rendered in English as "direct knowledge." Translator's note: In this translation I have rendered it as "superknowledge," reserving "direct knowledge" for *ñāṇa*.

228. M. III. 289–90. (The passages dealing with ears, nose, tongue, body, and mind and their related conditions follow the same pattern, so they have not been included here.) The final part of this passage dealing with the conditions that are to be realized with *abhiññā* also occurs at S. V. 51–53 and A. II. 247.
229. A. V. 106–7. Similar passages occur at A. IV. 338–39, 385–86. The latter also adds *saṅkappa* and *vitakka*, which "have mentality and physicality as object (*ārammaṇa*)." For *chandamūlakā*, cf. M. III. 16; S. III. 100–101.
230. A. II. 243; cf. It. 40.

Conclusion. The Four Noble Truths as Summary of the Buddhadhamma

1. M. I. 184–85.
2. *Dhammacakkappavattana Sutta*, Vin. I. 11; S. V. 422–23.
3. D. II. 90.
4. Translator's note: I have translated *dukkhasamudaya* as "cause of suffering" throughout this chapter, as per the Thai source text เหตุให้เกิดทุกข์. Other translations of the Pali include "source" or "arising" of suffering.
5. M. I. 379–80. The term *sāmukkaṁsikā dhammadesanā* is usually translated as "the lofty teaching," or "the teaching revered by all the Buddhas," or "the teaching that all the Buddhas themselves proclaim," unlike other teachings that are usually given in response to a question or in the course of a discussion.
6. A. IV. 384–85.
7. M. I. 428–31.
8. S. V. 437–38.
9. S. V. 434–35.
10. S. V. 435 (the phrase in parentheses is the commentary's explanation at SA. III. 299).
11. S. V. 433. (This is interpreted as cited in Vism. 495, but in the Thai recension of the canon the word *ariya* does not appear, so it would be translated "through becoming enlightened to these four noble truths as they are, the Tathāgata is called Arahant, Fully Self-Enlightened Buddha.")
12. Vism. 495. The Visuddhimagga cites the canon in explanation of the first interpretation: "Bhikkhus, the noble ones penetrate these truths; for that reason they are called 'noble truths,'" but this cannot be found in the current version of the Tipiṭaka. As for the fourth sense, *ariya* is usually

translated as "noble," but here he translates literally according to the Buddhavacana as "real truth."

13. As in the *Dhammacakkappavattana Sutta*: Vin. I. 10; S. V. 421-22; and also at Ps. II. 147-50; Vbh. 99-104.
14. See Vin. I. 1-5.
15. See Vin. I. 1-5.
16. M. I. 163-73, 240-9; M. II. 93, 211-12.
17. See, for example, S. II. 104-5.
18. Occurs in the *Dhammacakkappavattana Sutta*.
19. The three knowledges (*ñāṇa*) are given in the *Dhammacakkappavattana Sutta*.
20. M. III. 290; A. II. 247. In the Pali canon, the *bhāvetabbadhamma* (that is to say, *samatha* and *vipassanā*) are arranged before the *sacchikātabbadhamma* (knowledge and liberation), but here they are arranged the other way around to keep them in conformity with the arrangement of the four noble truths.
21. Vism. 512; VbhA. 88; PsA. I. 198.
22. Vism. 497-98; VbhA. 86; PsA. I. 54, 198 (the content is identical in all three volumes, being copied from one to the other.)
23. As in M. II. 214-23; A. I. 173; Vbh. 367-68; J. V. 232-43; J. VI. 206-11; JA. V. 237-41. *Issaranimittavāda* is also called *issarakaraṇavāda*, *issaranimmānavāda*, or *issarakuttivāda*. *Pubbekatavāda* should be clearly distinguished from the Buddhist teaching of *kamma*. The subject is well worthy of study. It seems that many Buddhists try to ignore this Buddhist teaching, but the fact that it is stressed so often in the texts shows its importance. If studied carefully it may help to clarify the principles of Buddhism a great deal. VbhA. 497 states that the first doctrine is that of the Niganthas (the Jains), the second that of the Brahmanists, and the third that of the *ājīvakas* (naked ascetics). In J. V. 239-41, *ucchedavāda* (nihilism) is included in this group of wrong views, making four altogether.
24. Ps. I. 27; Ps. II. 220.
25. Dh. verses 188-92. The Triple Gem comprises the three main principles that Buddhists should always bear in mind. Buddha = humanity (pointing to the highest potential that exists within all people); Dhamma = nature (the natural way of determinants, realization of which leads to the attainment of the state that transcends determinants); Saṅgha = society (the ideal community of noble beings, those who are established in various levels of knowledge of the truth of Dhamma and are walking the way of the Buddha).
26. In this regard, according to Buddhist practice, the truth must be acknowledged that for someone who is not a stream enterer, it is extremely difficult

to be able to help oneself mentally on a consistent basis. Thus, for people who are still hoping to take refuge in occult powers, divine intervention, and blind chance, the method of redirecting their hopes to the Dhamma is used, by transforming the mode of correction: instead of having people conduct ceremonies or praying to banish bad luck, they are encouraged to conduct a different kind of "banishing," in which one makes a sacrifice in a way that is of some benefit, such as a donation to some public benefit or working to perform some public benefit. Even a fortune teller whose mind is inclined to Buddhism may recommend that customers fix their bad fortune by donating a gift, observing morality, observing the observance days (*uposatha*), and so on.

27. It is a mistake to look on morality in merely negative terms. At worst, it is seen as consisting of prohibitions. A little broader outlook sees *sīla* as merely abstention, as in the term "abstaining" in the five precepts. Such views do not cover the entire breadth of the original meaning of the term. In the Saṅgha, for instance, *sīla* includes proper conduct between preceptor and preceptee, teacher and disciple, and more, as stated in the Mahākhandhaka and other sections of the Vinaya Piṭaka. For householders, *sīla* includes proper conduct between parents and children, between partners, and among friends, and is the basis for unity (*saṅgahavatthu*), as stated in the householders' *vinaya* (*gihivinaya*) of the *Siṅgālaka Sutta*.

Selected Bibliography

The references used throughout this book are mostly to the Pali Text Society publications in roman-script Pali language. Readers interested in doing further research can refer to the English translations published by Wisdom Publications and the Pali Text Society listed below. Readers can also find sutta translations online at Access to Insight (www.accesstoinsight.org) and Sutta Central (www.suttacentral.net).

Canonical Works Published by Wisdom Publications

Bhikkhu Bodhi, trans. *The Connected Discourses of the Buddha.* Boston, 2000.

Bhikkhu Bodhi, trans. *The Middle Length Discourses of the Buddha.* Boston, 2009.

Bhikkhu Bodhi, trans. *The Numerical Discourses of the Buddha.* Boston, 2012.

Bhikkhu Bodhi, trans. *The Suttanipāta.* Boston, 2017.

Walsh, Maurice C., trans. *The Long Discourses of the Buddha.* Boston, 2012.

Canonical Works Published by the Pali Text Society

Bhikkhu Bodhi, trans. *The Connected Discourses of the Buddha.* 2 vols. 2000, 2002. A translation of the Saṁyutta Nikāya.

Bhikkhu Ñanamoli, trans. *The Path of Discrimination.* Rev. 2nd ed. 2022. A translation of the Paṭisamhidāmagga, from the Khuddaka Nikāya.

Horner, I. B., trans. *The Collection of the Middle Length Sayings.* 3 vols. 1954, 1957, 1959. A translation of the Majjhima Nikāya.

Law, Bimala Churn, trans. *Designation of Human Types.* 1922. A translation of the Puggalapaññatti, from the Abhidhamma Piṭaka.

Masefield, Peter, trans. *The Udāna and the Itivuttaka.* 2013. Translations from the Khuddaka Nikaya.

Norman, K. R., trans. *The Elders' Verses*. 2 vols., 2nd ed. 2007. A translation of the Theragāthā and Therīgāthā, from the Khuddaka Nikāya.

Norman, K. R., trans. *The Group of Discourses*. 2nd ed. 2001. A translation of the Suttanipāta, from the Khuddaka Nikāya.

Norman, K. R., trans. *Word of the Doctrine*. 1997. A translation of the Dhammapada, from the Khuddaka Nikāya.

Rhys Davids, Caroline A. F., trans. *A Buddhist Manual of Psychological Ethics*. 3rd ed. 1993. A translation of the Dhammasaṅganī, from the Abhidhamma Piṭaka.

Rhys Davids, T. W. and Caroline A. F. Rhys Davids, trans. *Dialogues of the Buddha*. 3 vols. 1899, 1989 (4th ed.), 1921. A translation of the Dīgha Nikāya.

Shwe Zan Aung and Caroline A. F. Rhys Davids, trans. *Points of Controversy*. 2001. A translation of the Kathāvatthu, from the Abhidhamma Piṭaka.

Ven. U Narada, trans. *Discourse on Elements*. 1962. A translation of the Dhātukathā, from the Abhidhamma Piṭaka.

Ven. U Thittila, trans. *The Book of Analysis*. 1969. A translation of the Vibhaṅga, from the Abhidhamma Piṭaka.

Woodward, F. L., and I. B. Horner, trans. *The Minor Anthologies of the Pali Canon*. 3 vols. 1935, 1975, 1974. A translation of the sixth and seventh books of the Khuddaka Nikāya.

Commentarial Works Published by the Pali Text Society

Bhikkhu Ñanamoli, trans. *The Dispeller of Delusion*. 2017. A translation of the Vibhaṅga commentary.

Bhikkhu Ñanamoli, trans. *The Guide*. London, 1962. A translation of the Nettipakaraṇa.

Bhikkhu Ñanamoli, trans. *The Piṭaka Disclosure*. 1964. A translation of the Peṭakopadesa.

Masefield, Peter, trans. *Vimāna Stories*. 1989. A translation of the Vimānavatthu commentary.

Pe Maung Tin, trans. *The Expositor*. 1976. A translation of the Atthasālinī, a commentary on the Dhammasaṅgaṇī by Buddhaghosa.

Shwe Zan Aung and Caroline A. F. Rhys Davids, trans. *Compendium of Philosophy*. 1970. A translation of the Abhidhammatthasaṅgaha.

Other Works Published by the Pali Text Society

Horner, I. B., trans. *Milinda's Questions*. 1963. A translation of the Milindapañha.

Pe Maung Tin, trans. *The Path of Purity*. 1975. A translation of the Visuddhimagga.

Other Works by Bhikkhu P. A. Payutto, Published by the Buddhadhamma Foundation

Evans, Bruce, trans. *Buddhist Economics: A Middle Way for the Market Place*. Bangkok, 1994.

Evans, Bruce, trans. *Buddhist Solutions for the Twenty-First Century*. Bangkok, 2000.

Evans, Bruce, trans. *A Constitution for Living*. Bangkok, 1998.

Evans, Bruce, trans. *Toward Sustainable Science: A Buddhist Look at Trends in Scientific Development*. Bangkok, 1998.

Moore, Robin, trans. *Buddhadhamma: The Laws of Nature and Their Benefits to Life*. Bangkok, 2011.

Index

abhiññā (superknowledges), 344-45, 613, 618, 660, 808n227
absorptions. See *jhāna*
abyākatapañhā (unanswerable questions), 193, 316-17, 757n82
abyāpādasaṅkappa (thoughts of non-aversion), 491-92, 495, 496, 497, 499
access concentration. See *upacāra samādhi*
accidentalism, 88-89, 92, 265, 266, 712
acinteyya (unfathomable), 247-48, 251, 761n54
adhicittasikkhā (training in higher mentality), 386, 517, 565, 608, 725
adhipaññāsikkhā (training in higher wisdom), 386, 517, 725
adhisīlasikkhā (training in higher morality), 386, 504, 517, 724-25
ādīnava (fault, danger), 315, 441-45, 556
  Buddhavacana regarding, 52, 443-44
adinnādāna (stealing), 503, 506, 508, 521, 522, 526
advantages. See *sampatti*
agati (biases), 221
  four kinds of, 350, 530
Aggañña Sutta, 198, 791n60
aggregates. See *khandhas*
aging and death, 78, 118, 154-55, 158, 168, 173, 201
  Buddhavacana regarding, 191-92
agitation. See *uddhaccakukkucca*
ahaṁkāra (thoughts of "me"), 106, 141, 496
āhāre paṭikūlasaññā, (reflection on the loathsomeness of food), 637
ahetukadiṭṭhi. See accidentalism
ahetukavāda. See accidentalism
ājīvaparisuddhisīla (*sīla* of pure livelihood), 560
ākāsānañcāyatana (sphere of limitless space), 285, 340, 637-38, 657
ākiñcaññāyatana (sphere of nothingness), 285, 340, 638, 647, 657, 799n121
akiriyadiṭṭhi. See nihilism
akusala (unwholesome, unskillful), 211-12, 224-28
  Buddhavacana regarding, 228-37
  as catalyst for *kusala*, 221-22
  definitions of, 217-20
analysis, teaching of. See *vibhajjavāda*
anāgāmi (non returner), 291, 329-30, 337, 338, 684, 753n94
ānāpānasati (mindfulness of breathing), 392, 582, 637, 646-56, 799n117, 801n134, 802n144
  Buddhavacana regarding, 648-51
anattā (not self), 62-63, 70-71, 81-93, 140, 180, 429, 431, 752n64, 752n69

anattā (not self) (*continued*)
Buddhavacana regarding, 63-64, 82-83, 86, 92, 106, 112-13, 115-17, 193, 269-70, 430
commentarial extracts regarding 89-91, 97-99
concealment of 70-71
in the five khandhas, 32, 143
and *kamma*, 269-72
and *nirattā*, 93-99
practical value of, 111-12
anattalakkhaṇa, (characteristic of not-self), 65, 81
anicca (impermanence), 62-63, 69, 71-72, 92, 752n64,
Buddhavacana regarding, 63-64, 98, 112-13, 115, 117-22, 431, 432
commentarial extracts regarding, 97-98
concealment of 69
and *kamma*, 140
practical value of, 99-101, 107-10
reflecting on, 328, 431-33, 651
aniccalakkhaṇa (characteristic of impermanence), 65
annihilationism, 33, 88, 92, 93, 188-90, 755n45, 756n64, 756n66, 756n76
answering questions, 85-86, 165, 193-94, 464-70, 692-94
anupādisesanibbāna (*nibbāna* without remainder), 319-21, 338, 768n117
anupādisesapuggala (individual without remainder), 337-38, 342-43
See also arahant
anusaya (tendencies), 146-48
anussati (recollections), 636-37, 792n28, 801n135
appamāda (heedlessness), 104-5, 379, 528, 546, 579, 636, 662, 753n98, 792n16
Buddhavacana regarding, 99, 100-1, 110, 117, 122-23, 376, 382, 458-60, 574-77
appamaññā (limitless abidings), 637, 799n118, 800n131, 801n137, 807n202
appanāsamādhi (attainment concentration), 603-5, 645, 655, 657-61, 663, 800n13, 804n150, 808n227
See also *jhāna*
ārabbhavatthu (occasions for putting forth effort), 450-51
See also *kusītavatthu*
arahant, 93, 95, 164, 284, 290-91, 322-27, 334, 343-45, 373, 527, 616, 618, 635, 658, 669, 684, 768n117, 768n129, 771n164, 771n166, 772n171, 801-802n141
attributes of, 322-27
Buddhavacana regarding, 45, 50, 292-93, 316, 476, 623, 648
mentality of, 308-14
morality of, 300-8
types of, 343-45
wisdom of, 308-19
See also *anupādisesapuggala*; *ariyapuggala, asekha*; *nibbāna*
ārammaṇa (cognitive objects), 20, 34, 36, 39, 152, 425, 608
ariyapuggala (noble one), 330-43
eight kinds, 335-39
seven kinds, 339-43
See also arahant
ariyasacca. *See* four noble truths
ārogya (free of disease), 218, 284, 312
arūparāga (desire for the formless), 336
asaṅkhatalakkhaṇa (characteristics of the unconditioned), 67
āsava (outflows), 32, 116, 154-55, 179-80, 215-16, 275, 308, 392, 612, 616, 699, 755-56n62,
as conditioner for ignorance, 133, 151, 156
See also *āsavakkhayañāṇa*; *khīṇāsava*

āsavakkhayañāṇa (knowledge of cessation of the outflows), 344, 345, 617, 660, 686, 699
asekha (accomplished ones), 290, 337, 342-43, 770n157, 777n45, 778-79n22
See also arahant
asset. See *sampatti*
assāda ("sweet taste," attraction), 315, 441-45
assaddha (faithless), 310, 317
asubha (reflections on loathsomeness), 636, 676, 799n116, 799n119, 799n122
attachment. See *upādāna*
attainment concentration. See *appanā samādhi*
attakilamathānuyoga (self mortification), 294, 368, 697
attaññutā (knowing oneself), 404
attha (benefit, objective), 66, 365-66, 376-83, 404, 407, 436-41, 776n33
Buddhavacana regarding, 100-101, 122, 123, 274, 376
in three directions, 382-83
on three levels, 377-78
See also *attattha*; *diṭṭhadhammikattha*; *paramattha*; *paratha*; *samparāyikattha*; *ubhayattha*
atthaññutā (knowing the objective or result), 404
attattha (personal benefit), 303, 318, 382-83, 776n33
aversion. See *paṭigha*; *dosa*
avihiṁsāsaṅkappa (thoughts of non-hurtfulness), 491, 494, 497, 499
avijjā (ignorance), 86, 302, 311, 336, 754n25, 755n45
in the *paṭiccasamuppāda*, 132-33, 135, 144-45, 150, 151, 156-57, 158, 159-60, 166-67, 174, 178-82
āyatana (sense bases), 34-43, 583
Buddhavacana regarding, 43, 48-53, 161
in the *paṭiccasamuppāda*, 150, 152, 155, 156, 158, 167, 170
practical value of, 53-57
āyatana (sphere), 285-86
ayoniso-manasikāra, 86, 424, 676, 778n1, 781n61, 781-82n64, 785n115

Baptist, Egerton C., 761n56
becoming. See *bhava*
benefit. See *attha*
bhava (becoming), 151, 152, 153, 157, 159, 168, 175, 178
Buddhavacana regarding, 156
bhavacakka. See wheel of becoming
bhāvanā (cultivation), 293-95, 330, 380-81, 616, 643-46, 704-5, 709, 800n128
bhavataṇhā (desire for becoming), 160, 171, 175, 182, 424, 687, 709, 713, 755n48, 757n83
bhāvitacitta (cultivated in mind), 293, 308-14
Buddhavacana regarding, 295
bhāvitakāya (cultivated in body), 293, 294-300
Buddhavacana regarding, 295
bhāvitapaññā (cultivated in wisdom), 293, 314-19
bhāvitasīla (cultivated in conduct), 293, 300-8
bhāvitatta (cultivated ones), 291, 293, 764n30
bhayāgati (bias of fear), 350, 530
bhikkhus
difference in morality compared to laypeople, 508, 557-60
relations with householders, 410-11, 413, 534
right livelihood 535-39
biases. See *agati*

bījaniyāma (law of heredity), 140, 203-204, 206, 241-42
birth (*jāti*), 78, 151, 153-54, 157-58, 168, 175, 750n25
as a condition for aging and death, 173
blind men and the elephant simile, 288-89
bodhipakkhiyadhamma (requisites for enlightenment), 672, 677, 686, 806n188, 808n225
body, contemplation of, 636-37, 639, 680, 799n116, 799n117, 803n147
as foundation of mindfulness 573, 582, 650, 799n120, 801n135
See also *ānāpānasati*; *asubha*
bojjhaṅga (enlightenment factors), 213, 259, 296, 567, 583, 597-600, 661, 671, 673-82, 808n225
Buddhavacana regarding, 263, 475-76, 566, 597, 649, 673-74, 681-82
commentarial extracts regarding, 572, 602
bowing, 486
brahmacariya (higher life, holy life), 529
Brahmanism, 3-4, 761n59, 764n28
brahmavihāra, 340, 497, 637, 645, 748n29, 799n118, 801n137
Buddhadasa Bhikkhu, 184
Buddhaghosa Ācariya, 199-202, 661-62
See also Visuddhimagga
byāpāda (ill will), 220, 269, 607, 770n155, 784n93, 792-93n31
byāpādasaṅkappa (thoughts of ill will), 492, 493, 496, 497, 567

Cakkavatti Sutta, 196, 198
cakkavattivatta (duties of a universal emperor), 388, 534-35, 564, 729, 765n48
canker. See *āsava*; *āsavakkhaya-ñāṇa*
carita (disposition), 638-39, 755n45, 800n123.
See also *ducarita*; *sucarita*
caste system, 3, 9, 197, 277, 290, 331, 787-88n4
Buddhavacana regarding, 276-77
catudhātuvavaṭṭhāna (reflection on the four elements), 637
cause of suffering. See *dukkhasamudaya*
cessation. See *nirodha*; *dukkhanirodha*
cetanā (intention), 24-26, 35, 37, 157, 206-7, 209, 222-23, 666
Cetanā Sutta, 134
cetasika (mental concomitants), 45, 68, 745-46n2, 746n6
cetopariyañāṇa (knowledge of the minds of others), 345, 793n38
chanda (predilection for the good), 251, 260, 293, 301-2
chanda (zeal) 265, 565, 624, 625-26, 628, 666, 784n100
chandāgati (bias of liking), 221, 350, 498-500, 530
chanda samādhi, 630-31, 798n108
citta (mental application), 624-25, 626-28, 630
cittaniyāma (psychological laws), 140, 204, 206, 217, 222-24
cittānupassanā (contemplation of mind), 573, 582, 651, 680
clairaudience. See *dibbasota*
clairvoyance. See *dibbacakkhu*
clinging. See *upādāna*
coarse speech. See *pharusavācā*
conceit. See *māna*
conditionality. See *paccayakāra*
conditioned things. See *saṅkhārā*; *saṅkhatadhamma*
consciousness. See *viññāṇa*
contact. See *phassa*

continuity. See *santati*
conventional laws, 208, 217, 222-28, 237-41, 246, 759n11
conventional truth, 44, 45, 87, 748n33
  Buddhavacana regarding, 45-46
courses of skillful conduct. See *kusalakammapatha*
Creator, 13, 61, 81, 82, 83, 90, 96-97, 135-36, 140, 142-43, 205, 761n59.
  and *kamma*, 205
  See also God
Cūḷakammavibhaṅga Sutta, 252-55
cultivation. See *bhāvanā*
cutūpapātañāṇa (knowledge of the arising and passing away of beings), 309, 344, 660, 699

dakkhiṇeyyapuggala (persons worthy of offerings), 330-43, 770n157
  eight kinds, 335-39
  seven kinds, 339-43
dāna (giving), 332, 380, 381, 409, 508, 511-12, 521, 534, 555
danger, 710, 789n21
  Buddhavacana regarding, 458, 459-60, 571, 605, 710, 719
  See also *ādīnava*
death, 78, 117-22, 154-5, 158
  Buddhavacana regarding, 231, 235, 252-54, 324-25
deathlessness, 4, 122, 128, 284, 329, 353-54, 537, 688, 749n5
defect. See *vipatti*
defilements. See *kilesa*
delusion. See *moha*
dependent arising. See *paṭiccasamuppāda*
dependent origination. See *paṭiccasamuppāda*
Descartes, René, 85, 751n41
desire. See *kāmachanda*; *kāmarāga*; *taṇhā*
development. See *bhāvanā*
Dhamma teacher, qualities of. See *dhammadesakadhamma*
Dhammacakkappavattana Sutta, 368
Dhammacetiya Sutta, 323
dhammachanda (skillful desire). See *chanda*
dhammadesakadhamma (qualities of a Dhamma teacher), 411
dhammaniyāma (natural laws), 61, 62, 127, 140, 204-5, 758n7
dhammaññutā (knowing the principle or cause), 403-4, 783-4n86
dhammānudhammapaṭipatti (practicing in orderly progression), 437, 439, 783n85
  Buddhavacana regarding, 437-38, 438-39
dhammānusārī (one who follows through wisdom), 341, 669, 771-72n169, 743-44n188.
  See also *saddhānusārī*
dhammas (things), 65-68
dhammavicaya (contemplation of *dhammas*), 597, 598, 673, 674, 680, 793n32, 807n197
dhātu (elements), 196, 746n3, 758n85, 787n24
dibbacakkhu (clairvoyance), 344, 345, 613, 616-17, 660
dibbasota (clairaudience), 345, 605, 660
diligence, 243-44, 450-51, 545-46, 566-67, 792n16
  Buddhavacana regarding, 122-24, 450-51
disadvantages. See *vipatti*
discursive thought. See *vicāra*
disposition. See *carita*
distortions. See *vipallāsa*
diṭṭhadhammikattha (immediate/mundane benefit), 100-101, 376, 377, 379, 402, 403, 408, 519

diṭṭhadhammanibbāna (*nibbāna* in the here and now), 327, 752n64
diṭṭhadhammasukhavihāra (pleasant abiding in the present moment), 304, 614, 616, 648
divine abidings. See *brahmavihāra*
dosa (aversion, anger), 20, 25, 303, 576, 586, 595, 640
dosāgati (bias of anger), 350, 530
doubt. See *vicikicchā*
ducarita (bad conduct) 229, 234, 521
Ducasse, CJ, 761n57
dukkha, 47, 686
 Buddhavacana regarding, 83, 189-90
 as change, 138
 commentarial extracts regarding, 97-99
 concealer of, 69-70
 as a feeling, 39, 74, 75, 77, 79, 138, 152, 295
 in the four noble truths, 434-35, 696, 708, 709, 710-12
 kinds of, 77-81
 in the paṭiccasamuppāda, 131, 132, 154
 practical value of, 110-11
 in the three characteristics, 62, 63, 65, 73-77, 138-39, 431
 three kinds, 77
 twelve kinds, 78-79
 two kinds, 79-81
dukkhadukkhatā (the suffering that is a feeling), 77
dukkhalakkhaṇa (the characteristic of dukkha), 65, 73-75
dukkhanirodha (cessation of suffering), 130, 149, 697
Dukkhanirodha Sutta, 134
dukkhanirodhagāminī paṭipadā (way leading to the cessation of suffering), 259, 697, 704
dukkhasamudaya (cause of suffering), 130, 697, 704, 809n4
dukkhavedanā (unpleasant feeling), 39, 74, 75, 77, 79, 138, 152, 295

economics, 334, 538-39, 543-57, 563-64, 727
education, 482-91, 531, 554-45
effort. See *viriya*
eightfold path. *See* noble eightfold path
ekaggatā (one-pointedness), 45, 601, 608, 665, 794n49, 805n167
elements. See *dhātu*
emptiness, 117, 638, 795n54
enlightened beings. See *anāgāmi*; *arahant*; *bhāvita-*; *nibbāna*; *sakadāgāmī*; *sotāpanna*
enlightenment, 198, 326, 397, 412, 416, 428, 464, 661, 680, 684, 698-99, 759n26, 769n140
 Buddhavacana regarding, 52, 101, 123, 354, 368, 394, 442-43, 476, 519, 648-49, 691, 695, 698-700, 703, 706
 See also *bojjhaṅga*; *nibbana*; stream entry
enlightenment factors. See *bojjhaṅga*
equanimity. See *upekkhā*
escapes. See *vimokkha*
etadagga. *See* foremost disciples
eternalism, 33, 88, 92, 93, 188-89, 755n45, 756n63, 756n64, 756n66, 756n76
ethics. See *sīla*
external influences. See *paratoghosa*

faculties. See *indriya*
faith. See *saddhā*
faithlessness, 317, 766n80
false speech. See *musāvāda*
feeling. See *vedanā*
fetters. See *saṁyojana*
filial duties, 531-33

First Great Council, 307
five precepts, 348, 350, 504-8, 522-29, 721, 773n174, 776n30, 789n13, 789n16
  Buddhavacana regarding, 523-25
  criteria of severity, 526-28
floods. See *āsava*
fools, 274, 402-403, 405, 554
foremost disciples, 26, 305, 347, 528-29, 765n55
formations. See *saṅkhārā*
formless meditations, 327, 328, 336, 344, 637-38, 641, 647, 657, 771-72n169, 801n134
foundations of mindfulness. See *satipaṭṭhāna*
four noble truths, 31, 75-77, 111, 256, 259, 331, 341-42, 348, 583, 691-735
  Buddhavacana regarding, 31, 434, 474, 476, 691-95, 696, 698-99
  definition of, 695-97
  and *paṭiccasamuppāda,* 130, 150, 161, 697-703
  and right view, 474
  tasks in relation to, 703-9
  and *yoniso-manasikāra,* 434-36
friends, 408, 409, 410
  See also good friend
frivolous speech. See *samphappalāpā*

gatisampatti (favorable location), 242-46, 761n52
gativipatti (unfavorable location), 243-46, 761n52
generosity. See *dāna*
ghana (perception of mass), 69, 70
giving. See *dāna*
God, 94, 96, 135, 140, 143, 198, 205, 264, 513-15, 712, 718, 754n25, 794n48
  See also Creator
good and evil, 41, 198, 216-37, 513-14, 516, 721
  Buddhavacana regarding, 86, 419-20, 475
  and right view, 415, 475, 478-79
good friend. See *kalyāṇamitta*
goodwill. See *mettā*
government, 534-35, 544, 547, 562-64
greed. See *lobha*
groups, five. See *khandhas*

happiness. See *sukha*
heaven and hell, 249-52
  Buddhavacana regarding, 252-54
heedfulness. See *appamāda*
heedlessness, 104, 522, 669
  Buddhavacana regarding, 103, 122, 229, 262-63, 519, 524-25
hindrances. See *nīvaraṇa*
holy life. See *brahmacariyā*
hopelessness (*nirāsa*), 309-10, 766n80
  See also faithlessness
householders. See *kāmabhogī*

iddhi (psychic powers), 344, 613, 620, 634, 660, 798n106
  Buddhavacana regarding, 629
iddhipāda (pathways to success), 624-31, 798n106, 808n225
  Buddhavacana regarding, 629-31
ignorance. See *avijjā*
impediments. See *palibodha*
impermanence. See *anicca*
indeterminism, 88, 89, 92, 265, 712
indriya (faculties), 339, 341-42, 444, 667-69, 806n174, 808n225
  Buddhavacana regarding, 668
  development of, 294-300, 296-300,
Indriyabhāvanā Sutta, 297-300
indriyasaṁvara (restraint of the sense faculties), 56, 764n33
  Buddhavacana regarding, 296-97
  sīla of, 295, 559-60
initial thought. See *vitakka*

insight. See *vipassanā*
intention. See *cetanā*
intoxicants. See *surāmerayamajjapamādaṭṭhāna*
iriyāpatha (bodily postures), 69-70, 582, 800n129
issaranimittavāda (God-created theory), 712, 810n23

Jainism, 92, 257, 290, 810n23
jāti. *See* birth
jhāna, 327, 328, 340, 344, 601, 603, 617-18, 641, 645-46, 657-61
  benefits of, 620-21
  Buddhavacana regarding, 327, 384, 601, 604-5, 618, 647, 663, 698
  factors of, 663-66
  techniques for developing, 641, 647

Kālāma Sutta, 418-20
kālaññutā (knowing the time), 404
kālasampatti (favorable time), 242, 244
kālavipatti (unfavorable time), 242, 244
kalyāṇadhamma (good qualities), 352, 528, 765n48, 799n114
kalyāṇamitta (good friend), 399-420, 478, 634-35, 662, 722, 734, 766n16.
  Buddhavacana regarding, 400, 402-403, 407
  duties of, 414-18
  qualities of (*kalyāṇamittadhamma*), 403-14
  See also friends; good friend
kāmabhogī (householders), 467-69, 549-50
kāmachanda (sensual desire), 220, 606-7, 760n30, 770n155, 792-93n31, 795-96n66
kāmarāga (lust), 336, 770n155
kāmasaṅkappa (sensual thoughts), 492, 496
kāmasukhallikānuyoga (sensual indulgence), 368, 697
kāmesumicchācāra (sexual misconduct), 503, 506, 522, 526
kamma (karma), 12, 37, 203-78
  Buddhavacana regarding, 31, 210, 213, 214-15, 233-37, 241, 274-78
  cessation of, 255-63
    Buddhavacana regarding, 257-58, 261-63
  definition of, 208-11
  determining good and evil, 216-37
  that ends kamma, 255-63
  erasing of, 268-69
  fruition of, 237-55
    Buddhavacana regarding, 252-55
  as intention, 25-26, 35
  and not-self, 85-86, 89-90, 92, 189-90, 263-64, 269-72
  and the *paṭiccasamuppāda*, 151-52, 153, 157, 159, 162, 167, 172, 186
  practical value, 273-78
  results in future lives, 246-55,
    Buddhavacana regarding, 252-55
  on a social scale, 210-11, 238
  types of, 211-16
  wrong views regarding, 165-66, 264-68
  See also *vipāka*
kammaniyāma (law of *kamma*), 140, 204, 206-208, 217, 222-28, 237-42
kammassakatañāṇa (knowledge of what is and is not kamma), 415, 479
kammaṭṭhāna. *See* meditation objects
kāraṇa-manasikāra (thinking according to causes), 421-22, 781n58
karma. *See* kamma
kasiṇa (meditation device), 340, 604, 635-36, 637, 639, 641, 644, 799n115, 800n131, 801n134, 803n147
kāyānupassanā (contemplation of the body), 573, 582, 650, 680, 799n120, 801n135
kāyasakkhī ("witness in body"), 342, 772n169, 772n170

khandhas, 19-33
Buddhavacana regarding, 28-29, 31-32
interraction between, 28-31
practical value of, 32-33
khaṇika-samādhi (momentary concentration), 602, 606, 793n34
khīṇāsava (vanquisher of the outflows), 45, 290, 292, 312, 592, 768n123
kilesa (defilement), 87, 133, 158, 159, 162-63, 320, 527, 606, 611, 768n115
killing. See *pāṇātipāta*
knowledge, true and false, 44-48
kusala (skillful, wholesome), 212, 217, 221-22, 259, 422, 759n17
Buddhavacana regarding, 123, 228-29, 230-31, 233-34, 235
as catalyst for *akusala*, 103, 751n62
definition of, 217-20
kusaladhammachanda (skillful desire). See *chanda*
kusalakammapatha (skillful courses of action), 212, 256, 395, 506-7, 778n22
kusītavatthu (occasions for laziness), 448-49
See also *ārabbhavatthu*

laws of nature. See *niyāma*
laziness, 448-49
liberation, 277, 302, 309, 318-19, 343-45, 349, 364-67, 397-98
five levels of, 329
in the Three characteristics, 94-95, 101-3, 105-7
See also *nibbāna*
life after death, 250-52, 761n57
livelihood, 378-79
See also right livelihood
loathsomeness. See *asubha*
loathsomeness of food. See *āhāre paṭikūlasaññā*
lobha (greed), 492, 494, 760n31, 784n100, 795-96n66
Loka Sutta, 292-93
lokiyasammādiṭṭhi (transcendent right view), 478-80, 480-82
loving kindness. See *mettā*
lute simile, 568-69

macchariya (covetousness), 195, 349, 773n182
magga (path), 76, 361-62, 434, 436, 697, 705-6, 708, 709, 710, 717, 721.
See also noble eightfold path
magga (path attainment), 683, 769n140
mahābhūtarūpa (four great elements), 150, 746n3
Mahācakka Sutta, 294-95
majjhena dhammadesanā (middle teaching), 6, 187, 359, 360, 702, 756n70, 775n2
majjhimā paṭipadā (middle way of practice), 8, 361, 697, 721, 756n70
Buddhavacana regarding, 355
malicious speech. See *pisuṅāvācā*
Māluṅkyaputta Sutta, 692-94
mamaṁkāra (thoughts of "mine"), 106, 141, 496
māna (conceit), 106, 336, 496
mānānusaya (the conceit "I am"), 106, 496
Martin, A. R., 761n57
materiality. See *rūpa*
mattaññutā (knowing moderation), 404, 784n96
meanness. See *macchariya*
meditation. See *samādhi*
meditation objects, 635-42
memory and *sati*, 26-28
meritorious action. See *puññakiriyāvatthu*
metaphysics, 193-94, 757n82, 787-88n4
metta (goodwill), 411, 494, 604, 637, 639, 788n8
Buddhavacana regarding, 604-605
success and failure of, 221, 498-500

Middle Teaching. See *majjhena dhammadesanā*
Middle Way. See *majjhimā paṭipadā*
mind (*citta*), 45, 161, 745-46n2, 746n8, 758-59n9
application of (in the four *iddhipāda*), 624-25, 626-27, 628
contemplation of, 573, 582, 651, 680
distortion of, 46
mindfulness. See *sati*
mindfulness of the breathing. See *ānāpānasati*
moderation. See *mattaññutā*
moha (delusion), 20, 171, 303. See also *avijjā*
mohāgati (bias of delusion), 350, 530
momentary concentration. See *khaṇika samādhi*
Moore, Robin, x, xiii, 761n55, 765n55, 798n102
morality. See *sīla*
musāvāda (false speech), 503, 506-7, 508, 521, 522, 526

nāmarūpa (mind and body/mentality and corporeality), 131, 150, 152, 159, 161, 167, 175
nāmadhamma (mentality), 45, 66, 84, 745-46n2
ñāṇa (direct knowledge), 482, 683 705-6, 708, 807n197, 810n19
nanattasañña (perception of variation), 196, 340
natthikadiṭṭhi. *See* nihilism
natural laws. See *niyāma*
nekkhammasaṅkappa (thoughts of renunciation), 491, 494, 497
nevasaññānāsaññāyatana (state of neither perception nor non-perception), 285, 340, 638, 657, 799n121
nibbana, 45, 64, 67, 129, 281-354
Buddhavacana regarding, 281, 285-86, 287, 311, 316-17
commentarial extracts regarding, 67, 89
descriptions of, 282-85
kinds of, 319-22
levels of attainment, 327-43
qualities of arahant who has attained, 322-27, 343-45
state of attainment, 289-319
nihilism, 88-89, 187, 810n23
nimitta (sign), 598, 603, 641, 642, 643-45, 655-56, 676-77, 795n57, 800n126, 800n131, 804n150, 807n200, 807n201
nippariyāyadukkha (direct suffering), 79
nirāmisasukha (happiness independent of object), 107, 312, 716
nirattā (no self), 93-99
nirodha (cessation), 360
five levels, 328-29, 716-17
in the four noble truths, 359, 360, 434, 436, 697, 708, 709, 710
in the *paṭiccasamuppāda*, 130-32, 361
See also *kamma*, cessation of
nirodhasamāpatti (attainment of cessation concentration), 327, 618-19, 658
nissaraṇa (escape), 315-16, 441-45
nissaraṇanirodha (cessation of defilements through transcendence), 329, 717
nīvaraṇa (hindrances), 328, 583, 606-7, 666, 792-93n31, 765n41, 777n43, 781n61, 795-96n66
Buddhavacana regarding, 606, 609-12
niyāma (natural laws), 203-8, 758n2.
noble eightfold path, 259, 361, 363, 385, 473-689, 697, 708
Buddhavacana regarding, 261, 355,

368, 370-1, 372, 375-76, 400, 420-21, 575, 631, 696
connection to the Threefold Training, 383-94
noble truths. *See* four noble truths
non-returner. See *anāgāmi*
not-self. See *anattā*

old kamma philosophy (*pubbekatavāda*), 92, 257-58, 264, 712, 810n23
once-returner. See *sakadāgāmī*
one-pointedness. See *ekaggatā*
other-generationism (*parakāravāda*), 189, 762n71
outflows. See *āsava.*
Ovādapāṭimokkha (the cardinal teachings of all buddhas), 393

paccayakāra (conditionality), 132, 196-97, 200, 201, 753n1
paccayasannisitasila (*sīla* in use of supports), 560
padhāna (effort), 566-67, 625-26
palibodha (concerns, worries), 633-34, 797n92
pāmojja (gladness), 364, 367, 623, 804n161
pāṇātipāta (killing living beings), 198, 252, 503, 506, 521, 522, 526
paṇḍita. See sage
paññā (wisdom), 136, 314-19, 473-502, 793-94n43, 794n46
Buddhavacana regarding, 51-52, 101, 106, 114-15, 316-18, 405, 519, 663, 668, 716
of a stream enterer, 347-48
See also *yoniso-manasikāra*
paññavimutta (liberated through wisdom), 326, 342, 343, 345, 660, 771-72n169
paññāvuḍhidhamma (principles for growth in wisdom), 437
papañca (mental fabrication), 21-22, 43, 106
paramattha (ultimate benefit/truth), 46, 272, 320, 378, 379, 439, 748n33
paratoghosa (external influences), 398, 400-420
Buddhavacana regarding, 400, 402-403
See also *kalyāṇamitta*
parattha (benefit to others), 303, 318, 383, 776n33
parental duties, 531
parikamma-nimitta (preparatory *nimitta*), 644
pariyāyadukkha (indirect suffering), 79
parisaññutā (knowing company), 404
passaddhi (tranquility), 364, 671, 675, 677, 678, 679-80, 793n32, 804n161
past-action determinism. *See* old kamma philosophy
past lives, recollection of. See *pubbenivāsānussati*
patha-manasikāra (systematic thinking), 421, 781n58
path convergence (*maggasamaṅgi*), 476, 492, 682-89, 771n163
pathways to decline (*apāyamukha*), 388, 402, 530, 790n24
paṭibhāganimitta (replica nimitta), 603, 641, 644, 645, 656, 800n131
paṭibhānapaṭisambhidā (discernment of ready wit), 344
paṭiccasamuppāda (dependent arising), 127-202, 362-65, 747n13
Buddhavacana regarding, 127-29, 165-66, 193, 195, 475
dukkha in, 138-39
in everyday life, 164, 166-68, 173-78
factors of, 148-54, 166-68
and the four noble truths, 697-703
interaction between factors, 168-73
as a Middle Teaching, 187-94, 359, 187-88, 189-90, 191-92, 193-94, 195

paṭiccasamuppāda (dependent arising) (*continued*)
in one mind moment, 134, 199-202
and right view, 474, 475
on social scale, 195-98
over three lifetimes, 134, 151-64, 199-202
as world-origin theory, 135-37
and *yoniso-manasikāra*, 424, 428-29, 782n72
paṭigha (aversion), 311, 336, 770n155
pāṭimokkhasaṁvarasīla (sīla of restraint in the *Pāṭimokkha*), 559
paṭipassaddhinirodha (cessation of defilements through fruition attainment), 329, 717
paṭisambhidā (special knowledge), 343-44, 437
payogasampatti (favorable enterprise), 243, 244
payogavipatti (unfavorable enterprise), 243, 244
perception. See *saññā*
perception of solidity. See *ghana*
phala (fruit, attainment), 318, 684, 717, 769n140
pharusavācā (coarse speech), 269, 503, 507, 521
phassa (contact), 39, 85, 466, 688
Buddhavacana, 190, 261, 554
in the *paṭiccasamuppāda*, 150, 152, 167, 170-71, 175
pisuṅāvācā (malicious tale-bearing), 507, 521, 789n16
pīti (rapture), 364, 623, 650, 657, 664-65, 804n161, 805n167, 805n169
as enlightenment factor, 673, 675, 677, 678
present moment, 134, 181-82, 250, 455-60, 589-90, 593-96, 712
Buddhavacana regarding, 274-75, 419, 457-60
See also *diṭṭhadhammasukhavihāra*
problem solving, 347, 546, 694, 727-32
psychic powers. See *iddhi*
pubbekatavāda. See old kamma philosophy
pubbenivāsānussatiñāṇa (recollection of past lives), 345, 456, 660, 699
puggalaññutā (knowing the person), 404
puññakiriyā-vatthu (bases for meritorious action), 376, 379, 380-81
puthujjana (unenlightened being), 669, 721, 773-74n188

questions, types of, 465
See also *abyākatapañhā*

raft simile, 373-74
rapture. See *pīti*
recollection. See *sati*
recollections. See *anussati*
renunciation. See *nekkhammasaṅkappa*
restlessness. See *uddhaccakukkucca*
right action, 499, 506, 508, 521-22, 525-29, 529-34
Buddhavacana regarding, 503, 508, 523-25, 529
transcendent, 504
See also *sīla*
right concentration, 386, 600-89
Buddhavacana regarding, 601-602
See also *samādhi*
right effort, 565-72
Buddhavacana regarding, 565, 567-69, 570-72
four efforts (*padhāna*), 566-67, 570-71
See also *viriya*
right livelihood, 534-39
for *bhikkhus*, 335, 413
Buddhavacana regarding, 547-49

right mindfulness, 572-600
Buddhavacana regarding, 572, 577-78, 583, 587, 597
See also *sati*
right practice, 362-63, 437
Buddhavacana regarding, 370, 572, 574-77, 577-78, 583, 587, 597
right speech, 503, 506-7, 508, 521
transcendent, 504
right thought, 491-502
Buddhavacana regarding, 491-92, 500, 501-502
on two levels 491-92
right view, 395-96, 474-91, 774n191, 777n45, 777n48, 778n49, 780n48, 807n219
Buddhavacana regarding, 474-76, 214-16
definitions of, 477
factors of, 399-400, 470
importance of, 393-94
and kamma, 213-16
and learning, 482-91
mundane, 478-80
and *paṭiccasamuppāda*, 187-94
transcendent, 480-82
two levels of, 415-17, 475-76, 478-82
rites and observances, grasping at. See *sīlabbataparāmāsa*
root cause, 141-43
rūpa (physical form), 20, 82
See also *mahābhūtarūpa*
rūpa (visible object), 38
rūpadhamma (physicality), 89, 150. See also *nāmarūpa*
rūparāga (desire for form), 336

sadārasantosa (contentment with one's spouse), 522, 528-29, 789n19
saddhā (faith), 396-97, 418-20, 667, 669, 792n10, 794n48
Buddhavacana regarding, 418-20, 570
See also *tathāgatabodhisaddhā*
saddhānusārī (one who follows through faith), 341, 669, 771-72n169
See also *dhammānusārī*
saddhāvimutta (liberated through faith), 341-42, 771-72n169, 772-73n171
sage (*paṇḍita*), 101, 324, 378, 401
Buddhavacana regarding, 403, 405, 412
sakadāgāmī (once-returner), 291, 337, 338
sakkāyadiṭṭhi (own-body view), 335, 337, 347, 349, 350
samādhi (concentration)
and *ānāpānasati* (mindfulness of the breathing), 646-56
appanāsamādhi (attainment concentration), 603-5, 645, 657-63, 800n131, 804n150
attributes of, 608-12
benefits of, 612-21, 657-61
Buddhavacana regarding, 123, 601, 602, 603-604, 604-605, 624
component factors, 663-66
definition of, 600-601
development through *iddhipāda*, 624-31
development through *sati*, 631-32
as enlightenment factor, 673-75, 677-82
as *indriya*, 666-73
and the *jhānas*, 327, 328, 340, 344, 384, 601, 603, 604-605 617-18, 620, 641, 645-46, 647, 657-61, 693
khaṇikasamādhi (momentary concentration), 602, 605, 606, 621, 793n34
levels of, 602-606
and meditation objects, 635-42
methods for developing 621-46
mūlasamādhi (rudimentary concentration), 603-4

samādhi (concentration) (*continued*)
obstacles to, 606-607
systematic/traditional development of, 632-46
upacārasamādhi (access concentration), 603, 641, 645, 656, 805n167, 808-9n227
See also right concentration
samatha (calm), 388, 470, 490, 598, 660-61, 709, 746n31, 802n145, 810n20
sammā-ājiva. *See* right livelihood
sammādiṭṭhi. *See* right view
sammākammanta. *See* right action
sammappadhāna (right efforts), 566-67, 808n225
sammāsamādhi. *See* right concentration
sammāsaṅkappa. *See* right thought
sammāsati. *See* right mindfulness
sammāvācā. *See* right speech
sammāvāyāma. *See* right effort
sampajañña (clear comprehension), 582, 584-86, 588, 666, 782n68
samparāyikattha (further benefit), 100-101, 377-78, 519, 549
sampatti (advantage, endowment), 242-46, 761n52
samphappalāpā (frivolous speech), 269, 503, 507, 521, 524
saṁsāravaṭṭa (world of rebirth), 41, 55, 88, 164, 763n1
saṁyojana (fetters), 335-37, 583
samucchedanirodha (cessation of defilements though severance), 329, 716-17
samudaya (cause of suffering, or origination mode of the *paṭiccasamuppāda*), 161-64, 359-60, 434, 435, 697, 708, 709, 710, 712
Saṅgha (Order of bhikkhus), 306, 339, 557-60, 563, 571, 719, 728-29, 811n27
in the community, 124, 334-35, 410-11
saṅkhārā (all formations), 62, 65-67, 68
distinction from dhammas, 65-68
saṅkhārā (in the khandhas), 20, 24-26, 29-30, 68, 746n6, 747n13, 747n16, 748n29
as intention, 209
saṅkhārā (in the *paṭiccasamuppāda*), 130, 150, 151-52, 157, 159, 167, 174, 754n25
saṅkhāra-dukkatā (the suffering inherent in formations), 138-39
saṅkhatadhamma (conditioned things), 66-67, 749n3
saññā (perception), 20-23, 26, 29-30
distorted, 46, 47-48
and memory, 26-28
santati (continuity), 69
sappāya (conducive), 640, 642, 645, 800n129
sappurisa (true persons), 401, 402, 403-4, 542, 778-79n22, 791n59
sārāṇīyadhamma (conditions for social harmony), 348-49
sassatadiṭṭhi. *See* eternalism
sassatavāda. *See* eternalism
sati (mindfulness, recollection), 56, 455, 616, 792n16, 792n28, 793-94n43, 794n46, 806n195
benefits of, 590-93
Buddhavacana regarding, 577-78, 592-93, 670
as enlightenment factor, 597-600, 674, 677, 679
as heedfulness, 473-77
as *indriya*, 667, 670, 671-72
and memory, 26-28
in the present moment, 593-96
and *samādhi* development, 631-32
in samatha meditation, 598-60
social value of, 577-78

and wisdom development, 578-81
See also right mindfulness; *satipaṭṭhāna*
satipaṭṭhāna (foundations of mindfulness), 572-73, 581-88
Buddhavacana regarding, 572, 583, 587
sa-upādisesanibbāna (*nibbāna* with remainder), 338, 768n117
sa-upādisesapuggala (a person with remainder), 336, 338, 768n117, 770n157
Schweitzer, Albert, 788n8
sekha (initiate, learner), 334, 336, 337, 341-42, 348, 476, 765n48, 770n157, 773-74n188
self-generationism, 188
self-view, 32, 63, 64.
See also *māna*; *nirattā*; *sakkāyadiṭṭhi*
sense bases. See *āyatana*
sense contact. See *phassa*
sense restraint. See *indriyasaṁvara*
sensual desire. See *kāmachanda*; *kāmarāga*
sexual misconduct. See *kāmesumicchācāra*
shifting of position (*iriyāpatha*), 69-70
sīla (morality), 380, 503-64
Buddhavacana regarding, 101, 383-84, 392, 507, 519
arahants developed in, 300-308
in the economy, 543-49, 563-64
faith-based, 341
and the five precepts, 522-29, 521
four kinds of purity, 503-4, 508, 523-25, 529 559-60
in government, 562-63, 563-64
for householders, 516-34
and *kusalakammapatha* (skillful courses of action), 212, 256, 395, 506-7, 778n22
natural-order based, 509-16
social applications of, 529-34, 561-62
in a stream enterer, 348
theistic, 509-16
in the threefold training, 386, 390-91
wisdom-based, 341
See also right action; right livelihood; right speech
sīlabbataparāmāsa (grasping at rites and rituals), 117, 183-84, 185, 336, 347, 349, 434, 487
Siṅgālaka Sutta, 408-9
sitting posture, 652-53
six directions, 402, 409-12, 531-34
skillful action, bases of. See *puññakiriyāvatthu*
skillfulness. See *kusala*
sleepiness. See *thīnamiddha*
sloth. *See thīnamiddha*
Soṇa Sutta, 568-69
sotāpanna (stream enterer), 291, 329, 336-37, 338, 345-54, 771n164, 774n195
attributes of, 345-52
Buddhavacana regarding, 351, 352-54
stealing. *See adinnādāna*
Stevenson, Ian, 761n57
stinginess. See *macchariya*
stream enterer, stream entry. See *sotāpanna*
stress. *See dukkha*
subject-object view, distinction and unity, 190
sucarita (good conduct), 296-97, 521, 787n19
suffering. See *dukkha*
sukha (happiness), 54-55, 74, 310-14, 664
Buddhavacana regarding, 52, 99, 122, 323-24, 444, 547-49
for householders, 549-51
of a steam enterer, 349, 351
See also *nirāmisasukha*

sukkhavipassaka (one develops insight exclusively), 343, 345, 772n171
superknowledges. See *abhiññā*
surāmerayamajjapamādaṭṭhāna (indulgence in intoxicants), 522
Sutton, Joseph L., 788n8

tadaṅganibbāna (momentary *nibbāna*), 327, 783n79
tadaṅganirodha (temporary cessation of defilements through insight), 328-29, 716
taṇhā (desire), 259-60, 301
  in the *paṭiccasamuppāda*, 150, 153, 156-57, 158, 159, 167, 175, 755n45, 756n66, 757n83
  See also *bhavataṇhā*
tathāgatabodhisaddhā (faith in the Buddha's enlightenment), 519, 667, 800n127
teaching, 411-14, 532, 641-42
  Buddhavacana regarding, 412
  qualities of a Dhamma teacher, 411
telepathy, 617, 660
temperament. See *carita*
tevijja ([an arahant possessed of the] three knowledges), 344, 345
theistic determinism, 264, 265
thīnamiddha (sloth and torpor), 607, 792-93n31
three characteristics, the, 61-124
  Buddhavacana regarding, 62, 63-64, 112-24
  commentarial texts regarding, 97-99
  concealers of, 69-71
  definition of, 62-63
  practical value of, 99-107
  saṅkhāras in, 68
  and *yoniso-manasikāra*, 86
threefold training, 383-94
  Buddhavacana regarding, 383-84
  connection to the noble eightfold path, 385-94
tilakkhaṇa. *See* three characteristics, the
torpor. See *thīnamiddha*
Triple Gem, 717-20
  Buddhavacana regarding, 719
true person. See *sappurisa*

ubhatobhāgavimutta (liberated both ways), 342-43, 344-45, 660, 771-72n169
ubhayattha (benefit to both oneself and others), 383
ucchedadiṭṭhi. *See* annihilationism
ucchedavāda. *See* annihilationism
uddhaccakukkucca (restlessness and worry), 220, 607
uggahanimitta (learned nimitta), 644-45
ultimate truth, 44-45, 94
unconditioned, the, 66-67, 284, 287
  Buddhavacana regarding, 285
unfathomables. See *acinteyya*
unsatisfactoriness. See *dukkha*
unskillful thoughts, 447-55
unskillfulness. See *akusala*
unwholesomeness. *See akusala*
unwinding. See *vivaṭṭa*
unwise attention. See *ayoniso-manasikāra*
upacāra samādhi (access concentration), 603, 618, 645, 656, 686, 793n34, 795n57, 805n167, 808n227
upādāna (clinging), 94, 183-85
  Buddhavacana regarding, 146-48
  five khandhas, of 31-32
  four bases of, 183-85
  in the *paṭiccasamuppāda*, 150-51, 153, 156-57, 158, 167-68, 175, 184
upadhisampatti (favorable physical condition), 242, 244

upadhivipatti (unfavorable physical condition), 243, 244
upāya-manasikāra (thinking with skillful means), 421, 600, 781n56
upekkhā (equanimity), 39, 637, 746n4, 746n7, 748n29, 787n23, 787n26
as enlightenment factor, 675
as factor of *jhāna*, 665, 801n137, 805n167, 805n170
uppādaka-manasikāra (thinking for an objective), 422, 781n58
utuniyāma (physical laws), 203, 206

Vāseṭṭha Sutta, 210-11, 745n2
vaṭṭa (cycles), 154, 158-59
vedanā (feeling, sensation), 20, 24, 29-30, 39-41, 746n4, 746n6, 747n12, 747n13, 747n16, 748n28
contemplation of, 572, 573, 582
in the *paṭiccasamuppāda*, 150, 152, 157-64, 167, 170-71, 175
vibhajjavāda, 460-69, 782n72
vicāra (sustained application of mind), 657, 664, 675-76, 805n167
vicikicchā (doubt), 335, 337, 349, 607
vihiṁsāsaṅkappa (thoughts of hurting), 492
vikkhambhananirodha (cessation of defilements through *jhāna*), 328, 716
vīmaṁsā (analytical reflection), 625, 627-29, 630-31
vimokkha (escapes), 339-42, 771n166, 771n167, 806n178
eight levels of, 340
vinaya (discipline), 387-88, 514, 520-21, 777n37, 777n38
Vinaya (monks' discipline), 225, 797n90, 811n27
viññāṇa (consciousness), 286-87, 746n8, 747n13, 747n16
as *khandha*, 20, 22-23, 29, 30
in the *paṭiccasamuppāda*, 150, 151-52, 153, 157-64, 167, 174-75
viññāṇañcāyatana (sphere of limitless consciousness), 340, 637-38, 657
vipāka (kamma result), 90, 159, 161, 237-49, 252-55, 747n12, 747n13
on different levels, 237-38
vipallāsa (distortion), 46-48, 748n38
vipariṇāma-dukkhatā (suffering inherent in change), 138
vipassanā (insight), 343, 389, 470, 581-83, 598, 600 764n31, 766n86, 769n139, 781-82n64, 783n85, 793n34, 795n54, 802n145
vipatti (failure), 242, 243, 498, 536
viriya (effort), 560, 779n32
as enlightenment factor, 674-75, 779n32
as *iddhipāda*, 624, 626, 628, 661
as *indriya*, 339, 667, 792n10
See also right effort
virtue. See *sīla*
Visuddhimagga, 392, 401, 747n16, 770n160, 772n171, 780n49, 809n12
on the four noble truths 695-96, 710-12
on the *paṭiccasamuppāda*, 155, 199, 758n92,
on *samādhi*, 617-19, 632, 666, 670, 677, 798n106, 799 n115, 799n121, 799n122, 801-2n141, 803n148, 806n174, 808n227
on the three characteristics, 89-91, 101, 752n69
vitakka (initial application of mind), 657, 664, 675-76, 805n167, 809n229
vivaṭṭa (unraveling, unwinding), 41, 281, 424, 763n1
volition. See *cetanā*
volitional formations. See *saṅkhārā*

way leading to the cessation of suffering. See *dukkhanirodhagāminī paṭipadā*

wealth, 213-14, 467-69, 477-78, 547-49, 551-53
  limitations of, 277-78, 539-43, 553-54
wheel of becoming/existence/rebirth, 159
wholesomeness. See *kusala*
wisdom. See *paññā*
wise attention. See *yoniso-manasikāra*
wrong practice, 362, 363
  Buddhavacana regarding, 370
wrong thought, 492-93
wrong view, 182, 198, 264-65, 478, 768n134, 778n1
  Buddhavacana regarding, 165-66, 214-15, 265-66

yoniso-manasikāra (wise attention), 397-98, 420-71
  analysis *(vibhajjavāda)*, 460-69, 463
  analyzing by moments, 462-63
  analyzing component factors, 429-31, 461-62
  analyzing determinants, 428-29, 463
  for arousing virtues, 447-55
  on attraction, danger, and way out, 441-45
  Buddhavacana regarding, 420-21
  and considering alternatives, 463-67
  definitions of, 421-27
  and *dhammānudhammapaṭipatti* (ordered practice), 436-41
  importance of, 420-21
  kāraṇa-manasikāra, 421-22
  patha-manasikāra, 421
  in the present moment, 455-60
  and *sīla*, 499
  techniques for, 427-69
  on three characteristics, 431-36
  on true and false value, 445-47
  upāya-manasikāra, 421
  uppādaka-manasikāra, 422

About the Author and Translator

VENERABLE P. A. PAYUTTO* was born Prayudh Arayankun in 1938 in Suphanburi Province in Thailand. He became a novice monk at the age of thirteen, where he studied Pali and *vipassanā* meditation. He completed the highest level of Pali language studies (Parian 9) while still a novice and was consequently granted royal patronage for his ordination as a Buddhist monk (bhikkhu) in 1962, with the ordination name Payutto.

Venerable Payutto completed a bachelor's degree in Buddhist studies from Mahachulalongkorn Rajavidyalaya Buddhist University in 1962. Beginning in 1963 he served as associate dean of that university, until 1973 when he was appointed deputy abbot of Wat Phra Piren in Bangkok. After three years he left that position to further his academic studies.

In 1972 Venerable Payutto lectured on Buddhism and Thai Culture at the University of Pennsylvania; in 1976 he lectured on Buddhism at Swarthmore College; and in 1981 he was a research fellow in world religions at the Faculty of Divinity, Harvard University.

Venerable Payutto has received numerous awards, including honorary doctorate degrees from universities in Thailand and abroad, and the UNESCO Prize for Peace Education in 1994. Honorary doctorates include doctorates in Buddhists studies, liberal arts, education, philosophy, and science, reflecting the broad scope of his writings.

Buddhadhamma represents the venerable author's most famous work, but his publications in Thai are extensive, numbering in the hundreds and covering subjects as diverse as economics, science, politics, law, and social commentary, as well as clarifications of traditional Buddhist subjects such as the correct understanding of *kamma*, the proper kind of faith for a Buddhist, and skillful

*Ven. Payutto is also known by various ecclesiastical titles, including Phra Debvedi and Phra Dhammapitaka. At time of publication, he holds the title of Somdet Phra Buddhadhosacariya.

attitudes to technology and married life. Within Thai society, he has come to the fore with a voice of authority when there are challenges to the traditional Buddhist teachings.

BRUCE EVANS was born in 1952 in Melbourne, Australia. After wandering the hippie trail in the early 1970s, he developed a keen interest in Buddhism and traveled to Thailand in 1975 to further his knowledge and experience. There he met the famous Thai meditation teacher Venerable Ajahn Chah and was inspired to stay on, taking full ordination as a bhikkhu in 1976. He stayed at Ajahn Chah's monastery and branch monasteries for a total of seventeen years. During his time as a bhikkhu he became interested in translating Venerable Ajahn Chah's teachings into English, and he published three titles for free distribution: *A Taste of Freedom*, *Food for the Heart*, and *Living Dhamma*.

In the mid-1990s he developed an interest in translating the works of Venerable P. A. Payutto, impressed by his clear and authoritative explanations of the Buddha's teachings. He left the monkhood in 1997 and took up residence with his partner in Bangkok, where he worked for the Buddhadhamma Foundation translating and editing Buddhist texts, including *Buddhadhamma*. For various reasons, Bruce was unable to complete the final version of *Buddhadhamma* and returned to Melbourne with his family, where he worked for many years as an editor and managing editor at Lonely Planet Publications.

Since 2013 he has worked as a freelance translator and editor in Melbourne. During that time he revived his abridged version of *Buddhadhamma*, completely revising the translation in consultation with the venerable author. He continues to live in Melbourne, where he is focusing on reducing his freelance workload to concentrate more on Buddhist translations, an endeavor he has grown to love.